PEOPLES OF THE PAST AND PRESENT

PEOPLES OF THE PAST AND PRESENT

READINGS IN ANTHROPOLOGY

Jean-Luc Chodkiewicz
University of Manitoba

HARCOURT
BRACE

Harcourt Brace & Company

Toronto Montreal Fort Worth New York Orlando Philadelphia San Diego
London Sydney Tokyo

Canadian Cataloguing in Publication Data

Main entry under title:

Peoples of the past and present

Includes bibliographical references.
ISBN 0-7747-3214-8

1. Anthropology. 2. Ethnology. I. Chodkiewicz, Jean-Luc.

GN25.P46 1995 301 C93-095483-1

Publisher: Heather McWhinney
Editor and Marketing Manager: Daniel J. Brooks
Projects Co-ordinator: Megan Mueller
Director of Publishing Services: Jean Davies
Editorial Manager: Marcel Chiera
Supervising Editor: Semareh Al-Hillal
Production Manager: Sue-Ann Becker
Production Supervisor: Carol Tong
Copy Editor: Darlene Zeleney
Cover and Interior Design: Maher Design
Typesetting and Assembly: Howarth & Smith Typesetting & Printing Ltd.
Printing and Binding: Edwards Brothers Incorporated

Cover Art: *Maasai Messages*, watercolour by Canadian artist Irene Klar. Reproduced with the permission of the artist.

This book was printed in the United States of America.

    2   3   4   5   99   98

This book is dedicated to

Robert Francis Murphy
1924–1990

[...] behind every conscious motive there is a hidden agenda,
behind every social practice or institution there lies a covert
and undetected function, and after every great plan there
follows a series of wholly unintended and unanticipated
consequences. We must look, then, behind the façade of
appearances and the reality of common-sense experience in
order to reach the organization and flow of social life that
goes on beneath the surface.

R.F. Murphy, *An Overture to Social Anthropology*
(Englewood Cliffs, N.J.: Prentice Hall, 1979), p. 14.

Preface

This volume is intended to accompany your textbook in introductory anthropology, not to compete with its full and systematic coverage. The articles it contains, although they are not all written by anthropologists, illustrate many of the issues and viewpoints commonly discussed in the latest editions of the various available textbooks. The topical arrangement of the readings in this collection is also similar to that of most current textbooks for introductory courses, reflecting the "four-square" division of the field (biological anthropology, archaeology, cultural anthropology, and linguistic anthropology) so often honored in the breach in the research and practice of many modern anthropologists. To give just one example, the fast-developing field of applied anthropology would deserve some portion of that "square." The majority of the articles reproduced here were chosen from hundreds of books, journals, and magazine articles that have appeared over the last four decades. Older articles appear alongside original contributions published here for the first time. One function of the older articles is to dispel the illusion that only the latest is the best, or that only the anthropological research of this decade is useful and relevant to our basic understanding of human societies and cultures.

Whereas well-established facts and theories are the main fare of a textbook, a reader such as this one attempts to illustrate, comment, and speculate. To avoid creating an eclectic and disjointed collection of unrelated texts, I have combined articles unified by several themes, and provided introductory comments that highlight the links among the selections. So many choices had to be made among equally worthy anthropological contributions that, like any selection, this one does not contain every item of importance, but reflects, to an extent, its editor's preferences and perspectives. I wanted to present anthropology as a science in the making, and to emphasize the modern understanding and practice of "holism," which is not the so-called four-fields approach but a synthetic approach that distinguishes anthropology from all other social sciences. Although not all modern anthropologists find this approach equally useful and relevant, it has the advantage of promoting a logical and coherent framework for an initiation into the field of anthropology.

Anthropology is, first of all, a unique way of looking at the world, and the objective of an introductory course should be to illustrate and explain that world view. Anthropology does not have a monopoly on the study of humankind and its place in nature, but it has original contributions to make to that understanding. A leading concern in the selection of the articles in this reader was to introduce and emphasize problems of method, by providing illustrations of "sciencing," and not just scientific results. This emphasis on seeking knowledge rather than revealing accepted truths is intended to help students understand that there is much yet to be done: the purpose of their training is to enable them to dispel the confusions and fill the gaps of our present knowledge. No attempt was made to be comprehensive and to cover *all* the important points; that is the job of textbooks. Some of the more humanist, or postmodern, perspectives, for example, are underrepresented in this collection. Nevertheless, the present collection represents many of the anthropological perspectives embraced by modern leaders in the field. Other anthropologists, other ideas and theoretical positions have been or could be featured in other readers. As it is, *Peoples of the Past and Present* reflects different facets of modern anthropological research dedicated to making anthropology into the science that it could be, and that many anthropologists claim it is already becoming.

The articles chosen, as well as the comments that introduce the various sections, are not intended to be comprehensive or to settle issues, but to raise interest in them. Although they do not seek controversy for its own sake, they are often argumentative, intended to initiate a debate. The objective was to provide interesting illustrations of anthropological discoveries and points of view, in order to show that a scientific anthropology is an attractive and viable possibility.

Advances in other sciences — notably in biology, physics, and chemistry, but also in many of the new technologies that have been made available to us — help us to settle old issues, prompt us to raise new questions, and force us to reconsider cherished assumptions. Beginning students are often puzzled or discouraged by the argumentative self-analysis characteristic of the discipline, and by the "learning by debunking" illustrated by Stephen Jay Gould in Chapter 9. You may feel that, if the specialists cannot agree, then anything goes — you can believe whom you want. On the contrary, a point illustrated in many of the following selections is that we should *never* believe scientists. Science is not a matter of belief, but a self-correcting effort to develop workable explanations. We can use the discoveries of scientists only with caution, always aware that their interpretations are tentative and readily modified. Indeed, at any moment, it might be too late even to agree with them, because newer discoveries may have come along

to complement or replace the previous, hard-won knowledge. To some, this uncertainty is overwhelming and discouraging. To many others, including the present writer, it illustrates the excitement of "sciencing," an excitement that I hope you will come to share as you read this volume.

Five hundred years ago, Columbus made a fateful landing in the Caribbean, initiating the history of contact and interaction between the Old and the New World. This meeting of Indian bowmen with cavalry and guns is not properly described as a "culture contact": it was the start of a brutal conquest, assisted by pestilence and genocide. It is timely, so recently after the Quincentennial celebrations of this event, to reflect on the first "Americans" and their independent achievements: this is why many articles on the subject have been included in this reader.

Other articles in the collection are linked by their discussion of some aspect of reciprocity — ecological, economic, or political — which is present and important in all human societies. The discussion of social stratification in several of the articles and the focus on linguistic as opposed to alternative, nonlinguistic modes of communication in the second part of the book also distinguish *Peoples of the Past and Present* from other readers.

Acknowledgments

It is a pleasure to acknowledge my gratitude to the many people who helped me prepare this volume. First, I wish to thank the authors who allowed me to use their work, and their publishers. My students over many years have made insightful comments and raised important questions, which I have attempted to address in this book. I hope that it answers some of their questions, and raises challenging new ones. Anonymous reviewers have done an excellent job; their suggestions and criticisms guided much of my effort. I am particularly grateful to Dr. Gary Crawford of the University of Toronto, whose assistance in the late stages of preparation of the manuscript proved invaluable. Thanks also go to my colleagues at the University of Manitoba, especially Louis Allaire, Haskel Greenfield, Ellen Judd, Gregory Monks, and Hymie Rubenstein, who have read portions of the manuscript and provided many insightful and useful comments. I wish I could also hold them responsible for any mistake or inaccuracy remaining in the text, but I assume complete responsibility for the final manuscript. Finally, I am very grateful to my wife, Ruth Chodkiewicz, whose help and advice contributed so much to bringing this project to its conclusion.

Jean-Luc Chodkiewicz
University of Manitoba

A Note from the Publisher

Thank you for selecting *Peoples of the Past and Present: Readings in Anthropology*, by Jean-Luc Chodkiewicz. The author and publisher have devoted considerable time to the careful development of this book. We appreciate your recognition of this effort and accomplishment.

We want to hear what you think about *Peoples of the Past and Present: Readings in Anthropology*. Please take a few minutes to fill out the stamped reader reply card at the back of the book. Your comments and suggestions will be valuable to us as we prepare new editions and other books.

Brief Contents

Contents

PART TWO
Archaeology

on reviewing that evidence, he finds it unsatisfactory. Several recently discovered dating techniques have enabled researchers to correct faulty estimates and other errors that led to claims of pre-Clovis dates (older than 12,000 years) for some human remains. Owen shows that several dozen archaeological sites provide inconclusive evidence or can be proved to be much more recent than their discoverers had claimed.

18
Dating the First American / 129
PAUL G. BAHN

From *New Scientist*, 20 July 1991
Since 1984, new evidence has fueled the debate about the peopling of the New World. Bahn presents the discoveries of Brazilian archaeologist Niède Guidon, who has found rock art, stone tools, and charcoal samples at Pedra Furada, in Brazil, that date to earlier than 30,000 years ago. In Chile, at the Monte Verde site, Tom Dillehay has found many artifacts, including a stone flake and a core which he claims to be 33,000 years old. Richard MacNeish is also claiming pre-Clovis dates for his latest research site in New Mexico.

19
The Lost Civilization of the Maya / 133
T. PATRICK CULBERT

From *The Lost Civilization: The Story of the Classic Maya*, 1974
A review of previous explanations that attributed the collapse of the Maya civilization to a single major cause, be it overpopulation, warfare, or the breakdown of the long-distance trading system, finds them all wanting. Culbert uses a systems approach to reveal the interacting stresses that increased the frequency and severity of agricultural and political emergencies, until disaster finally struck. He concludes with the suggestion that the failure of the Maya should be a warning to modern civilizations.

20
Rethinking the Quincentennial: Consequences for Past and Present / 138
ALISON WYLIE

From *American Antiquity*, Vol. 57, No. 4, 1992
One important consequence of the conquest of the Americas, started in 1492, is that the

archaeologists reconstructing the history of the Amerindians are not Amerindians, but members of the dominant group. Many archaeological interpretations of past Amerindian cultures betray the political nature of archaeological practice and attest to the need for archaeologists to assume responsibility for the consequences of their work and findings.

21
Pixel Archeology / 141
NEIL McALEER

From *Discover* Magazine, August 1988
Ground-penetrating radar and many remote sensing devices mounted on satellites, planes, and even trucks have made possible the discovery of many important archaeological sites, from biblical sites to previously unknown settlements in the Sahara Desert, the Peruvian Andes, and the mountains of Costa Rica. These new techniques will revolutionize not only archaeological knowledge, but also the ways in which archaeological research is performed.

22
Gender, Politics, and American Archaeology / 145
JULIAN THOMAS

From *Anthropology Today*, Vol. 8, No. 3, June 1992
This review of two recent books suggests that a feminist critique of archaeology reveals it to be a male-dominated profession that has produced conclusions weakened by unverified assumptions about the respective roles of men and women in past societies. We can improve our reconstructions and our understanding of past societies by rejecting processual and ecological approaches, which emphasize the totality of the group and mask the asymmetrical social relations and processes that prevailed within it.

23
Who Owns the Past? / 148
DAVID HURST THOMAS

From *Natural History*, August 1990
This short essay analyzes some of the ethical, cultural, and political implications of the storage and exhibition of cultural artifacts from "have-not" countries in the museums of rich Western countries. The author explains why the demand for universal repatriation must be roundly rejected, and suggests several alternative ways of solving the problem.

have contributed to the formation of that heterogeneous blend that any society calls its "culture."

In spite of the isolation of nuclear families in North American societies, the wealthy and the poor still use extended kinship ties to their advantage.

The Mbuti Pygmies are hunters and gatherers in the tropical forests of Zaire. They hunt collectively for gazelles and the occasional elephant. The author discusses the maintenance and reproduction of the social order in terms of three constraints: dispersion, cooperation, and fluidity. Bands do not have chiefs. Inequality does not exist, and the Mbuti make a systematic effort to avoid all kinds of violence between individuals and between bands. They use a buffoon to draw attention away from serious quarrels, and they abandon guilty individuals to be punished by the forest, which is revered as a god and a life-giver.

This brief sketch of the life and achievements of Soŋi, a "Big Man" (*mumi*) from Bougainville, illustrates vividly the multiple aspects of egalitarian redistribution. Industrious, cunning, and friendless, Soŋi gains respect through calculating, planning, and coaxing and manipulating others to work hard and raise pigs for his feasts. Even the most successful feast in memory is no excuse to rest: the next one will be bigger!

Carneiro defines the state and analyzes the flaws in previous explanations for its emergence, all of them rooted in voluntaristic theories. Only a coercive theory, implying the use of force, is supported by the evidence, but, as Carneiro puts it, "while warfare may be a necessary condition for the rise of the state, it is not a sufficient one." Environmental circumscription is seen as another key condition: people who live in fertile valleys surrounded by mountains, seas, or deserts are prevented from escaping when they are defeated in war; they have no choice but to stay and accept political subordination to the victor. Examples from Peru and Amazonia show the effects of circumscription and other important factors contributing to state formation.

The state is both a provider of public services and a consumer of taxes. Political, religious, and military institutions demand increasing amounts of taxes, and when an economy can no longer support the increases, the state's only alternative is to conquer other states to garner their wealth, thus creating an empire, such as the Tiahuanaco empire of Peru. Overtaxing ultimately results in revolt, the destruction of the empire, and depopulation by starvation. Later, the survivors form villages, then chiefdoms, then states, then an empire, and a new cycle repeats the previous one.

The empires of the Incas in Peru and the Aztecs in Mexico were still thriving when the Spanish conquerors arrived and destroyed them. Carrasco emphasizes the similarities between these two economic and political systems. In both, the economy was politically directed. The Incas had unified their empire, but the Aztecs ruled a federation. In both, the rulers were economically powerful. Both empires comprised a multitude of ethnic groups and many local units, and were ruled by the emperor and his closest relatives.

Poverty is not a state of mind or the result of laziness. Hauch's analysis of Winnipeg's skid row residents reveals the self-perpetuating nature of the poverty of the destitute in affluent North American cities. They work, often hard and under dangerous conditions, in unskilled, casual jobs that are not permitted to become permanent. Their intermittent income forces them to pay daily rates for accommodation, which are far higher than monthly rates, or to endure life-threatening homelessness, even in the harsh Winnipeg winters. The practice of generalized reciprocity constitutes a valuable contribution to their survival, but it also exacts a high price: any windfall gain must be rapidly disbursed to avoid severe punishment for perceived miserliness. The solution comes in the form of apparently irrational drunken binges. Hauch explains how this behavior solves several of the economic and social problems of skid row residents.

themselves; their "exhaust" serves as precious manure and cooking fuel; the labor and the milk they provide are essential to the survival of millions of people. Moreover, their meat *is* consumed, by untouchables and non-Hindus, and herds are culled systematically. The sacredness of zebu cattle allows them to scavenge freely at no cost to their owners. The system is not flawless, but neither is it irrational.

forced acculturation was implemented in the aim of protecting capital in South Africa and pursuing the policy of Apartheid. Dutch Reformed Church missionaries converted large numbers of !Kung to Christianity. !Kung men were recruited to form paramilitary tracking units, and the South African army eventually gained total control of the San. The authors tackle the issue of the role of anthropology in face of such politically determined developments among indigenous peoples.

The poverty and underdevelopment of American Indians were a direct result of the development of the white-controlled national economy. The Bureau of Indian Affairs contributed actively to their poverty through mismanagement, by dealing with symptoms rather than causes, and by encouraging industries to use Indian resources, tax-free. The Indians did not receive the skills, capital, or counsel they would have needed in order to exploit successfully what had not been robbed from them. The Indians have been integrated into the U.S. political economy since they were conquered: That is at the root of their poverty.

A member of the Cree nation explains how it feels to have a dam built in one's backyard. She describes the traditional life of her people, which was conducted in relative harmony with one another and with nature. She then describes the high price that aboriginal people have paid for the hydroelectric megaprojects of recent years, from the loss of land and livelihood to the general dislocation of their society.

In Alaska, where 85 percent of state revenues come from oil and gas fields, the 7000 local Gwich'in succeeded in 1991 in their lobby to defeat a bill supported by the Bush administration to open for oil and gas exploration a large tract of coastal wetland bordering on a vast wildlife refuge. They were aided by the joint efforts of environmentalist and conservationist groups. In the process, they had to re-create long-forgotten political institutions, overcome dissension and animosities in their midst, and, eventually, take their distance from their new allies.

General Introduction: What Is Anthropology All About?

A great deal of romantic lore is attached to the word *anthropology*. For many people, it connotes the most diverse inquiries, from the study of "stones and bones" to the discovery of hidden treasures in the "Temple of Doom" or the tomb of Tutankhamen. Others think of studies of primates, or inquiries into the "sexual life of savages," or magazine articles on exotic rituals of manhood around the world. Many people see anthropology as a quaint sort of study of lost tribes or disappearing peoples, one that is largely irrelevant to the modern world. Most of these misconceptions tend to arise because anthropology is such a vast field of science, and encompasses so many other topics of research.

The term *anthropology* derives from two Greek words that, in combination, mean "the science of man." However, the term *man* is both too general, since it lumps together all kinds of different people, and too specific, since it excludes prehumans and other primates, which are an important subject of study in anthropology. Moreover, the term is sexist. We might better define **anthropology** as the comprehensive and comparative study of past and present human populations and their origins.

Now that we have a satisfactory definition of the term, we should consider what it is that makes anthropology different from other social sciences.

First, the anthropological approach is *comprehensive*: whereas the economist, the psychologist, and the biologist each may study only one aspect of a human population, the anthropologist seeks correlations among all its different aspects. If we were to represent a human population and its social system as a layer cake, as in the accompanying diagram, we could say that, whereas other social scientists each specialize in a single layer of the cake, anthropologists slice through the cake vertically, grasping within one inquiry ecological, economic, social, and ideological facts and interpretations. In other words, whereas other social sciences tend to be more analytical, anthropology strives for a synthesis: it tends to be more **holistic**, that is, to perceive and emphasize the totality, the whole, rather than the details of the parts. Put another way, a holistic approach does not permit the trees to conceal the forest. Holism is not a focus on discrete details, but a method of moving toward a synthesis.

Another important difference between anthropology and other social sciences is that anthropologists do not study only Western industrial societies. Instead, they study many societies distant from us in time (early hominids, first agriculturalists), space (Peruvian Indians, Chinese villagers), and life style (hunters-gatherers, cannibals, societies in which brothers share a wife). This means that anthropologists collect

The Holistic Perspective of Anthropology

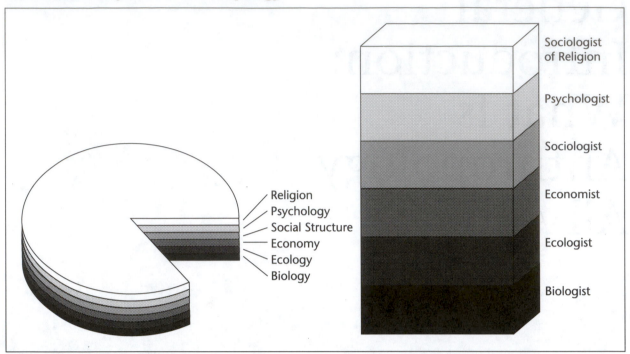

Whereas each of the specialized social sciences deals with "one layer of the pie," anthropologists tend to "cut a whole slice," to show the relationship between the layers.

facts about all kinds of peoples, past and present. Because of the *comparative techniques* they use, anthropologists can make generalizations about humankind that have greater scope and validity than the generalizations made by other social scientists, who do not have the anthropologist's experience of the diversity of human societies and cultures. For example, the social scientists of the past century responsible for such generalizations about "the nature of humankind" as "Humans are naturally aggressive" or "Humans dominate nature" or "Women have a more submissive temperament than men," and for claims concerning the importance of family or religion to human societies, would clearly have benefited from a knowledge of the many ways of being human, the many ways of organizing families, and the many ways of worshiping that have existed throughout the world. Thus, an important and useful characteristic of anthropology is that it involves **cross-cultural comparisons**.

You will notice, especially in the study of biological anthropology and archaeology, that the time frame of anthropology is much greater than that of the other social sciences. Most social scientists, even when they study "change" or "history", deal with only a few years, or a few decades at most. Even historians confine their

interests to a few centuries, and their entire frame of reference is less than 3000 years. Anthropology, however, deals with millions of years. Because of this extended time frame, anthropologists have the advantage of knowing the end result of many different "solutions" to the problems of countless, long-disappeared peoples. Some of these solutions were more successful than others: the past is littered with bones and garbage of failed societies. The better we know these past societies, the less we shall be condemned to repeat their errors. For example, the farmers of California and the Canadian Prairies could learn something of how to avoid economic and ecological disaster from the devastating effects of irrigation in the early agricultural societies of Mesopotamia and from the failure of the Mayan civilization (see Chapter 19). Cross-cultural comparisons reveal correlations among a number of characteristics of each social system, and those correlations suggest hypotheses about predictable interdependencies among certain variables. Out of such evidence arise possible explanations for the presence or absence of certain sociocultural characteristics. One of the first examples of this approach to anthropological analysis was proposed by Edward Tylor, who compared many societies and found a significant correlation between the custom of "mother-in-law avoidance" and the custom that requires a newly married couple to live with the bride's family (Tylor 1889). This sort of cross-cultural comparison among many past and present societies is the anthropological equivalent of the experimental method of the physicists.

These comments are not intended to draw an arrogant or invidious comparison of anthropology with other social sciences: all sciences are important. After all, using a telescope to look at the sky does not negate the importance of using a microscope to see something else. Anthropology is no "better" than any other social science, but it differs from all of them in its scope and objectives. The "panoramic" vision of humankind that is revealed by the anthropological perspective is original and most fascinating. Just as the most common objects look different and more interesting when you observe them through 3-D glasses or through a microscope, so anthropology should help you to see the world around you with new eyes, as a place more exotic and exciting to live in than you had ever imagined.

The subject matter of anthropology is so vast that it has become impossible for any individual anthropologist to analyze, with equal competence, the range of questions it addresses. Few can claim, for example, to be expert in the language of the Papuans, the dentition of *Australopithecus*, genetic polymorphisms, aboriginal creation myths, and the diversity of the rules forbidding incest. Neither superman nor Jack of all trades, an anthropologist tends to specialize, focusing on the study of only certain types of facts and problems related to the general field of anthropology. The scope and the goals of anthropology have expanded to such an extent that it has become futile to even attempt equal competence in all its aspects. Consequently, as the field has expanded, specializations among individual anthropologists have become narrower.

Many modern anthropologists tend to criticize as unrealistic and outmoded the holistic definition of the field proposed in this introduction. At the same time, newly developing fields such as medical anthropology and applied anthropology are superb examples of the kind of original and thought-provoking synthesis anthropologists advocate when they refer to their "holistic" approach. In this age of overspecialization, generalists are needed to "put Humpty-Dumpty back together again." It is often claimed that a specialist is somebody who knows much about very little: overspecialization is often a great obstacle to understanding the major patterns and processes. The holistic, panoramic approach of anthropology is one of its most precious contributions to science and to the planning of the future of our civilizations.

A compromise between the holistic approach and extreme specialization has been achieved by anthropologists subdividing their tasks within the loose boundaries of four main subfields. The accompanying chart shows the four main subdisciplines that result from this division of labor: biological (physical) anthropology, archaeology, linguistic anthropology, and cultural anthropology. These subdisciplines traditionally constituted the four major foci of interest to anthropologists. There are professional associations and journals linked to each of the four fields. The list of the four subfields corresponds to the outline of many textbooks and is reflected in the four main divisions of this reader. As many of the following comments and most of the selected readings will show, the simplistic division of anthropology into only four specialties is a useful first approximation of what anthropology is all about. Nevertheless, it is no longer an accurate description of the training or activities of many modern anthropologists.

Biological anthropology, sometimes referred to as **physical anthropology**, is the study of the evolution of primates, the appearance of the first humans, and the evolution of their diverse biological characteristics. This evolution continues today. More than just a study of old bones (paleontology), biological anthropology studies modern human biology and biological diversity. It is relevant to such contemporary concerns as explaining human biological diversity in ways that expose racist fallacies, discovering the origins and history of certain diseases, or even attempting to compute the shoe sizes of the next generation of soldiers in the armed forces.

Archaeology studies the material remains of the cultures of past human populations. Much like cultural anthropology, and borrowing from its theories and vast database, archaeology is an ethnology — that is, a comparative analysis of the social and cultural characteristics — of past societies. Like detectives, archaeologists catalog, describe, and analyze such evidence as tools, tombs, and garbage. They use these and many other clues to reconstruct the way of life of vanished peoples. Like ethnologists, archaeologists attempt to explain the diversity of cultural systems, the way they may have operated, and the way they changed and eventually disappeared. Furthermore, many of the concerns of cultural anthropologists are shared by archaeologists. Like cultural anthropologists, archaeologists

The Main Subdisciplines of Anthropology

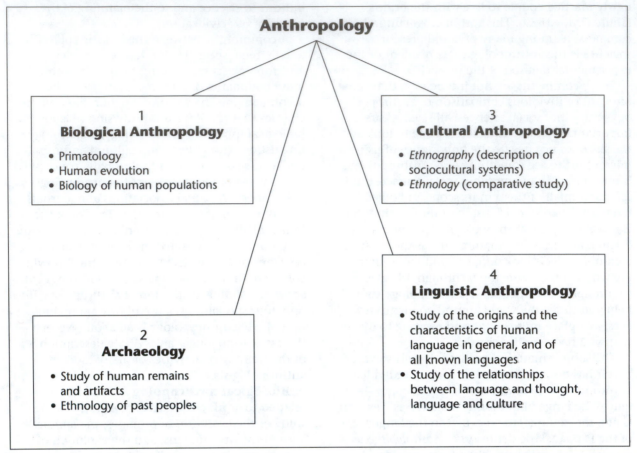

study ecology, social systems, and symbols, and they reflect upon their own cultural biases and theoretical presuppositions. Several chapters in this collection will illustrate how the study of the rise and fall of past societies and civilizations can serve as a cautionary tale relevant to modern political and social concerns.

The rapidly expanding field of **linguistic anthropology** (also known as **anthropological linguistics**) focuses on a defining characteristic of the members of our species: symbolic communication through language. It includes research on the origins of language and universal features of human language. It attempts as well to describe and explain the diversity of human languages and the relationship between language and culture. Some anthropological linguists specialize in the investigation of how and why chimpanzees and human children differ in their learning of linguistic signs; others contribute to research in the rehabilitation of speech impairments; and others still offer their expertise in devising signs that could be understood fifteen thousand years from now by our descendants, to

warn them, for example, of the dangerous radioactive mess that our generation is leaving behind.

Cultural anthropology is the study of the similarities and diversity of contemporary societies. A traditional distinction between **ethnography** — the description of societies — and **ethnology** — the analysis and explanation of social and cultural similarities and differences — has been abandoned by many, on the grounds that any description is inherently also a theoretical commitment, and that the distinction between description and analysis is consequently blurred. This point is discussed in detail in Chapters 20, 22, 31, and 32, which emphasize the distortions often found in "scientific" analyses of other cultures, resulting from the conscious and unconscious theoretical presuppositions and cultural biases of the researchers.

What North Americans call "cultural anthropology" tends to be more holistic in perspective and includes more topics than its British and French equivalent, which is called *social anthropology*. In addition to being a cross-cultural study of economic, social, political, and religious processes and institutions, it includes such specialties as **ecological anthropology**, **medical anthropology**, **applied anthropology**, and the very important field of symbolic anthropology. Symbolic anthropologists attempt to interpret the meanings of a society's beliefs, symbols, and values. **Symbols** are observable objects, sounds, actions, rituals, and so on, that refer to ideas outside themselves; examples include flags that are associated with given countries, the crucifix in Christian religions, and the use of the color black to indicate mourning. The symbols of different cultures differ, and all symbols may simultaneously refer to various different ideas or emotions.

If you have been reading carefully so far, you might be puzzled by an apparent contradiction: *How can anthropologists adopt a holistic approach and specialize at the same time?* Indeed, this is a topic of heated debate among anthropologists. Some argue that since it is impossible to be equally competent in all subdisciplines, we should be realistic and settle for specialization. Others claim that to do so would deprive anthropology of its greatest claim to originality, and that, in any event, "holism" implies a type of approach to research and explanation rather than an equally detailed knowledge of all subdisciplines. The approach and research tools of a biological anthropologist, for example, are not the same as those of a biologist studying the same specimen. This is because anthropologists include in their explanations of the biological adaptations of our ancestors many social and cultural factors, such as food sharing or the use of tools, that would be ignored in a purely biological study. Archaeologists routinely combine data and theory from the biological sciences, soil sciences, nuclear physics, and cultural anthropology, and use results from these disciplines to test many theories about society and culture. In other words, the synthesis of information about all aspects of human existence, from genetics to technology or beliefs, and of the knowledge about them provided by other, more specialized sciences, is an important and original characteristic of anthropology.

Despite the increasing tendency toward specialization among many anthropologists, it is notable that much of the new research in the areas of applied anthropology, medical anthropology, ethnicity, and gender roles, to name a few, exemplifies this kind of disciplinary synthesis. In the October 1992 issue of the *Anthropology Newsletter*, dedicated to the topic of "The Four

Fields: Myth or Reality," the editors invited a debate on the issue, and commented that

> Based on remarks printed throughout this *AN*, American anthropologists still credit the quality of their insights, research and teaching in one field to past and present influences of the remaining three. Trained in one subdiscipline, they still are affected by other parts of the whole. The persistent power of "Holism" continues today as American anthropology's essential and coveted reality. (Givens and Skomal 1992:1)

In fact, this holistic approach involves a panoramic view beyond the narrow borders of cultures and scientific disciplines. and represents anthropology's most original and important contribution to the solution of ecological, medical, social, and other problems. Anthropologists are becoming increasingly interested in the range of possible applications of their knowledge in the solution of practical problems. Superficial observers might consider archaeology, for example, to be too focused on a distant past to be relevant to modern concerns; they might reason that we have progressed so far beyond ancient cultures that they could not possibly have much to teach us. To illustrate that this is not the case, we could mention, among many examples of the contemporary relevance of archaeology, the work of Gomez Pompa and W. Rathje. Gomez Pompa is a Mexican archaeologist who has used his rediscovery of the techniques of cultivation of the Maya to help modern Mexican peasants improve the productivity and sustainability of their agricultural production. At the annual meeting of the American Anthropological Association in December 1992, archaeologist W. Rathje received the S.T. Kimball Award, a prize honoring anthropologists whose work has had an important impact on public policy: Dr. Rathje's systematic analysis of garbage landfills had resulted in legal action against advertisers guilty of misleading advertising because it proved that supposedly biodegradable packaging did not degrade in landfills.

Works Cited

Givens, David B., and Skomal, Susan. N. 1992. "The Four Fields: Myth or Reality?" *Anthropology Newsletter* (American Anthropological Association) 33, no. 7 (October 1992): 1.

Tylor, E.B. 1889. "On a Method of Investigating the Development of Institutions; Applied to Laws of Marriage and Descent." *Journal of the Royal Anthropological Institute* 18: 245–69.

PART ONE
Biological Anthropology

Introduction

An important focus of the subdiscipline of anthropology known as **biological anthropology**, or **physical anthropology**, is the study of human origins — the study of fossilized remains of extinct species in order to trace our lineage. Biological anthropologists also study contemporary nonhuman primates, and unravel the causes for the genetic, somatic, and physiological diversity of past and modern human populations. In addition, they study the interactions of biology with culture. For example, several readings in this section show that biological anthropologists are very much concerned with research on the relationship between genotype and behavior. This issue is relevant to understanding, for instance, why scientific evidence does not support racist stereotypes.

The beginnings of biological anthropology can be traced back to the work of such scholars as Blumenbach and Retzius, who carefully collected and measured many human skulls, starting the important study of **anthropometry** (the measurement of the body). They established racial classifications on the basis of their analysis of the skulls. However, the fundamental theoretical charter of biological anthropology was provided by the work of Alfred Wallace and Charles Darwin. Darwin did not invent the idea of evolution; he used that term very seldom, preferring to discuss what he called "descent with modification." In fact, the sociologist Herbert Spencer, among others, had already elaborated the concept of evolution and made it popular. Darwin borrowed from Spencer the expression "survival of the fittest." Nevertheless, in *The Origin of Species* (1859), Darwin increased scientific as well as popular acceptance and support for this idea by providing detailed and convincing evidence of what we now call evolution and by describing the major process that explains it: adaptation through natural selection. Thus, the "theory of evolution" was born.

Darwin's argument started with the fact that the members of any species of plants or animals do not all live together: they are scattered in groups, and each of these groups adjusts differently to its own particular environmental circumstances. Each of these groups — for example, rainbow trout living in different streams — is composed of individuals who mate with each other much more frequently than they mate with members of any other group: they form what biologists call a **breeding population**. The different populations of a species living in different environments become increasingly distinct from one another as each adjusts to its own specific environment. Since all populations reproduce much

faster than their food supply, many individuals die. Which one will die first — the fittest or the least fit? The mechanism that causes successive generations to be better and better adjusted is a weeding mechanism called **natural selection**, which eliminates the less well adjusted, the less "fit." Fitness is now measured functionally by reproductive success.

The result of all these adjustments, and of the weeding out through natural selection of the less successful ones, is the adaptation of the population to its own, changing environment. **Adaptation** is a random process: it has no goal and no direction. A characteristic that may have been adaptive for millions of years (like the large size of the dinosaurs) may suddenly become maladaptive if the environment changes. The carriers of maladaptive traits tend, statistically, to reproduce less successfully and to die earlier than better-adjusted individuals. A popular misconception that the "fit" have to eliminate the "unfit" can be corrected by pointing out that the measure of adaptive success is *reproductive success*.

The greater the diversity of a population, the greater is the choice for natural selection. When there are many varieties, many can be weeded out, but the possibility remains that at least some will be able to survive the culling process and reproduce. For a choice (selection) to be possible, it is necessary to have a diverse population. Diversity is a key to long-term survival, and natural selection operates on this diversity: it does not create it. Selection is simply the "culling of the herd," a random and opportunistic process. What was adaptive yesterday may become extremely maladaptive tomorrow, if the environment of that population changes, even in very subtle ways. Adaptation is only a momentary success, at best. If all the populations of a given species fail to adapt, that species becomes extinct. In fact, the majority of plant and animal species known to scientists are extinct.

The environment of a population is always changing: the climate may become colder or drier; other populations — competitors or pests — may be introduced; volcanic eruptions, fires, or floods may modify radically the chances of survival of populations that had been successful in that environment for a long time. Think about it: The very existence of humans in their present form is a result of chance associations of our ancestors with particular environmental circumstances. And those ancestors owed *their* very existence to the success of mammals on earth, which is linked to the extinction of dinosaurs, an event now explained by some scientists as the result of the chance collision of earth with a meteor! The point is that because all environments are always changing, no population is ever fully adapted: at any given time, it is either adapting or on its way to extinction. Shakespeare was wrong: The question, for anything alive, is "*To become* or not to be?"

Don't Believe Scientists!

Evolution is a theory, not a dogma. Scientists don't believe in it, and don't want you to, because, like any other scientific theory, although it represents the most satisfactory explanation so far, it is nonetheless subject to constant testing, revision, and refinement. Since Darwin, the theory of evolution has been altered dramatically by the introduction of genetics, which describes mechanisms for the transmission of existing characteristics and the emergence of new ones (recombination, mutations). More recently, biologists have also challenged the Darwinian notion that evolutionary changes are gradual. On the contrary, they argue, evolution is marked by long periods of stability followed by sudden and dramatic changes. This is the theory of **punctuated equilibrium**, of which S.J. Gould (Chapters 5 and 9) is an ardent proponent. The meteor that caused the dinosaurs to become extinct is an example of the kind of factor that can "punctuate" a period of equilibrium. Although it is constantly being updated and refined, the theory of evolution remains the fundamental basis of biological research. It has no valid *scientific* alternative.

Since the publication in 1859 of Darwin's *The Origin of Species*, controversy has greeted the theory of evolution in some religious circles. Some students perceive a contradiction between their religious beliefs and the basic scientific claim that modern human beings are animals who have evolved slowly from other animal species. A vocal minority of fundamentalist Christians now claims to have found in so-called creation science a sound and biblically correct alternative to the theory of evolution.

Belief and theory represent extremely different kinds of knowledge, distinguished by the kind of evidence that supports them. A belief is a subjective feeling of certainty that rests ultimately on the acceptance of a revelation. Beliefs are empirically untestable. Scientific theories are logical constructs that are intersubjectively agreed upon. They tie observations made in accordance with arbitrary rules of evidence into a web of causal connections. Religion and science adhere to different definitions of "truth," and their claims are supported by different kinds of evidence. Therefore, they cannot contradict each other, any more than two people broadcasting their opinions on different radio wavelengths can be said to be having an argument.

Scientists do not "believe" in the theory of evolution: they just agree that it is the best proven explanation for the diversity, the origins, and the changes characteristic of plant and animal species. Many of the following readings make clear that "sciencing" often requires a critical reevaluation of accepted facts and theories. Unlike beliefs, scientific theories are constantly and vigorously being challenged, without blasphemy. Mutual scrutiny and criticism among scientists are the sources of new discoveries and of the refinement of understanding that, with some self-indulgence, we call scientific "progress." Jared Diamond's "Voyage of the Overloaded Ark" (Chapter 1) demonstrates that the so-called creation science does not accept the rules of evidence and criticism that are fundamental to the scientific method, and does not explain even the facts that it accepts. The ark would have to have been gigantic to hold all the millions of species of cockroaches, chipmunks, dinosaurs, and so on, in the world, not to speak of what would have been an enormous food supply. Creationism is not just bad science: ironically, most leaders of the Jewish and Christian faiths also reject creation science as a distortion of the Bible.

We might also learn a lesson from another significant attack on the theory of evolution, made in the USSR during the 1930s by Soviet agronomist Trofim Lysenko, a charlatan who became Stalin's protégé and gained control over agriculture in the Soviet Union. Under his regime, the teaching of evolution and genetics in schools and universities was punished by deportation to Siberia. He denied the existence of genes and rejected "bourgeois" Darwinism in favor of the Lamarckian doctrine of the inheritability of acquired characteristics. Lysenko applied these beliefs to the "research" he directed in the aim of improving agricultural production. The countries that constituted the former USSR are only now recovering from the resulting backwardness in biological sciences; the crippling effects of Lysenko's ignorance on their agricultural production, however, are still being felt.

"A Giant Step for Mankind"

One of the primary mandates of biological anthropology is to explore human **phylogeny**, that is, our links with the rest of the animal kingdom. Until recently, guesses about the similarity and relatedness of different fossil forms were based mostly on comparisons of the shape of the bones that were left behind for anthropologists by scavengers and by many biological, chemical, and physical agents of decay. More recently, great advances in biology, notably in genetics, have provided invaluable information — information of a different order than subjective opinion about whether skull X resembles skull Y, both of which are broken and missing big pieces! It is thanks to contemporary analyses of genetic material, for example, that we know that only 1 or 2 percent of our genetic material is different from that of a chimpanzee.

The study of **primates** in their native habitats by researchers who have spent years living in their company has generated findings that contradict nearly every "scientific" statement made on the subject before these intensive field studies were undertaken. During the past few decades, work in the field of *primatology* has progressed considerably as a result of the concerted efforts, the courage, and the ingenuity of various researchers. The work of Jane Goodall and her associates among the chimpanzees of the Gombe National Park in Tanzania revealed those animals' ability to manufacture and use tools, as well as their frequent hunting expeditions and other important protocultural achievements. The tragic end of Dian Fossey focused international attention on her study and protection of mountain gorillas, whose only enemies are human. Biruté Galdikas, like Goodall and Fossey, was encouraged and financed by the famous paleoanthropologist Louis Leakey. She conducted a long study of the orangutans of Borneo (see Chapter 2). At a time when researchers are hypothesizing that orangutans are descended from *Sivapithecus*, making them more relevant to the study of human evolution, Galdikas has provided us with revolutionary insights into their physiology and behavior.

The hunt for fossils is far from over, as you will discover in "Lucy and the First Family" (Chapter 3); in fact, it has just begun. Most of the fossil species named and discussed in your textbooks are known only by fragments of scattered specimens. The luck and glory of Donald Johanson was to find not only the most complete skeleton (40 percent) of a hominid fossil, but also the very oldest skeleton of an **australopithecine** to be found to that date. Because the skeleton was so complete, much of the usual guesswork was taken out of the interpretation. According to Johanson, a crucial discovery was that Lucy was unmistakably bipedal: ironically, the first documented "giant step for mankind" was actually taken by a dwarf-sized hominid less than four feet (1.22 m) tall when she died, more than three million years ago.

Lucy was the first great find by Johanson's team, but their further discovery of a group of a dozen or more individuals, dubbed "the First Family,"

increased considerably our knowledge of ***Australopithecus afarensis***, because it provided concrete evidence of the differences between individuals resulting from sex and age variation. At that time, we knew much more about the skeleton of *Australopithecus afarensis* than about that of the more recent ***Homo erectus***. This was true until 1983, when the rivals of Johanson, the Leakey team, found a nearly complete skeleton of *Homo erectus* (KNM-WT 15000), near the western shore of Lake Turkana, in Kenya.

New technologies and discoveries in other sciences, such as physics, provide new tools for the analysis and interpretation of fossils, and for increasingly precise and reliable dating. We must always remember that "facts" cannot prove or disprove a theory. All scientific facts are **artifacts**: they never speak for themselves, and the information squeezed out of them is defined largely by our techniques of observation and by the questions we ask. In Chapter 4, Pat Shipman provides a telling example of the use of the electron scanning microscope to analyze the marks left on bones by our prehuman ancestors and other predators. This new evidence suggests that our ancestors were not hunters and killer apes: most of their meat was obtained by scavenging the leftovers of other predators better suited anatomically to hunt and kill. This kind of evidence is important for understanding the weakness of the claim that we are descendants of killer apes, a fallacy that is exposed by David Pilbeam in Chapter 7.

The next two articles illustrate again how the way we frame our questions predetermines the scope of our answers. The topics of the essays, by Stephen Jay Gould (Chapter 5) and Richard Klein (Chapter 6), overlap in their discussion of Neandertals (for an explanation of the variant spellings Neandertal/Neanderthal, see page 42 in Chapter 5). Their conclusions are compatible, but their different approaches illustrate the variety of techniques, methods, and insights that contribute to advances in the field of paleoanthropology. Together, they illustrate the saga of the position assigned to Neandertals in our ancestry: it is a story as full of twists and surprises as the best thriller. And the story is far from finished: in 1989, new Neandertal remains were found in France. These remains were closely associated with artifacts of the Chatelperronian, a culture that had, until 1989, been described as early Upper Paleolithic, produced by modern humans. Now, we must reclassify the Chatelperronian as a late Middle Paleolithic culture. Such discoveries frequently force archaeologists and biological anthropologists to reconsider their most cherished theories. Klein bases his argument on archaeological evidence, which suggests to him that about 40,000 years ago there was an abrupt shift in the behavior and culture of **Homo sapiens**, which he explains as probably a result of the changes in brain size and organization that separated modern humans from Neandertals.

Klein's essay does not discuss the main contentions of the geneticists led by the late Alan C. Wilson who proposed the *"African Eve" hypothesis.* Analysis of mitochondrial DNA, which is inherited from the mother alone, supports the hypothesis of African monogenesis — that is, that all modern humans are descended from African ancestors who lived about 200,000 years ago. One implication of that analysis is that Neandertals should be viewed not as our ancestors, but as distant cousins — a separate species. Another implication is that the biological diversity of modern human populations may be the result of very recent processes.

Nevertheless, serious objections to the African Eve hypothesis have recently surfaced, suggesting that the computations were skewed by the manner in which the computers were programmed: loading the data in a different order leads to different results, and the margin of error is so large that the results are not very useful anyway. The validity of these objections is accepted by prominent researchers, and suggests that yet another promising hypothesis will have to be adjusted to the facts.

Nature or Nurture?

You have learned so far that humans are animals, subject to all the laws of biology, and closely related to other primate species. You may have been reassured by the molecular biologists' claim that you missed being a chimp by nearly 2 percent of your genes, but don't rejoice too soon: there have been a number of bestsellers, such as Konrad Lorenz's *On Aggression* (1966) and Robert Ardrey's *African Genesis* (1961), suggesting that we are just apes who lost their body hair but kept their instincts for aggression, male dominance, and territoriality.

David Pilbeam points out in Chapter 7 that there are no facts to support the conclusions of Lorenz and Ardrey. The rigid enactment of genetic programs for male dominance, aggression, or territoriality presupposed by these authors is simply not observed in most interactions of monkeys and apes made in carefully controlled studies. These books slander the apes, whose patterns of behavior are mostly learned and mostly cooperative, and whose acts of aggression or submission toward members of their own species are mostly ritualized. All recent scientific studies of our primate relatives indicate that the contrast between "nature" (instinct) and

"nurture" (learned behavior) is not a valid one. It is not even useful for describing the animal realm, where many patterns of behavior, from bird songs to tool use by chimpanzees, are *transmitted* or *modified* by learning. Why should we attribute to human beings instincts more fixed and overwhelming than those of chimpanzees and gorillas? In fact, most anthropologists would agree that humans possess no behavior that is entirely fixed in their genes: humans have no instincts.

Many social scientists of the nineteenth century were racists. Not only did they divide existing human populations into so-called racial categories, but they also explained the diversity of cultures, social systems, and even psychological traits on this basis. Among them, we could mention the influential British anthropologists J.C. Pritchard and W. Lawrence, the German philosopher F. Hegel, the French sociologist A. Comte, and the French orientalist and philosopher Count J.A. de Gobineau (see Harris 1968, ch. 4, for more details). Advances in our scientific methodology, along with many discoveries in biology, helped anthropologists become champions of the opposite position — specifically, that the term *race*, in its popular meaning, is inaccurate and misleading in relation to humans. Racial classifications (like the ones you may have studied in junior high school) are based on **phenotype** — body size and proportions, skin color, hair type, and so on. By contrast, the scientific definition of race is based on **genotype** — the genetic potential of individuals, expressed only in part in their phenotype — and anthropologists have shown that this scientific definition of race cannot be applied to any human population.

Boyce Rensberger's essay (Chapter 8) demonstrates that the distribution throughout the world of biological traits, such as skin color or nose shape, is not random, and that it is best explained as a result of natural selection. Furthermore, biologists have discovered that for any specific trait, there is more variation among members of a so-called race than there is between separate "races." All humans are equally human, and the few, rather superficial differences among the body shapes and physiologies of contemporary human populations do not overlap precisely (for example, the distribution of nose shapes and skin colors among world populations do not coincide), and are certainly not explained by racial classifications. Race is a scientifically useless and socially dangerous four-letter word when it is applied to humans. However, it is also important to note that modern geneticists and other biologists hotly contest the notion of "hybrid vigor," which Rensberger defends here. At one time, there was a consensus among biologists in favor of this notion, but it is no longer considered a valid explanation.

We should also add to Rensberger's argument that if human races do not exist in a biological sense, they are nonetheless very important social realities. Racism is a social phenomenon, with social causes and painful consequences. It is thriving, despite its illegality, in Canada and the United States, where subtle discrimination and some spectacular incidents bring it to public consciousness from time to time. For millions of North Americans, racial discrimination is a painful reality that shapes their life expectancy, their job opportunities, their social status. For them, the knowledge that "races are dangerous myths" is of little consolation.

The fundamental errors of fact and reasoning of the biological determinists, be they "naked-apers" or racists, are explored with wit and clarity by Stephen J. Gould in his bestselling book *The Mismeasure of Man*. The conclusion of that book is included here as Chapter 9, and it constitutes a particularly valuable addition for its discussion of the methodological issues involved in the debate.

The bulk of the chapter focuses the reader's attention on yet another variant of biological determinism — **sociobiology** — which claims that the behavior of individuals is naturally selected to maximize their genetic contribution to the next generation. Since 1975, when E.O. Wilson popularized the theory in his *Sociobiology: The New Synthesis*, it has been adopted, usually in modified form, by many social scientists and biologists. A well-known Canadian supporter of sociobiology is psychologist Philippe Rushton of the University of Western Ontario (Rushton and Sorrentino 1981). In an address to the American Association for the Advancement of Science (Rushton 1989), which condensed several of his publications, Rushton claimed that approximately 50 percent of the variance in individual differences for both intelligence and personality is attributable to genetic makeup; that current evidence indicates that the races diverged at different times from common ancestors; and that the brains of Orientals, whites, and blacks differ in weight and volume. He claims further that blacks have a more uninhibited temperament and are more aggressive than members of the other races, but score lower in terms of technological development and family stability. Needless to say, serious anthropologists contradict every one of Rushton's claims. His use of the term *race* is without any scientific basis, as it is loosely applied to undefined populations (see Chapter 8), and most of his analysis also confuses the effects of race with the effects of racism. Of course, not all sociobiologists

support or even sympathize with Rushton's extreme position, a **racist** interpretation of the implications of sociobiological theory. But perhaps they are simply less consistent than Rushton: after all, the focus of sociobiology *is* the genetic determination of behavior.

This is the question that Gould addresses. He points to sociobiology's assumption that natural selection explains the origin and maintenance of specific adaptive behaviors, which are transmitted genetically. Examples of the "specific" patterns of behavior supposedly controlled by this genetic imperative include aggression, homosexuality, altruism, and spite. Gould compares this approach to explaining the fall of cannon balls by their "cannonballness" and the fall of feathers by their "featherness," rather than looking for an explanation at a higher, more general level, in the law of gravity. In human populations, natural selection favors the flexibility of behavior and its adaptability to different circumstances, rather than blind repetition of ancestral patterns. It is this requirement for flexibility and adaptability that explains why we have such a large and complex brain. Most of the behavioral traits discussed by sociobiologists were probably never subject to direct natural selection. Furthermore, human behavior patterns are constantly altered as a result of playful tinkering and experimentation and do not exhibit, in any society, the rigid predetermination assumed by sociobiologists. Gould expresses this point in his discussion of **neoteny**, the retention in adulthood of infantile characteristics. Neoteny, among other human characteristics, shows that humans remain basically children: playful, curious, and learning animals. (Neoteny is the retention in adulthood of more generalized and earlier characteristics of infants or fetuses of the same species or an ancestral species.)

In Chapter 10, a short essay on the career of the biological anthropologist Clyde Snow illustrates the applications of the methods and techniques of anthropology in the subdiscipline of forensic anthropology. This fast-paced story of many spectacular discoveries might inspire a vocation in the amateur sleuths among you. The point that should be emphasized is that the skills and techniques that helped to identify Josef Mengele and other criminals (the accuracy of those techniques was confirmed by DNA analysis in 1991) were used to describe Lucy and to reconstruct the face of Tutankhamen. In short, biological anthropology offers a great variety of research and career opportunities. Another example of the versatility and scope of the discipline is given in Chapter 11, which recounts the results of expeditions by Canadian forensic anthropologist Owen Beattie and arctic archaeologist James Savelle to King William Island to recover and analyze remains from the Franklin expedition of 1848. The two ships and 129 members of that expedition were lost during a search for the Northwest Passage. Beattie's team was able to confirm the tales of cannibalism connected with the tragedy, but also discovered proof that the members of the expedition had received lead poisoning from the solder in their food containers. They speculated that the poisoning probably contributed to the men's erratic behavior and subsequent death. The sophistication and detail of the results obtained on the basis of a few, scattered remains from a tragedy that took place nearly one and a half centuries ago explains the great demand for forensic anthropologists in criminal and accident investigations.

Works Cited

Ardey, R. 1961. *African Genesis: A Personal Investigation into the Animal Origins and Nature of Man*. New York: Atheneum.

Harris, M. 1968. *The Rise of Anthropological Theory*. New York: Crowell.

Lorenz, K. 1966. *On Aggression*. New York: Harcourt, Brace & World.

Rushton, J.P. 1989. "Evolutionary Biology and Heritable Traits (with reference to Oriental-White-Black Differences)." American Association for the Advancement of Science, Annual Meeting, San Francisco, 14–19 Jan. 1989.

Rushton, J.P., and R.M. Sorrentino, eds. 1981. *Altruism and Helping Behavior: Social, Personality, and Developmental Perspectives*. Hillsdale: Lawrence Erlbaum Associates, Publishers.

Wilson, E.O. 1975. *Sociobiology: The New Synthesis*. Cambridge, MA: Harvard University Press.

1
Voyage of the Overloaded Ark

JARED DIAMOND

"This monkey mythology of Darwin's is the cause of permissiveness, promiscuity, pills, prophylactics, perversions, pregnancies, abortions, pornotherapy, pollution, poisoning, and proliferation of crimes of all types."

That denunciation of Darwin wasn't thundered from the pulpit by an apoplectic (and alliterative) Victorian cleric in the first flush of outrage over evolution. Nor is its source the closing statement of William Jennings Bryan at the Scopes "monkey trial" in 1925. The words are those of Braswell Deen, presiding judge of the Georgia court of appeals, as propounded in lectures to law students, civic clubs, and church groups over the past five years. What has stirred him to such injudicious bombast?

An age-old argument about the ultimate mystery — the origin of the world, especially of living creatures, including ourselves. All peoples have their creation "myths." Ours is the Book of Genesis.

Most Americans interpret the Old Testament account symbolically, and accept the view of scientists that life sprang from inanimate matter, that modern species evolved from predecessors that became extinct, and that we're descended from an ape-like ancestor — "Darwin's monkey."

Yet in spite of the preponderance of evidence, a significant minority of Americans finds these conclusions anathema. To them, Genesis represents literal truth. According to a recent Gallup poll, nearly half of all Americans, including a quarter of all college graduates, believe that the world began 10,000 years ago, and that the simultaneous formation of man and all other species occurred soon thereafter. The most articulate spokesmen for this view assert it to be a scientific theory, which they term "creation science."

The debate over creation science has waxed and waned since 1859, when Charles Darwin published *Origin of Species*, and has heated up again in the past twenty years. It's not just a polite armchair discussion about beliefs, but a full-scale donnybrook that's being fought at school board meetings, in state legislatures, and in the courts. Creationists are demanding equal treatment for creation science and evolution in the classroom, and insist that textbooks either drop any mention of evolution or treat it as merely "a theory." Although the statutes were later tossed out as unconstitutional, Arkansas (in 1982) and Louisiana (1985) passed laws requiring equal teaching of creationism and evolution.

Scientists insist that creation science isn't science at all but disguised religious belief seeking illegal entry into our schools. Persuaded by an anti-creationist counteroffensive, Texas last year

From *Discover* Magazine, June 1985, pp. 82–92. © 1985 Discover Magazine. Reprinted with permission.

rescinded a creationist-inspired law requiring that biology texts carry a disclaimer to the effect that "evolution is treated as theory rather than fact." Still, several textbooks submitted by publishers for use in Texas schools this year have the cautionary words, and some make no mention of evolution at all. Teachers who unapologetically describe invisible atoms and the earth's revolution about the sun routinely waffle about evolution.

The stakes in this legal struggle are enormous. If the creationists are right, our children are being misled with shaky scientific theory masquerading as fact. Worse yet, morality is being undermined, since adherence to the Bible's ethical precepts, Judge Deen and other creationists believe, hinges on an acceptance of its literal correctness. If scientists are right, our children are being denied instruction in the central concept of the biological sciences, and their training for possible careers in agriculture and medicine is being jeopardized, as is America's international leadership in these areas.

Overlooked by both sides in this bitter struggle, forgotten by all but a few specialists, is creation science's venerable history, which may offer valuable lessons for our time. From the rise of modern biology in the 1600s until Darwin's day, almost all scientists believed that species were created by God, in part because of the scientists' intellectual heritage, in part because the evidence for a different view was still weak. And for two centuries, Europe's keenest minds valiantly and imaginatively tried to preserve the essentials of the biblical account in the face of disconcerting new evidence — until by the end of the nineteenth century their efforts finally collapsed.

The first of the great creation scientists was Athanasius Kircher (1602–1680), a German Jesuit who wrote some thirty learned books about everything from hieroglyphs to magnets. Like his contemporaries, he regarded Genesis not as a metaphor but as fact. Kircher was sure that science could only strengthen the faithful in their beliefs by making clear the ways in which the Lord worked his miracles.

As part of this noble effort, Kircher carefully examined the story of Noah's ark, calculating in exhaustive detail how the vessel must have been designed. From the ark's dimensions given in Genesis (300 cubits, which he interpreted as 450 feet), Kircher computed how many animals it might hold — after duly subtracting space for aisles, stairways, and ventilation hatches. He postulated three decks, each capable of contain-

ing three hundred stalls, some big enough to accommodate elephants. The top deck, or Ornithotropheion (from the Greek for bird storage area), held the birds, plus Noah and his family; the middle deck, or Bromatodocheion (food area), supplies; and the lower deck, or Zootropheion (animal area), the rest of the animals.

Ignoring fish and other creatures that didn't need an ark to survive the flood, Kircher proceeded to list all the rest of the animals he knew: about 130 kinds of mammals, 150 birds, and 30 snakes. He worked out the provisions they would require: smoked meat and chickens to feed the carnivores, grain and hay for the herbivores, seeds and berries for the birds, straw for bedding, and water. Noah and his three sons, along with their families, shared a kitchen and dining room, but they would need separate bedrooms. The manifest included bread and butter, oats and barley, and many other kinds of food for a journey that might last a year (Noah couldn't have known he would be afloat for only forty days and forty nights). In addition, Kircher provided the ark with ropes, tools, cloth, candles, and whatever else Noah might need to rebuild civilization when the ark came to rest.

For its time, the design of Kircher's ark represented a sophisticated application of the scientific method. He began with a specified set of assumptions (the ark's biblical dimensions, the number of crew and passengers, and their requirements for a year's voyage). He worked out the mathematical consequences (the necessary space and provisions), then compared these detailed predictions with reality. For Kircher, the Genesis account of Noah's ark was scientifically plausible.

In 1669 the Danish physician Nicholas Steno discovered specific evidence in support of a great flood. He found soil deposits in Italy similar to sediments on the sea floor, suggesting that what was now dry land may once have been inundated. Steno and the English scientist Robert Hooke independently recognized that fossils were remains of living animals that might have perished in the deluge. Most impressive of all, fossil seashells were discovered far inland, even atop mountains, which strengthened the belief that the whole earth had once been under water.

A serious problem soon developed, however. As Europeans explored Australia and the New World, they discovered enormous numbers of unknown species, from kangaroos and tapirs to hummingbirds. By the time Carl Linnaeus (1707–1778), the father of modern taxonomy, finished listing all creatures known to him, he had 15,000, including more than 40 times the number of large animals known to Kircher (today's estimate: 30 million species). Noah and his sons clearly couldn't house, feed, and tend this menagerie. Sadly, creation scientists watched the overloaded ark sink under its own weight.

Nevertheless, the eighteenth century's inventive creation scientists came up with ways of preserving the rest of Genesis. Linnaeus, a devout Swedish Protestant who viewed himself as the "publisher and interpreter of the wisdom of God," was also a superb biologist. He realized that mountains like snow-capped Kilimanjaro, rising from the hot African plains, were in effect miniature worlds. Tropical species live in the savannas at their bases. Temperate species dwell in the cool forests at higher elevations, and arctic ones in the cold tundra below the mountain's snow fields. Linnaeus reasoned that the Paradise where species were created was a high mountain — not Kilimanjaro but probably the biblical Mount Ararat. Each species could have been created in a suitable climate, at various elevations, and then have made its way to a part of the earth where it could live in comfort. With this script, Linnaeus salvaged the rest of Genesis, even while scuttling the ark.

Alas, Linnaeus's theory had its own fatal weaknesses. How could animals survive the rigors of changing climes while dispersing round the world from their mountain origin? Could reindeer setting out from Mount Ararat's snowy summit have made it to Lapland, across miles of hot desert, without dropping dead of heatstroke? And if animals really were created in pairs, as Genesis has it, how would they have survived predators? Wouldn't the first pair of lions have eaten the first pair of deer, then feasted on the first pair of zebra, then gobbled up all the other weaker animals as well, until the lions themselves starved to death?

These difficulties persuaded creation scientists to abandon another element of Genesis: a single center of creation. In its place, they devised multiple centers for the beginnings of life, an idea cogently set forth by the naturalist Eberhard Zimmermann in 1777. He had each animal created in the part of the globe where it now lives, with a full supply of food on hand. But just how many centers had God required? And where? As plant and animal specimens from all over the world came flooding into Europe, patterns emerged. Australia and New Guinea shared kangaroos, cassowaries, and eucalyptus trees, while South and Central America both had howler monkeys, toucans, and electric eels. By 1857 the British ornithologist Philip Sclater had divided the world into six biogeographical regions that he identified as the six centers of creation. So sound was his analysis that biogeographers today still recognize the same six regions, although they're now thought to reflect the changes in the earth's configuration caused by continental drift, which isolated groups of animals from one another, as well as to reflect movements of species and the birth of new ones, rather than being sites of a Genesis-type creation.

There was still worse news to come for creation scientists dismayed to learn that God had created life at six different locations. Many species were found to occur in two or more regions separated by impassable barriers. Moose, for instance, are just one of hundreds of species native to both Europe and North America (did God create them at the same time on opposite sides of the Atlantic?). In the American West, the little Uinta chipmunk lives in pine forests on the tops of 18 mountains. The territories are isolated by deserts in which the rodent couldn't possibly survive. Did God so love this chipmunk that he made it simultaneously in 18 places? If creation scientists could believe that the same species was created in many remote places, would they also claim that it was created at many separate times? The thought of God frantically churning out millions of species at billions of times and places made the whole theory of creation implausibly exhausting.

In 1846 the deeply religious British geologist Edward Forbes rescued creation science from this crisis with a brilliant argument. He realized there was considerable evidence that many parts of the earth were once covered by glaciers and that continents were linked in the past by so-called land bridges. Thus, if Europe and North America were formerly joined, he argued, a pair of moose created on either continent or even on the land bridge itself could have multiplied and its offspring could have wandered to the other continent before the link subsided beneath the sea. Similarly, in glacial times, the pine forests now confined to the cool tops of Utah's mountains had spread throughout a region that is now hot desert. Through these vanished forests, the progeny of the original pair of Uinta chipmunks scampered up their individual mountains, where they thrive today. In short, a single act of creation might have sufficed for each species, after all.

Forbes's clever theory won him a chair at Edinburgh University and the presidency of the British Geological Society. It also scooped Darwin, who had conceived a similar theory but failed to publish it quickly enough. (The cautious Darwin nearly repeated the error when he dawdled over putting his theory of evolution into print until Alfred Russel Wallace was about to publish a like idea.)

But the problems for creation science continued to grow. Sediments and fossils, whose discovery at first seemed to confirm the Genesis deluge, were proving more complicated. There wasn't just one covering of sediment, but many layers. Creationist geologists gave each the names we still use today: the Carboniferous, Triassic, Eocene, Pleistocene, to cite a few. Also, each layer contained a different set of fossils: dinosaurs in the Triassic, mammoths in the Pleistocene, and so on. The logical conclusion was that there had been a whole series of creations, and that the products of each one were swept away by a flood before the next. This theory appeared in its definitive form in a long preface that Harvard zoology professor Louis Agassiz wrote for his 1857 book *Contributions to the Natural History of the United States of America.*

But Agassiz couldn't even convince his fellow creation scientists. Geologists already knew that fossils aren't scattered at random in the strata at a given site. The deepest, and presumably oldest, layers hold the stony remains of such bizarre species as trilobites, while the uppermost, and youngest, contain fossils quite similar to modern species, like cave bears and the elephant-like mastodon. Here was evidence of a progression, from primitive creatures early in the earth's history to today's more complex ones.

Still more evidence for change came from the fossils dug up in a particular region, which often resembled the animals found in the area today. In Australia, fossils dating to the Pleistocene (the geological era immediately before the present) include the remains of giant kangaroos. In Asia, similarly aged beds contain mammoths. No one has ever found a fossil kangaroo in Asia or a mammoth relic Down Under (although fossil mammoths are so common in Asia that diggers once made selling tusks a big business). As the British essayist Robert Chambers wrote in 1844, it's absurd and degrading to expect God "to interfere personally and specially on every occasion when a new shellfish or reptile was to be ushered into existence."

Darwin helped sort out the confusion. First he convinced people of the fact of evolution. Second, he offered a theory, natural selection, to explain what causes it. Marshaling geological and fossil evidence, he showed that animals of each era were descendants of those of previous eras;

the ancestors of today's creatures, for example, are found in the fossils of the Pleistocene. Similarly, Darwin realized that there's a hierarchical relationship among living species. Species can be classified by their anatomy into closely related groups (genera), which can in turn be grouped into families, orders, classes, phyla, and kingdoms. The evidence is plain: we look a lot like chimpanzees, and progressively less like monkeys, leopards, fish, oysters, and cabbages.

Darwin's *Origin of Species* assembled this evidence so compellingly that within a decade almost all creation scientists accepted the fact of evolution. Darwin's theory of natural selection was slower to win acceptance, and its details are still debated today. It can be summarized as follows: Individual animals produce many offspring, but limitations of food and space, as well as predators, mean that only some survive. Occasionally variations occur in some offspring — Darwin didn't know why — that may enhance their ability to survive. These fitter creatures pass their characteristics (the concept of genes wasn't known in Darwin's day) to the next generation, which are therefore also better equipped to survive. Virtually all biologists agree with Darwin that natural selection accounts at least partly for evolution, although other factors may contribute as well.

Clearly, evolution didn't suddenly pop up as a theory put forth by cynical atheists seeking to undermine the Bible. On the contrary, it evolved from a literal belief in Genesis, as devout creationists tried to grapple with disturbing new evidence. By the time Darwin died, in 1883, his views had become sufficiently palatable to orthodox Christians that his body was honored by burial in Westminster Abbey.

Who, then, are the people who still deny the fact of evolution, who call themselves creation scientists and demand that textbooks give equal treatment to evolution and their creation science? Modern creationism is usually traced back to 1961, when John Whitcomb, a professor of the Old Testament at Grace Theological Seminary in Winona Lake, Indiana, and Henry Morris, a hydraulic engineer then at the Virginia Polytechnic Institute, published a book called *The Genesis Flood*, claiming that scientific evidence supported a literal view of Genesis.

Unlike their predecessors, most of today's creationists are based outside major universities, government, and industry. They usually operate under the aegis of private universities and institutes with Fundamentalist backing. The leading creationist publishing center is the Institute for Creation Research (ICR), which has been affiliated with Christian Heritage College and supported by the Scott Memorial Baptist Church. All three are located in the San Diego area. Morris is ICR's director, and its associate director is Duane Gish, a professor of natural science at Christian Heritage and an enthusiastic public defender of creationism. Competing creationist organizations include the Creation Science Research Center, San Diego; the Creation Research Society, Ann Arbor, Michigan; and the Bible-Science Association, Minneapolis.

The rival groups sound similar themes: that the earth is young; that out of nothing God suddenly created species, or the basic kinds of plants and animals now existing; that these species have remained more or less fixed, and no new ones have arisen since then; and that God created species by processes, called "special creation," that are no longer operating and so can't be investigated scientifically. Central to creationist ideology is a worldwide flood and Noah's ark.

Most creationists accept a figure for the age of the earth only slightly greater than that arrived at by the seventeenth-century English Old Testament scholar John Lightfoot. Using the ages of the patriarchs listed in Genesis, he calculated the exact moment of Adam's creation as 9 A.M., Friday, September 17, 4004 B.C.[1]

Creationists do a small amount of field research aimed at supporting the Genesis account. Within the past year, three competing teams have been seeking the remains of Noah's ark on Mount Ararat, on the Turkish–Soviet border: an ICR team; a High Flight Foundation team, led by former astronaut James Irwin; and an International Expeditions team, whose claim last August to have discovered the ark's resting place was ridiculed by the other groups. A March 1985 pamphlet published by ICR ("Acts and Facts") describes an expedition seeking evidence for living dinosaurs in Africa. The motivation for this search is "the tremendous impact the discovery of living dinosaurs would have on the evolution world view" (Discover, March).

What most disappoints me about today's creationists is their ignorance of their great predecessors, from Kircher to Agassiz. I had assumed that modern creationists would surely know the best arguments supporting their opinions, and that they would use biological discoveries since Darwin to build even stronger arguments. But no; they rarely cite the classical literature of creation science — if they're even

aware of it. In The Genesis Flood, Whitcomb and Morris try to demonstrate how a deluge could account for the known facts of geology and biology, but there isn't a mention of the refined flood theories involving multiple centers and varying times of creation invoked by earlier creation scientists. Whitcomb and Morris resort to a literal Noah's ark theory, similar to but much cruder than Kircher's, and abandoned by the devout creationists who succeeded him.

Modern creationists also have an outdated fondness for what is called argument from design. This holds that plants and animals are so exquisitely put together that they could only have been created by a master intelligence. However superficially appealing, the argument dissolves under close examination.

On the whole, though, the scientific efforts of creationists are feeble because they permit no middle ground: either one believes in evolution, and opens the door to atheism and immorality, or else one accepts Genesis literally and the moral truths it implies. Biologists can't have evolution and believe in God. In fact, Morris has written that the idea of evolution was originally handed down by Satan to the ancient Babylonians. Thus, today's creationists tend to dwell on the negative. They hope to show why evolution couldn't have occurred and they do little to prove the biblical story. Their attacks on evolution fall into four broad categories:

1. *Misinterpretations of science.* Especially common are attacks based on the second law of thermodynamics, which states that the universe tends to become less organized with time, or that entropy (a measure of disorganization) increases. Since evolution supposedly produces more highly organized species from simpler ones, Morris reasons that evolution violates the second law of thermodynamics and is impossible. However, Morris misinterprets the second law, which bans universal decreases in entropy but permits local ones. It would no more prevent the evolution of monkeys from bacteria than forestall the development of adults from babies. Evolution is ultimately driven by solar energy, just as adult development is driven by the energy in the milk and hamburgers that children consume.

2. *Superseded findings.* Creationists have attacked the age of the earth calculated by scientists by concentrating on some of the early uncertainties or inconsistencies in radioisotope dating. They seem unaware that this imprecision has largely been removed by subsequent research.

3. *Solved puzzles.* Darwin squarely confronted two major obstacles to the acceptance of evolution: the paucity of transitional forms in the fossil record (he postulated "missing links" between human beings and apes), and the evolution of extraordinarily complicated structures like the eye that seem beyond the powers of natural selection. In Origin of Species, he devoted much attention to the solution of these difficulties, and later biologists have given them even more attention. Yet creationists continue to raise these problems as if nothing had been written about them.

4. *Disagreements among scientists.* Because scientists frequently give conflicting explanations and often argue with each other over details, creationists cite these disagreements to undermine science's claim to have answered other questions. Creationists especially like to bring up disputes among biologists over the mechanisms underlying evolution to imply that the fact of evolution is in doubt.

The creationist attacks remind me of a type of problem that Mr. Bridgess, my high school math teacher, used to terrify us with in plane geometry exams. It was called "Find the Error in This Fallacious Proof." He would give us a 47-step proof that ended in some absurd conclusion, such as Every rectangle is a square. Each step was described in impeccable prose and seemed to follow logically from the one before. Only by going over the proof very carefully could we spot the incorrect assumption that had been subtly slipped in at step 19 by the canny Mr. Bridgess and that led to the false conclusion. In the same way, creationist attacks often combine scientific terminology and grammatically correct English with a logic flawed by a hard-to-spot fallacy.

In the light of their abysmal performance, can today's creationists call themselves scientists? The scientific method consists of observing the world, deducing an explanation for phenomena, comparing the predictions derived from these "models" with new observations, then modifying the explanation to account for discrepancies. Darwin's theories yielded thousands of predictions, some of which have been strikingly confirmed: genes, the dating of the fossil record, transitional forms between modern humans and apes. Other parts of Darwin's work have proved wrong and have been modified, such as his acceptance of Lamarck's view that some characteristics acquired after birth could be passed on to one's offspring. The creationists themselves are often schizophrenic about their scientific credentials. In one breath, they claim they're doing "creation science" (Gish and Bliss have written, "The creation model is at least as scientific as the evolution model"). In the next breath, they argue that creationism lies beyond the scientific method (Gish: "We cannot discover by scientific investigations anything about the creative processes used by the Creator").

As UCLA biologist Richard Dickerson says, the term "creation science" is an oxymoron — a phrase that contradicts itself, like full-length bikini or jumbo shrimp.

A tragic consequence of the contemporary creationist movement is its damaging impact on science teaching in schools. One can no more master biology while denying the fact of evolution than one can understand chemistry while refusing to admit the existence of atoms. Though creationists pretend to seek equal status for creation science and evolution in school curricula, their actual effect has been the omission or dilution of evolution in textbooks and courses. Schoolchildren are cruelly denied the background needed for careers in the biological sciences. The USSR offers a chilling example. The disastrous state of Soviet agriculture owes much to the late Trofim Lysenko, whose mad views on evolution led him to reject genetics, oppose the development of new wheat varieties, and block experimentation with hybrid corn.

A less publicized result of creationism is the damage it has inflicted on religion. Like Judge Deen, the creationists misguidedly link what they perceive as a widespread decay of morals in the U.S. with a belief in evolution and what they call scientific humanism. An instructive comparison is the damage that the Roman Catholic church inflicted on itself by condemning Galileo for his astronomical views. The fact of evolution is no more destructive to religion and morality than is the fact of the earth's revolution about the sun. What is destructive now, as in Galileo's time, is allying religion with ignorance. How can one respect a movement that adheres to interpretations discredited centuries ago — by men at least as devout as today's creationists? Fortunately, the danger is recognized by the religious majority: among the plaintiffs who successfully sued to overturn Arkansas's "creation science" law were leaders of the Catholic, Presbyterian, Episcopal, United Methodist, and African Methodist Episcopal churches, and members of the Southern Baptist clergy and Jewish organizations.

The creationists' either/or posture — literal creationism and morality, or else atheistic evolution and licentiousness — is wrong. Many

Catholics, Protestants, and Jews practice their religions *and* behave ethically *and* accept the fact of evolution. Indeed, Einstein and other scientists have been deeply religious, if not always in a strictly sectarian sense. The mystery of creation that lies beyond science isn't the evolution of millions of meticulously constructed species of bugs, but the very existence of the universe and its beautifully elusive laws. As theologian Paul Tillich asked, "Why is there something, when there could have been nothing?"

Note

1. Scientists reckon the age of the universe as 15 billion to 20 billion years. The sun and the planets were formed about 4.5 billion years ago. Trilobites appeared about 570 million years ago, and the dinosaurs vanished about 65 million years ago. Neanderthal man disappeared nearly 40,000 years ago, and the first walls of Jericho were built circa 8000 B.C.

2
The Relevant Ape

BIRUTÉ M.F. GALDIKAS

Perhaps the persistent presence of a subadult male orangutan prompted the brawny old "cheek padder" to turn on me. Whatever the cause, the big male could not have picked a less opportune time — assuming that there *is* a good time to be charged by 160 pounds of amorous wild primate intent on a few moments alone with his sexually receptive partner. The tea-coloured swamp water, up to my waist, was so clogged with vegetation that I could barely move. In my bogged-down state, I had already angered the male's intended, who had retreated to the rain-forest canopy and was kiss-squeaking loudly. Suddenly, the adult male grabbed two thick vines, swung down until he hung only a yard above my head, and glared into my eyes, so close that my nostrils tingled from the stale odour of orangutan sweat.

A decade of study in Indonesian jungles had taught me how rare it is for wild orangutans to so much as deign to look at a human. When they do, their eyes usually lock in for only an instant before they turn away. But I was not going to get off as lightly this time. The orangutan's gaze was hard and direct, his message clear: Leave us alone. Several seconds passed before he turned with what, in a human, could only be described as

disdain and climbed back into the canopy to join his mate.

I was left alone again, thankful that I was not another male orangutan, who would doubtless have been bloodied and bruised following such a confrontation. Still, once my heart rate had settled, I realized that the soggy encounter with the amorous orangutan was one of those infrequent victories for a field biologist studying a rare and furtive creature that makes its home in some of the world's most remote and inhospitable terrain. It was also a measure of how far my then husband, Rod Brindamour, and I had come since that evening in 1971 when we first arrived at Camp Leakey in Indonesian Borneo's Tanjung Puting Reserve. Camp might be a misnomer. Our first research station consisted of one decaying bark-walled thatched hut abandoned by hand-loggers who had been cutting illegally in the reserve.

At that time, I was a Ph.D student who had left my hometown, Toronto, to study anthropology at the University of California, and the consensus among primatologists was that orangutans, solitary apes from the deep swamps of central Borneo, would be unusually difficult to study. I was taken aside by one concerned professor who warned: "You know, you may be in for a big disappointment; you may spend three or four years in the jungle and only come across three or four orangutans." The late Louis Leakey, then my

From *Equinox*, May/June 1984, pp. 27–39. Reprinted with the permission of the author.

mentor, was even more blunt: "I'll give you 10 years. If you haven't contacted any orangutans in 10 years, I won't support you any longer." At one point, Leakey even urged me to study wild pygmy chimpanzees in Zaire instead. He thought they might be easier to contact.

But I was more fascinated by orangutans. Of the extant great apes, which also include chimpanzees and gorillas, orangutans are humanity's most distant cousins. They alone remain arboreal and do not exhibit any anatomical specializations for life on the ground, never having developed the knuckle-walking, or bipedalism, exhibited by their African ape cousins and human cousins. Orangutans stayed in the heart of the dank, dark nursery of all the primates: the tropical rain forest. Among the hominoids, which include humans, apes, and their ancestors, it is not people but orangutans that stand apart.

Orangutans are also separated from their African kin by the obscurity in which, until recently, they have lived. As early as the nineteenth century, naturalists realized that this intelligent ape was a solitary creature, unlike all other monkeys and apes, which are highly gregarious. The few scientific attempts to uncover details of the orangutans' unusual life style were stymied by the creatures' preferred habitats — swamps and tangled forests. The respected naturalist George Schaller wrote of wading armpit-deep in Sarawak swamps and catching an occasional glimpse of the elusive apes high in the canopy. In the end, he resorted to nest counts to estimate populations.

Because of such inexact methods, nobody knew how many wild orangutans survived. What was known was that thousands had been wantonly killed during colonial times. Others were shot as food by Borneo's aboriginal Dayak people. By the beginning of this century, orangutans were clearly a relict species confined to Sumatra and Borneo, a tiny corner of a range that once included vast portions of Southeast Asia and even parts of China. When I began my studies in the late 1960s, skeptics put wild-orangutan numbers at 2,000. When Walman Sinaga of the Indonesian Nature Protection Branch estimated that there might be 10,000 surviving orangutans, he was considered an incurable optimist.

The threat to the orangutans today no longer comes from being hunted with natives' blowguns for food — "Orangutan is tasty enough," a Dayak once told me, "but nothing like pork or civet." The species has even managed to survive decades of being slaughtered to obtain infants for zoos and for the pet trade. These two problems are now being controlled through laws. Unfortunately, today's crisis is of a different magnitude, one that cannot be overcome by vanishing into deep undergrowth or by retreating to the remote swamps. Orangutans can survive only in the rain forest. And those forests are being cut at such a rate that an area the size of Massachusetts falls each month. The orangutans' once remote haunts are now vulnerable to this creeping destruction.

The establishment of a rehabilitation centre at our camp was an attempt to combat at least some of the human-induced pressures on the species. As a first step, we wanted to dry up the market for captive orangutans. When Rod and I arrived, we were appalled to see orangutans in cages and on chains, even though such practices had been against the law for four decades. But these laws went unenforced by the local authorities. We hoped that providing a facility where the police could bring confiscated orangutans for rehabilitation in preparation for their release into the rain forest would be incentive for them to enforce the laws. Our idea worked. Within a week of arriving, we had convinced the head of the local forestry department to begin confiscating captive orangutans.

The first confiscated orangutan, a tiny male infant, became known as Sugito. We could not have released Sugito even if we had wanted to, since he clung furiously to whoever was near him when he was let out of his cage. After a few days in camp, he became more discriminating and clung only to me. I was thrilled, but life as a surrogate orangutan mother had distinct disadvantages, not the least of which was that an infant orangutan clings to its mother for four years. I could look forward to at least two more years of travelling about with a furry orange protuberance on my body.

Despite successes such as Sugito, some orangutan owners fought confiscation until their animals died in captivity. One former police chief said that his children would never forgive him if their pet orangutan was released in the wild. Soon afterward, a dog bit the orangutan on the arm. The wound became infected, and the limb had to be amputated. The orangutan died within weeks. It was much more gratifying when villagers sought us and voluntarily turned over their pets because they wanted to see them free in the forest. This soon began happening frequently.

Achieving our other goal — studying wild orangutans — was more difficult. For a time, it appeared that other primatologists might have been correct. Before we could study orangutans, we had to find them. The anxiety, frustration, and exhaustion of our first few months in the forest cannot be exaggerated. We had arrived in the middle of the wet season, and it rained incessantly. Leeches were so numerous that we lost track of how many we removed from our bodies in a day. Bloated with our blood, they fell out of our socks, dropped off our necks, and even squirmed out of our underwear.

The swamps that surrounded Camp Leakey became impassable, and the only easy way to reach dry ground was to hike one and a half miles over a narrow tongue of abandoned *ladang*, a rice field overgrown with grass and ferns. Even on sunny days, dew-laden elephant grass assured that our clothes were soaked before we reached the dry forests. To ease movement, Rod began hacking a network of trails through the trackless jungle of our 14-square-mile study area.

While Rod cut trails, I began searching for orangutans. But there were none to be found. There were numerous nests in trees, mute testimony that orangutans had rested here. Occasionally, I found remains of freshly eaten fruits. Still, as I trudged through our study area during those first weeks, I was beginning to wonder if we had travelled halfway around the world only to set up camp in the one corner of Borneo that was devoid of primates. My wondering stopped late in the afternoon when a bellowing sound exploded from the bush 50 feet away. Although orangutans are normally silent, the long-call of a male, when issued, is known to be the most intimidating sound in the Bornean forest. It begins with a series of low grumbles that peak into the bellowings which had stopped me in my tracks. The call, which could be compared to the sounds uttered by a cow having a nervous breakdown, gradually subsides into low rumbles and burbles. "The orangutan is sighing because his bride left him on his wedding night," according to local legend. Certainly, the orangutan's call has its mournful side, but it is the call's awesome quality that seems paramount to me. So, with the hair on the back of my neck erect, I forced myself to walk quickly away. Later, I learned that the caller had probably been so close that he watched from the forest floor as I retreated.

Twice while on the river in a dugout during those early weeks of our study, we did catch glimpses of wild orangutans. But as soon as we approached, they broke and dropped branches, then fled into the trees, vocalizing kiss-squeaks and hoots, moving into the deep river-edge swamps where we simply could not keep up to them. It never ceased to amaze me how animals weighing up to 175 pounds and bedecked with long bright orange hair could simply vanish into the forest canopy.

Gradually, over the months, I started finding and following wild orangutans. It soon became apparent that the orange apes were almost as solitary and certainly as arboreal as early naturalists had claimed. Adult males usually wandered the forests alone, and adult females were accompanied by only one or two dependent offspring. We saw some social interactions, some chance encounters at the tops of fruit trees. Occasionally, females travelled together for days, but most of the time, adult orangutans were alone, seemingly content to enjoy one of the animal kingdom's most lackadaisical existences — so lackadaisical that some aboriginal Borneo people say that orangutans can talk but refuse to for fear of being put to work. Orangutans prefer to stay in treetops and spend about two-thirds of each day eating, mostly fruit. The great intelligence that the wild orangutans exhibit as they make complex foraging decisions about which trees and vines to visit and as they manipulate branches and foliage to weave sleeping nests is not immediately obvious. Orangutans have a slow, relaxed style that belies how hard they really do work to extract maximum nutrients from tiny fruits.

In our second year of research, after we had begun to habituate several wild orangutans to the point where they usually ignored us, we followed an adult female continuously for 31 days. During that month, this female met other orangutans only five times. As we trailed her, I began to realize that I had inadvertently become very fond of my constant speechless companion in the trees, but the affection was in no way reciprocated. She did not even glance down at me most of the time. A few times, without the slightest warning, she dropped dead branches or snags that missed killing me by inches. It was clear that I needed her company more than she needed mine. When she nested alone on dark, rainy evenings, with the wind howling through the trees, I longed to grab her and shake her and ask: "Don't you ever get lonely?"

It took me a while to understand that loneliness has no meaning for a wild orangutan, a member of a semisolitary species that is usually alone more than 80 percent of the time. I almost envied her the intensity of her solitude, her capacity to be alone, and the self-contained way that she carried her universe within her. For me, as a member of a highly gregarious species, it was difficult to be always alone.

But sometimes, orangutans could be quite

social. Certainly the most important social relationship for adult males is consortship with sexually receptive females. One consorting pair stands out because the adult male was one of our most habituated wild orangutans. He was twice the size of his adolescent female consort, who had almost attained full size for her sex. Orangutans are, in fact, among the most sexually dimorphic of primates. The adolescent was sassy and uninhibited, still displaying the playfulness characteristic of immature orangutans. Not only was the adult male large and dignified, but also, like all adult males of his species, his awesome appearance was enhanced by huge cheek pads that framed the sides of his face and by a large throat pouch, which served as a resonator for the long-call.

Orangutans seem to recognize each other's calls, and males distribute themselves in such a way that they rarely meet. I have observed about 20 direct encounters among adult males in the wild; roughly half involved aggression or combat. But during this series of consortships, which spanned a one-year period, I saw no combats. No other adult male ever approached the loving couple. However, the adult male was irritated by subadult male orangutans — smaller and more agile than he in the trees — that lurked in the shadows behind tree trunks and dense foliage, following and observing the consorting pair. Sometimes he chased them away; sometimes he did not bother. The point was not so much to catch them but to keep them away from his consort.

I had watched this adolescent female a number of times before, and she was usually followed by subadult males. Now that she was in oestrus, however, she made her preference for the big cheek padder perfectly clear. She approached him, and I watched, stupefied, as she groomed his shoulder and arm for nine minutes straight — the longest grooming bout that I have ever seen among wild orangutans. Grooming has been called the social cement of primates. However, the semisolitary orangutans have little need for this cement because there is usually no other orangutan to groom.

The female then dangled from a branch in front of the male, sticking her lower quarters in his face. He seemed oblivious of the provocative sight. I wondered if he would pay more attention to her if she were older, more wrinkled, and a proven breeder. He had been consorting with her off and on for almost a year, and she still had not conceived. I assumed that adolescent sterility was to blame. Perhaps he was just wasting his time,

sharing his fruit trees with her. *She* certainly seemed to feel that way when she came out of oestrus, after five to ten days of consortship, because she departed, leaving him staring after her, moving in her direction in fits and starts and long-calling after her in vain.

Unfortunately, for the human observer who tries to chart the course of orangutans' lives, males and females diverge at adolescence — females generally stay in their natal areas, but the males leave. Males are so nomadic, it is difficult to document an individual's life. We can understand males only from the composite cross-sectional picture that comes from viewing numerous individuals at different stages of their lives. Sometimes they do come back; one adult male recently returned to the study area after an absence of seven years (generally, adult males are so distinctive that they can be recognized after being clearly seen just one time). Other adult males pass through only once. In fact, there are two patterns: males who stay in one general area of forest for several years or more and males who virtually never stop moving. The more resident males tend to be dominant.

The focus of male life is oestrous females. In most instances, if a female is not present when two adult males come face to face, one will run away, and the other will not expend much energy chasing him. But in the presence of oestrous females, there will be much aggression and combat. As two forest titans struggle for access to an oestrous female, one sees nature "red in tooth and claw." Some combats are over in a few minutes; others last half an hour; a few have taken several hours. Combats begin as two males advance toward each other — usually dropping to the ground if initially in the canopy — vocalizing, grappling, and biting. Then they pull apart and face each other. Bouts of staring are interspersed with short skirmishes. As a result of this aggression, most adult males resemble "walking wounded," sustaining deep cuts that frequently result in ripped cheek pads and lips, as well as stiff and missing fingers and toes. Blood is sometimes spilled and hair pulled out. But combats determine access to oestrous females; thus, during orangutan evolution, there was, indubitably, a premium placed on large size, fighting ability, and calling behaviour in males.

Females seem to prefer the big cheek-padded fully mature males, placing the smaller non-cheek-padded subadult males at a disadvantage. Subadults do not long-call to attract oestrous females as do adult males. Although they attempt to consort, subadults give way when an adult male appears. Subadult male reproductive tactics differ from the combat/consort manoeuvres of adult males. They rely on sneak copulations, when an adult male is momentarily distracted or distant from his female consort, and on forced copulations that are somewhat equivalent to rape.

In the face of raping subadult males, adolescent females seemed much calmer than adult females. One subadult male consorting with an aged adult female left her and raced off toward an adolescent female feeding some distance away. He entered her tree, grabbed her, and positioned her for intromission; there was a short struggle as she resisted, squealing in protest. The struggle was not particularly long or intense. A cynic might have said that the female was merely being "coy." While the male thrusted vigorously, the female resumed eating fruits with an expression on her face that suggested nothing of any particular moment was taking place.

Forced copulations between adult females and subadult males were a different story, however, with the females battling very hard and vocalizing loud, hoarse, grunting sounds heard at no other time. On a few occasions, they uttered very intense, high-pitched screams. Struggles were so fierce at times that one or both fell to the ground from the trees. Sometimes the female's dependent offspring — clinging infants or small juveniles — joined in the fight, biting the rapist.

As our research progressed, wild orangutans continued to surprise us. We soon realized that adult males spent a great deal of time on the ground; however, we did not fully understand the extent of their ground utilization until recently. During the first few years, we observed one adult male that foraged and locomoted on the forest floor up to six hours per day, while another adult male spent an average of two hours per day on the ground. The males seemed so comfortable and so much at ease on the forest floor, it was easy to forget, at times, that they were actually an arboreal species. Some males travelled more than half a mile terrestrially, barely stopping along the way; sometimes they sat on the ground, even lolled on it. Males in particular spent long hours on the ground looking for and feeding on termites. Adult females also ventured to the ground but never without a specific reason — whether to forage or to drink water from a swamp puddle or to escape from another orangutan — and averaged only three minutes per day.

A second aspect of our research, which forced us to rethink previously held views of orangutan biology, was the length of the birth interval.

When we went to Borneo, conventional wisdom dictated that wild orangutan females first gave birth at about 7 or 8 years of age, as they do in captivity, with birth intervals of two and a half to three years between successive offspring. Because wild orangutans, particularly the immature animals, are so much smaller than their well-fed, under-exercised conspecifics of the same age at zoos, it took us several years to realize that we were underestimating orangutan ages. What we had assumed to be a 1-year-old infant was actually 3 or 4 years of age, while a 10-year-old adolescent had looked to be 6 or 7.

One adolescent female, Georgina, was almost adult size when we encountered her for the first time. She gave birth in mid-1973, but it was not until mid-1981 that her second infant was born. In the meantime, she was monitored extensively, and she did not become pregnant. We knew this because, unlike the genitalia of many other primates, orangutan genitalia swell up only when females are pregnant, not when they are in oestrus. Georgina was not exceptional. The infants of other females were born at intervals of nine years. Thus, if an orangutan female first gave birth at 15 years of age — as the evidence suggests — then at eight-or nine-year intervals, she would be approximately 40 years old when had her fourth offspring. Our continuing research project at Tanjung Puting has documented several females with three surviving offspring, but our study has not yet been long enough to determine whether females give birth to four infants. Certainly, we did not expect such a long birth interval; it is unprecedented in wild-primate studies. It helps to explain why orangutan populations are extremely vulnerable. If orangutans are wiped out of an area, they simply cannot bounce back to their former numbers in a hurry. It takes decades to do so.

The years have rolled by. Sugito, our first rehabilitated orangutan, is long gone. As an adolescent, he started attacking people, and he caused such damage to camp equipment and supplies that during one of my absences from camp, Rod captured him and released him in a forest on another river. Sugito never made it back to camp, although for years, whenever a new orangutan was sighted near the feeding station, I would race over to see if it was Sugito. The last time I saw Sugito, he gripped my arm and literally tried to drag me up into the trees. But I gently pushed his hand away, and he let me go. He never fully understood that "mother" could not climb trees. When he was an infant, I had tried my best to do so, and sometimes, in a rather futile attempt to give him a "normal" orangutan infancy, we spent several hours in small trees with low horizontal branches.

Other ex-captive orangutans have found wild mates and given birth, coming back to camp with their infants. Many have totally returned to the wild.

Best of all, I no longer have to be mother to ex-captive orangutan infants. That role was taken over by some of the rehabilitated orangutans themselves, now grown to adolescence. Three adolescent females and one adolescent male adopted the last four released infants, carrying them, sharing night nests with them, and even allowing them to suckle their nipples. In the case of the adolescent females, lactation was probably induced. I remember the time when my thumb — approximately the size of a nursing orangutan's nipple — was suckled earnestly by three juvenile orangutans who regarded me as their mother. One of the three continued suckling my thumb until he was at least 8 years of age.

Most of the hand-raised male orangutans had to be relocated to other parts of the forest as they approached subadulthood. Due to their great familiarity with humans, they began testing men — and, to a limited extent, women — as though they were other male orangutans. But the females grew up and have offspring and are no particular problem to have around camp. Even in adulthood, many of them remain the gentlest creatures imaginable.

Our research has contributed to elevating the orangutan from academic obscurity to being one of the most thoroughly understood wild primates. We know that orangutans are not as rare as initially thought and that, to a degree, elusiveness had been misconstrued as scarcity. Current studies suggest that there are at least three times as many of the orange apes hidden in the depths of Indonesia's forests as was estimated a decade ago. Our research area in Tanjung Puting alone holds at least 1,000 of the great apes. At the same time, it has become evident that despite such heartening numbers, orangutan populations and the size of their habitats are decreasing rapidly. They are very much in danger of extinction. We have also learned that orangutans, while solitary much of the time, do not live in a social vacuum, as was once thought. Instead, they maintain complex relationships with other individuals, even though they may meet each other infrequently. Finally, orangutans have been found to be remarkably versatile eaters, consuming more than 330 different plants and insects. And, far from being totally arboreal, orangutans can be

found in the middle of shallow lakes, in young secondary forests, and, occasionally, even in fields up to half a mile from the nearest tree. In the absence of human interference, orangutans have demonstrated that they are extremely successful occupants of the tropical rain forest.

Now, however, this very success threatens to doom orangutans as a wild species. International forestry companies, which look upon rain forests not as valuable ecosystems but as mines from which to extract profits, are already cutting into vast tracts of habitat once occupied by the great orange apes. I distinctly remember the time when I and other members of the Orangutan Research and Conservation Project were guests of an American/Indonesian logging firm operating in eastern Borneo.

The American camp manager was cordial, in a down-home way, jovial and eager to demonstrate that "loggers aren't all bad." Indeed, he wasn't. He took a day off from his busy routine to show us the forest and the logging. It was clear that he has a deep personal appreciation of the forest's beauty, apart from his professional interest in exploiting it. He explained that instead of clear-cutting, his teams were using selective logging, where only 10 to 15 giants were taken per hectare, leaving the rest of the forest intact. However, the damage was not so much the cutting but, rather, the destruction caused as large machines dragged the felled logs through the forest to the nearest road. A young, smiling Dayak chain saw operator, with a red scarf jauntily tied around his head, appeared almost heroic as he pitted himself against a rain-forest giant. The saw began to bite, the dust to fly. I cringed involuntarily, looking at the doomed 120-foot-tall giant with a white X marked on its trunk.

I genuinely liked most of the people I met at the logging camp: the harried chief executive, with his rumpled suit and perpetually worried expression; the Malaysian agriculturist experimenting with various methods of planting cacao; the forestry faculty graduates still fresh-faced from school in Java and, in some ways, suffering almost as much cultural shock in the forest as the Americans. There was no evil there, and yet the fate of the orangutan in the vast tract of tropical rain forest that constitutes the logging concession is inextricably linked to the actions of this company.

Sadly, as this new threat pushes the orange apes closer to extinction, they are gaining a surprising importance to scientists. When I went to school, the orangutan was considered the "irrelevant" ape, in terms of understanding human evolution. But palaeontological finds have challenged the traditional ways in which we view our evolution. Robert Wilkie, who is a longtime supporter of orangutan research, occasionally sends me news and keeps me up to date. Not long ago, he forwarded several startling articles, which I thought about while following Georgina, a wild orangutan I have known for more than a decade. Palaeontologists and anthropologists are beginning to reexamine orangutans in the light of recent fossil finds of *Sivapithecus* and *Ramapithecus* remains. Although the matter is very controversial, these remains suggest that perhaps an orangutanlike creature may have been the common ancestor of the later hominoids and hominids. The orangutan may not be a specialized pongid after all but, rather, the ape that allows us to see what we humans left behind when we emerged onto the plains and savannas of this earth. Orangutans may also give us the best glimpse of the last common ancestor shared by pongids and hominids, great apes and humans. The orangutan is now declared a possible living fossil. We are not, after all, descended from a chimpanzee-like ancestor.

"What do you think about that, Georgina?" I asked, staring up into the canopy where Georgina sat with her second infant, Greg. I have known Georgina since she was a large adolescent, not yet pregnant with her first offspring, Gale. I remember when Georgina first descended from the forest canopy to stare for long minutes at Rod and me as if to determine who these rude intruders were.

Slow, gentle, quiet and nonshowy, Georgina continued to munch away on small, prickly fruits, displaying cognitive skills, in the way she collected and processed these fruits, that are equal to what is typically defined as tool use. Her new status as a relevant ape did not concern her in the least. Fruit was what mattered.

The sun was shining, the cicadas were humming, and the birds were singing. Although the equatorial sun beat mercilessly on the top of the forest canopy, down below, where Georgina and I sat, it was cool and damp. In the low light that filtered through the leaves, the world was a dark mix of greens and browns. After all, she and I — orangutan and human — were in the tropical rain forest, the last vestige of Eden. She never left the Garden of Eden, never lost her innocence. As a human, I am only slowly beginning to regain the innocence that our ancestors left behind somewhere in the perpetual twilight of the tropical rain forest.

3
Lucy and the First Family

DONALD C. JOHANSON and

MAITLAND A. EDEY

The Second Hadar Field Season

I went to the dining tent and got myself a cup of coffee. Drinking it, I found myself under a strong compulsion to put off paperwork and go out surveying instead. I knew I shouldn't. But at that moment Gray came in and began asking where Locality 162 was. Combined with the powerful feeling that this should be a day spent hunting fossils, that decided me. The papers could wait. Gray and I drove out of camp. Two hours later we found Lucy.

Lucy was utterly mind-boggling; there was no other way to describe her. She left the entire camp reeling. Everything about her was sensational. That nearly half of a complete skeleton should appear on the table of the anthropology tent, as her various parts were sorted out and laid in place, seemed incredible to the scientists even as they saw the evidence accumulating before their eyes.

Just as astonishing was the creature that was being assembled. It was not more than three and a half feet tall, had a tiny brain, and yet walked erect. Its jaw was V-shaped, not as rounded in

front as some of the other mandibles, and smaller than any of them. Furthermore, its first premolar had only a single cusp. The larger jaws had two-cusped premolars. Since the one-cusp condition is the more primitive and the two-cusp condition the more human, I came to the tentative conclusion that Lucy was different from the larger-jawed type. As I studied the fossils, it seemed to me that Alemayehu's jaws represented something very early on the *Homo* line, as the Leakeys had said, and that Lucy represented something else — possibly a very early representative of the australopithecines.

When bones are scarce, speculation about them can be as daring as one cares to make it, and no one can contradict the speculator. When bones become more numerous — when a single fossil is augmented by a large sample of fragments from a number of individuals — those fragments begin to make assertions about themselves that forbid some earlier speculations. The sheer increase of information cuts off a number of possibilities as to what they might be or what they might do. On the other hand, a good assemblage of bones increases the respectability of certain other speculations. On better evidence they improve themselves from merely hopeful guesses to logical probabilities. Once in a great while, a set of bones provides a certainty.

Lucy provided a certainty. Previous guesses about the presence or absence of early bipedalism

— those old arguments about whether *Australopithecus africanus* walked with a waddle, a scuffle, or a shuffle — were cut through with a brutal finality. Here was an ape-brained little creature with a pelvis and leg bones almost identical in function with those of modern humans. I remembered my timid conjectures about the knee joint of the year before, and my relief when Owen Lovejoy had reassured me about its resemblance to a modern human knee. Now I knew, with the certainty provided by this extraordinary fossil, that hominids had walked erect at three million b.c. More surprising yet, they had walked *before* their brains had begun to enlarge. There could no longer be any argument about that, or any conjecture over whether a certain leg bone and a certain skull did or did not belong to the same individual. Here they were, together, in one unbelievable skeleton.

But like all fossils that provide certainties, this one also posed some new questions. One of them virtually howled for an answer: If erect walking had been perfected before brain enlargement had taken place, what had caused erect walking? A popular guess for years had been that a combination of manual dexterity, increased tool-using, and brain development had forced certain apes up on their hind legs as a growing daily reliance on manipulation of objects encouraged them to stand erect so that they could carry more and more things around with them. One eloquent spokesman for this view was Sherwood Washburn of the University of California. He had argued persuasively in the 1960s that tool-using and brain enlargement came before bipedality, and probably had been responsible for its development.

Lucy destroyed that argument. I caught myself wondering what would replace it. That would be something to really tie up Owen Lovejoy for the next couple of years. I could not wait to show Lucy to Lovejoy. I wished I had more time to think about bipedalism myself, but Aronson was arriving at Hadar, and I would have to spend some time with him. I would also have to continue my own surveying, write a press release on Lucy for the Ethiopians, and then go to Addis to present it.

*   *   *

For five years I kept Lucy in a safe in my office in the Cleveland Museum of Natural History. I had filled a wide shallow box with yellow foam padding, and had cut depressions in the foam so that each of her bones fitted into its own tailor-made nest. *Everybody* who came to the Museum

— it seemed to me — wanted to see Lucy. What surprised people most was her small size.

Her head, on the evidence of the bits of her skull that had been recovered, was not much larger than a softball. Lucy herself stood only three and one-half feet tall, although she was fully grown. That could be deduced from her wisdom teeth, which were fully erupted and had been exposed to several years of wear. My best guess was that she was between twenty-five and thirty years old when she died. She had already begun to show the onset of arthritis or some other bone ailment, on the evidence of deformation of her vertebrae. If she had lived much longer, it probably would have begun to bother her.

Her surprisingly good condition — her completeness — came from the fact that she had died quietly. There were no tooth marks on her bones. They had not been crunched and splintered, as they would have been if she had been killed by a lion or a saber-toothed cat. Her head had not been carried off in one direction and her legs in another, as hyenas might have done with her. She had simply settled down in one piece right where she was, in the sand of a long-vanished lake edge or stream — and died. Whether from illness or accidental drowning, it was impossible to say. The important thing was that she not been found by a predator just after death and eaten. Her carcass had remained inviolate, slowly covered by sand or mud, buried deeper and deeper, the sand hardening into rock under the weight of subsequent depositions. She had lain silently in her adamantine grave for millennium after millennium until the rains at Hadar had brought her to light again.

That was where I was unbelievably lucky. If I had not followed a hunch that morning with Tom Gray, Lucy might never have been found. Why the other people who looked there did not see her, I do not know. Perhaps they were looking in another direction. Perhaps the light was different. Sometimes one person sees things that another misses, even though he may be looking directly at them. If I had not gone to Locality 162 that morning, nobody might have bothered to go back for a year, maybe five years. Hadar is a big place, and there is a tremendous amount to do. If I had waited another few years, the next rains might have washed many of her bones down the gully. They would have been lost, or at least badly scattered; it would not have been possible to establish that they belonged together. What was utterly fantastic was that she had come to the surface so recently, probably in the last year or two. Five years earlier, she still would have been buried. Five years later, she would have been gone. As it was, the front of her skull was already gone, washed away somewhere. We never did find it. Consequently, the one thing we really cannot measure accurately is the size of her brain.

Lucy always managed to look interesting in her little yellow nest — but to a nonprofessional, not overly impressive. There were other bones all around her in the Cleveland Museum. She was dwarfed by them, by drawer after drawer of fossils, hundreds of them from Hadar alone. There were casts of hominid specimens from East Africa, from South Africa and Asia. There were antelope and pig skulls, extinct rodents, rabbits and monkeys, as well as apes. There was one of the largest collections of gorilla skulls in the world. In that stupefying array of bones, I kept being asked, What was so special about Lucy? Why had she, as another member of the expedition put it, "blown us out of our little anthropological minds for months"?

"Three things," I always answered. "First: what she is — or isn't. She is different from anything that has been discovered and named before. She doesn't fit anywhere. She is just a very old, very primitive, very small hominid. Somehow we are going to have to fit her in, find a name for her.

"Second," I would say, "is her completeness. Until Lucy was found, there just weren't any very old skeletons. The oldest was one of those Neanderthalers I spoke of a little while ago. It is about seventy-five thousand years old. Yes, there *are* older hominid fossils, but they are all fragments. Everything that has been reconstructed from them has had to be done by matching up those little pieces — a tooth here, a bit of jaw there, maybe a complete skull from somewhere else, plus a leg bone from some other place. The fitting together has been done by scientists who know those bones as well as I know my own hand. And yet, when you consider that such a reconstruction may consist of pieces from a couple of dozen individuals who may have lived hundreds of miles apart and may have been separated from each other by a hundred thousand years in time — well, when you look at the complete individual you've just put together you have to say to yourself, 'Just how real is he?' With Lucy you know. It's all there. You don't have to guess. You don't have to imagine an arm bone you haven't got. You *see* it. You see it for the first time from something older than a Neanderthaler."

"How much older?"

"That's point number three. The Neanderthaler is seventy-five thousand years old. Lucy is approximately 3.5 million years old. She is the oldest, most complete, best-preserved skeleton of any erect-walking human ancestor that has ever been found."

That is the significance of Lucy: her completeness and her great age. They make her unique in the history of hominid fossil collecting. She is easy to describe, and — as will be seen — she makes a number of anthropological problems easier to work out. But exactly what is she?

The rest of [*Lucy: The Beginning of Humankind*, the book from which this text is taken] will be devoted to answering that question. Unique Lucy may be, but she is incomprehensible outside the context of other fossils. She becomes meaningless unless she is fitted into a scheme of hominid evolution and scientific logic that has been laboriously pieced together over more than a century by hundreds of specialists from four continents. Their fossil finds, their insights — sometimes inspired, sometimes silly — their application of techniques from such faraway disciplines as botany, nuclear physics, and microbiology have combined to produce an increasingly clear and rich picture of man's emergence from the apes — a story that is finally, in the ninth decade of this century, beginning to make some sense. That story could not even begin to be told, of course, until Charles Darwin suggested in 1857 that we *were* descended from apes and not divinely created in 4004 B.C., as the Church insisted. But not even Darwin could have suspected some of the odd turns the hominid story would take. Nor could he have guessed which apes we are descended from. Indeed, we are not entirely sure about that even today.

*   *   *

The Third Hadar Field Season: The First Family

We suspended work, and gathered the next morning to begin removal of Bush's fossil. Brill set up his equipment to photograph the operation. Also present was a French husband-and-wife movie team. The wife's name was Michèle. She was always enthusiastic about finding something, but she couldn't tell a fossil from the end of a Coca-Cola bottle. While we were working down at the bottom of a rather steep slope, she climbed halfway up to sit in the shade under a small acacia bush, and she practically sat on a couple of bones. "What are these?" she called out, holding them up. I climbed up to look at them and was bowled over. One was a hominid heel bone. The other was a femur exactly like the femur I had found two years before, except that it was nearly twice as large. All of this was photographed by Brill and by the French movie people — the first time ever that professional photographers have taken pictures of fossils actually being found. All the others that you see in books — *all* of them — are reenactments.

Finding teeth at the bottom of the slope and two other bones halfway up encouraged a closer scrutiny of it. Almost immediately other fragments were spotted. Looking on the other side of the acacia bush, I had the unnerving experience of picking up, almost side by side, two fibulas — the smaller of the two shin bones in the leg. Another Lucy? No, these were both right legs, indicating the presence of more than one individual. Meanwhile, others were shouting over finds of their own, all of them hominid. Fossils seemed to be cascading, almost as from a fountain, down the hillside. A near-frenzy seized us as we scrambled madly to pick them up.

For a little while I scarcely knew what I was doing. I had never seen anything like it. I had never *heard* of anything like it. We were like crazy people. Finally the heat got to us, and we settled down.

The bone-strewn slope was duly entered on the master map as site 333. The rest of the field season — and most of the next year's as well — we devoted exclusively to working it. First the entire hillside was combed systematically — not helter-skelter, as in that first insanely euphoric hour. Then the gravel surface was carried down the slope — tons of it — to be sifted, load by load, through coarse sieves. Ultimately the hillside would yield about two hundred teeth or pieces of bone. Duplication of specific parts made it clear that at least thirteen individuals were represented: men, women, and at least four children. It was not possible to fit many of the bones together into partially complete skeletons, as had been done with Lucy, because of the way they were jumbled and scattered down the slope. The possibility also cannot be ignored that considerably more than thirteen individuals may be represented.

Just as there is a residual faint hum or static buzz when a radio is turned on, so in Hadar there is a ubiquitous faint background "noise" of animal fossils. Collect anywhere, and fragments of animal fossil show up, more prominently in some places than in others, but nowhere are bits of stray animal bone entirely absent, attesting to the opportunities for deposition presented by the sheer passage of time, to the slowness of geological activity, to the incessant wandering and dying of unnumbered animals — back and forth, endlessly, while hundreds of feet of deposits are laid down over hundreds of thousands of years. What was odd about the material sifted from the 333 hillside was that animal fossils were virtually absent. The background scatter that normally could be expected to result from an intensive collecting effort in any fossil-bearing stratum was somehow missing; everything that came from that hillside was hominid.

How was this to be explained? Had an entire band suddenly been wiped out, so suddenly that there had been no time for the expected deposition of animal bones? It would seem so. The hominid fossils appeared to come from a common source in a stratigraphic horizon near the top of the slope. What was found lying on the slope was what had presumably washed out during the last few rainy seasons. This line of reasoning was strengthened when the horizon itself was found, and some preliminary excavation into the hillside produced nearly twenty more fossil pieces. The inference was clear that before erosion had begun to scatter the bones, they had all lain in close proximity, and therefore had presumably died together.

*   *   *

I discussed this problem with Taieb, who did his best, by studying the stratigraphy of the hillside, to see if there was any evidence of sudden flooding. He determined that all the bones came from a single stratum that consisted almost entirely of fine clay. The thinness of the layer suggested a single event like a flood. The clay did not; rushing water would have carried a mixture of larger particles. What could have happened, said Taieb, was that everything — bones, mud, sand — went down in a rush to a lake edge or some other flatter, more open area where the bones could have settled slowly and quietly, covered by finer material. Taieb stressed that while the foregoing may be logical, it is unprovable. Geology is wonderfully informative, thanks to sedimentation, volcanism, faulting, and so on, but it has not yet reached a stage of refinement that can interpret local events that took place overnight three million years ago. The strongest evidence for drowning, he continued, would have to be the absence of animal fossils. Animals would not have frequented a ravine inhabited by hominids, and thus would not have been caught with them in a catastrophe. By the time they began wandering about again in the vicinity, the hominids would have been safely buried in their layer of clay. That animals did eventually return is evidenced by the presence of their bones — background noise — in strata above the 333 clay layer.

That was as far as Taieb could go. The unique concentration of a hominid band remains a mystery. Its exact size will have to await final analysis of all the bones recovered so far, and the full excavation of the hillside, for I am confident of finding within it other bones in a far less disturbed state. I hope for another Lucy, perhaps a more nearly complete one. I hope for a better adult skull than Lucy provided. Most of all, I simply hope for more bones to build up my population sample. For there lies the true value of site 333. It provides a representative mix of sexes and ages that is in its way even more valuable than the priceless Lucy. Lucy is extraordinary, there is no question about that. She is like something seen during a lightning flash, her details lit by an unearthly clarity for just an instant. During that instant we take in a lot about her. We see her almost whole. But with nothing to compare her with, how do we figure out what she is? Is she representative of her kind? If so, her kind was extremely small. It had an odd lower jaw that came together in a V-shape at the front. Alemayehu's jaws were not V-shaped. Did they represent a different species? Were they like the new teeth and jaws from the 333 site, now dubbed the First Family? Between the anthropologists and answers to those questions lay the bones themselves, a vast jumble of them which had to be cleaned, sorted, described, and finally interpreted — a job that would take several years.

In December 1975 the third Hadar field season wound down. Taieb and his associates returned to France to spend the winter in mammal sorting, pollen analysis, and geological studies. Aronson and Walter returned to Cleveland loaded down with volcanic samples. I took the First Family to Addis Ababa and braced myself for the task of getting an exit visa for them.

Having run that gauntlet once before, I felt more confident this time. Taieb and I held the inevitable press conference to establish the importance of the fossils, then went the rounds of the ministries to secure the necessary papers. All went smoothly. I sailed through Customs and flew with Tom Gray to Nairobi to show the fossils to my friends Mary and Richard Leakey and to a number of other scientists who had been working as part of the Koobi Fora field team, several of whom I already knew. I also met for the first time some people who had been working for Mary

Leakey at Laetoli, a site in Tanzania a few miles south of Olduvai.

When I spread out the haul of new bones, they were an instant sensation. Nothing that combined their extreme antiquity, their remarkable quality and their profusion had ever been encountered before. There was an animated handing-round of fossils and a babble of discussion about them. Mary and Richard Leakey studied them with absorption and voiced the opinion that the First Family tended to confirm their conclusions reached during their visit to Hadar the year before: these were *Homo* fossils, albeit of a very primitive nature. Lucy, whom they had had a chance to examine by this time, was, they felt, something different. I was inclined to agree with them.

*   *   *

On January 29, Taieb and I went to the National Museum. There, at an elaborate ceremony featured by speeches, we handed over the entire Hadar hominid-fossil collection — more than 350 priceless bones — to Comrade Mammo Tessema, Keeper of the Museum.

I was well aware of the symbolic importance of this act, and what it meant for the future of paleoanthropology in Ethiopia. But at the very moment of relinquishment I felt a dreadful sense of loss. Lucy had been mine for five years. The most beautiful, the most nearly complete, the most extraordinary hominid fossil in the world, she had slept in my office safe all that time. I had written papers about her, appeared on television, made speeches. I had shown her proudly to a stream of scientists from all over the world. She had — I knew it — hauled me up from total obscurity into the scientific limelight. Finally, her bones, and all the others I was now giving away, had enabled me to launch a new interpretation of hominid evolution. Standing there in the Museum and listening to the acceptance speech, I felt like a parent signing away a child to an adoption agency. For a few minutes, amid all the handshaking and congratulation, I was quite desolated.

But that did not last long. The door that had been opened up for us by the Ethiopians was too wide and wonderful. The knowledge that we would be back with a full crew in the fall was too exciting. I know exactly what we are going to do and who is going to do it. I will take Tim White and Gerry Eck back to Hadar, with Kabete to cook for us. We will do nothing but survey for hominids — *nothing*. I will try to get some of those Kenyans who have done such magnificent work for Richard and Mary Leakey to join us. (Richard generously made the offer a few years ago, and I will take it up.) Kamoya Kimeu, for example, is eager to go. After seeing Lucy, he once said to me, "If you found that, think what *I* could find!"

Now that the Middle Awash sites have fallen back into our lap, Desmond Clark and a team of his will excavate there. What makes it potentially valuable is that *Homo erectus*, although spread all over Eurasia and Africa, and although he is a couple of million years younger than the Hadar fossils, is not really as well known anatomically as they are. There are some pretty good *erectus* skulls from here and there, and a lot of teeth, but not much else.

Most of what we know of *erectus* is cultural. His cave sites have been explored thoroughly. Clark Howell did that landmark study at the elephant-slaughter site in Spain. We know what *erectus* ate; we know that he cooked his food and made clothing. We know that he was an excellent hunter of large animals and that he made a variety of stone tools. We know that he showed a considerable amount of variability from place to place. What we don't know is just how or when — and perhaps, even *if* — he emerged out of *Homo habilis*.

We assume he did. We would like to prove it. We would like to find really good *erectus* fossils that sample a long period of time in one place. We would like to find them in association with their habitation sites, to see what they were doing all that time. We would like better dating. The middle Pleistocene is very poorly dated in Africa, but there are tuffs in the Middle Awash that should correct that. Desmond Clark and Jack Harris will be at the Middle Awash while we are at Hadar. I can't wait to see what they come up with, because *erectus* is such a strange and interesting character.

How does one account for *erectus'* sudden assumed jump out of *Homo habilis*? Was it actually all that sudden? Why was it made? Was it a matter of a quick evolutionary spurt taken in tandem with the development of a new and better tool culture? If so, where and why did that new culture start?

Then, an even more interesting question: why did that culture — and the man who made it — stagnate for another million years? *Homo erectus*, it is fairly clear, evolved practically not at all during that immense time. Then, suddenly, humanity took another spurt. About two hundred thousand years ago there occurred a second technological leap, and out of it rose *Homo sapiens*. The Middle Awash beckons because it may hold answers to both those questions.

4
Scavenger Hunt

PAT SHIPMAN

In both textbooks and films, ancestral humans (hominids) have been portrayed as hunters. Small-brained, big-browed, upright, and usually mildly furry, early hominid males gaze with keen eyes across the golden savanna, searching for prey. Skillfully wielding a few crude stone tools, they kill and dismember everything from small gazelles to elephants, while females care for young and gather roots, tubers, and berries. The food is shared by group members at temporary camps. This familiar image of Man the Hunter has been bolstered by the finding of stone tools in association with fossil animal bones. But the role of hunting in early hominid life cannot be determined in the absence of more direct evidence.

I discovered one means of testing the hunting hypothesis almost by accident. In 1978, I began documenting the microscopic damage produced on bones by different events. I hoped to develop a diagnostic key for identifying the post-mortem history of specific fossil bones, useful for understanding how fossil assemblages were formed. Using a scanning electron microscope (SEM) because of its excellent resolution and superb depth of field, I inspected high-fidelity replicas of modern bones that had been subjected to known

events or conditions. (I had to use replicas, rather than real bones, because specimens must fit into the SEM's small vacuum chamber.) I soon established that such common events as weathering, root etching, sedimentary abrasion, and carnivore chewing produced microscopically distinctive features.

In 1980, my SEM study took an unexpected turn. Richard Potts (now of Yale University), Henry Bunn (now of the University of Wisconsin at Madison), and I almost simultaneously found what appeared to be stone-tool cut marks on fossils from Olduvai Gorge, Tanzania, and Koobi Fora, Kenya. We were working almost side by side at the National Museum of Kenya, in Nairobi, where the fossils are stored. The possibility of cut marks was exciting, since both sites preserve some of the oldest known archeological materials. Potts and I returned to the United States, manufactured some stone tools, and started "butchering" bones and joints begged from our local butchers. Under the SEM, replicas of these cut marks looked very different from replicas of carnivore tooth scratches, regardless of the species of carnivore or the type of tool involved. By comparing the marks on the fossils with our hundreds of modern bones of known history, we were able to demonstrate convincingly that hominids using stone tools had processed carcasses of many different animals nearly two million years ago. For the first time, there was a firm link between

From *Natural History*, April 1984, pp. 22–27. Copyright 1984 American Museum of Natural History. Reprinted with permission.

stone tools and at least some of the early fossil animal bones.

This initial discovery persuaded some paleoanthropologists that the hominid hunter scenario was correct. Potts and I were not so sure. Our study had shown that many of the cut-marked fossils also bore carnivore tooth marks and that some of the cut marks were in places we hadn't expected — on bones that bore little meat in life. More work was needed.

In addition to more data about the Olduvai cut marks and tooth marks, I needed specific information about the patterns of cut marks left by known hunters performing typical activities associated with hunting. If similar patterns occurred on the fossils, then the early hominids probably behaved similarly to more modern hunters; if the patters were different, then the behavior was probably also different. Three activities related to hunting occur often enough in peoples around the world and leave consistent enough traces to be used for such a test.

First, human hunters systematically disarticulate their kills, unless the animals are small enough to be eaten on the spot. Disarticulation leaves cut marks in a predictable pattern on the skeleton. Such marks cluster near the major joints of the limbs: shoulder, elbow, carpal joint (wrist), hip, knee and hock (ankle). Taking a carcass apart at the joints is much easier than breaking or cutting through bones. Disarticulation enables hunters to carry food back to a central place or camp, so that they can share it with others or cook it or even store it by placing portions in trees, away from the reach of carnivores. If early hominids were hunters who transported and shared their kills, disarticulation marks would occur near joints in frequencies comparable to those produced by modern human hunters.

Second, human hunters often butcher carcasses, in the sense of removing meat from the bones. Butchery marks are usually found on the shafts of bones from the upper part of the front or hind limb, since this is where the big muscle masses lie. Butchery may be carried out at the kill site — especially if the animal is very large and its bones very heavy — or it may take place at the base camp, during the process of sharing food with others. Compared with disarticulation, butchery leaves relatively few marks. It is hard for a hunter to locate an animal's joints without leaving cut marks on the bone. In contrast, it is easier to cut the meat away from the midshaft of the bone without making such marks. If early hominids shared their food, however, there ought to be a number of cut marks located on the midshaft of some fossil bones.

Finally, human hunters often remove skin or tendons from carcasses, to be used for clothing, bags, thongs, and so on. Hide or tendon must be separated from the bones in many areas where there is little flesh, such as the lower limb bones of pigs, giraffes, antelopes, and zebras. In such cases, it is difficult to cut the skin without leaving a cut mark on the bone. Therefore, one expects to find many more cut marks on such bones than on the flesh-covered bones of the upper part of the limbs.

Unfortunately, although accounts of butchery and disarticulation by modern human hunters are remarkably consistent, quantitative studies are rare. Further, virtually all modern hunter-gatherers use metal tools, which leave more cut marks than stone tools. For these reasons I hesitated to compare the fossil evidence with data on modern hunters. Fortunately, Diane Gifford of the University of California, Santa Cruz, and her colleagues had recently completed a quantitative study of marks and damage on thousands of antelope bones processed by Neolithic (Stone Age) hunters in Kenya some 2,300 years ago. The data from Prolonged Drift, as the site is called, were perfect for comparison with the Olduvai material.

Assisted by my technician, Jennie Rose, I carefully inspected more than 2,500 antelope bones from Bed I at Olduvai Gorge, which is dated to between 1.9 and 1.7 million years ago. We made high-fidelity replicas of every mark that we thought might be either a cut mark or a carnivore tooth mark. Back in the United States, we used the SEM to make positive identifications of the marks. (The replication and SEM inspection was time consuming, but necessary: only about half of the marks were correctly identified by eye or by light microscope.) I then compared the patterns of cut mark and tooth mark distributions on Olduvai fossils with those made by Stone Age hunters at Prolonged Drift.

By their location, I identified marks caused either by disarticulation or meat removal and then compared their frequencies with those from Prolonged Drift. More than 90 percent of the Neolithic marks in these two categories were from disarticulation, but to my surprise, only about 45 percent of the corresponding Olduvai cut marks were from disarticulation. This difference is too great to have occurred by chance; the Olduvai bones did not show the predicted pattern. In fact, the Olduvai cut marks attributable to meat removal and disarticulation showed essentially the same pattern of distribution as the carnivore tooth marks. Apparently, the early hominids were not regularly disarticulating carcasses. This finding casts serious doubt on the idea that early hominids carried their kills back to camp to share with others, since both transport and sharing are difficult unless carcasses are cut up.

When I looked for cut marks attributable to skinning or tendon removal, a more modern pattern emerged. On both the Neolithic and Olduvai bones, nearly 75 percent of all cut marks occurred on bones that bore little meat; these cut marks probably came from skinning. Carnivore tooth marks were much less common on such bones. Hominids were using carcasses as a source of skin and tendon. This made it seem more surprising that they disarticulated carcasses so rarely.

A third line of evidence provided the most tantalizing clue. Occasionally, sets of overlapping marks occur on the Olduvai fossils. Sometimes, these sets include both cut marks and carnivore tooth marks. Still more rarely, I could see under the SEM which mark had been made first, because its features were overlaid by those of the later mark, in much the same way as old tire tracks on a dirt road are obscured by fresh ones. Although only thirteen such sets of marks were found, in eight cases the hominids made the cut marks *after* the carnivores made their tooth marks. This finding suggested a new hypothesis. Instead of hunting for prey and leaving the remains behind for carnivores to scavenge, perhaps hominids were scavenging from the carnivores. This might explain the hominids' apparently unsystematic use of carcasses: they took what they could get, be it skin, tendon, or meat.

Man the Scavenger is not nearly as attractive an image as Man the Hunter, but it is worth examining. Actually, although hunting and scavenging are different ecological strategies, many mammals do both. The only pure scavengers alive in Africa today are vultures; not one of the modern African mammalian carnivores is a pure scavenger. Even spotted hyenas, which have massive, bone-crushing teeth well adapted for eating the bones left behind by others, only scavenge about 33 percent of their food. Other carnivores that scavenge when there are enough carcasses around include lions, leopards, striped hyenas, and jackals. Long-term behavioral studies suggest that these carnivores scavenge when the can and kill when they must. There are only two nearly pure predators, or hunters — the cheetah and the wild dog — that rarely, if ever, scavenge.

What are the costs and benefits of scavenging compared with those of predation? First of all,

the scavenger avoids the task of making sure its meal is dead: a predator has already endured the energetically costly business of chasing or stalking animal after animal until one is killed. But while scavenging may be cheap, it's risky. Predators rarely give up their prey to scavengers without defending it. In such disputes, the larger animal, whether a scavenger or a predator, usually wins, although smaller animals in a pack may defeat a lone, larger animal. Bother predators and scavengers suffer the dangers inherent in fighting for possession of a carcass. Smaller scavengers such as jackals or striped hyenas avoid disputes to some extent by specializing in darting in and removing a piece of a carcass without trying to take possession of the whole thing. These two strategies can be characterized as that of the bully or that of the sneak: bullies need to be large to be successful, sneaks need to be small and quick.

Because carcasses are almost always much rarer than live prey, the major cost peculiar to scavenging is that scavengers must survey much larger areas than predators to find food. They can travel slowly, since their "prey" is already dead, but endurance is important. Many predators specialize in speed at the expense of endurance, while scavengers do the opposite.

The more committed predators among the East African carnivores (wild dogs and cheetahs) can achieve great top speeds when running, although not for long. Perhaps as a consequence, these "pure" hunters enjoy a much higher success rate in hunting (about three-fourths of their chases end in kills) than any of the scavenger-hunters do (less than half of their chases are successful). Wild dogs and cheetahs are efficient hunters, but they are neither big enough nor efficient enough in their locomotion to make good scavengers. In fact, the cheetah's teeth are so specialized for meat slicing that they probably cannot withstand the stresses of bone crunching and carcass dismembering carried out by scavengers. Other carnivores are less successful at hunting, but have specializations of size, endurance, or (in the case of the hyenas) dentition that make successful scavenging possible. The smaller carnivores seem to have a somewhat higher hunting success rate than the large ones, which balances out their difficulties in asserting possession of carcasses.

In addition to endurance, scavengers need an efficient means of locating carcasses, which, unlike live animals, don't move or make noises. Vultures, for example, solve both problems by flying. The soaring, gliding flight of vultures expends much less energy than walking or cantering as performed by the part-time mammalian scavengers. Flight enables vultures to maintain a foraging radius two to three times larger than that of spotted hyenas, while providing a better vantage point. This explains why vultures can scavenge all of their food in the same habitat in which it is impossible for any mammal to be a pure scavenger. (In fact, many mammals learn where carcasses are located from the presence of vultures.)

Since mammals can't succeed as full-time scavengers, they must have another source of food to provide the bulk of their diet. The large carnivores rely on hunting large animals to obtain food when scavenging doesn't work. Their size enables them to defend a carcass against others. Since the small carnivores — jackals and striped hyenas — often can't defend carcasses successfully, most of their diet is composed of fruit and insects. When they do hunt, they usually prey on very small animals, such as rats or hares, that can be consumed in their entirety before the larger competitors arrive.

The ancient habitat associated with the fossils of Olduvai and Koobi Fora would have supported many herbivores and carnivores. Among the latter were two species of large saber-toothed cats, whose teeth show extreme adaptations for meat slicing. These were predators with primary access to carcasses. Since their teeth were unsuitable for bone crushing, the saber-toothed cats must have left behind many bones covered with scraps of meat, skin, and tendon. Were early hominids among the scavengers that exploited such carcasses?

All three hominid species that were present in Bed I times (*Homo habilis, Australopithecus africanus, A. robustus*) were adapted for habitual, upright bipedalism. Many anatomists see evidence that these hominids were agile tree climbers as well. Although upright bipedalism is a notoriously peculiar mode of locomotion, the adaptive value of which has been argued for years (see Matt Cartmill's article, "Four Legs Good, Two Legs Bad," *Natural History*, November 1983), there are three general points of agreement.

First, bipedal running is neither fast nor efficient compared to quadrupedal gaits. However, at moderate speeds of 2.5 to 3.5 miles per hour, bipedal *walking* is more energetically efficient than quadrupedal walking. Thus, bipedal walking is an excellent means of covering large areas slowly, making it an unlikely adaptation for a hunter but an appropriate and useful adaptation for a scavenger. Second, bipedalism elevates the head, thus improving the hominid's ability to spot items on the ground — an advantage both to scavengers and to those trying to avoid becoming a carcass. Combining bipedalism with agile tree climbing improves the vantage point still further. Third, bipedalism frees the hands from locomotor duties, making it possible to carry items. What would early hominids have carried? Meat makes a nutritious, easy-to-carry package; the problem is that carrying meat attracts scavengers. Richard Potts suggests that carrying stone tools or unworked stones for toolmaking to caches would be a more efficient and less dangerous activity under many circumstances.

In short, bipedalism is compatible with a scavenging strategy. I am tempted to argue that bipedalism evolved because it provided a substantial advantage to scavenging hominids. But I doubt hominids could scavenge effectively without tools, and bipedalism predates the oldest known stone tools by more than a million years.

Is there evidence that, like modern mammalian scavengers, early hominids had an alternative food source, such as either hunting or eating fruits and insects? My husband, Alan Walker, has shown that the microscopic wear on an animal's teeth reflect its diet. Early hominid teeth have microscopic wear more like that of chimpanzees and other modern fruit eaters than that of carnivores. Apparently, early hominids ate mostly fruit, as the smaller, modern scavengers do. This accords with the estimated body weight of early hominids, which was only about forty to eighty pounds — less than that of any of the modern carnivores that combine scavenging and hunting but comparable to the striped hyena, which eats fruits and insects as well as meat.

Would early hominids have been able to compete for carcasses with other carnivores? They were too small to use a bully strategy, but if they scavenged in groups, a combined bully-sneak strategy might have been possible. Perhaps they were able to drive off a primary predator long enough to grab some meat, skin, or marrow-filled bone before relinquishing the carcass. The effectiveness of this strategy would have been vastly improved by using tools to remove meat or parts of limbs, a task at which hominid teeth are poor. As agile climbers, early hominids may have retreated into the trees to eat their scavenged trophies, thus avoiding competition from large terrestrial carnivores.

In sum, the evidence on cut marks, tooth wear, and bipedalism, together with our knowledge of scavenger adaptation in general, is consistent with the hypothesis that two million years ago hominids were scavengers rather than accomplished hunters. Animal carcasses, which contributed relatively little to the hominid diet, were not systematically cut up and transported for sharing at base camps. Man the Hunter may not have appeared until 1.5 to 0.7 million years ago, when we do see a shift toward omnivory, with a greater proportion of meat in the diet. This more heroic ancestor may have been *Homo erectus*, equipped with Acheulean-style stone tools and, increasingly, fire. If we wish to look further back, we may have to become accustomed to a less flattering image of our heritage.

5
A Novel Notion of Neanderthal

STEPHEN JAY GOULD

I am not insensible to the great American myth of wide-open western spaces (nurtured, in my formative experience, primarily by the closed domains of Hollywood backlots used for sets of B movies). Still, as a New Yorker now resident in New England, I tend to side with Frost on the correlation between good fences and good neighbors. Nonetheless, I must admit that, once in a while, the folks next door can actually outdo a resident on his own turf. I prefer T.H. Huxley or Charles Lyell — strictly as literature — to many Victorian novelists. Conversely, I regard one important area of my own profession as better enlightened by novelists than by scientists.

Science is constrained by its canons of evidence. Pure speculation, however reined by plausibility or pregnant with insight, does not lie within the rules of our game. But novelists are free, like Milton's "L'Allegro," the embodiment of good cheer:

> Come, and trip it as ye go
> On the light fantastic toe;
> And, in thy right hand lead with thee
> The mountain nymph, sweet Liberty.

(I was as happy as the namesake of this poem when I first read these lines during a dull college course, for they resolved one of those little puzzles that weighs, however lightly, on the intellect. I had never understood how you could "trip the light fantastic on the sidewalks of New York" because, in my streetwise parochialism, I had always pictured a traffic beacon.)

Many crucial events in life's history have provided no direct data for their resolution. Yet the art of plausible reconstruction has value to science because we must have frameworks to discipline our thoughts. Writers of fiction can enlighten us in this treacherous domain. No event so poor in evidence has so strongly captured our imagination as the meeting of Neanderthal and Cro-Magnon people in Europe some 30,000 years ago. The people of Cro-Magnon carved intricate figures of horses and deer and painted their caves with an esthetic power never exceeded in the history of human art. Some Neanderthals buried their dead with ceremony and may have adorned their bodies with ocher, but they had no concept (so far as we can tell) of representational art. We feel that something fundamental about our origin, and our "essence," must lie hidden in the character of this contact between our ancestors and our closest collateral relatives. But we have no data at all beyond the temporal and geographic overlap. We do not know if they murdered each other or met with the equivalent of a Paleolithic handshake, ignored each other or interbred.

From *Natural History*, June 1988, pp. 16–21. Copyright 1988 American Museum of Natural History. Reprinted with permission.

This combination of fascination and mystery has spawned a minor industry of novel writing — from William Golding (*The Inheritors*), who explored another aspect of human nature in *Lord of the Flies*, to more recent works of the Finnish paleontologist and novelist Bjorn Kurten (*Dance of the Tiger*) and the saga of Ayla as depicted by Jean Auel (*Clan of the Cave Bear* and sequels).

Let me cite just one example, at my own expense, of the novelist's power to enlighten. In the racist tradition, all too common and often unconscious, Cro-Magnons, as modern conquerors, are usually depicted as light-skinned, Neanderthals as dark. In *Meet Your Ancestors* (1945), for example, Roy Chapman Andrews wrote of the Cro-Magnon people:

> They have been called the finest physical types the world has ever produced. Probably their skins were white. In fact, if you saw a Cro-Magnon man on Fifth Avenue dressed in a sack suit and a Homburg you wouldn't give him a second glance [well, you probably would these days, for his out-dated apparel]. Or perhaps you might, if you were a woman, for artists depict him as a debutante's "dream man."

I had unconsciously adopted this stereotype in my mental picture of these people, but Bjorn Kurten's reconstruction explicitly depicts Neanderthal as white, Cro-Magnon as dark. This conjecture surely makes more sense — for Neanderthals were cold-adapted people living near the ice sheet of glacial Europe, while Cro-Magnons may have had a more tropical origin. Since we possess no direct data, a scientific treatise would have no basis for discussing the skin colors of these people. But a novelist is free, and Kurten's well-formed conjecture taught me something about prejudice and the hold of tradition.

For all their breadth and variation, however, one unchallenged assumption pervades the Neanderthal novels. The modes and reasons differ, but Cro-Magnons are superior, and they quickly prevail in all accounts. This contact of ca. 30,000 years ago is portrayed as the "first meeting" of primitive and advanced — and the Neanderthals rapidly succumb. Neanderthals are dazzled by the technological superiority of Cro-Magnons. Golding's primitives are awe-struck by a Cro-Magnon boat with sails, because they have never thought beyond a floating log when they needed to cross a river. Kurten's watch dumbfoundedly as a Cro-Magnon artist carves the likeness of an animal in wood. The brains of Auel's Neanderthals are so stuffed with memory that they cannot initiate anything new. Of the Cro-Magnon heroine Ayla, Auel writes, "In nature's way, her kind was destined to supplant the ancient, dying race."

This notion of *temporal succession* — superior supplanting primitive — is common to both major theories about the biological relationship of Cro-Magnon to Neanderthal. In one view, Neanderthals represent an ancestral stage in a progressive sequence of general advance toward modern humans. (The next step to Cro-Magnon then occurs outside Europe. Neanderthals become primitive survivors in a European backwater, and the emigrating Cro-Magnons wipe them out.) In the second view, Neanderthals are a side branch, not an ancestral stock. Yet their early division from an advancing central stock guarantees their backwardness and rapid defeat. Thus, even the novelists, with their maximal range of reasonable conjecture, have never challenged the cardinal premise of conventional wisdom — that modern people arrived in Eurasia far later than primitive Neanderthals, contacted them once, and quickly prevailed.

In this context, a report by H. Valladas and five colleagues generated astonishment in press accounts throughout the world ("Thermoluminescence Dating of Mousterian 'Proto-Cro-Magnon' Remains from Israel and the Origin of Modern Man," *Nature*, February 18, 1988, pp. 614–16). Neanderthals are a Eurasian group dating from about 125,000 to 150,000 years ago, for their first known occurrence, to about 30,000 years ago, for their supposedly singular replacement by modern Cro-Magnons. Anthropologists have puzzled for a long time over a few Eurasian sites that yield anatomically modern human remains but seem to be substantially older than the canonical 30,000-year date for contact and conquest. For example, the Qafzeh caves of Israel contain anatomically modern humans in association with species of rodents usually considered to have been victims of extinction during the early days of Neanderthal in Eurasia. Nonetheless, the presumption of nonoverlap between moderns and Neanderthals (until the crucial and momentary 30,000-year replacement) has been so strong that these sites have remained in limbo, usually rationalized in the literature as "probably" 40,000 years old or less.

Valladas and colleagues have confounded this tradition by reporting a date of 90,000 years for the anatomically modern humans of Qafzeh. You might cling to the old view by arguing that the Levant is not Europe and lies close to the favored

African source for modern human origins. Perhaps the Levant was a long staging ground for a western European invasion 60,000 years later. But this resolution will not work, because Israel and the Near East also house abundant and well-documented remains of classical Neanderthals clearly younger than the Qafzeh moderns. Thus, the geographic potential for contact between moderns and Neanderthals must have existed for nearly 60,000 years before the novelists' western European apocalypse. Yet moderns did not supplant Neanderthals.

I must admit that I am not fully confident about the 90,000-year date for Qafzeh because the technique of thermoluminescence dating (called TL in the trade), although applied in the most modern and meticulous way by Valladas and colleagues, includes some intrinsic, theoretical uncertainty. (Press accounts, in their lamentable tradition of reporting only claims, and omitting any critical discussion of procedure and methodology, have bypassed this issue entirely — and simply reported the 90,000-year date as though it possessed the factuality of a new fossil bone. I do so wish that this tradition could be broken. Science is a methodology for the testing of claims, not a list of oracular pronouncements about the nature of nature.)

As natural materials are exposed to ionizing radiation, both from the external environment and from the breakdown of isotopes in their own composition, they accumulate energy in the form of electrons trapped at defects in the crystal lattices of their constituent minerals. When the materials are heated, these electrons are driven off, often producing a visible "puff" of light, called thermoluminescence and first reported by Robert Boyle in October 1663 after he took a diamond to bed and warmed it against his naked body. (I shall refrain from the obvious vulgarities, but must report that Boyle considered his diamond as especially sensitive because he viewed his own constitution as "not of the hottest.") TL is not the ordinary red-hot glow of conventional heating, but a distinct emission of light at lower temperature caused by release of these trapped electrons. In any case, the intensity of the TL peak might measure the age of a sample since these electrons accumulate through time.

But how could we use TL to date ancient humans? Clays and flints record their own age, not the moment of human use. Unless, of course, human use has heated the materials and released their TL, thus setting the TL clock back to zero. The subsequent accumulation of new TL will then record the time since human heating.

Unsurprisingly, this method was first developed for dating pottery, since clays are fired at temperatures sufficiently high to release TL and reset the clock to zero. The method has been quite successful, but its application is neither straightforward nor unambiguous. In particular, no lawlike, universal rate governs the accumulation of TL; one has to measure the local influx of ionizing radiation from surrounding materials. This requires a firm knowledge of the postburial history of an artifact. In practice, gauges are usually buried for a year at sites where artifacts were found. The excess of an artifact's TL over this yearly dose should, in principle, determine its age.

But Neanderthals and early moderns didn't make pottery. However, they did occasionally drop flint tools and flakes into their fires. Thus, the reported TL dates at Qafzeh and other early sites are based on burned flints — and I am not entirely confident that human campfires invariably burned long enough or hot enough to reset the TL clocks to zero. However, I think that Valladas and colleagues have presented the best possible case, given intrinsic uncertainties of the method. They dated twenty flints from Qafzeh, and all fell in the narrow range of 82,400 to 109,900 years. Moreover, the associated mammalian fauna of Qafzeh, as previously mentioned, has been hinting for years that these anatomically modern humans predated the later Neanderthals of the Levant. (See M.J. Aitken, *Thermoluminescence Dating*, Academic Press, 1985. I also thank Tim White of Berkeley and John Shea of Harvard for their generous help in discussion and supplying references for several topics discussed in this essay.)

For the past thirty years or so, the main excitement in studies of human evolution has centered on discoveries about our early history — from the dawn of the first known australopithecine more than 3 million years ago, to the later transition to our own genus *Homo*, to the evolution and spread of *Homo erectus* from Africa throughout the Old World. The fascination of the opposite end — the much more recent origin of our own species, *Homo sapiens* — has received relatively little attention because no real breakthroughs have been made. This situation has changed dramatically in the last few years because two independent sources of data seem to be converging upon a firm, exciting conclusion that has been intensely surprising (but shouldn't be) to most people — *Homo sapiens* is the product of a relatively recent, discrete event of branching speciation in Africa, not the result of a continuous process of worldwide advance. The redating of Qafzeh provides a confirming link in this story — hence its status as the central item in this essay.

Genetics and paleontology are the partners of this reinterpretation. (For a good review of this important subject, see C.B. Stringer and P. Andrews, "Genetic and Fossil Evidence for the Origin of Modern Humans," *Science*, March 11, 1988, pp. 1263–68.) As discussed in my essay of June 1987, the genealogical tree of modern humans, as reconstructed from the evolution of mitochondrial DNA, contains two major branches: one with only Africans; the other with additional Africans, plus everybody else. This topology implies an African source for the most recent common ancestor. (Although origin in the Levant with multiple migrations back to Africa is not excluded, no data support this more complex reconstruction.) If we are willing to accept a constant rate for the evolution of mitochondrial DNA (unproved, but supported by data now available from other groups), then all non-African racial diversity in *Homo sapiens* is only 90,000 to 180,000 years old, while the common ancestral stock of all modern humans probably lived no more than 250,000 years ago, and perhaps a good deal more recently.

Genetic data cannot tell us what these ancestral people looked like or date their origin with certainty. Perhaps this ca. 200,000-year-old common ancestor was a brutish, small-brained fellow — and the selective blessings of mentality then promoted the evolution of modern characters in both great branches of our family tree. Only the direct evidence of paleontology can resolve this issue.

Happily, fossil data are beginning to suggest an interesting conclusion. The oldest-known anatomically modern humans are probably the South African remains from the Klasies River caves, dated at some 80,000 to 130,000 years old. The redate of Qafzeh indicates about the same age for anatomically modern humans in the Levant. We still do not know the form of the ca. 200,000-year-old common ancestor, but if Klasies and Qafzeh are essentially us, then at least we can say that half the history of our species involves little change of anatomy. Mired in my own biases of punctuated equilibrium, I rather suspect that the 200,000-year-old forebear won't look much different from us either.

Where does this reinterpretation leave Neanderthal, who looks quite a bit different from us — not the Alley Oop caveman primitive of legend, but different nonetheless. Neanderthals have been controversial ever since their first discovery in 1856. (They were found in a valley of the Düssel River named for the minor poet Neander. "Valley," in German, is *Tal* or, in an older spelling often used in the nineteenth century, *Thal*, hence chronic confusion over the variant spellings Neandertal and Neanderthal. In any case, the word was always pronounced "tal" whatever its spelling, and the common pronunciation with English "th" is just plain wrong — a good example of the common confusion between orthography and content.)

Some leading anthropologists have interpreted Neanderthal as a stage in a general trend to modern humans, hence as our direct ancestor. This view was defended by the Czech-born leader of American paleontology earlier in this century, Ales Hrdlička; also by Franz Weidenreich in the last generation and by C. Loring Brace in our own.

The extreme version of the alternative was presented by the great French anthropologist Marcellin Boule. In a series of detailed monographs on the well-preserved Neanderthal skeleton of La Chapelle-aux-Saints, Boule constructed the apish stereotype later assimilated by pop culture as the brutish, stoop-shouldered caveman — club in one hand, wife's hair in the other. Boule's Neanderthal, presented to the world just before World War I, slouched because he couldn't straighten his knees, bent forward because his backbone formed a single curve, slung his heavy head forward, and walked on the outer edge of his foot because his semi-prehensile big toe stuck out to the side and couldn't be used for proper support.

Boule's account was surely wrong, unfortunately mired in his own racist desire to compare these primitives with some modern groups that he wished to disparage, and partly based (though not so much as legend proclaims) on the arthritis, not the original anatomy, of his specimen. But in retrospect, bolstered by the redate of Qafzeh, Boule was probably right in his central claim — that Neanderthal is a branch of the human bush completely separated from *Homo sapiens*, and not at all part of our ancestry; and also that Cro-Magnons must have evolved elsewhere and lived contemporaneously with Neanderthals, long before their contact in western Europe some 30,000 years ago. The redating of Qafzeh is a vindication of Boule's primary conclusion:

> Now these Cro-Magnons, which seem to replace Neanderthals abruptly in our country, must have lived before then in another place, unless we are

willing to propose a mutation so great and so abrupt as to be absurd (from *Les hommes fossiles*, 1946 edition, p. 267).

Boule's Neanderthal was an apish primitive. Modern anatomical reconstructions reveal a stocky, heavy-set, cold-adapted skeleton with a brain as big as ours — a creature well designed for the climates of glacial Europe. But while Neanderthals have been promoted from primitive to merely different, they have not — and this is the crucial point — become more like us.

During the twenty years that I have studied this field, general consensus has ranked Neanderthal within our own species, as a cold-adapted European race, *Homo sapiens nean-derthalensis*. But if the dating of Qafzeh holds, and if the general view that ties all modern humans to a recent African root continues to gain strength, then this consensus must give way. If Neanderthals and modern humans lived in the Levant — and maintained their integrity without interbreeding — for 60,000 years before the great replacement in western Europe, then the two are separate species by the primary criterion of reproductive isolation. We shall have to return to the older view of Neanderthal as a separate species, *H. neanderthalensis*.

A much deeper issue underlies this entire debate. We are astonished to learn that all modern humans are products of a recent branching event in a single place, probably Africa. We are surprised that Neanderthal may be a separate branch of the human bush, not a more primitive ancestor. We are used to conceptualizing evolution as a tale of transformation within a continuous lineage — think of the museum parade of horses, from eohippus (fox-terrier sized, of course!) to Seabiscuit, or the line of human ascent from *Australopithecus*, naked in the African bush, to John Q. Businesssuit. Mired in this prejudice, for example, the *Auckland Sun* (February 19, 1988) reported the Qafzeh redating with this lurid leading paragraph (well, they do walk upside down out there in New Zealand, so maybe we shouldn't be surprised): "Evolutionary theories were turned back to front this week when scientists claimed modern humans existed before Neanderthal Stone Age cavemen."

We shall be truly wiser when we understand that the Qafzeh redate did not turn evolutionary theory upside down. Rather, the separation and prolonged simultaneous existence of Neanderthals and moderns as distinct species fits beautifully with a proper understanding of evolution. The only casualty of Qafzeh is a cultural prejudice for gradual, continuous advance as the canonical style of evolutionary change.

Evolution, at geological scales, is fundamentally about bushes and branching. Modern *Homo sapiens* and the extinct Neanderthals are two distinct branches, two contemporaneous species for most of their existence, if the data and arguments of this essay hold up to future scrutiny. Evolutionary trends usually work this way. The transition from reptiles to mammals, for example, is not the slow movement of a large population in lock-step from cold to warm blood, and from jawbones to earbones. Trends arise within a forest of distinct branches. Most of these branches die; a few are successful and produce more branches like themselves to fuel the transition. Trends are propagated by the differential birth and death of distinct branches, not the wholesale, gradual transformation of a single great entity. Mammals arose because the most mammallike species within a particular group of reptiles tended to live longer or branch off more daughter species. The robust australopithecines died; *Homo habilis* lived. Neanderthals became extinct; *Homo sapiens* survived.

Scientists are subject to the same biases of thinking; the press and general public hold no monopoly upon bloody-mindedness. Professional understanding of human evolution has long been hampered by a preference for viewing trends as the gradual transformation of "whole things," rather than the differential success of some kinds of little branches versus others. Stringer and Andrews, in the article cited previously, distinguished two basic views of human evolution. The "multiregional model" embodies the older view of trends as gradual transformation. It holds that *Homo sapiens* evolved over a large part of the Old World in a coordinated transition from African and Eurasian *Homo erectus*. Contact and gene flow was sufficient, according to this view, to forge *Homo erectus* from Nairobi to Beijing to Jakarta into a functioning whole, then gradually transformed by natural selection into modern humanity.

The second view, often called Noah's Ark among anthropologists, holds that most ancestral lines died, and that modern humans descend from a local group that eventually spread throughout the world. Everything discussed in this article — from the redating of Qafzeh to the status of Neanderthal to genetic and paleontological evidence for a common, temporally shallow root of all humanity in Africa — stands as a ringing confirmation of this second theory.

Yet as I advocate this second view with such delight (for it fits so well with my own preferences for punctuated equilibrium), I strongly reject its designation as Noah's Ark. I have no objection to flippancy or to biblical metaphor, but only to the inappropriate implications of this name. The Deluge was a disaster outside the ordinary course of nature. If all modern humans stem from the fortunate survivors of a debacle, then our evolution seems unusual among the trends of life's history. But nothing could be more ordinary than the derivation of a successful stock from a single event of branching. Evolution works this way nearly all the time.

Human unity is no idle political slogan or tenet of mushy romanticism (I speak of the biological meaning, not the ethical concept that science cannot touch). All modern humans form an entity united by physical bonds of descent from a recent African root; we are not merely the current state of a tendency, as the multiregional model suggests. Our unities are genealogical; we are an object of history. This insight is evolution's finest contribution to our greatest quest — the injunction inscribed as one of two cardinal precepts upon the Delphic oracle (according to Plutarch), and later invoked by Linnaeus as the very definition of the name he gave us, *Homo sapiens*: Know thyself.

6
The Archeology of Modern Human Origins

R I C H A R D   G .   K L E I N

Two competing hypotheses have long dominated specialist thinking on modern human origins. The first posits that modern people emerged in a limited area and spread from there to replace archaic people elsewhere. Proponents of this view currently favor Africa as the modern human birthplace. The second suggests that the evolution of modern humans was not geographically restricted, but involved substantial continuity between archaic and modern populations in all major regions of the occupied world. Based solely on the fossil record, both hypotheses are equally defensible, but the spread-and-replacement scenario is far more strongly supported by burgeoning data on the genetic relationships and diversity of living humans. These data imply that there was a common ancestor for all living humans in Africa between 280,000 and 140,000 years ago, and that Neanderthals and other archaic humans who inhabited Eurasia during the same interval contributed few, if any, genes to living people. I argue here that the spread-and-replacement hypothesis is also more compatible with a third line of evidence: the archeological record for human behavioral evolution.

The archeological record is geographically uneven, but where it is most complete and best-dated, it implies that a radical transformation in human behavior occurred 50,000 to 40,000 years ago, the exact time perhaps depending on the place. Arguably, barring the development of those typically human traits that produced the oldest known archeological sites between 2.5 and 2 million years ago, this transformation represents the most dramatic behavioral shift that archaeologists will ever detect. Based on evidence I will summarize, I think it almost certainly marks the advent of the fully modern way of doing things or, more precisely, of the fully modern ability to manipulate culture. The behavioral change is difficult to date precisely because it occurred beyond the effective limit of conventional radiocarbon dating, and alternative methods like accelerator mass spectometry (AMS) radiocarbon dating, thermoluminescence (TL), and electron spin resonance (ESR) are only now being applied or tested. Fresh dates and a fuller record may eventually show that the shift occurred earliest in Africa. However, even if this is not clear now, such radical and abrupt change is more consistent with population spread and replacement, as implied by the "Out-of-Africa" model, than it is with diffusion or independent invention, as required by the theory of multiregional continuity. The only potential incongruity between the archeological record and the current "Out-of-Africa" model is the date for the last common ancestor of modern humanity. If, as I suggest below, the origin of fully modern behavior was biologically founded, this date should probably be closer to 50,000 than to 140,000 years ago.

Because both the archeological and human fossil records are geographically variable, I proceed on a region-by-region basis. I also stress dating issues, which are as critical to the debate as the dated objects. Much of the discussion is broadly summarized in Figure 1.

Europe

The relevant archeological evidence in Europe is commonly divided between two great culture-stratigraphic complexes: the Middle Paleolithic, or Mousterian, between roughly 200,000 and 40,000 years ago, and the Upper Paleolithic, between roughly 40,000 and 10,000 years ago. Until recently, conventional radiocarbon dates could be used to argue that the Upper Paleolithic began 40,000 years ago in the east and only 35,000 years ago in the west. However, AMS radiocarbon dates on charcoal particles from very early Upper Paleolithic layers at l'Arbreda and El Castillo caves in northern Spain now show that the Upper Paleolithic was also under way in western Europe about 40,000 years ago. The likelihood that little time separates first appearances is supported by the remarkable similarity among the earliest universally accepted Upper Paleolithic assemblages throughout much of Europe. These assemblages are commonly assigned to the "early Aurignacian" Industrial Complex, which is characterized not only by uniquely shared stone artifact (endscraper and burin) types, but also by highly distinctive bone points.

The Upper Paleolithic is readily differentiated from the Mousterian by the following features:

1. Unlike Mousterian stone assemblages, which tend to be dominated by flakes, Upper Paleolithic assemblages generally include large numbers of well-made blades (flakes that are at least twice as long as they are wide and that require special effort or expertise to produce routinely.) Initially, the advantage of Upper Paleolithic blade technology may have been the additional amount of cutting edge it could extract from a single core. Subsequently, widespread Upper Paleolithic reliance on blades may have had more to do with shared history than with the need to economize on the use of stone.

2. Mousterian stone tools are mainly sidescrapers and denticulates that can be difficult to sort into discrete, nonoverlapping categories. In contrast, Upper Paleolithic tools commonly comprise endscrapers, burins (gravers), points, and other kinds of tools that are much easier to place within mutually exclusive, formally defined types and subtypes. In connection with this, the number and variety of palpably discrete tool types is much greater in the Upper Paleolithic. In fact, it has been cogently argued that many Mousterian tool types are not types at all, but simply different stages in the resharpening or refreshing of only a few fundamental types. The sum of the evidence suggests that, as compared to the Mousterian, Upper Paleolithic tool manufacture more often involved a well-formulated mental template of the complete end-product (as opposed to the simple image of an edge or point) and that Upper Paleolithic tools were used in a wider range of specialized, distinct activities. There was at least one major activity — the customary shaping of bone, antler, or ivory into formal artifact types — for which there is little or no evidence before the Upper Paleolithic. The abundance of burins in many Upper Paleolithic assemblages is probably tied to their importance in bone working.

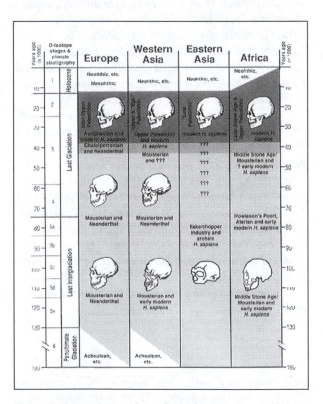

Figure 1 Approximate chronological arrangement of the major cultural units and fossil human types discussed in this paper.

3. Even the very earliest Upper Paleolithic people, unlike Mousterians, recognized bone, antler, and ivory as plastic materials that could be whittled, carved, or polished into a variety of useful artifact types. Formal bone artifacts occur in virtually every Upper Paleolithic site that preserves bone, whereas comparable Mousterian sites provide no standardized bone tools, only occasional bone fragments with traces of use as pounders, stone-tool retouchers or, perhaps, cutting boards. The failure of Mousterians (and all earlier people) to recognize the full artifactual potential of bone and similarly plastic raw materials is probably linked to another major difference — their failure to produce indisputable art objects such as beads or pendants. In contrast, art and items of personal adornment are an important aspect of even the earliest Upper Paleolithic. The later proliferation of art has been the subject of numerous studies.

4. Whereas Mousterian and earlier assemblages varied relatively little through time and space, the Upper Paleolithic, shortly after it appeared, rapidly differentiated into a wide range of regional and temporal variants. The degree of spatial and temporal heterogeneity in Upper Paleolithic artifact assemblages (or "cultures") is reminiscent of recorded history; in comparison, the relative homogeneity of the Mousterian and earlier cultures seems highly peculiar. The great variability of the Upper Paleolithic makes it more difficult to characterize than the Mousterian. Moreover, there will always be Upper Paleolithic sites that do not reveal the full range of Upper Paleolithic markers, such as well-made bone artifacts, art objects, or items of personal adornment. There is again a parallel with historically recorded, stone-tool using people, not all of whom worked bone extensively or manufactured art objects in materials that could survive for thousands or tens of thousands of years. However, the fundamental point is that the Mousterian and earlier industries are essentially invariant in these regards. They provide no compelling evidence that anyone before 40,000 years ago produced art or made formal artifacts in relatively durable plastic materials.

5. Finally, the Mousterian and Upper Paleolithic contrast in virtually every nonartifactual characteristic that archeology can detect. Thus, while both Mousterians and Upper Paleolithic people buried their dead, Upper Paleolithic graves tend to be significantly more elaborate. These graves are the first to suggest a burial ritual or ceremony, with its obvious implications of religion or ideology in the ethnographic sense of the term. Both Mousterians and Upper Paleolithic people used fire, but Upper Paleolithic fireplaces commonly reflect a much more refined knowledge of how to maintain and maximize heat production. Similarly, both Mousterians and Upper Paleolithic people probably built structures at open-air sites, but the evidence from Mousterian sites is vague, suggesting that Mousterian shelters were comparatively flimsy and informal. In contrast, many Upper Paleolithic sites have provided ruins implying substantial, well-built houses. Together with a more sophisticated mastery of fire, these ruins help explain how Upper Paleolithic people were able to colonize especially harsh environments in easternmost Europe and northern Asia where no one had lived before. Equally significant, Upper Paleolithic people were also the first to trade or transport large quantities of stone and, perhaps, other raw materials over more than a few kilometers. The mechanics of how this was done remain obscure, but the broad implication is that there was a more elaborate network of social relationships among neighboring groups. Conceivably, broader social networks were made possible by the development of fully modern linguistic capabilities, which arguably are signalled by many other Upper Paleolithic distinctions, such as the production of art.

The list of contrasts can be extended, and in each case the conclusion is not just that Upper Paleolithic people were qualitatively different, but also that they were behaviorally more advanced than Mousterians and earlier people in the same way that living people are. The evidence does not demonstrate that every known Upper Paleolithic trait was present from the very beginning. It is, in fact, only logical that many features, particularly those involving advances in technology, took time to accumulate. What the evidence does show is that, compared to their antecedents, Upper Paleolithic people were remarkably innovative and inventive; this characteristic, more than any other, is their hallmark. In the broad sweep of European prehistory, they were the first people for whom archeology clearly implies the presence of both "Culture" and "cultures" (or ethnicity) in the classic anthropological sense.

In light of the great behavioral contrast between Upper Paleolithic and Mousterian people, it is obviously relevant to ask if they belonged to different physical types. The answer is a qualified yes. Wherever diagnostic human remains have been found in a Mousterian context, they invariably come from Neanderthals. Similarly, virtually all human remains that have been found in Upper Paleolithic layers represent anatomically modern humans. The only clear exceptions to the rule are at two French sites, Arcy-sur-Cure and Saint-Césaire, where Neanderthal fossils are associated with artifacts of the early Upper Paleolithic Chatelperronian Industry. At Arcy-sur-Cure, the fossils comprise only isolated teeth, but at Saint-Césaire there is a partial skeleton of undeniable Neanderthal morphology.

Following François Bordes, most authorities agree that the Chatelperronian developed directly out of the preceding "Mousterian of Acheulean Tradition" in a limited area of northern Spain and western and central France. Mousterian roots are indicated by relatively abundant sidescrapers, denticulates, and other typical Mousterian stone tools, but assignment of the Chatelperronian to the Upper Paleolithic is clearly warranted by the frequent finding of well-made burins and end-scrapers and, especially at Arcy-sur-Cure, of equally well-made bone artifacts and beads or pendants. Similar Mousterian/Upper Paleolithic amalgams or transitional industries have been reported elsewhere — most notably, the Uluzzian of Italy and the Szeletian/Jerzmanovician of Central Europe. None, however, is as compelling as the Chatelperronian. In many cases, they could represent the inadvertent mixture of adjacent Mousterian and Upper Paleolithic layers during excavation, which is clearly not the case for the Chatelperronian.

One possible interpretation of the Chatelperronian is that it reflects or anticipates the evolution of Mousterian-making Neanderthals into fully modern Upper Paleolithic people. However, this explanation faces at least two serious objections. First, unlike the Chatel-perronian artifacts that accompany the Neander-thal skeleton at Saint-Césaire, there is nothing transitional or intermediate about the skeleton. It is as classically Neanderthal as any Mousterian skeleton. This is doubly significant, for TL dates on associated burnt flint artifacts indicate that the skeleton may date from only 36,000 years ago. Even if this date is slightly too young, it would still leave too little time for Neanderthals to have evolved into modern people.

The second problem is that the Chatelperronian was coeval with the early Aurignacian, which has no obvious local antecedents and which eventually replaced the Chatelperronian throughout its range. Broad contemporaneity is indicated by the apparent overlap between the Saint-Césaire TL date and the north Spanish AMS radiocarbon dates cited earlier. Temporal overlap is indicated even more directly by the interfingering of Chatelperronian and early Aurignacian levels at El Pendo Cave in northern Spain and at Le Piage and Roc de Combe shelters in France. Aurignacian truncation of the Chatelperronian is shown at many sites. In western Europe, the physical identity of the early Aurignacians, dating to as much as 40,000 years ago, remains to be established, but the later ones, living around 30,000 years ago, were classic "Cro-Magnons" with no obvious trace of Neanderthal ancestry. The early Aurignacians of central Europe were very robust, but also indisputably modern. Under the circumstances, perhaps the most plausible, if not fully persuasive interpretation of the Chatelperronian (and of analogous Mousterian/Upper Paleolithic blends elsewhere, to the extent that they are genuine), is that it reflects the diffusion of Upper Paleolithic traits into an otherwise Mousterian context. The most obvious source of that diffusion would be the contemporaneous early Aurignacian.

As already indicated, the early Aurignacian is the earliest indisputable Upper Paleolithic over much of Europe and in most places it seems to have replaced the Mousterian more or less abruptly. Its remarkable uniformity and syn-chroneity over a vast area clearly suggest that it was the product of a rapidly expanding popula-tion. The expansion it most likely reflects is the entry into Europe of modern humans from outside. There are obstacles to this interpretation — the Chatelperronian (and, to the degree they are genuine, broadly analogous Mousterian/Upper Paleolithic "transitional" industries elsewhere) is clearly one; the occur-rence of a very different (non-Aurignacian) early Upper Paleolithic tradition in easternmost Europe (essentially the former European USSR or Europe east of the Carpathian Mountains) is another. Still, on balance, widespread replacement of nonmodern Mousterians by modern Aurignacians is certainly the most plausible scenario. In sum, the European archeological evidence surely supports the spread-and-replacement theory of modern human origins more strongly than it does the multiregional alternative.

Asia (Including Australasia)

For present purposes, Asia is usefully divided between western and eastern parts roughly along longitude 80°E. In vernacular terms, the western part comprises the Near (or Middle) East and adjacent parts of Central Asia. The eastern part includes the eastern portion of the Indian sub-continent and the area yet further east that Europeans have long called the Far East. Archeologically, from the time between 1.4 and 1 million years ago when people first left Africa, western Asia appears to have been a kind of crossroads between Africa and Europe, sharing many features with both. In contrast, from very early on, eastern Asia appears to have been unique, as if it were following its own distinct historic-evolutionary trajectory. For the last 200,000 to 100,000 years that are of special concern here, the contrast between east and west is suggested not only by archeology, but also by the human fossil record. Before 50,000 to 40,000 years ago, when western Asia was variably occu-pied by Neanderthals who perhaps derived from Europe or by very early moderns who arguably derived from Africa, eastern Asia seems to have been occupied by a distinctive human type that was neither Neanderthal nor modern.

The west Asian archeological evidence bearing on modern human origins comprises the same two culture-stratigraphic units as in Europe: the Mousterian or Middle Paleolithic before about 40,000 years ago and the Upper Paleolithic afterward. The Upper Paleolithic is distinguished from the preceding Mousterian by essentially the same features as in Europe, including the manu-facture of formal bone artifacts and art objects or items of personal adornment. The best available dates indicate that the west Asian Upper Paleolithic began roughly 40,000 years ago, at about the same time as in Europe. If fresh dates eventually show that the Upper Paleolithic was present somewhat earlier in western Asia, a subsequent movement to Europe would be implied. In support of this possibility, western Asia has provided the most convincing case for the evolution of Upper Paleolithic blade technol-ogy from a sophisticated, but still typically Mousterian, flake technology. The evidence, which comes from Boker Tachtit in the Negev Desert of Israel, involves progressive change toward Upper Paleolithic core technology and a concomitant increase in Upper Paleolithic tool types within a sequence that, by means of uranium-series disequilibrium and conventional radiocarbon dates, has been tentatively bracketed between 47,000 and 38,000 years ago.

Upper Paleolithic human remains are scarce in western Asia, but where they occur they are anatomically modern. Especially noteworthy is a child's skull from a very early Upper Paleolithic

layer at Ksar Akil, Lebanon. Radiocarbon dates from overlying layers and the associated artifacts indicate that the skull is probably at least 37,000 years old. The thoroughly modern morphology of the skull thus suggests that all later Upper Paleolithic people were also modern, as in Europe. However, in sharp contrast to Europe, the makers of Mousterian tools included both Neanderthals and people commonly regarded as early modern humans. Neanderthal/Mousterian associations are especially well-documented at Tabun, Amud, and Kebara Caves in Israel, at Shanidar Cave in Iraq, and at Teshik-Tash Cave in Uzbekistan. Early modern/Mousterian associa-tions are demonstrated at Skhul and Qafzeh Caves in Israel.

Explanations for the occurrence of both modern humans and Neanderthals in a Mousterian context depend heavily on dating. Relative dating based on flake thickness and breadth ratios suggests that the early moderns from Skhul and Qafzeh postdate the local Neanderthals. This raises the possibility that modern people evolved from Near Eastern Neanderthals. However, a rash of TL dates on burnt flints and ESR dates on nonhuman dental enamel implies either that early moderns and Neanderthals coexisted locally from before 100,000 years ago until after 60,000 years ago or, perhaps, that Neanderthals actually replaced early moderns at the beginning of the Last Glaciation, roughly 75,000 years ago. Replacement might have been possible because, unlike the fully modern makers of Upper Paleolithic artifacts, early moderns had no obvious behavioral advan-tage over the Neanderthals, whereas the Neanderthals had short distal-limb segments and other traits indicating that they may have been especially adapted to cold.

Some of the TL and ESR dates contradict correlations among sites that are strongly sug-gested by faunal and artifact similarities, climatic stratigraphy, and uranium-series disequilibrium dates. It thus seems increasingly likely that some of the TL and ESR dates are incorrect, perhaps because they were based on incorrect estimates of the annual radiation dose received by the dated materials. Nonetheless, in aggregate, the dates all but preclude an evolutionary link between the Near Eastern Neanderthals and early modern people. Instead, given the proximity to Africa of Qafzeh and Skhul, the two Israeli sites that have provided early moderns, the dates can be used to argue either that the Qafzeh/Skhul people were the descendants of an immigrant early modern African population or that populations on the immediate periphery of Africa shared in the African evolution of modern humans. Equally important, the Near Eastern data indicate either that modern anatomy evolved before modern behavior or that the anatomical modernity of the Qafzeh/Skhul people and their African contemporaries has been overstated. As a group, the Qafzeh/Skhul fossils exhibit remarkable variability in the expression of fully modern features and, in some important respects, such as strongly developed browridges and large teeth, they tend to resemble more archaic people. Both cranially and postcranially, they clearly make far better ancestors for later modern people than the Neanderthals do. However, it seems reasonable to suppose that the reason their behavior was not fully modern is that they were not yet fully modern biologically — perhaps, above all, neurologically.

The picture in eastern Asia is very different, although the difference may in part reflect the lower intensity of research and the less uniform standard of investigation and reporting. Certainly, there is no evidence that a typically Upper Paleolithic blade technology was ever introduced to southern China and adjacent southeast Asia. Pope has argued that a relatively crude flake-and-chopper technology continued there, largely unchanged, from the time of classic *Home erectus*, before 250,000 years ago, until 12,000 to 10,000 years ago or even later. Equally important, he points out that there is no evidence for the relatively abrupt appearance of formal bone artifacts, art, sophisticated graves, or other innovations that indicate a behavioral metamorphosis in the west around 40,000 years ago. However, the impression of remarkable continuity and conservatism in the Far East is based on only a small number of excavated sites, often poorly dated and unevenly described, and it may not be sustained as research expands. One hint of what may have actually happened comes from Sri Lanka, to the southwest, where recent excavations in Batadomba Iena Cave have uncovered sophisticated stone tools ("geometric microliths"), formal bone artifacts, and modern human remains in a layer radiocarbon-dated to roughly 28,500 years ago.

The pattern that may eventually emerge is also suggested by the relatively well-known archeological record of northeast Asia (Siberia and adjacent regions), to the north, and even more strongly, by the record of Australasia, to the southeast. The harsh climatic conditions of northeast Asia seem to have largely precluded occupation until sometime between 35,000 and 20,000 years ago,

when anatomically modern people making Upper-Paleolithic-like stone tools, formal bone artifacts, and art objects or ornaments appeared widely. Substantial houses and fireplaces like those of their western contemporaries help explain how these people could live where no one had before. They also buried their dead in graves that resembled western ones in complexity. Stone artifact assemblages imply that the same broadly "Upper Paleolithic" complex penetrated southward to Mongolia, north China, Korea, and Japan. It may be represented at the famous Upper Cave at Zhoukoudian near Beijing, if the sparse artifacts and more abundant human remains recovered there are actually about 18,000 years old, instead of 11,000 years (or less).

The situation in Australasia (including New Guinea and Tasmania, which were connected to Australia throughout most of the period in question) is even more directly relevant, for the first Australasians surely came from southeast Asia. The initial colonization of Australasia apparently occurred 50,000 to 40,000 years ago. This event might itself be regarded as an index of behavioral innovation in that it manifestly required the development of watercraft that could cross at least 90 km of open sea. A modern skull from a layer radiocarbon-dated to roughly 40,000 years ago at Niah Cave, Borneo, may represent the parent population, although it is possible that the skull lay in an intrusive (more recent) grave that was not detected in the excavation. The very earliest Australians are not well-documented, but at least those who lived after 30,000 years ago were fully modern. They produced formal bone artifacts, art objects or ornaments, and relatively elaborate graves that broadly recall those of their far western contemporaries.

The same vagueness and uncertainty that characterize the Chinese and southeast Asian archeological evidence also tend to mark the regional human fossil record. Except by extrapolation from northeast Asia and especially Australia, the pattern of human evolution between 200,000 and 10,000 years ago remains speculative. Frequently cited fossils from Dali, Maba, Xujiayao, and Jinnui Shan (Yinkou) in China may imply the existence before 40,000 years ago of a distinct Asian population that was archaic to broadly the same degree as the Neanderthals, although markedly different from them in detail. However, none of these fossils is convincingly dated and their artifactual associations remain hazy. The same is true of most indisputably "early modern" human remains from China and southeast Asia, perhaps most notably including the famous Wajak skulls from Java. In sum, with regard to modern human origins, the Far East may seem exceptional not so much because it differed in important respects from western Asia, Europe, and Africa, but because it has provided far less evidence.

Africa

It is heuristically useful to divide Africa, like Asia, into two major parts, although, from a paleoanthropological perspective, they differ far less than do the two major regions of Asia. The two parts are north Africa, comprising especially the Nile Valley and the coastal regions north of the Sahara Desert, and sub-Saharan Africa, or Africa south of the Sahara. In north Africa, the archeological residues bearing on modern human origins are basically similar to those in western Asia and Europe, and are conventionally assigned to the same major culture-stratigraphic units — the Middle Paleolithic (earlier) and the Upper Paleolithic (later). Based primarily on radiocarbon dates from Cyrenaica (northern Libya), the Upper Paleolithic appears to have begun about 40,000 years ago, at roughly the same time as in western Asia and Europe.

In sub-Saharan Africa, the relevant archeological materials are commonly divided between the Middle Stone Age (MSA) and the Later Stone Age (LSA) (Fig. 2). The MSA occupied roughly the same time interval as the Middle Paleolithic, between approximately 200,000 and 40,000 years ago and it is very similar to the Middle Paleolithic in stone tool technology and typology. Typological schemes that have been employed for Middle Paleolithic tools apply equally well (or poorly) to MSA pieces. Moreover, MSA assemblages exhibit the same relatively limited degree of variability through time and space. Like their Middle Paleolithic counterparts, MSA people do not seem to have recognized bone, ivory, and shell as substances that could be worked into formal artifact types, and they left no evidence of art. If MSA assemblages had been found in Europe or western Asia, they would surely have been assigned to the Middle Paleolithic. The terminological distinction mainly reflects scholarly tradition and geographic distance.

The LSA is more difficult to characterize, partly because, like the broadly contemporaneous Upper Paleolithic, it was somewhat more internally variable. There is also the problem that early LSA assemblages, dating between at least 40,000 years ago and roughly 20,000 years ago, remain poorly

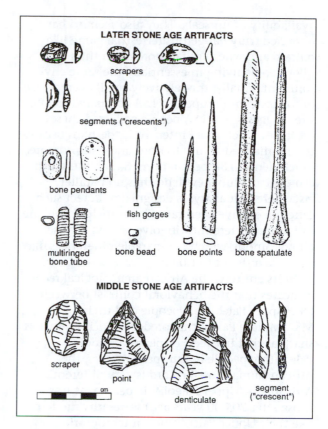

Figure 2 Typical Middle Stone Age and Later Stone Age artifacts (redrawn from originals by J. Deacon).

known or described. For the moment, it can be said that, like the Upper Paleolithic, the LSA differs from what preceded it by the presence of well-made, standardized bone artifacts and art objects or items of personal adornment. The well-known LSA assemblages that postdate 20,000 years ago tend to be distinguished by various kinds of microlithic pieces that were probably mounted or inserted in bone or wooden handles or shafts. Hafts with microliths still in place have been found in some relatively recent LSA sites. Based on ethnographic analogy, some of the microlithic pieces and associated bone artifacts in LSA sites were probably parts of composite arrows, while other bone and stone artifacts were probably used for fishing. There is no artifactual evidence for the bow and arrow or for fishing gear in the MSA.

The artifactual contrasts that suggest a significant behavioral difference between LSA and MSA people are mirrored in contrasts between the animal remains they discarded at southern African sites. Thus, fish bones abound at coastal LSA sites, but are all but absent from comparably located MSA sites. Similarly, only LSA people clearly recognized seasonal variability in the availability of fur seals. They also seem to have obtained truly dangerous terrestrial game like buffalo and wild pigs far more often than did MSA people living in essentially the same environment. Finally, the relatively small average size of tortoises and limpets in LSA compared to MSA sites suggests that LSA people collected these creatures much more intensively, perhaps because their enhanced ability to hunt and fish promoted much denser LSA populations. So far, the southern African faunal evidence has no parallel elsewhere, but analyses designed to detect such differences have been rare. The principal ones are in Europe, where they involve far less diverse faunas among which comparable differences may be more difficult to isolate.

In its entirety, the African archeological record indicates that the behavioral contrast between LSA/Upper Paleolithic people and their MSA/Middle Paleolithic predecessors is at least as sharp as that between Upper and Middle Paleolithic people in Europe. However, the African human fossil record is very different. African LSA/Upper Paleolithic people (at least those after 20,000 years ago) were fully modern, like their Upper Paleolithic contemporaries, whereas African MSA/Middle Paleolithic people differed appreciably from the Neanderthals and, in all observable respects, approached modern people far more closely. Admittedly, many relevant African fossils are not firmly dated, but others, in particular those from the Klasies River Mouth Cave complex in South Africa and from Dar-es-Soltan Cave 2 in Morocco are probably as well-fixed in time as any European Neanderthal remains.

At Klasies River Mouth, stratigraphic and geochemical observations place the most important human specimens firmly within global oxygen-isotope stage 5 (the Last Interglaciation, in the broad sense), before 75,000 years ago. At Dar-es-Soltan 2, the human fossils are associated with the Aterian variant of the Middle Paleolithic, which almost certainly lies beyond the range of conventional radiocarbon dating. The Aterian is commonly associated with evidence of much moister climate, and within the time range when the Aterian must have existed, the last time that climate was that moist was within stage 5. Arguably then, the Dar-es-Soltan 2 fossils are broadly comparable in age to those from Klasies River Mouth.

The fossil evidence from Klasies River Mouth, Dar-es-Soltan, and other sites clearly supports genetic evidence that modern people originated in Africa and subsequently replaced more archaic

people elsewhere. Moreover, like the broadly comparable human remains from Qafzeh and Skhul caves in Israel, the African fossils may imply that modern anatomy evolved before modern behavior. It might be argued that the apparent disjunction results from an incorrect reading of the archeological record and that the African MSA/Middle Paleolithic complex actually provides evidence for a behavioral change or advance that could be linked to the appearance of anatomically modern people.

In north Africa, the change could be signalled by the Aterian Industry, which, unlike the Middle Paleolithic (or Mousterian) in the narrow sense, contains numerous retouched tools with stems and tangs. In southern Africa, the change could be marked by the relatively abrupt appearance of the Howieson's Poort MSA variant within long MSA sequences at numerous sites south of the Limpopo River. The Howieson's Poort is distinguished from the MSA before and after mainly by the presence of well-made segments ("crescents") and other backed tools that recall similarly shaped, but much smaller LSA pieces (Fig. 2). The function of Aterian tangs and Howieson's Poort backing has not been directly established. But if they were to facilitate hafting, then either separately or together, the Aterian and the Howieson's Poort might indicate the kind of innovative ability that is more conspicuously reflected in Upper Paleolithic/LSA assemblages. However, it is only in tangs and backed pieces, respectively, that the Aterian and Howieson's Poort are distinctive. In all other fundamental characteristics, including basic stone-working technology and the absence of formal bone artifacts and art, neither industry stands out within the more general MSA/Middle Paleolithic complex.

Equally important, the Howieson's Poort and possibly also the Aterian were succeeded by less distinctive MSA/Middle Paleolithic variants and, based on stratigraphic superposition alone, the Howieson's Poort clearly postdates the oldest modern or near-modern human fossils in southern Africa, perhaps by 20,000 years or more. In this respect, it recalls the Amudian or "Pre-Aurignacian" Industry of Lebanon, Israel, and possibly Libya, which is likewise sandwiched between otherwise typically Middle Paleolithic industries and which clearly antedates the early modern human fossils of Qafzeh and Skhul by a long interval. Based on an elevated frequency of blades and Upper Paleolithic stone-tool types, the Amudian has sometimes been seen as a harbinger of the Upper Paleolithic, but A.J. Jelinek has argued that it is simply a relatively distinctive Middle Paleolithic variant. It seems reasonable to regard the Aterian and Howieson's Poort in the same light.

How, then, should the apparent lag of modern behavior behind modern form be understood? As in the Near East, the answer may be that the lag is more apparent than real, and that African MSA/Middle Paleolithic people are more appropriately characterized as "near-modern," or as the most probable immediate ancestors of fully modern people. The Dar-es-Soltan skull can be distinguished from virtually all modern humans by the size and structure of its brow ridge, while the Klasies River Mouth fossils are remarkably variable, especially in the chin region, in their expression of fully modern morphology. Arguably then, it was the subsequent evolution of fully modern people (with fully modern brains?) that made fully modern behavior possible, and it was the competitive advantage conferred by such behavior that allowed fully modern people to replace the Neanderthals and equally archaic people beginning 40,000 years ago or somewhat before.

If this hypothesis is correct, we should expect to find the earliest evidence for fully modern behavior in Africa. Unfortunately, the search may prove difficult, because in both northern and southern Africa many deeply stratified sites like Dar-es-Soltan and Klasies River Mouth exhibit long occupational hiatuses between Middle Paleolithic/MSA layers that probably antedate 40,000 years ago, and Upper Paleolithic/LSA layers that postdate 20,000 years ago. The reason is probably that African human populations were drastically reduced by widespread hyperaridity in the middle of the Last Glaciation. Attempts to document the earliest LSA or the MSA/LSA transition will probably have to target relatively limited areas where conditions remained more mesic and where archeological visibility was thus maintained. At the moment, based on a small number of excavations, it appears that these conditions may be best met in equatorial east Africa. It is there, perhaps, that searches for the earliest behaviorally modern humans should concentrate.

Summary and Conclusions

The archeological evidence bearing on modern human origins is uneven and incomplete, but wherever it is full enough for judgement, it suggests that a major transformation in human behavior occurred about 40,000 years ago. Prior to this time, human form and human behavior evolved hand in hand, very slowly over very long time intervals. Afterward, evolution of the human form all but ceased, while the evolution of behavior or, perhaps more precisely, the evolution of culture, accelerated dramatically. Considering all the available fossil and archeological evidence, I think the behavioral breakthrough probably reflects the last in a long series of biologically based advances in human mental and cognitive capacity. The special importance of this final advance was that it launched the fully modern human ability to manipulate culture as an adaptive mechanism. Fossil and genetic evidence suggest that the crucial neural change occurred in Africa, but this is not essential to my basic reasoning. My view is simply that if the change had occurred in Europe, students of modern human origins would be Neanderthals talking about the peculiar people who used to live in Africa.

It is of course possible to interpret the archeological evidence differently than I have here. One possibility raised by Soffer is that the relatively abrupt behavioral metamorphosis that occurred about 40,000 years ago has little or nothing to do with biological change. Instead it might reflect a radical transformation in social relations, including, primarily, the development of the nuclear family as the fundamental productive unit and of modern notions of kinship and descent to relate individuals and groups. The major problem I see with this hypothesis is that it offers no explanation of why the radical social transformation happened. I think it is far more economical to tie the basic behavioral shift, which may have included major changes in social organization, to a neurological change that occasioned the modern human ability to manipulate culture. Admittedly, this idea rests on changes in craniofacial morphology that need have no neurological correlates, and thus may prove difficult or impossible to test in the fossil record. However, it follows logically from the notion that selection for larger and presumably more sophisticated brains was a vital aspect of human evolution for a very long time before the origin of modern humans and from the observation that earlier advances in human behavior, from the Oldowan to the Acheulean to the Middle Paleolithic, corresponded broadly to changes in brain size and, probably, brain organization.

A second, more fundamental objection to the archeological interpretation I have offered is that it misrepresents the archeological evidence and that this evidence actually suggests widespread regional continuity rather than an abrupt shift about 40,000 years ago. At base, the principal recent proponents of this perspective are less concerned about the actual evidence than they are about the archeological paradigms that are used to understand it. Thus, they argue that the apparent contrast between Middle and Upper Paleolithic artifact assemblages may in large measure be a result of the differing typological systems by which the assemblages are commonly described. I take their point, but I believe that essential differences in the artifacts force the use of different systems and that the resulting contrast reflects prehistoric reality, not simply archeological (mis)perception. More generally, I believe that the most important obstacle to progress on the issue of modern human origins is evidentiary, not epistemological. New ideas and perceptions are welcome, but I think that what we need most of all is a much larger number of well-dated fossils and archeological sites.

Acknowledgments

This paper was revised and abridged from a manuscript prepared for the 14th Annual Spring Systematics Symposium at the Field Museum of Natural History, 11 May 1991. I thank O. Bar-Yosef, J.G. Fleagle, D.K. Grayson, F.E. Grine, M. Stoneking, and R.H. Tuttle for criticisms and suggestions.

7
The Naked Ape: An Idea We Could Live Without

DAVID PILBEAM

Last fall CBS Television broadcast a National Geographic Special, in prime time, called "Monkeys, Apes, and Man." This was an attempt to demonstrate how much studies of primates can tell us about our true biological selves. In a recent *Newsweek* magazine article, Stewart Alsop, while discussing problems of war, stated that nations often quarrel over geopolitical real estate when national boundaries are poorly defined: his examples were culled from areas as diverse as the Middle East, Central Europe, and Asia. One of his introductory paragraphs included the following:

> The animal behaviorists — Konrad Lorenz, Robert Ardrey, Desmond Morris — have provided wonderful insights into human behavior. Animals that operate in groups, from fish up to our ancestors among the primates, instinctively establish and defend a territory, or turf. There are two main reasons why fighting erupts between turfs — when the turfs are ill-defined or overlapping; or when one group is so weakened by sickness or other cause as to be unable to defend its turf, thus inviting aggression.

Here Alsop is taking facts (some of them are actually untrue facts) from the field of ethology

From *Discovery*, Vol. 7, No. 2, 1972, pp. 63–70. © 1972 Peabody Museum of Natural History, Yale University. Reprinted with the permission of Yale University.

— which is the science of whole animal behavior as studied in naturalistic environments — and extrapolating directly to man from these ethological facts as though words such as *territoriality, aggression*, and so forth describe the same phenomena in all animal species, including man.

Both these examples from popular media demonstrate nicely what can be called "naked apery." When Charles Darwin first published *The Origin of Species* and *The Descent of Man*, over 100 years ago, few people believed in any kind of biological or evolutionary continuity between men and other primates. Gradually the idea of man's physical evolution from ape- or monkey-like ancestors came to be accepted; yet the concept of human behavioral evolution was always treated with scepticism, or even horror. But times have changed. No longer do we discriminate between rational man, whose behavior is almost wholly learned, and all other species, brutish automata governed solely by instincts.

One of the principal achievements of ethologists, particularly those who study primates, has been to demonstrate the extent to which the dichotomy between instinct and learning is totally inadequate in analyzing the behavior of higher vertebrate species — especially primates. Almost all behavior in monkeys and apes involves a mixture of the learned and the innate; almost all behavior is under some genetic control in that its development is channelled — although the amount of channelling varies. Thus, all baboons of one species will grow up producing much the same range of vocalizations; however, the same sound may have subtly different meanings for members of different troops of the same species. In one area, adult male baboons may defend the troop; those of the identical species in a different environment may habitually run from danger. Monkeys in one part of their species range may be sternly territorial; one hundred miles away, feeding ranges of adjacent groups may overlap considerably and amicably. These differences are due to learning. Man is the learning animal par excellence. We have more to learn, take longer to do it, learn it in a more complex and yet more efficient way (that is, culturally), and have a unique type of communication system (vocal language) to promote our learning. All this the ethologists have made clear.

Studies of human behavior, at least under naturalistic conditions, have been mostly the preserve of social anthropologists and sociologists. The anthropological achievement has been to document the extraordinary lengths to which human groups will go to behave differently from other groups. The term *culture*, a special one for the anthropologist, describes the specifically human type of learned behavior in which arbitrary rules and norms are so important. Thus, whether we have one or two spouses, wear black or white to a funeral, live in societies that have kings or lack chiefs entirely, is a function not of our genes but of learning; the matter depends upon which learned behaviors we deem appropriate — again because of learning. Some behaviors make us feel comfortable, others do not; some behaviors may be correct in one situation and not in another — forming a line outside a cinema as opposed to the middle of the sidewalk, for example; singing rather than whistling in church; talking to domestic animals but not to wild ones. The appropriate or correct behavior varies from culture to culture; exactly which one is appropriate is arbitrary. This sort of behavior is known as "context dependent behavior" and is, in its learned form, pervasively and almost uniquely human. So pervasive is it, indeed, that we are unaware most of the time of the effects on our behavior of context dependence. It is important to realize here that although a great deal of ape and monkey behavior is learned, little of it is context dependent in a cultural, human sense.

In the past ten years there has been a spate of books — the first of the genre was Robert Ardrey's *African Genesis*, published in 1961 — that claim first to describe man's "real" or "natural" behavior in ethological style, then go on to explain how these behaviors have evolved. In order to do this, the authors use primate societies as models of earlier stages of human evolution: primates are ourselves, so to speak, unborn. *African Genesis, The Territorial Imperative, The Social Contract*, all by Ardrey; *The Naked Ape* and *The Human Zoo*, by Desmond Morris; Konrad Lorenz's *On Aggression*; the exotic *The Descent of Woman*, by Elaine Morgan; plus Antony Jay's *Corporate Man*, without exception, for some reason approach the bestseller level. All purport to document the supposedly surprising truth that man is an animal. The more extreme of them also argue that his behavior — particularly his aggressive, status-oriented, territorial and sexual behavior — is somehow out of tune with the needs of the modern world, that these behaviors are under genetic control and are largely determined by our animal heritage, and that there is little we can do but accept out grotesque natures; if we insist on trying to change ourselves, we must realize that we have almost no room for maneuver, for natural man is far more like other animals than he would care to admit. Actually, it is of some anthropological interest to inquire exactly why this naked apery should have caught on. Apart from our obsessive neophilia, and the fact that these ideas are somehow "new," they provide attractive excuses for our unpleasant behavior toward each other.

However, I believed these general arguments to be wrong; they are based upon misinterpretation of ethological studies and of the rich variety of human behavior documented by anthropologists. At a time when so many people wish to reject the past because it has no meaning and can contribute nothing, it is perhaps a little ironic that arguments about man's innate and atavistic depravity should have so much appeal. The world *is* in a mess; people *are* unpleasant to each other; that much is true. I can only suppose that an argument about the inevitability of all the nastiness not only absolves people in some way of the responsibility for their actions, but allows us also to sit back and positively enjoy it all. Let me illustrate my argument a little.

Take, for example, one particular set of ethological studies — those on baboons. Baboons are large African monkeys that live today south of the Sahara in habitats ranging from tropical rain forest to desert. They are the animals that have been most frequently used as models of early human behavior; a lot of work has been done on them, and they are easy to study — at least those living in the savannah habitats thought to be typical of the hunting territories of early man.

They are appealing to ethologists because of their habitat, because they live in discrete and structured social groups, and because they have satisfied so many previous hypotheses.

Earlier reports of baboon behavior emphasized the following. Baboons are intensely social creatures, living in discrete troops of 30 to 50 animals, their membership rarely changing; they are omnivorous, foraging alone and rarely sharing food. Males are twice as big as females; they are stronger and more aggressive. The functions of male aggression supposedly are for repelling predators, for maintaining group order, and (paradoxically) for fighting among themselves. The adult males are organized into a dominance hierarchy, the most dominant animal being the one that gets his own way as far as food, grooming partners, sex, when to stop and eat, and when and where the troop should move are concerned. He is the most aggressive, wins the most fights, and impregnates the most desirable females. Females, by the way, do little that is exciting in baboondom, but sit around having babies, bickering, and tending to their lords. Adult males are clearly the most important animals — although they cannot have the babies — and they are highly status conscious. On the basis of fighting abilities they form themselves into a dominance hierarchy, the function of which is to reduce aggression by the controlling means of each animal knowing its own place in the hierarchy. When groups meet up, fighting may well ensue. When the troop moves, males walk in front and at the rear; when the group is attacked, adult males remain to fight a rearguard action as females and young animals flee to safety in the trees.

Here then we have in microcosm one view of the way our early ancestors may well have behaved. How better to account for the destructiveness of so much human male aggression, to justify sex differences in behavior, status seeking, and so forth. I exaggerate, of course, but not too much. But what comments can be made?

First, the baboons studied — and these are the groups that are described, reported, and extrapolated from in magazine articles, books, and CBS TV specials — are probably abnormal. They live in game parks — open country where predators, especially human ones, are present in abundance — and are under a great deal of tension. The same species has been studied elsewhere — in the open country and in forest too, away from human contact — with different results.

Forest groups of baboons are fluid, changing composition regularly (rather than being tightly closed); only adult females and their offspring remain to form the core of a stable group. Food and cover are dispersed, and there is little fighting over either. Aggression in general is very infrequent, and male dominance hierarchies are difficult to discern. Intertroop encounters are rare, and friendly. When the troop is startled (almost invariably by humans, for baboons are probably too smart, too fast, and too powerful to be seriously troubled by other predators), it flees, and, far from forming a rearguard, the males — being biggest and strongest — are frequently up the trees long before the females (encumbered as they are with their infants).

When the troop moves it is the adult females that determine when and where to; and as it moves adult males are not invariably to be found in front and at the rear. As for sexual differences, in terms of functionally important behaviors, the significant dichotomy seems to be not between males and females but between adults and young. This makes good sense for animals that learn and live a long time.

The English primatologist Thelma Rowell, who studied some of these forest baboons in Uganda, removed a troop of them and placed them in cages where food had to be given a few times a day in competition-inducing clumps. Their population density went up and cover was reduced. The result? More aggression, more fighting, and the emergence of marked dominance hierarchies. So, those first baboons probably were under stress, in a relatively impoverished environment, pestered by humans of various sorts. The high degree of aggression, the hierarchies, the rigid sex-role differences, were in a sense abnormalities. In one respect, troop defense, there is accumulating evidence that male threats directed toward human interlopers occur only after troops become habituated to the observers, and must therefore be treated as learned behavior too.

Studies on undisturbed baboons elsewhere have shown other interesting patterns of adult male behaviors. Thus, in one troop, an old male baboon with broken canines was the animal that most frequently completed successful matings, that influenced troop movements, and served as a focus for females and infants, even though he was far less aggressive than, and frequently lost fights with, a younger and more vigorous adult male. Here, classical dominance criteria simply do not tie together as they are supposed to.

The concept of dominance is what psychologists call a unitary motivational theory: there are two such theories purporting to explain primate social behavior. These are that the sexual bond ties the group together, and that social dominance structures and orders the troop. The first of these theories has been shown to be wrong. The second we are beginning to realize is too simplistic. In undisturbed species in the wild, dominance hierarchies are hard to discern, if they are present at all; yet workers still persist in trying to find them. For example, Japanese primatologists describe using the "peanut test" to determine "dominance" in wild chimpanzees by seeing which chimp gets the goodies. Yet what relevance does such a test have for real chimp behavior in the wild, where the animals have far more important things to do — in an evolutionary or truly biological sense — than fight over peanuts? Such an experimental design implies too the belief that "dominance" is something lurking just beneath the surface, waiting for the appropriate releaser.

Steven Gartlan, an English primatologist working in the Cameroons, has recently suggested a different way of analyzing behavior, in terms of function. Each troop has to survive and reproduce, and in order to do so it must find food, nurture its mothers, protect and give its young the opportunity to learn adult skills. There are certain tasks that have to be completed if successful survival is to result. For example, the troop must be led, fights must be stopped, lookouts kept, infants fed and protected; some animals must serve as social foci, others might be needed to chase away intruders, and so on. Such an attribute list can be extended indefinitely.

If troop behavior is analyzed in a functional way like this, it immediately becomes clear that different classes of animals perform different functions. Thus, in undisturbed baboons, adults, particularly males, police the troop; males, especially the subadults and young adults, maintain vigilance; adult females determine the time and direction of movement; younger animals, especially infants, act as centers of attention.

Thus a particular age-sex class performs a certain set of behaviors that go together and that fulfill definite adaptive needs. Such a constellation of behavior attributes is termed a role. Roles, even in nonhuman primates, are quite variable. (Witness the great differences between male behaviors in normal baboon troops and those under stress.) If dominance can come and go with varying intensities of certain environmental pressures, then it is clearly not innately inevitable, even in baboons. Rigid dominance

hierarchies, then, seem to be largely artifacts of abnormal environments.

What is particularly interesting in the newer animal studies is the extent to which aggression, priority of access, and leadership are divorced from one another. Although a baboon may be highly aggressive, what matters most is how other animals react to him; if they ignore him as far as functionally important behaviors such as grooming, mating, and feeding are concerned, then his aggression is, in a social or evolutionary sense, irrelevant.

I want to look a little more closely at aggression, again from the functional point of view. What does it do? What is the point of a behavior that can cause so much trouble socially?

The developmental course of aggressive behavior has been traced in a number of species; among primates it is perhaps best documented in rhesus macaques, animals very similar to baboons. There are genetical and hormonal bases to aggressive behavior in macaques; in young animals, males are more aggressive, on the average, than females, and this characteristic is apparently related to hormonal influences. If animals are inadequately or abnormally socialized, aggressive behaviors become distorted and exaggerated. Animals that are correctly socialized in normal habitats, or richly stimulating artificial ones, show moderate amounts of aggression, and only in certain circumstances. These would be, for example, when an infant is threatened, when a choice item is disputed, when fights have to be interrupted, under certain circumstances when the troop is threatened, and occasionally when other species are killed for food.

Under normal conditions, aggression plays little part in other aspects of primate social life. The idea that the function of maleness is to be overbearingly aggressive, to fight constantly, and to be dominant makes little evolutionary sense.

How about the extrapolations from primates to man that the "naked apers" are so fond of? Take, for example, dominance. Everything that I have said about its shortcomings as a concept in analyzing baboon social organization applies to man, only more so. Behaviors affecting status-seeking in man are strongly influenced by learning, as we can see by the wide variation in human behavior from one society to another. In certain cultures, status is important, clear-cut, and valued; the emphasis placed on caste in Hindu society is an obvious example. At the opposite extreme, though — among the Bushmen of the Kalahari Desert, for example — it is hard to discern; equality and cooperativeness are highly valued qualities in Bushman society, and hence learned by each new generation.

I've used the term "status-seeking" rather than "dominance" for humans, because it describes much better the kind of hierarchical ordering one finds within human groups. And that points to a general problem in extrapolating from monkey to man, for "status" is a word that one can't easily apply to baboon or chimp society; status involves prestige, and prestige presupposes values — arbitrary rules or norms. That sort of behavior is cultural, human, and practically unique.

As we turn to man, let's consider for a while human groups as they were before the switch to a settled way of life began a mere — in evolutionary terms — 10,000 years ago. Before that our ancestors were hunters and gatherers. Evidence for this in the form of stone tool making, living areas with butchered game, camp sites, and so on, begins to turn up almost 3 million years ago, at a time when our ancestors were very different physically from us. For at least 2½ to 3 million years, man and his ancestors have lived as hunters and gatherers. The change from hunting to agricultural-based economies began, as I said, just over 10,000 years ago, a fractional moment on the geological time scale. That famous (and overworked) hypothetical visiting Martian geologist of the 21st century would find remains of hunters represented in hundreds of feet of sediments; the first evidence for agriculture, like the remains of the thermonuclear holocaust, would be jammed together in the last few inches. Hunting and gathering has been a highly significant event in human history; indeed, it is believed by most of us interested in human evolution to have been an absolutely vital determinant, molding many aspects of human behavior.

There are a number of societies surviving today that still live as hunters and gatherers; Congo pygmies, Kalahari Bushmen, and Australian Aborigines are three well-known examples. When comparisons are made of these hunting societies, we can see that certain features are typical of most or all of them, and these features are likely to have been typical of earlier hunters.

In hunting societies, families — frequently monogamous nuclear families — are often grouped together in bands of 20 to 40 individuals; members of these hunting bands are kinsmen, either by blood or marriage. The band hunts and gathers over wide areas, and its foraging range often overlaps those of adjacent groups.

Bands are flexible and variable in composition — splitting and reforming with changes in the seasons, game and water availability, and whim.

Far from life being "nasty, brutish, and short" for these peoples, recent studies show that hunters work on the average only 3 or 4 days each week; the rest of their time is leisure. Further, at least 10 percent of Bushmen, for example, are over 60 years of age, valued and nurtured by their children. Although they lack large numbers of material possessions, one can never describe such people as savages, degenerates, or failures.

The men in these societies hunt animals while the women gather plant food. However, women often scout for game, and in some groups may also hunt smaller animals, while a man returning empty-handed from a day's hunting will almost always gather vegetable food on his way. Thus, the division of labor between sexes is not distinct and immutable; it seems to be functional, related to mobility: the women with infants to protect and carry simply cannot move far and fast enough to hunt efficiently.

Relations between bands are amicable; that makes economic sense as the most efficient way of utilizing potentially scarce resources, and also because of exogamy — marrying out — for adjacent groups will contain kinsmen and kinsmen will not fight. Within the group, individual relations between adults are cooperative and based upon reciprocity; status disputes are avoided. These behaviors are formalized, part of cultural behavior, in that such actions are positively valued and rewarded. Aggression between individuals is generally maintained at the level of bickering; in cases where violence flares, hunters generally solve the problem by fission: the band divides.

Data on child-rearing practices in hunters are well known only in Bushmen, and we don't yet know to what extent Bushmen are typical of hunters. (This work on Bushman child-rearing, as yet unpublished, has been done by Patricia Draper, an anthropologist at the University of New Mexico, and I am grateful to her for permitting me to use her data.) Bushman children are almost always in the company of adults; because of the small size of Bushman societies, children rarely play in large groups with others of their own age. Aggression is minimal in the growing child for two principal reasons. First, arguments between youngsters almost inevitably take place in the presence of adults and adults always break these up before fights erupt; so the socialization process gives little opportunity for practicing aggressive behavior. Second, because of the reciprocity and cooperativeness of adults, children have few adult models on which to base the learning of aggressiveness.

Thus, the closest we can come to a concept of "natural man" would indicate that our ancestors were, like other primates, capable of being aggressive, but they would have been socialized culturally in such a way as to reduce as far as possible the manifestation of aggression. This control through learning is much more efficient in man than in other primates, because we are cultural creatures — with the ability to attach positive values to aggression-controlling behaviors. Thus, Bushmen value and thereby encourage peaceful cooperation. Their culture provides the young with non-violent models.

Other cultures promote the very opposite. Take, for example, the Yanomamö Indians of Venezuela and Brazil; their culture completely reverses our ideals of "good" and "desirable." To quote a student of Yanomamö society: "A high capacity for rage, a quick flash point, and a willingness to use violence to obtain one's ends are considered desirable traits." In order to produce the appropriate adult behaviors, the Yanomamö encourage their children, especially young boys, to argue, fight, and to be generally belligerent. These behaviors, I should emphasize, are learned, and depend for their encouragement upon specific cultural values.

Our own culture certainly provides the young with violent, though perhaps less obtrusive, models. These, I should emphasize again, are to a great extent learned and arbitrary, and we *could* change them should we choose to do so.

So far we have seen that fierce aggression and status-seeking are no more "natural" attributes of man than they are of most monkey and ape societies. The degree to which such behaviors are developed depends very considerably indeed upon cultural values and learning. Territoriality likewise is not a "natural" feature of human group living; nor is it among most other primates.

As a parting shot, let me mention one more topic that is of great interest to everyone at the moment — sex roles. Too many of us have in the past treated the male and female stereotypes of

our particular culture as fixed and "natural": in our genes, so to speak. It may well be true that human male infants play a little more vigorously than females, or that they learn aggressive behaviors somewhat more easily, because of hormonal differences. But simply look around the world at other cultures. In some, "masculinity" and "femininity" are much more marked than they are in our own culture; in others, the roles are blurred. As I said earlier, among Bushmen that are still hunters, sex roles are far from rigid, and in childhood the two sexes have a very similar upbringing. However, among those Bushmen that have adopted a sedentary life devoted to herding or agriculture, sex roles are much more rigid. Men devote their energies to one set of tasks, women to another, mutually exclusive set. Little boys learn only "male" tasks, little girls exclusively "female" ones. Maybe the switch to the sedentary life started man on the road toward marked sex role differences. These differences are almost entirely learned, and heavily affected by economic factors.

So much of human role behavior is learned that we could imagine narrowing or widening the differences almost as much or as little as we wish.

So, what conclusions can be drawn from all this? It is overly simplistic in the extreme to believe that man behaves in strongly genetically deterministic ways, when we know that apes and monkeys do not. Careful ethological work shows us that the primates closely related to us — chimps and baboons are the best known — get on quite amicably together under natural and undisturbed conditions. Learning plays a very significant part in the acquisition of their behavior. They are not for the most part highly aggressive, obsessively dominance-oriented, territorial creatures.

There is no evidence to support the view that early man was a violent status-seeking creature; ethological and anthropological evidence indicates rather that pre-urban men would have used their evolving cultural capacities to channel and control aggression. To be sure, we are not born empty slates upon which anything can be written; but to believe in the "inevitability of beastliness" is to deny our humanity as well as our primate heritage — and, incidentally, does a grave injustice to the "beasts."

8
Racial Odyssey

BOYCE RENSBERGER

The human species comes in an artist's palette of colors: sandy yellows, reddish tans, deep browns, light tans, creamy whites, pale pinks. It is a rare person who is not curious about the skin colors, hair textures, bodily structures, and facial features associated with racial background. Why do some Africans have dark brown skin, while that of most Europeans is pale pink? Why do the eyes of most "white" people and "black" people look pretty much alike but differ so from the eyes of Orientals? Did one race evolve before the others? If so, is it more primitive or more advanced as a result. Can it be possible, as modern research suggests, that there is no such thing as a pure race? These are all honest, scientifically worthy questions. And they are central to current research on the evolution of our species on the planet Earth.

Broadly speaking, research on racial differences has led most scientists to three major conclusions. The first is that there are many more differences among people than skin color, hair texture, and facial features. Dozens of other variations have been found, ranging from the shapes of bones to the consistency of ear wax to subtle variations in body chemistry.

The second conclusion is that the overwhelming evolutionary success of the human species is largely due to its great genetic variability. When migrating bands of our early ancestors reached a new environment, at least a few already had physical traits that gave them an edge in surviving there. If the coming centuries bring significant environmental changes, as many believe they will, our chances of surviving them will be immeasurably enhanced by our diversity as a species.

There is a third conclusion about race that is often misunderstood. Despite our wealth of variation and despite our constant, everyday references to race, no one has ever discovered a reliable way of distinguishing one race from another. While it is possible to classify a great many people on the basis of certain physical features, there are no known feature or groups of features that will do the job in all cases.

Skin color won't work. Yes, most Africans from south of the Sahara and their descendants around the world have skin that is darker than that of most Europeans. But there are millions of people in India, classified by some anthropologists as members of the Caucasoid, or "white," race who have darker skins than most Americans who call themselves black. And there are many Africans living in sub-Saharan Africa today whose skins are no darker than the skins of many Spaniards, Italians, Greeks, or Lebanese.

What about stature as a racial trait? Because they are quite short, on the average, African Pygmies have been considered racially distinct from other dark-skinned Africans. If stature, then, is a racial criterion, would one include in the same race the tall African Watusi and the Scandinavians of similar stature?

The little web of skin that distinguishes Oriental eyes is said to be a particular feature of the Mongoloid race. How, then, can it be argued that the American Indian, who lacks this epicanthic fold, is Mongoloid?

Even more hopeless as racial markers are hair color, eye color, hair form, the shapes of noses and lips, or any of the other traits put forth as typical of one race or another.

No Norms

Among the tall people of the world there are many black, many white, and many in between. Among black people of the world there are many with kinky hair, many with straight or wavy hair, and many in between. Among the broad-nosed, full-lipped people of the world there are many with dark skins, many with light skins, and many in between.

How did our modern perceptions of race arise? One of the first to attempt a scientific classification of peoples was Carl von Linné, better known as Linnaeus. In 1735, he published a classification that remains the standard today. As Linnaeus saw it, there were four races, classifiable geographically and by skin color. The names Linnaeus gave them were *Homo sapiens Africanus nigrus* (black African human being), *H. sapiens Americanus rubescens* (red American human being), *H. sapiens Asiaticus fuscusens* (brownish Asian human being), and *H. sapiens Europaeus albescens* (white European human being). All, Linnaeus recognized, were members of a single human species.

A species includes all individuals that are biologically capable of interbreeding and producing fertile offspring. Most matings between species are fruitless, and even when they succeed, as when a horse and a donkey interbreed and produce a mule, the progeny are sterile. When a poodle mates with a collie, however, the offspring are fertile, showing that both dogs are members of the same species.

Even though Linnaeus's system of nomenclature survives, his classifications were discarded, especially after voyages of discovery revealed that there were many more kinds of people than could be pigeonholed into four categories. All over the world there are small populations that don't fit. Among the better known are:

- The so-called Bushmen of southern Africa, who look as much Mongoloid as Negroid.
- The Negritos of the South Pacific, who do look Negroid but are very far from Africa and have no known links to that continent.
- The Ainu of Japan, a hairy aboriginal people who look more Caucasoid than anything else.
- The Lapps of Scandinavia, who look as much like Eskimos as like Europeans.
- The aborigines of Australia, who often look Negroid but many of whom have straight or wavy hair and are often blond as children.
- The Polynesians, who seem to be a blend of many races, the proportions differing from island to island.

To accommodate such diversity, many different systems of classification have been proposed. Some set up two or three dozen races. None has ever satisfied all experts.

Classification System

Perhaps the most sweeping effort to impose a classification upon all the peoples of the world was made by the American anthropologist Carleton Coon. He concluded there are five basic races, two of which have major subdivisions: Caucasoids; Mongoloids; full-size Australoids (Australian aborigines); dwarf Australoids (Negritos — Andaman Islanders and similar peoples); full-size Congoids (African Negroids); dwarf Congoids (African Pygmies); and Capoids (the so-called Bushmen and Hottentots).

In his 1965 classic, *The Living Races of Man*, Coon hypothesized that before A.D. 1500 there were five pure races — five centers of human population that were so isolated that there was almost no mixing.

Each of these races evolved independently, Coon believed, diverging from a pre–*Homo sapiens* stock that was essentially the same everywhere. He speculated that the common ancestor evolved into *Homo sapiens* in five separate regions at five different times, beginning about 35,000 years ago. The populations that have been *Home sapiens* for the shortest periods of time, Coon said, are the world's "less civilized" races.

The five pure races remained distinct until A.D. 1500; then Europeans started sailing the world, leaving their genes — as sailors always have — in every port and planting distant colonies. At about the same time, thousands of Africans were captured and forcibly settled in many parts of the New World.

That meant the end of the five pure races. But Coon and other experts held that this did not necessarily rule out the idea of distinct races. In this view, there *are* such things as races; people just don't fit into them very well anymore.

The truth is that there is really no hard evidence to suggest that five or any particular number of races evolved independently. The preponderance of evidence today suggests that as traits typical of fully modern people arose in any one place, they spread quickly to all human populations. Advances in intelligence were almost certainly the fastest to spread. Most anthropologists and geneticists now believe that human beings have always been subject to migrating and mixing. In other words, there probably never were any such things as pure races.

Race mixing has not only been a fact of human history but is, in this day of unprecedented global mobility, taking place at a more rapid rate than ever. It is not farfetched to envision the day when, generations hence, the entire "complexion" of major population centers will be different. Meanwhile, we can see such changes taking place before our eyes, for they are a part of everyday reality.

Hybrid Vigor

Oddly, those who assert scientific validity for their notions of pure and distinct races seem oblivious of a basic genetic principle that plant and animal breeders know well: too much inbreeding can lead to proliferation of inferior traits. Crossbreeding with different strains often produces superior combinations and "hybrid vigor."

The striking differences among people may very well be a result of constant genetic mixing. And as geneticists and ecologists know, in diversity lies strength and resilience.

To understand the origin and proliferation of human differences, one must first know how Darwinian evolution works.

Evolution is a two-step process. Step one is mutation: somehow a gene in the ovary or testes of an individual is altered, changing the molecular configuration that stores instructions for forming a new individual. The children who inherit that gene will be different in some way from their ancestors.

Step two is selection: for a racial difference, or any other evolutionary change to arise, it must survive and be passed through several generations. If the mutation confers some disadvantage, the individual dies, often during embryonic development. But if the change is beneficial is some way, the individual should have a better chance of thriving than relatives lacking the advantage.

Natural Selection

If a new trait is beneficial, it will bring reproductive success to its bearer. After several generations of multiplication, bearers of the new trait may begin to outnumber nonbearers. Darwin called this natural selection to distinguish it from the artificial selection exercised by animal breeders.

Skin color is the human racial trait most generally thought to confer an evolutionary advantage of this sort. It has long been obvious in the Old World that the farther south one goes, the darker the skin color. Southern Europeans are usually somewhat darker than northern Europeans. In North Africa, skin colors are darker still, and, as one travels south, coloration reaches its maximum at the Equator. The same progressions hold in Asia, with the lightest skins to the north. Again, as one moves south, skin color darkens, reaching in southern India a "blackness" equal to that of equatorial Africans.

This north-south spectrum of skin color derives from varying intensities of the same dark brown pigment called melanin. Skin cells simply have more or less melanin granules to be seen against a background that is pinkish because of the underlying blood vessels. All races can increase their melanin concentration by exposure to the sun.

What is it about northerly latitudes in the Northern Hemisphere that favors less pigmentation and about southerly latitudes that favors more? Exposure to intense sunlight is not the only reason why people living in southerly latitudes are dark. A person's susceptibility to rickets and skin cancer, his ability to withstand cold and to see in the dark may also be related to skin color.

The best-known explanation says the body can tolerate only a narrow range of intensities of sunlight. Too much causes sunburn and cancer, while too little deprives the body of vitamin D, which is synthesized in the skin under the influence of sunlight. A dark complexion protects the skin from the harmful effects of intense sunlight. Thus, albinos born in equatorial regions have a high rate of skin cancer. On the other hand, dark skin in northerly latitudes screens out sunlight needed for the synthesis of vitamin D. Thus, dark-skinned children living in northern latitudes had high rates of rickets — a bone-deforming disease caused by a lack of vitamin D — before their milk was routinely fortified. In the sunny tropics, dark skin admits enough light to produce the vitamin.

Recently, there has been some evidence that skin colors are linked to differences in the ability to avoid injury from the cold. Army researchers found that during the Korean War blacks were more susceptible to frostbite than were whites. Even among Norwegian soldiers in World War II, brunettes had a slightly higher incidence of frostbite than did blonds.

Eye Pigmentation

A third link between color and latitude involves the sensitivity of the eye to various wavelengths of light. It is known that dark-skinned people have more pigmentation in the iris of the eye and at the back of the eye where the image falls. It has been found that the less pigmented the eye, the more sensitive it is to colors at the red end of the spectrum. In situations illuminated with reddish light, the northern European can see more than a dark African sees.

It has been suggested that Europeans developed lighter eyes to adapt to the longer twilights of the North and their greater reliance on firelight to illuminate caves.

Although the skin cancer–vitamin D hypothesis enjoys wide acceptance, it may well be that resistance to cold, possession of good night vision, and other yet unknown factors all play roles in the evolution of skin colors.

Most anthropologists agree that the original human skin color was dark brown, since it is fairly well established that human beings evolved in the tropics of Africa. This does not, however, mean that the first people were Negroids, whose descendants, as they moved north, evolved into light-skinned Caucasoids. It is more likely that the skin color of various populations changed several times from dark to light and back as people moved from one region to another.

Disease Origins

The gene for sickle cell anemia, a disease found primarily among black people, appears to have evolved because its presence can render its bearer resistant to malaria. Such a trait would have obvious value in tropical Africa.

A person who has sickle cell anemia must have inherited genes for the disease from both parents. If a child inherits only one sickle cell gene, he or she will be resistant to malaria but will not have the anemia. Paradoxically, inheriting genes from both parents does not seem to affect resistance to malaria.

In the United States, where malaria is practically nonexistent, the sickle cell gene confers no survival advantage and is disappearing. Today only about 1 out of every 10 American blacks carries the gene.

Many other inherited diseases are found only in people from a particular area. Tay-Sachs disease, which often kills before the age of two, is almost entirely confined to Jews from parts of Eastern Europe and their descendants elsewhere. Paget's disease, a bone disorder, is found most often among those of English descent. Impacted wisdom teeth are a common problem among Asians and Europeans but not among Africans. Children of all races are able to digest milk because their bodies make lactase, the enzyme that breaks down lactose, or milk sugar. But the ability to digest lactose in adulthood is a racially distributed trait.

About 90 percent of Orientals and blacks lose this ability by the time they reach adulthood and become quite sick when they drink milk.

Even African and Asian herders who keep cattle or goats rarely drink fresh milk. Instead, they first treat the milk with fermentation bacteria that break down lactose, in a sense predigesting it. They can then ingest the milk in the form of yogurt or cheese without any problem.

About 90 percent of Europeans and their American descendants, on the other hand, continue to produce the enzyme throughout their lives and can drink milk with no ill effects.

Consider, for example, that long before modern people evolved, *Homo erectus* had spread throughout Africa, Europe, and Asia. The immediate ancestor of *Homo sapiens, Homo erectus,* was living in Africa 1.5 million years ago and in Eurasia 750,000 years ago. The earliest known forms of *Homo sapiens* do not make their appearance until somewhere between 250,000 and 500,000 years ago. Although there is no evidence of the skin color of any hominid fossil, it is probable that the *Homo erectus* population in Africa had dark skin. As subgroups spread into northern latitudes, mutations that reduced pigmentation conferred survival advantages on them and lighter skins came to predominate. In other words, there were probably black *Homo erectus* peoples in Africa and white ones in Europe and Asia.

Did the black *Homo erectus* population evolve into today's Negroids and the white ones in Europe into today's Caucasoids? By all the best evidence, nothing like this happened. More likely, wherever *Homo sapiens* arose it proved so superior to the *Homo erectus* populations that it eventually replaced them everywhere.

If the first *Homo sapiens* evolved in Africa, they were probably dark-skinned; those who migrated northward into Eurasia lost their pigmentation. But it is just as possible that the first *Homo sapiens* appeared in northern climes, descendants of white-skinned *Homo erectus.* These could have migrated southward toward Africa, evolving darker skins. All modern races, incidentally, arose long after the brain had reached its present size in all parts of the world.

North–south variations in pigmentation are quite common among mammals and birds. The tropical races tend to be darker in fur and feather, the desert races tend to be brown, and those near the Arctic Circle are lighter colored.

There are exceptions among humans. The Indians of the Americas, from the Arctic to the southern regions of South America, do not conform to the north–south scheme of coloration. Though most think of Indians as being reddish-brown, most Indians tend to be relatively light skinned, much like their presumed Mongoloid ancestors in Asia. The ruddy complexion that lives in so many stereotypes of Indians is merely what years of heavy tanning can produce in almost any light-skinned person. Anthropologists explain the color consistency as a consequence of the relatively recent entry of people into the Americas — probably between 12,000 and 35,000 years ago. Perhaps they have not yet had time to change.

Only a few external physical differences other than color appear to have adaptive significance. The strongest cases can be made for nose shape and stature.

What's in a Nose

People native to colder or drier climates tend to have longer, more beak-shaped noses than those living in hot and humid regions. The nose's job is to warm and humidify air before it reaches sensitive lung tissues. The colder or drier the air is, the more surface area is needed inside the nose to get it to the right temperature or humidity. Whites tend to have longer and beakier noses than blacks or Orientals. Nevertheless, there is great variation within races. Africans in the highlands of East Africa have longer noses than Africans from the hot, humid lowlands, for example.

Stature differences are reflected in the tendency for most northern peoples to have shorter arms, legs, and torsos and to be stockier than people from the tropics. Again, this is an adaptation to heat or cold. One way of reducing heat loss is to have less body surface, in relation to weight or volume, from which heat can escape. To avoid overheating, the most desirable body is long limbed and lean. As a result, most Africans tend to be lankier than northern Europeans. Arctic peoples are the shortest limbed of all.

Hair forms may also have a practical role to play, but the evidence is weak. It has been suggested that the more tightly curled hair of Africans insulates the top of the head better than does straight or wavy hair. Contrary to expectation, black hair serves better in this role than white hair. Sunlight is absorbed and converted to heat at the outer surface of the hair blanket; it radiates directly into the air. White fur, common on Arctic animals that need to absorb solar heat, is actually transparent and transmits light into the hair blanket, allowing the heat to form within the insulating layer, where it is retained for warmth.

Aside from these examples, there is little evidence that any of the other visible differences among the world's people provide any advantage. Nobody knows, for example, why Orientals have epicanthic eye folds or flatter facial profiles. The thin lips of Caucasoids and most Mongoloids have no known advantages over the Negroid's full lips. Why should middle-aged and older Caucasoid men go bald so much more frequently than the men of other races? Why does the skin of Bushmen wrinkle so heavily in the middle and later years? Or why does the skin of Negroids resist wrinkling so well? Why do the Indian men in one part of South America have blue penises? Why do Hottentot women have such unusually large buttocks?

There are possible evolutionary explanations for why such apparently useless differences arise.

One is a phenomenon known as sexual selection. Environmentally adaptive traits arise, Darwin thought, through natural selection — the environment itself chooses who will thrive or decline. In sexual selection, which Darwin also suggested, the choice belongs to the prospective mate.

In simple terms, ugly individuals will be less likely to find mates and reproduce their genes than beautiful specimens will. Take the blue penis as an example. Women might find it unusually attractive or perhaps believe it to be endowed with special powers. If so, a man born with a blue penis will find many more opportunities to reproduce his genes than his ordinary brothers.

Sexual selection can also operate when males compete for females. The moose with the larger antlers or the lion with the more imposing mane will stand a better chance of discouraging less well-endowed males and gaining access to females. It is possible that such a process operated among Caucasoid males, causing them to become markedly hairy, especially around the face.

Attractive Traits

Anthropologists consider it probable that traits such as the epicanthic fold or the many regional differences in facial features were selected this way.

Yet another method by which a trait can establish itself involves accidental selection. It results from what biologists call genetic drift.

Suppose that in a small nomadic band a person is born with perfectly parallel fingerprints instead of the usual loops, whorls, or arches. That person's children would inherit parallel fingerprints, but they would confer no survival advantages. But if that family decides to strike out on its own, it will become the founder of a new band consisting of its own descendants, all with parallel fingerprints.

Events such as this, geneticists and anthropologists believe, must have occurred many times in the past to produce the great variety within the human species. Among the apparently neutral traits that differ among populations are the following:

Ear Wax

There are two types of ear wax. One is dry and crumbly and the other is wet and sticky. Both types can be found in every major population, but the frequencies differ. Among northern Chinese, for example, 98 percent have dry ear wax. Among American whites, only 16 percent have dry ear wax. Among American blacks the figure is 7 percent.

Scent Glands

As any bloodhound knows, every person has his or her own distinctive scent. People vary in the mixture of odoriferous compounds exuded through the skin — most of it coming from specialized glands called apocrine glands. Among whites, these are concentrated in the armpits and near the genitals and anus. Among blacks, they may also be found on the chest and abdomen. Orientals have hardly any apocrine glands at all. In the words of the Oxford biologist John R. Baker, "The Europids and Negrids are smelly, the Mongoloids scarcely or not at all." Smelliest of all are northern European, or so-called Nordic, whites. Body odor is rare in Japan. It was once thought to indicate a European in the ancestry and to be a disease requiring hospitalization.

Blood Groups

Some populations have a high percentage of members with a particular blood group. American Indians are overwhelmingly group "O" — 100 percent in some regions. Group A is most common among Australian aborigines and the Indians in western Canada. Group B is frequent in northern India, other parts of Asia, and western Africa.

Advocates of the pure-race theory once seized upon blood groups as possibly unique to the original pure races. The proportions of groups founds today, they thought, would indicate the degree of mixing. It was subsequently found that chimpanzees, our closest living relatives, have the same blood groups as humans.

Taste

PTC (phenylthiocarbamide) is a synthetic compound that some people can taste and others cannot. The ability to taste it has no known survival value, but it is clearly an inherited trait. The proportion of persons who can taste PTC varies in different populations: 50 to 70 percent of Australian aborigines can taste it, as can 60 to 80 percent of all Europeans. Among East Asians, the percentage is 83 to 100 percent, and among Africans, 90 to 97 percent.

Urine

Another indicator of differences in body chemistry is the excretion of a compound known as BAIB (beta-amino-isobutyric acid) in urine. Europeans seldom excrete large quantities, but high levels of excretion are common among Asians and American Indians. It has been shown that the differences are not due to diet.

No major population has remained isolated long enough to prevent any unique genes from eventually mixing with those of neighboring groups. Indeed, a map showing the distribution of so-called traits would have no sharp boundaries, except for coastlines. The intensity of a trait such as skin color, which is controlled by six pairs of genes and can therefore exist in many shades, varies gradually from one population to another. With only a few exceptions, every known genetic possibility possessed by the species can be found to some degree in every sizable population.

Ever-Changing Species

One can establish a system of racial classification simply by listing the features of populations at any given moment. Such a concept of race is, however, inappropriate to a highly mobile and ever-changing species such as *Homo sapiens*. In the short view, races may seem distinguishable, but in biology's long haul, races come and go. New ones arise and blend into neighboring groups to create new and racially stable populations. In time, genes from these groups flow into other neighbors, continuing the production of new permutations.

Some anthropologists contend that at the moment American blacks should be considered a race distinct from African blacks. They argue that American blacks are a hybrid of African blacks and European whites. Indeed, the degree of mixture can be calculated on the basis of a blood component known as the Duffy factor.

In West Africa, where most of the New World's slaves came from, the Duffy factor is virtually absent. It is present in 43 percent of American whites. From the number of American blacks who are now "Duffy positive" it can be calculated that whites contributed 21 percent of the genes in the American black population. The figure is higher for blacks in northern and western states and lower in the South. By the same token, there are whites who have black ancestors. The number is smaller because of the tendency to identify a person as black even if only a minor fraction of his ancestors were originally from Africa.

The unwieldiness of race designations is also evident in places such as Mexico, where most of the people are, in effect, hybrids of Indians (Mongoloid by some classifications) and Spaniards (Caucasoid). Many South American populations are tri-hybrids — mixtures of Mongoloid, Caucasoid, and Negroid. Brazil is a country where the mixture has been around long enough to constitute a racially stable population. Thus, in one sense, new races have been created in the United States, Mexico, and Brazil. But in the long run, those races will again change.

Sherwood Washburn, a noted anthropologist, questions the usefulness of racial classification: "Since races are open systems which are intergrading, the number of races will depend on the purpose of the classification. I think we should require people who propose a classification of races to state in the first place why they wish to divide the human species."

The very notion of a pure race, then, makes no sense. But, as evolutionists know full well, a rich genetic diversity within the human species most assuredly *does*.

9
Fallacies of Biological Determinism

STEPHEN JAY GOULD

Learning by Debunking

Science advances primarily by replacement, not by addition. If the barrel is always full, then the rotten apples must be discarded before better ones can be added.

Scientists do not debunk only to cleanse and purge. They refute older ideas *in the light of* a different view about the nature of things.

If it is to have any enduring value, sound debunking must do more than replace one social prejudice with another. It must use more adequate biology to drive out fallacious ideas. (Social prejudices themselves may be refractory, but particular biological supports for them can be dislodged.)

We have rejected many specific theories of biological determinism because our knowledge about human biology, evolution, and genetics has increased. For example, Morton's egregious errors could not be repeated in so bald a way by modern scientists constrained to follow canons of statistical procedure. The antidote to Goddard's claim

that a single gene causes feeble-mindedness was not primarily a shift in social preferences, but an important advance in genetical theory — the idea of polygenic inheritance. Absurd as it seems today, the early Mendelians did try to attribute even the most subtle and complex traits (of apolitical anatomy as well as character) to the action of single genes. Polygenic inheritance affirms the participation of many genes — and a host of environmental and interactive effects — in such characters as human skin color.

More importantly, and as a plea for the necessity of biological knowledge, the remarkable lack of genetic differentiation among human groups — a major biological basis for debunking determinism — is a contingent fact of evolutionary history, not an a priori or necessary truth. The world might have been ordered differently. Suppose, for example, that one or several species of our ancestral genus *Australopithecus* had survived — a perfectly reasonable scenario in theory, since new species arise by splitting off from old ones (with ancestors usually surviving, at least for a time), not by the wholesale transformation of ancestors to descendants. We — that is, *Homo sapiens* — would then have faced all the moral dilemmas involved in treating a human species of distinctly inferior mental capacity. What would we have done with them — slavery? extirpation? coexistence? menial labor? reservations? zoos?

Similarly, our own species, *Homo sapiens*, might have included a set of subspecies (races) with meaningfully different genetic capacities. If our species were millions of years old (many are), and if its races had been geographically separated for most of this time without significant genetic interchange, then large genetic differences might have slowly accumulated between groups. But *Homo sapiens* is tens of thousands, or at most a few hundred thousand, years old, and all modern human races probably split from a common ancestral stock only tens of thousands of years ago. A few outstanding traits of external appearance lead to our subjective judgement of important differences. But biologists have recently affirmed — as long suspected — that the overall genetic differences among human races are astonishingly small. Although frequencies for different states of a gene differ among races, we have found no "race genes" — that is, states fixed in certain races and absent from all others. Lewontin studied variation in seventeen genes coding for differences in blood and found that only 6.3 percent of the variation can be attributed to racial membership. Fully 85.4 percent of the variation occurred within local populations (the remaining 8.3 percent records differences among local populations within a race). As Lewontin remarked (personal communication): if the holocaust comes and the members of a small tribe deep in New Guinea forests are the only survivors, almost all the genetic variation now expressed among the innumerable groups of our four billion people will be preserved.

This information about limited genetic differences among human groups is useful as well as interesting, often in the deepest sense — for saving lives. When American eugenicists attributed diseases of poverty to the inferior genetic construction of poor people, they could propose no systematic remedy other than sterilization. When Joseph Goldberger proved that pellagra was not a genetic disorder, but a result of vitamin deficiency among the poor, he could cure it.

Biology and Human Nature

If people are so similar genetically, and if previous claims for a direct biological mapping of human affairs have recorded cultural prejudice and not nature, then does biology come up empty as a guide in our search to know ourselves? Are we after all, at birth, the *tabula rasa*, or blank slate, imagined by some eighteenth-century empiricist philosophers? As an evolutionary biologist, I cannot adopt such a nihilistic position without denying the fundamental insight of my profession. The evolutionary unity of humans with all other organisms is the cardinal message of Darwin's revolution for nature's most arrogant species.

We are inextricably part of nature, but human uniqueness is not negated thereby. "Nothing but" an animal is as fallacious a statement as "created in God's own image." It is not mere hubris to argue that *Homo sapiens* is special in some sense — for each species is unique in its own way; shall we judge among the dance of the bees, the song of the humpback whale, and human intelligence?

The impact of human uniqueness upon the world has been enormous because it has established a new kind of evolution to support the transmission across generations of learned knowledge and behavior. Human uniqueness resides primarily in our brains. It is expressed in the culture built upon our intelligence and the power it gives us to manipulate the world. Human societies change by cultural evolution, not as a result of biological alteration. We have no evidence for biological change in brain size or structure since *Homo sapiens* appeared in the fossil record some fifty thousand years ago. (Broca was right in stating that the cranial capacity of Cro Magnon skulls was equal if not superior to ours.) All that we have done since then — the greatest transformation in the shortest time that our planet has experienced since its crust solidified nearly four billion years ago — is the product of cultural evolution. Biological (Darwinian) evolution continues in our species, but its rate, compared with cultural evolution, is so incomparably slow that its impact upon the history of *Homo sapiens* has been small. While the gene for sickle-cell anemia declines in frequency among black Americans, we have invented the railroad, the automobile, radio and television, the atom bomb, the computer, the airplane and spaceship.

Cultural evolution can proceed so quickly because it operates, as biological evolution does not, in the "Lamarckian" mode — by the inheritance of acquired characters. Whatever one generation learns, it can pass to the next by writing, instruction, inculcation, ritual, tradition, and a host of methods that humans have developed to assure continuity in culture. Darwinian evolution, on the other hand, is an indirect process: genetic variation must first be available to construct an advantageous feature, and natural selection must then preserve it. Since genetic variation arises at random, not preferentially directed toward advantageous features, the Darwinian process works slowly. Cultural evolution is not only rapid; it is also readily reversible because its products are not coded in our genes.

The classical arguments of biological determinism fail because the features they invoke to make distinctions among groups are usually the products of cultural evolution. Determinists did seek evidence in anatomical traits built by biological, not cultural, evolution. But, in so doing, they tried to use anatomy for making inferences about capacities and behaviors that they linked to anatomy and we regard as engendered by culture. Cranial capacity per se held as little interest for Morton and Broca as variation in third-toe length; they cared only about the mental characteristics supposedly associated with differences in average brain size among groups. We now believe that different attitudes and styles of thought among human groups are usually the nongenetic products of cultural evolution. In short, the *biological* basis of human uniqueness leads us to reject biological determinism. Our large brain is the biological foundation of intelligence; intelligence is the ground of culture; and cultural transmission builds a new mode of evolution more effective than Darwinian processes in its limited realm — the "inheritance" and modification of learned behavior. As philosopher Stephen Toulmin stated: "Culture has the power to impose itself on nature from within."

Yet, if human biology engenders culture, it is also true that culture, once developed, evolved with little or no reference to genetic *variation* among human groups. Does biology, then, play no other valid role in the analysis of human behavior? Is it only a foundation without any insight to offer beyond the unenlightening recognition that complex culture requires a certain level of intelligence?

Most biologists would follow my argument in denying a genetic basis for most behavioral *differences* between groups and for *change* in the complexity of human societies through the recent history of our species. But what about the supposed constancies of personality and behavior, the traits of mind that humans share in all cultures? What, in short, about a general "human nature"? Some biologists would grant Darwinian processes a substantial role not only in establishing long ago, but also in actively maintaining now, a set of specific adaptive behaviors forming a biologically conditioned "human nature." I believe that this old tradition of argument — which has found its most recent expression as "human sociobiology" — is invalid not because biology is irrelevant and human behavior reflects only a disembodied culture, but because human

biology suggests a different and less constraining role for genetics in the analysis of human nature.

Sociobiology begins with a modern reading of what natural selection is all about — differential reproductive success of individuals. According to the Darwinian imperative, individuals are selected to maximize the contribution of their own genes to future generations, and that is all. (Darwinism is not a theory of progress, increasing complexity, or evolved harmony for the good of species or ecosystems.) Paradoxically (as it seems to many), altruism as well as selfishness can be selected under this criterion — acts of kindness may benefit individuals either because they establish bonds of reciprocal obligation, or because they aid kin who carry copies of the altruist's genes.

Human sociobiologists then survey our behaviors with this criterion in mind. When they identify a behavior that seems to be adaptive in helping an individual's genes along, they develop a story for its origin by natural selection operating upon genetic variation influencing the specific act itself. (These stories are rarely backed by any evidence beyond the inference of adaptation.) Human sociobiology is a theory for the origin and maintenance of *specific, adaptive behaviors* by *natural selection*[1]; these behaviors must therefore have a *genetic basis*, since natural selection cannot operate in the absence of genetic variation. Sociobiologists have tried, for example, to identify an adaptive and genetic foundation for aggression, spite, xenophobia, conformity, homosexuality, and perhaps upward mobility as well.

I believe that modern biology provides a model standing between the despairing claim that biology has nothing to teach us about human behavior and the deterministic theory that specific items of behavior are genetically programed by the action of natural selection. I see two major areas for biological insight:

1. *Fruitful analogies*. Much of human behavior is surely adaptive; if it weren't, we wouldn't be around any more. But adaptation, in humans, is neither an adequate, nor even a good argument for genetic influence. For in humans, as I argued above, adaptation may arise by the alternate route of nongenetic, cultural evolution. Since cultural evolution is so much more rapid than Darwinian evolution, its influence should prevail in the behavioral diversity displayed by human groups. But even when an adaptive behavior is nongenetic, biological analogy may be useful in interpreting its meaning. Adaptive constraints are often strong, and some functions may have to

proceed in a certain way whether their underlying impetus be learning or genetic programming.

For example, ecologists have developed a powerful quantitative theory, called optimal foraging strategy, for studying patterns of exploitation in nature (herbivores by carnivores, plants by herbivores). Cornell University anthropologist Bruce Winterhalder has shown that a community of Cree-speaking peoples in northern Ontario follow some predictions of the theory in their hunting and trapping behavior. Although Winterhalder used a biological theory to understand some aspects of human hunting, he does not believe that the people he studied were genetically selected to hunt as ecological theory predicts they should. He writes (personal communication, July 1978):

> It should go without saying ... that the causes of human variability of hunting and gathering behavior lie in the socio-cultural realm. For that reason, the models that I used were adapted, not adopted, and then applied to a very circumscribed realm of analysis.... For instance, the models assist in analyzing what species a hunter will seek from those available *once a decision has been made to go hunting* [his italics]. They are, however, useless for analyzing why the Cree still hunt (they don't need to), how they decide on a particular day whether to hunt or join a construction crew, the meaning of hunting to a Cree, or any of a plethora of important questions.

In this area, sociobiologists have often fallen into one of the most common errors of reasoning: discovering an analogy and inferring a genetic similarity (literally, in this case!). Analogies are useful but limited; they may reflect common constraints, but not common causes.

2. *Biological potentiality vs. biological determinism.* Humans are animals, and everything we do is constrained, in some sense, by our biology. Some constraints are so integral to our being that we rarely even recognize them, for we never imagine that life might proceed in another way. Consider our narrow range of average adult size and the consequences of living in the gravitational world of large organisms, not the world of surface forces inhabited by insects. Or the fact that we are born helpless (many animals are not), that we mature slowly, that we must sleep for a large part of the day, that we do not photosynthesize, that we can digest both meat and plants, that we age and die. These are all results of our genetic construction, and all are important influences upon human nature and society.

These biological boundaries are so evident that they have never engendered controversy. The contentious subjects are specific behaviors that distress us and that we struggle with difficulty to change (or enjoy and fear to abandon): aggression, xenophobia, male dominance, for example. Sociobiologists are not genetic determinists in the old eugenical sense of postulating single genes for such complex behaviors. All biologists know there is no gene "for" aggression, any more than for your lower-left wisdom tooth. We all recognize that genetic influence can be spread diffusely among many genes and that genes set limits to ranges; they do not provide blueprints for exact replicas. In one sense, the debate between sociobiologists and their critics is an argument about the breadth of ranges. For sociobiologists, ranges are narrow enough to program a specific behavior as the predictable result of possessing certain genes. Critics argue that the ranges permitted by these genetic factors are wide enough to include all behaviors that sociobiologists atomize into distinct traits coded by separate genes.

But in another sense, my dispute with human sociobiology is not just a quantitative debate about the extent of ranges. It will not be settled amicably at some golden midpoint, with critics admitting more constraint, sociobiologists more slop. Advocates of narrow and broad ranges do not simply occupy different positions on a smooth continuum; they hold two qualitatively different theories about the biological nature of human behavior. If ranges are narrow, then genes do code for specific traits and natural selection can create and maintain individual items of behavior separately. If ranges are characteristically broad, then selection may set some deeply recessed generating rules; but specific behaviors are epiphenomena of the rules, not objects of Darwinian attention in their own right.

I believe that human sociobiologists have made a fundamental mistake in categories. They are seeking the genetic basis of human behavior at the wrong level. They are searching among the specific products of generating rules — Joe's homosexuality, Martha's fear of strangers — while the rules themselves are the genetic deep structures of human behavior. For example, E.O. Wilson writes: "Are human beings innately aggressive? This is a favorite question of college seminars and cocktail party conversations, and one that raises emotion in political ideologues of all stripes. The answer to it is yes." As evidence, Wilson cites the prevalence of warfare in history and then discounts any current disinclination to fight: "The most peaceable tribes of today were often the ravagers of yesteryear and will probably again produce soldiers and murderers in the future." But if some peoples are peaceable now, then aggression itself cannot be coded in our genes, only the potential for it. If innate only means possible, or even likely in certain environments, then everything we do is innate and the word has no meaning. Aggression is one expression of a generating rule that anticipates peacefulness in other common environments. The range of specific behaviors engendered by the rule is impressive and a fine testimony to flexibility as the hallmark of human behavior. This flexibility should not be obscured by the linguistic error of branding some common expressions of the rule as "innate" because we can predict their occurrence in certain environments.

Sociobiologists work as if Galileo had really mounted the Leaning Tower (apparently he did not), dropped a set of diverse objects over the side, and sought a separate explanation for each behavior — the plunge of the cannonball as a result of something in the nature of cannonballness; the gentle descent of the feather as intrinsic to featherness. We know, instead, that the wide range of different falling behaviors arises from an interaction between two physical rules — gravity and frictional resistance. This interaction can generate a thousand different styles of descent. If we focus on the objects and seek an explanation for the behavior of each in its own terms, we are lost. The search among specific behaviors for the genetic basis of human nature is an example of *biological determinism*. The quest for underlying generating rules expresses a concept of *biological potentiality*. The question is not biological nature vs. nonbiological nurture. Determinism and potentiality are both *biological* theories — but they seek the genetic basis of human nature at fundamentally different levels.

Pursuing the Galilean analogy, if cannonballs act by cannonballness, feathers by featherness, then we can do little beyond concocting a story for the adaptive significance of each. We would never think of doing the great historical experiment — equalizing the effective environment by placing both in a vacuum and observing an identical behavior in descent. This hypothetical example illustrates the social role of biological determinism. It is fundamentally a theory about limits. It takes current ranges in modern environments as an expression of direct genetic programming, rather than a limited display of much broader potential. If a feather acts by featherness, we cannot change its behavior while it remains a feather. If its behavior is an expression of broad rules tied to specific circumstances, we anticipate a wide range of behaviors in different environments.

Why should human behavioral ranges be so broad, when anatomical ranges are generally narrower? Is this claim for behavioral flexibility merely a social hope, or is it good biology as well? Two different arguments lead me to conclude that wide behavioral ranges should arise as consequences of the evolution and structural organization of our brain. Consider, first of all, the probable adaptive reasons for evolving such a large brain. Human uniqueness lies in the flexibility of what our brain can do. What is intelligence, if not the ability to face problems in an unprogramed (or, as we often say, creative) manner? If intelligence sets us apart among organisms, then I think it probable that natural selection acted to maximize the flexibility of our behavior. What would be more adaptive for a learning and thinking animal: genes selected for aggression, spite, and xenophobia; or selection for learning rules that can generate aggression in appropriate circumstances and peacefulness in others?

Secondly, we must be wary of granting too much power to natural selection by viewing all basic capacities of our brain as direct adaptation. I do not doubt that natural selection acted in building our oversized brains — and I am equally confident that our brains became large as an adaptation for definite roles (probably a complex set of interacting functions). But these assumptions do not lead to the notion, often uncritically embraced by strict Darwinians, that all major capacities of the brain must arise as direct products of natural selection. Our brains are enormously complex computers. If I install a much simpler computer to keep accounts in a factory, it can also perform many other, more complex tasks unrelated to its appointed role. These additional capacities are ineluctable consequences of structural design, not direct adaptations. Our vastly more complex organic computers were also built for reasons, but possess an almost terrifying array of additional capacities — including, I suspect, most of what makes us human. Our ancestors did not read, write, or wonder why most stars do not change their relative positions while five wandering points of light and two larger disks move through a path now called the zodiac. We need not view Bach as a happy spinoff from the value of music in cementing tribal cohesion, or Shakespeare as a fortunate consequence of the role of myth and epic narrative in maintaining hunting bands. Most of the behavioral "traits" that sociobiologists try to explain may never have been subject to direct natural selection at all —

and may therefore exhibit a flexibility that features crucial to survival can never display. Should these complex consequences of structural design even be called "traits"? Is this tendency to atomize a behavioral repertory into a set of "things" not another example of the same fallacy of reification that has plagued studies of intelligence throughout our century?

Flexibility is the hallmark of human evolution. If humans evolved, as I believe, by neoteny, then we are, in a more than metaphorical sense, permanent children. (In neoteny, rates of development slow down and juvenile stages of ancestors become the adult features of descendants.) Many central features of our anatomy link us with fetal and juvenile stages of primates: small face, vaulted cranium and large brain in relation to body size, unrotated big toe, foramen magnum under the skull for correct orientation of the head in upright posture, primary distribution of hair on head, armpits, and pubic areas. In other mammals, exploration, play, and flexibility of behavior are qualities of juveniles, only rarely of

adults. We retain not only the anatomical stamp of childhood, but its mental flexibility as well. The idea that natural selection should have worked for flexibility in human evolution is not an ad hoc notion born in hope, but an implication of neoteny as a fundamental process in our evolution. Humans are learning animals.

Note

1. The brouhaha over sociobiology during the past few years was engendered by this hard version of the argument — genetic proposals (based on an inference of adaptation) for specific human behaviors. Other evolutionists call themselves "sociobiologists," but reject this style of guesswork about specifics. If a sociobiologist is anyone who believes that biological evolution is not irrelevant to human behavior, then I suppose that everybody (creationists excluded) is a sociobiologist. At this point, however, the term loses its meaning and might as well be dropped. Human sociobiology entered the literature (professional and popular) as a definite theory about the adaptive and genetic basis of specific traits of human behavior. If it has failed in this goal — as I believe it has — then the study of valid relationships between biology and human behavior should receive another name. In a world awash in jargon, I don't see why "behavioral biology" can't extend its umbrella sufficiently to encompass this legitimate material.

10
No Bone Unturned

PATRICK HUYGHE

Clyde Snow is never in a hurry. He knows he's late. He's always late. For Snow, being late is part of the job. In fact, he doesn't usually begin to work until death has stripped some poor individual to the bone, and no one — neither the local homicide detectives nor the pathologists — can figure out who once gave identity to the skeletonized remains. No one, that is, except a shrewd, laconic, 60-year-old forensic anthropologist.

Snow strolls into the Cook County Medical Examiner's Office in Chicago on this brisk October morning wearing a pair of Lucchese cowboy boots and a three-piece pin-striped suit. Waiting for him in autopsy room 160 are a bunch of naked skeletons found in Illinois, Wisconsin, and Minnesota since his last visit. Snow, a native Texan who now lives in rural Oklahoma, makes the trip up to Chicago some six times a year. The first case on his agenda is a pale brown skull found in the garbage of an abandoned building once occupied by a Chicago cosmetics company.

Snow turns the skull over slowly in his hands, a cigarette dangling from his fingers. One often does. Snow does not seem overly concerned about mortality, though its tragedy surrounds him daily.

"There's some trauma here," he says, examining a rough edge at the lower back of the skull. He points out the area to Jim Elliott, a homicide detective with the Chicago police. "This looks like a chopping blow by a heavy bladed instrument. Almost like a decapitation." In a place where the whining of bone saws drifts through hallways and the sweet-sour smell of death hangs in the air, the word surprises no one.

Snow begins thinking aloud. "I think what we're looking at here is a female or maybe a small male, about thirty to forty years old. Probably Asian." He turns the skull upside down, pointing out the degree of wear on the teeth. "This was somebody who lived on a really rough diet. We don't normally find this kind of dental wear in a modern Western population."

"How long has it been around?" Elliott asks.

Snow raises the skull up to his nose. "It doesn't have any decompositional odors," he says. He pokes a finger in the skull's nooks and crannies. "There's no soft tissue left. It's good and dry. And it doesn't show signs of having been buried. I would say that this has been lying around in an attic or a box for years. It feels like a souvenir skull," says Snow.

Souvenir skulls, usually those of Japanese soldiers, were popular with U.S. troops serving in the Pacific during World War II; there was also a trade in skulls during the Vietnam War years. On

From *Discover* Magazine, December 1988, pp. 39–45. © 1988 Discover Magazine. Reprinted with permission.

closer inspection, though, Snow begins to wonder about the skull's Asian origins — the broad nasal aperture and the jutting forth of the upper-tooth-bearing part of the face suggest Melanesian features. Sifting through the objects found in the abandoned building with the skull, he finds several loose-leaf albums of 35-millimeter transparencies documenting life among the highland tribes of New Guinea. The slides, shot by an anthropologist, include graphic scenes of ritual warfare. The skull, Snow concludes, is more likely to be a trophy from one of these tribal battles than the result of a local Chicago homicide.

"So you'd treat it like found property?" Elliott asks finally. "Like somebody's garage-sale property?"

"Exactly," says Snow.

Clyde Snow is perhaps the world's most sought-after forensic anthropologist. People have been calling upon him to identify skeletons for more than a quarter of a century. Every year he's involved in some 75 cases of identification, most of them without fanfare. "He's an old scudder who doesn't have to blow his own whistle," says Walter Birkby, a forensic anthropologist at the University of Arizona. "He knows he's good."

Yet over the years Snow's work has turned him into something of an unlikely celebrity. He has been called upon to identify the remains of the Nazi war criminal Josef Mengele, reconstruct the face of the Egyptian boy-king Tutankhamen, confirm the authenticity of the body autopsied as that of President John F. Kennedy, and examine the skeletal remains of General Custer's men at the battlefield of the Little Bighorn. He has also been involved in the grim task of identifying the bodies in some of the United States' worst airline accidents.

Such is his legend that cases are sometimes attributed to him in which he played no part. He did not, as the *New York Times* reported, identify the remains of the crew in the *Challenger* disaster. But the man is often the equal of his myth. For the past four years, setting his personal safety aside, Snow has spent much of his time in Argentina, searching for the graves and identities of some of the thousands who "disappeared" between 1976 and 1983, during Argentina's military regime.

Snow did not set out to rescue the dead from oblivion. For almost two decades, until 1979, he was a physical anthropologist at the Civil Aeromedical Institute, part of the Federal Aviation Administration in Oklahoma City. Snow's job was to help engineers improve aircraft design and safety features by providing them with data on the human frame.

One study, he recalls, was initiated in response to complaints from a flight attendants' organization. An analysis of accident patterns had revealed that inadequate restraints on flight attendants' jump seats were leading to deaths and injuries and that aircraft doors weighing several hundred pounds were impeding evacuation efforts. Snow points out that ensuring the survival of passengers in emergencies is largely the flight attendants' responsibility. "If they are injured or killed in a crash, you're going to find a lot of dead passengers."

Reasoning that equipment might be improved if engineers had more data on the size and strength of those who use it, Snow undertook a study that required the meticulous measurement of some of the most admired flesh-bearing skeletons in the world. When Snow's report was issued in 1975, Senator William Proxmire was outraged that $57,800 of the taxpayers' money had been spent to caliper 423 young airline stewardesses from head to toe. Yet the study, which received one of the senator's dubious Golden Fleece Awards, was firmly supported by both the FAA and the Association of Flight Attendants. "I can't imagine," says Snow with obvious delight, "how much coffee Proxmire got spilled on him in the next few months."

It was during his tenure at the FAA that he developed an interest in forensic work. Over the years the Oklahoma police frequently consulted the physical anthropologist for help in identifying crime victims. "The FAA figured it was a kind of community service to let me work on these cases," he says.

The experience also helped to prepare him for the grim task of identifying the victims of air disasters. In December 1972, when a United Airlines plane crashed outside Chicago, killing 43 of the 61 people aboard (including the wife of Watergate conspirator Howard Hunt, who was found with $10,000 in her purse), Snow was brought in to help examine the bodies. That same year, with Snow's help, forensic anthropology was recognized as a specialty by the American Academy of Forensic Sciences. "It got a lot of anthropologists interested in forensics," he says, "and it made a lot of pathologists out there aware that there were anthropologists who could help them."

Each nameless skeleton poses a unique mystery for Snow. But some, like the second case awaiting him back in the autopsy room at the Cook County morgue, are more challenging than others. This one is a real chiller. In a large card-board box lies a jumble of bones along with a tattered leg from a pair of blue jeans, a sock shrunk tightly around the bones of a foot, a pair of Nike running shoes without shoelaces, and, inside the hood of a blue wind-breaker, a mass of stringy, blood-caked hair. The remains were discovered frozen in ice about 20 miles outside Milwaukee. A rusted bicycle was found lying close by. Paul Hibbard, chief deputy medical examiner for Waukesha County, who brought the skeleton to Chicago, says no one has been reported missing.

Snow lifts the bones out of the box and begins reconstructing the skeleton on an autopsy table. "There are two hundred six bones and thirty-two teeth in the human body," he says, "and each has a story to tell." Because bone is dynamic, living tissue, many of life's significant events — injuries, illness, childbearing — leave their mark on the body's internal framework. Put together the stories told by these bones, he says, and what you have is a person's "osteobiography."

Snow begins by determining the sex of the skeleton, which is not always obvious. He tells the story of a skeleton that was brought to his FAA office in the late 1970s. It had been found along with some women's clothes and a purse in a local back lot, and the police had assumed that it was female. But when Snow examined the bones, he realized that "at six foot three, she would probably have been the tallest female in Oklahoma."

Then Snow recalled that six months earlier the custodian in his building had suddenly not shown up for work. The man's supervisor later mentioned to Snow, "You know, one of these days when they find Ronnie, he's going to be dressed as a woman." Ronnie, it turned out, was a weekend transvestite. A copy of his dental records later confirmed that the skeleton in women's clothing was indeed Snow's janitor.

The Wisconsin bike rider is also male. Snow picks out two large bones that look something like twisted oysters — the innominates, or hipbones, which along with the sacrum, or lower backbone, form the pelvis. This pelvis is narrow and steep-walled like a male's, not broad and shallow like a female's. And the sciatic notch (the V-shaped space where the sciatic nerve passes through the hipbone) is narrow, as is normal in a male. Snow can also determine a skeleton's sex by checking the size of the mastoid processes (the bony knobs at the base of the skull) and the prominence of the brow ridge, or by measuring the head of an available limb bone, which is typically broader in males.

From an examination of the skull he concludes that the bike rider is "predominantly Caucasoid." A score of bony traits help the forensic anthropologist assign a skeleton to one of three major racial groups: Negroid, Caucasoid, or Mongoloid. Snow notes that the ridge of the boy's nose is high and salient, as it is in whites. In Negroids and Mongoloids (which include American Indians as well as most Asians) the nose tends to be broad in relation to its height. However, the boy's nasal margins are somewhat smoothed down, usually a Mongoloid feature. "Possibly a bit of American Indian admixture," says Snow. "Do you have Indians in your area?" Hibbard nods.

Age is next. Snow takes the skull and turns it upside down, pointing out the basilar joint, the junction between the two major bones that form the underside of the skull. In a child the joint would still be open to allow room for growth, but here the joint has fused — something that usually happens in the late teen years. On the other hand, he says, pointing to the zigzagging lines on the dome of the skull, the cranial sutures are open. The cranial sutures, which join the bones of the braincase, begin to fuse and disappear in the mid-twenties.

Next Snow picks up a femur and looks for signs of growth at the point where the shaft meets the knobbed end. The thin plates of cartilage — areas of incomplete calcification — that are visible at this point suggest that the boy hadn't yet attained his full height. Snow double-checks with an examination of the pubic symphysis, the joint where the two hipbones meet. The ridges in this area, which fill in and smooth over in adulthood, are still clearly marked. He concludes that the skeleton is that of a boy between 15 and 20 years old.

"One of the things you learn is to be pretty conservative," says Snow. "It's very impressive when you tell the police, 'This person is eighteen years old,' and he turns out to be eighteen. The problem is, if the person is fifteen you've blown it — you probably won't find him. Looking for a missing person is like trying to catch fish. Better get a big net and do your own sorting."

Snow then picks up a leg bone, measures it with a set of calipers, and enters the data into a portable computer. Using the known correlation between the height and length of the long limb bones, he quickly estimates the boy's height. "He's five foot six and a half to five foot eleven," says Snow. "Medium build, not excessively muscular, judging from the muscle attachments that we see." He points to the grainy ridges that appear where muscle attaches itself to the bone. The most prominent attachments show up on the teenager's right arm bone, indicating right-handedness.

Then Snow examines the ribs one by one for signs of injury. He finds no stab wounds, cuts, or bullet holes, here or elsewhere on the skeleton. He picks up the hyoid bone from the boy's throat and looks for the telltale fracture signs that would suggest the boy was strangled. But, to Snow's frustration, he can find no obvious cause of death. In hopes of identifying the missing teenager, he suggests sending the skull, hair, and the boy's description to Betty Pat Gatliff, a medical illustrator and sculptor in Oklahoma who does facial reconstructions.

Six weeks later photographs of the boy's likeness appear in the *Milwaukee Sentinel*. "If you persist long enough," says Snow, "eighty-five to ninety percent of the cases eventually get positively identified, but it can take anywhere from a few weeks to a few years."

Snow and Gatliff have collaborated many times, but never with more glitz than in 1983, when Snow was commissioned by Patrick Barry, a Miami orthopedic surgeon and amateur Egyptologist, to reconstruct the face of the Egyptian boy-king Tutankhamen. Normally a facial reconstruction begins with a skull, but since Tutankhamen's 3,000-year-old remains were in Egypt, Snow had to make do with the skull measurements from a 1925 postmortem and X-rays taken in 1975. A plaster model of the skull was made, and on the basis of Snow's report — "his skull is Caucasoid with some Negroid admixtures" — Gatliff put a face on it. What did Tutankhamen look like? Very much like the gold mask on his sarcophagus, says Snow, confirming that it was, indeed, his portrait.

Many cite Snow's use of facial reconstructions as one of his most important contributions to the field. Snow, typically self-effacing, says that Gatliff "does all the work." The identification of skeletal remains, he stresses, is often a collaboration between pathologists, odontologists, radiologists, and medical artists using a variety of forensic techniques.

One of Snow's last tasks at the FAA was to help identify the dead from the worst airline accident in U.S. history. On May 25, 1979, a DC-10 crashed shortly after takeoff from Chicago's O'Hare Airport, killing 273 people. The task facing Snow and more than a dozen forensic specialists was horrific. "No one ever sat down and counted," says Snow, "but we estimated ten thousand to twelve thousand pieces or parts of bodies." Nearly 80 percent of the victims were identified on the basis of dental evidence and fingerprints. Snow and forensic radiologist John Fitzpatrick later managed to identify two dozen others by comparing postmortem X-rays with X-rays taken during the victim's lifetime.

Next to dental records, such X-ray comparisons are the most common way of obtaining positive identifications. In 1978, when a congressional committee reviewed the evidence on John F. Kennedy's assassination, Snow used X-rays to show that the body autopsied at Bethesda Naval Hospital was indeed that of the late president and had not — as some conspiracy theorists believed — been switched.

The issue was resolved on the evidence of Kennedy's "sinus print," the scalloplike pattern on the upper margins of the sinuses that are visible in X-rays of the forehead. So characteristic is a person's sinus print that courts throughout the world accept the matching of antemortem and postmortem X-rays of the sinuses as positive identification.

Yet another technique in the forensic specialist's repertoire is photo superposition. Snow used it in 1977 to help identify the mummy of a famous Oklahoma outlaw named Elmer J. McCurdy, who was killed by a posse after holding up a train in 1911. For years the mummy had been exhibited as a "dummy" in a California funhouse — until it was found to have a real human skeleton inside it. Ownership of the mummy was eventually traced back to a funeral parlor in Oklahoma, where McCurdy had been embalmed and exhibited as "the bandit who wouldn't give up."

Using two video cameras and an image processor, Snow superposed the mummy's profile on a photograph of McCurdy that was taken shortly after his death. When displayed on a single monitor, the two coincided to a remarkable degree. Convinced by the evidence, Thomas Noguchi, then Los Angeles County coroner, signed McCurdy's death certificate ("Last known occupation: Train robber") and allowed the outlaw's bones to be returned to Oklahoma for a decent burial.

It was this technique that also allowed forensic scientists to identify the remains of the Nazi "Angel of Death," Josef Mengele, in the summer of 1985. A team of investigators, including Snow and West German forensic anthropologist Richard Helmer, flew to Brazil after an Austrian couple claimed that Mengele lay buried in a grave on a São Paulo hillside. Tests revealed that the stature, age, and hair color of the unearthed skeleton were consistent with information in Mengele's SS files; yet without X-rays or dental records, the scientists still lacked conclusive evidence. When an image of the reconstructed skull was superposed on 1930s photographs of Mengele, however, the match was eerily compelling. All doubts were removed a few months later when Mengele's dental X-rays were tracked down.

In 1979 Snow retired from the FAA to the rolling hills of Norman, Oklahoma, where he and his wife, Jerry, live in a sprawling, early-1960s ranch house. Unlike his 50 or so fellow forensic anthropologists, most of whom are tied to academic positions, Snow is free to pursue his consultancy work full-time. Judging from the number of miles that he logs in the average month, Snow is clearly not ready to retire for good.

His recent projects include a reexamination of the skeletal remains found at the site of the Battle of the Little Bighorn, where more than a century ago Custer and his 210 men were killed by Sioux and Cheyenne warriors. Although most of the enlisted men's remains were moved to a mass grave in 1881, an excavation of the battlefield in the past few years uncovered an additional 375 bones and 36 teeth. Snow, teaming up again with Fitzpatrick, determined that these remains belonged to 34 individuals.

The historical accounts of Custer's desperate last stand are vividly confirmed by their findings. Snow identified one skeleton as that of a soldier between the ages of 19 and 23 who weighed around 150 pounds and stood about five foot eight. He'd sustained gunshot wounds to his chest and left forearm. Heavy blows to his head had fractured his skull and sheared off his teeth. Gashed thigh bones indicated that his body was later dismembered with an axe or hatchet.

Given the condition and number of the bodies, Snow seriously questions the accuracy of the identifications made by the original nineteenth-century burial crews. He doubts, for example, that the skeleton buried at West Point is General Custer's.

For the last four years Snow has devoted much of his time to helping two countries come to terms with the horrors of a much more recent past. As part of a group sponsored by the American Association for the Advancement of Science, he has been helping the Argentinean National Commission on Disappeared Persons to determine the fate of some of those who vanished during their country's harsh military rule:

between 1976 and 1983 at least 10,000 people were systemically swept off the streets by roving death squads to be tortured, killed, and buried in unmarked graves. In December 1986, at the invitation of the Aquino government's Human Rights Commission, Snow also spent several weeks training Philippine scientists to investigate the disappearances that occurred under the Marcos regime.

But it is in Argentina that Snow has done the bulk of his human-rights work. He has spent more than 27 months in and around Buenos Aires, first training a small group of local medical and anthropology students in the techniques of forensic investigation, and later helping them carefully exhume and examine scores of the *desaparecidos*, or disappeared ones.

Only 25 victims have so far been positively identified. But the evidence has helped convict seven junta members and other high-ranking military and police officers. The idea is not necessarily to identify all 10,000 of the missing, says Snow. "If you have a colonel who ran a detention center where maybe five hundred people were killed, you don't have to nail him with five hundred deaths. Just one or two should be sufficient to get him convicted." Forensic evidence from Snow's team may be used to prosecute several other military officers, including General Suarez Mason. Mason is the former commander of the I Army Corps in Buenos Aires and is believed to be responsible for thousands of disappearances. He was recently extradited from San Francisco back to Argentina, where he is expected to stand trial this winter.

The investigations have been hampered by a frustrating lack of antemortem information. In 1984, when commission lawyers took depositions from relatives and friends of the disappeared, they often failed to obtain such basic information as the victim's height, weight, or hair color. Nor did they ask for the missing person's X-rays (which in Argentina are given to the patient) or the address of the victim's dentist. The problem was compounded by the inexperience of those who carried out the first mass exhumations prior to Snow's arrival. Many of the skeletons were inadvertently destroyed by bulldozers as they were brought up.

Every unearthed skeleton that shows signs of gunfire, however, helps to erode the claim once made by many in the Argentinean military that most of the *desaparecidos* are alive and well and living in Mexico City, Madrid, or Paris. Snow recalls the case of a 17-year-old boy named

Gabriel Dunayavich, who disappeared in the summer of 1976. He was walking home from a movie with his girlfriend when a Ford Falcon with no license plates snatched him off the street. The police later found his body and that of another boy and girl dumped by the roadside on the outskirts of Buenos Aires. The police went through the motions of an investigation, taking photographs and doing an autopsy, then buried the three teenagers in an unmarked grave.

A decade later Snow, with the help of the boy's family, traced the autopsy reports, the police photographs, and the grave of the three youngsters. Each of them had four or five closely spaced bullet wounds in the upper chest — the signature, says Snow, of an automatic weapon. Two also had wounds on their arms from bullets that had entered behind the elbow and exited from the forearm.

"That means they were conscious when they were shot," says Snow. "When a gun was pointed at them, they naturally raised their arm." It's details like these that help to authenticate the last moments of the victims and bring a dimension of reality to the judges and jury.

Each time Snow returns from Argentina he says that this will be the last time. A few months later he is back in Buenos Aires. "There's always more work to do," he says. It is, he admits quietly, "terrible work."

"These were such brutal, coldblooded crimes," he says. "The people who committed them not only murdered; they had a system to eliminate all trace that their victims even existed."

Snow will not let them obliterate their crimes so conveniently. "There are human-rights violations going on all around the world," he says. "But to me murder is murder, regardless of the motive. I hope that we are sending a message to governments who murder in the name of politics that they can be held to account."

11
Did Solder Kill Franklin's Men?

WALTER KOWAL, OWEN B. BEATTIE,
HALFDAN BAADSGAARD, and PETER M. KRAHN

One of the greatest mysteries of Arctic exploration is the loss of the 129 crewmen and officers of the Sir John Franklin expedition (1845–48) in search of a North-West Passage. As part of a forensic investigation of recently discovered human remains from the expedition, atomic absorption analysis yielded levels of lead in tissues consistent with acute lead intoxication. These findings indicate that it was exposure to toxic levels of lead that adversely affected the health, judgement, and ultimate survival of the expedition members. It has been hypothesized that food preserved in soldered tins was the source of the high lead levels. Because lead isotopes do not fractionate in biological systems, their ratios within human tissues are a reflection of the ratios from the contaminating source. Matching lead isotope ratios would indicate that the lead in the human remains came from the soldered tins. We have carried out isotope studies of lead from the human remains and tins to test the hypothesis.

The materials used in the analyses were collected from Beechey and King William Islands, Northwest Territories, Canada. Bone samples from Inuit and caribou from the same time period and geographical area, and with the same depositional characteristics, were analysed to evaluate the concentration and isotope composition of lead from the local environment. Samples of modern human bone and solder from food tins manufactured in the 1880s were included as additional controls.

The results of the lead isotope analyses are presented in the accompanying figure. The variation in the isotope ratios of the Franklin expedition samples is only slightly greater than the analytical uncertainty. The mean $^{206}Pb/^{204}Pb$, $^{207}Pb/^{204}Pb$ and $^{206}Pb/^{204}Pb$ ratios, with 1σ uncertainty, (for the tissue samples ($n = 9$) were 18.46 ± 0.03, 15.64 ± 0.01, 38.48 ± 0.04 and, for the solder samples ($n = 10$) 18.46 ± 0.02, 15.64 ± 0.01, 38.50 ± 0.04). The slight spread in lead isotope values was expected as not all of the lead present in the tissues would have been acquired during the expedition.

Differential environmental exposures before the expedition would have assured a wide variety of isotopic ratios in the tissues of the various crewmen. The close clustering of isotope ratios, however, indicates that most of the lead in the tissues came from a single dominant source as the variability seen in the ratios is consistent with that observed when a small amount of lead from one source is mixed with a large amount of lead from another source; only a slight shift occurs in

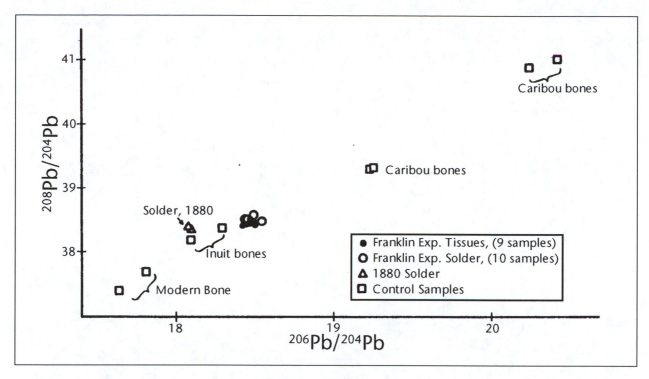

Lead isotope analyses, carried out by thermal ionization mass measurement using a VG-Micromass-30 mass spectrometer. The measured lead isotope ratios were corrected for mass fractionation, as determined by repeat analyses of U.S. National Bureau of Standards NBS SRM 981 standard lead. The precision of the lead isotope ratios was established by replicate analyses and indicated a variation of one part per thousand at the 95 percent confidence level. Error limits are indicated (approximately) by the size of the circular symbols.

the isotopic ratios from that of the dominant contributor.

The isotope composition of lead in the tissues from the expedition members does indeed closely match that of the solder from the food tins. We conclude, therefore, that the toxic lead levels thought to be responsible for the demise of the expedition members were derived from the tinned foods.

PART TWO
Archaeology

Introduction

In 1859, in his *Origin of Species*, Darwin hypothesized that modern humans were distantly related to nonhuman ancestors. It was in the same year that the discoveries of Jacques Boucher de Perthes were recognized by the Royal Society. Since the 1830s, this French customs official had been excavating stone tools along with the remains of extinct animal species in quarries near Abbeville, in northern France. Soon, similar discoveries made in England, France, and Holland confirmed the great antiquity of humankind. The evidence from geology, which Charles Lyell had shown how to interpret, had proved that the earth was at least several hundred thousand years old. Darwin's theory of adaptation through natural selection added strength to these archaeological discoveries, and forced many scientists to reject the Christian theological explanations that had until then been taken for granted. They could no longer accept Archbishop James Ussher's sophisticated calculations, or John Lightfoot's even more precise claim, based on a careful reading of the Bible, that man was created at 9 A.M., on October 23, in the year 4004 B.C. Many earlier discoveries of bones and flint tools, which had until then been dismissed as oddities, since they did not fit into any known context, were now reinterpreted correctly as evidence of the existence of prehistoric humans. This development gives credence to the claim that facts cannot "speak" to us unless we have a proper theory in the context of which to grasp their message.

If you were to examine the garbage of your neighbors, you would find wrappers, food remains, newspapers, condoms, TV dinners, liquor bottles, and other refuse. With a bit of imagination, you could learn very much from this collection about your neighbors' eating, drinking, and spending habits; their hobbies; their sexual activity; and even their political preferences. You could learn so much about them, in fact, that your investigation of their garbage would legally constitute an invasion of privacy. Archaeologists are detectives who seek clues about the life styles of societies of the past in tombs, ruins, and ancient garbage pits. Some archaeologists, like W. Rathje, even study the landfill sites of modern North America. Their discoveries improve our understanding of the fossilization of deposits, and are relevant to solving various ecological problems, such as calculating the precise amount and rate of decomposition of different kinds of refuse and determining whether recycling works and whether our basic assumptions about waste disposal are correct.

Archaeological research often involves digging up the shattered remains of past cultures. What archaeologists often find are broken pots, discarded tools, kitchen rubbish, and various other leftovers. However, the goal of their activity is to describe and explain as thoroughly as possible the behavior, settlement patterns, technologies, activities, social organization, art, religion, and other aspects of the lives of past peoples.

Archaeology is the scientific study of the material remains of human cultures. In this book, we shall concern ourselves mostly with the remains of past cultures. These can be cultures of the quite recent past, as in the case of Rathje's excavations of modern North American garbage pits, or of the historical past. The archaeologists who fill the gaps in our knowledge of historical events — analyzing, for example, the ruins and garbage of a plantation or the remains of an old fort or trading post built by the early European invaders of the American continent — are called **historical archaeologists**. Others specialize in the monumental and artistic heritage of early civilizations in the ancient Mediterranean world: they often refer to themselves as *classical archaeologists*. Many of them are art historians or classical scholars. The training and approach of Egyptologists, who focus on Egypt's early periods, are similar to those of classical archaeologists. One specialty that is making increasingly important contributions as the result of the new technologies available to its practitioners is *marine archaeology*, which deals with sites and materials found underwater. The Great Lakes, for example, hold thousands of shipwrecks, and many requests for archaeological permits in Ontario are for the exploration of those submerged remains. Archaeologists who specialize in the study of extinct people who left no written documents — particularly those who lived before the invention of writing — are commonly called **prehistoric archaeologists**.

It should be noted that the distinctions we have just described are not always useful, since many archaeologists are active in more than one of these fields, and all are in many ways doing the same job as cultural anthropologists. They study human societies and cultures, but focus on the material evidence for cultural and social change over the millennia.

The analysis of many past societies and their cultures, made possible by archaeological methods and techniques, is an essential element of the solution of many anthropological problems. This becomes self-evident when one considers that prehistory constitutes more than 99 percent of the duration of humanity's existence on earth. The analysis of prehistoric societies helps us to answer questions such as the following: *When, where, how,* and *why* did agriculture replace a hunting-gathering existence? Was it invented only once, or many times? When, where, how, and why did the first city appear? The first state? Cross-cultural comparisons of societies that followed one another in sequence help us to identify various trends and regularities in cultural evolution.

Besides its factual and theoretical contribution to anthropology, archaeology is also relevant to the solution of many practical modern problems. Several readings in this section will show you how we can learn from the mistakes of our ancestors. Typically, archaeologists' findings connected with ecological disasters of the past support the validity of modern ecologists' predictions about the consequences of such problems as overpopulation, resource depletion, and pollution. However, archaeology also discovers evidence of various successes that can benefit societies today. For example, the governments of Bolivia, Colombia, and Mexico have raised the standard of living of some of their peasants by reintroducing pre-Columbian techniques of cultivation that were rediscovered by archaeologists.

In many countries, archaeological remains are a source of national pride and tourist dollars. However, there is a darker side to this public interest. Many kinds of archaeological artifacts, from stone arrow-points to Mayan carvings and Peruvian pottery, are routinely displaced from their context and damaged or destroyed by tourists, amateurs, treasure hunters, greedy collectors, and professional looters. The careless removal of artifacts from the context that could have explained them represents a significant loss to the discipline. Archaeologists do not claim as private property the artifacts they discover: the true value of those artifacts lies in their contribution to our knowledge of human history. Thus, the "curse" of archaeologists comes not from the Egyptian mummy of horror movies but from the hordes of amateur diggers and pilferers who destroy crucial evidence. I should hasten to emphasize that careful amateurs have made, and continue to make, numerous and splendid contributions to archaeological research. Just to mention a few of the more famous examples, amateur archaeologists were responsible for the discovery of the caves of Lascaux and the prehistoric site of Pincevent in France, as well as of the Fell Cave in Tierra del Fuego.

One of the constraints on the study of archaeology is that the evidence of the past is very incomplete. Important information is often lacking because the evidence for it has been destroyed either by natural forces, such as decay and erosion, or by people. Many archaeological sites have been destroyed in the recent past; for example, ancient camp sites have been plowed over and ancient monuments have been used as quarries for building supplies. Because stone, unlike bone, wood, or cloth, does not rot or decay, the cultural remains of our earliest ancestors that we are most likely to find are those made of stone. (Until recently, archaeologists attributed the flint tools found by Boucher de Perthes around Abbeville to *Homo erectus*, but some now suggest that early *Homo sapiens* may have made them.) Metal artifacts, from later periods, are also often well preserved and present in sufficient numbers to be useful as markers of certain styles and cultures.

During the nineteenth century, a great popular interest in the collection of "antiquities" and a better understanding of the meaning and value of flint tools and other such "oddities" resulted in numerous, and enormous, collections of archaeological artifacts. To make sense of his own collection, C.J. Thomsen, the curator of a Danish Museum, divided it up into three separate sections, according to material type, and he suggested that the arrangement reflected a succession of cultural periods, which he called the Stone Age, the Bronze Age, and the Iron Age. Thomsen's classification was immediately accepted, together with its evolutionary assumptions.

In 1865, British scientist Sir John Lubbock proposed a significant improvement when he distinguished the old stone age — the **Paleolithic** — from the new stone age — the **Neolithic**. Polished stone tools and pottery appeared during the Neolithic period. Modern archaeologists still use these terms, but over the years, a wealth of new information, much of it discovered in the course of systematic archaeological excavations, contributed to the introduction of important refinements. The Paleolithic is now subdivided into the *Lower Paleolithic*, the *Middle Paleolithic*, and the *Upper Paleolithic*, and each of these periods is known for a variety of cultural traditions. Another period, the **Mesolithic**, has been introduced into the European sequence, following the Paleolithic: many technological innovations were made during this transitional period. The term *Neolithic* is still used, but rather improperly: We shall see later that, rather than referring to a "new stone age," the term has been used by modern archaeologists since V. Gordon Childe in reference to a period whose key innovation they consider to be the domestication of plants and animals. They describe early agricultural societies as Neolithic, even in the absence of polished stone tools.

Today we know that many nonhuman animals also use tools. We define tools as objects that are not part of the user's body but that serve to manipulate the user's environment to acquire or modify resources or energy. Eagles dropping stones on ostrich eggs, Galapagos finches using twigs to catch insects in tree holes, chimpanzees using twigs to catch termites — all are examples of animals using tools. The latter example is most significant, because the chimpanzees also select and prepare the twigs according to optimal length and shape; consequently, we can no longer make the arrogant claim that humans alone are "tool makers." Nevertheless, when our early hominid ancestors started to depend on tools as their primary means of survival, they set themselves apart from all other animals, and triggered innumerable changes in their ecology, and even in their biology. Because of the interrelationships of the various aspects of human and prehuman life in the course of such profound transitions, it is understandable that biologists, archaeologists, cultural anthropologists, and even linguists commonly pool their resources to attempt to unravel this long forgotten past. JoAnn Gutin's essay "Who Peopled the Planet?" (Chapter 12), which starts this section and links it to the previous one, provides vivid examples of collaborations among geneticists, paleontologists, archaeologists, and linguists to discover the movements of humans and their ancestors that can explain the distribution of artifacts and languages on earth.

Until the 1950s, archaeologists had often contented themselves with endless descriptions, classifications, and chronologies. They described sites and artifacts, not people. They shied away from reconstructing a way of life or theorizing about cultural change. Sally Binford and Lewis Binford emphasized on the contrary that "one goal of prehistory is the accurate description of past *patterns of life*" [emphasis added]. Precise descriptions and typologies of tools are very useful, but they do not tell us how those tools were used by their makers. A successful approach to determining the latter is to start the analysis from the point of view of the tasks to be performed — hunting, cutting, or cooking, for example. These tasks each require different tools and are often performed in different places. Therefore, the number of each type of tool found at different sites gives us a hint about the kind of site we are studying — permanent settlement, butchering site, or overnight camp. Lewis Binford also studied living hunters and gatherers for the techniques they employed and the "archaeological remains" they left behind of their camps and settlements: he visited the Nunamuit Eskimo, the Navajo, and the Australian Aborigines. The study of modern people to understand extinct cultures is called **ethnoarchaeology**. Binford also pioneered experiments in the manufacture of stone tools and

their actual use in butchering animals, cleaning hides, and other tasks. His message was that archaeology is a science about peoples, not a collection of antiquities. With his famous essay entitled "Archaeology as Anthropology" (1962), Binford became the leading spokesman for what we call the "New Archaeology."

Since that time, new methodological concerns and the availability of new technologies, such as electron microscopes (Chapter 4) and earth satellites (Chapter 21), have spawned not one but several "newer" archaeologies. Nevertheless, as we see in Lawrence Keeley's essay (Chapter 13), the goal remains to describe the lifestyle of early human populations. Keeley shows how microscopes can help decipher the kind of use to which Paleolithic stone tools were put, thereby increasing the precision of our knowledge beyond the wildest dreams of archaeologists even two decades ago.

In Part One, Biological Anthropology, we learned that bipedal locomotion preceded the development of large brains: the foot came first! The discovery of *Australopithecus afarensis* and of the 3.7-million-year-old footprints of Laetoli settled that question. Bipedal locomotion freed the hands for acquiring, carrying, and sharing food, as well as for using tools. These tools could accomplish many tasks, such as grasping, tearing, or cutting — functions that big teeth and powerful jaws had performed before the emergence of bipedal locomotion. Rather than being used as a crushing vise, the skull came to serve primarily as a brain case. Since the cleverest tool-using and tool-making hominids had an adaptive advantage over others, and since brain size and intelligence are to some extent linked, natural selection favored bigger-brained individuals. Archaeologists indeed find evidence of such trends. As we analyze, in turn, the tool kits of *Homo habilis*, *Homo erectus*, and *Homo sapiens neanderthalensis*, we note an increase in the number of types of tools and a marked increase in the efficiency of their production; at the same time, the skeletal evidence indicates an increase in brain size. It has been calculated that whereas 40 cm of cutting edge could be made from 1 kg of flint in the Lower Paleolithic, more than 4 m could be made from the same amount of flint by the end of the Middle Paleolithic. After the appearance of our own subspecies, *Homo sapiens sapiens*, cultural innovations ceased to be tied to variations in brain characteristics. The explanation of why neither a Cro-Magnon individual nor your grandfather could have invented minicomputers and space-stations is cultural, not biological.

The oldest type of stone tool was made more than two million years ago, probably by *Homo habilis*. Called a "pebble tool" or "chopper," this tool looks like a smooth stone with a few chips broken off at one end. Louis Leakey, who discovered both pebble tools and *Homo habilis* remains at his excavations at Olduvai Gorge (starting in 1931), named that tool-making technique Oldowan after the site at which the tools were found. Many tools similar to the **Oldowan** assemblages have been found in other parts of Africa, India, and China.

In tools found at Olduvai Gorge and many other sites, we observe that, over time, more and more flakes are chipped away from the stone. In an innovation called bifacial technology, stone flakes were chipped alternately from two sides of a flat stone. This trend eventually produced so-called hand axes that were thinner and more pointed at the end and had sharp but wavy cutting edges. Little evidence points to the actual use of these tools as axes, but, as Keeley demonstrates in Chapter 13, they were very useful for cutting and scraping. Because the first "hand axes" were found in a quarry in the French village of Saint-Acheul, they are called **Acheulian** hand axes. In Europe, they are associated with the prehuman culture of *Homo erectus*,

who lived between 1.8 million years B.P. (before the present) and 300,000 years B.P. in Africa and Europe, as well as with early *Homo sapiens*. Although there were *Homo erectus* populations in East Asia as well, they were associated with choppers and chopping-tool traditions. In Africa and Europe, smaller tools made from stone flakes, probably used to work on wood or animal hides, are found together with Acheulian hand axes. Evidence for the existence of wooden tools appears in England and in Germany, where remnants of spears have also been found.

Another significant cultural innovation of *Homo erectus*, which emerged roughly half a million years ago, was the controlled use of fire. The use of fire gave *Homo erectus* populations warmth, light, protection, and the ability to cook, setting them well apart from all other animals. Cooking extended considerably the variety of local resources that could be digested as food; its implications for health, nutrition, and dentition were significant.

The number and variety of stone tools made from **flakes** increased dramatically during the next major

The stone age is now! Stone tools are not obsolete, as shown by this contemporary New Guinean, who prefers stone axes to steel for the delicate carving of his canoe and war shield. He is pictured making a stone axe, using a technique that was known to Homo erectus *more than a million years ago. Source: Jean-Luc Chodkiewicz.*

archaeological period, the Middle Paleolithic. Although some **core tools** are also associated with this period, tools made from flakes removed from the larger stones predominate in the Mousterian–**Levalloisian** tool assemblages of *Homo neanderthalensis*. The significant technological innovation represented by all these flake tools is that they were chipped, with a single blow, from a lump of flint — known as a "tortoise-shell core" — that had been specially prepared to predetermine the shape of the flakes.

In Chapter 6, Richard Klein outlined five technological and cultural differences between the first modern humans and their immediate predecessors. Stone-tool technology changed substantially with the emergence of modern humans. Chapters 12 through 18 describe and explain some of the fascinating accomplishments of early *Homo sapiens sapiens*. Chapters 14 and 15 focus on what we can learn about their beliefs and thought processes from their artistic expressions; Chapter 16 evaluates the mixed blessing of agriculture; and Chapters 17 and 18 deal with the expansion of humans into a previously unoccupied area, the New World.

The early *Homo sapiens sapiens* whose cultures are grouped under the rubric "Upper Paleolithic" were very clever and efficient hunters who benefited from a favorable change in climatic and ecological conditions. In southern Europe, especially southern France and Spain, they painted magnificent frescoes on the walls of caves, notably at Lascaux and Altamira, which specialists date at about 15,000 B.P. Paul Bahn describes artifacts at least 5000 years older, such as the "Dancing Venus of Galgenberg" (Chapter 14), and suggests that a long artistic tradition preceded the "Gravettian period" famous for the "Venus figurines." Roger Lewin discusses a new hypothesis that claims to explain the rock frescoes at such famous Magdalenian sites as Lascaux and Altamira (Chapter 15): It suggests that the frescoes were neither examples of hunting magic nor sexual symbols, but rather representations of the hallucinations of shamans in a state of trance. This is not likely to be the last word on the subject.

The Magdalenian culture was the last hurrah of the Paleolithic hunters and gatherers. The last glaciation of the Pleistocene (traditionally called "Würm" in Western Europe) ended by 12,000 B.P.; with that transition, the climate changed rapidly, some types of vegetation were replaced by others, and many big game species, such as the mammoth, disappeared. The Mesolithic peoples of Europe focused on fishing and collecting seafood when the hunting of large herd animals became less efficient. They built permanent villages and started to use hunting dogs, bows and arrows, fish hooks, harpoons, skis, boats, and paddles. They manufactured very different kinds of stone tools from those that their predecessors had used: either very small tools (microliths) or very large ones (macroliths), such as the axes they used to exploit the forests that were now invading the vast prairies of Europe.

Meanwhile, in a region extending from modern Iraq, Iran, Syria, and Turkey to Egypt, other human innovations started a chain of events that was to change the face of the earth. Several populations in these regions started to shift their subsistence pattern from hunting and gathering to producing. In a relatively short time — a wink by the geological time scale — they settled in villages, then became herders and cultivators; all the while, their populations grew in size at an unprecedented rate. The basis of their subsistence became the exploitation of domesticated plants, such as wheat, barley, peas, and lentils, and animals, such as pigs, sheep, goats, and cattle. In a few millennia, the expanding populations had built cities and started the first civilizations in this area, which we commonly designate as the "Fertile Crescent."

It was British archaeologist V. Gordon Childe who alerted archaeologists to the fact that the radical change in life style resulting from plant and animal domestication was a much more significant characteristic of the **Neolithic** period than the appearance of polished stone tools. Gordon Childe thought that the agricultural revolution occurred only once, in the Middle East, and then spread to other parts of the world, where either the seeds or the idea of cultivation were transmitted to other people. This theory is now rejected, as archaeologists have found evidence of independent "agricultural revolutions" in Southeast Asia, China, Meso-America, and South America. Although modern archaeologists agree with Gordon Childe's claim that the Neolithic way of life was in large part diffused to Europe, they also point out that Europeans did not just accept blindly the inventions made elsewhere — they contributed significant inventions of their own. Furthermore, we find evidence in Israel that certain seeds that would be domesticated later were already being used routinely by 18,000 B.P. Thus, the shift in subsistence strategy appears to have taken nearly ten thousand years — hardly sudden enough to be called a "revolution." That is why most modern archaeologists refer to this complex of events and processes by the less romantic expressions "development of agriculture" and "agricultural transition."

Our understanding of the slow process of domestication of plants and animals, and the associated shift in subsistence strategy, has increased, not only because we have gathered much additional data, but also, and perhaps more importantly, because our theories and approaches are more sophisticated and rigorous. A major contribution to this refinement of method was proposed by the geographer Carl Sauer, who introduced an ecological approach to the problem in a long essay entitled *Seeds, Spades, Hearths and Herds* (1952). A decade later, Lewis Binford's demographic analysis suggested that population increase led to resettlement into areas where potential domesticates were found. The overflow of successful and overpopulating Mesolithic groups forced them to colonize these new areas, and to change in order to cope with scarcity. More recently, Lewis Binford and Kent Flannery, among others, made skillful use of the systems approach, which emphasizes the interrelationships among the parts of a system, and holds that a change in any one part affects all the others. From this perspective, the simplistic "causal arrows" of previous explanations are replaced by complex webs of causal relationships, some of which are mutually reinforcing ("feedbacks"). This suggests that explanations relying on a single cause, such as Gordon Childe's claim of a sudden, major climatic change, are never sufficient and seldom correct. Many recent books on the topic of the development of agriculture, such as Cowan and Watson 1992 and Gebauer and Price 1992, illustrate a diversity of local archaeological sequences and ecological processes associated with the origins of agriculture in different parts of the world, which had been underestimated by earlier theories.

Was the shift to agriculture a wonderful example of progress, providing humankind with more and better food, leisure, and well-being? Anthropologists doubt it. In Chapter 16, Jared Diamond points out that even today's hunters and gatherers have a more varied and abundant diet than most agriculturalists; moreover, they enjoy more leisure time and better health. (This point will be explained further in Marvin Harris's essay in Chapter 33, "Murders in Eden.") Skeletal evidence of malnutrition, disease, and shorter life span suggests that, in Neolithic populations, most people worked harder and lived less comfortably than their hunting-and-gathering ancestors. In other words, whatever the benefits of turning to food production, the costs were high. The "agricultural revolution" was not a success story on the theme of people coming to dominate nature. It was more akin to a counterrevolution: A penalty for overpopulation, it led eventually to war, inequality, and oppression.

An important point made by Diamond is that the way of life of hunters–gatherers is sustainable. By controlling both the size of their population and every individual's volume of consumption — conspicuous consumption and the hoarding of wealth are social crimes — they protect themselves from "development." Although development may give more power to some (for a while), it can never be sustainable. Once certain Neolithic populations started to develop, and thereby to increase rapidly both in size and power, the rest of the world had no choice but to join them, or to be conquered. Ecologists might agree that "the meek shall inherit the earth," but the political reality is that the powerful will take it away from them! The expression "sustainable development," made popular by the Brundtland Commission in its report, entitled *Our Common Future* (1987), is a contradiction in terms, and a dangerous nonsense. Archaeologists studying the remains of the first civilizations in Iraq confirm Diamond's message.

Thorkild Jacobsen and Robert M. Adams (1958) performed a lengthy archaeological and ecological investigation of agriculture and population settlement in a portion of the flood plain of the Tigris River. The area between the Tigris and Euphrates rivers is called **Mesopotamia**, a Greek word that means "the land between rivers." The authors focused their attention on irrigation practices. They found that, to feed expanding populations, agriculture had to be expanded beyond the natural limits of narrow and shifting river valleys. The building of ever-larger irrigation systems emerged as a superb example of the domination of civilization over nature. An unintended effect of irrigation, however, is that salts dissolved in the soil are left on its surface after irrigation waters evaporate, poisoning the soil and creating an agricultural "dead zone" that can eventually lead to the starvation of the population and the destruction of its society. In addition to the working of such effects in Mesopotamia, silt deposits soon came to clog all the artificial water systems, and the maintenance of the canals and dams became increasingly expensive and, ultimately, futile. When political upheavals and military destruction added to these burdens, the system collapsed: the region of fertile growth became an uninhabited, man-made desert, wrought of human activity. The very same ecological mistakes are being made today in Canada and the United States, where farmers draw on aquifers (layers of rock or soil that hold reserves of water) *as if there were no tomorrow*. Indeed, there may not be one if such practices continue.

The New World

All major human biological evolution took place in the Old World: Africa, Asia, and Europe. None of our hominid ancestors lived in what is now known as

America. The first "Americans" were *Homo sapiens sapiens*. The evidence supporting the claim that the first Americans were of Asian origin is compelling. They were Upper Paleolithic hunters who followed herds of mammoth, musk ox, reindeer, and other game across the vast plain of Beringia. This land bridge between Asia and America was at times 1500 km wide; it was a busy link between continents, criss-crossed by many species of mammals. At times, it was submerged, as it is now, when melting glaciers raised the level of the oceans. Biological and archaeological evidence also suggests that humans crossed over to America not just once but on several occasions, whenever the emergence of Beringia and the corridors in the Alaskan glaciers made the crossing possible.

All modern archaeologists would agree with this story, so far; where they diverge, primarily, is in estimating the date of the first arrivals. Chapters 17 and 18 exemplify the kinds of debates that develop in archaeology. Although those debates can be heated, archaeologists do agree that humans had arrived by at least 12,000 B.P., because the remains of the Clovis big game hunters of that period are abundant, well studied, and precisely dated. But were the Clovis people the first Americans? In the 1970s, Paul Martin claimed that they had to have been, since their superior tools and hunting techniques were sufficient to cause the extinction of horses, mammoth, camels, and many other species in a short time. Although it is true that many species became extinct at the end of the Pleistocene in the Old World as well, many more disappeared in the Americas — specifically, 31 entire *genera*. Other archaeologists simply point out that there is no strong evidence of pre-Clovis human occupation in terms of well-dated sites at which humans and tools are associated. One such archaeologist is Roger Owen, who details and criticizes some of the evidence most frequently cited by supporters of a more ancient human presence in America (Chapter 17). Among the ardent supporters of a pre-Clovis human occupation of the Americas, archaeologist Richard MacNeish claims to have found dates between 14,000 B.P. and 20,000 B.P. for different strata of a Peruvian site. Owen and other critics of MacNeish question the reliability of his dating techniques and object to his interpretation of when a "crude tool" is a human-made artifact and when it is simply a product of natural processes.

Owen's interpretation of the evidence available at the time that he wrote the essay, in 1984, is devastating, in that he focuses on well-known finds of human bones or artifacts and shows that, in every case, the dating or the interpretation of the evidence was wrong or unreliable. The essay has

caused much controversy, because many archaeologists find that it unjustifiably denigrates the accomplishments of seasoned researchers. Furthermore, other kinds of evidence support the claim that humans arrived in the New World much before 12,000 B.P. For example, as you will have learned in Chapter 12, even linguists suggest that the great diversity of languages of the New World and their differences from the languages of the Old World could not have arisen in such a short time.

Actually, however, Owen does not necessarily disagree with those archaeologists who are convinced that new evidence will ultimately be discovered to prove that humans arrived in America as early as 20,000 B.P. or even 25,000 B.P. The point of his controversial essay is only that, *as of 1984*, precise and reliable scientific evidence to support the theory had not yet been provided. Richard MacNeish continues to disagree: in February 1992, he presented dramatic evidence at the annual meeting of the American Association for the Advancement of Science. He had found human palm and finger prints on clay in a 28,000-year-old layer in South America, and several hearths in various layers, some of which he dated at 38,000 years. In Chapter 18, Paul Bahn, writing in 1991, summarizes some of the new evidence from Pedra Furada, in Brazil, and Monte Verde, in Chile, which is claimed by some researchers to prove a human presence as early as 30,000 years ago. A few of the major opponents of the hypothesis of a pre-Clovis peopling of the New World are being swayed by the new evidence. However, these claims, like earlier ones, will have to be investigated thoroughly. After all, as Owen's essay demonstrates, many recent interpretations of similarly promising archaeological discoveries have proved to be unconvincing or simply erroneous.

It is important to note Richard MacNeish's fascinating and extremely important discovery that the domestication of plants and animals was achieved independently by the native peoples of Central and South America. MacNeish studied sites in the state of Tamaulipas and in the Tehuacán Valley, both in Mexico, where, stratum by stratum, a slow, 5000-year-long process was revealed in which nomadic hunters and gatherers were gradually transformed into agriculturalists, whose staples were maize, beans, and squash, all domesticated locally. The great handicap of these New World agriculturalists was that, unlike their counterparts in the Middle East, they had no herbivores (grass-eating animals such as cattle, goats, and sheep) suitable for traction or milk production. Horses and camels had thrived in great numbers in the New World, but the last of them had been exterminated by human hunters just a few thousand years before, and there were no suitable replacements. The Mexicans domesticated turkeys, ducks, and bees. The Peruvians, who domesticated potatoes, cotton, and possibly maize, did have guinea pigs and llamas (a relative of the camel), but neither could pull a plow or a cart. These and other ecological differences between the Americas and the Middle East explain why the beginnings of the development of agriculture and civilization were so different in the two areas. In the Americas, with a few exceptions (along seashores), settlement in villages followed the domestication of plants, whereas the reverse was true in the Middle East. Until the appearance of the first villages, the rate of technological and ecological change was also much slower in the Americas. After the settlement of villages in Mexico, and again in South America, social stratification, cities, states, and ecological problems followed one another in a sequence that parallels that which occurred in the Old World.

Archaeological discoveries such as the ones just noted, which document the processes that led up to the development of New World civilizations, contradict a convenient myth that was accepted in the United States until the nineteenth century. According to this myth, the enormous artificial mounds found in various parts of North America were built by highly civilized nations that had peopled the continent *before the Indians* and had been destroyed by the Indians in bloody wars. This version of events is even incorporated as an article of faith in the Book of Mormon. Excavations of one of the mounds were carefully performed and documented by Thomas Jefferson, who concluded correctly that they were burial mounds built by Indians, and not war memorials. (Jefferson published his results in France in 1784.) Over the years, other studies of many of the mounds dotting the American countryside, such as Prufer's "The Hopewell Cult" (1964), confirmed the conclusions of the late American statesman and amateur archaeologist.

The **Maya** of Southern Mexico and Guatemala, discussed in Chapter 19, are among the best studied prehistoric peoples in America. The achievements of their civilization are so impressive, the conditions of their doom so difficult to unravel, that they have sparked the imagination of scholars and the general public alike. They built magnificent temples, whose carvings and frescoes are considered impressive and sophisticated by modern standards. Their mathematical system incorporated the concept of zero, which even the Greeks and Romans failed to conceive. The Maya had complex calendars and a hieroglyphic writing system that, thanks to computers and human ingenuity, modern scholars are now

deciphering with increasing success. At one time, archaeologists thought that the civilization's huge ceremonial centers were built by devoted villagers who living far away; the collapse of the civilization might then have been attributed simply to the fact that people were not going to church anymore. However, that explanation was disproved by archaeologists who documented the depopulation of the countryside around Tikal, one of the major centers. At least a million Maya died at the time of the collapse. Furthermore, during the last two decades in particular, remote-sensing devices, scanners, and various types of radars have revealed to archaeologists a totally different picture: The Mayan ceremonial centers were surrounded by sizable cities; the "jungle" that had been cut away by earlier generations of archaeologists was composed of overgrown orchards; and a large and dense population had practiced sophisticated and extremely productive techniques of agriculture. Although the most famous period of Mayan civilization, that of the "Classic Maya," flourished only between A.D. 250 and A.D. 900, it was the culmination of at least 3000 years of continuous tradition, which has now been documented by archaeologists.

After such a long history of success, what caused the demise of the Maya? Although it is by no means likely to be the last word on the subject, Patrick Culbert's analysis reflects a consensus among modern archaeologists. Rather than attributing the fall of the civilization to any single cause, such as overpopulation, an invasion, or the breakdown of long-distance trading, Culbert proposes a systemic approach in which the interaction of different kinds of interrelated processes led to the amplification of deviations away from equilibrium. The same causes that contributed to the success and prosperity of the Mayan civilization, taking the system from one equilibrium to another, richer one, also brought about its demise.

Culbert's analysis is consistent with more recent work in archaeology. In *The Dynamics of Apocalypse: A Systems Simulation of the Classic Maya Collapse*, (1985), John W.G. Lowe provides a lengthy review of previous attempts to explain the demise of the Maya. His conclusion reads in part:

[Gordon R.] Willey and [Demitri B.] Shimkin's ... comprehensive model of the collapse probably remains the definitive account of the subject to date. As they describe it, the structure of Late Classic ecology and society gave rise to a number of processes: burgeoning elite demands, increasing class tension, increasing competition between ceremonial centers, subsistence and health problems associated with rising population density, and external pressures of both an economic and military kind. Eventually these external stresses and internal pressures overloaded the regulatory apparatus. [The resulting] "coincidence of an array of disturbing factors — trade disruptions, social unrest, agricultural difficulties, disease — appears to have coalesced to administer a shock to the Maya polity, around 9.17.0.0.0 (A.D. 771) to 9.18.0.0.0 (A.D. 790), which exceeded the recuperative capacity of the Maya Lowland sociocultural system, especially in its capacity of elite"...

An extended critique of the model seems inappropriate since in a very real sense this volume began as an attempt to formalize the ideas contained therein. Perhaps, though, the essence of the appeal of the Willey-Shimkin formulation, its ability to be all things to all people, is also its greatest shortcoming. Almost every Mayanist, myself included, can find his/her opinion of the collapse embedded somewhere in the Willey-Shimkin formulation; in particular, most systems explanations of the collapse are more or less in accord with the summary chapter of P. Culbert's *The Classic Maya Collapse* (1973). They tend, however, to give greater weight to particular parts of that formulation while deemphasizing other parts (p. 110).

Just like the civilizations of Mesopotamia, the Maya wanted bigger and better: they developed their civilization to death. The parallels with modern industrial civilization are too obvious to be missed. Culbert elaborates on this point, and shows in passing that archaeologists may not be explaining only the past; alas, they may also be predicting the future.

In Chapter 20, Canadian archaeologist Alison Wylie reflects on the Quincentennial of the discovery of the American continent by Europeans. Her argument is typical of the new awareness among archaeologists that their work cannot be considered an objective, value-free fact-finding mission. Archaeologists have lost their innocence: they have become aware that they are responsible for the political implications of their work and their findings.

The short article by Neil McAleer in Chapter 21 is an informative report on some of the sophisticated new technologies that have become available to archaeologists. Several kinds of remote-sensing devices improve our ability to discover new sites invisible to the naked eye, such as the Mayan canals in the jungle. Such instruments made possible the discovery in 1992 of the lost city of Ubar (2800 B.C. to A.D. 100), buried in the deserts of Oman. Of equal or even greater importance are techniques that may enable archaeologists to analyze the elemental structure of artifacts without having to move or destroy them. Archaeologists are well aware of the

inevitable destruction of evidence that had taken place each time they excavated a new site; hence, this technological innovation may have profound repercussions on their work. Computers also make possible the analysis of complex information presented, for instance, in pictures: each picture element (pixel) can be retrieved and analyzed in ways that earlier generations of archaeologists would not have dreamed possible.

The most important changes that have taken place in archaeology during the last decade do not result from new gadgets, but from a new approach. In Chapter 22, Julian Thomas raises some of the issues that trouble modern archaeologists. This essay, a review of two books recently published by archaeologists, starts with the provocative claim that "archaeology has increasingly begun to see itself as a political practice." Recently, some archaeologists have started to rebel against the systematic and objective approach of the New Archaeology of Binford and his followers. Those who have regrouped under the banner of "Post-Processual Archaeology" point out that the so-called objectivity of systemic archaeologists concealed many prejudices and ethnocentric concepts, and that it was often accompanied by insensitivity to the beliefs and aspirations of the people studied, or of their contemporary descendants (Hodder 1986). Thomas examines two contributions to this debate with commendable serenity, given the emotional tone of the claims and counterclaims presented by certain defenders of the old New Archaeology and those who declare it obsolete by calling themselves "Post-Processual" archaeologists.

Finally, in Chapter 23, David H. Thomas presents some of the debate surrounding the gathering of cultural artifacts from poor countries for the collections of museums of rich countries. In this brief piece, he manages to make us aware of the complex ethical and political issues involved.

Works Cited

Binford, L. 1962. "Archaeology as Anthropology." *American Antiquity* 29: 425–41.

Cowan, C.W., and P.J. Watson, eds. 1992. *The Origins of Agriculture: An International Perspective.* Washington, D.C.: Smithsonian Institution Press.

Culbert, T.P., ed. 1973. *The Classic Maya Collapse.* Albuquerque, N.M.: University of New Mexico Press.

Gebauer, A.B., and T.D. Price, eds. 1992. *Transitions to Agriculture in Prehistory.* Madison: Prehistory Press.

Hodder, I. 1986. *Reading the Past: Current Approaches to the Interpretation of Archaeology.* New York: Cambridge University Press.

Jacobsen, T., and R.M. Adams, 1958. "Salt and Silt in Ancient Mesopotamian Agriculture." *Science* 128: 1251–58.

Lowe, J.W.G. 1985. *The Dynamics of Apocalypse: A Systems Simulation of the Classic Maya Collapse*. Albuquerque, N.M.: University of New Mexico Press.

Prufer, O. 1964. "The Hopewell Cult." *Scientific American* (Dec.) 235–43.

Sauer, C. 1952. *Seeds, Spades, Hearths and Herds*. Washington, D.C.: American Geographical Society.

World Commission on Environment and Development (Brundtland Commission). 1987. *Our Common Future*. New York: Oxford University Press.

12
Who Peopled the Planet?

JOANN C. GUTIN

Reconstructing the events that got prehistoric humans all over the globe is like keeping a litter of puppies in a basket. Every time order seems imminent, some crucial element wriggles away. The potential chaos has different guises. Sometimes a new laboratory technique upends the conventional wisdom, then is itself upended. Sometimes a new archeological site rattles an old timetable, then slinks, invalidated, into obscurity. Sometimes a specialist from another discipline looks at the problem and says, in effect, "sorry to be a nuisance, but according to what we know in our department, your solution can't possibly be right." All these things, and more, have happened in the last decade. Brush fires — to change metaphors — have flared on every continent. For Old World prehistorians the heat has been fairly intense for the past five or six years. At issue has not been whether the earliest hominids evolved in Africa 3 million to 4 million years ago: fossils have made that, by now, beyond debate. Nor has there been any question that a subset of those hominids (in the shape of heavy-browed *Homo erectus*) left Africa about a million years ago; hand axes and fossils scattered throughout the Old World prove they were there. The mystery is whether those *Homo erectus* populations gave rise to us. That is, it's a mystery

unless you ask Milford Wolpoff. "This is no mystery," says the University of Michigan paleoanthropologist happily. "This thing is solved."

The background to his contentment is as follows. For years, Wolpoff had been studying *Homo erectus*, confident — as were many others in the field — that it was *H. erectus* who established the human beachhead in the temperate zone, *H. erectus* who gave rise, more or less, to modern European, Middle Eastern, and Asian populations.

That commonsense scenario — European *H. erectus* evolving into modern Europeans, Asian *H. erectus* into modern Asians — was badly shaken in 1987. That was when several biochemists from the University of California at Berkeley presented the phenomenon called mitochondrial Eve, in a six-page paper in *Nature* that abruptly turned the Old World evolutionary debate on its head. The research team, led by the late Allan Wilson, based its conclusions on genes, not bones, and asserted that there had been not one but two radiations out of Africa. The first was indeed by *Homo erectus*, but that one apparently didn't take. It was the second radiation — at about 200,000 years ago — that counted; those emigrants were our ancestors. They displaced the previous tenants by fair means or foul, did not interbreed with them, and thus could rightfully lay claim to the title of ancestral person.

In a trice Eve became the hottest new evolutionary player since Lucy — that is, *Australo-*

pithecus afarensis, the oldest upright human ancestor we have evidence of — and *H. erectus* became a footnote. Wolpoff, convinced that the fossil record provided no support for the paleo-invasion envisioned by the Berkeley group, picked up the cudgels and became *H. erectus*'s point man, defender of the fossil faith.

The Berkeley biologists based their startling conclusion on an examination of the DNA in mitochondria. Mitochondria are a cell's energy factories; every human cell contains them, and every mitochrondrion contains its own bit of DNA. However, your mitochondrial DNA (mtDNA) differs from the DNA in the nucleus of your cells in one essential respect: you got all of it from your mother. When an egg is fertilized, the sperm's tiny mitochondrion is reabsorbed; thus all of us — male and female — contain exclusively maternal mtDNA.

Because mtDNA doesn't undergo mixing, the differences between, say, your mtDNA and that of your great-grandmother will be due to the accumulation of mutations. Most researchers believe that mutations pile up in the mtDNA of all organisms with an average statistical regularity; this is the so-called molecular clock. All else being equal, the genetic distance between you and your third cousin — or between the average human and the average chimpanzee — is a measure of how long ago each pair shared a common ancestor. (In the first case, four generations; in the second, 5 million years.)

The Berkeley group examined mtDNA from 147 women of various ethnic groups and found surprisingly little variation among them — much less than the ticking molecular clock would have produced had their African, Asian, and European ancestors been evolving in relative isolation since the days of *H. erectus*. Furthermore, the mtDNA that looked oldest — that, broadly speaking, had the most mutations — came from the women of African ancestry. According to the best estimates of mutation rate, that branch appeared to be about 200,000 years old. Q.E.D.: A small population of Africans had given rise to all modern humans.

The traditional paleoanthropological donnybrook ensued, the Berkeley researchers defended themselves energetically, and as recently as early 1992 it looked as though many anthropologists had been converted. Even the decidedly unconvinced — Milford Wolpoff, for example — had lost heart. "If you had asked me even a year ago," he says, "I'd have said this argument is never going to be resolved. I figured it would always be sort of a muddle, and we'd never know what actually happened."

So why is this man smiling now? Because he's just heard a lecture in which a geneticist — a laboratory scientist well equipped to confront the Berkeley group on its own intellectual turf — has demolished the group's methodology. "In one careful hour that guy pulled the rug out from everything the Eve hypothesis people ever said," chortles Wolpoff. "My mouth is still hanging open at the implications of this work. That guy is a ticking time bomb."

Alan Templeton, Washington University geneticist and the incendiary device in question, doesn't sound like a ticking time bomb. He sounds more like an affable scientist who is, despite all the comfort he's brought to the fossil forces of Wolpoff and company, still enthusiastic about the potential of mtDNA. But he's even more enthusiastic about precise statistical analysis. "I think there's a lot of information in mitochondrial DNA," he asserts, "lots of biologically and statistically significant data to be drawn from it. The thing is, the analytical techniques need to be as good as the data."

In his view the analytical techniques that uncovered Eve weren't. For one thing, there was a problem with the way the Berkeley group used the computer program to create their genetic trees. Templeton says it could have generated millions of equally plausible trees depending on the order in which the data were introduced. The program's instructions tell you to do multiple runs with random orders of data introduction. Wilson did only one; or as Wolpoff growls, "Templeton just read the owner's manual that came with their program. When you run it right, there's no support for Eve."

There is more. Templeton, more circumspect by nature than Wolpoff, is at pains to make clear that the statistics and mathematics available for examining evolutionary questions are evolving themselves, and those he used in his critique hadn't been developed when Eve debuted. Yet the bottom line now is that neither hypothesis — African origins or take-no-prisoners invasion — is necessarily supported by mtDNA.

Templeton believes there's a lot more ambiguity in the dates than the Berkeley scientists hoped: an order of magnitude, in fact. We had a mitochondrial ancestor, but she lived somewhere between a hundred thousand and a million years ago, by his reckoning. "The Berkeley group always acknowledged there was an error margin," he says. "I just figured out a mathematical way to see how large it was." (Wolpoff is a bit blunter, as is his wont: "So you have a clock that can tell you it's either 4 A.M. or noon. What good is that?")

What Templeton visualizes involves neither a late, explosive radiation out of Africa nor strict local evolution, but something in between. Humans probably did move out of Africa into the rest of the Old World, and they did evolve there, but there was always enough contact between the continents to muddy the mitochondria. It was restricted, to be sure. "I'm not saying Europeans and Asians were randomly mating with one another," Templeton emphasizes. But, he points out, even a little trickle would do the job. "Look at the Grand Canyon — water erodes rock, given enough time. In terms of human generations, we're talking about a great deal of time here."

So Templeton is not rejecting Eve entirely. "I'm just saying we don't know where she lived, we probably never will, and it's not that relevant in an evolutionary sense. All human populations have been evolving as a single entity as far back as the mitochondria go." Our genes are a geographic mosaic: "Even if the source of our mitochondria is Africa, our hemoglobin gene (which is contained in nuclear DNA) may come from an Asian ancestor, or our Y chromosome from Europe."

To muddy the ancestral waters and challenge the Eve theory further, last June another group announced the results of its research on two skulls found in China in 1989 and 1990. The skulls show a mix of *Homo erectus* and early *Homo sapiens* features that might indicate that a transition to modern humans was taking place in Asia at the same time as in Africa, thus lending support to the Wolpoff camp.

While the raucous Old World debate rages on, in North America another puppy is trying to squirm out of the basket. This one has nothing to do with new laboratory techniques. In North America the would-be escapee is a linguist, an expert in languages who says politely but firmly that the current timetable for the migration of humans into North America is wrong: it is "hopelessly, impossibly" too short.

That timetable is one of the more durable phenomena in archeology. It's stayed intact since the early 1950s, when radiocarbon dating became a practical reality, and it reflects the widespread consensus that modern humans entered the New World via the now submerged Bering land bridge not much earlier than 12,000 years ago. Those Siberian immigrants and their descendants were dubbed Paleo-Indians, ancestors of nearly all native Americans.

Often referred to as the Clovis chronology, after a site in New Mexico where the stone tools of these pioneers were first discovered, it is, like many fifties phenomena, approaching a rather tired middle age. It's no longer exciting, but nothing much better has come along to replace it. Over the past several decades, many initially exciting pre-Clovis claims have arisen, only to fizzle spectacularly. A bone tool from the Yukon had a claimed date of 27,000 years, for example; that shrank to a measly 1,350 when the tool was redated. Stones from California that resembled ancient African chopping tools once received the Paleolithic imprimatur of Louis Leakey; now they're considered ecofacts — naturally fractured stone.

Nevertheless, new contenders appear. Sites in the running since the mid-1980s include at least three in South America, a couple in the United States, and another in the Yukon. The oldest claimed date is 32,000 years, for a site in northeastern Brazil excavated by a French-Brazilian team. The ancient hearths found in the Pedra Furada rock shelter would, if verified, nearly triple the duration of *H. sapiens* in the New World. Some archeologists, however, question whether the areas that yielded the dates are really hearths and not just naturally burned patches.

At any rate, given the slightly fusty aura surrounding Clovis, it was rather a relief when in 1986 an academic troika of physical anthropology, genetics, and linguistics gave the old scenario a much-needed shot in the arm. The physical anthropology — dental studies of American Indians, Asians, and Pacific Islanders — pointed to late colonization, probably in three waves. The genetics — a comparison of blood antibody types of three groups — corroborated it. But it was the third member of the trio — the linguistics — that particularly engrossed archeologists.

Linguists have always been puzzled by the extraordinary diversity of native American languages. The native languages of coastal California alone, for example, include representatives of more than a dozen language families (the northern Mediterranean coast, which is roughly six times as long, contains only two). Remarkably, some 1,000 distinct native American tongues have been described, and as many have probably been lost since European colonization.

Complexity of any kind takes time to accumulate, and language complexity is no exception.

Over time, languages evolve into modern versions of themselves or, like Latin, branch into several distinct tongues. The crux of the linguistic conundrum in North America has always been this: How much time did it take for all those languages to develop, particularly if they were, as most specialists believed, very distantly related at best?

The Clovis-friendly linguistic classification that answered the question was produced by Joseph Greenberg (an unorthodox scholar from Stanford whose ordering of the African linguistic picture had met with universal acclaim). His solution? All of these languages *were* related, he said. The first Paleo-Indians, suggested Greenberg, all spoke a common "proto" language when they drifted across the land bridge 12,000 years ago.

Using a technique he calls mass comparison, Greenberg looked for similarities in categories of words — the water category, for example, might include *lake, pond*, and *swamp* — in as many native languages as were recorded. He found them where specialists had not, and on this basis defined three great language groupings in North America. (The more conventional tally is somewhere around 140.) Two were unremarkable, one containing 9 and the other 34 languages, but the third, called Amerind, was both gigantic and controversial. It contained all the other tongues.

Three language families, three colonizations, 12,000 years — all the pieces fit. One hundred forty distinct language families, 140 distinct colonizations — as Greenberg himself has remarked, "There would have had to be a traffic controller at the Bering Strait."

Greenberg's economical solution left most historical linguists gasping for breath. Inferring the existence of a 12,000-year-old common ancestor was suspect, they thought. Orthodox historical linguists look at separate languages and compare the individual components that make up the various grammatical categories like case and tense. Even with that kind of painstaking research, they can't reconstruct a proto-language any older than 8,000 years. At that time depth, the comparative method — what one linguist calls "our flickering flashlight into the past" — can't distinguish between similarities due to relatedness and those due to borrowing or accident.

Enter Berkeley linguist Johanna Nichols. She doesn't claim that a chronology based on language evolution can provide more than ballpark figures — but if she's right, she says, "the Clovis chronology is in the whole wrong ballpark."

Nichols's approach is different from either mass vocabulary comparison or the conventional historical method. To decide how old a group of languages is, she looks at overall grammatical categories that don't change or spread rapidly over time — traits like whether there are separate cases for subject and object, or if the verb goes at the end or the beginning of the sentence. These sets of resemblances are better measures of time than are word similarities, she maintains, because they're unlikely to be borrowed wholesale or to attain the same frequency in two groups of languages simply by chance. By this yardstick, the Greenbergian picture of North America seems unlikely. Every conceivable language typology is represented, suggesting that chances of relatedness at 12,000 years are slim.

However, Nichols's most tantalizing question is not "How many?" but "How long?" What does language say about the antiquity of humans in America? In a 1990 paper that has the small linguistics community abuzz, Nichols contends there is a roughly clocklike regularity to the tempo at which languages give rise to daughter languages. She bases this claim on language history: specifically, on her survey of how the living and extinct languages, language families, and reconstructed protolanguages of the Northern Hemisphere have behaved. Nichols has observed two things: most families give rise to between one and three individual daughter languages (the mean language birthrate is 1.6 per family), and they do it about every 6,000 years. With those two datum points, Nichols has devised a way to wring a chronology out of the North American mélange. She has created, in effect, a language clock.

Its mechanism is deceptively simple. Nichols merely divides the 140 distinct North American groups by 1.6; this, she says, takes her back one linguistic generation, or 6,000 years, to approximately 88 ancestor groups. Another division, and she's back 12,000 years, at the threshold of the Clovis chronology, with 55 distinct families. That date, she believes, is unreasonable — for one thing, there's no evidence in either Siberia or Alaska for the population size and social complexity the number of language families implies.

On the other hand, if all the native American languages come from one language brought to the continent in a single migration, the language clock says it must have happened 50,000 years ago. Nichols cheerfully admits that the number is "off the wall." More realistic, she thinks, is the idea of a number of linguistically distinct colonizations — perhaps ten — over the past 30,000 years or so.

But the puzzlement remains. If humans have been here that long, and in the fairly substantial numbers it takes to keep a language alive, why are there so few — and ambiguous — early archeological sites? Nichols is, frankly, stumped. "It's highly" — she searches, vainly, for the mot juste — "strange. The linguistic evidence points very clearly to a great time depth, and the accepted archeology doesn't." Brightening, she adds, "I suppose there's always the hope that convincing archeological evidence will be found."

As Sherlock Holmes once said, when you've eliminated the impossible, whatever remains — however improbable — is the truth. Nichols knows full well that her results are unsettling, but she sticks by her grammatical guns. Exact dates are problematic, but linguistics is "absolutely unambiguous in regard to ballparks," she says firmly. "The New World has been inhabited for tens of millennia."

13
The Functions of Paleolithic Flint Tools

LAWRENCE H. KEELEY

Almost the only evidence of man's presence on the earth for a period of more than half a million years is vast numbers of stone tools. Some are made of basalt, some of quartzite or quartz, and some of the volcanic glass obsidian. In many places the majority are made of flint. As soon as these objects were recognized as man's handiwork they were assigned names based on guesses about their probable function. The French began the process with *coup-de-poing*, which in English became "hand axe." A multitude of other functional names followed: "end scraper," "side scraper," "blade," "point," "burin," and the like. Although generations of prehistorians have used such names, there has been scarcely any tangible evidence on what purposes the stone tools actually served.

Over the past 15 years students of early man have grown sufficiently dissatisfied with this state of affairs to do something about it. The result has been the development of a methodology known as microwear analysis, which reveals the functions of many early flint implements. The evidence is almost indelibly recorded in the form of microscopic traces of wear on the working edges of the flint.

From *Scientific American*, Vol. 237, November 1977, pp. 108–26. Copyright © 1977 Scientific American, Inc. All rights reserved. Reprinted with permission.

One reason for the current lively interest in the function of stone tools is that progress in the methods of absolute dating, such as carbon-14 analysis, has freed many prehistorians from two former preoccupations. The first was, in the absence of absolute dating, the construction of relative chronologies. The second was closely related to the first: it was the search for "cultural" similarities between assemblages of stone tools from different areas. Such similarities aid in the construction of interlocking regional chronologies. Early in the 1960s a new school of prehistorians began to offer fresh hypotheses to explain the variations between and within regional assemblages of tools.

In this view the variations were attributable less to chronological and cultural differences and more to differences in function. For example, the new school sought to explain the differences between the kinds of tools present in two roughly contemporaneous assemblages in terms of the different kinds of activity the tools' users could have pursued in the two places. Proponents of this school argued that in attributing such differences to "cultural" distinctions between two unrelated groups the older school was misreading the evidence.

A vital prerequisite to the testing of the functional hypotheses was a detailed knowledge of what the artifacts were used for and how. In 1964 *Prehistoric Technology*, a summary of the studies of tool function conducted by the Russian prehistorian S.A. Semenov, was published in an English translation. Semenov and his colleagues at the Leningrad Academy of Sciences had established the fact that tools of even the hardest stone retained actual traces of their use in the form of polishes, striations, and other alterations of the tools' working edges. More often than not the traces of wear were visible only at quite high magnifications. It seemed to scholars in Britain and America that at last the means were in hand for pursuing just the kind of information about tool function that the new hypotheses required.

Semenov's functional interpretations of the uses of Paleolithic and later stone implements unearthed in the USSR were fascinating but also tantalizing. He had not included a detailed account of the methodology that formed the basis for his interpretations. To make matters worse, the particular kinds of microscopic equipment employed by Semenov were then available only in the USSR, and so the translator had omitted most of the few technical details Semenov had included in his original.

As a result a number of prehistorians outside the USSR proceeded to do microwear analysis armed only with the translation of Semenov's book and stereoscopic microscopes that often had a maximum magnification of 80 diameters. In addition to this technical handicap the implements these workers selected for study were made from stone materials quite unlike those found in the USSR. Disappointment and disillusionment followed as one investigator after another found Semenov's results impossible to substantiate.

This situation, however, was scarcely surprising. For one thing, in most cases the investigators could not even see microwear features such as the polishes and striations Semenov had observed because the magnifications they were working with were far too low. For another, the low-magnification wear features they could see (primarily edge damage, the small breaks and flake scars on the working edge of the tool) did not allow precise and unambiguous interpretations of tool function. Many investigators came to the conclusion that Semenov's interpretations were suspect and that microwear analysis simply did not work. Nevertheless, the demand for information about the functions of stone tools ensured that the research would continue.

As a result of this chain of events investigators outside the USSR concentrated on studies of the edge damage that could be observed with low-powered stereomicroscopes and ignored the polishes and striations that only begin to be visible at a magnification of 200 diameters. Many edge-wear studies sensibly relied on experiments. Modern replicas of Paleolithic implements were made and were used in various ways to work on a wide range of materials in order to determine whether the resulting traces of wear differed from material to material. Most of these programs, however, involved too few experiments, controlled too few variables, and were too limited in scope to achieve anything useful.

The one adequate program employing the low-magnification approach to the analysis of edge damage was conducted at Harvard University by Ruth Tringham and her students. When the results of the work were published in 1974, the chief demonstrable distinction proved to be one between work on "hard" materials (such as bone, antler, and wood) and work on "soft" materials (such as meat, hides, and nonwoody plant materials). No reliable criteria were found for distinguishing between different methods of working, such as scraping, whittling, sawing, cutting, and the like. It was also impossible to distinguish between, on the one hand, edge-damage scars resulting from the actual use of an implement and, on the other hand, small scars created in the course of manufacture or by the implement's rubbing against other hard materials during millenniums of burial.

I first undertook research in microwear in 1972 after a review of the literature in the field and some preliminary studies. These preliminaries convinced me that I should employ a wider range of microscope magnifications and techniques than others had. I began with a program of experiments designed to provide a framework for analysis of the functions served by particular sets of flint implements from English sites of the Lower Paleolithic: 500,000 to 100,000 years ago.

I had three microscopes at my disposal: a light stereomicroscope with a range of magnifications between 6 and 50 diameters, a light microscope with a range between 50 and 1,000 diameters, and my principal research instrument, a microscope with an incident-light attachment and a range between 24 and 400 diameters. I also made occasional use of a scanning electron microscope, mainly for magnifications above 500 diameters.

After making replicas of Paleolithic stone implements I conducted a series of nearly 200 tests, processing a variety of foodstuffs and other materials in many different ways. I also subjected certain implements to the kinds of natural wear that are likely either to make microscopic scars similar to those made by human use or to erase such scars. Along this same line I was able, thanks to the availability of large numbers of Paleolithic implements that had been subjected to wear by soil movements, chemical weathering, and abrasion by water-borne and wind-borne sediments, to compare this natural kind of wear with my experimental results.

The key finding that emerged from those tests was that microwear polishes on the working edges of modern replicas become visible at magnifications between 100 and 400 diameters under illumination striking the sample at an angle of 90 degrees to the optical axis of the microscope. The different kinds of polish can readily be distinguished from one another. Whether the activity was cutting or whittling wood, cutting bone, cutting meat, or scraping skins, I found that each produced a characteristic kind of work polish.

The work polishes proved to be durable: they could not be removed from my replica implements even with chemical cleaning. I applied caustics that ran the full pH spectrum from an extreme base (sodium hydroxide) to an extreme acid (hydrochloric) without effect. The same was true with various organic solvents. I concluded that the work polishes represent real and permanent alterations in the microtopography of the flint. Accordingly similar polishes seemed likely to have survived unaltered on flint artifacts of great age. This being the case, it should be

possible to infer from the traces of microwear observable on a Paleolithic tool just what use that particular tool had served.

The distinctive microwear polishes can be described as follows:

Wood polish: The tool edge shows a polish that is consistent in appearance regardless of whether the wood being worked is hard, soft, fresh, or seasoned. The polish is also the same regardless of the manner of tool use. It is very "bright," reflecting a considerable percentage of the incident illumination, and very smooth in texture. Because the polish first develops on the elevated parts of the microtopographic surface of the flint its gross appearance is affected by that topography up to the point where the contact area becomes completely polished. Thus if the original topography of the flint is coarse, the polish in its initial stages will be distributed in a netlike pattern. If the flint is fine-grained, the polish is soon evenly spread. Regardless of the distribution, the polish has a constant bright, smooth character.

Bone polish: The tool edge is bright, but the polish has a rough, uneven texture that lacks the smoothness characteristic of wood polish. One distinctive feature of the rough texture of bone polish is the presence of numerous pits on the otherwise bright surface. Bone polish develops more slowly than wood polish. On a modern replica, even after prolonged use, the polish is

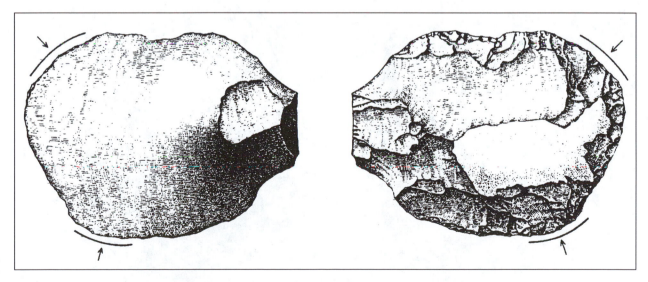

Paleolithic flake tool, a "side scraper" from Hoxne, an Acheulean site in England, was among some 800 flint implements examined for evidence of microwear by the author. The top of the flake (right) still shows some of the outer surface (lighter area) of the nodule of flint the flake was struck from. Lines and arrows indicate the working edges of the tool. Prehistorians have assumed that scrapers were used to process animal hides. Microwear traces found on the flake lend support to such an assumption.

seldom very extensively developed. My experiments revealed no consistent differences between the polishes on tools used to work cooked bone and those on tools for working uncooked bone, or between the polishes on tools used to work bone belonging to different species of animals.

Hide polishes: Here the tool edges do not develop a single distinctive kind of polish. The hide polishes differ depending on the material being worked. They range from a relatively bright polish with a greasy appearance (produced by working fresh wet hide) to a dull matte polish (produced by working dry hide or leather). The differences are attributable to variations in the quantity of lubricants present in the animal skin at different stages. A fresh hide gradually creates a polish not unlike that created by the cutting of meat. As the hide becomes progressively drier it contains progressively less lubricant, and the tool polish not only develops faster but also is duller and less greasy in appearance. If the hide is fully dried or tanned, the polish is quite dull and shows an extreme matte texture. Regardless of these differences in polish all hide-working tools show two characteristic kinds of microwear. One is relatively severe attrition of the working edge of the implement, that is, removal of flint by

means other than breakage or scratching. This attrition gives the stone implement a markedly rounded edge. The other characteristic is the development of shallow and diffuse linear surface features that run parallel to the direction in which the tool is moved. These diffuse linear marks are similar to the striations caused by other kinds of materials, but they cannot be mistaken for such striations, which are much more prominent.

Meat polish: The tool edge that is used to slice meat and other soft animal tissue develops a microwear polish rather like the polish produced by working fresh hide. This polish is easily distinguished, however, from the polishes created by the working of dry hide, bone, antler, wood, and nonwoody plant materials. Pronouncedly greasy, it is at the same time dull rather than bright. Thus, with respect to brightness, the contrast between meat polish and an unaltered flint surface is slight. For this reason meat polish does not show up well in photomicrography. The distinction is nonetheless clear to the eye. The grainy texture characteristic of raw flint is replaced by a matte texture that, although it seems to preserve the original surface microtopography, has actually transformed the elevations

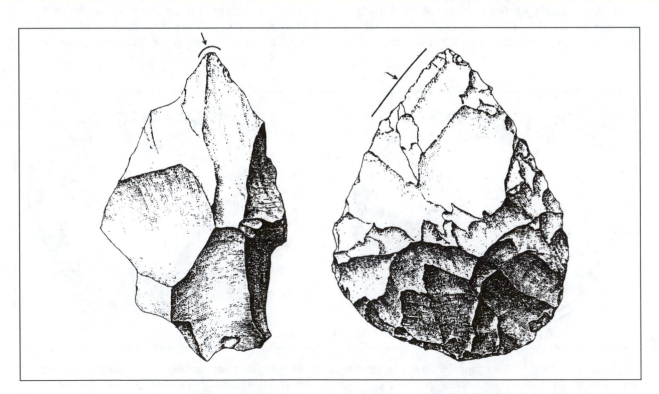

Bifacial tools from two Lower Paleolithic sites in England are a "chopper" from Clacton-on-Sea (left) and a "hand axe" from the Acheulean site Hoxne. Lines and arrows locate their working edges. The microwear analysis shows they served different functions.

and depressions into a semicontinuous surface. Tools that show meat polish also frequently bear short, narrow striations.

Antler polishes: The edges of tools used to work antler exhibit one or another of two distinctive polishes. The difference depends on how the tool was used. Scraping, planing, or graving antler leaves a very bright and smooth polish. Sawing antler, however, leaves a polish like bone polish; it is bright but pitted. In its early stages of development smooth antler polish is sometimes virtually indistinguishable from wood polish. When it is further developed, the polished surface displays small scattered depressions, giving it a pockmarked appearance that is quite different both from a wood polish and from the stronger surface pitting characteristic of the rougher antler polish. My experiments with antler were conducted almost entirely with samples that had been soaked for a day or two in water. Dry antler is so hard that stone tools used to work it are dulled by edge damage before anything has been accomplished. Water-soaked antler, however, is quite easy to work.

Nonwoody plant polishes: The edges of tools used to cut nonwoody plant stems, such as grasses or bracken, acquire a "corn gloss." The characteristic feature is a very smooth, highly reflective surface with a "fluid" appearance. If any striations are present, they often appear to be "filled in." At the same time the polished surfaces of the working edge develop curious comet-shaped pits. As the term implies, corn gloss is most commonly found on the flint sickles used by Neolithic farmers to harvest domesticated species of the grass family. As I was to discover, however, some nonwoody plants were cut in Lower Paleolithic times, and the cutting tools developed the same kind of gloss.

Work polishes alone enable the investigator to infer what materials were processed with various flint implements. If one is to determine how the implements were used, however, one must rely on several other kinds of microwear evidence. Perhaps most important are the distribution and orientation of such linear wear features as striations. Other kinds of evidence include the location and nature of edge damage and the location and extent of the polished working portions. All such evidence must be considered in relation to the general size and shape of the tool. In the broadest terms, once an inventory of the various kinds of microwear evident on a particular implement has been made, one then asks how the tool must have been handled to acquire the observed features. For example, microwear traces on both sides of a working edge, combined with striations that run parallel to the edge, are the strongest kind of evidence that the implement was used for sawing or cutting. Analysis of the work polish should then indicate what material was sawed or cut.

Having established six broad categories of polishes, I was prepared to apply my experimental results to selected Paleolithic artifacts. A skeptical colleague suggested, however, that I first submit my analytical technique to a blind test. The colleague, Mark H. Newcomer of the University of London, had strong doubts about the validity of microwear analysis. We agreed that he would make several replicas of flint tools and then work on various materials with them. After recording what he had done with the tools and then cleaning them, he would send them to me for analysis. Thereafter we would meet and compare my inferences with his records of the actual uses. Newcomer made 15 replicas of ancient flint tools and did various kinds of work with a total of 16 tool edges.

The results of the blind test were instructive. To be sure, the number of implements was small. Nevertheless, I identified the working portions of the tool edge in 14 edges of the 16. For 12 of the edges I was able to reconstruct the mode of tool use and for 10 of them to infer the kind of material worked.

Some of the inferences were remarkably close to the mark. For example, Newcomer had skinned a hare with a double-edged tool, using one of the edges for the actual skinning and the opposite edge to sever those parts of the limbs that remained with the skin during hide preparation. I identified the wear on the skinning edge as meat-cutting polish. (I had no way of knowing that in this instance the meat was less than a millimeter below the skin.) The microwear on the opposite edge I interpreted as the result of breaking a joint.

With another implement, Newcomer had cut fresh meat resting on a wood cutting board. I was able to distinguish between the microwear caused by the cutting of the meat and the incidental wear caused by the contact between the flint and the cutting board.

Even some of my misinterpretations were not unreasonable. For example, Newcomer had used the edge of one flint tool to cut frozen meat, which leaves few traces of wear. He had cut the meat on a wood board, however, and contact with the board did leave discernible traces. I interpreted the resulting microwear as characteristic of an implement used very delicately on wood. Since Newcomer's tests were the first check on the validity of high-resolution microwear analysis, I found the results quite encouraging.

It was now time to apply the technique to selected Paleolithic artifacts. Three classic British sites of the Lower Paleolithic period met the desired criteria. First, flint implements from all three sites are well preserved; they have not accumulated the surface patina that would conceal or destroy the evidence of microwear, and they have usually escaped damaging natural abrasion. Second, all the artifacts had been recently excavated, ensuring that their stratigraphic position in the ground had been recorded under strict controls and that they had been carefully handled and stored to eliminate the

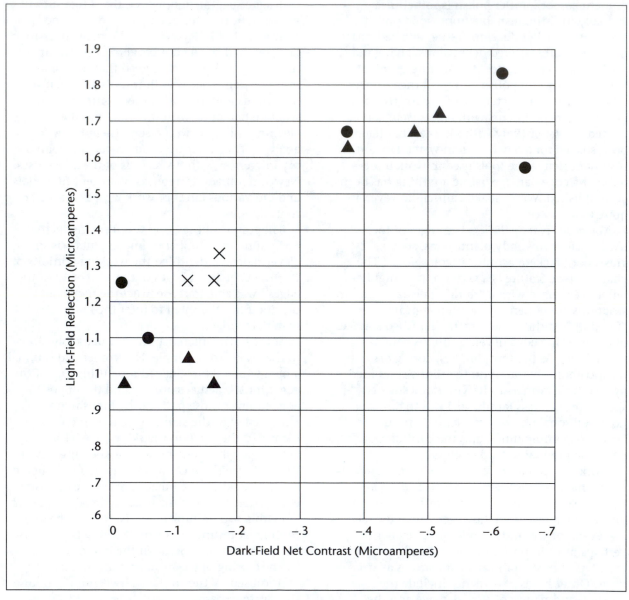

Relative brightness of various work polishes is shown in this reflectivity graph as a function of two measurements. The ordinate values indicate the amount of light reflected from a standard area of polished surface under normal light-field illumination, as registered in microamperes on a photometer. The abscissa values indicate differences between the reflectivity of polished and unpolished surfaces of an implement under dark-field illumination: the smaller the difference, the rougher the texture of the polished surface. The brightest and smoothest of the work polishes were the "corn glosses" produced by cutting nonwoody plant stems rich in plant opal. Dots indicate the readings on Neolithic flint sickle blades from Syria; the triangles, the readings on Neolithic blades from Bavaria. Among the dullest and roughest of the work polishes were the ones formed on modern replicas by work on greasy hide (triangles); the polishes produced by work on dry hides (dots) were rougher but brighter. Polishes produced by working wood (crosses) were smoother and brighter.

danger of post-excavation damage. The sites were at Clacton-on-Sea in Essex (the "Golf Course site"), at Swanscombe in Kent (the "Lower Loam"), and at Hoxne in Suffolk (mainly the "Lower Industry").

The Clacton site has given the name Clactonian to an entire Lower Paleolithic flint-tool industry that flourished some 250,000 years ago during the early stages of the Mindel-Riss interglacial period. The distinctive flake tools of the Clactonian industry were made by striking rather coarse flakes off nodules of flint and trimming a few of the flakes into the desired shape. Some of the leftover "cores" of flint were also employed as tools.

The Lower Loam at Swanscome is a somewhat later Clactonian site, occupied during the same Mindel-Riss interglacial period. The stone artifacts from the Lower Loam include tools made of flakes. Hoxne, a still later site, has yielded refined tools worked on both sides. These "bifacial" implements are typologically assigned to the Acheulean, a Lower Paleolithic industry named after Saint-Acheul, the site in France where such implements were first found. The Hoxne strata also contain an abundance of flint flakes, many of them the waste left over from production of the bifacial tools.

The total number of artifacts in suitable condition for microwear analysis was not large. The Clacton group included 144 tools from a layer of gravel at the Golf Course site and 102 from a layer of marl. Some of the flakes could be fitted into the original core from which they had been struck, indicating that they had been made on the spot. Taken together with microwear evidence that the flake tools had been used for butchering, woodworking, hide-working, and some work on bone, this suggests that the Golf Course site was probably occupied for some time rather than being a transient hunters' camp. The predominant activities at the site were woodworking and butchering.

Of the artifacts from Clacton that I examined, 22 were the coarse bifacial tools that are traditionally classified as choppers. Microwear indicates that only two of the 22 had actually been used as tools. This is a utilization rate of 10 percent, about half the rate for the flakes found at the site. Of the flakes from the gravel, 22 percent showed traces of use; of those from the marl, 16 percent did. The relative ratios suggest that the Clacton toolmakers were primarily interested in using their flint cores to turn out flakes, as opposed to bifaces.

Sixty-six flake tools from the Lower Loam at Swanscombe were in suitable condition for microwear analysis. Of these only four actually showed traces of use. The microwear characteristics shown by the four flakes were much like those visible on flake tools from Clacton. The Swanscome sample is too small, however, to allow any conclusion from this coincidence.

The artifacts from Hoxne included one group of tools (Lower Industry, Layer 3 West) with little or no abrasion damage. I studied the entire assemblage from that layer, numbering 408 implements. I also analyzed a random sample of artifacts from other Lower Industry and Upper Industry strata. The Acheulean industry at Hoxne, with its emphasis on the manufacture of bifacial tools, is marked by large quantities of flakes that must be counted as potential implements even though most of them are surely the debris of toolmaking, too thin-edged and fragile to be made into flake tools. Indeed, microwear analysis reveals that only 9 percent of the flakes from all the Lower Industry levels actually show evidence of wear.

The makers of the Hoxne tools used them for butchering, woodworking, hide-working, and for boring wood and bone. Interestingly enough, some were also used to slice or cut plant material other than wood. These hunters may have gathered reeds or bracken for bedding. The butchering was not done exclusively with flake tools: two of the Lower Industry "hand axes" showed the polish characteristic of butchering implements.

Among the Upper Industry tools at Hoxne were a small number of the flake implements that are traditionally called "side scrapers" and are presumed to have played a role in the dressing of hides. The microwear on these tools lends support to the guess of the traditionalists; most of the side scrapers show the polish characteristic of hide-working tools.

To cite one further example of microwear analysis, a bifacial tool from Clacton was found to show wood polish on its working surface. Further examination revealed utilization damage that could only have come from a rotary motion such as boring: the tool had been turned in a clockwise direction at the same time that downward pressure was being applied. Similar wear patterns also appear on flake tools that were used for boring. The patterns suggest that the Clacton woodworkers of perhaps 200,000 years ago were consistently right-handed.

The seeming wastefulness represented by the 9 percent rate of flake utilization at Hoxne may be more apparent than real; most of the flakes were biface-manufacture waste and unsuitable for use as tools. The prodigal use of flint at Clacton cannot be similarly explained away as the debris of bifacial-tool production. Perhaps at both sites much of the waste is better explained by the fact that chalk flint, an excellent raw material for the making of stone tools, can be found easily almost anywhere in southeastern England: in river gravels, on beaches and other superficial deposits, and, of course, in exposures of the chalk itself.

The microwear analysis of work polishes on this group of Lower Paleolithic implements provides the first direct and unequivocal evidence of the kinds of human activity that took place at English campsites roughly 250,000 years ago. Such findings make it clear that a new and rewarding method of archaeological research has finally come of age. It is now possible, assuming that the tools have been suitably preserved, to determine in most instances not only how ancient flint tools were but also what they were used on.

It seems very likely, although it remains to be proved, that microwear that can be interpreted in similar ways is present on tools made from stone materials other than flint, such as obsidian, chert, and even fine-grained basalts and quartzites. I have found this to be true of one fine-grained chert from southern Africa: experiments show that the material retains microwear polishes that are directly comparable to those found on chalk flint. The information derived from future microwear studies should enable prehistorians to discuss with increasing confidence the technology and economy of early man.

14
Age and the Female Form

PAUL G. BAHN

Archaeologists in Austria have discovered one of the world's earliest known sculptures, in the form of the oldest dated female figurine. The find is remarkable not merely for its antiquity but also for the artistic sophistication it displays.

Since 1941 the loess sediments of the Galgenberg site, near Krems, have been known to contain bones of Ice Age mammals (including reindeer and mammoth) together with abundant charcoal and flint flakes. New excavations in a nearby vineyard, directed by Christine Neugebauer-Maresch for the Österreichisches Bundesdenkmalamt, led to the discovery in September 1988 of the fragments of the female figurine. Charcoal samples from the same layer have produced radiocarbon dates of 29,200 to 31,190 years before present (B.P.).

The "Dancing Venus of Galgenberg," as the sculpture has been dubbed, is 7.2 cm long, and carved in green serpentine. Unlike the well-known "Venus figurines" of the Ice Age, such as that from Willendorf in Austria (found almost exactly 80 years earlier to the day), the Galgenberg specimen is flattish rather than

From *Nature*, Vol. 341, 23 November 1989, pp. 346–47. Copyright © 1989. Macmillan Magazines Ltd. Reprinted with permission. (Bibliographic documentation contained in the original text is omitted here. Interested readers should consult the original publication.)

carved in the round; its shape was probably predetermined by the stone used, because serpentine often occurs in slabs. The figure has not been polished, and its surface shows the marks of tools and erosion.

The right arm and the legs are supported at both ends, while the left arm appears to be folded back at the elbow. Body weight is supported primarily on the left leg, while the right leg rests on a slightly higher support. The right hand is placed on the hip. This pose causes the left breast to be depicted almost in profile, while the right is in very low relief because of the stone's flatness. The vulva is marked (a feature rare in Ice Age depictions of females), and in further contrast to many of the better known "Venus figurines" there is no hint of obesity or of an emphasis on breasts and buttocks. The figure is more or less anatomically accurate, except for the thickened limbs which are probably as thin as the artist dared carve them without making the sculpture unduly fragile.

There are two important points about the Galgenberg figurine. First, it is at least 5,000 years older than the "Gravettian period" to which most "Venus figurines" are usually, often unjustifiably, assigned; most of the Western European specimens have no archaeological context whatsoever, and are merely assumed to be Gravettian, whereas dated specimens in Eastern Europe in fact span a period from about 23,000 to 12,000 years B.P.

Second, the Galgenberg carving is the result of considerable technological skill — the stone is rather delicate and brittle, and the head, left arm, and breast could all easily have broken off. In addition, the two openings (under one arm and between the legs) would have required a delicate boring operation; the later "Venus figurines" are normally static, solid symmetrical figures with no perforations and no protruding limbs.

The sophistication revealed in both technology and composition can only be the end-result of a long tradition in carving (perhaps of perishable materials). The same conclusion had already been reached from study of the contemporary or even older ivory carvings of animals and humans from West Germany (Vogelherd, Geissenklösterle, Hohlenstein-Stadel) and perhaps also the ivory human figurines from Brassempouy in France. These objects, the oldest figurative carvings known at present, simply cannot represent the "first art," which must therefore have appeared long before.

In this respect, the Acheulian female "figurine" from Berekhat Ram, Israel, may provide a crucial clue. Dating to between 230,000 and 800,000 years B.P., it is a small scoria pebble whose shape, naturally resembling a "Venus figure," may have been modified by several grooves. Whether or not it was modified, its very presence at Berekhat Ram implies that the occupants of the site recognized its iconic properties, and therefore that an interest in the female form is one of the most enduring features of mankind.

15
Stone Age Psychedelia

ROGER LEWIN

A visit to the Cave of Lascaux in southwest France is an arresting experience. Colourful and often realistically posed images of bulls, deer, horses, and many other animals cover large areas of Lascaux's extensive passageways and chambers, making it by far the most prolifically decorated of all known caves from the Upper Paleolithic, the period between 35,000 and 10,000 years ago. The style of these powerful images looks strongly familiar to Western eyes, so much so that the late French archaeologist André Leroi-Gourhan suggested that they represent "the origins of Western art," painted as they were some 17,000 years ago, at the height of the Magdalenian period.

Yet this is clearly not the case. Representational painting and engraving all but disappeared at the end of the Magdalenian, in the so-called Azilian era. It was replaced by schematic images and patterns, a different mode of expression. Many of the techniques that had been applied in Lascaux, such as perspective and a sense of movement, had to be reinvented in Western art, during the Renaissance.

A closer look at the walls of Lascaux reveals the geometric patterns, such as grids, lines of dots, and nested curves, scattered among the animal images and in some cases superimposed on them. Such "signs" are not a normal accompaniment of most Western art, but are a constant component of Upper Paleolithic art. They are also one its greatest enigmas. For the late Abbé Breuil, France's greatest prehistorian, these geometric patterns represented hunting paraphernalia, including traps, snares, even weapons. This fitted in with his interpretation of the art as "hunting magic." Leroi-Gourhan included them in his notion of a structural duality in the Upper Paleolithic art. Dots and strokes were male signs, he said, while ovals, triangles, and quadrangles were female signs.

Recently a South African archaeologist, David Lewis-Williams, has suggested that neither interpretation is correct. They are, he says, images plucked from a mind in the state of hallucination, a sure sign of shamanistic (medicine man) art. His argument is based on a study of San (Bushman) art, in southern Africa, and on a neuropsychological model that might be basic to much human image-making in hunter-gatherer societies, including those of the Upper Paleolithic.

Lewis-Williams developed the neuropsychological model with his colleague Thomas Dowson. The shamanistic interpretation goes too far for some scholars. Lewis-Williams's thesis "is very important in many ways," says Margaret Conkey, an archaeologist at the University of California,

Berkeley. "But I'd shy away from any kind of monolithic explanation, anything that claims to explain everything."

Nevertheless, Lewis-Williams and Dowson's thesis is receiving a cautious welcome in continental Europe. At a major symposium held last year in France to commemorate the 50th anniversary of the discovery of Lascaux, Lewis-Williams was the only speaker invited who did not come from France or Spain. "We are taking what he says very seriously," says Jean-Philippe Rigaud, director of Prehistoric Antiquities of the Aquitaine, Bordeaux.

Lewis-Williams's thesis is as surprising as it is seductive. Prehistoric rock art is relatively common in southern Africa, where it goes back as far as 27 000 years, a full ten millennia before Lascaux, at the Appollo-11 cave in Namibia. In many ways, the African art is much more schematic and contains more human figures than the European art, but it includes the same kinds of geometric signs. San art is a recent part of this body of images in southern Africa, and for a long time it was considered to be principally narrative and decorative, with a small element of mythological depiction.

Lewis-Williams's interest in the interpretation of southern African prehistoric art goes back several decades, and he remembers some of the abortive approaches to trying to understand the art. "We were pretty naive," he now laments, recalling an idea from the late 1960s that quantification was the answer. "We thought that all we had to do was count various features of the paintings, and some sort of pattern would emerge and explain itself to us." Lewis-Williams and his colleagues had not realised that it was very difficult to know exactly what was significant enough to be counted and what could be ignored. "We discovered later on, when we learned what the art was really about, that many of the key elements in the paintings simply weren't on our lists," he says. "Things like the bending forward posture, or the arms-back posture. It didn't occur to us that these were important, but now we know better."

Making no progress with the quantification approach, Lewis-Williams and his colleague Patricia Vinnicombe decided to look to ethnography for inspiration, specifically to the traditional stories of the Kalahari San. The last of the images here were painted about 120 years ago, at the fringes of recent history. Although the Kalahari San were 1500 kilometres from the sites of the prehistoric images they had been studying, Lewis-Williams and Vinnicombe hoped to draw some insight from their art.

Prominent among San images was the eland, just as it was over large parts, but not all, of southern Africa. In what way was the eland important? Immersion in Kalahari ethnography and anthropological theory suggested that the eland was a symbol with multiple meanings. The eland turned up in all kinds of contexts, in the girl's first puberty ritual, the boy's first kill, in marriage ritual, in rainmaking, in healing rituals, everywhere. But Lewis-Williams made his first real discovery as he assembled his dissertation, eventually published as a book, *Believing and Seeing*.

"When I was doing the book, I could find only a few pictures of the girl's puberty dance, only a few of the boy's first kill, the marriage ceremony, depictions of events in people's lives," Lewis-Williams explains. "But when I got to the shamanistic chapters, rainmaking and so on, there were more pictures than I could accommodate. It was one of those cases where the data challenged the theory." The art was not principally narrative and decorative, as people had supposed. It was dominated by shamanism. But the next step of discovery was decisive, for it set in train a most unlikely but highly productive line of investigation.

"I used to take copies of the pictures home with me, prop them up on the mantlepiece, and contemplate them for days, hoping I'd see something in them that would give me a clue," remembers Lewis-Williams. "Then, one day, I was looking at a picture in which there was a dying eland and a man apparently holding its tail. The man had hoofs, like the eland; his hair was standing out, like the eland's hair; his legs were crossed, in imitation of the eland's legs. I suddenly saw that the dying eland was a metaphor for the dying medicine man. Shamans are said to 'die' when they enter the spirit world through trance. And the dying eland is a source of potency. The penny dropped, and I thought, how could I have been so dumb not to see it before?"

Not only were the images produced in a shamanistic context, but they were its very essence. They were not meant to depict the shaman carrying out rainmaking, healing, or whatever his speciality was. They were a product of the trance that the shaman enters to perform these functions.

Shamans may induce a trance by various techniques, including drugs and hyperventilation, but it is almost always in the context of rhythmic singing, dancing, and clapping by groups of women. As trance deepens, the shamans begin to tremble, their arms and whole body vigorously vibrating. They may also bend over as if in pain, and need the support of a staff. They are "dying," visiting the spirit world beyond this world. They are also hallucinating. Later, the shamans of the past painted the images.

It was the workings of the mind during this altered state of consciousness, this hallucination period, that intrigued Lewis-Williams. So he turned to the neuropsychological literature. There he learnt of the stages of trance, and of the nature of hallucination that the trance produces. Research stretching back over half a century had identified the occurrence of so-called entoptic phenomena, shimmering, incandescent, moving patterns produced within the visual system in early trance states. These entoptic images take geometric forms, such as grids, parallel lines, zigzags, dots, spirals, nested sets of curves, and filigrees.

In deeper trance states, these geometric images may be construed as real images, depending on the state of mind and cultural background of the individual involved. As one researcher put it: "Thus the same ambiguous round shape on initial perceptual representation can be 'illusioned' into an orange (if the subject is hungry), a breast (if he is in a state of heightened sexual drive), a cup of water (if he is thirsty), or an anarchist's bomb (if he is hostile or fearful)." The San commonly see nested curves as a honeycomb, something that is extremely important to these people as honey is a great delicacy.

Moving into a yet deeper stage of trance is often accompanied, according to laboratory reports, by an experience of a vortex or rotating tunnel that seems to surround the subject. The external world is progressively excluded and the inner world grows more florid. Iconic images may appear on the walls of the vortex, often imposed on a lattice of squares, like television screens. Frequently there is a mixture of iconic and geometric forms. Experienced shamans are able t plunge rapidly into deep trance, where they manipulate the imagery according to the needs of the situation. Their experience of it, however, is a world they have come briefly to inhabit; not a world of their own making, but a spirit world they are privileged to visit.

Hallucination in this deepest of the trance stages can become quite bizarre, with human and animal forms combining, forming chimeras or part animal, part human therianthropes. One early experimenter reported the transformation of a human head into a cat's head. Another described his experience this way: "I thought I was a fox, and instantly I was transformed into that animal. I could distinctly feel myself a fox, could see my long ears and bushy tail, and by a sort of introversion felt that my complete anatomy was that of a fox."

From these and other details of the neuropsychological literature, Lewis-Williams and Dowson developed what they call their three-stage model, which corresponds to the three, increasingly deep, trance stages. The model included an identification of specific entoptic images and of their perception and manipulation. The model was meant to predict what images would look like, in a general sense, if indeed they had been generated as the result of a trance state. The first thing that was necessary was to test the model against known shamanistic art.

"It had seemed apparent that San art had indeed been shamanistic art, and we were able to support this idea when we interviewed the old lady in the Transkei," says Lewis-Williams. "She was the daughter of a shaman, and she told us how she had seen the images done, how people used the images, turned to face them, touching them to receive potency. It all seemed to us to be about as firm a confirmation as we could hope for that San art was shamanistic."

It was important that Lewis-Williams and Dowson could test their model against known shamanistic art, otherwise they might have found themselves trapped in circular arguments. The presence in San art of the six specified entoptic forms, the mix of geometric and iconic images, and the importance of therianthropes are strongly indicative of shamanism, say the South African researchers: "We take [it] ... to be an initial confirmation of the validity of our model."

What of Upper Paleolithic art? Interpretation of its "meaning," a highly culturally bound concept, has moved through two major stages and is in the infancy of its third. The first stage, championed by the Abbé Breuil, was that of sympathetic hunting magic, beginning early this century and continuing until the early 1960s, when the Abbé died. The second stage focused on how images of different types of animals are distributed in different parts of the caves, and the association of images with one limb or the other of a sexual duality. This was the view of Leroi-Gourhan and Arlette Laming-Emperaire. By the time Leroi-Gourhan died in 1986, his theory had already begun to weaken. No single authority has since emerged to dominate the field, and no single explanation dominates. The very diversity of interpretations offered today suggests that the images themselves may have had many different meanings for the people of the Upper Palaeolithic. It was into this new intellectual setting that Lewis-Williams and Dowson ventured when they decided to apply their neuropsychological model to Upper Palaeolithic art.

"The neuropsychological model orders and fits Upper Palaeolithic art as well as it does San art," says Lewis-Williams. "The 'fit' is by no means simple; it is in fact highly complex, and this increases confidence in the conclusion that it does not result from chance." For instance, all six entoptic forms are to be found in Upper Palaeolithic art, although this does not account for all geometric forms in the caves. The presence of the forms associated with altered states of consciousness was, however, an encouraging sign, an apparent confirmation of stage one hallucination and associated images.

Stage two, the construal of entoptic forms, proved more difficult to identify. Nevertheless, Lewis-Williams and Dowson suggest that the exaggerated curved ibex horns with a zigzag outer margin in the Pyrenean cave of Niaux might qualify. So, too, might similarly exaggerated horns of ibex on a stone lamp from the cave of La Mouthe in the Dordogne. The South African researchers also cite paintings and engravings of mammoths in Rouffignac, also in the Dordogne, in which tusks of various animals appear as nested curves. These, and other, suggestions are tentative, admit Lewis-Williams and Dowson, but they "expect examples as convincing as the San ones to come to light."

Stage three, the most complex of all, provides stronger evidence. Looking for combinations of iconic and geometric images, Lewis-Williams and Dowson cite the famous horses of Peche Merle, in which red and black dots were placed within the black outlines of these animals. With the more enigmatic images of therianthropes, there are strong parallels between San and Upper Palaeolithic art. Often in the past, such images had been interpreted as hunters or shamans wearing masks. This does not explain the common occurrence of therianthropes with hoofs as feet. It was once suggested that therianthropes were the product of a "primitive mentality" that had "failed to establish definitive boundaries between humans and animals."

Lewis-Williams and Dowson acknowledge that during certain rituals shamans of the Stone Age may have used animal adornments, but argue that the overall nature of therianthropic images is strongly consistent with stage three trance. This holds good for paintings and engravings in Upper Palaeolithic art, as it does for San art.

Therianthropes represent a small but arresting proportion of Upper Palaeolithic images. The most famous example is the so-called sorcerer in the cave of Les Trois Frères, in the French Pyrenees. Deep underground, in a cramped cavern, the sorcerer dominates the space. Denis Vialou, of the Institute of Human Palaeontology in Paris, has studied the cave in detail, and describes the image like this: "The body is uncertain, but is some kind of large animal. The hind legs are human, until above the knees. The tail is some kind of canid, a wolf or a fox. The front legs are abnormal, with human-like hands. The face is a bird's face, odd, with deer's antlers." Unusually for Upper Palaeolithic images, the sorcerer is staring directly out of the wall, a full-face stare that transfixes the spectator.

Below the sorcerer are several heavily engraved panels, a riot of animal figures with no apparent order, no pattern. In the midst of all this is another human/animal figure, again with human hind legs. Human hind legs on animals are common in Upper Palaeolithic art, as are hoofs on otherwise human figures. This therianthrope is standing upright, with a bison's body and the head of a bison, with horns but a somewhat human face. The front legs are odd, in the same way as the sorcerer's forelimbs. This individual is holding something that might be a bow or a musical instrument. "Directly in front of this image is an animal," explains Vialou. "It has reindeer hind legs and rear end, showing female sex prominently displayed, the only one known in Upper Palaeolithic art. The rest of the body is bison, the head turned, looking back over its shoulder at the first individual. Something special is going on between these individuals, I'm sure of that."

Something similar is to be seen in Lascaux. The very first beast in the stampede in the Hall of Bulls is an enigma. Known as the Unicorn — wrongly, because it has two very straight horns — this beast has a swollen body on thick limbs, and a head of no known animal. There are six circular markings on the body, and the partial outline of a horse. Look at the head again, squint, and the profile snaps into that of a bearded man. It is a curious image, one that Lewis-Williams and Dowson believe fits very well into the kind of therianthropes hallucinated during stage three trance.

In arguing that Upper Palaeolithic art conforms to the three-stage neuropsychological model, and is therefore shamanistic, the South

African researchers do not claim to have explained the meaning of the images. "Meaning is always culturally bound," say Lewis-Williams and Dowson. "What we are pointing to are neurological mechanisms that underlie shamanistic art, wherever it is produced. How people construe and manipulate entoptic images, and what kind of iconic images they depict, all this will be influenced by the cultural context." It is like working with a given palate of paints, from which any desired image may be constructed. The meaning of the images remains elusive, but knowing the art is shamanistic — if indeed it is — at least offers a more secure foundation from which to analyse it.

If Upper Palaeolithic art is shamanistic then, Lewis-Williams and Dowson suggest, there might be a clue to the origins of image making, the origin of the notion that two-dimensional lines can represent three-dimensional objects. Prehistorians and psychologists have speculated on this issue for decades, wondering about the mental processes that would be required to provide the key innovation. One idea, recently revised, is that the production of representational images grew out of nonrepresentational marks, that it was a progressive process, a maturing of cognitive abilities and insights. The suggestion that the art is shamanistic makes this unnecessary. Image making, suggests Lewis-Williams, might have derived directly from the experience of hallucination itself.

For instance, some of the studies on hallucinations report that the images, both geometric and iconic, often appear to exist on surfaces, as if projected onto the wall or ceiling. "Pictures painted before your imagination," commented one observer. In a more naturalistic context, shamans often perceive their hallucinations as if they were on rock surfaces. This is natural, because the rock surface represents an interface between the real world and the spirit world, a passageway between the two. "They see the images as having been put there by the spirits, and in painting them, the shamans say they are simply touching and marking what already exists," explains Lewis-Williams. "The first depictions were therefore not representational images in the way you or I think of them. They were fixed mental images of another world."

16
The Worst Mistake in the History of the Human Race

JARED DIAMOND

To science we owe dramatic changes in our smug self-image. Astronomy taught us that our earth isn't the center of the universe but merely one of billions of heavenly bodies. From biology we learned that we weren't specially created by God but evolved along with millions of other species. Now archaeology is demolishing another sacred belief: that human history over the past million years has been a long tale of progress. In particular, recent discoveries suggest that the adoption of agriculture, supposedly our most decisive step toward a better life, was in many ways a catastrophe from which we have never recovered. With agriculture came the gross social and sexual inequality, the disease and despotism, that curse our existence.

At first, the evidence against this revisionist interpretation will strike twentieth-century Americans as irrefutable. We're better off in almost every respect than the people of the Middle Ages, who in turn had it easier than cavemen, who in turn were better off than apes. Just count our advantages. We enjoy the most abundant and varied foods, the best tools and material goods, some of the longest and healthiest lives, in history. Most of us are safe from starvation and predators. We get our energy from oil and machines, not from our sweat. What neo-Luddite among us would trade his life for that of a medieval peasant, a caveman, or an ape?

For most of our history we supported ourselves by hunting and gathering: we hunted wild animals and foraged for wild plants. It's a life that philosophers have traditionally regarded as nasty, brutish, and short. Since no food is grown and little is stored, there is (in this view) no respite from the struggle that starts anew each day to find wild foods and avoid starving. Our escape from this misery was facilitated only 10,000 years ago, when in different parts of the world people began to domesticate plants and animals. The agricultural revolution gradually spread until today it's nearly universal and few tribes of hunter-gatherers survive.

From the progressivist perspective on which I was brought up, to ask "Why did almost all our hunter-gatherer ancestors adopt agriculture?" is silly. Of course they adopted it because agriculture is an efficient way to get more food for less work. Planted crops yield far more tons per acre than roots and berries. Just imagine a band of savages, exhausted from searching for nuts or chasing wild animals, suddenly gazing for the first time at a fruit-laden orchard or a pasture full of sheep. How many milliseconds do you think it would take them to appreciate the advantages of agriculture?

The progressivist party line sometimes even goes so far as to credit agriculture with the remarkable flowering of art that has taken place over the past few thousand years. Since crops can be stored, and since it takes less time to pick food from a garden than to find it in the wild, agriculture gave us free time that hunter-gatherers never had. Thus it was agriculture that enabled us to build the Parthenon and compose the B-minor Mass.

While the case for the progressivist view seems overwhelming, it's hard to prove. How do you show that the lives of people 10,000 years ago got better when they abandoned hunting and gathering for farming? Until recently, archaeologists had to resort to indirect tests, whose results (surprisingly) failed to support the progressivist view. Here's one example of an indirect test: Are twentieth-century hunter-gatherers really worse off than farmers? Scattered throughout the world, several dozen groups of so-called primitive people, like the Kalahari Bushmen, continue to support themselves that way. It turns out that these people have plenty of leisure time, sleep a good deal, and work less hard than their farming neighbors. For instance, the average time devoted each week to obtaining food is only 12 to 19 hours for one group of Bushmen, 14 hours or less for the Hadza nomads of Tanzania. One Bushman, when asked why he hadn't emulated neighboring tribes by adopting agriculture, replied, "Why should we, when there are so many mongongo nuts in the world?"

While farmers concentrate on high-carbohydrate crops like rice and potatoes, the mix of wild plants and animals in the diets of surviving hunter-gatherers provides more protein and a better balance of other nutrients. In one study, the Bushmen's average daily food intake (during a month when food was plentiful) was 2,140 calories and 93 grams of protein, considerably greater than the recommended daily allowance for people of their size. It's almost inconceivable that Bushmen, who eat 75 or so wild plants, could die of starvation the way hundreds of thousands of Irish farmers and their families did during the potato famine of the 1840s.

So the lives of at least the surviving hunter-gatherers aren't nasty and brutish, even though farmers have pushed them into some of the world's worst real estate. But modern hunter-gatherer societies that have rubbed shoulders with farming societies for thousands of years don't tell us about conditions before the agricultural revolution. The progressivist view is really making a claim about the distant past: that the lives of primitive people improved when they switched from gathering to farming. Archaeologists can date that switch by distinguishing remains of wild plants and animals from those of domesticated ones in prehistoric garbage dumps.

How can one deduce the health of the prehistoric garbage makers, and thereby directly test the progressivist view? That question has become answerable only in recent years, in part through the newly emerging techniques of paleopathology, the study of signs of disease in the remains of ancient peoples.

In some lucky situations, the paleopathologist has almost as much material to study as a pathologist today. For example, archaeologists in the Chilean deserts found well-preserved mummies whose medical conditions at time of death could be determined by autopsy (*Discover*, October). And feces of long-dead Indians who lived in dry caves in Nevada remain sufficiently well preserved to be examined for hookworm and other parasites.

Usually the only human remains available for study are skeletons, but they permit a surprising number of deductions. To begin with, a skeleton reveals its owner's sex, weight, and approximate age. In the few cases where there are many skeletons, one can construct mortality tables like the ones life insurance companies use to calculate expected life span and risk of death at any given age. Paleopathologists can also calculate growth rates by measuring bones of people of different ages, examine teeth for enamel defects (signs of childhood malnutrition), and recognize scars left on bones by anemia, tuberculosis, leprosy, and other diseases.

One straightforward example of what paleopathologists have learned from skeletons concerns historical changes in height. Skeletons from Greece and Turkey show that the average height of hunter-gatherers toward the end of the ice ages was a generous 5'9" for men, 5'5" for women. With the adoption of agriculture, height crashed, and by 3000 B.C. had reached a low of only 5'3" for men, 5' for women. By classical times heights were very slowly on the rise again, but modern Greeks and Turks have still not regained the average height of their distant ancestors.

Another example of paleopathology at work is the study of Indian skeletons from burial mounds in the Illinois and Ohio river valleys. At Dickson Mounds, located near the confluence of the Spoon and Illinois rivers, archaeologists have excavated some 800 skeletons that paint a picture of the health changes that occurred when a hunter-gatherer culture gave way to intensive maize farming around A.D. 1150. Studies by George Armelagos and his colleagues then at the University of Massachusetts show these early farmers paid a price for their new-found livelihood. Compared to the hunter-gatherers who preceded them, the farmers had a nearly 50 per cent increase in enamel defects indicative of malnutrition, a fourfold increase in iron-deficiency anemia (evidenced by a bone condition called porotic hyperostosis), a threefold rise in bone lesions reflecting infectious disease in general, and an increase in degenerative conditions of the spine, probably reflecting a lot of hard physical labor. "Life expectancy at birth in the pre-agricultural community was about twenty-six years," says Armelagos, "but in the post-agricultural community it was nineteen years. So these episodes of nutritional stress and infectious disease were seriously affecting their ability to survive."

The evidence suggests that the Indians at Dickson Mounds, like many other primitive peoples, took up farming not by choice but from necessity in order to feed their constantly growing numbers. "I don't think most hunter-gatherers farmed until they had to, and when they switched to farming they traded quality for quantity," says Mark Cohen of the State University of New York at Plattsburgh, co-editor, with Armelagos, of one of the seminal books in the field, *Paleopathology at the Origins of Agriculture*. "When I first started making that argument ten years ago, not many people agreed with me. Now it's become a respectable, albeit controversial, side of the debate."

There are at least three sets of reasons to explain the findings that agriculture was bad for health. First, hunter-gatherers enjoyed a varied diet, while early farmers obtained most of their food from one or a few starchy crops. The farmers gained cheap calories at the cost of poor nutrition. (Today just three high-carbohydrate plants — wheat, rice, and corn — provide the bulk of the calories consumed by the human species, yet each one is deficient in certain vitamins or amino acids essential to life.) Second, because of dependence on a limited number of crops, farmers ran the risk of starvation if one crop failed. Finally, the mere fact that agriculture encouraged people to clump together in crowded societies, many of which then carried on trade with other crowded societies, led to the spread of parasites and infectious disease. (Some archaeologists think it

was crowding, rather than agriculture, that promoted disease, but this is a chicken-and-egg argument, because crowding encourages agriculture and vice versa.) Epidemics couldn't take hold when populations were scattered in small bands that constantly shifted camp. Tuberculosis and diarrheal disease had to await the rise of farming, measles and bubonic plague the appearance of large cities.

Besides malnutrition, starvation, and epidemic diseases, farming helped bring another curse upon humanity: deep class divisions. Hunter-gatherers have little or no stored food, and no concentrated food sources, like an orchard or a herd of cows; they live off the wild plants and animals they obtain each day. Therefore, there can be no kings, no class of social parasites who grow fat on food seized from others. Only in a farming population could a healthy, non-producing élite set itself above the disease-ridden masses. Skeletons from Greek tombs at Mycenae c. 1500 B.C. suggest that royals enjoyed a better diet than commoners, since the royal skeletons were two or three inches taller and had better teeth (on the average, one instead of six cavities or missing teeth). Among Chilean mummies from c. A.D. 1000, the élite were distinguished not only by ornaments and gold hair clips, but also by a fourfold lower rate of bone lesions caused by disease.

Similar contrasts in nutrition and health persist on a global scale today. To people in rich countries like the United States, it sounds ridiculous to extol the virtues of hunting and gathering. But Americans are an élite, dependent on oil and minerals that must often be imported from countries with poorer health and nutrition. If one could choose between being a peasant farmer in Ethiopia or a Bushman gatherer in the Kalahari, which do you think would be the better choice?

Farming may have encouraged inequality between the sexes, as well. Freed from the need to transport their babies during a nomadic existence, and under pressure to produce more hands to till the fields, farming women tended to have more frequent pregnancies than their hunter-gatherer counterparts — with consequent drains on their health. Among the Chilean mummies, for example, more women than men had bone lesions from infectious disease.

Women in agricultural societies were sometimes made beasts of burden. In New Guinea farming communities today I often see women staggering under loads of vegetables and firewood while the men walk empty-handed. Once while on a field trip there studying birds, I offered to pay some villagers to carry supplies from an airstrip to my mountain camp. The heaviest item was a 110-pound bag of rice, which I lashed to a pole and assigned to a team of four men to shoulder together. When I eventually caught up with the villagers, the men were carrying light loads, while one small woman weighing less than the bag of rice was bent under it, supporting its weight by a cord across her temples.

As for the claim that agriculture encouraged the flowering of art by providing us with leisure time, modern hunter-gatherers have at least as much free time as do farmers. The whole emphasis on leisure time as a critical factor seems to me misguided. Gorillas have had ample free time to build their own Parthenon, had they wanted to. While post-agricultural technological advances did make new art forms possible and preservation of art easier, great paintings and sculptures were already being produced by hunter-gatherers 15,000 years ago, and were still being produced as recently as the last century by such hunter-gatherers as some Eskimos and the Indians of the Pacific Northwest.

Thus with the advent of agriculture an élite became better off, but most people became worse off. Instead of swallowing the progressivist party line that we chose agriculture because it was good for us, we must ask how we got trapped by it despite its pitfalls.

One answer boils down to the adage "Might makes right." Farming could support many more people than hunting, albeit with a poorer quality of life. (Population densities of hunter-gatherers are rarely over one person per ten square miles, while farmers average 100 times that.) Partly, this is because a field planted entirely in edible crops lets one feed far more mouths than a forest with scattered edible plants. Partly, too, it's because nomadic hunter-gatherers have to keep their children spaced at four-year intervals by infanticide and other means, since a mother must carry her toddler until it's old enough to keep up with the adults. Because farm women don't have that burden, they can and often do bear a child every two years.

As population densities of hunter-gatherers slowly rose at the end of the ice ages, bands had to choose between feeding more mouths by taking the first steps toward agriculture, or else finding ways to limit growth. Some bands chose the former solution, unable to anticipate the evils of farming, and seduced by the transient abundance they enjoyed until population growth caught up with increased food production. Such bands outbred and then drove off or killed the bands that chose to remain hunter-gatherers, because a hundred malnourished farmers can still outfight one healthy hunter. It's not that hunter-gatherers abandoned their life style, but that those sensible enough not to abandon it were forced out of all areas except the ones farmers didn't want.

At this point it's instructive to recall the common complaint that archaeology is a luxury, concerned with the remote past, and offering no lessons for the present. Archaeologists studying the rise of farming have reconstructed a crucial stage at which we made the worst mistake in human history. Forced to choose between limiting population or trying to increase food production, we chose the latter and ended up with starvation, warfare, and tyranny.

Hunter-gatherers practiced the most successful and longest-lasting life style in human history. In contrast, we're still struggling with the mess into which agriculture has tumbled us, and it's unclear whether we can solve it. Suppose that an archaeologist who had visited us from outer space were trying to explain human history to his fellow spacelings. He might illustrate the results of his digs by a 24-hour clock on which one hour represents 100,000 years of real past time. If the history of the human race began at midnight, then we would now be almost at the end of our first day. We lived as hunter-gatherers for nearly the whole of that day, from midnight through dawn, noon, and sunset. Finally, at 11:54 P.M., we adopted agriculture. As our second midnight approaches, will the plight of famine-stricken peasants gradually spread to engulf us all? Or will we somehow achieve those seductive blessings that we imagine behind agriculture's glittering façade, and that have so far eluded us?

17
The Americas: The Case against an Ice-Age Human Population

ROGER C. OWEN

Archaeology is the study of discovered evidences of prehistoric human activity used to reconstruct, understand, and date human life of earlier times. Research has proven beyond doubt that humans lived, loved, and died millions of years ago in Africa, Asia, and Europe. So, when did the first inhabitants arrive and begin to develop the first native American cultures? Curiously, despite agreement regarding the other continents, American experts differ by as much as several hundred thousand years. In this article, which asks "Were humans in the Americas prior to 12 ky ago," we shall explore the character of the evidence, the nature of the "proof," and the role of skepticism in archaeological inquiry. [*Note:* "ky" means "thousands of years"; 28 ky = 28,000 years. *Ed.*]

When I began library research for this article I believed specialists had proved that humans first arrived in the Americas at least 30 ky ago. I had so written in a textbook. But upon examination of source after source, hundreds in total, I gradually became an "agnostic" and then a strong

From Fred H. Smith and Frank Spencer, eds., *The Origins of Modern Humans: A World Survey of Fossil Evidence*, pp. 517–63. Abstract, modified by author. Copyright © 1984 Alan R. Liss Inc. Reprinted with the permission of Wiley-Liss, a division of John Wiley & Sons, Inc. (Bibliographic documentation contained in the original text is omitted here. Interested readers should consult the original publication.)

"skeptic." I did not find a single published source that convinced me, or that had convinced all other skeptics, that humans were in the Americas pre-12 ky ago. They may have been here, but those pleistocene travellers may have so few and so scattered in time and space we may never find the convincing "smoking gun" of scientific proof.

Linguists and physical anthropologists do not lend support to great antiquity for America's prehistoric human populations. Two prominent linguists, M. Swadesh and J. Greenberg, concluded that the great multiplicity of languages spoken by native Americans needed no more than 15 ky or as few as 12 ky to produce the diversity exhibited in the nineteenth century.

Great physical heterogeneity developed in Africa, Asia, and Europe during millions of years of human occupancy. Native Americans in 1492, on the other hand, exhibited notable physical homogeneity. This lack of diversity led one early observer to write, "If you had seen one Indian, you had seen them all." Native Americans' physical characteristics in recent times, including their teeth, bones, blood types, gene ratios, and other features, indicate a relatively recent relationship between native Americans and people of east Asia. A.B. Harper suggests no more than 15 ky for a time of separation of American and Siberian populations. A.M. Brues argues that insufficient time had elapsed since their arrival, perhaps only 15 ky or so, to produce a distinctive native American physical type distinct from contemporary Asians.

Tens of thousands of fossilized human bones have provided irrefutable proof that humans (hominids) lived on the continents of the Old World for millions of years. In the Americas, no equivalent evidence has been found. Seven finds of human skeletal material have been offered as of more than 12 ky age. In the past decade, each of these purported ancient bones ("Sunnyvale," the Del Mar bones [*aka* "Scripps Estate," "La Jolla," or "San Diego Man"], the Taber child, the Otovalo skeleton, the Los Angeles bones, the Yuha burial, the Midland bone, and the Laguna Beach bones) has been shown to have been of less than 10 ky age. It is scarcely credible that any substantial occupation of the Americas pre-12 ky ago could leave behind so few human bones for our study. Following on the end of the pleistocene, from 10 ky to the present, human bone is a common archaeological find. It is important for the reader to be aware that throughout the twentieth century, most anthropological authorities have accepted as fact and so written (including the present author) that the Americas have been occupied for tens of thousands of years. The highly esteemed dean of Americanist archaeology, Gordon Willey, summed up this professional consensus when, in 1966, he wrote:

> ...I think it likely that the "pre-projective point" horizon is a reality and that man first crossed into America as far back as 40,000 to 20,000 B.C.

Proponents of "early, early" Americans often are not academically trained archaeologists, although some are, and have not been trained in the rigorous interpretive techniques insisted upon by trained scientists. Many are personally committed to proving early dates rather than, as scientists must be, dedicated to discovering evidences that permit the community of scholars to enter into the debate and to shape the interpretation, chips falling where they may.

Following Vance Haynes, a prominent critic of "early, early man in America" hypotheses, I'll divide the archaeological evidences into an Early (pre-28 ky), a Middle (28–12 ky), and a Late Paleo-American epoch (12 ky to present).

The Early Paleo-American Period (pre-28 ky)

Among the archaeological sites reported by their claimants to possess human or cultural remains

greater than 28 ky are: in California, Calico Mts. — Simpson and Leakey; the Texas Street Site near San Diego — G.F. Carter; Yuha Pinto Wash — Childers and Minshall; China Lake — E.L. Davis; Santa Rosa Island — P.C. Orr; in the Yukon Territory, Old Crow Basin — Irving and Harington, Morlan, Bonnichsen; in Nevada, Tule Springs; in Texas, Lewisville; and an additional handful of sites in Mexico, Nicaragua, and elsewhere. Not one of these sites has produced evidence that will meet the minimum criteria for establishment as valid proof.

Many are too poorly described in the literature to permit debate on their significance (Calico Mts., Santa Rosa Island, Texas Street, China Lake). One either believes or rejects the claims based upon brief published notes and verbal communiques from their proponents. Tule Springs and Lewisville are known to have been misdated and to be of relatively recent origin. Old Crow Basin, where elephant bone "tools" are the primary "artifacts" recovered, has generated debate over the possibility that humans might have given up use of stone as a raw material in favor of bone. L.S. Binford has criticized this proposal as "having produced a series of modern myths." Many specialists have concluded that these bone "artifacts" were produced by natural forces, not by humans.

Few, if any, experts regard the Early Paleo-American Period as established.

The Middle Paleo-American Period (28–12 ky)

Most anthropologists who have published an opinion have accepted the probability, if not the certainty, that humans were present in the Western Hemisphere during all or most of the time between 28 and 12 ky ago. Among them are F. Bordes, R. Chard, J. Comas, D. Dummond, A.D. Krieger, W.S. Laughlin, R. MacNeish, C.W. Meighan, I. Rouse, F. Wendorf, H.M. Wormington, and G. Willey. Nonetheless, a growing number of critics are coming to believe that neither the Early nor the Middle Paleo-American Periods have been unequivocally demonstrated and may never be. In 1983, D. Stanford summed up what is still needed to prove a pre-Clovis presence:

> If I could find one clearly stratified site with some busted mammoth bones, a couple of crude flake tools, and a single human bone, all in unquestionable association with a charcoal hearth dated 19,500 years ago — I'd have my dream.

Several dozen locations have been proposed as evidences of a Middle Paleo-American population. Many possess an early date with doubtful tools, or a date with a tool or two associated but with the possibility that the tools belong to a later horizon and have drifted downward, as Stanford has discovered at the Dutton Site.

Tlapacoya. Eighteen localities have been excavated in the environs of the Cerro de Tlapacoya, Mexico, between 1965 and 1973. Interdisciplinary teams believe they have defined a cultural sequence evidenced by an obsidian projectile point, obsidian flakes, and three hearths associated with a sequence of C-14 dates from 24 to 15 ky. C.V. Haynes believes the C-14 dates to be valid for the site but is concerned about the association of the dated material, a log and a single obsidian blade.

Pikimachay Cave. R.S. MacNeish, in 1967, sought preceramic sites in highland Peru, near Ayacucho:

> The long hill we were descending had a number of bad hairpin curves in it, so I was paying attention to the driving. In fact, I didn't look up until the road wound to the north away from the basin. When I looked up, there it was! Halfway up a large rounded hill full of ancient terraces was a huge dark cave, highlighted by the morning sun shining on the surrounding cliffs.

Thus was discovered one of the most significant Paleo-American sites in the Americas: Pikimachay Cave (piki = flea, machay = cave). Herein, MacNeish has delineated 13 superimposed zones that appear to contain 43 definable phases of occupancy extending in time from Spanish days to perhaps 23 ky ago. The levels of greatest interest are Pacacaisa (23 ky) and Ayacucho (14 ky). He has recovered scrapers, spoke shaves, worked flakes, and other apparent tools. Of these, MacNeish remarked: "The material is extremely crude with the majority made from volcanic tufa (*sic*) — (actually tuff), that does not show evidence of man's work very clearly." Of the same "tools" Haynes wrote:

> At Pikimachay Cave there are now several C-14 dates above and below the 14,000-B.P. level which are stratigraphically consistent, but all dates are from bone, a material notorious for being contaminated. I do not believe the lower levels to be cultural but the 14 ky level cannot be dismissed entirely.

In review of the earliest level in Pikimachay Cave, Thomas Lynch calls attention to a disagreement MacNeish has had with geologists as to which strata in the cave represent glacial advance or retreat, a controversy that, if MacNeish is correct, must be resolved by concluding that the glacial sequence around the cave is different from that of Europe and North America. As already noted, Lynch has concluded that no solid evidence exists in South America of a pre-14 ky human occupation.

Valsequillo (Hueyatlaco). In 1962, C. Irwin-Williams and J.A. Camacho began excavation around the Valsequillo Reservoir, near Puebla, Mexico, where large quantities of paleontological and archaeological materials had been recovered. Bifacially chipped projectile points, blades, and a "pseudo-fluted" point resemble specimens from El Inga, Ecuador, and a bipointed projectile point is similar to some Plano points (Late Paleo-American, 9.5–7.5 ky) such as Lerma, Cascade, and others. These artifacts were associated stratigraphically with the bones of horse, camel, elephants, and of other extinct animals. Another group of artifacts, "crudely edge-worked points," reminds Irwin-Williams not of any other New World tool complex but rather of Old World Upper Paleolithic materials.

Dates of 21.85 and 9.15 ky from C-14 on freshwater shell have been obtained, a dating ambiguity that leaves the precise date of the site in substantial doubt. An absence of charcoal, heavy mineralization of the bones, and very complex "stream bed" stratigraphy composed of gravels that might be as much as 200 ky old, combine to defy easy confirmation of a pre-Clovis age. Haynes believes Valsequillo possesses some of the best evidence of a late Wisconsin human presence in the Americas but, on the other hand, he notes that, apart from the dates, the sites illustrate no cultural materials that could not be quite recent.

Meadowcroft Rockshelter. Meadowcroft Rockshelter, Pennsylvania, which since 1973 has been meticulously excavated by a team directed by J.M. Adovasio, is a deeply stratified, multicomponent site located in southwestern Pennsylvania. Eleven strata have been defined within which firepits, ash and charcoal lenses, large burned areas, as well as refuse and storage areas have been identified. Adovasio believes the site to have been first occupied 19 ky ago, then intermittently until historic times. Radiocarbon dates for lower Stratum IIa, which Adovasio believes to be the oldest, range from 10.85 to 17.65 ky. Over 400 items have been discovered from this stratum and there is no question as to their cultural nature.

Dates in the cave for the earliest levels have been derived from charcoal using C-14. Haynes believes that this charcoal may have been contaminated by older carbon brought into the lower levels by ground water. He and others have called attention to the absence in the cave of any evidence of other than a Holocene flora or fauna, a condition regarded as unlikely for a site that, if correctly dated at 19 ky ago, would have been only a short distance from the leading edge of the continental ice mass. Fossil pollens from a source near Meadowcroft indicate that the area was dominated by tundra with spruce forests 19–12 ky ago but no evidence of such a flora is found in the Meadowcroft deposits. Furthermore, all of the Meadowcroft cultural assemblage falls within an acceptable Clovis pattern. The only real indicator of great age in the cave is in the C-14 dates from sediment 70 cm or less in thickness. Haynes believes Meadowcroft to be no older than Clovis, if as old.

Despite these criticisms, Adovasio and his colleagues stand their ground and insist that Meadowcroft constitutes the best evidence recovered so far for a pre-Clovis occupation anywhere in the New World.

The Timlin Site. Claims have been made since the early 1970s that early "Paleolithic" tools were to be found in the Catskill Mountains at the Timlin Site, near Cobleskill, New York. Dismissed by a number of authorities as preposterous, the claims have generally been taken lightly. But further excavation at the site by A.L. Bryan in 1979, although not supportive of earlier claims, did find cores and flakes at a level that might be 16 ky old, although, according to Bryan, dates from the site are contradictory. No detailed report is yet available on this site.

Pollen profiles suggest a date of between 14 and 13 ky for the level in which the cultural material was found. Bracketing C-14 dates on mammal bone support approximately this age also: 12.9 and 15 ky.

The Selby and Dutton Sites. Extensive excavation in 1979 of these two Pleistocene fossil beds in eastern Colorado by D. Stanford discovered what to him appeared to be four classes of evidence of human presence among the abundant remains of 24 or more extinct Pleistocene vertebrate species. These classes of evidence were: (1) bone expediency tools, (2) flaked bone, (3) bone processed to extract marrow, and (4) at Dutton, seven tiny stone flakes. Geological considerations suggest an age of approximately 15 ky ago for the materials.

But because the existence of any bone "tool kits" in the Americas has been seriously challenged, further proof of the existence of one at these locations is required. Furthermore, since the Dutton site possesses a Clovis occupational level, and the seven tiny stone flakes underlay that, there exists the possibility that they are of Clovis origin. Also, at Dutton, Stanford believed he might have found an artifact associated with broken camel bone in a stratum 16 ky old, but further work proved the tool to be lying at the bottom of a gopher hole. Stanford appears to be no longer sure that the recovered fractured bones form part of a human tool kit. Perhaps the Selby and Dutton sites warrant removal from the ranks of pre-Clovis candidates.

Wilson Butte Cave. Wilson Butte Cave on the Snake River in southern Idaho was reported by R. Gruhn in 1961. Three artifacts — a biface, a blade, and a "burinated" flake — were recovered from the lowest level, Stratum C, a water-laid sand, a level that yielded C-14 dates to 14.55 ky, obtained from numerous bones of small animals found in the layer. Haynes suggests that the artifacts might have been carried into the lower level by rodent activity within the cave. C.M. Aikens, summarizing the archaeology of the region, regards the dates from Wilson Butte Cave as "controversial"; the artifact group is too limited to be meaningfully assessed.

The El Jobo Complex (Taima-Taima). The El Jobo Complex of coastal Venezuela was first defined in 1956 by J.M. Cruxent and I. Rouse from surface-collected material. The "type" tool is a long lanceolate projectile point with a thick cylindrical cross section. El Jobo points have been found associated with bones of mastodon, glyptodon, and other extinct forms at a waterhole site at Muaco, and elsewhere. Burned bone from Muaco was dated to 14–16 ky but because modern glass co-occurs in the deposit, there is suspicion that it has been seriously mixed. There is no question regarding the cultural character of El Jobo artifacts. If it were not for their association with Pleistocene fauna and with pre-Clovis dates, the El Jobo tools could fall within the typological range of post-Clovis blade complexes, referred to as "Plano."

Taima-Taima, also a waterhole site, was excavated by Bryan and Gruhn in 1976 in order to confirm previously reported associations between extinct fauna and El Jobo artifacts. They uncovered the semi-articulated remains of a young mastodon with an El Jobo point midsection in its pubic cavity, apparently killed and butchered by humans. In the vicinity of the mastodon skeleton, and presumed by Gruhn and Bryan to be the intestinal contents of the animal, were fragments of sheared wood twigs, twigs which have yielded four C-14 dates ranging from 14.2 to 12.98 ky.

If the interpretations of Gruhn and Bryan are correct, there must have been an elephant hunting, non–Clovis point–using adaptation in northern Venezuela 13 ky ago. But mucky earth — past, intermittent, or present — can lead to movement in soils and their contents, the extent of which would be impossible to know. Plodding large animals in search of drink, ravenous predators attacking game, humans digging for water (or archaeological workers in search of evidences of Paleo-hunters), burrowing animals, or simply the natural movement associated with bog formation will result in displacement of soil contents beyond the ability of even the most meticulous workers to recapitulate. Haynes, Lynch, and others have criticized these and other dates and associations derived from materials obtained from waterholes.

D.F Dincauze questions the association of the fragment of the El Jobo point with the mastodon bones on another basis. She reasons that, as both are found together on an impermeable floor at the base of old spring deposits, they could have moved down separately to become co-residents of the bottom at different times, up until about 10 ky ago, when a soil formed which seals the deposit below it. Thus, neither their relationship to each other nor the age of either is really certain.

The Blue Fish Caves. Two small caves, in northeast Yukon Territory, Canada, were test excavated by Cinq-mars from 1978 to 1981, and revealed late Pleistocene faunal remains. Lithic cultural evidence consists of an angle burin made on a retouched chert blade, flakes, and a possible micro-blade fragment. In addition to these stone items, all made of rock exotic to the caves, two mammal tibiae, polished primarily at one end, were found, as well as other bones which appeared to show human modification. Distribution of faunal remains within the cave also suggests human agency to Cinq-mars.

It is surprising that so little evidence of human presence in Beringia exists. If Clovis hunters prove to be the first Americans it would be reasonable to expect that their ancestors were in Beringia by 15 ky ago. But the Blue Fish Cave materials scarcely prove it. The data are too modest, the evidence for mixing in the deposits substantial, the conclusions regarding a human presence perhaps premature.

Monte Verde. Several seasons of multidiscipli-nary research at the Monte Verde site in south-central Chile have convinced T. Dillehay and his collaborators that they have recovered a tool kit associated with mastodon-hunting people of 14–12 ky ago. Archaeological materials include fragmentary remains of perhaps six mastodons of various ages, with some bones possibly modified; wood and plant remains; one hundred or more lithic items, most showing minimal, if any, modification; charcoal; plus a possible feature. A C-14 date obtained from bone (12.35 ky) and one from wood (13.03 ky) are believed to date human presence.

Due to the quality of excavation and research at Monte Verde, and the complexity of the remains, this site must be regarded as a leading candidate for pre-Clovis age. But, all of the evidence was recovered around an old stream course, thus there is the possibility that all are fortuitously associated. Perhaps supporting such an interpretation are the mastodon remains. Dillehay believes they represent a cultural event. Just how likely it is that a group of primitive hunters perhaps lacking projectile points could drop a whole family of elephants in a small area is a matter for conjecture. An alternative explana-tion for this collection of bones might be that water-action or nonhuman predators deposited them into a back-water or lair. Although the flow of the stream today is slight, weather disruptions in the area, for example, exceptional quantities of snow and rain due to periodic shifts by the Pacific Ocean current "El Nino" can bring massive water flow (as Americans learned in 1983 [and 1993 — Ed.]).

Another complicating factor at Monte Verde might be the materials used for dating, especially the wood. C.W. Meighan reports that in the Chilean desert he recovered charcoal that gave a date of 5 ky on a site otherwise known to be only 2 ky old. Apparently, the ancient people were burning fossil wood. More work is under way at Monte Verde, so final interpretations are not yet available.

The Levi Site. During the 1960s and again during the 1970s, H.L. Alexander excavated a long, narrow rock shelter near Austin, Texas. He uncovered five strata, from recent at the top to Clovis at the next to bottom. The bottom stra-tum, Zone I, contains crude flakes, polished bones, a small hammerstone, use flakes, and burned bones. Hackberry seeds from the Clovis level provide a C-14 date of 13.75 ky, while from Zone I, beneath the Clovis level, a hackberry date of 12.83 ky and a C-14 date from bone collagen of 10.825 ky were obtained. There is evidence that the Pedernales River may have flooded the cave in times past and mixed its contents. So all of the material in Stratum I could be from the Clovis occupation.

Table 1 Archaeological Evidences of Paleo-American Period Occupation

Name/ Location	Earliest Date(s)	Method(s)	Cultural Materials	Critics	Status
The Early Paleo-American Period Locations (28 ky ago and more)					
a. Calico Mts. Site, CA	202 ky	Geologic	Flakes/cores	Haynes and others	Questioned[a]
b. Texas Street, San Diego, CA	200 ky +	Geologic	Flakes/cores/hearths	Kreiger	Questioned[c]
c. Yuha Pinto Wash, CA	50 ky	Geologic/C-14	Choppers/scrapers	—	Uncertain[f]
d. Old Crow Basin, Yukon Terr, Canada	Mid-Pleistocene 27 ky	C-14 Geologic	Fractured bone "tools"	—	Questioned[c]
e. China Lake, CA	42.35 ky	Uranium Series	Flakes	MacNeish	Questioned[c]
f. El Bosque, Nicaragua	30 ky	C-14 and others	Flakes	—	Uncertain[f]
g. El Cedral, Mexico	33.3 ky	C-14	Scrapers/modified bones	—	Uncertain[f]
h. Santa Rosa Island, CA	40 ky	C-14	Mammoth bones/scraper	—	Uncertain[f]
i. Lewisville, TX	38 ky +	C-14	Hearths/stone tools—Clovis pt.	Heizer/Brooks/Haynes	Rejected
j. Tule Springs, NV	32 ky	C-14	Obsidian flake/biface chopper	Shutler and others	Rejected[d]
k. Tlapacoya, Mexico	24 ky	C-14 Geologic	Obsidian pt./hearths	Haynes	Questioned[d]
l. Pikimachay Cave, Peru	23 ky	C-14	Stone "tools"	Haynes, Lynch	Uncertain[c]
m. Valsequillo, Mexico	21.85 ky	C-14	Points/scrapers	—	Uncertain[c,d]
n. Meadowcroft, Rock-shelter, PA	19 ky	C-14	Tool kit/hearths	Haynes	Uncertain[b]
o. Timlin Site, NY	16 ky	C-14	Cores/flakes	—	Uncertain[f]
p. Selby, Dutton Sites, CO	15 ky	Geologic	Bone tools/flakes	—	Rejected[f,e,c]
q. Wilson Butte Cave, ID	14.55 ky	C-14	Biface/blade	Haynes/Aikens	Uncertain[d,e]
r. El Jobo Complex, Venezuela	14.2 ky	C-14	El Jobo pts.	Haynes/Lynch	Questioned[d]
s. Blue Fish Caves, Yukon Terr, Canada	14 ky	C-14	Flakes	—	Uncertain[f]
t. Monte Verde, Chile	14 ky	C-14	Flakes/modified bones	—	Uncertain[f]
u. The Levi Site, TX	13.75 ky	C-14	Flakes	—	Uncertain[f]
v. Fort Rock Cave, OR	13.2 ky	C-14	Pts./scrapers/milling stones	—	Possible[d]
w. Los Toldos, Argentina	12.65 ky	C-14	Scrapers/flakes	Lynch	Questioned[d,e]
x. Malakoff Heads, TX and Mexico	Pleistocene	Geologic	Modified boulders	Agogino	Uncertain[b]
The Late Paleo-American Period (12 ky ago)					
a. The Clovis Complex (dozens of locations throughout hemisphere)	12 ky	All methods	Fluted pts./complete tool kit	None	Demonstrated
b. The Folsom Complex	11 ky	All methods	Fluted pts./complete tool kit	None	Demonstrated
c. The Plano Complex (hundreds of locations)	9.5 ky	All methods	Large blades/complete tool kit	None	Demonstrated

[a] Poor dates, human presence questioned.
[b] Poor dates, human presence unquestioned.
[c] Good dates, human presence questioned.
[d] Good dates, human presence unquestioned, but association between dates and human presence questioned.
[e] Good dates, but cultural evidence too sparse to permit conclusions.
[f] Conclusions too recent to permit careful assessment or too little evidence so far published to permit careful evaluation.

Fort Rock Cave. Two projectile points, several scrapers and gravers, plus a milling stone and a fragment of a handstone or manno (common Archaic Period tools) were found resting on Pleistocene lake gravels in Fort Rock Cave, Oregon. Nearby, also on ancient lake gravels, was a concentration of charcoal from which a date of 13.2 ky was obtained. In question is the degree of association between the dated charcoal and the artifacts; corroborating evidence is needed.

Los Toldos. The stratified Los Toldos caves, located in southern Patagonia, Argentina, have been excavated since the early 1950s. A date from hearth charcoal of 12.65 ky appears to date an industry at the bottom of Cave 3, an industry that consists mostly of scrapers and flakes but that may include a unifacial point. Lynch believes the early date to be valid but the apparently associated artifacts to be too few in number to permit sound interpretation.

The Malakoff Heads. Five apparently modified boulders, ranging in weight from 31 to 135 pounds, have been recovered by various people at various times in south Texas and in nearby Mexico. None was found in situ by professional investigators. The possibility apparently exists that the first three found may have been in association with Pleistocene fauna in a terrace that dates from 200 ky ago to as recent as 5–7 ky. Although undatable, and as likely of Archaic as Paleo-American age, A.D. Krieger included them among his evidence of pre-Clovis Americans.

The Late Paleo-American Period (12–7.5 ky)

The Clovis Complex (12–11 ky). Evidences of human presence south of the retreating glacial masses are abundant and unambiguous beginning around 11.5 ky ago. Dozens of excavated sites in Canada, in the United States, and a few in Latin America testify to the presence of people hunting mammoths and other now extinct animals throughout the hemisphere at that time. They possessed a complex tool kit marked by a fluted, lanceolate stone projectile point that has come to be known as a Clovis point, a projectile point type that F. Bordes once labeled "the first American patent." At places such as Blackwater Draw, at Lehner and Naco, perhaps at Sandia Cave, and at many other locations, abundant Clovis fluted projectile points, scrapers, chopping tools, gravers, knives, and hammerstones, as well as fragments of bone tools provide testimony to

the existence of a technology and culture comparable in general contour to those known for Old World humans of the Upper Paleolithic.

C.V. Haynes and P.S. Martin, along with many other scholars, believe the progenitors of the Clovis adaptation to have come from Asia via Beringia. In Asia, their cultural antecedents may have been the Dyuktai Complex or, as Haynes believes more likely, the Mal'ta-Afontova, either of which possessed complex lithics, including bifacially flaked stone blades. They entered Beringia perhaps 20 ky ago in pursuit of game animals during a time when steppe-tundra united Siberia and Alaska across Beringia. As the steppe-tundra and the Pleistocene megafauna began to decline 15 ky or so ago, these ancient hunters were led further to the southeast away from Beringia until, ultimately, 12 ky or so ago, they passed south of the ice sheets through the MacKenzie Corridor and burst into the northern plains of North America. Here they would encounter abundant and relatively easy prey. A rapid spread and successful adaptation for the Clovis people is indicated by a date for a fluted point from Fell's Cave at the tip of South America of approximately 11 ky, only 0.5 ky after the earliest known date for Clovis to the north. In North America, from Borax Lake in California to the Shoop Site in Pennsylvania, a number of stratified sites containing Clovis material provide an abundant, if incomplete basis for reconstructing their ancient way of life, as C.V. Haynes and others have attempted.

The appearance of Clovis kill sites in the archaeological record is dramatic and relatively abrupt. It is as if humans and elephants suddenly confronted each other for the first time; the result of the confrontation was to be the extinction of this whale of the land by 11 ky, little more than 0.5–1 ky after the first known kill. Within 2 ky or so of their postulated arrival, the Clovis-descendent people witnessed, and perhaps precipitated, the extinction of 31 genera of animals; some 90 percent of the hemisphere's total of animals by body weight. Whatever its cause, as the "Pleistocene extinction" proceeded, new adaptations become evident in the archaeological record.

The Folsom Complex (11–9 ky). The Folsom Complex, primarily associated with the giant wide-horned bison (*Bison antiquus*), is characterized by a fluted point, slightly smaller than the typical Clovis, exhibiting a high degree of technical competence in its careful flaking around the deep channel bifacial flutes. In general, except for the difference in the projectile points, the Folsom tool kit closely resembles that of Clovis. Folsom sites tend to be larger than those of Clovis and, although originally defined in the high Plains to the east of the Rocky Mountains, a number of fluted point sites of approximately the same age are known from eastern North America as well (Bull Brook, MA; Debert, Nova Scotia; Port Mobil, NY; The Quad Site, VA; and others).

The Plano Adaptation (9.5–7.5 ky). As the retreat of the glaciers continued, and as the post-Pleistocene biotic community underwent change in the direction of its modern composition, regional Paleo-American adaptations become apparent. The diagnostic tool of the different Plano cultures continues to be large projectile points with regionally variable shapes, often lanceolot but never fluted. Stone-chipping technology remains excellent, tool kits complex, and sites large.

Shifts in climate and in the character of the faunal community forced upon these descendants of the earlier Paleo-Americans an ever more archaeologically apparent reliance upon plant food resources. As the Paleo-American epoch ends, and the Archaic Period begins, culture adaptations are detectable in the archaeological record that will still be practiced by the native American people of the sixteenth century, when Europeans begin to describe the pattern and variety of native American cultures.

Discussion

Americanist archaeology has faced a dilemma since the 1960s, when the tacitly accepted presence of humans in the Americas prior to the Clovis hunters was challenged by the questions and possible alternative answers offered by C.V. Haynes and P.S. Martin. Professional response to this dilemma has been bidirectional: (1) proponents of the pre-Clovis position have intensified their activities or, at least, their publication rates, and (2) critics of the pre-Clovis proponents have become more vocal and direct in rejection of data put forward as evidence. In the effort to identify the earliest Americans, the issues are becoming clearer than at any time since that of Hrdlička.

The controversy as to who and when were the first Americans has reached what Kuhn has called the "paradigm debate" state in the development of a science; a time when conflicting points of view, or paradigms, should be examined in the light of available data in order to develop lines of reasoning which will link data into bodies of evidence that support one of the contending points of view or "paradigms." If the notion of

paradigm can be overdone, it has useful applications in archaeology, a discipline that rarely has made explicit the assumptions or procedures that have led to the conclusions reached. But, as the "new archaeology," with its emphasis upon logical positivism, has come to dominate the field, examination of underlying paradigms has become more common.

It is possible to detect at least four paradigms, or points of view, being employed in the analyses and conclusions drawn from existing data on Early Man in the Americas.

Paradigm 1: Humans of a premodern *H. sapiens* or even *H. erectus* variety spread across Beringia and into North America more than 40 ky ago utilizing a simple percussion-flaked chopper/scraper stone technology.

A.L. Bryan, E.L. Davis, G.F. Carter, R. Gruhn, L. Leakey, H.L. Minshall, R.S. MacNeish, R.D. Simpson, and others (including most or all the reporters of work done at Old Crow Basin), who accept as valid Calico Mountain, Texas Street, the Yuha site, and any other data of purported Sangamonin age, employ this paradigm. It is by no means a new point of view. Quite the contrary. F.W. Putnam, in the last two decades of the nineteenth century, while Curator of the Peabody Museum, had a great interest in proving, as Boucher de Perthes had done for Europe, that humans had occupied the Americas during the Pleistocene. Belief by some in an early Pleistocene American paleolithic has continued since Putnam's time.

To accept Paradigm 1, it is necessary to work from the following assumptions: (1) early *H. sapiens* or earlier forms of the genus *Homo* entered the Americas; (2) while adaptively radiating into the Western Hemisphere, they lost the capacity or will to practice the systematic chipping of stone that would produce a recognizable tool kit; (3) they did not utilize caves; (4) they did not bury their dead; (5) they did not systematically use hearths, etc.

With the understanding of worldwide cultural evolution developed by anthropologists during the past half century, it is difficult to believe that an ancient American society and culture born of the Paleolithic of the Old World would lack its parents' most common archaeological evidence — stone tools. This is especially true in the light of archaeological research in China that has readily provided satisfactory evidence of human presence there for the past half million years or more.

It is a fact that some humans have employed relatively little rock in the face of its relative absence, as in the rainforests, but no such scarcity would afflict Beringians. Perhaps adaptive radiation into and across Beringia brought about cultural and social chaos of a kind we shall never understand. But if we may judge from known Paleo-arctic cultures, such as Akmak, with its skilled use of stone, it is clear that existence in arctic or subarctic ecological contexts does not mandate cessation of the use of stone as a raw material or diminution of the technical skill with which it is worked.

At present, there is little reason to employ Paradigm 1. Not a single datum exists that requires assumption of any of these parameters. As MacNeish remarked regarding purported 40 ky dates for mammoth bone, charcoal, and putative human tools on Santa Rosa Island:

> We seem to be coming close to getting some good dates on Early Man, but knowing exactly what his artifact assemblages were or how they fit into any stage or model eludes us for the most part.

If one must make the type of assumptions listed above (obviously without regard for the peaceful rest — wherever he may be — of William of Occam), then one has left behind concern for scientific parsimony and probability and entered another interpretative realm. Paradigm 1, despite its endurance through the years and notwithstanding the intellectual perseverance of its proponents, requires too many assumptions poorly supported by existing evidence and is, consequently, of little explanatory value.

Paradigm 2: Anatomically modern *H. sapiens* spread across Beringia from Asia and into the Americas during early or middle Wisconsin times, perhaps 30 ky or more ago but perhaps as recently as 15–20 ky; were possessed of a simple tool kit perhaps lacking lithic elements; and either died out or became ancestors of later hunters, including the Clovis people.

J.M. Adovasio, J.L. Bada, R. Berger, M.W. Childers, and P.C. Orr are some whose interpretations of their materials are based upon this second interpretative paradigm. Use of Paradigm 2 does not require the assumption of a premodern *sapiens* morphological type, so the absence of other than fully modern human bones in the Americas is not an embarrassment. But, otherwise, it requires many of the same assumptions as does Paradigm 1. Because nowhere in the Americas has a flaked stone tool kit of middle or upper Paleolithic quality been found that dates to the pre-Clovis time, some explanation of its absence must be made. This absence is a particu-

lar embarrassment because, in northeast Asia, the earliest Dyuktai sites (18 ky or older) provide bifacially worked oval knives, subprismatic pebble cores, Levallois tortoise cores, scrapers, burins, and other artifact types associated with abundant remains of mammoth, wooly rhinoceros, bison, and other large mammals — thus meeting evidentiary criteria for establishing the presence of humans there and then. Furthermore, Australia, apparently peopled for the first time 30 ky or more ago, provides adequate artifacts and associations to permit a clear definition of a human presence there as well.

The confidence of proponents of Paradigm 2 rests heavily upon acceptance of dates derived from techniques in which more conservative specialists have little confidence: AAR; C-14 testing of calcium carbonate or the apatite fraction, for example; or upon trust that once deposited in the ground, cultural materials will not move from the location and associations that obtained millennia ago. If AAR dates are wildly wrong, or if dates taken on bone apatite cannot be trusted, or if some archaeological deposits in places such as Pikimachay, Meadowcroft, and Wilson Butte Cave have undergone even slight mixing of strata, then support for either Paradigm 1 or 2 becomes very tenuous. In no case are the data sufficient to approximate the evidentiary requirements met by archaeological complexes of much greater age elsewhere in the world. Use of Paradigm 2 is based more upon faith than upon evidence.

Paradigm 3: Sometime after 20 ky but before 12 ky ago, humans, possessed of a tool kit characterized by large nonfluted projectile points distinctive from, earlier, and perhaps ancestral to the Clovis complex, came south from Beringia and peopled many parts of the Western Hemisphere.

Some assumptions utilized by those who would employ Paradigm 3 are: (1) 12 ky ago, some force, as yet unspecified, muddles the American archaeological record; (2) humans, as predators, had little noticeable effect upon the biotic community until joined or succeeded by the Clovis hunters 11.5 ky ago; (3) they did not bury their dead; (4) they did not make hearths; (5) they did not systematically use caves, etc.

Bryan (although he appears to prefer Paradigm 1) believes there exists a "stemmed point tradition," prior to as well as contemporaneous with the Clovis hunters, a tradition that, if he is correct, would validate this paradigm. In the stemmed-point tradition Bryan includes Mount Moriah points from Smith Creek Cave, Nevada; Taima-Taima; Bird's "fishtailed points" from

Patagonia; perhaps Lake Mohave stemmed points; Los Toldos; and others. But none of these so far has been found in contexts unambiguously of Middle Paleo-American age.

Humans must have entered Beringia by 12–20 ky ago at least; consequently, it would not be surprising to find areas south of the ice-sheets occupied by them during this time period as well. But, surprisingly, not a single site provides substantial, unequivocal evidence of such a presence. The sites to which Bryan alludes as possible representatives of a cultural tradition that precedes and is then contemporaneous with Clovis all provide either incomplete or controversial proof, at best. On the other hand, it is possible that all these sites are, in fact, later than Clovis. None possesses cultural, paleontological, or other attributes that force ascription of pre-Clovis dates.

Paleo-ecologists have pointed out that it is inconceivable that humans could be present in a habitat and not have a substantial and detectable impact upon the ecosystem. Although in a recent symposium a group of these specialists apparently accepted the presence of humans in Beringia and perhaps throughout the hemisphere by at least 35 ky ago, they, inconsistently, could point to no such evident impact upon the Western Hemisphere's ecosystems before 10–12 ky ago.

An enduring problem that may never be resolved for the period just preceding 12 ky ago is that which apparently intruded into the interpretation of the Dutton site (see above): If there is a Late Paleo-American occupation at a location, it is almost certain that, due to small animal or human activity, or natural soil movement, or other disruptions, some cultural material will drift downward into what might otherwise be sterile, noncultural levels, or older paleontological beds, or even into genuinely older cultural strata. It is unlikely that, given the inherent lack of precision of C-14 dating, the dawn of Clovis could ever be separated through use of it from a cultural stratum one or two thousand years older, particularly if the only major differences are temporal not cultural.

Paradigm 4: The first Americans south of the continental glaciers were the Clovis hunters, approximately 12 ky ago.

To accept and employ Paradigm 4, the following assumptions must be made: All putative earlier Paleo-American data are a result of either "background noise," which naturally exists in the ground; or faulty application of dating techniques; or faulty association of cultural materials with properly dated noncultural materials; or faulty identification of ecofacts as artifacts; or, perhaps, occasionally, excessive zeal on the part of some pre-Clovis partisans prepared to believe, however thin the evidence. All of the assumptions that underlie Paradigm 4 appear warranted and are being utilized by a growing number of Americanist archaeologists.

Conclusions

If Paradigm 4 is effective as an explanation of who and when were the first Americans, then (1) its application should constantly satisfy and agree with accepted tenets of scientific archaeology; (2) all new data should be explained within its assumptions; and (3) other appropriate lines of scientific reasoning, when applied to the same question, should reach the same conclusions. When any of these conditions are not met, the paradigm should be changed.

From the end of the nineteenth century, when natural science standards began to be applied to Americanist archaeology, it took approximately 30 years to demonstrate the reality of a Late Paleo-American cultural horizon. In the half century since, application of ever more rigorous and precise techniques and methods has resulted in the delineation of subsequent American prehistory concordant with that known from elsewhere in the world: Early foragers and hunters were followed by village-dwelling plant utilizers who, in their turn, were succeeded by urban, agricultural, "civilized," people. Success in solving the puzzle of American prehistory has rested directly upon the continued application of ever more rigorous techniques and methods in assessment of data. Today, although much of the content of native American prehistory remains to be learned, its general outline is well understood. There are no "Mysterious Moundbuilders" to be explained and, if "lost" cities may still be found, the pattern of urbanization in the prehistoric Americas is basically known. Archaeological fieldwork, wherever it is conducted in the Americas, employing universally recognized cannons of archaeological research, regularly brings further support to the general proposition. To date, scientific archaeology has not been able to demonstrate a pre-Clovis occupation of the Americas.

If an Early or Middle Paleo-American occupation is to take its place within the framework of existing scientific Americanist archaeology, then it is time to find answers to a number of specific questions: (1) If the hemisphere has been occupied for more than 12 ky, where are the cultural remains that worldwide archaeological knowledge would lead us to expect: stone tools and tool kits, skeletal material, living areas, etc.? (2) Where are the American equivalents to Old World Middle and Upper Paleolithic sites? Why are there not lower levels at such likely places as Ventana Cave, Danger Cave, the Koster Site, or ancient human remains at the La Brea Tar Pits? (3) Where are the early Beringian sites? (4) If present, why did Early or Middle Paleo-Americans not have some detectable impact upon the Pleistocene fauna? (5) Why, as new evidences of a pre-Clovis occupation of the Americas are offered by proponents, are older ones eliminated? (6) Why cannot the Early and Middle Paleo-American archaeological record be expected to meet the worldwide evidentiary standards of scientific archaeology? (7) If the evidence of pre-Clovis people in the Americas were to be present in the hemisphere, would not scientific archaeology, practiced with the great intensity that has characterized research in North America for the past half century, have found it by now?

Failure to provide convincing answers to any of these questions is further evidence of the utility of Paradigm 4: Clovis hunters were the first Americans.

18
Dating the First American

PAUL G. BAHN

"I climbed down the rope to the bottom of the shaft, 80 feet below, and then realised that bees were heading my way in a squadron. I hid behind some rocks, but they eventually found me, and I had to get out fast." Niède Guidon grimaces at the memory. "I certainly climbed up faster than I came down," she jokes, describing how she emerged from the chasm of Sansão, her head and arms enveloped in Brazil's extraordinarily aggressive "killer bees." Despite 200 stings on that occasion, and a long drive over dirt roads to the nearest hospital, she not only survived but continues to work in the cave, though now in protective clothing and headgear.

Killer bees are not the only hazard faced by this tough 58-year-old Brazilian archaeologist. Over the past 20 years she has carried out an amazing programme of work in Piauí, one of Brazil's poorest and most arid regions. In the course of this research, she has found herself at the centre of the fiercest debate in American archaeology today: when did people first enter the New World?

Guidon started by studying biology and natural sciences at the University of São Paulo; later she studied prehistory in France. In 1963 she was working in a museum at São Paulo when one day the mayor of the remote little town of São Raimundo Nonato came to the museum and showed her photographs of some rock art in his area of Piauí. The art depicted hunting scenes and acts of sex and violence. It was so different in style to the art with which Guidon was familiar, which was mostly geometric, that she resolved to investigate.

After a period of exile in France to escape the military dictatorship which took over Brazil in the 1960s, she visited São Raimundo Nonato in the 1970s. Over the next two decades, she continued to explore, survey, and excavate the area with a growing team of international assistants. Since her first archaeological explorations by mule or donkey, she has recorded 346 sites in the region, 280 of which contain rock art.

Guidon's sites are in a part of Piauí that is characterised by cactuses and soaring sandstone cliffs, with huge rock shelters hollowed into their bases. One of the largest shelters, known as Pedra Furada ("perforated rock," after a natural arch nearby), is profusely decorated from one end to the other with red, and sometimes white, paintings representing humans as dynamic little stick figures, along with large birds, and animals such as deer, armadillo, and capybara, the world's largest rodent. Here and there one can see rarer depictions such as a crab, or a tiny hunting scene.

From *New Scientist*, 20 July 1991, pp. 26–28. Copyright 1991 *New Scientist*. Reprinted with permission.

At other sites there are scenes of sex and violence. Studies of style, motif, and superimposition (where one layer of art rests upon another) led Guidon and her French colleague Annemarie Pessis to divide the region's art into three phases, but they had no idea how old the paintings might be.

So they started to excavate at the foot of the decorated panels in several sites, most notably at Pedra Furada in 1978. They explored successive occupation layers, rich in stone tools and charcoal from campfires. Unfortunately, all bones have totally disintegrated in the sandstone shelters. As she dug down, Guidon sent off charcoal samples from different layers to the Centre des Faibles Radioactivités in Gif-sur-Yvette, the foremost radiocarbon laboratory in France. The first results were not unusual: 6000 years old, even 12 000 years old. Soon, however, she became convinced there had been a mistake; the results were 23 000 and 29 000 years old. Since then, charcoal aged 32 000 years and even 48 500 years has been uncovered — all the dates emerging in a coherent sequence. The dates have been confirmed by the Beta Analytic Laboratory in Florida.

To understand Guidon's shock, bear in mind that for decades a fundamental dogma of all archaeology in the New World was that people first entered America no earlier than 12 000 years ago, at a time when the Ice Age had lowered sea levels sufficiently to expose an 85-kilometre land bridge across the Bering Strait, linking Siberia and Alaska. This theory goes back to the 1930s when Edgar Howard and John Cotter of the University Museum in Philadelphia discovered long stone projectile points near Clovis in New Mexico. These Clovis points are finely flaked spear points and were used to kill prehistoric big game such as bison and mammoth. When radiocarbon dating became established as an archaeological tool, in the 1950s, tests revealed that the spear points were about 12 000 years old. The Clovis hunters were accepted by most archaeologists as the first Americans.

Claims for earlier human occupation of the New World have surfaced sporadically ever since. Even Louis Leakey, famous for his work on early humans in East Africa, declared that California had evidence for occupation about 200 000 years ago. Most archaeologists, however, believe that the alleged stone tools at his site in the Calico Hills are "geofacts," that is, stone shaped by natural processes. Only one of the claims advanced has stood up to intense scientific scrutiny.

Scholars Divided

In the 1970s, James Adovasio of the University of Pittsburgh carried out a series of impeccable excavations in the rock shelter of Meadowcroft in Pennsylvania. He produced more than 50 coherent radiocarbon dates stretching back to 14 500 years ago. This is older than the official start of Clovis — though not enormously so in archaeological terms — making Meadowcroft the earliest definite site of occupation in North America so far. Since people would have had to cross North America to reach the south, so the argument goes, it follows that people could not possibly have settled in South America before this date. Yet Guidon's Brazilian evidence seems to indicate otherwise.

When Guidon, after waiting to amass more dates, finally published her claims in *Nature* in 1986 (vol. 321, p. 769), there were reverberations throughout the archaeological world. Scholars immediately divided into three camps: some longtime supporters of pre-Clovis occupation of the New World, such as Alan Bryan of the University of Alberta and Robson Bonnichsen of the University of Maine, were perfectly willing to accept her results; most archaeologists advised caution while awaiting fuller publication; and some expressed the gravest doubts about her data. It is the last group, particularly Thomas Lynch of Cornell University, which has tended to make its voice heard most loudly, although none of Guidon's most vociferous critics has been to see her evidence at first hand. Yet she is not possessive about the sites of her finds, and is eager for others to come and investigate — even to dig their own sites in the region.

Radiocarbon dates from a different South American site, Monte Verde in Chile, have added fuel to the debate. Tom Dillehay of the University of Kentucky started to excavate at Monte Verde in 1977. He found charcoal and wood that date to about 13 000 years ago. Even more remarkable, he uncovered charred wood that has been dated to about 33 000 years ago. Dillehay now says that he has "unequivocal" evidence that a flake and core (a lump of stone from which flakes have been removed), dating from about 33 000 years ago, were made by humans (*American Antiquity*, vol. 56, p. 333).

Monte Verde is a waterlogged site, which means that it is excellent for preserving organic materials that normally decompose. As he excavated, Dillehay also uncovered pieces of worked wood (probably used as digging sticks), wooden mortars, and wooden spear tips. He also found the remains of wooden hut foundations and evidence of plants that were probably used for food and medicine. All this suggests that while the Clovis community specialised in big-game hunting with sophisticated stone points, the people here lived by foraging, in particular for plant foods. Dillehay also discovered crude flaked tools, suggesting that the Monte Verde community used stone tools with little or no deliberate shaping.

Guidon's claims tend to be taken less seriously than those from the Chilean site. This is caused, in part, by her lack of publication (Dillehay's first monograph, published by the Smithsonian Institution in Washington, DC, has already appeared), but it is hard not to suspect that her gender and nationality may also be significant factors in this attitude.

Guidon is an archaeologist with a solid training in geology. She is contemptuous of critics who claim that her site's layers are disturbed by water action, and that her charcoal is natural rather than produced by people. However, her main evidence, the 12 000 stone implements found at Pedra Furada, is ambiguous. The upper layers of the site, dating to 10 000 years ago or less, contain clearly worked tools made of a flint brought from 16 kilometres away. But in the lower levels, the contentious ones, there are only quartz and quartzite pebbles, which eroded out of the cliff tops above. Why didn't the earlier occupants seek out and exploit the flint used by the more recent people? (In the Old World, people were using flint hundreds of thousands of years ago.) Most of the early "pebble tools" could have been produced by natural breakage. Guidon's critics, therefore, dismiss all her early material.

Red Figures on the Walls

But Guidon has uncovered other evidence. There are a few pieces from her most ancient layers, 5 metres down, which were almost certainly produced by people more than 30 000 years ago, according to Hansjürgen Müller-Beck of Tübingen University, a leading expert in Ice Age studies, who visited the site last year. Pedra Furada has also yielded 110 "campfires," concentrations of charcoal within crude arrangements of stones, which are difficult to explain away. Guidon has made similar finds of charcoal and tools, with similar dates, at other shelters in the region showing that Pedra Furada is not a freak site. At Sitio do Meio, for example, charcoal from a

hearth was dated to about 14 000 years ago. And charcoal taken from Caldeirao dos Rodrigues was found to date from about 18 000 years ago.

There is also the matter of rock paintings. Pieces of the sandstone walls constantly flake off and fall, even today. At Pedra Furada, some of the pieces which fell in ancient times still have painted figures on them. So dating the layer onto which they fell provides a minimum age for the art. Pedra Furada has one slab with a little red human figure from a layer which dates from at least 10 000 or 12 000 years ago. A slab from a lower level, dating from 17 000 years ago, bears two red lines which are very probably from a painted figure.

Most amazing of all is an excavation at a rock shelter called Perma where, as the occupation layers were stripped away, red figures were exposed on the walls of the shelter; they had survived burial for thousands of years. Dates from the layers that masked them indicate that they too must have been made at least 12 000 years ago. They match those of Pedra Furada in style, and constitute the oldest known paintings in America.

It now seems likely that America's first settlers came down the coast from Siberia in boats, rather than across the land bridge and through an ice-free corridor in Canada. Recent work in northern Australia indicates that this voyage would have posed few problems even as far back as 61 000 years ago.

Last year, Richard Roberts of the University of Wollongong, together with Rhys Jones and M. Smith of the Australian National University, working at a site called Malakunanja II in the Northern Territory, dated some sandy deposits associated with stone tools. They used thermoluminescence dating to find the age of the deposits, a technique which gauges the age of sediments by measuring the quantity of light released when minerals are heated. The dates obtained suggested that people first entered Australia 45 000 or even 61 000 years ago. Since the continent has not been joined to Southeast Asia by a land bridge at any time during the past 3 million years, the shortest journey would have entailed eight sea voyages, seven of them about 32 kilometres long, and the final lap to Australia at least 88 kilometres. Clearly, people at that time were already competent seafarers and possessed sturdy craft. Their traces in North America were probably limited to the immediate coastal area, and would have been drowned by the subsequent rise in sea level at the end of the Ice Age, about 10 000 years ago.

There is a slight chance that evidence may emerge in the north to support Guidon's claims. In a small cave on a military reservation in New Mexico's Chihuahua desert, Richard "Scotty" MacNeish, an American archaeologist, claims to be uncovering remains which might rival Pedra Furada in antiquity. MacNeish is a former bush pilot who studied the origins of agriculture and maize cultivation in the Tehuacán Valley in Mexico in the 1960s. He has been excavating at Pendejo cave, whose unfortunate name is a Spanish word for the male member, and has come across layers containing ash, bones of extinct animals, and stone tools. He also claims to have found a clay-lined hearth.

MacNeish sent samples of charcoal to the University of California at Riverside and bone to the Lawrence Livermore Laboratory to be dated. The lowest levels, well over 24 000 years old according to the first radiocarbon dates, include many pieces of stone from the cave roof. While most, if not all, of these pieces are geofacts, MacNeish is convinced that some were brought in from outside or shaped by human hand. Robson Bonnichsen, who has visited the site, has expressed cautious interest in one or two pieces. MacNeish himself believes that his new site counters all previous objections of critics, but the initial reaction among more conservative archaeologists is that they have heard this many times before, and sometimes from this same excavator.

MacNeish continues with his excavation, and his site — being far more accessible than Guidon's — will be visited and assessed by the most vehement critics. It remains to be seen whether Pendejo will prove valid, and become the site that finally breaks the "Pre-Clovis barrier" in North America. In the meantime, Brazil is where the dates come from.

19
The Lost Civilization of the Maya

T. PATRICK CULBERT

As soon as the facts of the Maya collapse became evident, archaeologists were attracted to the problem and began to suggest reasons for it. The reasons advanced fall into several different categories. The first category may be called catastrophic, since it includes sudden, natural disasters that were beyond the control of Maya culture. Among catastrophes suggested are earthquakes, climatic change, epidemics, and hurricanes. Earthquakes can be rejected as a likely cause, for there is no geological reason to believe that they have ever been severe in the Maya lowlands. Climatic change, disease, and hurricanes are still considered possible factors in the collapse of the system. A second major class of reasons may be termed ecological. Although varying in details, all ecological explanations share the idea that the Maya overpopulated and overfarmed their limited rain forest environment, with the result that their subsistence system failed. The thesis of overpopulation seems well justified, and subsistence failure remains a strong theme in present ideas about the collapse.

I will term the final class of explanations "social," since such explanations involve interaction within the social system rather than interaction between man and nature. The present revolt theory of J. Eric Thompson advances the idea that an increasingly burdensome exploitation of the lower class led to outright rebellion and destruction of the elite levels of society. Invasion hypotheses would also be social explanations, since they attempt to explain the collapse as a result of conflict between the Maya and people outside the lowlands. Civil war hypotheses, based on the assumption that the Maya led to their own collapse by fighting among themselves, are similar. Other social explanations are trade hypotheses that suggest that the Maya collapse was triggered by a breakdown of long-distance trading systems. These explanations can, of course, be combined in a variety of ways, and there has been a tendency through time to move from single-cause theories to theories of a domino sort, in which a starting cause is seen as leading to a whole series of reactions that together resulted in the collapse.

For more than two generations archaeologists, in their attempts to understand the Maya collapse, based their efforts on a search for possible causes. A particular case would be advanced — invasion, for example — and argument would follow about whether or not the cause had occurred. Since data were usually not good enough to prove that the cause had or had not happened, or whether, if it had happened, it had

Excerpted from T. Patrick Culbert, *The Lost Civilization: The Story of the Classic Maya*, pp. 111–17. Copyright © 1974 T. Patrick Culbert. Reprinted with the permission of HarperCollins Publishers.

preceded or followed the collapse, no real solutions could be achieved. In fact, articles about the collapse written in the late 1960s included almost nothing (except additional facts) that was not present in articles from the 1930s.

This was the context in which a group of specialists agreed in 1970 to meet at the School of American Research for a seminar specifically devoted to the problem of the Maya collapse. This seminar was a turning point in my own thinking and led to my approaching the problem in ways that are reflected throughout this book [*The Lost Civilization* (1974)]. It was moreover, I feel, a milestone for Maya studies as a whole. The key to the formulation that resulted was the realization that no explanation of the collapse of a social system can be achieved without a clear understanding of the way the system operated. This led us to reexamine Classic Maya culture and to challenge many previously held ideas about the Maya. The eventual model of the collapse that we achieved concentrates less upon "causes" like those listed above and more upon the stresses that were inherent in the very fabric of Late Classic Maya society.

In a summary article that draws together the ideas of all the participants of the Maya Collapse Seminar, Gordon R. Willey and Demitri B. Shimkin advance the idea that Late Classic Maya society was subject to a series of internal stresses that could only be worsened by a continuation of the very trends that had made the society successful. Most of these stresses have been discussed in previous chapters, but they must be brought together again to emphasize the complex ways in which they are interrelated.

Population was rising rapidly during the Maya Late Classic and would have increased demands for all commodities, but it would at the same time have supplied an increasing labor force. Since nutritional levels and sanitation — which can relate to checks on population growth — would have been better for the elite class than for commoners, it is not unlikely that elite levels of society were growing even more rapidly than lower levels.

Agricultural production would have been a point of stress at high population densities. Even if the Maya were still capable of expanding production by some of the means discussed in Chapter 4, such expansion must have been increasingly demanding in terms of the amount of labor it consumed. In addition, agriculture probably faced situations in which some of the techniques available for short-term expansion, such as

decreasing the fallow cycle, may have presented risks of long-term deterioration of farming lands.

The *ability to respond to subsistence emergencies* would have been overtaxed by the stresses mentioned above. Even in relatively tolerant climates, crop losses occur from time to time and must be countered if disaster is to be avoided. Unless enough reserve food is stored locally to make up for temporary deficits, importation, which involves problems in trade and transportation, becomes necessary. High population and stress in the agricultural system would increase both the frequency and the magnitude of agricultural emergencies, which would then consume already critical wealth and manpower supplies as well as increasing the competition between political units.

Malnutrition and *disease* were additional stress factors for the Maya. Malnutrition could result from stresses in the agricultural system that decreased either total food supply or the quantity of key dietary components such as protein. Disease was an ever-present possibility; many diseases, such as intestinal troubles of either bacterial or parasitic origin, were probably endemic in the Maya population. Malnutrition, if it occurred, could have raised the rates and severity of endemic diseases from levels quite acceptable for continued population survival to levels that would contribute to decline. Both malnutrition and disease would have the effect of reducing the labor output, thus potentially feeding the problem of an increasing shortage of labor back to the already stressed and labor-dependent agricultural system.

Competition between political units would increase as a result of increased population densities and consequent shortages of land and other resources. If competition took the form of warfare, additional stresses on all units would result, although a victorious power might temporarily improve its position at the expense of vanquished units. A more important, if more subtle, sort of competition was peaceful competition between centers for wealth and status (and associated economic advantages), which they would seek to achieve by lavish ceremonial displays, including the construction of even larger ceremonial centers. That investment in such competition was disastrously wasteful of manpower and resources and yielded no tangible returns may seem obvious to us, but there is no reason to think that the Maya so regarded it. Consumption in ceremonialism was part of a system that had worked well for many centuries.

Centers that had excelled ceremonially had been rewarded by status and power and indirect benefits that contributed to their well-being. To expect a centuries-old system with demonstrated advantages to be dumped at a moment of stress would show little understanding of human conservatism or of the self-serving demands of power groups that become associated with any large system.

Increased investment in the elite levels of society would have been demanded at the same time that there were stresses at all levels. The fact that the elite class probably grew more rapidly than lower classes would have necessitated larger investments simply to maintain the *status quo*. Adding to this, increasing needs for competition among centers and expanding emergency facilities would have resulted in a rapid escalation of demands upon those who supported the elite. Since the principal commodity that the lower classes have to contribute is labor (whether expended in food production, crafts, or military service), the primary burden would have fallen upon manpower supplies that were already under stress from other directions.

Management capabilities of the directorial class of Maya society must have been severely stressed. Every increment of expansion in the population and in the economic system would have added to the tasks of record keeping, tax collection, and transmission and enforcement of management directives. There is no indication that Maya society attempted any major innovations in its managerial system, and it may have tried to get by with methods suited only for a much smaller society.

The foregoing stress system is such that a difficulty in one part of the interaction network can easily spread to cause difficulties in other parts, which then feed back to increase the problem. Once this interconnection is obvious, the question of cause becomes less interesting. Pressure or a minor crisis at any of a number of sensitive points could set the entire cycle in operation, and it is far more important to understand the way in which the system reacted than to search for the starting point of the reaction. In a sense, the reasons for the Maya collapse are inherent in the system and are the same reasons that for many centuries led to growth and success.

The final touch to an understanding of the Classic Maya downfall can be added by turning to concepts from general systems theory. Systems theory is a field that attempts to comprehend the properties of complex systems by stressing the *interrelationships* between parts rather than by the more common practice of analyzing parts in isolation.

Complex systems are of many kinds. Some are extremely stable and contain sets of regulatory (deviation-counteracting) mechanisms that, by acting like thermostats in a heating system, keep variables such as population, economics, and so on, close to steady values. Other systems are growth systems, in which parts are connected by growth (deviation-amplifying) loops in which an increase in one part causes an increase in a second part, which feeds back to cause further increase in the first part, and so on *ad infinitum*.

The continual expansion of the Maya — in population, in size and number of sites, and in complexity — shows all the characteristics of a growth system. So far so good; this concept may help us to understand Maya development up to the time of the Late Classic, but what does it have to do with the collapse? To clarify this part of the problem, it is necessary to introduce another property of growth systems — the overshoot mode. No system can grow indefinitely, since if it did, it would eventually absorb all the energy and matter in the universe. Consequently, growing systems meet one of two fates. Some reach equilibrium; growth slows and eventually ceases, and the system becomes a stable system in which further change is minimal. Other systems, rather than achieving equilibrium, outgrow their resources and "overshoot." When this happens, many of the same cycles that caused growth reverse themselves and the system declines. A simple example may help to illustrate the concept. Consider the expansion of a city into a new area. People begin to move into the area and soon, because of the population, businesses and industries are attracted. Jobs from business and industry attract more people, who attract more business and so on. Eventually, however, as the area becomes older and more crowded, some people (usually well-to-do members of the community) begin to move out to other new areas. With loss of some wealth, businesses may begin to close or move elsewhere, further weakening the economic and population base, and the whole cycle may accelerate in the new (and opposite) direction. This is a case of overshoot, and the result can be downward revision to a point at which growth may start over again.

I feel that the Maya collapse is an exemplary case of overshoot by a culture that had expanded too rapidly and had used its resources recklessly in an environment that demanded careful techniques of conservation. The Maya outran their resource base, not only in terms of farming capabilities, but also in terms of organizational capabilities, the ability to distribute goods, and the ability to use manpower efficiently. Growth cycles reversed, and the resource base was so badly overstrained that the cycle of decline for the Maya could not be stopped, short of the final resting point of near depopulation. The ravaged land offered little potential for repopulation, and the rain forest home of the Maya still remains an unpopulated wilderness with only the silent remains of the vast temple centers to remind the visitor of its once great past.

Are the Maya simply an historical curiosity of concern only to those with an antiquarian passion for the strange and long-forgotten? A few years ago even many of those involved in Maya studies might have agreed that such was the case. But if the analysis that the Maya were victims of overshoot in a growth cycle is correct, their relevance to the present may be far greater. Recently a group of scientists from the Club of Rome, an informal organization of experts concerned with the future environment of our planet, simulated the future of the world by computer techniques. The results reported in *The Limits to Growth* are sobering indeed. The near future, like the recent past, inevitably holds unprecedented world population growth and economic expansion as well as rapidly accelerating use of natural resources and generation of the pollutants associated with technology. Then the skyrocketing curves of growth level off and begin to turn downward, at first slowly and then in an ever-accelerating cycle of decline that stabilizes only after it has reached very low levels. The computer curves are easy to interpret but hard to accept. If they are correct, a frightening percentage of the world's population faces extinction in the next few centuries. There is no guarantee, of course, that the computer projections are correct and many reputable scientists have raised objections about the data and methods involved. Worldwide data are extremely difficult to assemble with any pretense at accuracy; computer simulations demand a series of shaky assumptions; it is next to impossible to make allowance in projections for possible breakthroughs in technology. We can certainly argue about the accuracy of projections about the future, but we ignore them only at our peril.

At this point, we can close the circle to the Maya once again. The curves that we could estimate for the Maya rise and decline would look very much like the Club of Rome's computer simulations of the modern world. If we ourselves stand at the edge of a precipice — our entire world endangered by the possibility of a global overshoot — can we say any longer that the fact that the Maya overpopulated, overexploited their environment, and disappeared from the earth bears no relationship to modern problems? Instead, should we not ask whether the knowledge and information we can glean from a study of the Maya failure can be applied to our own situation? Given an understanding of the forces that destroyed earlier civilizations, can we not look at ourselves and our society and marshal our talents and energies in a determined effort to avoid a world collapse — a collapse from which there might be no return for the human race?

Three ceremonial centers of the Maya. Ceremonial centers were important marketplaces and political forums; usually, many houses, or even cities, surrounded them.

Temple of the Inscriptions at Palenque, Chiapas. This building has become a center of attention in recent years in connection with major advances in Maya glyph identification and decipherment. In 1952, Alberto Ruz l'Huillier discovered a funerary crypt at the base of the pyramid. It contained the remains of Lord Shield Pacal, who ruled Palenque from 615 A.D. to 683 A.D. The construction of the Temple of the Inscriptions was probably begun in 672 A.D. and completed in 682 A.D. Source: Reproduced with the permission of Stan Freer.

Overview of the Ball Court, Pyramid of the Magician, and nunnery quadrangle at Uxmal, all built at different times. The Pyramid of the Magician consists of five temples, constructed one over the other. The oldest is dated at 590 A.D. (±50). The Ball Court dates to 649 A.D., according to glyphs inscribed on the ball rings. Uxmal was the major site in the Puuc zone of the Maya, and exhibits some of the finest masonry in the Maya region. Source: Reproduced with the permission of Stan Freer.

The Caracol (observatory) in the foreground and the Castillo (castle) in the central ground. These buildings, found at Chichén Itzá, were completed in the Late Maya Classic stage, between 600 A.D. and 900 A.D. The circular tower is 14.4 m (48 ft.) high. The Caracol was built to align with the vernal equinox on March 21, as well as with the setting of the moon at its greatest southern and northern declinations. Like the Caracol, the Castillo has a long history at Chichén Itzá and reflects both Maya and Mexican cultures. Source: Reproduced with the permission of Stan Freer.

20
Rethinking the Quincentennial: Consequences for Past and Present

ALISON WYLIE

The events marked by the Quincentennial have been called by many names: "a collision of worlds" (the title of a special 1991 issue of *Newsweek*); an "encounter"; an "invasion," followed by a "half millennium of land-grabs and one-cent treaty sales"; a disaster waiting to happen as land and resource and market pressures in the so-called Old World set in motion 500 years of colonial adventurism in the Americas characterized by the mass enslavement, deportation, displacement, and exploitation of indigenous populations not only in the Americas but in Africa and Asia as well; and, notoriously, the "discovery" of a vast, "virginal" continent waiting to be civilized. Living as I have this past year in Berkeley — recently declared a Columbus-free zone — I have been somewhat insulated from this last sort of Quincentennial name-calling. Last Fall the city sponsored various "pre-invasion" parties, and on October 12, 1992, Berkeley celebrated "Indigenous Peoples' Day," in anticipation of 1993, which the United Nations has declared the "Year of the Indigenous People." A different kind of celebration, this — one that marks "the miracle of survival of those remaining Native people, religions, cultures, languages, medicines, and values," and that "memorialised those who did not survive the invasion of 1492," to borrow Suzan Harjo's words. This sort of reaction to the Quincentennial is by no means the preserve of so-called special-interest groups; it is shared by such organizations as the National Council of Churches, and a wide range of human-itarian groups and human-rights activists, as well as by virtually all of the First Nations represented among the two million Native Americans living in the United States today.

There are still, of course, plenty of vocal advocates of the notion that Columbian contact has largely benefited "mankind," that it has resulted in progressive developments that were well worth the price they exacted. In this vein Raymond Sokolov, a historian of foodways, counters commentators like Harjo, insisting that the "entirely new world" forged in North America (which he describes as a "mammoth achieve-ment" of the "American way") is now the acknowledged center of gravity in world politics. The tables have been turned on former coloniz-ers; "the rest of the world looks to us for ideas and fashions," which are a unique blend of the cultures that came into sustained contact after 1492. Sokolov urges us to "raise a glass — of bourbon, rum, or Coke — and wish [ourselves] a happy 500th." I am sure any of you who have been drawn into the Quincentennial activities of

From *American Antiquity*, Vol. 57, No. 4, 1992, pp. 591–94. Reprinted with the permission of the Society for American Archaeology. (Bibliographic documentation contained in the original text is omitted here. Interested readers should consult the original publication.)

the past year share my sense of having stumbled into a minefield.

The fact is, however, that archaeologists working in the Americas — especially archaeologists working on late prehistoric and historic periods — are implicated in the negotiation of this minefield whether they want to be or not. Archaeology is intimately involved in the construction of "authoritative" stories about this Columbian past and, more to the point, archaeological evidence and interpretation have been used to legitimate the whole range of cultural aspirations and political and economic agendas that have been articulated in response to the Quincentennial.

Certainly there is no shortage of cases in which archaeology has both embodied racist and nationalist agendas and been used to articulate and promote them; B.G. Trigger's important paper, "Archaeology and the Image of the American Indian" (1980), demonstrates how profoundly and unreflectively Eurocentric and racist the broad sweep of archaeological thinking has been in and about North America. And yet, as is often said, archaeology has enormous potential to counter these "mythologies" (as D.H. Thomas refers to them). Indeed, it is inescapable that the archaeological record — and the results of archaeological investigation and interpretation of this record — are the only bases we have for understanding many of the cultures that European conquistadors and explorers encountered at contact, given how profoundly contact disrupted indigenous oral traditions, and it is our only hope for understanding the vast majority of populations that have been enmeshed in the processes of colonization that followed, given the extraordinarily limited reach of documentary history where they are concerned. As we break the fascination with monuments and art — as we explore the democratizing power of archaeology conceived as a science of garbage — this critical potential has begun to be realized. Archaeology does have the capacity to counter what many repudiate as revisionist strategies, whereby history is crafted in such a way that (intentionally or not) it serves to legitimate "the bloodshed and destruction ... to deny that genocide that was committed ... and to revive policies of assimilation." Indeed, as R. Handsman has argued, archaeology has sometimes proven to be a very effective tool in unmasking and dislodging the "colonialist discourse of invisibility" that has persisted since contact (cf. Williams's views on the analysis of ethnogenesis [in *American Antiquity* 57, no. 4 (1992)]). And, increasingly, it

bears witness to powerful and persistent strategies of resistance by which Native Americans and African Americans actively manipulated the systems of oppression and exploitation to which they were subjected, a dimension of the legacy of contact that has been systematically obscured in ways Jalil Sued-Badillo ... [discusses] with reference to the Caribbean [in the same issue of *American Antiquity* as noted above].

Two things follow from this entanglement of archaeology in the very construction — the perpetuation — of Columbian consequences today. The first is that when you deal with such a complex of plural, fractured subject positions as are represented in virtually any component of the Columbian legacy, you cannot reasonably expect simple, one-dimensional models — such as are the staple of racist and nationalist ideologies — to be credible. For empirical and conceptual, as well as political reasons, old ideals of seeking a single, comprehensive, "true" account of the past must give way to something like the cubist approach urged by D.H. Thomas in his introductions to Volumes 1 and 3 of *Columbian Consequences* (1989, 1991). This point arises directly from reflection on the sheer diversity of perspectives represented among accounts of the course and consequence of contact that have been based on archaeological evidence; as contributions to the *Columbian Consequences* volumes make clear, systematic, scientific methods of inquiry cannot be counted on to deliver a single, comprehensive, uniquely authoritative account of the past. In some cases new and divergent perspectives stand as a corrective to established views. They decisively undermine assumptions and claims that were previously thought plausible; they prove that the "Image of the American Indian" projected by many long-entrenched archaeological interpretations is simply wrong — empirically unsustainable — judged in terms internal to the disciplines that produced it. But in a good many other cases the alternatives reflect divergent perspectives that are not straightforwardly reducible to, or displaced by, one another. Thomas urges a "cubist" approach that resists the pressure to construct "single-point version[s] of the 'truth' — the way it really was" and endorses a strategy of viewing "events of the past from multiple directions simultaneously," through the "prism of the intricate [and radically diverse] lifeways that came into conflict," recognizing that this will necessarily yield "not one, but multiple histories." I would argue that this is by no means an endorsement of a facile constructivism, but that is another issue. The relevant point here is simply that a much wider range of possibilities, of "versions," must be taken into account when considering the circumstances and consequences of contact. It must be recognized that any contestation of the Eurocentrism and racism of Quincentennial "celebrations" also initiates what R. Handsman has described as "a relentless and necessary critique of the disciplines and institutions normally thought to be supportive and protective of the heritages of native people."

This brings me to the second, and central, point that frames the program of the 1992 Plenary Session. It is that nothing could make more visible, more inescapable, the profoundly *political* nature of archaeological practice than the role it has played in Quincentennial reconstructions. There is no avoiding the fact that, however esoteric and inaccessible you may strive to make it, archaeological discourse — written and oral — does do work in the world. What the Quincentennial throws into relief is the need for archaeologists to take responsibility for the work their research does in a world that is structured by classist, racist, and sexist politics. This is not a new theme, nor does it appear only in the work of self-identified "critical" and theoretical archaeologists.[1] One of the strongest and most challenging statements I know is due to William Y. Adams, writing on "Science and Ethics in Rescue Archaeology" most of a decade ago. He objects that, while archaeologists have often been clear about their responsibility to science and their own discipline, "they do not seem to be aware that they have any other responsibilities": they betray "a moral myopia not much different from that of the nineteenth century treasure-seeker ... both engaged in excavation — which is to say, destruction — of archaeological sites for narrowly defined objectives of their own, disregarding any interest which other scholars, or the lay public, may have had in the same sites." Coming to terms with this myopia — recognizing and substantially changing it — is exactly the challenge that has crystallized in the issues to do with repatriation/reburial and First Nations' interests in Native heritage taken up [in *American Antiquity* 57, no. 4 (1992)] by Vine Deloria. What the

Quincentennial makes clear, in the cacophony of voices that contest and celebrate it, is just how complex the responsibility is that archaeologists bear at this juncture: as W.Y. Adams observes, archaeologists do, "in truth, [have] many publics with many interests, and most of them are as legitimate as ours." This, in turn, underlines the urgent need to accelerate the process of engaging these publics, not so much with the aim of educating them about archaeology as with that of "educat[ing] ourselves" about the *consequences* that flow from the practice of archaeology in the "postcolonial" contexts of all of our lives.

It is to be hoped that the process of "rethinking the Quincentennial," which was marked by the 1992 Plenary Session, will have profound consequences for future practice; it is, indeed, [as Suzan Harjo put it,] "time to begin an era of respect and rediscovery, to find a new world beyond 1992." Where the specifically *archaeological* prospects for such an era are concerned, the papers [published in *American Antiquity* 57, no. 4 (1992)] by Vine Deloria, Jalil Sued-Badillo, and Brackette F. Williams provide rich food for thought in the form of insights both about presuppositions that must yet be critically scrutinized and about constructive possibilities for opening dialogue, finding common cause, and building an archaeology that actively engages the politics of its practice.

Notes

This paper was originally presented as one of two introductory statements (the other by David Hurst Thomas) at the Plenary Session of the 57th Annual Meeting of the Society for American Archaeology (Pittsburgh, April 9, 1992). The Plenary Session — "Rethinking the Quincentennial: Consequences for Past and Present" — also included presentations by Jalil Sued-Badillo, Vine Deloria, and Russell G. Handsman.

1. Where North American archaeology is concerned, I have in mind the sort of arguments developed in the literature of "critical" archaeology, e.g., M.P. Leone and R.W. Preucel's discussion of "Archaeology in a Democratic Society" (1992), in which they argue that, "when archaeology is cited in a public context, one of its purposes is to legitimize a dominant position ... [often by masking or glossing over the actual conditions of existence]"; R. Handsman's insistence that "archaeologists must be socially responsible both for the effects that their work has on the lives and heritage of Native Americans and for what their actions and writings say to others"; and Potter's critique of "plantation archaeology," among many others.

21
Pixel Archeology

NEIL McALEER

In the foothills of Mount Hebron, midway between the Gaza Strip and the Dead Sea, stands a prominent seven-acre mound called Tell Halif. The region is on the edge of a desert; for most of the year the only moisture comes from fog drifting inland from the Mediterranean. Yet Tell Halif, as archeologist Joe Seger of Mississippi State University has found, has been inhabited on and off for more than 5,000 years. Some scholars think it was the biblical city of Ziklag, where David lived after he was cast out by Saul and before he became king of Israel.

Seger and his colleagues have been excavating Tell Halif for more than a decade. Their work, like most archeology, is incredibly painstaking. They must dig without knowing whether they will find something, and slowly enough that if they *do* find something, they won't destroy it. Last July, however, the researchers at Tell Halif began using a tool that promises to save them considerable time and trouble. It's a kind of archeologist's divining rod: microwave radar that can "see" underground.

With the new tool, it took Seger's team only a few days to hit pay dirt. The radar signal showed a strong echo above one spot in a large unexcavated area of the site, indicating the presence of an underground object that was a good reflector of microwaves. Most members of the team were reluctant to start digging — no one had expected to find anything in that part of the tell — but Jim Doolittle, a specialist from the U.S. Soil Conservation Service who was operating the instrument, stuck to his guns because, he recalls, "the signature was so strong and distinct."

Finally they brought in the picks and hoes, and, sure enough, about two feet down, the diggers found something: a large rock. The skeptics crowed, and professional "discussions" broke out again. But then, says Doolittle, "just as we were looking at the stone, some dirt started falling in beneath it. My heart started beating like crazy. There was a shaft below!"

Doolittle and the others stuck a ladder into the shaft and climbed down about 12 feet. "I was petrified," he recalls. "It was spooky, very dark." The bottom of the shaft opened onto a large, dusty chamber, 30 feet long by 15 feet wide by 11 feet high, cut out of the soft limestone bedrock. The walls were coated with several layers of limestone plaster. The chamber was empty; it was clearly not a tomb. It turned out to be a water cistern built 2,500 to 3,000 years ago, around the time of King David, by farmers who had to store the life-giving water of the rainy season for use in the long dry months.

Ground-penetrating radar, as the system used at Tell Halif is called, is not new; it was first employed by the Army in Vietnam to find enemy hideouts and mines. Nor is "remote sensing" in its broadest sense a new technique in archeology. Aerial photographs of Stonehenge were taken from a balloon as long ago as 1906; Charles Lindbergh and his wife scouted archeological sites in several flights over the Yucatán in 1929 and 1930; and in the 1960s Robert McCormick Adams, now secretary of the Smithsonian Institution, photographed ancient sites in Iraq with an old Leica camera mounted on a kite-like parafoil.

What *is* new is the widespread application of the modern electronic remote-sensing techniques to archeological research. Ground-penetrating radar is just one example. As Seger's group showed, beaming radar pulses into the ground and measuring the echo is a good way of finding buried artifacts in arid areas. Microwaves, which tend to be absorbed by water molecules, penetrate dry sand even better than they do roast beef; and they are strongly reflected by man-made objects.

But archeological objects can reveal themselves in parts of the electromagnetic spectrum other than microwaves. They can also be seen by the infrared radiation — the heat — they emit, or even in the way they reflect sunlight. The ground above a buried stone wall, for instance, may be a touch hotter than the surrounding terrain because the stone absorbs more heat. With a sensitive electronic detector one can measure the excess thermal radiation. The spectrum of sunlight reflected by Earth's surface, on the other hand, contains information about the composition of the surface, and it may reveal traces of past human activities, such as agriculture.

Using instruments mounted on trucks, blimps, airplanes, and satellites, archeologists are beginning to hunt for such clues. With satellite sensors they can survey an entire region and determine where undiscovered archeological sites are most likely to be found. From airplanes they can get a closer look and actually discover new sites. On the ground they can map unexcavated areas of a site and even find new artifacts — like the cistern at Tell Halif.

All this is a far cry from traditional archeology. For one thing, it involves the heavy use of computers, which convert the mass of numeric data gathered by electronic sensors into decipherable images. Even on computer-enhanced images, though, archeological clues may be extremely subtle and in some cases invisible to the untrained eye. "Archeologists are just beginning to become familiar with these techniques," says Fritz Hemans, director of archeological applica-

tions at Boston University's Center for Remote Sensing. "The problem is a lack of expertise."

Yet most archeologists agree that a revolution is under way — one that may ultimately have as much impact as the discovery, 42 years ago, that regular, clocklike decay of radioactive carbon atoms could serve to measure the precise age of ancient artifacts. "We don't know where remote sensing is going to lead," says James Wiseman, chairman of Boston University's archeology department. "But even now it represents the kind of scientific breakthrough for archeology in the second half of the twentieth century that radiocarbon dating was in the first half."

No one has felt the remote-sensing breakthrough more keenly than Tom Sever, a NASA archeologist, and Payson Sheets of the University of Colorado at Boulder. For several years Sheets has been studying the culture of an Indian people that flourished between 3000 B.C. and A.D. 1500 — predating and outlasting both the Maya and the Aztecs — in the mountains of northwestern Costa Rica. The region is dominated by a 5,000-foot-high volcano called Arenal. In ten devastating eruptions over the past 4,000 years, Arenal has repeatedly deposited thick layers of ash over the jungle and thereby preserved the culture's artifacts.

Finding the artifacts under all that ash, though, is not easy. Sever, who has made remote sensing his specialty, arranged for a specially equipped NASA airplane to survey the Arenal region in late 1984 and early 1985. Flying some 1,000 feet off the ground, the investigators collected radar data and took infrared photographs. The radar's microwave beam could not penetrate the wet ground of the tropical forest, but on the infrared photographs, Sheets and Severs noticed some unnatural-looking straight lines where the composition of the surface was different.

Soon after the two archeologists began digging, they realized they had found something significant. Buried as much as five feet deep in volcanic ash was a network of footpaths. Several led to a large cemetery on the crest of the continental divide, overlooking the Pacific. Sheets had already found the cemetery, which dates from roughly 1,000 years ago. But the discovery of the paths was an important step toward understanding the daily comings and goings of a society that left no written records.

Sever and Sheets continued to investigate. During a flight last February, they began collecting data with an ultrasensitive infrared detector called the Thermal Infrared Multispectral Scanner. The scanner can detect temperature differences of less than 0.2 degree Fahrenheit; it can see the minute heat given off by the wake of a boat. Sever has demonstrated the instrument's archeological promise at Chaco Canyon, a famous Anasazi Indian site in northwestern New Mexico, where he found buried walls, prehistoric roadways, and ancient agricultural fields. "Where circumstances are right," says Sever, "you can even estimate the dimensions of buried stone features."

The data from Arenal haven't been analyzed yet, but Sever and Sheets are confident. "There'll be further footpath detections, I'm sure of that," says Sheets. "I'm also optimistic about detecting new cemeteries." To mark graves in their cemeteries, the Arenal people hauled large rocks, some weighing as much as 100 pounds, up the paths from a river several miles away. On the image produced by the scanner, the thermal signature of those now-buried slabs should stand out.

Remote sensors can't always pinpoint an artifact; sometimes they just give archeologists a general idea of where to look. That's what happened in the case of one of the most celebrated remote-sensing discoveries, which took place in the Sahara in 1981. Actually, the first part of the discovery occurred in a U.S. Geological Survey laboratory in Flagstaff, Arizona, where researchers were analyzing the vast data streams collected by a radar instrument carried into orbit by the space shuttle *Columbia*. The radar images showed that under the sands of southern Egypt and northwestern Sudan, in a region where it now rains about once every 50 years, there were ancient river-beds, some wider than the Nile.

Months later an expedition to the region confirmed that the radar had penetrated the sand and bounced off limestone bedrock at a depth of around five feet. Along the shores of the radar rivers the excavators found the shells of a species of land snail that can only survive in a moist, tropical climate. Equally striking, they found thousands of Stone Age human artifacts (hand axes and the like) as much as 300,000 years old. Hence researchers now believe that the eastern Sahara has at times been wet — and inhabited.

In Mexico's remote, poorly mapped Yucatán peninsula, home of the Maya, the same logic applies: to find human artifacts, look for water. In this case, though, since the Mayan civilization fell only 11 centuries ago, archeologists can look for existing bodies of water rather than extinct

riverbeds. The Thematic Mapper, a multispectral scanner on Landsat satellites that records reflected sunlight in seven visible and infrared bands, is well suited to the purpose.

Recently Charles Duller of NASA's Ames Research Center, working with Maya expert Edward Kurjack of Western Illinois University, put together the first Landsat mosaic of the entire northern Yucatán. (Kurjack has a special appreciation for the grand view from space; he's been hoofing through the scrub and dense tropical growth of the Yucatán for 25 years.) What the images showed was more surface water in the region than anyone had imagined. Much of the water is in cenotes: circular sinkholes in the limestone bedrock that connect to the underground water table. The Maya often settled near these natural wells. "Some of these water sources were found for the first time," says Duller. "And experience tells us that eighty percent of the time, where you find water, you'll find ruins."

The Landsat instrument does not have the resolution to see crumbling Mayan buildings from space; the smallest details it can distinguish are 100 feet across. So Kurjack's next step is to take a closer look at some promising areas. He and Sever are hoping to fly a blimp over the Yucatán. "What we're planning to do," says Kurjack, "is take a system that includes a thermal scanner as well as a multispectral scanner and mount it on a dirigible. With the kind of resolution we should get, the results might be spectacular."

From the blimp's cruising altitude of 1,500 feet or less, the instruments should detect not only ruins, but individual stones. What's more, unlike an airplane, a blimp can hover over a site and examine it in detail. A 90-foot-long, two-man blimp is ready and waiting, but Kurjack and Sever still need funding, as well as permission from Mexico.

If ever an archeological project cried out for remote sensing, it is the study of the pre-Incan civilization that made its home in the cloud forests of the Peruvian Andes. Gran Pajaten and Cerro Central are the most prominent of several known sites in the valley of the Rio Abiseo; Gran Pajaten is believed to have been inhabited from about 400 B.C. to A.D. 1475, shortly after the founding of the Incan empire. Research teams that have trekked into the remote mountainous jungle during the 1980s have found more than 200 structures, many with intricate stone carvings. The evidence suggests that hundreds of square miles of steep mountain slopes were once densely populated.

Yet only about one square mile of the terrain around Gran Pajaten has been surveyed so far, and the Cerro Central area hasn't been mapped at all. It would take generations of archeologists to complete the task on foot; remote sensing is the only hope. "Remote sensors will allow us to begin to identify the types of sites and settlement patterns that would be impossible to discern from the ground," says Thomas Lennon of the University of Colorado, who led the first archeological expedition to Cerro Central in 1985. Although the thick clouds and jungle canopy of the region often block the sensors' view, NASA has recently obtained a cloud-free Landsat image. Lennon is also hoping to get a picture from France's SPOT satellite, which has substantially better resolution than Landsat.

In many ways, the ideal instrument for surveying the Rio Abiseo region would be the Shuttle Imaging Radar, the same device that discovered the riverbeds under the Sahara. According to the radar's principal designer, Charles Elachi of the Jet Propulsion Laboratory, an updated version will be flying on the shuttle in the early 1990s. The new instrument will beam microwaves at three frequencies instead of just one. That will allow it to simultaneously image an arid surface and penetrate beneath it to two different depths. "From orbit," says Elachi, "we will be able to determine how deep features are, whereas in the past we had to go into the field and do soundings." In wet regions like the Rio Abiseo valley, the radar would not see underground; but it might penetrate both the cloud cover and the thick forest canopy and perhaps reveal uncharted ruins.

The shuttle radar will not be the last word in remote-sensing technology. Other sensors are already being developed at the Jet Propulsion Laboratory. Some of them promise to make the scanners on *Star Trek* (Mr. Spock's "tricorder," say) seem downright realistic.

One device, called the High-Resolution Imaging Spectrometer, should go aloft on a polar-orbiting satellite by the mid-1990s. It will monitor reflected sunlight in the visible and infrared range and break it down into 200 narrow bands (the Landsat Thematic Mapper uses seven). The more detailed spectra it will provide should allow researchers to identify the light signatures of individual chemicals.

"We can acquire all the information that is available in the reflected signal — nothing escapes us," says Alexander Goetz of the University of Colorado, who directed work on the new spectrometer when he was at the Jet Propulsion Laboratory. "And through it we'll determine the chemical composition of what's on the ground. We'll be able to go to any point of the image, pull out that picture element, and have the computer plot a spectrum for it. Or we can ask the computer to search the millions of pixels for a particular substance by having it check a library of known spectral signatures." The product of all these satellite data will be rough chemical maps of various regions of Earth. Archeologists will then be able to scan the maps for evidence of early human activity.

A modified version of this instrument, mounted on an aircraft, could survey a given region with incredible resolution, analyzing the chemistry of objects just a few feet across. And Elachi thinks an even smaller version of the device may eventually be built. "Every archeological site could have its own portable instrument to carry into the field," he says. "You could go into the tombs of the pharaohs, scan paintings or other artifacts, and learn what material or mixture of materials was used to make them. You then could tell when they were made and who made them — all without touching the artifacts."

22
Gender, Politics, and American Archaeology

JULIAN THOMAS

Over the past decade or so, archaeology has increasingly begun to see itself as a political practice. Long ago, archaeologists like V. Gordon Childe demonstrated both personal political commitment and a desire to write accounts of the past informed by their political views. However, it has been with the ebb of positivist approaches, dedicated to establishing a single "true" and objective past, that the way has been opened for writings which emerge from a variety of oppositional standpoints. As the stranglehold of white males on the discipline has come to be recognized, women and ethnic groups have begun to demand the right to construct their own pasts, while many of the white males themselves have proved increasingly willing to incorporate issues of power, resistance, and identity into their analyses. While these developments are global in scope, many of the early attempts to theorize an archaeology concerned with gender, class, race, and ideology took place in Britain. However, several recent books demonstrate the existence of a strong radical tradition in the archaeology of the United States. Two particu-

From *Anthropology Today*, Vol. 8, No. 3, June 1992, pp. 12–13. Reprinted with the permission of the Royal Anthropological Institute of Great Britain and Ireland. (Bibliographic documentation contained in the original text is omitted here. Interested readers should consult the original publication.)

lar volumes have recently emerged in Blackwell's new "Social Archaeology" series, edited by Ian Hodder. The work contained in both books represents not simply a political point of view, but an epistemological challenge to orthodox archaeological positions which issues out of the confrontation between conventional archaeological practice and personal ideals.

In this respect, the recent impact of feminism upon archaeological thought has been illuminating. Archaeology remains a profoundly androcentric discipline, although it is one in which a great many of the practitioners (if not those who hold positions of power) are women. Consequently, a great number of archaeologists share the experience of feeling excluded both from the professional practices and the interpretations to which they contribute, and in many cases have become politicized by this. In the example of the volume edited by J.M. Gero and M.W. Conkey, *Engendering Archaeology: Women and Prehistory*, this has the interesting consequence that a concern with feminism and the role of women in past societies leads to a series of very different conclusions. The appearance of the book prompts the question of why it has taken so long for such a coherent statement of the content and philosophy of a feminist archaeology to emerge.

Perhaps the answer is that, more than any other approach within the human sciences, feminism does fundamental damage to the established traditions of working within archaeology, a point recognized here in both the introduction and a clear and measured piece by Alison Wylie. What distinguishes the different contributors to the volume is the extent to which they are prepared to follow through the lines of reasoning which are set up by a feminist critique. As the title implies, one of the fundamental concerns of the book is to move beyond a gender-neutral writing of the past to a recognition that past social processes were engaged with in different ways by women and men. In several cases this is achieved in the context of an account which remains sympathetic to ecological and systematic approaches, and to cross-cultural generalization. Thus Watson and Kennedy consider the adoption of domesticated plant resources in the Eastern Woodlands of North America by setting up a series of assumptions concerning the presumed role of women in "egalitarian" societies. However, as Claassen points out in her paper, this engendering of the archaeological record does not merely provide new answers to old questions, but causes us to ask new questions. Principally, if one is prepared to adopt the essentially realist argument that archaeological evidence was produced by gendered human beings, and thus to move beyond that which is empirically testable, is not such a reliance upon these cross-cultural assumptions rather insecure? Where assumptions are made about the character of gender relations in generalized entities like "egalitarian," "simple agricultural," or "stratified" societies, is there not a danger of imposing the ethnographic present on the past? This may be better than assuming that modern western gender roles are natural and eternal, but still does not allow the past to be "different."

Others of the contributors are more willing to consider gender as a process of social categorization which is both historically and culturally contingent. Indeed, the focus upon women's roles in productive processes in Conkey's, Hastorf's, Brumfiel's, and Gero's papers actively opens the question of the extent to which the differentiation of tasks within society is productive of gender relations, rather than a sexual division of labour being based upon an extant gender system. So for instance, Conkey suggests that certain sites where people gathered into large groups on a seasonal basis in the Upper Paleolithic, and where a variety of craft activities were practised, may have provided a context for the emergence, negotiation and contestation of gender identities. In this respect, these contributions mark a major advance in the potential of

archaeology to construct significant statements about past social relations, by concentrating in new ways upon the material evidence. Here, spheres of material practice all too often pigeonholed as eternal and unchanging, or as "responses" to changing ecological conditions (food production and cooking, crop processing, weaving), are recognized as having been actively involved in the flux of social relationships. In particular, one can point to Christine A. Hastorf's imaginative use of bone isotope measurements and distributions of plant remains in order to make inferences concerning the circumscription of female roles with the expansion of the Inka empire [see her article "Dietary Reconstruction in the Andes: A New Archaeological Technique," *Anthropology Today*, December 1985]. One might argue that it is because of their background and training in social and cultural anthropology that American archaeologists are increasingly starting to use the evidence provided by "scientific" technologies in rather more inspired ways than many of their British counterparts.

However, as Wylie persuasively demonstrates, this does not exhaust the potential impact of feminism upon archaeology. For feminism also represents a concerted critique of academic practice, questioning the structures of power within the discipline. This can take the form of recognizing the male domination of the career structure and of particular aspects of archaeology, as with Gero's depiction of experimental archaeology as a close relative of "Iron John"–style male bonding practices, "rugged men doing primal things." But beyond this, the recognition that "objective," "scientific" language and research procedures often serve to mask androcentric preconceptions working at a deeper level can lead to a mistrust of accepted modes of academic discourse. In several cases, this emerges as a desire to write archaeology in a new way. Both Tringham and Spector end their chapters by introducing a narrative section, weaving a story of women's experience in the Balkan Neolithic or amongst the nineteenth century Eastern Dakota around the existing material evidence. Both recognize that this is a position which they have reached through a rejection of over-formal research programmes, and one is left wondering whether "storytelling" is indeed the only rhetorical move which one ends up with, having rejected objective description.

The Archaeology of Inequality, by contrast, edited by R.H. McGuire and R. Paynter, brings to bear on the archaeology of historic America a series of approaches to ideology and power derived from marxism and post-structuralism. As Mary Beaudry and others argue here, it has often been the case that the role of material evidence has been underrated in the historic era. This is partly a consequence of the existence of a textual record of past events, which tends to relegate artefacts to the status of mere illustrative material. However, there is also the difficulty of finding a context for material culture studies in the global processes of recent history. McGuire and Paynter take the view that such a contribution would prove difficult to make as long as archaeology was dominated either by morphology and typology or by cultural ecology. Both the culture–historic archaeology of the period before 1960 and more recent "processual" approaches tended to represent societies as undivided totalities, governed exclusively by large-scale processes, whether of cultural drift and diffusion or of group adaptation. Only where asymmetrical social relations and processes of change internal to society begin to be recognized does the value of an archaeology written "from the bottom up," and concerned with the details of small scale interaction, begin to be recognized. In a useful introduction, McGuire and Paynter adopt a position influenced by Abercrombie, Hill, and Turner's critique of the Althusserian "dominant ideology thesis" and by Foucault's account of power. Thus they come to see power as heterogeneous, and exercised from multiple centres, while knowledge too is produced and manipulated differentially across the social field. Material culture is thus bound up with the negotiation of social position, and with resistance as well as with domination. This point is well demonstrated by Ferguson's study of colonial South Carolina, which uses material culture to demonstrate the active resistance of the slave population. Despite efforts to erase ethnic identity, the Colono Ware pottery used by the slaves documents the survival of West African ways of serving and eating food.

Two or three of the papers in the volume are more effective as social history than as archaeology, displaying a less sophisticated attitude toward the material evidence. But at its best, the book demonstrates the potential of archaeology as counter-memory or alternative history. Thus McDonald *et al.* use archaeological methods of investigation to uphold Northern Cheyenne oral testimony concerning the outbreak of 1879 against the "official" military history. Here the potential of archaeology to support accounts of the past which question orthodoxy, and as a weapon which can be deployed by disadvantaged groups, is demonstrated. It is not theory alone which enables this to take place, but the material resistance offered by the archaeological evidence itself: it can quite simply demonstrate that dominant interpretations are fictitious.

There remains the worrisome question of the extent to which archaeologists should presume to "speak for" indigenous groups, although in this case the project was clearly a collaborative one. It seems likely that in the near future groups like native North Americans will begin to write their own accounts of the past based upon archaeological evidence, and we may then expect the discipline to become a genuine field of political contestation. McGuire's own chapter effectively makes the links between the small scale of analysis and the global context. His study of architecture in nineteenth and twentieth century Broome County begins with the crisis of American capitalism, Fordism, and industrial democracy, and focuses gradually in upon the details of town planning, factory layout, and gravestone design.

Both of these books are thus important contributions, not simply because they demand that archaeologists look beyond the artefacts to the social relationships within which they were enmeshed, but because they require us to return to material things and look at them in new ways.

23
Who Owns the Past?

DAVID HURST THOMAS

A review of The Return of Cultural Treasures, *by Jeanette Greenfield, Cambridge University Press, 1990, 361 pp., illus., and* The Ethics of Collecting Cultural Property: Whose Culture? Whose Property? *edited by Phyllis Mauch Messenger, University of New Mexico Press, 1990, 266 pp., illus.*

Ambrose Bierce, that wry nineteenth-century satirist, defined the term *prehistoric* as "belonging to an early period and a museum." And until very recently, Bierce had it about right. Most of the tangible, portable record of our human past did indeed belong to one museum or another.

Most of the world's great museums already had huge collections in Bierce's day. Despite a mid-twentieth century "birth of conscience" regarding the expropriation of antiquities from other countries, museum stockpiles have continued to expand. An American Association of Museums survey disclosed that between 1960 and 1963, a new museum sprouted up every three or four days. By the 1980s, the United States and Canada could boast more than twenty-one museums for every million people.

It was in the museums of natural history and ethnology that most of us first bumped into the Third World. Through the high-security glass, we peered at our first Maya stelae, took in our initial Egyptian mummy, and stared down at our first Pygmy. Hermetic cases paraded seemingly endless rows of originals — enigmatic Chinese jades, deadly Amazon blowguns, and ingenious Eskimo harpoons. Through the decades, museums showed the "civilized world" how vast, complex, and bizarre the human experience has been. To urbanite and rural fairgoer alike, the museum served up what the Third World was really like. While today's television might capture better images, only a museum could flaunt the real thing.

The Third World now wants the real things back. While research and exhibition still dominate daily curatorial life, the corridors of today's museums are echoing with strange new jargon: Repatriation of patrimony, Restriction of imports and exports, and Rights retained by relevant parties — what philosopher Karen Warren terms the three Rs of cultural property disputes. The modern museum community is under siege, and the ground rules governing museum collections are evolving as we speak.

Two new books highlight this escalating skirmish. *The Return of Cultural Treasures* takes a rational and well-reasoned, if resolute, stand. Author Jeanette Greenfield, brandishing a Cambridge Ph.D. in international law, steers the reader through the tangled world of purloined patrimony. She begins, of all places, in Iceland, by reciting in exhaustive detail the legal, political, diplomatic, and social contentions that ultimately culminated in the controversial 1971 return by Denmark of the *Flateyjarbók* and *Codex Regius*, the most valuable manuscript treasures of Iceland's medieval literature. Although conflict arose at every turn, Icelandic self-respect and pride ultimately won out over Danish jurisprudence.

Few readers may know of Iceland's triumph, but everyone will recognize Greenfield's second case study — the tiff surrounding the Elgin Marbles (or, as the Greek nationals insist on calling them, the Parthenon Marbles). By whatever name, this 247-foot-long marble frieze, lifted nearly two centuries ago from the Parthenon and now firmly ensconced in the Duveen Gallery of the British Museum, has become without question the *cause célèbre* of cultural return cases. The Greek Minister of Culture (and former actress) Melina Mercouri argues that these sculptures symbolize Greece itself, that they constitute part of Greece's psychological landscape. Sir David Wilson, dogged director of the British Museum, counters that any such return — and most particularly that of the Elgin Marbles — would smack of "cultural fascism."

While recognizing that world history reveals an "intricate web of universal plunder" and "the cannibalization of cultures," Greenfield joins a growing chorus of concerned scholars who urge that certain kinds of objects should be returned immediately to their countries of origin. Citing both logical and legal grounds, she argues that Third World museums should own some of the objects in the national museums of the West, that some of the Benin bronzes should find their way into African museums, and that the Rosetta stone — clearly collected as a spoil of war — should perhaps be on display in Cairo rather than in London.

A rather different approach surfaces in *The Ethics of Collecting Cultural Property: Whose Culture? Whose Property?* This edited work attempts to define the range of conflicting perspectives on the ownership and preservation of the artifacts of past cultures. Contributors include several archeologists and museum administrators, a self-described "active art dealer," a curator of pre-Columbian art at Princeton University, an attorney specializing in art law, and a professor of philosophy.

This cast of characters is simultaneously the book's strength and its greatest weakness. Although the legally oriented pieces tend to drag a bit, many of the contributions are lively and persuasive. I was, however, disappointed to find that a volume emphasizing a diversity of ethical, legal, and intellectual issues would be so narrowly focused. Not a single native voice is heard, an omission that itself promises to fuel the debate. Granted, the occasional scholar attempts to summarize the native perspective. But such third-party recapitulation constitutes the problem, not the solution. Why, in a volume entitled *The Ethics of Collecting Cultural Property: Whose Culture? Whose Property?*, are aboriginal, indigenous, and Third World people not articulating their own positions?

The larger debate over "who owns the past" has taken a number of curious turns recently, and both books succeed in highlighting the issues. In one sense, the dispute reflects the split between "have" and "have-not" constituencies. But more is involved than an international game of "finders-keepers." Underlying and cross-cutting such intuitive dichotomies are complex sets of conflicting claims and counterclaims, sometimes between the claimants themselves.

We find, for example, an encroaching sense of "pan-ism." Seeking to defend the British Museum's claim to the Elgin Marbles, the Parliamentary Assembly of the Council of Europe passed a resolution stressing "the unity of the European cultural heritage." In effect, a quickening "pan-European perspective" was employed to vindicate strictly British privilege. In their ultimate futile attempt to retain the Icelandic manuscripts, a band of Danish university lecturers claimed that the texts were more properly viewed as a "pan-Scandinavian treasure." That the manuscripts happened to be written in Icelandic, they argued, was mere historical happenstance. A similar pan-Indian mandate is increasingly cited by a vocal and self-appointed minority to justify claims on complex issues of reburial of skeletal material and repatriation of items of cultural heritage. In each case, a covering pan-ism is interjected to warrant exclusive access to the past, too often ignoring the diverse and even fractious communities actually represented.

Both volumes also address the alarming increase in the looting of archeological sites. Charles S. Koczka, former senior special agent for the U.S. Customs Service, spells out in graphic detail the complication, emphasizing that illegal art traffic may today be second only to the drug trade in international crime. David Pendergast, a field archeologist with extensive experience, thinks that the well-organized looting crews operating in Belize today are "larger than any ever mustered by archaeologists." Unless site destruction can be curbed, the future of the past is dim indeed.

The museum community has been surprisingly slow to condemn the looting of archeological sites and the marketing of illegally obtained antiquities. Nevertheless, responsible museums today uniformly refuse to accept artifacts illegally imported from the country of origin; the more sapient also decline to display illegitimate artifacts. At the American Museum of Natural History, for instance, curators are explicitly forbidden by the trustees from authenticating or appraising any artifacts. The Museum Shop refuses to sell antiquities in any form, and *Natural History* magazine will not accept advertising for antiquities, regardless of how acquired.

As the museum community is increasingly drawn into active participation in conservation efforts, maintenance of biodiversity, and investigating global climate change, it would seem worthwhile to alert the viewing public about ongoing site destruction and potential losses of human heritage. Still, when was the last time you saw an exhibition even mention the evils of archaeological thievery and art smuggling?

The fortunate exception was the May 1983 exhibition, "Stolen Treasures — Missing Links," mounted by the National Geographic Society in Washington, D.C. It consisted of five hundred pre-Columbian pieces seized by American customs agents in the previous two years. After touring eight major museums nationwide, the artifacts were returned to Peru as part of a bilateral agreement to return such property recovered at U.S. borders. We need more exhibits of this sort. Museums are too often viewed as compulsive institutions, functioning only to retain their collections — getting the most artifacts and sitting on them. Museums need to demonstrate how the interrelated objectives of collecting, conserving, and disseminating can serve the greater public, both at home and abroad. Museums can indeed serve a global, increasingly pluralistic community if they are willing to accept the challenge.

Consider the experiences of Margaret Mead in the Admiralty Islands of Melanesia. In 1928, during her first year of curatorship at the American Museum, Mead went to live at Pere village, on the island of Manus, where she made an extensive collection of nearly one thousand artifacts, mainly bowls, arm and ear ornaments, belts, cloth, betel bags, and spears. She subsequently installed many of these artifacts in the Peoples of the Pacific Hall at the American

Museum; the rest were cataloged and conserved as part of the overall research collection.

Mead returned to Manus in 1953, to work amid a society she said had simply "slipped over thousands of years of history in just the last twenty-five years." Part of her research strategy involved showing the Manus people her photographs from 1928, to illustrate the "old way." The grown men were generally amused at the photographs of their now-dead elders, particularly the ornaments of dogs' teeth, the obsidian-pointed spears, and the shell-bedecked phalluses. But for the younger men, the old ornaments, the slit-drum, the spears and daggers — now all abandoned — had become symbols of pure evil. Not only had the material culture passed into disuse but the people of Pere village themselves had deliberately destroyed most of it, had pitched their past wholesale into the sea in a gesture designed to make way for the new social and economic order.

When Margaret Mead died in November 1978, the Manus people declared the traditional week of mourning, which customarily ends with the presentation of gifts to the family of the deceased. To make this presentation, John Kilipak of Pere village traveled to New York to present a necklace of newly minted coins to Mead's American Museum family (see "Pere Mourns Margaret Mead," *Natural History*, November 1979).

Mead had first encountered Kilipak in 1928, when she described him as "a lively fourteen-year-old." Kilipak was a key informant during her 1953 stay there, and he appears throughout Mead's book *New Lives for Old*. While in New York, Kilipak expressed great interest and pride in the traditional artifacts on display. Noting that traditional material culture had virtually vanished in the Admiralty Islands, Kilipak remarked that the Margaret Mead collection constitutes, in a very real sense, the only tangible vestige of their "old ways." Rather than berating the museum community for retaining such rare artifacts or pressing a repatriation claim, Kilipak emphasized that the artifacts would have been destroyed had Mead not collected them. He also expressed pride that the surviving Manus artifacts were deemed so important, employing the neo-Melanesian pidgin term for "museum": house-look-look-belong-all (*haus-lukluk-bilong-ol*).

The Manus case points up the fallacy of extremist thinking with regard to cultural properties. We must roundly reject the demands for universal repatriation; taken to their illogical extreme, these arguments would insist that every Picasso hang in Spain, that all Leonardos be repatriated to Italy, and that every archeological artifact be returned to its country of origin.

At the opposite extreme, some major museums still take an ultraconservative, no-return-under-any-circumstance position. I know of one university-based curator who has even formulated a secret "doomsday plan," in which Native American skeletal collections and associated funerary items would be shuttled between campus labs, like so many MX missiles. That way, the bad guys would be unable to find anything to repatriate.

Such capricious extremes only exacerbate the problem. The enlightened are attempting to define a middle ground for cultural heritage claims by employing a long-term, good-faith, case-by-case assessment of specific objects in their specific cultural context. Each object must be evaluated according to its own particular history, including the specific circumstances of its acquisition, plus such factors as the ability of the home country to house, conserve, protect, study, and display anything that is returned. Long-term loans, museum training for indigenous and Third World interns, and cooperative exhibition programs are all tools for defining this new, interactive museum posture.

The issue revolves around the ownership of the past — not just the objects of the past but also the broader perceptions of that past. Although ample doses of empathy and self-restraint are required on both sides of the cultural fence, today's museum can still achieve the Manus ideal — truly becoming a "house-look-look-belong-all."

PART THREE
Linguistic Anthropology

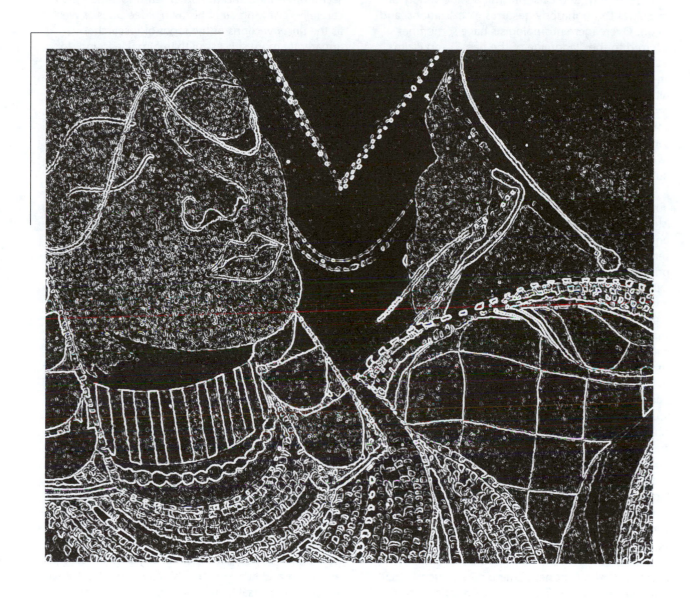

Introduction

A characteristic that distinguishes human beings from all other animals is their innate potential for acquiring **language**. We all know that many animals communicate with each other; most of us have seen dogs and cats transmit a wide variety of messages through body gestures, vocalizations, and so on. Overeager entomologists have sometimes referred to the "language of the bees," and claims have been made that some apes, such as Washoe and Koko, have a wide range of linguistic abilities. Although it is certainly true that all animals, and probably even plants, employ a variety of means of communication, including chemical, tactile, auditory, or gestural signals, none uses a linguistic mode of communication, at least not in the absence of human intervention.

Language did not appear all of a sudden among our ancestors. Like the rest of our human characteristics, it had antecedents in the biology and physiology of our nonhuman primate ancestors. It makes sense to study the linguistic potential of nonhuman primates, because, in the wild, they frequently exhibit complex methods of communication, involving up to four senses — touch, smell, sight, and hearing — at once. But while scientists agree that chimpanzees and gorillas are able to communicate much information, they know that neither group uses language. The problem, then, has been to discover whether these primates could acquire a linguistic mode of communication. Many scientific journals, as well as magazines and films, have publicized certain researchers' claims that apes trained by them had achieved linguistic communication: they possessed extensive vocabularies, used a grammar, and made creative use of language. Skeptics have responded by stating that, even if confirmed, the linguistic achievements of these elaborately trained laboratory specimens are not equal even to those of the average three-year-old human child. In his review of two books on the subject, Martin Gardner (Chapter 24) suggests that none of the existing films and studies about "talking apes" has ever, in fact, established their linguistic competence.

Gardner refers to the theories of prominent linguists, such as Noam Chomsky, who maintain that chimpanzees are unable to learn syntax. Chomsky holds that the major types of linguistic ability reflect a uniquely human, and innate, universal grammar. Gardner recounts the experience of H.S. Terrace, a psychologist who determined to prove, once and for all, that Chomsky was wrong. He trained a chimpanzee, which he named Nim Chimpsky, to use American Sign Language (ASL). He made a point of keeping his methodology as rigorous as possible, in order to avoid the kinds of criticisms that had been leveled against earlier, similar research. Initially dismayed by his lack of success, Terrace eventually came to understand the secret of Washoe and the other "talking" apes, after carefully reviewing all of his own videotapes as well as the *uncut* versions of the tapes of researchers apparently more successful than him. He found, for example, that all of Washoe's filmed multisign statements *followed* similar sign sequences made by her teachers. The makers of the films that had ostensibly proved that chimps could talk had edited out not only the initial prompting of the researchers, but also hundreds of nonsense combinations of signs. They preserved only the lucky hits for the record. To use a simple analogy, a cat running back and forth across a piano keyboard might eventually "hit" on something resembling a few bars of Beethoven's "Moonlight Sonata," but that does not make the cat a musician. The secret of Washoe was out: wishful interpretations combined with creative editing had bestowed syntactic ability upon unsuspecting apes. "At this time, supporters of the apes have not yet proved to the satisfaction of their critics that genuine symbolic behavior is occurring, much less anything resembling syntactic patterning or creative linguistic use" (Dobrovolsky 1987, 431). It cannot be ruled out, however, that rigorously conducted research might one day prove that apes have, in Gardner's words, "a dim awareness of syntax."

Nonlinguistic means of communication, such as gesturing or body posture, whether among humans or nonhumans, are severely limited in the amount of communication they allow, the range of messages they are able to convey, and the number of variations on those messages they permit. Although language is only one of a wide variety of means of communication, it is a special and uniquely human one. It allows communication about any real, possible, or impossible aspect of any kind of reality, anywhere and at any time. This characteristic, called semantic universality, is typical of all human languages, without exception. One aspect of **semantic universality** is *productivity*: the speakers of all human languages can create new messages that have never been uttered before, and can modify them into an unlimited number of variations.

Only humans can speak, and no animal other than a human can be taught to speak: your pet parrot may be able to imitate some of the sounds of human language, but it cannot converse with you. Human language is made possible by certain features of the brain and vocal tract of *Homo sapiens*

sapiens that are genetically transmitted and unique to humans. Nonetheless, there is no such thing as "natural language." Many examples of children deprived of normal contact and interaction with other human beings have shown that, without the experience of using language actively — that is, of making requests and responding to requests — language is not learned and the ability to learn it wanes after the first few years of life. Moreover, thousands of different, mutually unintelligible, languages are spoken on earth at any given time. It is cultural experience and learning, not "nature," that determine whether language will be learned and whether that language will be Spanish, Chinese, Cree, or another of the thousands of alternatives.

Not only do humans have many different languages, but all languages change considerably over time. A fascinating aspect of linguistics is the study of the relationships among existing languages, as well as between spoken and extinct languages. *Historical linguistics* describes the "family trees" of known languages, and uses some rigorous and well-tested techniques to study linguistic changes and to reconstruct extinct languages. Most linguistic changes develop gradually, and are not made consciously. **Phonemes**, for example, are arbitrary units of sound used in each language to mark differences in meaning, although these phonemes do not have a meaning by themselves. Linguists distinguish the phonemes of a language, but most people speaking that language are oblivious to their existence. In each utterance, the speakers combine the phonemes of their language into meaningful units (**morphemes**), which are in turn combined following unconscious grammar rules to form messages that can be understood by all speakers of this language. Over the generations, the speakers of a language unconsciously drop or modify certain phonemes, according to rules that linguists are later able to discern. The study of such changes over time allows linguists to understand the relationships among different languages and thereby to contribute to the reconstruction of migration routes and of the cultural connection among peoples separated by time and space. In Africa, the Americas, and Oceania, archaeologists and linguists have collaborated to reconstruct paths and sequences of migrations and diffusion. In Chapter 25, Philip Ross discusses some of the issues that are debated by modern linguists who attempt to reconstruct the complex links among languages that have not been spoken for millennia. An important aspect of this essay is that it reflects the constant dialogue between linguists and biological anthropologists, archaeologists, and cultural anthropologists.

Language and Culture

The fact that all human languages have semantic universality means that anything that can be said in one language can, in some way, be said in any other human language. In that sense, all human languages are said to be "functionally equivalent," or equally perfect: no human language is "better" than another. Nevertheless, the ease or difficulty of translation between two languages varies with the differences between the natural, social, and cultural environments of their speakers: How would a North American explain snow to a tropical-forest dweller? "holidays" to a traditional !Kung hunter who has never experienced a nine-to-five job? the carbon-14 dating technique to an Australian Aborigine living according to traditional ways?

In the 1940s, the following question a major concern of anthropological linguists: Is language determined by culture or does the language of a group of people mold and determine their thoughts and perceptions? The anthropologist and linguist who conceived this question was Edward Sapir. One of his students, Benjamin L. Whorf, suggested that the speakers of different languages live in different "thought worlds." Whorf studied the language of the Hopi Indians and compared it with several European languages to prove the existence of parallels between grammatical categories and the culture of a group of people. He formalized his answer to Sapir's question about the relationship of language, thought, and reality in what is often called the **Sapir–Whorf Hypothesis**. According to this hypothesis, language is not simply an encoding process for expressing our ideas, but rather a shaping force that determines, in part, our thinking and our behavior. Whorf claimed that the language spoken by a group of people structures their perceptions and the way they think.

Modern anthropologists and linguists generally disagree with Whorf: they suggest instead that the language of a group of people tends to reflect and reveal their common interests and perceptions, their social structure and ecology. A recent textbook of linguistics summarizes the verdict at this point in the debate: "The repeated failure of experimental attempts to uncover systematic shaping effects for language has drastically reduced the credibility of the Sapir–Whorf Hypothesis" (O'Grady 1987). Consider, for instance, that speakers of Gaelic, such as the Welsh, and speakers of many Native American language, have a single word to refer to the colors that speakers of English distinguish with the names *blue* and *green*. Does that mean that they perceive these colors differently and react differently to this part of the color spectrum? Carefully controlled experiments have proven that, although the labeling of colors differs from language to language, the perception of color by their speakers does not. The essay by Robbins Burling (Chapter 26) illustrates another fascinating aspect of this debate. It seems that all languages assign color terms with much less arbitrariness than had been suspected until recently, and even their differences in this matter follow certain predictable patterns. For example, any language that labels only five colors on the spectrum invariably lists black, white, red, yellow, and green. Languages that label six points on the color spectrum always add blue to the list. Human biology, culture, and ecology determine in part the perception and categorization of colors by humans. Findings pertaining to issues such as these contribute to an ongoing debate concerning the existence of underlying *universals of human languages*.

Although anthropological linguists study the universal characteristics of language, they also explore the phenomenon that all humans do not speak the *same* language. More than 4000 languages are now spoken in the world, but this is a small fraction of all the different languages known to have been spoken in the past. The multiplicity of languages interferes with communication: why does it persist? After all, if the function of language is to communicate, why do all humans not speak "God's French," "the Queen's English," or some other single language?

Besides communication, a language has many other functions, one of which is to *prevent* communication, that is, to exclude certain "others." The language of a group of people is the main vehicle of their culture, and often symbolizes it, as a flag symbolizes a country. This is an important reason behind the political battles that have been waged along linguistic lines in Belgium, Canada, and several African countries, among many others. Within any given language, as well, various sorts of distinctions are symbolized or maintained through the display of certain linguistic characteristics. Anyone who has heard the famous Watergate tapes — replete with bleeps deleting expletives — knows that, in the United States, the leaders speak "like the masses"; the same cannot, however, be said of Great Britain. In his famous play *Pygmalion*, George Bernard Shaw illustrated the importance of language in maintaining Britain's class distinctions: all it takes to transform a lowly flower girl into a respectable lady is to replace her Cockney speech with the upper-class dialect. (This is not to say that linguistic characteristics have no social implications in America — variations in dialect certainly do become associated with class in many countries.)

Shaw's play also touches on another linguistic–social convention: in the course of becoming a lady, Eliza learns that she must remain silent, in a feminine and demure way, while men talk. The issue of differences in the linguistic performance of men and women in all societies is taken up in Chapter 27, by Mary Ritchie Key. One example of such a difference in English-speaking countries is found in the conventions surrounding curses and obscenities: whereas young men learn that they will appear more adult if they swear, young women learn that swearing will detract from their femininity. Similarly, in many languages, the speech patterns of men and women differ not only in vocabulary, but also in certain aspects of syntax (sentence structure) and phonology. Although such differences have long been noted, the explanations provided for them — largely by men — have often been based on sexist attitudes. Key points out that well-known linguists and anthropologists alike have fallen into this trap. To demonstrate the arbitrariness and fragility of the gender distinctions made in English, she analyzes some of the difficulties that arise in translating religious terms associated with the beliefs of the Aztecs of Mexico. For example, since the Aztecs' supreme being is a single being comprising dual aspects — masculine and feminine, singular and plural — its translation defies the simplistic gender distinctions of the English language.

There was a time when speakers of English innocently believed that *grass* referred simply to the green ground-cover that is food for sheep and cows; that *pot* referred to a kitchen utensil; and that to be *gay* was a social grace. Such shifts in the meaning of words are taking place constantly, but not all of them are unconscious, or unplanned. The short article from *The Seattle Times* reproduced in Chapter 28 illustrates the phenomenon of linguistic manipulation. Sally Macdonald lists examples of the "doublespeak" (reminiscent of NEWSPEAK in George Orwell's novel *Nineteen Eighty-Four*) that was used by the U.S. Defense Department in an effort to rally the American public behind the Gulf War. Words such as *clean* were associated with war, *smart* with bombs, and *surgical strike* with the slaughter of hundreds of soldiers huddled in a bunker. Commercial language offers analogous examples of linguistic manipulation — for instance, *pre-owned car* for "used car" and *free gifts* for what amounts to "bait." Language can be used to manipulate public opinion and distort peoples' perception of reality; in short, words can be chosen for their propaganda value more than their accuracy. In spite of the use of language to deceive, however, we do still use it effectively to tell the truth as well. The name of the science of anthropology is derived, in part, from *logos*, the Greek word for "language": a science is first and foremost an attempt to create a precise language that can be used to describe a range of phenomena and processes.

Works Cited

Dobrovolsky, M. 1987. "Animal Communication." Chap. 16 in *Contemporary Linguistic Analysis: An Introduction*, edited by William O'Grady and Michael Dobrovolsky. Toronto: Copp Clark Pitman.

O'Grady, W. 1987. "Semantics: The Study of Meaning." Chap. 7 in *Contemporary Linguistic Analysis: An Introduction*, edited by William O'Grady and Michael Dobrovolsky. Toronto: Copp Clark Pitman.

Orwell, G. 1949. *Nineteen Eighty-Four: A Novel*. New York: Harcourt and Brace.

Shaw, G.B. 1918. *Pygmalion, Play in Five Acts*. London: Constable & Co.

24
Monkey Business

MARTIN GARDNER

A review of Nim: A Chimpanzee Who Learned Sign Language, *by Herbert S. Terrace, Knopf, 1980, 303 pp., and* Speaking of Apes: A Critical Anthology of Two-Way Communication with Man, *edited by Thomas A. Sebeok and Donna Jean Umiker-Sebeok, Plenum, 1980, 469 pp.*

Remember the great tumult during the Sixties about talking dolphins? Because a dolphin brain is larger than ours, could it be that porpoises are potentially as bright as we are, maybe more so? John C. Lilly seriously tried teaching English to these clever little whales and for a time actually believed he had taught dolphins to mimic human speech. Like the black races of Africa, Lilly once said, porpoises are on the brink of becoming Westernized, a revolution with unpredictable consequences. "If dolphins come to understand our cold war," he warned, "we don't know how they will proceed to operate."

After Lilly became convinced that several of his Florida porpoises had committed suicide, he abandoned his watery research to wander off into the jungles of parapsychology and Eastern mysticism. He reported fantastic encounters with extraterrestrial intelligence. He told reporters that

dolphins were using ESP to "infiltrate" human minds. Eventually it became clear to almost everybody, as it had been all along to "establishment" biologists, that Lilly's research was hopelessly flawed, and that the whale mind, though wondrous and unique, is not much more so, if at all, than the mind of a pig or an elephant. The lovable dolphins swam away from the press and television, leaving in their wakes a batch of careless books and TV documentaries, and surely the worst movie (*The Day of the Dolphin*) ever directed by Mike Nichols.

As the dolphin flap faded, a new media enthusiasm began to gather momentum. At the University of Nevada, Allen and Beatrice Gardner succeeded in teaching ASL (American Sign Language) to an infant female chimpanzee named Washoe. For the first time in history, it was loudly proclaimed, a lower primate had mastered a language in which it could talk to humans.

"Talk" and "language" are, of course, fuzzy terms with wide spectrums of meaning. A bluejay "talks" to other birds when it warns them of a cat. A cat "talks" when it asks to be fed by rubbing against your calf. Dogs communicate by barking, growling, whimpering, wagging their tails, and leaving symbolic messages on fire hydrants. Even so, the world was astounded by Washoe's ability to understand hundreds of sign gestures, especially by her ability to combine signs in ways that suggested a rudimentary grasp of grammar.

The best-known instance of Washoe inventing a phrase was when her teacher, Roger Fouts, had taken her out in a rowboat and a swan glided by. Fouts signed "What's that?" Washoe, knowing the signs for water and bird, responded with "water bird." There were many other two-word combinations mastered by Washoe: *Washoe sorry, Roger tickle, you drink*, and so on.

Other researchers soon were teaching other visual languages to young chimps. In California, David Premack symbolized words with plastic tiles of different shapes and colors. His star pupil, Sarah, became almost as famous as Washoe. Like Washoe, Sarah seemed to create significant phrases. David's wife, Ann, wrote a book called *Why Chimps Can Read*.

In Georgia, Duane Rumbaugh tried a new tack. He had a computer built with a console of keys bearing patterns that represented words. A chimpanzee named Lana was taught to speak in this computer language of "Yerkish," named for the Yerkes Primate Center in Atlanta where Rumbaugh did his work. Lana, too, apparently combined signs in meaningful sequences. She called a cucumber a *green banana*. She called an orange an *orange apple*.

The achievements of Washoe, Sarah, and Lana have now been surpassed, so it is claimed, by the fabulous linguistic feats of Koko, a female gorilla trained since 1972 by a psychologist, Francine ("Penny") Patterson, in Stanford. It is not hard to understand why Penny — young, pretty, with long blond hair — has received such enormous publicity. What could be more dramatic than color photographs of Beauty and the Beast, heads together, raptly chattering to one another? Patterson wrote a cover story (the cover photo of Koko was snapped by Koko) for *National Geographic* (October 1978) titled "Conversations with a Gorilla." The pair graced the cover of *The New York Times Magazine* (June 12, 1977). In *Koko, A Talking Gorilla*, a stirring film documentary that opened last December in Manhattan, Koko does a fine job of acting like a gorilla, but otherwise the film is mostly flimflam.

There is another reason for Penny's growing fame. Her claims for ape intelligence far exceed those of any other trainer. For one thing, Koko loves to make up rhymes: *Squash wash, do blue, bear hair*, and so on. (She has learned English vocalizations by hearing Penny repeat them, and by using a typewriter speech synthesizer designed by the Stanford mathematician Patrick Suppes.) Once Koko made up the poem: *Flower pink, fruit stink — fruit pink stink*. Here is a sampling of Koko's skill in inventing clever metaphors: *Elephant baby* (for a Pinocchio doll), *eye hat* (mask), *finger bracelet* (ring), *white tiger* (zebra), *fake mouth* (nose).

A reporter asked Koko whom she liked best, Penny or her assistant. According to Penny, Koko looked back and forth, then diplomatically signed, "Bad question." On another occasion Penny asked, "What are you afraid of?" Koko: "Afraid alligator." Koko had never seen a live alligator. Penny thinks this shows how researchers can learn new facts about apes now that they can ask them questions.

According to Eugene Linden (who wrote a popular book about talking apes), in a wildly laudatory article ("Talk to the Animals," *Omni*, January 1980), when Koko was asked where you go when you die she signed, "Comfortable hole bye." Once when Penny became exasperated by the number of toys Koko had broken Penny muttered, "Why can't you be normal like any other kid?" Koko, says Linden, signed "Gorilla."

From the beginning large numbers of experts on animal behavior have been deeply skeptical of these extraordinary claims, but their animadversions appeared only in technical journals. Now the secret is out. Two books have been published, one popular, one technical, that give a strong case for the view that apes do not comprehend sign sequences in any way essentially different from a dog's understanding of such commands as "Sit up and shake hands" or "Go get the newspaper."

Nowhere on the jacket of *Nim* or in the book's advertising does the publisher so much as hint that the book severely criticizes practically all earlier work with talking apes. Even the author, Herbert Terrace, a psychologist at Columbia University, plays down his doubts at the start of his book, though there is a reason. When he began training Nim Chimpsky, a baby male chimp named in honor of Noam Chomsky, he had high hopes of confirming the earlier findings. His book is an informal narrative, with marvelous photographs, about four years that he and his many assistants spent in teaching ASL to Nim. Not until Chapter 13, after Nim has returned to his birthplace in Oklahoma, does Terrace see the light.

Terrace's complete disenchantment did not descend until he began to study his own extensive videotapes. Here are some of the things he learned:

Nim rarely initiated signing. Ninety percent of his signing was in response to gestures by teachers.

Half of Nim's signs imitated part or all of what a teacher had just signed. In many cases his teachers were astonished to see how often they had unconsciously started a sign that Nim had noticed.

If Nim wanted something he first grabbed, signing only when the grab failed. He never initiated signs except when expecting such rewards as food, hugs, and tickling.

Most of Nim's phrases were random combinations of signs, usually involving *me, hug*, and *Nim* — signs that fitted with almost all other signs, and which he had learned were likely to elicit favorable reactions.

Unlike children when they start to talk, Nim constantly interrupted teachers. He never learned the two-way nature of conversation. Researchers have attributed such interruptions to an ape's eagerness to talk.

Nim's mistakes were more often the confusing of signs similar in form rather than similar in meaning.

When Nim began to extend sentences beyond two or three words he simply added a string of nonsense words, usually repeating earlier signs. For example: "Give orange me give eat orange me eat orange give me eat orange give me you." This in contrast to the longer utterances of children which expand the sense of shorter ones.

Nim never signed to another chimpanzee who knew ASL unless a teacher was present to coax him.

Nim Chimpsky finally convinced Terrace that Noam Chomsky, the most distinguished of skeptical linguistics experts, was right. Although apes have a remarkable memory that enables them to master hundreds of visual signs, Terrace believes there is no evidence yet that they understand any kind of syntax. Of course this may be true also of very young children, but children quickly go on to form sentences that require a firm grasp of the rules of form. When an ape learns to put a few signs together there is no reason, says Terrace, to suppose it is doing anything essentially different from a pigeon that has been taught to obtain food by pecking four differently colored buttons in a specific order regardless of how the buttons are arranged.

When Terrace examined the videotapes of other researchers he found the same disturbing features. In many cases of film released for public viewing and for fund raising, episodes had been edited so that initial promptings were not seen. A Nova documentary called *The First Signs of Washoe* consistently followed this practice. Uncut versions of the same episodes showed that every one of Washoe's multi-sign statements came after similar signs by teachers.

"Can an Ape Create a Sentence?" is the title of Terrace's report in *Science* (November 23, 1979). His reluctant answer is no. "Apes can learn many isolated symbols (as can dogs, horses, and other nonhuman species), but they show no unequivocal evidence of mastering the conversational, semantic, or syntactic organization of language." Of the earlier researchers only Rumbaugh so far seems impressed by Terrace's analysis. His own work, he told *The New York Times* (October 21, 1979) has been pushing him toward similar views.

Speaking of Apes, edited by linguist-semiotician Thomas A. Sebeok and anthropologist Donna Jean Umiker-Sebeok, is a much needed anthology of important articles on both sides of the intensifying controversy over the capacities of apes for language. It is impossible to discuss such a wide variety of papers so I will concentrate mainly on the long introductory article, "Questioning Apes," by the Sebeoks. Both are at Indiana University's Research Center for Language and Semiotic Studies, of which Thomas Sebeok is chairman. Their introduction is the most powerful indictment in print of the early work on talking apes.[1]

Psychologists have a term, "experimenter effect," that covers all the insidious ways a researcher's strong convictions can unwittingly distort data. The Sebeoks first remind us of obvious ways that scientists in any field can be unconsciously motivated to get positive results. The stronger the results the faster their career advances, and the more likely will their work attract funding. Assistants are strongly motivated to please an employer who pays their salary, and success often advances their own careers. If the work is controversial there is a tendency for research teams to form a cluster of insiders deeply suspicious of outsiders. They become, as the Sebeoks put it, a "dedicated group of enthusiastic workers, one that constitutes a tightly knit social community with a solid core of shared beliefs and goals in opposition to outside visitors.... In fact, it is difficult to imagine a skeptic being taken in as a member of such a 'team.'"

Within this frame the Sebeoks see a variety of curious ways in which talking-ape results are easily twisted in the direction of belief. Consider, for example, the "Clever Hans effect." The term comes from a classic 1907 study by Oskar Pfungst, a German psychologist, of a famous performing horse of the day who could answer difficult questions, including arithmetical problems, by pawing the ground. In most cases of such performing animals (there have also been "learned" dogs, pigs, and even geese), a trainer tells the animal when to stop by secret cueing, such as a slight sniff, but in the case of Hans, Pfungst was able to prove by ingenious tests that the horse had learned to respond to subliminal cueing on the part of spectators.

Talking-ape researchers have tried to exclude the Clever Hans effect, but the Sebeoks show convincingly that the effect is omnipresent. There is no evidence, they maintain, that successful teachers had any training in controlling unconscious facial movements, breathing rhythms, bodily tensions and relaxations, and so on. Some reactions, such as eye-pupil size, are probably uncontrollable. Pfungst reported his inability to avoid cueing Hans no matter how hard he tried.

Talking apes seldom perform well for strangers. Believers explain this by an ape's emotional attachment to certain teachers, but it is as readily explained by assuming that over the years apes develop a special sensitivity to unconscious reactions peculiar to a loved human and which they naturally fail to perceive if someone new tries to talk to them. Could it be, the Sebeoks ask, that the best trainers are those most expressive in unconscious cueing? A study of unedited films shows that ape teachers are, in the authors' words, "anything ... but stone faced." Even uncropped still photos reveal obvious cueing. The Sebeoks cite some horrendous instances in the photos illustrating Patterson's *National Geographic* article, and in Mrs. Premack's book.

Concerning the famous Washoe-swan incident, both Terrace and the Sebeoks point out what should have been obvious at once. Washoe may simply have signed "water," then noticed the bird and signed "bird." It is unlikely that Fouts could have concealed his elation. Washoe, observing this social reward, would henceforth associate the double sign with a swan.

There is no solid evidence that an ape has ever invented a composite sign by understanding its parts. In the course of several years an ape will put together signs in thousands of random ways. It would be surprising if it did not frequently hit on happy combinations that would elicit an immediate Clever Hans response. No teacher has bothered to record all the nonsense combinations

produced by an ape, but every lucky hit is sure to be reinforced by cues of approval, and to go into a teacher's records, reports, books, and lectures.

Even when an ape has memorized a sign it often makes errors in reproducing it. When this happens, the Sebeoks point out, ape teachers have a battery of excuses. Instead of a mistake it becomes a joke or a lie or an insult. Patterson is especially prone toward this kind of subjective evaluation. She asks Koko to sign drink. Koko touches her ear. Koko is joking. She asks Koko to put a toy under a bag. Koko raises it to the ceiling. Koko is teasing. She asks Koko what rhymes with sweet. Koko makes the sign for red, a gesture similar to the one for sweet. Koko is making a gestural pun. She asks Koko to smile. Koko frowns. Koko is displaying a "grasp of opposites." Penny points to a photograph of Koko and asks, "Who gorilla?" Koko signs "Bird." Koko is being "bratty."

The *National Geographic* article reproduces a crayon picture by Koko that is captioned "Representational Art." Its black squiggles, says Penny, are spiders. An orange scrawl is Koko's drinking glass. A similar tendency to overhumanize ape behavior, though less blatant, infects all the earlier work. It is little different from the firm belief of sentimental pet owners that a beloved cat, or even a parrot, understands almost everything you say to it.

It is possible, of course, that apes do have a feeble talent for creating meaningful composite signs, but by the principle of Occam's razor, the Sebeoks insist, should we not accept simpler explanations first? So far there is no reason to suppose that Koko's remarkable utterances are anything more than responses to unwitting cueing on Penny's part, or to Penny sifting out from thousands of nonsense combinations those that make sense to *her*, not to Koko. An objective evaluation of a phrase like "bad question" cannot be made without a videotape of the scene to make sure the details are correctly recalled, and without knowledge of how many of the ape's unlearned and spontaneous two-word combinations are nonsense. Otherwise we have nothing more than a collection of anecdotes.

Some researchers, especially Premack, have tried "double blind" tests to rule out Clever Hans effects, and whenever these controls were tight the ape's ability dropped almost to chance. Much is made of the slight deviations from chance, but the Sebeoks list numerous ways in which bias could have slipped into these efforts to exclude it. We are not told what controls were placed on photographers. Reports often fail to note the presence of others who happened to be around but were deemed too irrelevant to mention. One-way windows eliminate visual cues but not sound cues. Details are sparse about randomizing procedures and the rules followed in scoring.

There are religious beliefs — in the West notably those of the Catholic Church and conservative Protestantism — that make it necessary to assume that human beings have an immortal soul denied to the beasts that perish. Mortimer J. Adler wrote a book a few years ago called *The Difference of Man and the Difference It Makes* in which he enlarges on Thomist arguments that the ability to understand syntax is one of the main ways a human mind differs from the mind of a beast. At the time Adler wrote his book the dolphin language flap was in full swing, and Adler made much of the fact that if we ever succeed in conversing with a whale his thesis will be undermined. If the book has a new edition you can be sure Adler will underplay porpoises and concentrate his dialectical fire on apes.

It is good to understand that this sort of metaphysical objection to talking apes, reinforced by Revelation, is not behind the views of Chomsky, Terrace, the Sebeoks, or any other major critic.

What they are saying is much simpler. Contemporary humans and apes are terminal branches on the tree of evolution. Transitional types that flourished over the millennia during which human beings acquired the ability to talk are no longer available for study. Chomsky believes that evolution gave to humans, as it did not give to any living lower primates, a capacity for language that is deeply interlocked with the inherited structure of their brains.

Little is gained by quibbling over the meaning of "language." As Chomsky says in his contribution to the Sebeok anthology, this is a conceptual not a scientific question. If you define flying, he writes, as rising into the air without the aid of special equipment and landing some distance away, then human broadjumpers can fly about thirty feet. Chickens do slightly better — about three hundred feet.

Suppose, Chomsky continues, we label the four colors pecked by pigeons with four words: *Please-give-me-food*. "Do we want to say that pigeons have the capacity for language, in a rudimentary way? This is much like the question whether humans can fly, almost as well as chickens though not as well as Canada geese. The question is not clear or interesting enough to deserve an answer."

The central empirical question can be simply put. Do apes have the ability to link visual signs in ways that justify saying they are using syntax? Yes, say most of the researchers and many outsiders. Jane H. Hill, an American anthropologist, closes her contribution to *Speaking of Apes* by writing: "It is unlikely that any of us will in our lifetime see again a scientific breakthrough as profound in its implications as the moment when Washoe ... raised her hand and signed 'come-gimme' to a comprehending human."

No, say some researchers and a growing number of outsiders. If no, Chomsky concludes, then a study of ape signing can be expected to cast as little light on human language or conversely as a study of human jumping can cast light on the mechanism of bird flight or conversely. One can teach two pigeons to bat a ball, writes Ms. Hill, quoting a familiar aphorism, but is it ping-pong? She thinks it unjust to apply this skepticism to talking-ape research. Chomsky holds the opposite opinion.

No one can rule out the hope that as talking-ape research continues, under better controls, it may turn out that apes do have a dim awareness of syntax. If so, then the researchers will have made a point even though it may not be a big one. At the moment, however, the situation seems little different from that which confronted biologists a century ago. Here is how Darwin summed it up in a section on language in *The Descent of Man*:

> As the voice was used more and more, the vocal organs would have been strengthened and perfected through the principle of the inherited effects of use; and this would have reacted on the power of speech. But the relation between the continued use of language and the development of the brain has no doubt been far more important. The mental powers in some early progenitor of man must have been more highly developed than in any existing ape, before even the most imperfect form of speech could have come into use....

Note

1. Thomas Sebeok's earlier anthology, *How Animals Communicate*, was reviewed the *The New York Review of Books* by J.Z. Young, March 9, 1978.

25
Hard Words

PHILIP E. ROSS

In the beginning there was the word. Ask Merritt Ruhlen what it was and he will reply: *tik.* That simple monosyllable was what prehistoric man may have named finger. Ruhlen says it comes down to English as *toe* and to Latin as *digit*. He refuses to put a date on the root, although others argue, on genetic evidence, that it goes back perhaps 100,000 years.

Ruhlen, an unaffiliated linguist, is one of a small group of radical researchers who believe they can hear echoes of ancient voices. He thinks it is possible to trace all the world's languages back to a single source spoken in the distant past, a tongue not heard since well before the first horse was broken and the first dog was brought unflinching to the campfire. Others are content to trace language back to roots current perhaps 12,000 to 15,000 years ago, before the development of agriculture.

That all the several thousand languages spoken by the world's four billion people sprang from a common root is a powerful idea indeed. It is the linguistic parallel of the "Eve hypothesis" formulated by Allan C. Wilson, Mark Stoneking, and Rebecca L. Cann of the University of California at Berkeley, who compared samples of DNA to trace the entire human population back to a single woman in Africa perhaps 150,000 years ago. It

may even rival the importance of the grand unified theory now being sought by physicists. But, like its counterparts in other disciplines, the monogenesis of language is hard to prove.

For nearly two centuries, scholars have been grouping languages into families, some 200 in all. Some families, known as isolates, contain only a single member: Basque, a language still spoken in the Spanish and French Pyrenees, is the best-known example. But most contain a number of languages whose similarities point to their descent from a common ancestor, the protolanguage of the family. The most ancient protolanguages that all linguists accept are believed to have been spoken about 7,000 years ago.

To comparative linguists who have devoted entire careers to a painstaking study of one group of languages, the idea that the families themselves might be compared and their far more ancient roots discerned seems impossibly ambitious. If the tree of language could in fact be traced to far deeper roots, then the trunks on which most specialists have labored would seem mere twigs on a vaster tree.

Shouted Down

Yet that is precisely what two groups of researchers are doing. The first serious effort to trace the branches of human language back to a 12,000-year-old Neolithic trunk was made nearly

30 years ago by the Soviet linguists Vladislav M. Illych-Svitych and Aaron B. Dolgopolsky. The two scholars, at first working independently, eventually linked six families of languages to trace a hypothetical ancestor that they called Nostratic, derived from the Latin for "our" (language). Together these families transmit the cultural heritage of three-quarters of humankind.

In the United States, Joseph H. Greenberg of Stanford University began comparing families of languages in the 1950s. His most sweeping work, *Language in the Americas*, was published in 1987. In that book, Greenberg classified the myriad languages of the Americas into three groups, each with its own ancient antecedents. He thus united three-quarters of the language families that are known to exist or to have ever existed.

Even before it was published, Greenberg's analysis came under attack. In 1986 a preview of his book appeared in *Current Anthropology*. That inspired Lyle Campbell, who teaches Native American languages at the University of Louisiana, to write that Greenberg's classification should be "shouted down" so as not to mislead anthropologists into wasting time trying to confirm it.

But the strongest opposition to the Nostraticists and to Greenberg and his associates comes from the traditional comparative linguists who specialize in the Indo-European family of languages. This family is thought to be descended from a single speech last spoken in the fourth or fifth millennium B.C.

All specialists agree that by the dawn of history, about 4,000 years ago, proto-Indo-European had fragmented into a dozen branches, two of which, Anatolian and Tocharian, left no survivors. By the Middle Ages, Germanic, Italic, Celtic, Baltic, Slavic, Albanian, Greek, Armenian, Iranian, and Indic had differentiated into a plethora of modern tongues, several of which have since ridden through the world on the shoulders of conquerors, farmers, merchants, and missionaries, becoming the native speech of every second human being.

Indo-European study has its origin in the systematic, if rather fanciful, classifications of the sixteenth and seventeenth centuries, when theologians first attempted to prove the biblical account of the confusion of tongues at Babel by tracing all languages to biblical Hebrew. Secular etymologies were tried as early as the seventeenth century, notably by Gottfried Wilhelm Leibniz, the co-discoverer of calculus.

But linguists like to date their field to its first great achievement, the argument propounded in 1786 by Sir William Jones, a scholar and jurist. He observed of Sanskrit, Greek, and Latin that "no philologer could examine them all three without believing them to have sprung from some common source, which, perhaps, no longer exists."

Jones's immediate successors were the Dane Rasmus Rask and the Germans Franz Bopp and Jacob Grimm, one of the Brothers Grimm of fairy-tale fame. Grimm was the first to call general attention to systematic sound differences in words having similar meanings from different Indo-European groups. He noted that such modern members of the Germanic family as English and German have an *f* and *v* in places where the other groups have a *p*. For example, English and German say *father* and *vater*, whereas Latin has *pater* and Sanskrit gives *pitar-*. A web of such sound shifts, as they are called, was subsequently found to have left marks in many other languages.

The comparative technique attained nearly modern form in the mid-nineteenth century in the work of August Schleicher, who first charted language families as branches on a tree. Schleicher was also the first scholar to attempt to reconstruct languages by inferring their words from later forms, a laborious process that has been likened to triangulation. He even imagined how these words might have produced sentences in combination with grammatical markers, which he also reconstructed.

Historical linguists look for analogies that they then test against a range of criteria to determine whether the analogy is a form that descended directly from the two languages' last common ancestor. Such forms are called cognates. But in language, where change is the rule and words are traded, modified, and discarded, reconstructing true meanings is a complex process.

At the foundation of this method is the idea that two languages can be genetically related even if they have no cognates in common. If language A shares cognates with language B, which in turn shares cognates with language C, all three must be kin. Yet one can imagine that the lexicons of A and C might not overlap. Kinship refers to the history of a language, not to its content.

Traditional linguists compare only a few languages at a time, seeking commonalities and reconstructing roots. So far the Indo-Europeanists have reconstructed a vast lexicon of words spoken well before writing was invented. Such reconstructions often tell more about early cultures than can be learned from their material artifacts.

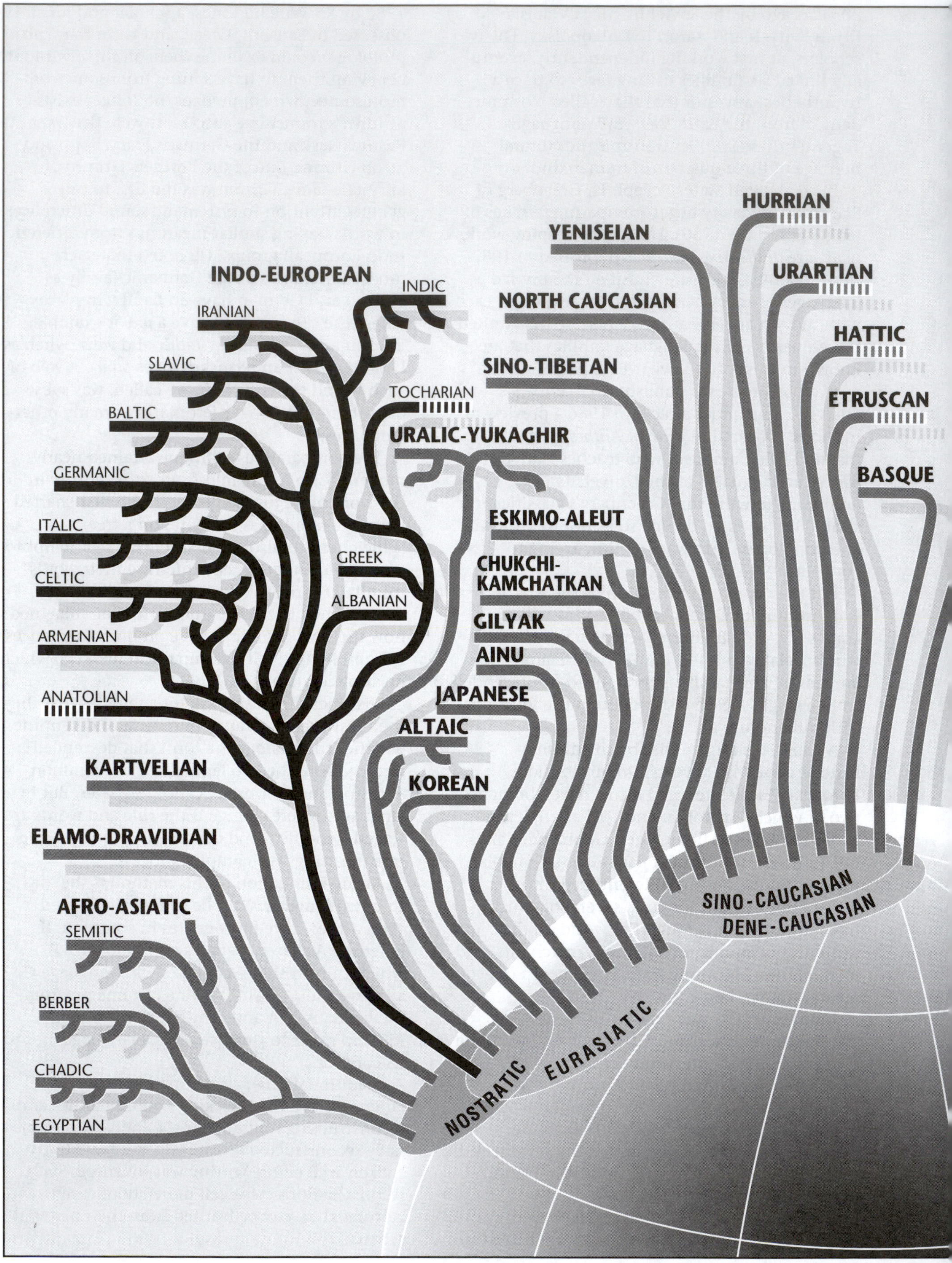

INDO-EUROPEAN
INDIC
IRANIAN
SLAVIC
BALTIC
GERMANIC
ITALIC
CELTIC
ARMENIAN
ANATOLIAN
GREEK
ALBANIAN
TOCHARIAN
KARTVELIAN
ELAMO-DRAVIDIAN
AFRO-ASIATIC
SEMITIC
BERBER
CHADIC
EGYPTIAN

YENISEIAN
NORTH CAUCASIAN
SINO-TIBETAN
URALIC-YUKAGHIR
ESKIMO-ALEUT
CHUKCHI-KAMCHATKAN
GILYAK
AINU
JAPANESE
ALTAIC
KOREAN

HURRIAN
URARTIAN
HATTIC
ETRUSCAN
BASQUE

NOSTRATIC
EURASIATIC
SINO-CAUCASIAN
DENE-CAUCASIAN

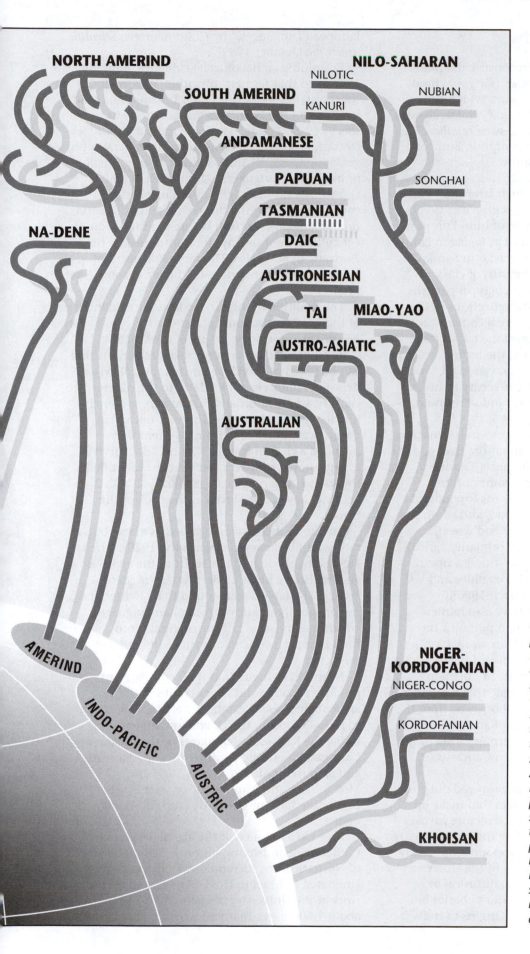

NORTH AMERIND

SOUTH AMERIND

NILO-SAHARAN

NILOTIC

KANURI

NUBIAN

ANDAMANESE

NA-DENE

PAPUAN

SONGHAI

TASMANIAN

DAIC

AUSTRONESIAN

TAI   **MIAO-YAO**

AUSTRO-ASIATIC

AUSTRALIAN

AMERIND

INDO-PACIFIC

AUSTRIC

NIGER-KORDOFANIAN

NIGER-CONGO

KORDOFANIAN

KHOISAN

Genealogical chart relates entire families of languages to proposed superfamilies. The Indo-European family, for example, appears in black; it includes English in its Germanic branch (top left). Some Soviet linguists group the family with six others in the controversial Nostratic superfamily (bottom left). An alternative superfamily, Eurasiatic, has also been proposed. None of the superfamilies and not all of the families are accepted as proved by the majority of linguists. Families, such as Etruscan, and subfamilies, such as Anatolian, that have no living languages appear as dashed lines.

Prehistoric Patriarchs

Consider, for example, the reconstructed Indo-European word for father: *p'tēr-*. Linguists modeled this root from derived forms, which comparative studies have shown to signify the male head of a household, as in the Latin *pater familias*. Thus do we know that the speakers of Indo-European formed patriarchal communities.

Similarly, linguists think the Indo-European word for god was *deiw-os*, which later shows up in Latin as *deus*. In combination with *p'tēr-*, it designated the patriarchal god of Indo-European religion: *Dyeu p'ter-*. It survived as *Jupiter* in Latin, *Zeus patēr* in Greek, and *Dyaus pitar* in Sanskrit.

By such means can some myths of classical cultures be reconstructed to archetypal patterns, themselves anthropomorphic reflections of the way Indo-Europeans lived. "The reconstructed words *deiw-os* and *Dyeu p'ter-* alone tell us more about the conceptual world of the Indo-Europeans than a roomful of graven idols," wrote Calvert Watkins of Harvard University in his introduction to a dictionary of Indo-European roots.

Indeed, the reconstructed proto-Indo-European vocabulary speaks volumes about the lives of those who spoke it. Soviet linguists Thomas V. Gamkrelidze and V.V. Ivanov point out, for example, that the numerous words for domesticated animals, such as dogs, cows, and sheep, as well as for crops, such as barley and wheat, indicate that the cultures were primarily agricultural [see "The Early History of Indo-European Languages," by Thomas V. Gamkrelidze and V.V. Ivanov; *Scientific American*, March 1990].

Gamkrelidze and Ivanov have also reinterpreted the linguistic evidence to pinpoint the location at which Indo-European arose. Its homeland has been variously placed in the steppes of Russia and the forests of northern Europe. But the two Soviets argue that a number of words seemed to have been borrowed from the non-Indo-European languages of ancient Mesopotamia, specifically eastern Anatolia (now part of Turkey) and the southern Caucasus (in Soviet Georgia).

From there the protolanguage spread out and differentiated into the languages that make up this group today. The traditional picture invokes conquering horsemen imposing their language by force. But another scenario, propounded recently by archaeologist Colin Renfrew of the University of Cambridge, depicts a gradual diffusion of language borne not by the warrior's chariot but by the farmer's plow [see "The Origins of Indo-European Languages," by Colin Renfrew; *Scientific American*, October 1989].

Examining archaeological evidence, Renfrew concluded that farmers' offspring, moving just a short distance away from their birthplaces, could have spread the languages across Europe in the space of 1,500 years. As people moved out of contact, their speech changed, from generation to generation, into distinct dialects, then mutually unintelligible languages. Although it would appear that no such agricultural mechanism could have guided the dispersion and differentiation of languages spoken before the invention of agriculture, Renfrew says he is intrigued by the Nostratic hypothesis. "The more I've heard of Nostratic, the more interested I have become," he says.

The traditional linguists believe the evidence of their reconstructions is trustworthy. Reconstructions, they say, meet the strictest definitions of science: they make predictions that can be tested positively against empirical evidence. A famous example dates to the nineteenth century, when Ferdinand de Saussure, a French linguist, deduced that the Indo-European languages were descended from a system that included a class of sounds that had not survived in any known tongue. Later scholars identified the sounds as laryngeal consonants, so called because they are produced at the back of the throat.

Saussure's theory was regarded as a neat but rather artificial construct until the 1920s, when archaeologists dug up tablets from the archives of ancient Hittite kings at Hattusas, in modern Turkey. The tablets were found to be written in the previously unknown Anatolian languages, which preserve some of the original proto-Indo-European consonants that Saussure had predicted.

Nostraticists argue that their comparisons produce equally valid insights into far more ancient cultures. Nostratic is held to be ancestral to Indo-European, the Dravidian languages of India, the Kartvelian languages of the southern Caucasus, the Uralic family (including Finnish and Samoyed), Altaic (such as Turkish, Mongolian), and Afro-Asiatic or, as it is sometimes called, Hamito-Semitic (such as Arabic, Berber).

Illych-Svitych died at the age of 31 years in a traffic accident, leaving his projected dictionary of Nostratic roots incomplete. Dolgopolsky, who emigrated to Israel in the 1970s, carried on the work at the University of Haifa. He now has about 1,600 roots, many of which carry cultural

A Discipline Where Caution Prevails

Linguists tend to conservatism, and not without some justification. More than most other scholars, linguists are besieged by amateurs advancing potentially embarrassing notions. Most of these amateurs are merely harmless drudges in the grip of a private theory. But there also was Adolf Hitler, who used a strange combination of Darwinism and Indo-European linguistics to support his ideology of an Aryan superrace.

With the taint of World War II, it is perhaps not surprising that many historical linguists are now quick to dismiss any attempt to find connections between genes and language. Even linguists who specialize in matters besides classification tend to be leery of any idea that might hint at racist implications.

Take the theory about Creole languages propounded nearly 10 years ago by Derek Bickerton of the University of Hawaii. Bickerton studied the common languages created by immigrants to island communities and found that they changed strikingly between the first and second generation of speakers. First-generation speakers cobble together structurally cumbersome codes called pidgins, whereas their children create complete languages called Creoles. Bickerton argued that all Creoles share structural features that reflect innate patterns of mind.

That's not the equalitarian idea it might seem to be at first, says Mark R. Hale of Harvard University. "That Creoles somehow preserve a structure innate in children under the age of two is, in a way, racist or can be used for that," he says. Might not the invariant syntax of Creoles prove, rather, the unity of humankind? "I think that is what Bickerton intended," Hale replies, after a pause. "But there is the danger that others might put another construction on it. Remember, these Creoles are spoken by brown people, the children of slaves and indentured laborers."

Even studying the words used for colors can get a linguist into political trouble. In 1968 Paul Kay and Brent Berlin of the University of California at Berkeley set out to test the belief that people perceive the world wholly through the conceptual grid of language. The extreme position held that a Russian, for example, might be conditioned by his language to see a color as light blue or dark blue, whereas an American might see it as plain old blue, for which a single English word exists.

Kay and Berlin found that it does not work that way. "Languages that lump many colors together under one color term tend to lump in the same way," Kay observes. "Some people haven't forgiven me to this day," he says. "Some even argued that my theory had racist implications — not the universalist aspect, but the calling attention to the varying number of color terms. The languages of Colonial oppressors tend to have more words for color than those of the oppressed."

Woe, too, to a biologist who links languages to population groups. Stanford University geneticist Luigi L. Cavalli-Sforza was attacked for correlating the frequency with which certain genes appear in populations to the languages those populations speak. He thinks genes and language diverged at the same time — when populations split apart — and that some splits date to the settling of the earth by modern *Homo sapiens*.

It was Charles Darwin who first linked the evolution of languages to biology. In *The Descent of Man* (1871), he wrote, "The formation of different languages and of distinct species, and the proofs that both have been developed through a gradual process, are curiously parallel." But linguists cringe at the idea that evolution might transform simple languages into complex ones.

Today it is believed that no language is, in any basic way, "prior" to any other, living or dead. Language alters even as we speak it, but it neither improves nor degenerates. Modern English may be better than Old English for a discussion of physics, but this tells us nothing about the potential resources of either tongue.

Earlier generations of linguists had no such reservations about ranking languages. In the nineteenth century August Schleicher classified them according to their structures.

Schleicher said that "isolating" languages, such as Chinese, used simple elements and were thus more "primitive" than "agglutinating" languages, such as Turkish, which builds its words from distinct forms. He put "inflecting" languages like German higher because their words vary with function. He ranked Sanskrit highest because its inflections were so elaborate. The system failed even on its own terms, however, by elevating the languages of many hunter-gatherers above those of the linguists themselves.

baggage comparable to that in the reconstructed lexicon of Indo-European.

The differences, however, are much more interesting: Nostratic has many words for plants but none for cultivated varieties or for the technologies of cultivation. Similarly, it has words for animals but does not differentiate between domestic and wild. From these absences of data, scholars tentatively conclude that the language was spoken before the emergence of agriculture and animal husbandry.

It would therefore appear that speakers of Nostratic were hunter-gatherers. Vitaly Shevoroshkin, a former associate of the Soviet Nostraticists now teaching at the University of Michigan, observes that the vocabulary includes words like *haya*, which meant the running down of game over a period of days. Still, he notes that words for fairly permanent shelters indicate that the Nostrates (as he calls them) lived in villages for which some tentative archaeological evidence exists.

To arrive at those conclusions, however, the Nostraticists are accused of taking shortcuts that traditional Indo-Europeanists consider unacceptable. The traditionalists admit that the Soviet linguists indeed reconstruct the requisite web of sound shifts and try to reconstruct protowords according to accepted rules. But, they maintain, the Nostraticists compare poorly sifted data and accept as cognates words from different languages that might owe their resemblances to chance or simple linguistic borrowing.

The Nostraticists reply that they minimize chance resemblances by seeking complex sound correspondences and that they rule out borrowing by examining words that are particularly unlikely to be borrowed. These so-called stable words denote concepts believed to be common to all languages — body parts, for example, or natural objects such as the sun and the moon.

Lost in Static

"It is certain that the word for house is much less stable than the word for hand, because the whole system of architecture and house building can be replaced, and the words with them," says Sergei Starostin, a Soviet linguist. "It is known that you borrow things and the words that describe them. But you do not borrow *hand*; it does not happen."

That's not good enough for the Indo-Europeanists. "I'm not saying the Nostraticists are wrong. I'm saying they haven't shown that they are right," declares Eric P. Hamp of the University of Chicago, one of the world's leading historical linguists. Hamp and other conservative linguists argue that the information left over from long-dead languages must tend, like the signal broadcast by a distant radio statio, to be drowned in the static of random linguistic change.

For their part, the radicals say Hamp and his like-minded colleagues take potshots at Nostratic and related theories without making a reasoned response. "I have repeatedly urged Hamp and Calvert Watkins at Harvard to publish their objections to Nostratic," says Alexis Manaster Ramer of Wayne State University. "Both of them attended a conference on these things, as discussants, in 1984 in Ann Arbor, and I repeatedly challenged both of them to state specifically what the hell they were objecting to, and they wouldn't."

In an interview, however, Hamp is voluble enough to maintain a crackling telephone conversation for six hours without a break and energetic enough to regard his imminent retirement as a chance to do still more research. He readily wrings out citations from "your schoolboy Latin" and "your Homeric Greek" without considering that his interlocutor may have little of the one and less of the other.

Nor is he reticent as his listens to the Nostratic root for dog, wolf, namely *küjna/qüjna*. "That alternation between *k* and *q* is already unacceptable," he says. "We do that with an occasional form, but only when we think we know the phonological system." When he hears the root's proposed meaning, *dog, wolf*, he dismisses the entire exercise. "I would say they're playing very fast and loose with the semantic content," he says. "From all we know of proto-Indo-European, the word for dog was used for the domesticated thing, which apart from its zoological classification had a social content. Somebody who says, 'We'll just move *dog* over into *wolf*' has a consummately naive view of the world."

What about in the Neolithic world of Nostratic? "If Nostratic was spoken at a time when the dog was just being domesticated, then it would be perfectly reasonable" to combine the concepts, Manaster Ramer argues. Dolgopolsky adds: "I just don't think [Hamp's] right that we aren't as accurate."

If the Nostraticists bend the rules of the game, Greenberg and his group break them. That's because Greenberg does not even bother to reconstruct roots. Instead Greenberg works with large groups of languages at once — a process he calls multilateral comparison. Compare, he says, the 25 major languages of modern Europe according to the sounds they use to signify nine basic concepts — one, two, three, head, eye, ear, nose, mouth, and tooth.

Under *one*, you find most of the words falling into one class or another. The similarity between *vienas* and *viens* in Lithuanian and Latvian is striking. Under *two* some of the foggier boundaries become clear — such as *dau, dau,* and *do,* for Breton, Irish, and Welsh, respectively. "By the time you get through, you've got three main groups: Indo-European, Finno-Ugric, and Basque," Greenberg says. "Then you can divide Indo-European into Romance, Baltic, Slavic, Germanic, and Albanian."

Greenberg says his multilateral comparison is so powerful that it will find relationships among languages even when the data available are rather thin. He first applied the method nearly 30 years ago to a reclassification of the African languages — many of them rather poorly documented. His

work won him praise, even from some of his most ardent critics. His success may have encouraged him to enter into the greatest snake pit of his life, the notoriously diverse languages of the New World.

When he classified American languages, Greenberg divided them first into Eskimo-Aleut and Na-Dene, which has members in the Pacific Northwest and the southwestern United States, such as Navaho. Both groups are generally accepted. But the specialists bitterly attack Greenberg's third group, which he dubbed Amerind, in which he throws the hemisphere's many other language families.

While Nostratic raises the traditionalists' hackles to half-mast, Greenberg's Amerind thesis completes the job. The reason is the apparent ease with which his system solves one of the thorniest problems in contemporary anthropology. There are 150-odd Native American language

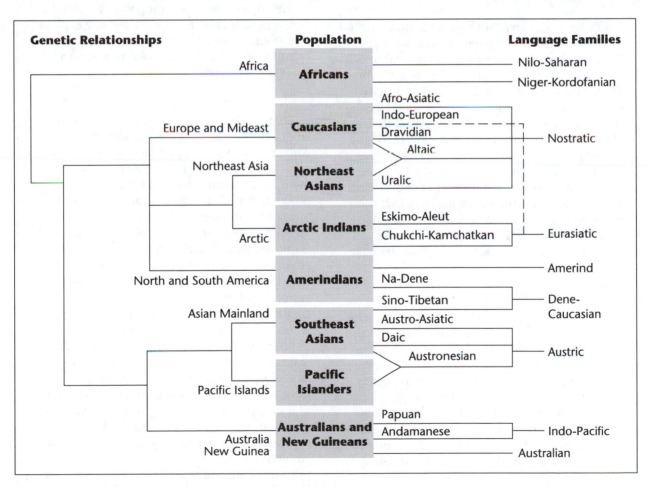

Genetic and linguistic histories roughly correspond because both diverge when populations split apart to form isolated communities. The genetic closeness of populations is shown by their distance from a common branching point (left); their linguistic closeness is depicted in a similar chart of language families and superfamilies (right). Source: Based on work by Luigi L. Cavalli-Sforza, Merritt Ruhlen.

families, each apparently as different — the specialists say — as Indo-European is from Sino-Tibetan. Yet the Old World has only 40-odd families, despite the much more ancient history of settlement that ought to have produced more linguistic diversity, not less.

Moreover, crucial data vanish whenever a speaker's death puts an end to the last language of a given family, and there are not enough linguists (or funding) to describe the dying tongues. Linguists estimate that half of the world's 6,000 existing languages will die out in the next century. No one is even sure how many there might have been. "Even when you have five living speakers left, you don't see linguists rushing around with an ambulance and a tape recorder," says Thomas L. Markey, who has recently organized conferences on Indo-European and Nostratic studies.

Even without attempting to reconstruct ancient tongues, Greenberg insists that his method is illuminating the distant past. And a growing number of scientists in other disciplines agree. Two early converts were Stephen L. Zegura and Christy G. Turner II of the University of Arizona. They had studied genetic and dental variation among Native Americans independently of Greenberg. When they heard him lecture on his preliminary findings for Native American languages, they told him that his results closely matched their own. When the biological and linguistic classifications were plotted on a map, they roughly coincided. The main discrepancies came in the Native American populations of the Pacific Northwest, which apparently had a tangled history.

Are Humans Born to Speak?

Language is the great human invention — if it is an invention at all. Noam Chomsky of the Massachusetts Institute of Technology thinks it isn't. He believes that language is as innate in the infant as flight is in the eaglet and that children do not so much learn language as develop it spontaneously in response to a stimulus. "Very few people are concerned with the origin of language because most consider it a hopeless question," Chomsky says.

Indeed, the question had generated so much talk and so little knowledge by 1866 that the Linguistic Society of Paris banned its discussion. The ban failed long before Chomsky came along, however, and many theories have been advanced:

- The bow-wow theory: Early words may have formed by onomatopoeia, as in *bow-wow* for dog, *cuckoo* for the familiar bird, and *whoosh* for a puff of wind.
- The pooh-pooh theory: Emotional interjections such as *pooh, bah*, and *harrumph* may have constituted early words.
- The yo-he-ho theory: When many people coordinated their exertions to haul a rope or roll a stone, they may have had recourse to ritualized chants that eventually acquired meaning.
- The la-la theory: Some sounds may have originated in play, as in children's singing or lovers' cooing.

- Oral gestures: Early speakers may have used their lips to point, creating vowel shifts that distinguish close from far. This may explain the shifts heard in the English words *this* and *that* and in French *voici* (here it is) and *voilà* (there it is).

That, of course, begs the question of why language arose at all. Derek Bickerton of the University of Hawaii speculates in his recent book *Language and Species* that the development of the brain produced language as a by-product. Neural structures that allowed early hominids to abstract from their perceptions a "secondary representation" of the world improved their capacity to adapt to their environment. These structures then might have enabled them to attach meaning to gestures and sounds, producing a primitive language that had no syntax, the ordering of words that defines human language.

Primitive language would have been full of words signifying meaning but would have lacked grammatical elements. Because it would have evolved much earlier than syntax, traces of it may perhaps be found in the gesturing of apes that have been taught the elements of sign language. Bickerton speculates that feral children also provide an inkling of what primitive language was like because they were isolated in the crucial early years when syntax normally develops. Supposed "wolf children" rescued from the wilds of India early in this century could learn many things, but they never advanced much beyond the verbal ability of a normal two-year-old.

The jump from primitive language to syntactic language is hardest of all to explain. Bickerton offers a tentative argument that concludes that "a single genetic event might indeed have been enough to turn protolanguage into syntacticized language." He concludes by noting that all the prerequisites for language — larger brain, improved vocal tract, new neural linkages — involve changes in the anatomy of the head.

Chomsky, too, agrees that the event must have happened abruptly in evolutionary terms because syntax reflects an inborn pattern of great intricacy. He thinks this innate ability explains why any child can learn any language without making the grammatical mistakes that one would expect if no preprogrammed structure were at hand.

Human language ability could have emerged suddenly when some genetic event knitted together a panoply of traits that had evolved for other purposes, Chomsky and others say. One such trait may have been the conscious control of vocalizations. Dogs bark when the mood seizes them; chimpanzees at least try to choke back impolitic calls, although with indifferent success. Humans, however, can lie through their teeth.

Another adaption may have been the ability to decode vocalizations. The very best telegraphists have never been able to absorb Morse code at the rate at which even a half-attentive child can extract meaning from dialogue. Our brains, it appears, are adapted to process vocal modulations.

The modulations themselves have remarkable richness, in part because of the unusual shape of the human vocal tract. Philip Lieberman of Brown University notes that this shape makes humans the only mammals incapable of drinking and breathing at the same time. The drawback is that it is not uncommon for humans to choke to death while eating.

The increased risk of choking would seem to have been offset by the improved articulation made possible by our vocal tract. The Neanderthals, in contrast, had a vocal tract resembling that of an ape, according to Lieberman's reconstruction of the fossil evidence. If so, then they would have been rather inarticulate, a failing that might explain why they died out and *Homo sapiens* survived.

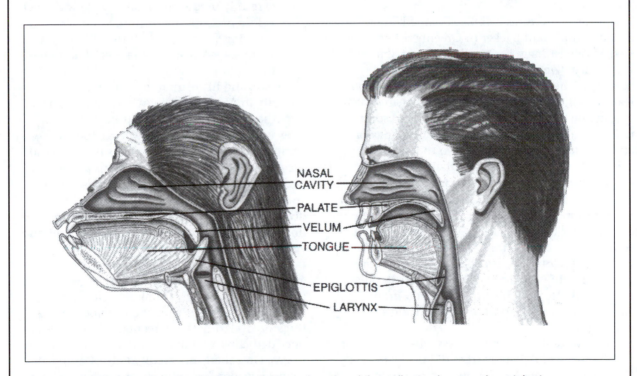

NASAL CAVITY
PALATE
VELUM
TONGUE
EPIGLOTTIS
LARYNX

Nonhuman primates such as the chimpanzee (left) *can breathe while swallowing because the epiglottis and velum form a watertight seal. In humans* (right) *the position of the larynx makes this feat impossible. Source: Philip Lieberman.*

Early Americans

Greenberg and his two collaborators published their findings jointly in 1986 and concluded that the ancestors of Native Americans must have immigrated in at least three discrete waves over the land bridge that once connected Siberia to Alaska. They could not rule out more than three, because additional implanted languages and genes might have left no traces. Exactly which communities of Asia contributed to these waves is hard to say, although Soviet linguists, working independently, have suggested a link between Na-Dene and the languages of northern Caucasia.

Further genetic evidence in support of Greenberg's Amerind hypothesis has since been provided by Douglas C. Wallace of Emory University. "Data we published this year indicate that Greenberg's hypothesis seems correct," Wallace said in an interview in late November. "Our data show, I feel strongly, that the paleo-Indians — Amerinds — are one group."

The combination of genetic and linguistic analysis works particularly well in America, Wallace adds, because it was a blank slate. "The first immigrants who came over the land bridge did not encounter another culture," he says. "I'm not surprised that there are ambiguities in the Old World, because there have been so many mixtures."

But those mixtures can be explained, argues another important backer of Greenberg's hypothesis, geneticist Luigi L. Cavalli-Sforza of Stanford University. "Genes have no direct effect on language," he notes, "but the language that you learn depends on where you were born and with whom you were born — your family and social milieu. If a group separates, both the gene pool and the language will diverge, so the history of genes and of language is essentially the same."

Cavalli-Sforza is a venerable worker in his field, as Greenberg is in his, and he too has come under fire for supporting the Amerind theory. He went even further three years ago, when he published a study finding correlations between the frequency with which certain genes appear in populations and the families of languages that those populations speak. He took his linguistic data from Greenberg's classification of all the world's languages.

There were some notable cases where details of the linguistic and genetic trees did not match, Cavalli-Sforza says. Each, however, can be explained as the result of the replacement of one language by another, or the interchange of genes. Hungary provides a good example of language replacement: although its people are genetically like their European neighbors, they speak a language from a non-Indo-European family, adopted in the Middle Ages from Hungary's Magyar conquerors. African Americans have similarly undergone both language replacement and partial gene replacement. Not everybody accepts these explanations. "Linguists can test word resemblances to see if they result from common descent or just from borrowing, but I don't see how Cavalli-Sforza can do the same for his genetic patterns," Manaster Ramer says.

But to get a true picture of ancient demographic patterns, Cavalli-Sforza has laid particular emphasis on studying those populations that are believed to have borrowed less of their language and of their genes. "In aboriginal populations, there is no complete blurring," he says. "Traces of the common history remain, going back, as far as I can tell, to the original settling of the earth, perhaps as much as 100,000 years ago."

Mitochondrial Eve

That estimation reflects the Eve work of Allan Wilson and his colleagues. The genes they studied to trace humanity's common genetic inheritance were encoded on DNA of the mitochondria, intracellular organelles that convert glucose into a more readily used form of energy. Because such DNA is inherited strictly from the mother, without being scrambled with the father's genes during mitosis, "Mitochondrial Eve" had to be a woman.

Wilson and his team found more genetic diversity in Africa than anywhere else, so they hypothesize that Eve and her tribe lived there. They estimated the dates on the basis of two comparisons: one among humans from around the world and one between humans as a group and chimpanzees. The DNA is then used as a "molecular clock," calibrated by the estimated divergence between the human and chimpanzee lineages (which split off more than five million years ago).

Yet all the corroboration provided by the geneticists and archaeologists cannot sway Indianists such as Lyle Campbell. He rejects Greenberg's position with the vehemence of a litigator, declaring that Greenberg's theory is at once derivative and unsupported. "I don't want to give Greenberg any credit at all," Campbell snaps. The idea "was already around; we were working on it all along. This doesn't address the problem of whether these verbal similarities are due to historical reasons or to other things."

Campbell also dismisses Greenberg's word lists as worthless and his grammatical patterns as illusory. These patterns, which Greenberg regards as "conclusive," are clearest in the case of two pronominal markers, *n-*, denoting the first person, and *m-*, denoting the second person. Campbell says that these markers are absent in many of the languages Greenberg classes as Amerind and that they are present in many he excludes. Because they are easy-to-pronounce nasals, he adds, the sounds are likely by chance to end up as grammatical markers. He also invokes the argument of "nursery talk" to link each sound to the concept it denotes.

Whether or not the Nostraticists and Greenberg are playing fast and loose with the rules, the hypothesis of the monogenesis of language is one that most linguists believe to be plausible. Indeed, the appearance of language may define modern *Homo sapiens* and explain why our species apparently did not interbreed with contemporaries like the Neanderthals. It is a horrifying scenario: the hominids without language would have seemed subhuman.

Monogenesis is not an issue that is likely to go away. The question of the origin of language is of preeminent importance; the history of language bears on the trading of goods, the migration of peoples, and the evolution of ideas. Every discovery — by comparative linguists of whatever school — pushes back the borders of what is considered the irrecoverable past.

26
Colorful Languages

R O B B I N S   B U R L I N G

The semantic studies so far considered [in preceding chapters of Burling's *Man's Many Voices*] have rested upon a more or less explicit assumption that events in the world present an essentially undifferentiated continuum to our most naive perceptions. Only our language, we have presumed, forces us to divide up this continuum into lexically labeled classes that are mutually contrasting. It has been thought that each language makes its own distinctions, which need have little to do with the distinctions made by other languages. Our perceptual abilities are supposed to be too flexible and too complex to impose any particular categorization upon the world's events.

The classic domain used to persuade skeptics of this doctrine has been that of color. The color spectrum is surely a physical continuum, for the possible wave lengths of visible light show no sharp breaks from the red end to the blue end of the spectrum, only a continuous intergradation of ever changing hues. From this physical fact, it has seemed to follow that only the arbitrary characteristics of a particular language could impose divisions upon the continuum, and only the lexical labels for various segments would separate one region from its neighbors.

From Robbins Burling, *Man's Many Voices: Language in Its Cultural Context*, pp. 45–48. Copyright © 1970 Holt, Rinehart and Winston, Inc. Reprinted with permission.

Investigations by Brent Berlin and Paul Kay now suggest, however, that all languages share certain common features in color assignment, and even differences that do exist are by no means random.

If you offer a man a chart of colors, ranging across the spectrum from red on the left to blue on the right and varying on the vertical scale from the lightest to darkest shades so that they reach a maximum of white at the very top and black at the bottom, you can ask him to do two related but by no means identical tasks. Either task might be expected to indicate the meaning of his color terms. You can ask him to indicate the range of each of his terms by drawing boundaries on the chart that separate the areas referred to by each. To make this request is to assume that all of the thousands of discriminable colors can be assigned to one of the basic color terms of the language, though some colors will be much closer than others to a border. The request to draw borders seems a reasonable one, but people often have considerable difficulty with it. They debate about marginal colors and struggle over the exact range of some terms. If asked on a later occasion to repeat the task they may give quite different results from their first attempt. Their difficulties suggest that the bordering regions between the terms are not very well-defined.

If, instead, a man is asked to indicate the particular points on the chart that represent the truest *red*, the truest *green*, and so forth, he will generally have a much easier time. He can quickly indicate the spot that is a *real red* (if he is a speaker of English), another that is a *real yellow*, and still another that is a *real orange*. If asked later to repeat his performance he is likely to duplicate his own work quite closely, and different speakers of a language agree better with one another upon the designation of these focal points than they do on the location of the borders between the terms.

This much is consistent with the idea that our language imposes its own classification upon a continuous range of hues. Some colors (those near the center of a term's range) might be relatively easy to code, while those along the borders would pose more difficulties. The startling result of Berlin and Kay's study is that speakers of all languages seem to place the foci of their color labels at very nearly the same spots on the color chart. Borders are more variable from one language to another, though perhaps not a great deal more variable than from one speaker of the same language to another or even between repeated trials by the same person, but the foci remain in one place. Color terminology seems not to be assigned so arbitrarily as we have always imagined.

This identity of color foci does not mean that all color terminologies are identical. Some languages have more basic terms than others and thereby code more foci, but those terms that a language does have will have their foci at the same locations as other languages. Furthermore, if a language has, for instance, five basic color terms, these five will always have their foci at the same places (white, black, red, green, yellow), and if a sixth term is added it will always be added at the focus of blue.

We can hardly doubt that all people with normal vision are physiologically capable of discriminating the same colors. An impoverished color vocabulary does not mean impoverished vision, and whatever a man's language may be, he can refine his reference to color by forming complex phrases or by citing particular colored objects. But, to be counted as a basic color term, a word must be a single lexical item (not a construction such as *light blue, lemon-colored,* or *the color of the rust on my aunt's old Chevrolet*). It must not be merely a subdivision of a higher-order term (such as *scarlet* or *crimson,* which are unquestionably varieties of *red*); it must be applicable to more than a restricted range of objects (unlike *blond,* which is rarely used for anything except hair or wood); and it must be used and accepted readily by all speakers of the language or dialect (unlike *beige* or *chartreuse*). It is in their number of

basic terms that languages differ, not in the foci of those they have or in the ability to give more precise descriptions of colors when this must be done.

Languages have been reported with no more than two basic color terms, and these always have their foci at black and white. It may help an English speaker to think of these terms as if they translate our own *dark* and *light,* but when a Jalé of the New Guinea highlands is asked for the truest *siŋ* he will indicate the color we refer to as *black,* and when asked for the truest *hóló* he will point to white. (An English speaker would presumably indicate black and white as the foci of his own *dark* and *light*.) The Jalé have more specialized terms that are used in restricted contexts. *Mut* means "red soil." *Pianó* is the name of a plant that can produce a green dye. But these are not basic color terms since they are not broadly applicable to all objects.

Languages with three basic color terms always add the third one at the focus that we call *red*. Most of the warm colors — yellows, oranges, and browns — may be included under red at this stage, but its focus is still a proper red. When a language has four basic color terms, three still have their foci at black, white, and red, but the fourth may be either at yellow or at green. The fifth term adds the one missed at the previous stage, so that all languages with exactly five terms have "black," "white," "red," "yellow," and "green." The focus of the sixth term is always at blue, which becomes differentiated from green and black, and the focus of the seventh term is brown, which refines the terminology for the warm colors. Up to this point, with the exception of variability in adding "yellow" and "green," it appears that people do not have a term late in the list unless they have all the earlier terms. They do not have a term for brown unless they also have one for blue, and they do not have one for blue unless yellow and green are also labeled.

To these seven terms, English adds four others, which can be considered basic: *grey, pink, orange,* and *purple*. Terms with the same foci as these are also found in other languages, but it does not seem to be possible to arrange these final four foci in any fixed order of acquisition. None of these final four appears unless all of the earlier seven are also present, but they are not mutually ordered among themselves.

Perhaps the most astonishing and controversial claim about this sequence is that it correlates rather closely with the level of cultural and technological complexity. Languages with two terms are confined to people with the simplest level of technology, such as the New Guinea Jalé. At the other extreme, the only languages known to have terms for all eleven foci are from Europe and east Asia, where the people have long histories, and great complexity in their culture and technology. Between these extremes are people like the Tiv, a rather simple African tribe of Nigeria, with three terms; the Hanunóo tribe of the Philippines, with four; the Eskimo, with five; some rather complex African tribes, with six; and the Malayalam of southern India and the Burmese, with seven.

For present purposes, however, it is not so much the differences between the systems that are important as their underlying similarity, for the common features of all color terminologies insistently suggest that the spectrum does not form a perceptual continuum after all. The physical determinants of color — wave length and degree of purity or mixture of different wave lengths — certainly vary continuously, but it is difficult to imagine how the world's languages could be so consistent in the colors they code by basic terms if our underlying perceptual skills did not impose a discontinuity upon the spectrum and break it up into perceptually distinct chunks. In a sense these chunks are sitting there, waiting for a label.

27
Male and Female Language

MARY RITCHIE KEY

There is a good principle, which has created
order, light, and man;
and a bad principle, which has created chaos,
darkness, and woman.

— attrib. to Pythagoras

The separation of the roles of male and
female undoubtedly goes back to the
beginnings of the history of human beings
for very obvious reasons: child-bearing functions.
It is a safe assumption that differences in the
language of male and female also go back to the
beginning of language, though we have to realize
that much of history is lost in this aspect of
human affairs, as well as in all other facets of
human conduct.

Language is in a constant state of flux; today
the focus is upon changes in the area of male and
female linguistic behavior. People are taking a
second look at language forms which they have
been using automatically all their lives. What was
always there is now being examined carefully
with pink and blue glasses. A great deal of experimentation is taking place during these transi-

tional stages and while some of what is being
tried today will remain in common usage, other
forms will be dropped along the way. What is
happening today is a general liberation of the
language. All of this is rather fascinating and
frightening; nevertheless, it is spiced with humor.
The purported "phallacies about the movement"
are being avidly discussed and there was a long
and tense argument about "pronoun envy" at
one of our prestigious institutions. A radio
newscaster reported that a suit was being filed on
the basis of sex discrimination because a woman
was turned down for a job as Santa Claus. He
quipped that, "In order to go HO, HO, HO, it is
not necessary to be a HE, HE, HE!" A recent stage
production was named "Adam and Even." A
prominent feminist published "Quotations from
Charwoman Me." Humor is a non-threatening
way that human beings have to deal with the
world about them. It functions as a safety valve
for situations too difficult to trust oneself with.
Magnificent puns and plays on words have
emanated from this focus upon male/female
problems, which all students of language will
appreciate. In any case, it is quite apparent that in
these times, a woman is not apt to take a "broad"
view of things, and many hope that fewer men
do.

The first time that I became aware of male/
female differences in languages, I was in Bolivia
as a linguistic consultant visiting different villages

studying the various Indian languages spoken. I landed at a little village, which probably isn't on your map, where the Ignaciano Indians have been living for centuries. Up until that time not much was known about their language, and I was to verify some of the linguistic data which had been collected. The linguist who had written down this material was a male, and I was reading from his field notes. I sat down on a tree stump surrounded by large pottery vessels and chickens and children, and I read off the phonetically transcribed vocabulary items. My informant was an affable woman who was bilingual and could tell me in Spanish what the words meant. When I came to a certain form, she started laughing, and I thought she was going to fall off her stool from amusement! We soon discovered that the word which I had read was from the vocabulary of men — a word which females never articulated.

It was several years later when I began teaching a course on varieties of language that I began to focus again on the differences between male and female linguistic behavior. It soon became apparent to me that this distinction in language is a certain universal just as the sex role is universal, and that linguistic sex distinctions undoubtedly occur in every language of the world. Interestingly enough, however, they have not been reported upon widely. Of the some four to five thousand languages of the world, I can find linguistic statements about sex distinctions in fewer than a hundred.

Societies cannot exist without language. Yet in spite of this universality, and even though Plato and Aristotle and other great minds throughout the centuries have commented on language, the science of language, or linguistics, is a fairly recent discipline. Only in the last century or two has linguistics (previously philology) been accepted as a discipline in its own right on university campuses. But the differentiated use of language by male and female is more than just a matter of linguistic forms; it is the *use* of these forms in society. It is the sociological choice and function of these forms. In the early development of linguistics, scholars were so busy trying to find symbols for the sounds they found in languages and to define subjects and predicates that they did not have time to become involved in the interdisciplinary efforts necessary to systematically describe the sociologically important male and female differences. In addition, the differences that occur are often very subtle and abstract, and though everyone responds to them, they are not readily identified. If you ask your friend, "How do men and women talk differ-

ently?" the answer is likely to be something vague: "Well, I don't know ... do they? ... why, I suppose they do!"

Although extensive systematic studies on male/female linguistic distinctions were not made until this century, some language studies from very early times did make brief mention of sex differences. [Elizabethan scholar and educationist Richard] Mulcaster in 1582 commented on the differences in pronunciation by males and females and related these differences to refined and vulgar language. It is probably not an unrelated fact in Mulcaster's life that he also advocated education for girls. Writers on the French language in 1688 and around 1700 made similar observations about female pronunciation. The volubility attributed to women speakers was noted by Swift in 1735, and a generation later Lord Chesterfield commented on women's fondness for hyperbole: a very small gold snuff-box was "vastly pretty, because it was so vastly little." Oscar Wilde continued the observations on women's speech: "Women are a decorative sex. They never have anything to say, but they say it charmingly."

Sometimes it is easier to observe differences objectively when the subject matter is not our own. This seems to be the case in linguistic studies of male/female language, because the first statement I find with substantial data about these differences is on the American Indian languages Carib and Arawakan, recorded by Raymond Breton in *Dictionaire Caraibe-Français* [sic] in 1665. Throughout the nineteenth century descriptions are largely on "the women's language" of these exotic, aboriginal peoples. Travelers, historians, and philologists, such as Karl Wilhelm von Humboldt, enjoyed commenting on these esoteric tribes where the men and women had different languages! It has never been true that males and females had completely different languages, for the societies could not have existed as such.

In this century, language scholars, notably the famous Danish scholar Otto Jespersen and the great linguist Edward Sapir, began more extensive studies of male and female language differences. These scholars, however, were bound by their cultural preconceptions and distortions, as all human beings are, and this is reflected in their otherwise scholarly treatments of "women's language." Jesperson spoke of feminine weaknesses and Sapir included women's speech in his study of "abnormal types of speech." Greenough and Kittredge, highly respected English scholars, spoke of "feminine peculiarities." In discussions of the German language, it was said that, "Women naturally have certain peculiarities in their German as in other languages...."

It was shortly before this time that some scholars had come to the conclusion that genius could only be a masculine trait. This was "documented" by Weininger, along with his other ideas that women did not have souls and that they were incapable of true love. Not all great thinkers were hospitable to the idea that women did not have souls; for example, George Bernard Shaw: "Men are waking up to the perception that in killing women's souls they have killed their own." To be fair, one should say that Jespersen tried to have a more balanced perspective about genius — and he pointed out that "idiocy is more common among men," another myth that he would have been unable to prove. Nevertheless, these ideas about intellectual potential influenced the statements about language and promulgated weird conclusions: the vocabulary of a woman is smaller; male language is more constructive, useful, and abstract; male language has more complex, embedded constructions, while female language is simple-minded with much emotional emphasis. It should be remembered here that these distorted and stereotyped judgments were not restricted to sex differences. Varieties of languages had not yet been studied scientifically, and the anthropologically and sociologically oriented recognition of *differences*, without value judgments of good/bad and normal/peculiar, was only beginning to be established in the study of human beings and their behavior.

When Sapir published his study of abnormal speech types of the Nootka language in 1915, he included the speech of fat people, dwarfs, hunchbacks, lame people, left-handed people, circumcised males, cowards, and women, as well as baby talk. No one questioned that some of these categories are not abnormal. (I have to admit that I didn't immediately see the incongruity of including women's speech in *abnormal* types!) An enlightened awareness will challenge that kind of classification. Analogous to this is a recent study on mental health that showed double standards being applied in judging for male and female what is normal, healthy behavior. This orientation of looking at language variation as different cultural and sociological types, and the development of linguistics in its maturing stages has led to the establishing of a sub-discipline in linguistics called *sociolinguistics*. This branch of linguistics studies the infinite varieties of language within language: age differences, cultural differences, occupational vocabulary, slang, styles of speech and writing, and many others, but including, of course, sex differences in language. Before the development of sociolinguistics, linguists were not truly ready to talk about male/female differences because none of these differences operates alone and without intricate connections to other variables. The little girl rolling her eyes and inveigling an ice cream cone from a tall adult male is, indeed, using female language, but she is also using pre-school language; familial language (he is her father); and dramatic language (the scene occurs in public). Now that linguists are more sophisticated in methodology and evaluations, we can look forward to enlightened language descriptions in the future.

Besides these obvious state-of-the-art reasons that we do not have much information on actual male/female differences in language, there are other realisms we have to face. Scientists are human beings and they sometimes bury ideas they cannot cope with. A case in point is the study of sex origin and development in the fetus. Recent information leads to the conclusion that all human fetuses are originally female but that, upon some of them, an active organizer substance called androgen operates to cause the development of a male. In fact, a rather good case could be made that mankind's first speech, "Madam, I'm Adam," is, indeed, backwards, in more ways than are apparent at the surface structure. I will refer to this again when the matter of gender/sex analysis is discussed under linguistic structures.

Another area that is difficult or impossible to cope with is the collection of discomforting vocabularies in linguistic behavior. A real investigation of the linguistic behavior of male and female would treat areas of tyranny, discrimination, and power displays, and involve some usage which is very distasteful to certain people. One has to have a pretty strong stomach to read through the vocabulary collected on females as sex objects. It would appear that philologists and linguists through the years, keen enough to have observed these offensive distinctions, might have avoided further investigation as an area they could not cope with for the same reasons that prison language had not been documented in earlier years. A further difficulty in research and understanding of the phenomenon of human behavior is the climate of the society around the research institutions. The other day on the radio a news commentator spoke about the recently published love letters of Winston Churchill. He was extolling the life-long love affair of the Churchills, but lamented that, among other things, the rivalry between male and female today is destroying the beautiful love relationships of male and female! This kind of distorted logic fortifies and perpetuates the myths and scares off timid researchers. What isn't recognized in that kind of sentimental propoganda is that it is the myths/misconceptions and untruths that separate male and female and inhibit communion and understanding.

Human beings are always interested in explanations of the phenomena that exist and move around us. From the time youngsters learn to speak, they start asking, "Why?" Scientists continue the tradition and work to find theoretical explanations for the data they observe. Explanations for sex roles are glibly passed off as child bearing or at least related to child bearing and nurturing. Linguistic differences are not so easily explained away by innate sexual differences. That is, linguistic differences cannot be explained as physiological. There are perhaps some differences in the brain which are not yet understood (I shall discuss this later). The only physiological difference in the actual speech apparatus is the size and length of the vocal folds (vocal cords), which control pitch and quality of voice. This does not account for the fact that some women speak lower than some men and male/female linguistic behavior can still be distinguished. Most of the differences noted have to do with vocabulary choice and grammatical devices, neither of which has anything to do with the physiology of speech mechanisms. One phonetician found in his studies of the vocal apparatus a performance behavior that remains curiously unexplained. More men than women can roll up the edges of the tongue! This articulatory virtuosity, however, never occurs in language sounds, and one might conclude that the advantages are dubious, since there doesn't seem to be much demand for people who can curl up the edges of the tongue. If, then, the physiological differences are minimal, why are the culturally learned differences so ubiquitous? Scholars have attempted to explain "women's language" in various ways, such as historical, sociological, psychological, and religious. Sir James Frazer, at the beginning of this century, attempted to explain the origin of gender in language. Kraus, a psychoanalyst, spent considerable effort in compiling the hypotheses of various writers up to 1924 concerning the phenomena of male/female differences in languages. Then she proceeded, as expected out of Vienna, to give the *real* reason! — the psychoanalytic explanation. Royen later criticized Freud for his exaggerated sexualistic

doctrines in relation to the science of language. Probably, most of the differences can be explained on the basis of role expectancies and beliefs (myths?) of society: *Man Does, Woman Is*. Throughout the millennia women have accepted this with the dignity of futility.

In truth, explanations must go far beyond our present imaginations into the beginnings of relationships between human beings. People have had to eat to survive. Hunting at times took the males away from the camp fire and the family circle — however that family might have been constituted at that time. Hunting language would soon have been distinguished as one aspect, and a male one, of the material culture of the people. After a time it would result that the entire economic system of the society would similarly find its own language. Thus, economics in language would have been an early important association. Whatever was barterable was the precursor of money, in itself a special kind of communication. The exchange of goods soon incorporated females and all of this involvement of economics, kinship and marriage, and communication or language is undoubtedly the foundation of other varieties in language based on status and sex. It is significant that a recent book on marriage is entitled *Pigs, Pearlshells, and Women*. Robert Graves succinctly observed: "Marriage, like money, is still with us; and, like money, progressively devalued. The ties between these two male inventions get closer and closer." George Bernard Shaw also commented on the "commercial interpretation of marriage" and, further, noted that a "marked difference is made in price between a new article and a secondhand one" — the "damaged goods" syndrome. This is paralleled in linguistic terms for women who are not virgins.

While the development of economics and all that is entailed was essential for the survival of the human race, supernatural or religious beliefs quickly followed. Basic distinctions in belief systems have to do with living and non-living beings and things, and their interdependency. At this point it looks simple enough — we think we know what is living and what isn't. But it is not that easy; societies — and languages — classify the parts of the world differently. Most of the time they overlap, but it is the grey areas of non-agreement in the thinking of human beings which cause us to ponder. For example, a moldy fungus would be a living organism to a scientist, but not to a rubber hunter in the Amazon jungle. However, the large tree standing near the third bend of the river is a supernatural "living" being to the rubber hunter, but is not a living being to

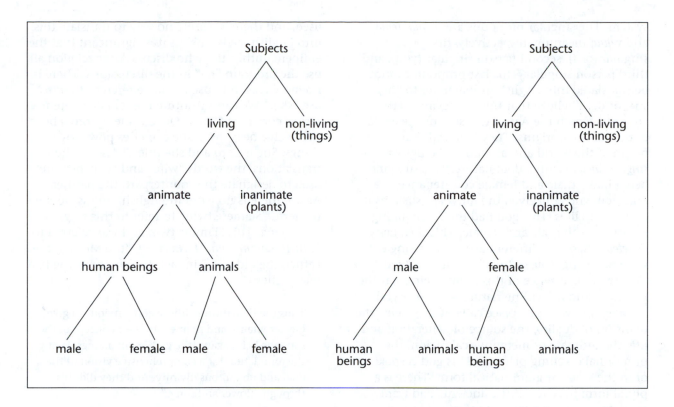

many sophisticated scientists. Male human beings have souls, but, variously — depending upon the group making the judgment — tables, giraffes, Indians, trees, pets, fetuses, insects, and women *don't* have souls. Thus, *categories* are supremely important in controlling the behavior of human beings. In subtle, at times almost imperceptible ways, classificatory systems correlate with language structures and control the syntax of language as they control other behaviors of people. In languages, there is a very close relationship between gender and animate/inanimate distinctions. Compare the two accompanying diagrams.

Which represents more closely the facts of the universe? Which is the more basic category: human beings/animals or male/female? It should be noted that these diagrams are not necessarily correct for all languages. They are based on English categories and language.

To show how these concepts can be completely misunderstood even by highly intelligent people, I quote a renowned scholar of the last century. In discussing the Arawak language of Guiana, he noted two genders, which he called masculine and neuter. This kind of linguistic gender classification has nothing to do with diminishing females. Nevertheless, he mistakenly observed:

A peculiarity ... is that [Arawak] only has two genders ... masculine and neuter. Man or nothing was the motto of these barbarians. Regarded as an index of their mental and social condition, this is an ominous fact. It hints how utterly destitute they are of those high, chivalric feelings, which with us centre around women.

All of the Indo-European languages except Armenian have masculine and feminine grammatical categories of gender in their linguistic systems. In some, as we will see later, the gender system is very predominant — every tree, table, chair, and stone has either a masculine, feminine, or neuter assigned to it. In others, such as English, the gender system is evident only in a few pronouns: she and he, his and her. In order to grasp the significance of gender-consciousness in our world view, it is useful to go outside of the Indo-European languages and see how other people and languages deal with gender. This also we will discuss [in a later chapter of *Male/Female Language*], but here I want to deal with this aspect of language and the origins of human beings. The Aztec language is a good example, because we know something of the Aztecs' ancient beliefs and it is a language which does not have masculine and feminine gender in the grammatical system. The singular pronouns are: *nejua, tejua,* and *yejua,* meaning, respectively, first person singular (or I), second person singular (you), and third person singular. This last pronoun cannot be translated into English. It may refer to "he, she, or it." I believe that this is relevant to the concepts which the Aztecs devised for the explanation of their origins. They believed that the origin of the world and all human beings was *one single principle* with a dual nature. This supreme being had a male and female countenance — a dual god who conceived the universe, sustains it, and creates lifes. This god had the regenerating ability of both male and female. This dual deity, *Ometeotl,* had two different aspects of a single supreme being. *Ome* = "two" and *teotl* = "god." The dynamic essence of this divine being was the feminine and masculine nature — a *whole* god.

Ometeotl dwelt in a place called *Omeyocan*: "the mansion of duality, the source of generation and life, the ultimate or metaphysical region, the primordial dwelling place...." This god is spoken of in the singular grammatical form. There is a plural form in Aztec, if the ancients had wanted to use it, but they referred to this god in the singular. At the same time this singular divine being is described as having a partner, which means "equal" or "a thing which fits or adjusts with some other thing" or "that which improves a thing or makes it more complete."

Besides the gender difficulty in rendering these ideas into English, there is the difficulty of the multitudes of gods being *one god.* Do we use "is" or "are"? Note that I have not used either pronoun referent "he" or "she" so far, in reference to this Aztec god. There is nothing in the Aztec language to indicate which gender should be used, and there is simply no way to translate this into English. Nevertheless it is significant that the eminent authorities who discuss Aztec religion all use the pronoun "he" in the discussions. There is no more reason to use the male referent than to use "she." We can substitute the female referent just as correctly: "She is Queen, she is Lord, above the twelve heavens ... she exercises power over all things. She is Lord and she rules." Also in the translations, the words "wife" and "consort" are used to designate the counterpart, the partner. Again, there is no word in English, unless we use the term "Siamese twin" to refer to this single dual being. This Siamese twin god was referred to as *in Tonan, in Tota, Huehueteotl,* "the Mother, the Father, the old god." In fact, this divine being had many titles:

> Thus the tlamatinime [the sages], anxious to give greater vitality and richness to their concept of the supreme being, gave [the god] many names, laying the foundation for a comprehensive vision of the dual and ubiquitous divinity. And they did this through "flower and song."

Thus, attempts at explanations and theoretical discussions continue — and will continue as long as human beings like to talk with each other and ask questions. In reality, what we must deal with now, whether or not we know the explanation, is that for whatever the reasons, male and female linguistic behaviors differ from each other. In the atmosphere of today's thinking in terms of *Human Liberation,* surely the greatest and most profound of all revolutions, we are even now witnessing linguistic change of male and female behavior.

28

Armed Situation Impacts Severely, Linguistics-wise: War Is Hell on Plain Speaking

SALLY MACDONALD

SEATTLE — The nation's best camouflage artist is the U.S. Defense Department, which gave us an "armed situation" — not war — in the Persian Gulf.

So say the nation's English teachers, who gave the department their annual Doublespeak Award for language meant to bamboozle, befuddle, and obfuscate. The award was announced yesterday by the National Council of Teachers of English, meeting in Seattle through Wednesday.

War is hell on words, according to the English teachers. So are business, government, advertising, and technology.

The Gulf War — like its predecessor in Vietnam, when the first Doublespeak Awards were given — was rich in euphemisms, says William Lutz, a Rutgers University professor and chairman of the organization's Committee on Public Doublespeak.

Bombing attacks against Iraq were "efforts" and warplanes were "weapons systems" or "force packages." When pilots went out on bombing missions they were "visiting a site." Buildings were "hard targets"; people were "soft" ones.

The bombs didn't kill. They "degraded, neutralized, attrited, suppressed, eliminated, cleansed, sanitized, impacted, decapitated, or

took out" targets. Killing the enemy was "servicing the target."

The allies were also guilty as charged by the teachers. The government of Saudi Arabia, unable to accept female soldiers from the United States, called them "males with female features."

The awards have been made since 1974, when Col. David Opfer, U.S. air attache in Cambodia, exploded to reporters, "You always write it's bombing, bombing, bombing. It's not bombing! It's air support!"

This year's second prize goes to Rep. Newt Gingrich, R-Ga, who heads a group that published the booklet "Language: A Key Mechanism of Control" for the use of Republicans in office. The Republicans are told to use "optimistic, positive governing words" to characterize the Republican vision — words like "environment, peace, freedom, fair, flag, family, and humane."

To "define our opponents," the booklet advises, use words like "betray, sick, pathetic, lie, liberal, hypocrisy, permissive attitude, self-serving."

President Bush, Secretary of State James Baker, and Secretary of Defense Richard Cheney share the English teachers' third prize, for muddy statements on arms control in the Middle East.

In February, Baker said the time had come to reduce arms flow to the Middle East, and on May 29, the president announced an arms-control plan. But the next day Cheney announced the

From *The Seattle Times*, 23 November 1991. Reprinted with permission.

185

sale of weapons to Israel, the United Arab Emirates, and Bahrain, saying, "We simply cannot fall into the trap of ... (saying) that arms control means we don't provide any arms to the Middle East."

According to Lutz, doublespeak is language that only pretends to communicate. "It is language that makes the bad seem good, something negative appear positive, and something unpleasant appear attractive, or at least tolerable."

People have been trying to talk without communicating since the times of the Romans, Lutz said. "Julius Caesar 'pacified' Gaul; he didn't conquer it."

Commissioner David Kessler of the federal Food and Drug Administration received the group's annual Orwell Award for Distinguished Contribution to Honesty and Clarity in Public Language. Kessler was honored for taking on food manufacturers who use deceptive labels to claim their products are fresh, cholesterol-free, low-fat, and light.

The award is named for George Orwell, the English author who introduced the concept of governmental doublespeak in 1949 in his futuristic novel, *1984*.

Americans aren't the only ones practicing the art of misinformation. In Canada, the recession was a period of "negative growth." Bald men in Japan were "hair disadvantaged." In England, members of Parliament who failed to be re-elected were "deselected."

PART FOUR

Cultural Anthropology

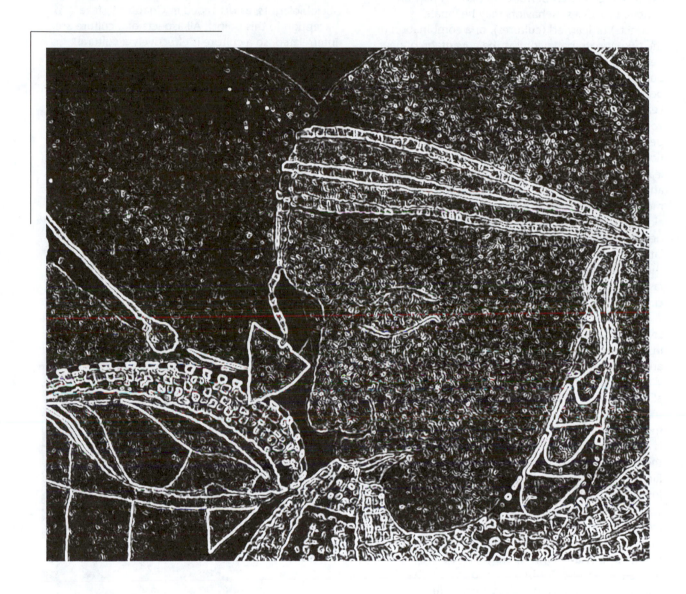

Introduction

An important aspect of the interactions between animals and their environment is behavior. The repertoire of behaviors of some species is more complex than that of others. The development and expansion of such repertoires depend in part on genetic processes. Behaviors may be innate (instincts) or learned (cultures), or a combination of the two. Innate behavior has the advantage of near-perfect continuity from one generation to the next, but, as we saw in our discussion biological anthropology, no human behavior is entirely innate. Learning also contributes to continuity; however, as you may have noticed on exam days, it is never 100 percent effective: errors, forgetfulness, and innovations are bound to arise. A great advantage of learning is that it assists in responding to change and new stresses in the environment at a much more rapid rate than would be possible with instinct alone. Consider the simple example that millions of people over the centuries have learned to use the latest inventions of brilliant innovators with whom they have no genetic connection. Natural selection favors good learners, and what humans learn is the *culture* of their *society*.

A **society** is a group, including people of both sexes and at least three generations, who share institutions and are largely dependent on one another for their survival and well-being. A **culture** is an abstraction, a scientific artifact, that comprises all the patterns of behavior, thoughts, and feelings that are acquired through symbolic learning by the members of a group of people. Because a "culture" is an abstraction, you cannot visit a culture, and there can be no such thing as "cultural contact." Richard Lee and Susan Hurlich, in Chapter 55, and Joseph Jorgensen, in Chapter 56, point out that what earlier anthropologists used the term *contact of cultures* to describe was really cases of people with guns meeting, and overpowering, people with bows and arrows. Many anthropologists, notably archaeologists and museologists, refer to the "material culture" of groups of people, which includes the artifacts manufactured by them and typical of their culture. As Leslie White pointed out, what is cultural is not the object itself, but the customs, ideas, and symbols associated with the manufacture and use of that object: "Culture is a traditional organization of objects (tools, and things made with tools), ideas (knowledge, lore, beliefs), sentiments (attitudes toward milk, homicide, mothers-in-law, etc.), and the use of symbols" (White 1947, 165).

Cultural anthropology studies this most typically human characteristic: the learning, use, and transmission of culture. Untold numbers of books and essays by anthropologists reveal considerable disagreement on what would be the most accurate or the most useful definition of "culture." Nevertheless, they generally agree on the main points of the definition proposed above — namely, that all human groups have a culture; that it is an essential component of their adaptation; and that it is learned socially, not inherited genetically (some sociobiologists, as discussed in Chapter 9, take exception to this point). All aspects of a culture are interrelated, so a culture is effectively a cultural *system*, not a crazy quilt of patches and pieces. A culture is composed largely of shared symbols. Because the most complex system of symbols is found in language, language is the essential tool for the elaboration and transmission of culture. As discussed in the previous section, all humans are genetically programmed with the potential to learn language, but they speak many different languages. Similarly, all humans are born with the potential to learn culture, but which culture they will learn is determined only by the social group in which they are reared and educated, and not by their biological background.

The process whereby individuals learn the behavioral patterns, symbols, beliefs, and values of

Sori man. Dress codes are examples of cultural differences that may be maintained by the enforcement of rigid rules. It would be shocking for North American students or professors to attend class dressed like this Sori of New Guinea, who displays his nose and ear ornaments. His bark belt and penis sheath would not be considered decent clothing in North America. Source: Jean-Luc Chodkiewicz.

their society is partly conscious and partly unconscious. Anthropologists call this process of transmitting the culture of a group from one generation to the next **enculturation**. **Diffusion**, by contrast, is the transmission of cultural traits from one society to another: it is a mechanism that promotes cultural change. If a Chinese villager teaches his son to eat with chopsticks, that is an example of enculturation, but if a French patron asks the owner of a Chinese restaurant to show him how to do it, that is an example of diffusion. Ralph Linton's essay, in Chapter 29, illustrates the multiplicity of diffused traits that have been woven into the fabric of "American" culture. It also illustrates the tendency of many people to reject, despise, and denigrate foreign ideas and ways of life. The narrow-minded nationalism that Linton ridicules in this essay is an example of **ethnocentrism** — the idea, supported by a mixture of beliefs and feelings, that one's own culture is superior to others and that foreign ways of life, values, and ideas are less rational, less "human." An extreme form of ethnocentrism is racism.

Ethnocentrism is an unscientific attitude, which is reflected, for example, in the use of such terms as "primitives," "savages," "pagans," or "heathens" in reference to other peoples. Most of us are guilty of having used terms such as these at one time or another; indeed, all of us are, to some extent, ethnocentric. Why is it that such an irrational attitude is so pervasive? It may be because people find it necessary to defend the integrity of their own culture; indeed, the values, goals, and models for action of every culture are always, in some way, incompatible with those of others. Ethnocentrism is, in that sense, adaptive, because it contributes to the maintenance of cultural diversity. "*Vive la différence!*" (Long live difference!) is not just a slogan: it is an adaptive rule of thumb.

Anthropologists strongly oppose the unscientific, superior attitude associated with ethnocentrism, and one of the important objectives of introductory courses in anthropology is to help students become more tolerant of cultural differences. This objective is often sought through the perspective of cultural relativism. **Cultural relativism** is a philosophical approach whereby other people's customs, beliefs, and institutions are evaluated strictly in terms of the social and cultural context within which they occur, and not in terms of the values and customs of the observer. It is important to understand that this attitude of respect for social and cultural differences represents a scientific rather than a moral commitment. For example, anthropologists who find the perspective of cultural relativism useful to the process of recording, analyzing, and explaining the presence of cannibalism, slavery, or male dominance in a given society do not have to approve of those

institutions — indeed, modern anthropologists normally do not.

The study of cross-cultural similarities and differences is one of the main objectives of cultural anthropology. There are many ways to be human, and many ways of understanding humanity: anthropologists attempt to know them all! In this sense, archaeology is just one way of studying culture, using techniques appropriate to people of the past, who cannot speak for themselves. As noted in the general introduction, the traditional distinction between **ethnography**, the description of cultures, and **ethnology**, the comparative analysis of and theories about culture, is rather obsolete. No anthropologist today would publish a "purely descriptive" ethnography. Such an attempt would be doomed to failure in any event, as the very selection of the facts to be described and the words chosen to describe them are themselves dictated by an implicit perspective or theory. All scientific facts are artifacts: they are human inventions based on assumptions and developed with the aid of theoretical tools. Observers who delude themselves into believing that their reporting is value-free or theory-free must be viewed as naive and unreliable. This idea is central to the concerns of the so-called post-processual archaeologists and postmodern anthropologists, but it is by no means unique to them.

Anthropologists study all human societies and cultures, not just exotic ones. In the following chapters, you will find anthropological analyses of Winnipeg's skid row and U.S. soap operas, as well as of Mexican Indians and Australian Aborigines. If anthropologists appear to specialize in the study of "primitive," nonindustrial peoples, this is mostly by default, because other social scientists have not bothered to do so. We must study the sociology of the Yir Yoront of Australia (Chapters 53 and 54) and the economy of the Miskito Indians of Nicaragua (Chapter 35) not because the study of these societies is the preserve of anthropologists, but because sociologists and economists have not done so. Furthermore, anthropologists bring to their analyses an attitude that is seldom evident in the work of other, more specialized, social scientists: the **holistic approach**. You will discover in each of the following chapters that, while focusing on some ecological issue or kinship problem or political institution, the author includes in the analysis many other aspects of the social and cultural system. Rather than trying to be an ecologist and an economist and a sociologist, as well as a linguist, the anthropologist attempts to show the *relationships among* the various aspects of the society and cultural system of a group of people.

Since the famous work of Bronislav Malinowski (1922) among the Trobrianders, anthropologists have gathered their data by sharing the life of the people they study and participating in their activities. Not satisfied with simple answers to questionnaires or with creating lists of "cultural traits," anthropologists attempt to observe daily routines and the processes of social life at work. This requires travel, adjustment to sometimes trying physical conditions, and, of course, acceptance by the people under study. This typically anthropological method of observation is called **participant observation**. The complex and often disconcerting ways in which anthropologists collect their information is illustrated in Allyn Maclean Stearman's description of her fieldwork among the Yuquí Indians of Bolivia (Chapter 30). Her strong personality and her experience working for the Peace Corps contributed to the success of her adjustment to the discomforts of life with poor people in the middle of a tropical forest, as well as to her eventual acceptance by the Yuquí. None of her academic courses prepared her directly for the experience.

To become accepted by their hosts, anthropologists must acquire a status that is considered appropriate in that society. Most anthropologists admit to having been thought of initially as helpless buffoons, more ignorant than any child of the most elementary techniques and rules of etiquette. Admired or useful personal qualities may help to upgrade the anthropologist to the status of pet or mascot and, eventually, of friend, at least in the eyes of a few people. Not all attempts to do fieldwork succeed, and more than a few budding anthropologists have lost their health or given up on their career, or both, as a result of difficult fieldwork experiences.

Their research objectives, combined with the variety and nature of local beliefs and customs, guide anthropologists in the building of their social image in the community under study. Normally, they do not try to become too thoroughly identified with members of the group, because in many societies taboos or other social customs applying to group members could interfere with the collection of needed information. For example, it is often the case that women cannot attend certain rituals or talk "innocently" to men, and men are never allowed to spend a long time observing or talking to another man's wife or daughter. The fieldworker must try to gauge how much deviance from local social norms the community will tolerate. Like any successful stage actor, the anthropologist must deliver a convincing and well-timed performance to be effective, only this performance must generally be sustained for months at a time and under difficult conditions: it can take its toll on both the health and the personality of the anthropologist. For many

anthropologists, the fieldwork for their doctoral research is an exhilarating but also a humbling experience, a sort of **rite of passage**. Some of the frustrations, difficulties, and joys of fieldwork are reflected in Allyn Stearman's report of her experiences among the Yuquí. She is explicit in her description of the misunderstandings that can arise between the anthropologist and the people observed. Richard Lee's adventure in the Kalahari Desert (Chapter 34) also shows how difficult it can be for the anthropologist to forget his or her own value system, and how easy it can be, even for an experienced researcher, to become the brunt of a vastly amusing cultural joke.

In Chapter 31, Michael Levin invites us to consider another aspect of the activities of ethnographers — namely, that their publications label their hosts, and that those labels can affect considerably not only the group's self-confidence, but also the way it will be perceived by larger, more powerful groups. A slightly different theoretical approach, a slight change of focus in the topic of research, and the resulting description of and labels attached to the observed group could be significantly different. Which description is more accurate? Which one is it more ethical to publish? Anthropologists have not always understood the gravity of their responsibility to the people they study. Levin makes it clear that ethnographers must consider what the political, moral, and other consequences of choosing to publish one "truth" over another might be.

Whereas anthropologists use *words* to convey the experiences of another culture, museums use *things* to achieve the same end. In her provocative essay in Chapter 32, Julie Cruikshank shows that both have often failed in the endeavor. Both museum collections and ethnographic details are selected on the basis of certain policies, theories, and preferences that are not those of the people who provide the "cultural artifact," be it a song, a myth, or a drum. The meaning of both words and things is distorted when they are presented outside their social and cultural context. Moreover, many ethical issues are raised when the dominant, wealthy social groups that own museums collect and control the cultural treasures of less powerful people. Both anthropologists and museum curators are now rethinking their traditional attitudes and strategies.

Works Cited

Malinowski, Bronislav. 1922. *Argonauts of the Western Pacific*. London: Routledge & Sons.

White, L.A. 1947. "Evolutionism and Anti-Evolutionism in American Anthropology." *Calcutta Review* 105: 30–40.

29
One Hundred Per Cent American

RALPH LINTON

There can be no question about the average American's Americanism or his desire to preserve this precious heritage at all costs. Nevertheless, some insidious foreign ideas have already wormed their way into his civilization without his realizing what was going on. Thus dawn finds the unsuspecting patriot garbed in pajamas, a garment of East Indian origin; and lying in a bed built on a pattern which originated in either Persia or Asia Minor. He is muffled to the ears in un-American materials: cotton, first domesticated in India; linen, domesticated in the Near East; wool from an animal native to Asia Minor; or silk whose uses were first discovered by the Chinese. All these substances have been transformed into cloth by methods invented in Southwestern Asia. If the weather is cold enough he may even be sleeping under an eiderdown quilt invented in Scandinavia.

On awakening he glances at the clock, a medieval European invention, uses one potent Latin word in abbreviated form, rises in haste, and goes to the bathroom. Here, if he stops to think about it, he must feel himself in the presence of a great American institution: he will have heard stories of both the quality and frequency of

foreign plumbing and will know that in no other country does the average man perform his ablutions in the midst of such splendor. But the insidious foreign influence pursues him even here. Glass was invented by the ancient Egyptians, the use of glazed tiles for floors and walls in the Near East, porcelain in China, and the art of enameling on metal by Mediterranean artisans of the Bronze Age. Even his bathtub and toilet are but slightly modified copies of Roman originals. The only purely American contribution to the ensemble is the steam radiator, against which our patriot very briefly and unintentionally places his posterior.

In this bathroom the American washes with soap invented by the ancient Gauls. Next he cleans his teeth, a subversive European practice which did not invade America until the latter part of the eighteenth century. He then shaves, a masochistic rite first developed by the heathen priests of ancient Egypt and Sumer. The process is made less of a penance by the fact that his razor is of steel, an iron-carbon alloy discovered in either India or Turkestan. Lastly, he dries himself on a Turkish towel.

Returning to the bedroom, the unconscious victim of un-American practices removes his clothes from a chair, invented in the Near East, and proceeds to dress. He puts on close-fitting tailored garments whose form derives from the skin clothing of the ancient nomads of the Asiatic

From Ralph Linton, *The Study of Man*, pp. 325–27. © 1936, renewed 1964. Reprinted with the permission of Prentice-Hall, Englewood Cliffs, New Jersey.

steppes and fastens them with buttons whose prototypes appeared in Europe at the close of the Stone Age. This costume is appropriate enough for outdoor exercise in a cold climate, but is quite unsuited to American Summers, steam-heated houses, and Pullmans. Nevertheless, foreign ideas and habits hold the unfortunate man in thrall even when common sense tells him that the authentically American costume of gee string and moccasins would be far more comfortable. He puts on his feet stiff coverings made from hide prepared by a process invented in ancient Egypt and cut to a pattern which can be traced back to ancient Greece, and makes sure they are properly polished, also a Greek idea. Lastly, he ties about his neck a strip of bright-colored cloth which is a vestigial survival of the shoulder shawls worn by seventeenth-century Croats. He gives himself a final appraisal in the mirror, an old Mediterranean invention, and goes downstairs to breakfast.

Here a whole new series of foreign things confronts him. His food and drink are placed before him in pottery vessels, the popular name of which — china — is sufficient evidence of their origin. His fork is a medieval Italian invention and his spoon a copy of a Roman original. He will usually begin the meal with coffee, an Abyssinian plant first discovered by the Arabs. The American is quite likely to need it to dispel the morning-after effects of over-indulgence in fermented drinks, invented in the Near East; or distilled ones, invented by the alchemists of medieval Europe. Whereas the Arabs took their coffee straight, he will probably sweeten it with sugar, discovered in India; and dilute it with cream, both the domestication of cattle and the technique of milking having originated in Asia Minor.

If our patriot is old-fashioned enough to adhere to the so-called American breakfast, his coffee will be accompanied by an orange, domesticated in the Mediterranean region, a cantaloupe, domesticated in Persia, or grapes, domesticated in Asia Minor. He will follow this with a bowl of cereal made from grain domesticated in the Near East and prepared by methods also invented there. From this he will go on to waffles, a Scandinavian invention, with plenty of butter, originally a Near-Eastern cosmetic. As a side dish he may have the egg of a bird domesticated in Southeastern Asia or strips of the flesh of an animal domesticated in the same region, which have been salted and smoked by a process invented in Northern Europe.

Breakfast over, he places upon his head a molded piece of felt, invented by the nomads of Eastern Asia, and, if it looks like rain, puts on outer shoes of rubber, discovered by the ancient Mexicans, and takes an umbrella, invented in India. He then sprints for his train — the train, not the sprinting, being an English invention. At the station he pauses for a moment to buy a newspaper, paying for it with coins invented in ancient Lydia. Once on board he settles back to inhale the fumes of a cigarette invented in Mexico, or a cigar invented in Brazil. Meanwhile, he reads the news of the day, imprinted in characters invented by the ancient Semites by a process invented in Germany upon a material invented in China. As he scans the latest editorial pointing out the dire results to our institutions of accepting foreign ideas, he will not fail to thank a Hebrew God in an Indo-European language that he is one hundred per cent (decimal system invented by the Greeks) American (from Americus Vespucci, Italian geographer).

30
Fieldwork among the Yuquí

ALLYN MACLEAN STEARMAN

A Preliminary Visit

I first considered the possibility of doing research among the Yuquí while I was preparing to undertake a restudy of the Sirionó Indians. A colleague in Bolivia, German anthropologist Jürgen Riester, had been corresponding with me and suggested I look into the Yuquí as well. Riester wrote that it was believed the recently contacted Yuquí were related to the Sirionó but that few people other than missionaries had spent much time among this group. Since I was anticipating a preliminary site visit to Bolivia in 1982 prior to a more lengthy stay, he suggested I try to make a side trip to the Yuquí camp. Riester cautioned me, however, that the New Tribes Mission, the mission group working with the Yuquí, discouraged outsiders from coming to the Chimoré.

My initial contact with the New Tribes missionaries working with the Yuquí was at the mission home in Cochabamba. Although I had expected to leave the Yuquí segment of my research until the end of the trip, when I arrived in Bolivia I was told by a mission official in Santa Cruz that the senior couple at the Yuquí camp would be leaving shortly for a year's "furlough."

From Allyn Maclean Stearman, *Yuquí: Forest Nomads in a Changing World*, pp. 1–10. Copyright © 1989 Holt, Rinehart and Winston, Inc. Reprinted with permission.

If I wanted to visit the Chimoré, he explained, I would need their approval first. I quickly flew from Santa Cruz to Cochabamba, where I met John and Helen Porter, who were scheduled to leave Bolivia the following day. They interviewed me briefly and then arranged for the mission pilot to take me to the Chimoré on an already scheduled flight. By radio they were able to communicate with missionary Hank Monroe at the camp, and it was agreed I would stay at the home of Mike and Mary Daniels while they were away from the Chimoré. The Daniels, the camp's newest missionary couple, were to be gone for a week at a conference and would fly out on the plane that was taking me in. It was also decided that I would take my meals with the schoolteacher, Mariano Ichu, and his family.

After a short flight over the mountains from Cochabamba, I arrived at the Yuquí camp. The Daniels greeted me quickly as they boarded the plane for the return flight to Cochabamba. The only missionary remaining was Hank Monroe, a man I judged to be in his late 50s or early 60s.

I settled myself into a spare room on the first floor of the Daniels' two-story house, keeping an eye on things and checking to make certain the old kerosene refrigerator had fuel and was operating properly. During the time I was alone in the house I met Monica,[1] a Yuquí woman about my age who had been twice widowed as a result of hostile encounters with outsiders. Recently, the

Yuquí camp had been relocated to avoid seasonal flooding; as a woman without the assistance of a spouse, Monica had been unable to complete the move. Her eldest son, Jaime, had taken off about half the tin roofing from her old place and carried it to the new site, where he had erected support poles and a roof frame; but the house remained unfinished while he worked on his own dwelling. I volunteered to help Monica finish her house.

Monica knew a few words of Spanish, I was learning some Yuquí, and gestures filled in the gaps. I immediately determined that Monica knew how to use an axe, was strong as an ox, and would be a willing working companion. However, as the two of us began gathering materials for the house, our efforts were embarrassingly reminiscent of an old Laurel and Hardy movie. I took charge of designing the form the house would take, since I had had some previous experience in house construction. Monica's expertise lay in locating the materials we would require. Most of the wood we needed would come from a tall, stately palm called *pachiuba (Socratea exorrhiza)*, which could be split into boards for walls and a sleeping platform. With axes, machetes, and Monica in the lead, we started off into the forest.

Monica found a stand of four *pachiuba* palms a short distance from her house site. I looked up into the crowns and saw that there was a good bit of tangle and growth there that might impede the trees' fall. I pointed out the problem to Monica, who seemed to understand but appeared unconcerned. I shrugged my shoulders. We took turns chopping and soon the pithy wood core was cut through. We heard the final crack as the tree gave way, both of us stepping away from the trunk. Nothing happened. Our tree was hanging there, swinging like a 30-foot pendulum. Monica plucked at her hair and muttered *"Eturã biti!"* a favorite Yuquí phrase used when things are not going well. We both grabbed the trunk to try to pull it free and soon were swinging back and forth like bell ringers. But the tree was stuck fast. Then Monica indicated we should chop down the next palm, using the weight of that tree to break loose the first. It seemed like a good idea so once again we began cutting. Our aim was perfect, and our second palm fell into the first but succeeded only in knocking it down to a 45° angle. Now we had two trees hung up. The plan this time was to climb up the leaning trunks and jump on them. Many *Eturã biti*s later we decided that this technique was not going to work either. But Monica refused to give up. We cut down the last two trees, felling them on top of the others, having finally achieved a pile of four *pachiubas* inextrica-

bly entwined in the surrounding vegetation. By now we had spent most of the morning cutting down trees and had nothing to show for our labor. Monica motioned for me to follow. We would try a new location.

We moved to the edge of the small swamp behind the Yuquí camp that was filled with *chuchillo (Gynerium sagittatum)* reed and some large trees. There was a good-sized *pachiuba* among the trees, but I estimated that if we cut it properly, it would fall clear. True to form, Monica was swinging her axe harder than I and before we realized it, the tree was falling off center. We watched it drop into the crown of a tree nearby. Discouraged, I squatted down and rested my head in my arms. From a short distance away, I heard chopping. Looking up, I saw Monica attacking an enormous hardwood growing at the edge of the swamp.

Her plan again evidently was to use the weight of this tree to knock the *pachiuba* loose. But if this tree fell the wrong way, it would land in the middle of her half-completed house. I grabbed Monica's arm and indicated the problem. She nodded, smiled, and resumed cutting. At that moment, the schoolteacher's son appeared to tell me that lunch was ready and to come quickly before the food got cold. I needed little urging to leave Monica to her impending disaster.

After lunch with the Ichu family, I made my way with trepidation back to the Yuquí camp. As I came down the trail, I saw Monica busily roasting a plantain at a small fire in her unfinished house. I was greatly relieved to see that both she and the house were safe. She smiled at me and we walked back to where she had been cutting on the huge tree. As we stood on the edge of the swamp, my mouth fell open in wonderment. Monica had succeeded in dropping the big hardwood into the crotch of another large tree, pinning the *pachiuba* between them. I decided we would call it a day and returned to the Daniels' house.

The following day Monica and I were at it again, only now we had fortunately broken our streak of bad luck in felling trees. With several good *pachiubas* on the ground, Monica showed me how to make palm boards, a skill I had not learned in the region where I had previously worked. It was a laborious chore, taking strength and patience to pound the palm trunks with the broad head of the axe and to make hundreds of small vertical cuts along the trunk until it could be split open and flattened. Then the pithy core had to be peeled loose, leaving the hard palm wood exterior intact. The palm pith was full of needle-like fibers, and soon Monica's and my hands were sore from punctures. At this point, I walked back to the Daniels' house and borrowed a pair of cotton work gloves I had seen in the storeroom. The work was much easier with the gloves since not only was I protected from the spiny fibers, but I could get a better grip on the wet pith. After a while, I handed the gloves to Monica, who seemed delighted to try them. She struggled a moment before I realized she had never had on gloves before. While understanding how they worked, Monica was unable to get her fingers in the holes properly. Soon we were laughing uproariously as we both tried to get the gloves over those ten stubborn fingers.

By the end of the week, the house was progressing well but still needed a good deal of work. I was enjoying my time with Monica and the opportunity to get to know a few other Yuquí as well. Thus when the Daniels returned, I decided, with their consent, to remain a while longer. They were grateful for my efforts with the old refrigerator and that I had kept the house swept and clean during their absence. Mike and Mary Daniels were new to the field, this being their first assignment. They were pleasant people from my home state of California, and we seemed to find a number of shared experiences. I helped Mary around the house when I was not out with Monica, and assisted her with the clinic. She seemed overwhelmed by this responsibility since she had been given little training in medical work and was having to learn by experience. She was genuinely thankful one morning when I happened to be present to help out when Daniel, Monica's youngest son, sliced all of his toes across the bottom on a serrated *chuchillo* leaf while he was out hunting.

Mary expressed regret that I was not taking meals with them but explained that those arrangements had been made by others. I told her that I was enjoying eating with the Ichu family and was getting to know both Mariano and Leonarda quite well. They were a typical indigenous peasant family very much like the people I had worked with as a Peace Corps volunteer. At first, Leonarda was shy and embarrassed around me, fearful that I would scorn her food, which, she explained, was "not like what the missionaries eat." I laughed and said that I had spent many years eating food just like she prepared and enjoyed it very much. She relaxed and soon we were good friends. I tried to arrive for our main meal (at noon) early enough to help with the food preparation. There in the kitchen with Leonarda and the several Yuquí women who were

always present, we would discuss the day's events. I have found that kitchens are always excellent places to do fieldwork since women are most at ease there and engage in free, unstructured conversation with few inhibitions. I also came to realize that Leonarda was very lonely at the Chimoré, having no one enough like her for her to feel comfortable. The missionary women were involved in their own activities and found Leonarda "native" like the Yuquí. Thus, while they were always kind to her, they had little in common. For Leonarda, the Yuquí were just as strange to her as she was to the missionaries. She spent a great deal of time with the Yuquí women teaching them to cook, sew, and bake, but did not understand them and found their ways and treatment of her savage at times.

Monica and I worked on her house for another week or so, finishing the roof, walls, and sleeping platform. During all this, the Daniels were entertained by my tales of Monica's and my exploits in house building. During the evening hours Mike would engage me in conversations of a religious nature, which after a while I found draining, especially after a long day of physical exertion in the heat and humidity of the forest. But he was also interested in broadening his own knowledge and of sharing my perceptions of the Yuquí. I found that both he and Mary were trying very hard to be "good missionaries" but still were struggling to learn Spanish. Yuquí, they said, seemed insurmountable. Mike was a large man with a jovial nature but lacking in manual skills. He had brought in a piece of finished mahogany to try to repair the Yuquí's broken machete handles. When he saw that I was good with my hands, Mike asked if I would teach the Yuquí men to make the new handles. There was a big palm wood shed behind the Daniels' house that had a great many tools in maddening disarray, but in looking for a hammer and pliers to work on Monica's house, I had found what I needed. The Yuquí men had access to the tool shed as well, were frequently in there tinkering with their guns, and so had a knowledge of what was available. The old workshop served our purposes well, and before long I had a veritable production line of men cutting out handles, making rivets from nails, and wrapping the finished products with wire for additional strength. During all this, the young headman, Leonardo, asked me if I would teach him to make a canoe paddle. Mike found us a board of the right length and thickness, but it was a dense hardwood and seemed to take forever to cut out and shape. The result was a bit heavy but nonetheless a fine paddle, which

Leonardo and I worked on diligently for several days until it was smooth to the touch. I was pleased when I returned a year later to see that he had the paddle in his house, now darkened from use but still intact.

Before leaving Bolivia, the Porters had told me of the existence of the mission's "Culture File," a compilation of cultural data on the Yuquí spanning almost ten years. When I had finished with Monica's house, I asked the Daniels if I could see the file. Hank brought it to the house one evening, and I realized what a mine of information it was. I then began what was to be, between other chores, a ten-day task of copying verbatim all of the information the file contained. I remember pausing one morning, as writer's cramp began to take its toll, to reflect that with a few nickels and a photocopying machine, I could have completed the entire project in about 15 minutes.

I left the Chimoré to continue with a related research project after having spent five weeks with the Yuquí and the New Tribes missionaries. It had been an interesting experience in many respects and I was eager to return for a more lengthy stay.

Preparing for Fieldwork

Having completed a preliminary site survey, I applied for a leave from my university teaching duties the following year. Once funding was secured, I wrote to the Chimoré to tell them of my plans to spend half of my year's leave with the Yuquí. In a letter from Hank, I learned that the Daniels had taken another post and had been replaced by a different couple, Bill and Jane Brown. Hank also mentioned that the Porters would return in August.

I took a bush plane to the Chimoré camp on September 9, 1983, and was surprised to hear that the Porters had not yet arrived but would do so that same afternoon. Having been told by the other missionaries that the Porters would be there momentarily, I waited at the missionary end of camp to greet them. But the flight was delayed, and when the plane finally landed, it was dusk. By the time we had finished welcoming back the Porters so that Leonarda, Mariano, and several of the Yuquí were free to help me carry my gear back to the Yuquí camp, it was nearing sundown. I knew that it would now be impossible to cut *chuchillo* reed for tent poles (I had been forced to leave them behind because of weight limitations) so I settled for an abandoned house Leonarda and

the Yuquí showed me. The former occupants, Humberto and Gloria, had squabbled with their neighbors and moved to another location, where they built a new house. Leonarda and the Yuquí helped me fashion a sleeping platform where I put up my mosquito net. Monica brought a burning brand from her house and started a fire. I made tea, shared the kilo of cheese I had brought as a gift with everyone present, and went to bed. A cold front had passed through earlier in the day and the night was chilly. I climbed onto my makeshift bed and zippered myself into my mosquito net. I was totally enclosed, giving me a sense of security that nothing would crawl in with me despite my poor shelter. Once inside my sleeping bag, I closed my eyes, trying to imagine that I was in more familiar surroundings. How many times before I had experienced the same sensation, as have other anthropologists on that first uncertain night in the field. I pondered what surely lay ahead of me: the good, the bad, the unknown. Also as before, I wondered what it was that brought me here, to give up the comforts of home and the warmth of my family in exchange for the small, nagging hardships and that hollow feeling of loneliness. Before falling asleep, I mused ruefully that anthropology was somehow much more romantic after the fact, when one was standing in the safe neutrality of a classroom.

After consulting with the missionaries and the Yuquí about a house site, I spent the next several days clearing brush. While I was busy preparing the area for my house, I received a visit from a young Bolivian man living with our only neighbor, a Yuracaré named Francisco Blanco. He needed work, he explained, and asked if I would consider hiring him to build my house. This seemed like a stroke of good fortune. We worked out an acceptable daily wage, and the young man, Oscar, began to cut and set palm posts. A few of the Yuquí men would stop by to help us now and then, but would take off without notice to hunt or fish. Oscar rapidly became disgruntled with their lack of dependability and was also beginning to suffer under the strain of the young girls' almost constant teasing while he was working. One day he failed to show up. I followed the trail upriver to Francisco's house, where I found Oscar. He looked embarrassed to see me but explained that he had found "other work" and would not be able to complete the house. I paid him for his labor and left. The Yuquí men and women helped me finish the house, and I moved in three weeks after construction had begun, much longer than I had anticipated. With the tent tied inside the house frame and off the ground, I had achieved a relatively bug-free, rain- and wind-resistant workplace. I could now begin fieldwork in earnest.

The Yuquí

While doing fieldwork among the Ik (pronounced "eek") of Uganda, Africa, anthropologist Colin Turnbull challenged the old anthropological myth that the researcher will like and admire the people he or she is studying. A corollary of this assumption is that to the uninformed outsider who does not "understand" the culture, a group may seem hostile, unresponsive, or stoic, or may have any number of less admirable characteristics; but to the trained observer who truly knows "his or her" people, these attributes are only a façade presented to outsiders. What Turnbull finally had to concede, however, was that overall the Ik were not a very likeable people. His portrait of the Ik as selfish, uncaring, and uninterested even in the survival of their own children is understandable when he describes their history of displacement, social disruption, and the constant threat of starvation. Nonetheless, an intellectual understanding of the factors contributing to Ik personality and behavior did not make it any easier for Turnbull to deal emotionally with the day-to-day interactions of fieldwork.

For me, knowing of Turnbull's situation alleviated some of my own anxieties in dealing with the Yuquí. As was Turnbull's, my previous field experiences among other peoples had been very positive. In the anthropologist's terms, this meant that I was accepted quite rapidly as a friend and that my informants were open and cooperative. The Yuquí did not fit any of these patterns. But like Turnbull, I understood something of the Yuquí past and thus on an intellectual level could comprehend that since they were a hunted, beleaguered people being threatened with extinction I could not expect them to be warm, friendly, and welcoming. Still, on an emotional level it was very difficult to cope with my frequent feelings of anger and resentment at having to put up with their teasing, taunting, and testing on an almost daily basis. My only consolation was that while I was often the brunt of this activity, so were they themselves. I am uncertain whether I finally came to understand the Yuquí, or simply became hardened to their particular way of dealing with the world. By doing favors for people, I incurred their indebtedness, and these debts could be translated into favors owed. How I chose to collect was up to me. As favors

mounted, I found that relationships with individual Yuquí were better. Then came the challenges. Could I be easily duped or taken advantage of? At first, I extended kindnesses gratuitously and was mocked. I learned to show my anger and stubbornness, to demand something in return for a tool lent or a service provided. Rather than alienate the Yuquí, this behavior (which I found difficult and distasteful throughout my stay) conferred prestige. The more I provided and then demanded in return, the more the Yuquí were willing to accept me. In the Yuquí world, as in any other, respect must be earned. But unlike many other peoples, for the Yuquí, kindness alone is not enough. In the end it is strength that is valued and that earns respect.

This lesson was driven home one day when I was physically assaulted by one of the young women, Susana. I had taught the children to sing a few old songs that I could play on a battered guitar given to one of the older lads by a colonist upriver. Their favorite was "Oh, Suzanna!" But because it was in English, Susana, the Yuquí woman, was uncertain if it was meant to tease her. One afternoon as we were all seated on a log singing, she suddenly leaped on me, laughing, but also quite serious about establishing her dominance. Although it was done in fun, I quickly realized that much more was at stake. Susana outweighed me by at least 30 pounds, and I soon found myself in the infamous Yuquí choke hold I had read about in the mission's "Culture File." Susana's strong thumb and fingers were wrapped around my windpipe. I could feel the tears well up in my eyes, the fear beginning to creep in that she would hold on until I passed out. If I did, I knew, I would be an object of ridicule. Still, I restrained myself, a lifetime of parental admonitions and the moral teachings of my own culture forbidding me to respond with violence. Then I experienced the sensation that everything was becoming quiet. I could see mouths laughing but the only sound was my own heart pounding. From some deep place within, the need to fight back overcame all of my inhibitions; I could feel the adrenaline begin to clear my head. I reached up with one hand and grabbed Susana just as she had me, but at the same time pulling her free arm behind her back. Now there was a different look in her eyes. The laughing stopped. I could feel her windpipe resisting my grip but tightened down even more. I was both exhilarated and disgusted by my actions. Finally, I rolled her off me, laughing as I did. There was no real victor, but at least I had held my own. For the next several days, the Yuquí admired the bruises on my neck like some badge of courage. We continued singing "Oh, Suzanna!" without further incident.

I also began to realize that my behavior was as carefully scrutinized by the Yuquí as theirs was by me. This scrutiny was more than just curiosity or even judgment. Once I had been accepted as a person of some worth and value, a status that took great energy on my part to achieve, the Yuquí began to consider my responses to given situations with thought and reflection. They are a people insecure in this new world of theirs. There is an innate comprehension that much of their old understanding of the world no longer applies. Because they are a very small group that has

experienced long-term reduction in population and has lost much of its original culture, there is very little of their tradition that they are willing to fight for. Like the Ik of Africa, for many generations the Yuquí have had little time to do much other than try to stay alive. This in itself is a brutalizing experience, as Turnbull found in Uganda, a way of life that can rob people of much of their basic humanity.

Note

1. All of the Yuquí have taken Spanish names now rather than continue to use their given names in Yuquí. These are the names they are known by, and so I will use them as well. Children no longer are given names in their own language.

31
Cultural Truth and Ethnographic Consequences

MICHAEL LEVIN

Fieldwork in an increasingly literate world presents new dilemmas for anthropologists. The information recorded in ethnographies may have consequences in the cultures and for the people with whom the ethnographer has worked. The political system of the peoples' nation may be able to use ethnographic information, and the politics of the local community can be affected by the permanent record an ethnography creates. This paper uses an old baseball story as a metaphor for the decisive powers of the ethnographer, and illustrates the issues with four instances calling for decisions from fieldwork in southeastern Nigeria.

To speak of the position of an anthropologist as being between two cultures is by now a truism. The very distance of these cultures allowed this place between them to be a comfortable position; at one time it was possible to learn from, and about, one culture and speak and write in and to members of another and be secure that, like East and West for Kipling, "never the twain shall meet." Those cultures themselves were also quite limited: a primitive world or place and an academic, scholarly community. The comfort of these limited worlds has been lost; the security of

From *Culture*, Vol. 11, No. 1–2, 1991, pp. 93–99. Reprinted with the permission of the Canadian Anthropology Society/Société Canadienne d'Anthropologie. (Bibliographic documentation contained in the original article is omitted here. Interested readers should consult the original publication.)

separation no longer exists. Regretting the loss of this comfortable division is merely nostalgia, surely one of the more tawdry of sentiments. Our world is not now divided, nor can we even think it is, if we wished to, between the expanding rational Western civilization and those peoples, cultures, and nations being drawn into this world system willy-nilly. Our informants now have interests, rights, reputations, and a place in this world, and these matters are issues of contention for them as for us. Our informants now read our books; they comment on our views, our understandings, our portraits of them and their culture. They adopt new perspectives, new concepts; they invent themselves and others. The monopoly on conceptualization — the one-way flow of definition, the unilateral power of definition, the unique privilege of translation, the power to capture another culture — is now a contested field. The two audiences are now more truly contestants, and both must be kept in mind.

The different expectations, interests, and feelings of these two audiences in the telling of our cultural or historical stories are not easy to accommodate. The need to balance the sense of identification or connectedness one might have with the aspirations and destinies of people with whom one worked against the ideals of scholarship is demanding but may be possible. This possibility may require more than one form of anthropological writing.[1]

Other readers, not party to this relationship of understanding and mutual respect, can use our work. Among these readers may be officials in their governments and in international agencies, whose purposes are likely to be not so scholarly. Our local friends and people from those parts in agencies of government have differing interest from others in the capital city, and those from dominant, majority cultures in the state in question may have competing interests or desire confirmation of the superiority of urban culture. I am suggesting, however tentatively, that what an anthropologist says and writes might have some impact, that there are some moments when our ethnography can have consequences and where the cultural truth is perhaps indefinite, or fluid, and may be inappropriately defined, made concrete and specific, by how we write about it.[2] If we as anthropologists recognize our multiple audiences, we can become cautious when aware of situations where the impact of an anthropologist's work, the consequences of our ethnography, although not usually seen as particularly potent in the world of affairs, politics, business, and development can have real effects. The metaphor of the baseball umpire nicely illustrates the situations I have in mind. A baseball story suggests the powers of the umpire.

It's an umpires' convention; three umpires are standing aside conversing. The most junior remarks "Baseball, nuthin' but balls and strikes. I calls 'em as I *sees* 'em." After a pause the umpire with somewhat more experience says, "Baseball, nuthin' but balls and strikes. *I* calls 'em as they *are*." Finally the senior umpire says, "Baseball, nuthin' but balls and strikes, and *they ain't nothin'* till I calls 'em."

There are limitations to the role described in this little joke about powers of definition and reality, but it conveys well enough the relation of perception, definition, and choice.[3] The origin of the word "umpire" is in Old French *nomper, nonper* "not one of a pair (of contestants)"; it's a position structurally not unsimilar to Georg Simmel's *tertius gaudens*, the happy third. This place of anthropologists, being between two cultures, is it a happy place? It was once a comfortable position; is it still? The anthropologist is a third person whose position is today more and more likely to be described as the troubled third, faced with being an intermediary between two audiences which have quite different criteria for approval and success. Because these audiences remain unequal in their capacity to affect our lives, the responsibility to our informants becomes more demanding, not less.[4]

It is through the publication of what we find in fieldwork that we discover the potency of anthropological description and the range of our umpirical discretion. In my fieldwork experience there are a number of moments when I have faced that umpirical decision "what should I call 'em?" Some of those moments which stand out are moments of realization, moments when my preconceptions of Bette[5] life, or social structure, or history were rattled by statements or responses of Bette people. Although the baseball story really applies only to the last of the four moments I'll recount here, the question of what I as an anthropologist *calls 'em* might have wider consequences in all four instances than I might intend, or expect, and certainly more than I would wish.

My first encounter occurred very early as I was being shown around the village in the first few days. I had come from the New World with a copy of the recently published *Peasants*, by Eric Wolf (1966), under one arm and my mosquito net under the other. I wanted to write about African cultivators as peasants. We, I, had all read about the traditional segmentary systems, but few ethnographies recognized the transformations that *had* to be taking place, but were not acknowledged in the literature. And the way to do it seemed to be to test one *structural category* against another, in this case, segmentary opposition of local groups against corporate peasant community. Lloyd Fallers had written a suggestive, but short, article on the question, but the issue was unresolved. Works from southern and east Africa suggested possibilities, but they were cast, in what seemed to a brash graduate student, archaic language, or seemed to be special cases. P. Mayer's *Townsmen or Tribesmen* (1961) seemed to deny the individuality of people, the reality of social change, to emphasize the displaced and inappropriate character of such people, to echo the earlier contempt for educated and political Africans. William Watson's *Tribal Cohesion in Money Economy* (1958) was a study of remittances by, and absences of, miners, and the effects of these factors in a bounded reserve-like community. In 1957, Kenneth Little wrote [in *American Anthropologist*] about *landschaftmen* associations, tribal voluntary associations, in African towns. Such organizations did not seem particularly African or arising out of that tradition, but more a concomitant of migration to the city, being present in remarkably similar form as representations of sentiment and cooperation in immigrant associations in the New World. These works, impressive in their own right, seemed only to extend the cultural divisions into the city, but did not deal with emerging, modern forms of rural social organization. *Peasants*, on the other hand, was somehow more contemporary, more modern; it importantly took into account the relationship of individuals and communities with the larger economy and society, and with the state. It might allow for the study of the nature and direction of change in a rural African community. It was invested with some important theoretical implications. West Africa on the world map in Wolf's brilliant little book was shaded to show peasants, but the references were sparse. There were two, to Forde's work in Yakö and some work on the Ashanti. And there was reference to the work of French geographers and agronomists, whose use of the term *paysan* was quite uncritical. So there was a place for this kind of modelling.

This was my plan when I arrived in this village with a mixed agricultural economy. I met with people, the chief, elders, school teachers, the local literate adults, and I attended the frequent meetings of savings groups in the first few days while setting up a household and engaging an assistant. One of those early Sundays, as I have said, as I was being shown around the village, a man said to me, "It's a shame you have come so late. It will be difficult to understand us. We used to live together, one brother next to another. Now we have moved away from the old homes and are scattered. It will be difficult for you to understand us." What good to me was Wolf's wonderful structural category: agnatic kinship was the beginning of explanation and interpretation. Lineages, in the sense of groups agnatically defined, were some aspect of life. Concepts which embraced kinship and collectivity were used. Did lineages exist? The problem became, what form did they take? What was to become of the categories of ceremonial and rent funds? peasant coalitions? and peasant ecotypes?[6]

This was the problem in the specific sense. Broadly, it was one of preconceptions and intentions. I had theoretical preconceptions, perhaps theoretical presumptions. Should these preconceptions determine my perceptions? Was I to call *'em* something they were not? Was I to see a social formation, *peasants*, where some other social formation was working?[7]

It was not only the conscious models of society, against which we, as anthropologists, have been warned by scholars as diverse as Marvin Harris and Claude Lévi-Strauss, that made me doubt the utility of the peasant concept in this setting. In southeastern Nigeria the main products are food stuffs, making the economic dimension much less clear and less structured than where crops are non-consumable export crops like cotton or coffee. In many ways the concept *peasants* did not help organize the information I was getting. Setting up two models, however, peasants and segmentary systems, forced my attention to what was being said and done.

It became clear, that to use this model, I would be making of these people "paper peasants," who, out of perversity or lack of true consciousness, do not fit the theory. I must begin with what the Bette people *say* — if I dare use the term, *their discourse*. It must be what they say that comes first. It is here that there is some chance of beginning to say something that means something to them as Bette and is valid for me as an anthropologist. These communities are becoming occupationally differentiated, yet residence, rights, property, and, at some levels, collective action are expressions of tradition, expressions of segmentary forms of solidarity or of forms of communalism — that is, lineages and clans.

At the same time it is not their Bette-ness, their essence, which is of interest, but their development in the Nigerian context, their use of tradition, of their social relationships, of their culture to act within the state and secure their rural and their national place that is important. To describe local communities as peasants would imply a uniformity of village structure and an extreme degree of individualization which does not represent present realities. The collective action of individuals is mediated through and organized on the basis of kinship-defined relationships. In S.F. Moore's words, they "...have neither broken with their past nor have they reproduced it."

What seemed like a crass comment marked the second moment of new understanding. I was told "money is a good thing." But this was not a crass comment; it went straight to the heart of vital daily relationships. The novelty of this statement struck me immediately: the corrupting dimension of money is what one hears about most often. P.J. Bohannon had reported, in 1959, that the Tiv thought that money had spoiled the system of exchange and undermined distinct values found in pre-monetary spheres of exchange. Yet Bette men and women thought money and the bride-price it allowed them to pay liberated them from an oppressive exchange system of marriage. In this system of concrete exchanges the only equivalent of a woman was another woman. The oppression of the system was felt in the connection imposed between pairs of marriages and in father–daughter and brother–sister relationships. Money allowed divorce. A wife could stay with her husband, despite his sister's leaving hers. Without money a father, a brother, had to force a daughter or sister to stay married, to stay with her husband, or he had to surrender his own wife to her family. Certainly in this situation marriage was a contingent relationship!

My awareness of the novelty of linking the approval of money as a progressive innovation with the possibility to pay bride-price was heightened once back in Canada listening to various levels and forms of feminist argument. Was the welcomed relative liberation of Bette men and women from the bonds of custom to be appreciated as such, or are they misguided, victims of false consciousness, not realizing the oppression capitalism is visiting on them?

What should I be calling these beliefs, these cultural practices? Are they balls or strikes? Has money liberated women and their brothers and husbands? If a woman says she knows that she is properly married when her husband has paid something to her father is she deluded? Must I impose our dichotomy between the personal and the material to be correct? Am I to insist to people who are quite poor by world standards that money is corrupting? I think they would think me a particularly naive kind of preacher.

Clearly, everyday relationships, everyday life, was being affected by the consequences of world system expansion, of capitalist penetration, of colonialism, but linking such broad macro-categories to the possibilities of divorce in Bette was an awkward problem. The problem again was found not in the experience of Bette people but in diffuse and undifferentiated categories, such as capitalism and colonialism, which lead to undifferentiated judgements. Such concepts, when used as a variable, as in the sense of the phrase "capitalism causes ..." or "as a result of colonialism ...," also keep the background against which local changes take place out-of-focus, fuzzy and indistinct.

One solution is to approach the issue more specifically and in a more focused way as monetization itself, and to emphasize comparison with the system of the past. In this specific situation money *is liberating*. And it is especially liberating when you can substitute it for persons.

This issue has two aspects: one is the anthropological audience which disapproves of the impact of our Western culture on other cultures; the other is a full understanding of this stated appreciation for money in the political context that never considered British rule legitimate. Appreciating the utility of multi-purpose money is not the same as approving of everything new,

of everything European. Acknowledging that some rational recognition and valuation of change can be made both by informants, in this case, Bette people, and by anthropologists is important in such an analysis.[8]

This encounter of competing interpretations also raises the whole question of the romantic view of the past, pre-colonial, pre-capitalist society. Is every aspect of tradition worth preserving? Is all change corrupting? Is any desire to change inauthentic? Evaluating change is beyond the scope of this paper.

The third moment was more one of confusion of roles and naivety about communication. It arose over the issue of "the creation of states." (Nigeria as of 1989 has twenty-one states. The number has increased from twelve, created out of the four regions in 1967.) This question brought into confrontation questions of theory versus questions of power, local aspirations, and political practice. Nigeria was set up by the British as three regions; later, one was divided, making four regions. The minorities question has pre-dated independence, with the major concern of minorities being their subjugation in some sense by the larger ethnic groups which were the majorities in each region. Each region had been centred around one majority ethnic group. In the Eastern Region this was the Igbo. The minority peoples of this area had sought a separate state for many years, going back to the period of nationalist agitation before independence in 1959. The first campaigns were for a large state, basically a division of the region into Igbo and non-Igbo states. Later, when the region was divided into four states, Imo, Anambra, Rivers, and Cross River, the campaign shifted to arguing for a division of Cross River State into two, a division that has recently been effected. There is a theory of development underlying this argument that is quite simple. Its central premise is that development is achieved through the multiplication of the structures of the state. This question is not a hypothetical one; it is a question of solidarity: to doubt the aspirations is to be disloyal. To doubt that more government jobs for "our boys and girls" is important is to be hopelessly naive if not unsympathetically cruel. At a certain point in the last civilian regime in Nigeria (1979–1983) local governments (formerly divisions) were multiplying, at least on paper, at a phenomenal rate. One state had subdivided its 17 Local Government Areas (formerly Divisions, equivalent to Municipalities) into 54! One LGA kept the dump truck to carry the gravel for roads, and the other got the grader to spread it! I voiced some restrained academic doubts about this wasteful proliferation of bureaucracy and was told very firmly that I was wrong — that a new state was necessary and that I did not understand. I left it at that, thinking we had had a nice chat over beer and nothing more. A few weeks later someone not present at my original conversation (and I thought not connected to the people I had been with) stated that he had heard I was against the new state! What I had seen as a bar-room political theory was real-world political practice. I realized immediately that I could only lend some vague authority to dissenting opinion, but not do any good. This was a question of team loyalty, and I had better stay with the team that had already brought me so far.

When I returned in 1987 to Nigeria to do some more detailed work on village history, I was told "now you could say we are three sons of one father." This was the fourth moment of realization. The village is divided into three segments, none named eponymously, and the three segments operate as equal political parts of the village. In my early period of fieldwork there, only for about six months until the outbreak of the Biafran War, I had not worked on historical questions as such, but on language, kinship terminology, residence, and related questions. I had learned that two of the segments had a ritual society, a deity, and an associated dance that the third did not, but I had thought little of it.

Although it was clear the villagers were aware of the slave trade on the coast of what is now Nigeria, slavery and slaves were not mentioned even in private. Nor was slavery or trade in slaves given much importance in the ethnographic literature on West African peoples, although as a "status" of some persons and as a privileged activity of some men it was mentioned almost in passing. Perhaps its illegality prevented the investigation of its presence by white anthropologists.[9]

By the late 1970s, however, the incredible growth of publication and debate on slavery forced one to recognize the hidden inequalities even in vociferously egalitarian communities.

This statement "now you could say we are three sons of one father" by one of the elderly men in the course of more detailed inquiries into the village history drew my attention by his careful qualification of the claim to common ancestry. Why *could one say* we are three sons of one father? Why did not one simply say we are the sons of one father! And why *now*? What did one say *then*? The account went on to describe the origins of the village, one of the ancestors being a foundling, the others being brothers. Later I was told candidly and in the hearing of a member of "the foundling" segment that the ancestors of this segment had been slaves of one of the other segments.

I continued the series of interviews over the next few weeks and confirmed this information. I thought this was a marvellous transition to write about: the change from a free-slave community to an egalitarian-free community. But in this village writing was no longer an innocent process of recording peoples' statements, the facts, making a realist ethnography. At the very end of my stay, the very morning I was leaving, two retired school teachers approached me and made a request. They knew it was not a simple request. They asked that I write very carefully about what I had learned. It could do a great deal of damage, they said. This was not a heartfelt simple plea from someone who might be stigmatized by being labelled. It came from both sides of the divide. Nor was it a request that I distort the historical truth. Somehow I had to come to terms with telling the truth and avoiding the ethnographic consequences.[10]

I had considered this sentence "now you could say we are three sons of one father" as an alternative title for this paper, because the implications of the decisions made about this question are so intertwined with theoretical problems of temporality, history, and literacy. It also raises most acutely what we may call, perhaps belabouring the metaphor, the umpirical dilemma. In one reading of it there is no doubt this statement is a clean uncomplicated pitch, a good straightforward fastball, belt-high and across the plate. A strike! Another reading of it, a crucial understanding, is that the request for discretion in labelling part of the village as *slaves*, which I would be doing if I wrote that they are descendants of slaves, is also a pitch, but a change-up, sinking, down low and inside. If I were the batter I would have to go for it. But is it a ball or a strike?

What kind of umpire am I going to be, what kind of umpire should I be? Shall I call 'em as they *are*, compressing time and making the past more important in the present by labelling *in print* some of my friends and scholarly co-workers? Shall I call 'em as I see 'em, showing progress and the triumph of universalistic values over oppression and cultural difference, but still stigmatizing by identifying *in print* with the slave label, identifying *in print* some members of this village community that has been so good to me? Or shall I be the umpire "makin' 'em somethin' when I call 'em," equals to their "brothers," or inferiors to their "brothers," putting this history into print making it more important in the present than it already is and extending this history that some wish to forget into the future by giving it permanence in a village Domesday Book?

These moments of realization of the ethnographic consequences are personal, but exemplify the broadening implications and uses of ethnography. It is in the awareness of the open context that literacy brings to the uses of ethnography that we must write about the cultural truth. All consequences cannot be anticipated; some can. What is certain is that the uses of ethnography and its consequences are not in the control of its authors, nor of its subjects. Only the unpredictability of its consequences is certain. I do not want to suggest that ethnography can dominate politics, nor that the anthropologist can, or should, have some dominant role in the lives of the people he or she writes about, but that ethnography can have many uses and therefore requires care in its preparation. The revelation of cultural truth must take into account the ethnographic consequences, and they may not be trivial.

Notes

1. Renato Rosaldo's *Culture and Truth* (Boston: Beacon Press, 1989) was published after this paper was written. Chapter 2, "Beyond Objectivism," distinguishes the forms of writing that ethnography can take and deals with the understandings of these forms of writing by these two audiences, the anthropologists and the ethnographic subjects. His essays have been immensely useful in revising this paper.

2. Scholarly anthropological culture may be seen as driven by the needs of academic careers and by a popular culture that has few limits on what may be said and published. There is a temptation to renounce the pressure that comes from this culture, but such a renunciation of the consequences of literacy seems to me to be but an unrealistic attempt to maintain innocence in the face of change, to say one is totally outside of events. To choose not to speak at all about some aspects of a culture studied, or experiences that reflect badly on it, or illegal acts of individuals is a different, but related, question.

3. Those who consider there are few ambiguities in sports and that most of the variation comes from an excessive zeal for winning might consider other baseball rules, such as the balk rule. To

explore the umpire analogy a comparison with the much more limited roles and powers of the umpire in cricket is instructive.

4. On dyads and triads, see G. Simmel's *The Sociology of Georg Simmel* (1950). Simmel raises the possibility of the non-partisan using his "...position for purely egoistic interests." One of the interests which drives anthropologists is the furtherance of their careers by publishing, and publishing in a culture which values the printed product. Nigerians in rural communities are well aware of the value of theses, books, etc., in university life and of the material benefit accruing to those who publish.

5. The Bette (biti, as in Eng. *bit*) live at the northern boundary of Obudu Local Government Area, Cross River State, Nigeria, neighbouring the Tiv, and speak a Bantoid language. Fieldwork was carried out for varying lengths of time from 1967 until, most recently, July 1987.

6. I had been able to write of peasant aspects of social relations in Cameroun, where classic commodities, cocoa, and coffee are grown, and I could trace the inflation of ceremonial expenditures, primarily funereal feasts and bride-price, following the rise of cocoa prices. Yet the reviewer in the *American Anthropologist* of the book *Peasants in Africa*, in which my paper had appeared, reported an African student asking querulously, but not unjustly, "Why do they call our farmers peasants? Peasants is a derogatory term." Perhaps this unhappiness with such social categories or labels is the consequence categories have in this kind of analysis, of labelling people as social categories and making the past relations of people, their culture and history, invisible. Bernard S. Cohn makes a similar comment: "Those anthropologists who continued to be interested in the transformation of societies, either in the right wing mode of modernization or the left wing mode of revolution, discovered that they were studying 'peasant societies,' and this enabled them to continue indexing features without worrying too much about the content and context of civilizations they were studying."

7. There are other ways, more scholarly, of putting this dilemma: Were my perceptions to be driven by theory? Should I choose the academic audience with an investment in concepts and theory over the local sense of reality? This debate is neither a brief nor a simple one.

8. This argument for a close examination of the impact of the world system, capitalism in its specifics, is in some ways parallel to suggestions made in "Imagining the Whole: Ethnography's Contemporary Efforts to Situate Itself," by George Marcus [*Critique of Anthropology* 9, no. 3 (1989) 7–30] of ways to efface the macro–micro dichotomy.

9. This contrasted with my experience later in Cameroun, where the recognizable epithet *ninga* was used to refer to those of slave descent. In Cameroun, slavery was spoken about openly and it was marked by degrees of distance, personal, linguistic, and ethnic, but in Nigeria, the topic was suppressed.

10. The ambivalence toward public representation of slavery was a more general Nigerian attitude. I own two carvings which have been deliberately disfigured by cutting away the bindings at the mouth, although the ropes or shackles at the ankles and wrists remain. This disfiguring of the sculptures was explained as a reaction to the knowledge that slavery was illegal and had been abolished.

32
Oral Tradition and Material Culture

Multiplying Meanings of "Words" and "Things"

JULIE CRUIKSHANK

Museums have occupied an ambiguous place in North American anthropology since Boas set them adrift from the disciplinary mainstream early in the century. After a decade of intense involvement with the American Museum of Natural History, Boas resigned in 1905, convinced that it was impossible to represent culture adequately through such a restricted part of heritage as physical object. When he departed, he took with him his fledgling science of anthropology, and in the decades that followed, material culture studies gradually became segregated and associated with museum anthropology while university anthropologists moved on to study behavior and ideology. Museums were further marginalized in anthropology once they became identified as a material manifestation of colonial encounters from which many anthropologists now seek distance.

A contested issue in contemporary anthropology centres on how best to convey, in words, the experience of another culture. Increasingly, museums face similar challenges about the use of *things* to represent culture, particularly when

From *Anthropology Today*, Vol. 8, No. 3, June 1992, pp. 5–9. Reprinted with the permission of the Royal Anthropological Institute of Great Britain and Ireland. (Bibliographic documentation contained in the original article is omitted here. Interested readers should consult the original publication.)

material objects displayed in exhibits convey conflicting symbolic messages to different audiences. This paper arises from my interest in juxtaposing two seemingly restricted ethnographic approaches — analysis of oral tradition and analysis of material culture. It also considers how indigenous peoples in Canada are making spoken words and material objects central to debates about cultural property and representation of culture.[1]

Representing Culture through Words and Things

In the short history of anthropology, analyses of spoken words and of material objects have usually been compartmentalized. Yet there are a surprising number of parallels: both were originally treated as *objects* to be collected; then attention shifted to viewing words and things in *context*; recently they have been discussed as aspect of cultural *performance*, just as now they are often referred to as cultural *symbols* or as cultural *property*.

The analogy has obvious limitations, given the ambiguous boundary distinguishing utterance from object. Spoken words, embodied in ordinary speech, may be ephemeral physical processes. But they become *things* when they appear on paper or on artefacts or when they are recorded in magnetic or digital codes on tapes or disks, or in film or videotape. Material objects, especially the portable kind found in museums, can have meanings read into them quite different from those their makers intended, but those meanings tend to be framed, interpreted, understood in words. Yet this blurred distinction underscores the parallel ways in which verbal utterances and material objects are used both to symbolize the past and to stake out positions in discussions about cultural representation, copyright of oral narratives, and ownership of cultural property. Museums, with their collections of artefacts, folksongs, and folklore have so often been compared with archives, though, that it is worth examining the parallels.

Two recent incidents sparked by exhibitions at Canadian museums are instructive because they show the multiplicity of stories viewers read into the material world of "things," especially when those things are exhibited in museums. A 1987 exhibition at the Glenbow Museum in Calgary, *The Spirit Sings*, focussed on the artistic traditions of Native Canadians. According to the curator, Julia Harrison, one objective was to draw attention to how much of this artistic heritage is housed in foreign museums; another was to educate the Canadian public about the richness of that heritage. The exhibition came under intense criticism for exhibiting indigenous heritage as art rather than exposing the colonial underpinnings still governing relationships between Native people and Canadian institutions. Protestors objected that major funding for the exhibit came from Shell Oil, a company drilling on lands claimed by the Lubicon First Nation in northern Alberta. In November 1987, the Canadian Ethnology Society debated and passed a resolution supporting the boycott.

In 1990, the Royal Ontario Museum in Toronto mounted an exhibition, *Into the Heart of Africa*, which called attention to Canada's complicity in colonizing Africa. Curator Jeanne Cannizzo attempted to document the cultural arrogance of Canadian soldiers and evangelists in Africa, and to demonstrate the contradictions involved in "collecting" culture — tracing the life history of objects "... from ritual object to missionary souvenir and finally to museum specimen...." Both the subtlety of the message and the absence of a clear coalition with Africans in Toronto resulted in a boycott of the exhibit by groups claiming to represent Africans and charging that the exhibit was racist. Sympathetic observers suggest that the curator's error was to use irony. No matter how clever the curatorial narrative, the message seems to be, the authority of the outside observer is suspect.

The more museums become the scapegoat for the sins of objectification in anthropology, the more directly they re-enter anthropological debate, possibly because they embody so clearly the sets of social relationships in which the entire discipline is embedded. As we near the end of the century, museums and anthropology are once again discussing the same issues. Because museums are institutions open to the public, they often occupy the front lines in that debate.

A critical problem involves situating museums within a larger anthropological discourse. Until recently, a conventional way to explicate one's research interests was to begin by acknowledging the anthropological ancestors — Boas or Malinowski, or perhaps Evans-Pritchard or even Julian Steward — then framing one's own questions within a web of kinship created from that sometimes unwieldy scaffolding. Currently, the convention involves distinguishing oneself from earlier anthropologists, alluding to the crisis of representation, making appropriate linkages with critical theory, deconstruction, and postmodernism, and locating oneself in theory from *outside* anthropology. Such a truncated summary shows how brief anthropology's history is: most of the "pioneers" also drew on theory from outside anthropology because they were inventing the discipline. Ultimately, though, casting the net ever wider within the western intellectual tradition in order to represent non-western cultures more adequately raises troublesome issues.

Museums and anthropology are undeniably part of a western philosophical tradition, embedded in a dualism which becomes problematic as a conceptual framework for addressing issues of representation. Entrenched oppositions between "self/other," "subject/object," "us/them" inevitably leave power in the hands of the defining institution. If anthropology museums provide a convenient focus for examining the control of cultural representations, this should not mask the fact that the same issues permeate late twentieth-century society. Museums may house and maintain "legal ownership" of personal and ceremonial property, providing a powerful representation of indigenous peoples' feelings of powerlessness. But governments are under pressure to work out equitable settlements for Native communities which have been denied their legal, contractual rights to land and to grant those communities greater political autonomy. Indigenous peoples do not define land rights, self-government, control of material culture, or control of images in ethnographic monographs, fiction, and film as separate issues with distinct boundaries.

Anthropological discourse, like any other, proceeds primarily by re-examining the boundaries of categories formerly taken to be self-evident. "Words" and "things" seem to stand at opposite ends of a spectrum — the one associated with linguistic expression of ideas, the other with physical manifestation of ideas; the one ongoing and changing and the other arrested in glass boxes.

Objects

In the earliest years of anthropology, words and things were treated as *objects* to be collected; the Linnaean concept of material objects as natural history specimens parallels the folklorist's notion of narrative plots as collectible, mappable, comparable things. F. Boas, early on, considered them to be "pre-existing" attributes of culture, somehow pure because they seemed to him less influenced by the ethnographic observer than other aspects of culture. Museums and folklore journals built up their independent collections for "later study."

Yet this notion of putting words and things in museums and archives as though they are discrete, unmediated, objective artefacts is one that continues to be contentious. Renato Rosaldo has been critical of the ways some historians equate oral testimony with archival records that can be stored for eventual use. He argues that oral history has only one purpose — reconstitution of the past, not collection for its own sake, that oral traditions are texts to be heard, not documents to be stored — cultural forms that organize perceptions about the past, not "containers of brute facts." Similarly, D. Cole and N.J. Parezo each demonstrate that museum collections don't "just happen" as the general public assumes. They are shaped by explicit objectives of the collector and the funding institution. Their meaning frequently requires an understanding of the social conditions under which they were collected as well as the conditions under which they were produced and used.

Anthropological writing about the social life of *things* still seems less self-conscious than writing about *words*, possibly because words have come under the deconstructive eye of linguists while objects remain a relatively unanalysed common-sense category of western culture. Critical attention to objects, though, is opening up parallel discussions about how we constitute material culture. Analyses of the ways "things" are embedded in social relations or of how objects become commodities help to revise perspectives about what constitutes an object in the first place.

Context

As anthropologists began to look at the social and cultural settings from which words and things were being gathered, notions of *context* became increasingly important. This emphasis exacerbated the contradictions inherent in collecting detached assemblages of objects and narratives to represent something as complex as culture. An initial response was to try to reconstruct context — dioramas and stuffed animals in museums, summaries of dates and places dutifully reported with narratives. But none of these directly acknowledged that physical things and words wrenched from their social and cultural setting become part of another semiotic sphere that cannot be redressed by contextual padding. The contradiction drove Boas from museums, though he never acknowledged it as completely in his continuing work with oral tradition.

Boas was hardly alone in this willingness to see texts as having a life of their own. Octavio Paz discusses how European colonial expansion spawned early fascination with recording texts; this, in turn, formed the foundation for later collecting of "primitive" art. Chronicles recorded by Spanish conquistadores and missionaries, Chinese texts studied by Jesuits and eighteenth century philosophers, and Sanskrit texts that preoccupied German Romantics were all interpreted from the cultural distance of the armchair, just as indigenous art would be later. Malinowski, a better fieldworker than Boas, was more critical of the tendency to study narrative on paper, rather than for its function in real life: "It is easier to write down a story than to observe the diffuse, complex ways in which it enters into life, or to study its function by the observation of the cast social and cultural activities into which it enters. And this is the reason why we have so many texts and why we know so little about the very nature of myth" [B. Malinowski, *Myth in Primitive Psychology*, 1926, p. 111].

The notion of context continues to be troublesome in anthropology. It is no longer sufficient to be sensitive to the setting and situation in which an object is collected or a story is heard. We have also to understand its continuing life. And to do that we need to develop ways of *retaining* the setting. Storytellers are well aware of this in northern Canada; for example, some elders order accounts of their life experiences by incorporating ancient narratives to explain contemporary events in their own lives. Many of the explanatory stories they tell were recorded almost a century ago by ethnographers who thought they were recording a disappearing folklore. Hearing such stories in 1990 from living narrators, suggests convincingly that these are not so much the "same stories" as ongoing ideas, continually reinvested with new meaning.

Likewise, the idea that objects are unique, discrete entities raises questions about what constitutes an object in different cultural settings. A notion underlying much of museum practice, that objects in museums are frozen in time and are primarily evidence of the past, is not universally shared. In many non-western cultures they are understood to be not inert things, but to have life histories that do not stop when they enter museums. A Trobriand kula necklace or a Northwest Coast copper, for example, accumulates value during its life. Following a recent theatrical performance at the University of British Columbia's Museum of Anthropology, Okanagan actor Sam Bob commented on his ambivalence about performing there: "I wonder whether the things here are really happy? I wonder how they feel about being here?" Objects and words both have ongoing stories; their meaning cannot be fully captured in a synchronic analysis.

Performance

A further shift in analyses of both material and oral traditions gives greater place to the ongoing social life in which both occur — the growing attention to performance. Increasingly, museums are becoming centres for cultural performance of indigenous music, dance, and political statement, attracting audiences who may have concerns very different from readers of ethnography.[2] This presents both ideological and practical problems for museums where the primacy of the object has long been a fundamental principle, and where conservators have a mandate requiring them to minimize alteration to objects. A conservator at the University of British Columbia's Museum of Anthropology has had to confront a range of decisions: from the claims of performance artists that their creativity is inhibited if they must avoid physical contact with the totem-poles, to the less visible effects resulting when a performance creates vibrations or when large audiences crowd the exhibits and subject them to accidental touching. Performance is an interactive process and at best it centres on social relationships between objects and people, a direction some museums are clearly acknowledging as central. But this may call for a significant re-evaluation of museum practice.

In the field of verbal arts, a wide public is losing interest in attempts to represent the world realistically in a causally connected, continuous, seamless, linear narrative. Native oral traditions have roots in procedures and methods different from written literary texts. Increasingly, indigenous writers are experimenting with literary forms, redefining ethnographic authority on their own terms, and challenging images of their cultures presented by nonwestern writers, filmmakers, and anthropologists.[3] In Canada, museums are one of the locations where discussion of these issues occurs.

Aboriginal peoples have demonstrated a masterful ability to mount symbolic protests drawing attention to asymmetrical social relations. Museums, holders of symbols, have an opportunity to host debates about cultural representation and even to point out contradictions in the complex relationship between object, performance, and meaning.

Symbol

Approaches by anthropologists, museum professionals, and indigenous peoples converge (and conflict) most closely in definitions of culture that focus on ideas about symbol and meaning. In the 1970s, Clifford Geertz argued that culture could be understood objectively by studying the public symbols which members of society use to communicate worldview and values. The meanings of those symbols are embedded in social relations and the project of anthropology is to explicate the balance between locally understood meanings of social worlds and the independent existence of social relations. More often than not, meanings are contested. Fowler, for example, discusses how in one Native American community, people from different age groups have different interpretations of which objects are "sacred" and which "profane," with younger people often giving greater latitude to those boundaries than do their elders. Meanings of symbols may also be unconscious; British observers sometimes point to Canadian state symbolism — ranging from crowns of royalty to Inuit carvings and Northwest Coast totem poles — as an unverbalized attempt to distinguish Canada from its neighbour to the south.

Objects can make powerful statements about legitimacy. Curators may display and describe objects thoughtfully in terms of their aesthetic, ceremonial, or historical importance. Those same objects may be experienced simultaneously as symbols of family heritage by some members of indigenous communities and as symbols of cultural oppression by those who are critical of their location in institutions seen to have participated in colonial encounters. Still others may see material culture as a strategic resource which can be used to communicate an ideology of cultural identity in negotiations with governments who deny their existence as autonomous cultural groups.

Social relations of class also generate contested meanings, with western-educated professionals of indigenous ancestry choosing to, or being expected to, speak on behalf of indigenous communities. Indigenous communities are no less complex than other communities, nor do they exist outside state and society where class is an important element in social relations. Hence, contested meanings become especially problematic for museums located in urban centres and affiliated with universities where hegemonic values prevail.

Again, there are parallels with oral tradition. If the growing emphasis on the importance of the indigenous voice poses pitfalls, perhaps the greatest is its centrifugal force toward essentialism, the attribution of ideas and concepts to "the indigenous voice" when the words are actually being supplied by a Eurocentric ideology. Indigenous writers legitimately claim the right to add their voices to discussions about culture, because their voices are so rarely represented in written texts. However, if their audience credits individual writers with representation of a generalized "Native Voice," their entire project is undermined. The furore over who has the right to tell and publish Native stories is experienced very differently by Canadian First Nations who have a concept of the social location of stories in community, and by those non-Native writers who see authorship as an index of individual creativity and speak in terms of "travel of the imagination." Indigenous writers, mindful of both arguments, sometimes find themselves caught in the middle in this issue.

Cultural Property

Words and things intervene decisively in definitions of culture, a problematic concept in anthropology and one gaining new meanings and significance in discussions about representation. Entire books have been written charting the definition of culture in anthropology, where it is conventionally treated as a set of ideas, concepts, and values that give people competence as members of their society. But the term *culture* is increasingly up for grabs. It is becoming part of political discourse, particularly in countries like Canada, New Zealand, and Australia.[4] Indigenous peoples are developing their own definitions, which often differ markedly from definitions given either by anthropologists or by members of the general public.

Despite Boas's protestations, museums by their nature tend to emphasize an idea of culture based in physical objects. Object-based definitions of culture present particular problems in the museum with which I am most familiar, the Museum of Anthropology at the University of British Columbia. In British Columbia, there is a strong representational tradition of monumental coastal art, and that is the tradition that dominates MOA. It reflects an impressive variety of beautifully carved totem-poles, masks, and wooden boxes, made possible at least partly by the coincidence of a rich marine environment and the availability of cedar. The intensive exploitation of coastal waters and annual salmon runs permitted sedentary communities and the kind of accumulation of wealth that could support specialists who addressed their talents to the creation of large and complex carvings. Often spoken of as Northwest Coast "art," these works are also complex statements about social and ceremonial workings of the communities in which they were created.

The arts of the interior part of the province, and particularly the northern interior, are equally complex but harder to display. Successful harvesting of resources on the interior plateau required mobility. It was important to keep material possessions to a minimum so that only essentials were carried from place to place. More important than the physical object was the ability to re-create a snare or a container or a house when and where it was needed. Intellectual culture was carried in one's head rather than on one's back. Archaeologists have sometimes remarked that were it not for oral tradition, remarkably little could be known about the past of subarctic peoples because so much of their material culture perished. Speaking of the southeastern Yukon, W.B. Workman comments that "It is humbling to realize how much of this transforming trade was carried on in perishables and how scanty the archaeological record for it is in view of its documented significance. Almost invariably we will underestimate the volume of trade in the prehistoric record in this area, given the likelihood that much of it was also in perishable items...." [*Prehistory of the Aishihik Kluane Area, Southwest Yukon Territory*, 1978, p. 94] Oral tradition is a complex and intricate art form in the Yukon, critical for passing on essential information. It weighs nothing and can accompany a traveller anywhere, but it rarely appears in museums.

In an introductory undergraduate course I teach at the Museum of Anthropology, a Native student from the interior of British Columbia once explained that she would like to write a paper about the culture of her own people, but that since she understood that it was *coastal* peoples who had culture, she would be unable to do so. Her perspective comes at least in part from messages given by museums. Museums are cultural products of western societies, where fetishization of "things" leads to an object-dominated aesthetics. A definition of culture that promotes representational art inevitably does so at the expense of other definitions.

Reinventing Museums

An axiom of social science is that how we situate ourselves says a lot about the kind of analysis we make. If museums are to become a forum for public discussion of symbols, we have to reconstitute our idea of material culture as an analytical tool to include social relations as well as other voices.

In many parts of North America, attention is shifting from metropolitan museums to the activities of community-based museums, and the possibilities of collaboration between these two kinds of institutions in oral history projects, exhibition display, education, and research. Smaller museums may find themselves better situated than large museums to contribute analytical and practical strategies to discussions about representation. In the Yukon Territory, northwestern Canada, the Yukon Historical and Museum Association has been hosting annual conferences based on a collaborative model since

1980. Each year a theme is chosen: subarctic archaeology, subarctic material culture in museum collections, and aboriginal maps are examples from recent years. Academics, museum educators, and aboriginal people are invited as participants, and a forum is created to try to integrate indigenous knowledge with western scholarship. With the local museums association overseeing loans of material culture from metropolitan museums and archives, these sessions provide a venue for discussing a range of topics where indigenous oral tradition may contribute to an understanding of material culture. These conferences have generated further projects funded by both territorial and federal levels of government, employing elders, young people, anthropologists, and archaeologists to undertake collaborative projects in Yukon communities.

Another model for collaboration comes from the Museum of Anthropology at the University of British Columbia. This museum holds collections of Salish weavings, including 3,000-year-old basketry retrieved by archaeologists from wet sites at Musqueam. The Musqueam weavers, a group of indigenous women interested in studying and re-learning old techniques and reintegrating weavings into a ritual context, approached the museum to study its collections. With the assistance of curator Elizabeth Johnson and other museum staff, they prepared their own exhibition of contemporary weaving, including the words of weavers in labels and catalogue. The process provided a context for communication between weavers, visitors, and the Musqueam community, underscoring a point made too rarely in museums — that these are evolving traditions, not specimens of extinct arts.

The Makah Cultural and Research Center provides a striking example of ongoing collegiality between a community museum and university-based archaeologists. In 1947, an archaeological site was identified at the old Makah village of Ozette on the Olympic Peninsula in the state of Washington, USA. A landslide approximately 550 years ago engulfed the site, sealing some 2,000 years of continuous occupation from normal climatic processes. Excavation over the next eleven years revealed 55,000 artefacts — mostly made of wood or wood products — and 40,000 structural remains. Well aware of the issues surrounding the site, the Makah Tribal authority at Neah Bay obtained funding to engage in collaborative research with Washington State University. They built their own museum where the artefacts are housed and displayed and went on to develop language and cultural programmes at the centre. Research, exhibition, and education programmes have developed an evolving relationship between community and researchers.

Coalitions between community and museum do more than merely smooth jagged relations. They also contribute methodological insights. The most clearly formulated, finely tuned ethnographic projects inevitably become reformulated and take unanticipated directions as soon as one takes collaborative research seriously, not as consultation but as central to methodology. Collaboration reinforces the lesson that we should be prepared to be surprised by the results of our research, or there is no point in doing it. Such an approach also suggests convincingly that theory should *intervene* at the interface between scholarship and community, rather than remain a framework for structuring research. Any theoretical and methodological guidelines that emerge from collaboration will have to be based as firmly in indigenous traditions as in anthropological narratives.

Notes

1. I would like to thank Michael Ames, John Barker, Jonathan Benthall, Miriam Clavir, Marjorie Halpin, Elizabeth Johnson, Nancy Marie Mitchell, and unnamed reviewers for comments on an earlier version of this paper, and for ongoing discussion of these issues.

2. During the spring and summer of 1991, for example, the Museum of Anthropology at the University of British Columbia co-sponsored a land claims forum drawing several hundred people each evening, hosted a forum on the issue of Native writers and writing, and provided the venue for a dance performance written and developed as a collaboration between a Gitksan artist and a non-Native choreographer. The Royal British Columbia Museum in Victoria, B.C., recently purchased a Nuu-chah-nulth screen from the collection of Andy Warhol and hosted a major ceremony held by the family to mark the return of the screen from New York to the Northwest Coast where it was made.

3. Two journals recently established in Canada, *Trickster: A Magazine of New Native Writing*, published in Toronto, and *Gatherings: The En'owkin Journal of First North American Peoples*, published by Theytus Books in Penticton, British Columbia, have attracted national attention. In the United States, these issues are addressed directly in a number of publications, including Coltelli's (1990) edited volume of interviews with Native American writers who explore their own convictions about the location of cultural voice.

4. It is worth noting that the concept of culture is equally contested within anthropology. Some anthropologists see culture as *enabling* people to function in society, others see culture as an ideological construct that disables people by preventing their objective analysis of reality. Still others argue that it is *reality* that is culturally constructed while others that culture is fundamentally a system of classification.

SECTION ONE
The Material Basis of Social Life

Introduction

Although the culture of a group of people is essentially a set of shared symbols, values, and beliefs, anthropologists point out that it also provides human groups with their most important adaptive tools. In cold countries, humans do not grow fur: they make a coat. To cross water, humans do not grow flippers and gills: they build a boat. You can think of millions of such examples, all of which demonstrate that humans solve culturally the problems of biological adaptation to specific ecosystems that other animals solve, over time, through **somatic** variation — that is, changes in the body (*soma*, in Greek). Culture is **extrasomatic**: it is not to be found in any individual body or brain; it is not transmitted genetically. The American anthropologist Leslie White (1959) emphasized this point, viewing culture as not only extrasomatic, but even "superorganic." A century after Darwin demonstrated that humans are part of the animal kingdom, White was one of the anthropologists who were "busy re-erecting a barrier between man and the rest of the animal kingdom" (Alland 1967, 192).

Should we view culture, which is learned and not transmitted genetically, as independent of biology? Should we also distinguish biological evolution from cultural evolution, as though they were separate processes? Many anthropologists do, while conceding that this distinction is not quite satisfactory. In fact, there is a fundamental reason to avoid it, which

Alexander Alland expressed succinctly: "To consider culture as extrasomatic does not require us to abandon the biological model of evolution, since behavior based on culture must still solve basically biological problems" (1967, 87).

Cultural models guide human populations in their production of goods and services, in the exchange of the fruits of their labor, and in the patterns of reproduction of their population and social systems. Whereas ecologists and **ecological anthropologists** focus on the relationship between populations and their living and nonliving environment, **economic anthropologists** focus on the patterns of exchange between people. As we shall see later, kinship specialists and **political anthropologists** deal with realities that seem quite removed from these mundane, material problems. The advantage of using a holistic approach that links these different facets of human culture is illustrated in the following readings through a focus on the phonemenon of **reciprocity**. From one chapter to the next, reciprocity is discussed as a technique, a mechanism to control production and consumption, a mode of exchange, and a social institution central to kinship.

No society can survive the destruction of its ecological base, as the great rulers of Mesopotamia, Teotihuacán, and Tikal learned the hard way. Any society that destroys its ecological base is not progressing, but endangering itself: ecological busts do not bring about cultural booms. One of the puzzles that anthropologists confront is that many

The Sori prepare to go hunting. They spend most of the year on hunting and gathering trips, coming back to their villages of three houses on frail stilts to rest or to work one small slash-and-burn garden. Among the Sori, as among the majority of societies, it is usually the men who carry and use the weapons of hunting and war. Source: Jean-Luc Chodkiewicz.

of the small, egalitarian societies they study have exploited the same resources, in the same location, generation after generation for thousands of years: in other words, their way of life has proved *sustainable*. By contrast, great civilizations have come and gone at a rapid rate, and today, deserts are often found where they had briefly thrived.

Some critics sneer at anthropologists for this (apparently) hopelessly romantic notion that small, egalitarian societies are more sustainable and better adapted than large, stratified ones. Actually, even some anthropologists have cast doubt on anthropological reports, such as those by Marshall Sahlins (1972) and Richard Lee, of groups of hunters and gatherers living in a kind of time warp, isolated and in their "original affluence." We now know that several previously accepted examples of successful hunting and gathering societies were not quite what they seemed: The Siriono of Bolivia are descendants of agriculturalists who took refuge in an inhospitable environment; the Mbuti and other pygmies of Africa (see Chapter 40) have long been involved in trade with agricultural neighbors; and the San speakers of

South Africa had practiced some farming and herding even before this century. Practically all of them have now completely abandoned their nomadic, foraging life style.

In a recent book, *Land Filled with Flies* (1991), Edwin N. Wilmsen argues that the !Kung San (discussed in Chapters 33, 34, and 55) were transformed by contact and interaction with other South African people over the course of the last thousand years. He suggests that they practiced herding, trading over long distances, and some farming until the nineteenth century, when the advance of colonialism in South Africa forced them to become marginal, nomadic hunters and gatherers. Wilmsen's work embodies typical aspects of *postmodernism* in anthropology, including the rejection of "false" categories — which, according to postmodernists, are the result of the unacknowledged idealogical biases of anthropologists — and the interpretation of tribal peoples as victims of capitalist domination. Unlike the majority of anthropologists, postmodern anthropologists do not claim to be in the business of testing hypotheses: they reject their predecessors'

Woman the Hunter. Although anthropologists have discussed at length Man the Hunter, they have until recently given less attention to woman the gatherer and still less to the many instances in which women actually hunt. This Wayana Amerindian woman, from French Guiana, in South America, is about to shoot a capybara (a hundred-pound rodent). The Wayana consider hunting to be a man's business, but women sometimes take over when their husbands are sick or absent. Some husbands are proud of their wives' hunting skills. Source: Jean-Luc Chodkiewicz.

assumption that it is *possible* for anthropologists to be scientific or objective. The followers of this recent movement propose instead that we produce a kind of literary analysis of cultural events or patterns — in their terminology, a "text." Only time will tell if this approach of substituting intuition for deduction will advance our understanding of other societies and their cultures.

In Chapter 16, we presented Jared Diamond's explanation for the rise of less stable but bigger and more powerful state societies. He suggested that the domestication of plants and animals made possible a relaxation of population controls, and that it also promoted social stratification and the development of the state. Subsequently, policies were employed that systematically encouraged overpopulation, increasing both the political power of states and the wealth of their leaders, since larger populations

meant more subjects, more laborers, more taxpayers, and more soldiers. Increasingly sophisticated technologies made possible, for a while, the increased production of food and other necessities, as well as of luxuries. The consequences of the resulting overconsumption were erosion, pollution, and the depletion of resources. If you cut the branch on which you've made your nest, you're in trouble, and a "better" technology — an electric saw, perhaps? — will only make you fall faster. We know what the outcome was for the great civilizations of the past: Mesopotamia, with its fertile fields, buried under sand dunes; the magnificent ruins of Maya cities rotting under tropical forests in desolate solitude.

Even today, when the earth is overpopulated with six billion people, of whom at least a billion are hungry at any given time, many state societies continue to encourage overpopulation. Rather than imposing punitive luxury taxes on babies, our state gives us baby bonuses and tax rebates for making more of them! The harsh measures that the governments of certain countries have adopted from time to time — for example, the recent government campaigns of sterilization that led to riots in India, or China's "one child" policy — are not only distasteful, but infringe on some of our basic human rights. However, overpopulation and famine deprive a population of *all* human rights, to which the starving masses of the Sudan and Somalia have sadly attested.

"Murders in Eden" (Chapter 33), by Marvin Harris, explains how our hunting and gathering ancestors prevented or postponed the destructive effects of overpopulation. Archaeology shows that our pre-agricultural ancestors lived in small and well-fed groups, too scattered to make possible the spread of epidemics. As we have already read in Chapter 16, research on modern-day hunters and gatherers shows that they have better nutrition, better health, and more leisure time than their agricultural neighbors. When hundreds of thousands of African agriculturalists and pastoralists were starving during recent severe droughts, the !Kung Bushmen of the Kalahari Desert, described by Richard Lee in Chapter 34, lived comfortably. In Chapter 33, Harris presents evidence of the lack of *natural* controls on population growth among our hunting–gathering ancestors. By modern standards, the current population increase of 0.5 percent per year among the Bushmen of Botswana appears ridiculously small. Nevertheless, as Harris points out, if their ancestors had allowed their population to increase at that rate for the last 10,000 years of the old stone age, by 10,000 B.C. their population would have exceeded 600 billion trillion people! We can therefore conclude that, until recently, they could not have allowed even such a modest rate of population increase, and that, since natural checks on population growth were insufficient, *cultural* checks had to have been present. In the absence of modern contraceptive pills and devices, it is probable that the practice of infanticide, and perhaps most commonly female infanticide, was the precondition of the ancient hunting–gathering societies' sustainability.

Richard Lee's "Eating Christmas in the Kalahari" (Chapter 34) is an amusing illustration of the indirect cultural controls that force individuals to respect the rules of reciprocal exchange and equality with other members of the group. Unlike **barter**, reciprocity is a universal concept of exchange, normally requiring that givers and receivers maintain the pretense that they do not care about the value of the items exchanged and do not even expect gifts in return. In the Kalahari Desert where the !Kung live, hunting is a chancy business: long periods of failure can follow the occasional success. In addition, in such a hot climate, the storage problem is acute. Consequently, if you don't have a refrigerator, the best place to store your extra meat is perhaps in the stomach of your friends. Thus, reciprocity solves, without complex technologies, the practical problems of waste and potential food poisoning, and results in an ecologically more efficient way of distributing food. The conventions associated with reciprocity — in particular, that of denying that a bigger gift has greater value than a small one — allow lucky and unlucky, skilled and less skilled hunters to go on helping one another without competitiveness and hard feelings. In societies guided by principles of "generalized reciprocity," sharing is taken for granted, and people often fail to express any particular appreciation for gifts. This, too, can serve to discourage overproduction: what is the point of hunting more than anyone else, if one is neither allowed to keep the kill, nor praised or thanked for giving it away? Such checks are critical: it is easy to see that a "Rambo in the bush" would quickly overhunt and jeopardize the livelihood of the community by wasting, and risking extermination of, the available game. The joke played at Lee's expense can thus be seen as part of a custom essential to the maintenance of the !Kung's social system and ecological balance.

When reciprocity is replaced by barter or money exchanges, overproduction, depletion, and hunger are likely to follow in short order. In Chapter 35, Bernard Nietschmann illustrates this process vividly in his account of the demise of turtles and Miskito Indians in Nicaragua. His story represents only the latest in a series of boom-and-bust cycles resulting from contact between the Miskito Indians and French, English, then American aliens and their market economies. Resources that had supported subsistence for the Miskito became market commodities, with a price tag and a death warrant. The diet and consequently the health of the Miskito have suffered, and even kinship relations have become strained as a result of stingy meat distribution. Their communities have decayed to the level of neighborhoods, then of lonely groups of isolated, mutually indifferent nuclear families. The article aptly illustrates the ecological consequences of certain social and economic institutions.

In closing, it should be noted that anthropologists have also discovered the shocking reality that it is not uncommon for reciprocity to be employed in the service of maintaining or increasing the exploitation of the poor by the rich. "Give me your watch, and I shall give you the time of day" — since giver and receiver are supposed to be oblivious to any asymmetries in exchanges, reciprocity between rich and poor is allowed to exist regardless of the exploitative nature of the transaction. In many countries of Latin America, there is a special tie, a ritual kinship, between the parents and godparents of a child, called **compadrazgo**. This tie of ritual kinship entails reciprocity, and when the tie is asymmetrical, it can be shown to conceal class differences and a deliberate exploitation of the poor (Chodkiewicz 1976).

Works Cited

Alland, A. 1967. *Evolution and Human Behavior.* Garden City: Natural History Press.

Chodkiewicz, J.L. 1976. *Fictive Kinship and Real Politics.* Ann Arbor, Mich.: University Microfilms.

Sahlins, M. 1972. *Stone Age Economics.* Chicago: Aldine Publishing Co.

White, L. 1959. *The Evolution of Culture.* New York: McGraw-Hill.

33
Murders in Eden

MARVIN HARRIS

The accepted explanation for the transition from band life to farming villages used to go like this: Hunter-collectors had to spend all their time getting enough to eat. They could not produce a "surplus above subsistence," and so they lived on the edge of extinction in chronic sickness and hunger. Therefore, it was natural for them to want to settle down and live in permanent villages, but the idea of planting seeds never occurred to them. One day an unknown genius decided to drop some seeds in a hole, and soon planting was being done on a regular basis. People no longer had to move about constantly in search of game, and the new leisure gave them time to think. This led to further and more rapid advances in technology and thus more food — a "surplus above subsistence" — which eventually made it possible for some people to turn away from farming and become artisans, priests, and rulers.

The first flaw in this theory is the assumption that life was exceptionally difficult for our stone age ancestors. Archaeological evidence from the upper paleolithic period — about 30,000 B.C. to 10,000 B.C. — makes it perfectly clear that

hunters who lived during those times enjoyed relatively high standards of comfort and security. They were no bumbling amateurs. They had achieved total control over the process of fracturing, chipping, and shaping crystalline rocks, which formed the basis of their technology, and they have aptly been called the "master stoneworkers of all times." Their remarkably thin, finely chipped "laurel leaf" knives, eleven inches long but only four-tenths of an inch thick, cannot be duplicated by modern industrial techniques. With delicate stone awls and incising tools called burins, they created intricately barbed bone and antler harpoon points, well-shaped antler throwing boards for spears, and fine bone needles presumably used to fashion animal-skin clothing. The items made of wood, fibers, and skins have perished, but these too must have been distinguished by high craftsmanship.

Contrary to popular ideas, "cave men" knew how to make artificial shelters, and their use of caves and rock overhangs depended on regional possibilities and seasonal needs. In southern Russia archaeologists have found traces of a hunters' animal-skin dwelling set in a shallow pit forty feet long and twelve feet wide. In Czechoslovakia winter dwellings with round floor plans twenty feet in diameter were already in use more than 20,000 years ago. With rich furs for rugs and beds, as well as plenty of dried animal dung or fat-laden bones for the hearth, such

From Marvin Harris, *Cannibals and Kings: The Origins of Cultures,* Chapter 2, pp. 9–17. Copyright © 1977 Marvin Harris. Reprinted with the permission of the author and Random House, Inc.

dwellings can provide a quality of shelter superior in many respects to contemporary inner-city apartments.

As for living on the edge of starvation, such a picture is hard to reconcile with the enormous quantities of animal bones accumulated at various paleolithic kill sites. Vast herds of mammoth, horses, deer, reindeer, and bison roamed across Europe and Asia. The bones of over a thousand mammoth, excavated from one site in Czechoslovakia, and the remains of 10,000 wild horses that were stampeded at various intervals over a high cliff near Solutré, France, testify to the ability of paleolithic peoples to exploit these herds systematically and efficiently. Moreover, the skeletal remains of the hunters themselves bear witness to the fact that they were unusually well-nourished.

The notion that paleolithic populations worked round the clock in order to feed themselves now also appears ludicrous. As collectors of food plants they were certainly no less effective than chimpanzees. Field studies have shown that in their natural habitat the great apes spend as much time grooming, playing, and napping as they do foraging and eating. And as hunters our upper paleolithic ancestors must have been at least as proficient as lions — animals which alternate bursts of intense activity with long periods of rest and relaxation. Studies of how present-day hunters and collectors allocate their time have shed more light on this issue. Richard Lee of the University of Toronto kept a record of how much time the modern Bushman hunter-collectors spend in the quest for food. Despite their habitat — the edge of the Kalahari, a desert region whose lushness is hardly comparable to that of France during the upper paleolithic period — less than three hours per day per adult is all that is needed for the Bushmen to obtain a diet rich in proteins and other essential nutrients.

The Machiguenga, simple horticulturalists of the Peruvian Amazon studied by Allen and Orna Johnson, spend a little more than three hours per day per adult in food production and get less animal protein for this effort than do the Bushmen. In the rice-growing regions of eastern Java, modern peasants have been found to spend about forty-four hours per week in productive farm work — something no self-respecting Bushman would ever dream of doing — and Javanese peasants seldom eat animal proteins. American farmers, for whom fifty-and-sixty-hour work weeks are commonplace, eat well by Bushman standards but certainly cannot be said to have as much leisure.

I do not wish to minimize the difficulties inherent in comparisons of this sort. Obviously the work associated with a particular food-production system is not limited to time spent in obtaining the raw product. It also takes time to process the plants and animals into forms suitable for consumption, and it takes still more time to manufacture and maintain such instruments of production as spears, nets, digging sticks, baskets, and plows. According to the Johnsons' estimates, the Machiguenga devote about three additional hours per day to food preparation and the manufacture of essential items such as clothing, tools, and shelter. In his observations of the Bushmen, Lee found that in one day a woman could gather enough food to feed her family for three days and that she spent the rest of her time resting, entertaining visitors, doing embroidery, or visiting other camps. "For each day at home, kitchen routines, such as cooking, nut cracking, collecting firewood, and fetching water, occupy one to three hours of her time."

The evidence I have cited above leads to one conclusion: The development of farming resulted in an increased work load per capita. There is a good reason for this. Agriculture is a system of food production that can absorb much more labor per unit of land than can hunting and collecting. Hunter-collectors are essentially dependent on the natural rate of animal and plant reproduction; they can do very little to raise output per unit of land (although they can easily decrease it). With agriculture, on the other hand, people control the rate of plant reproduction. This means that production can be intensified without immediate adverse consequences, especially if techniques are available for combating soil exhaustion.

The key to how many hours people like the Bushmen put into hunting and collecting is the abundance and accessibility of the animal and plant resources available to them. As long as population density — and thus exploitation of these resources — is kept relatively low, hunter-collectors can enjoy both leisure and high-quality diets. Only if one assumes that people during the stone age were unwilling or unable to limit the density of their populations does the theory of our ancestors' lives as "short, nasty, and brutish" make sense. But that assumption is unwarranted. Hunter-collectors are strongly motivated to limit population, and they have effective means to do so.

Another weakness in the old theory of the transition from hunting and collecting to agriculture is the assumption that human beings naturally want to "settle down." This can scarcely be true given the tenacity with which people like the Bushmen, the aborigines of Australia, and the Eskimo have clung to their old "walk-about" way of life despite the concerted efforts of governments and missionaries to persuade them to live in villages.

Each advantage of permanent village life has a corresponding disadvantage. Do people crave company? Yes, but they also get on each other's nerves. As Thomas Gregor has shown in a study of the Mehinacu Indians of Brazil, the search for personal privacy is a pervasive theme in the daily life of people who live in small villages. The Mehinacu apparently know too much about each other's business for their own good. They can tell from the print of a heel or a buttock where a couple stopped and had sexual relations off the path. Lost arrows give away the owner's prize fishing spot; an ax resting against a tree tells a story of interrupted work. No one leaves or enters the village without being noticed. One must whisper to secure privacy — with walls of thatch there are no closed doors. The village is filled with irritating gossip about men who are impotent or who ejaculate too quickly, and about women's behavior during coitus and the size, color, and odor of their genitalia.

Is there physical security in numbers? Yes, but there is also security in mobility, in being able to get out of the way of aggressors. Is there an advantage in having a larger cooperative labor pool? Yes, but larger concentrations of people lower the game supply and deplete natural resources.

As for the haphazard discovery of the planting process, hunter-collectors are not so dumb as this sequence in the old theory would suggest. The anatomical details in the paintings of animals found on the walls of caves in France and Spain bear witness to a people whose powers of observation were honed to great accuracy. And our admiration for their intellects has been forced to new heights by Alexander Marshak's discovery that the faint scratches on the surface of 20,000-year-old bone and antler artifacts were put there to keep track of the phases of the moon and other astronomical events. It is unreasonable to suppose that the people who made the great murals on the walls of Lascaux, and who were intelligent enough to make calendrical records, could have been ignorant of the biological significance of tubers and seeds.

Studies of hunter-collectors of the present and recent past reveal that the practice of agriculture is often forgone not for lack of knowledge but as a matter of convenience. Simply by gathering acorns, for example, the Indians of California probably obtained larger and more nutritious harvests than they could have derived from planting maize. And on the Northwest coast the great annual migrations of salmon and candlefish rendered agricultural work a relative waste of time. Hunter-collectors often display all the skills and techniques necessary for practicing agriculture minus the step of deliberate planting. The Shoshoni and Paiute of Nevada and California returned year after year to the same stands of wild grains and tubers, carefully refrained from stripping them bare, and sometimes even weeded and watered them. Many other hunter-collectors use fire to deliberately promote the growth of preferred species and to retard the growth of trees and weeds.

Finally, some of the most important archaeological discoveries of recent years indicate that in the Old World the earliest villages were built 1,000 to 2,000 years before the development of a farming economy, whereas in the New World plants were domesticated long before village life began. Since the early Americans had the idea for thousands of years before they made full use of it, the explanation for the shift away from hunting and collecting must be sought outside their heads. I'll have more to say about these archaeological discoveries later on.

What I've shown so far is that as long as hunter-collectors kept their population low in relation to their prey, they could enjoy an enviable standard of living. But how did they keep their population down? This subject is rapidly emerging as the most important missing link in the attempt to understand the evolution of cultures.

Even in relatively favorable habitats, with abundant herd animals, stone age peoples probably never let their populations rise above one or two persons per square mile. Alfred Kroeber estimated that in the Canadian plains and prairies the bison-hunting Cree and Assiniboin, mounted on horses and equipped with rifles, kept their densities below two persons per square mile. Less favored groups of historic hunters in North America, such as the Labrador Naskapi and the Nunamuit Eskimo, who depended on caribou, maintained densities *below* 0.3 persons per square mile. In all of France during the late stone age there were probably no more than 20,000 and possibly as few as 1,600 human beings.

"Natural" means of controlling population growth cannot explain the discrepancy between these low densities and the potential fertility of the human female. Healthy populations interested in maximizing their rate of growth average eight pregnancies brought to term per woman. Childbearing rates can easily go higher. Among the Hutterites, a sect of thrifty farmers living in western Canada, the average is 10.7 births per woman. In order to maintain the estimated 0.001 percent annual rate of growth for the old stone age, each woman must have had on the average less than 2.1 children who survived to reproductive age. According to the conventional theory such a low rate of growth was achieved, despite high fertility, by disease. Yet the view that our stone age ancestors led disease-ridden lives is difficult to sustain.

No doubt there were diseases. But as a mortality factor they must have been considerably less significant during the stone age than they are today. The death of infants and adults from bacterial and viral infections — dysenteries, measles, tuberculosis, whooping cough, colds, scarlet fever — is strongly influenced by diet and general body vigor, so stone age hunter-collectors probably had high recovery rates from these infections. And most of the great lethal epidemic diseases — smallpox, typhoid fever, flu, bubonic plague, cholera — occur only among populations that have high densities. These are the diseases of state-level societies; they flourish amid poverty and crowded, unsanitary urban conditions. Even such scourges as malaria and yellow fever were probably less significant among the hunter-collectors of the old stone age. As hunters they would have preferred dry, open habitats to the wetlands where these diseases flourish. Malaria probably achieved its full impact only after agricultural clearings in humid forests had created better breeding conditions for mosquitoes.

What is actually known about the physical health of paleolithic populations? Skeletal remains provide important clues. Using such indices as average height and the number of teeth missing at time of death, J. Lawrence Angel has developed a profile of changing health standards during the last 30,000 years. Angel found that at the beginning of this period adult males averaged 177 centimeters (5'11") and adult females about 165 centimeters (5'6"). Twenty thousand years later the males grew no taller than the females had formerly grown — 165 centimeters — whereas the females averaged no more than 153 centimeters (5'0"). Only in very recent times have populations once again attained statures characteristic of the old stone age peoples. American males, for example, averaged 175 centimeters (5'9") in 1960. Tooth loss shows a similar trend. In 30,000 B.C. adults died with an average of 2.2 teeth missing; in 6500 B.C., with 3.5 missing; during Roman times, with 6.6 missing. Although genetic factors may also enter into these changes, stature and the condition of teeth and gums are known to be strongly influenced by protein intake, which in turn is predictive of general well-being. Angel concludes that there was "a real depression of health" following the "high point" of the upper paleolithic period.

Angel has also attempted to estimate the average age of death for the upper paleolithic, which he places at 28.7 years for females and 33.3 years for males. Since Angel's paleolithic sample consists of skeletons found all over Europe and Africa, his longevity estimates are not necessarily representative of any actual band of hunters. If the vital statistics of contemporary hunter-collector bands can be taken as representative of paleolithic bands, Angel's calculations err on the low side. Studies of 165 !Kung Bushman women by Nancy Howell show that life expectancy at birth is 32.5 years, which compares favorably with the figures for many modern developing nations in Africa and Asia. To put these data in proper perspective, according to the Metropolitan Life Insurance Company the life expectancy at birth for non-white males in the United States in 1900 was also 32.5 years. Thus, as paleodemographer Don Dumond has suggested, there are hints that "mortality was effectively no higher under conditions of hunting than under those of a more sedentary life, including agriculture." The increase in disease accompanying sedentary living "may mean that the mortality rates of hunters were more often significantly lower" than those of agricultural peoples.

Although a life span of 32.5 years may seem very short, the reproductive potential even of women who live only to Angel's 28.7 years of age is quite high. If a stone age woman had her first pregnancy when she was sixteen years old, and a live baby every two and a half years thereafter, she could easily have had over five live births by the time she was twenty-nine. This means that approximately three-fifths of stone age children could not have lived to reproductive age if the estimated rate of less than 0.001 percent population growth was to be maintained. Using these figures, anthropological demographer Ferki Hassan concludes that even if there was 50 percent infant mortality due to "natural" causes, another 23 to 35 percent of all potential offspring would have to be "removed" to achieve zero population growth.

If anything, these estimates appear to err in exaggerating the number of deaths from "natural" causes. Given the excellent state of health the people studied by Angel seemed to enjoy before they became skeletons, one suspects that many of the deceased died of "unnatural" causes.

Infanticide during the paleolithic period could very well have been as high as 50 percent — a figure that corresponds to estimates made by Joseph Birdsell of the University of California in Los Angeles on the basis of data collected among the aboriginal populations of Australia. And an important factor in the short life span of paleolithic women may very well have been the attempt to induce abortions in order to lengthen the interval between births.

Contemporary hunter-collectors in general lack effective chemical or mechanical means of preventing pregnancy — romantic folklore about herbal contraceptives notwithstanding. They do, however, possess a large repertory of chemical and mechanical means for inducing abortion. Numerous plant and animal poisons that cause generalized physical traumas or that act directly on the uterus are used throughout the world to end unwanted pregnancies. Many mechanical techniques for inducing abortion are also employed, such as tying tight bands around the stomach, vigorous massages, subjection to extremes of cold and heat, blows to the abdomen, and hopping up and down on a plank placed across a woman's belly "until blood spurts out of the vagina." Both the mechanical and chemical approaches effectively terminate pregnancies, but they are also likely to terminate the life of the pregnant woman. I suspect that only a group under severe economic and demographic stress would resort to abortion as its principal method of population regulation.

Hunter-collectors under stress are much more likely to turn to infanticide and geronticide (the killing of old people). Geronticide is effective only for short-run emergency reductions in group size. It cannot lower long-term trends of population growth. In the case of both geronticide and infanticide, outright conscious killing is probably the exception. Among the Eskimo, old people too weak to contribute to their own subsistence may "commit suicide" by remaining behind when the group moves, although children actively contribute to their parents' demise by accepting the cultural expectation that old people ought not to become a burden when food is scarce. In Australia, among the Murngin of Arnhem Land, old people are helped along toward their fate by being treated as if they were already dead when they become sick; the group begins to perform its last rites, and the old person responds by getting sicker. Infanticide runs a complex gamut from outright murder to mere neglect. Infants may be strangled, drowned, bashed against a rock, or exposed to the elements. More commonly, an infant is "killed" by neglect: the mother gives less care than is needed when it gets sick, nurses it less often, refrains from trying to find supplementary foods, or "accidentally" lets it fall from her arms. Hunter-collector women are strongly motivated to space out the age difference between their children since they must expend a considerable amount of effort merely lugging them about during the day. Richard Lee has calculated that over a four-year period of dependency a Bushman mother will carry her child a total of 4,900 miles on collecting expeditions and campsite moves. No Bushman woman wants to be burdened with two or three infants at a time as she travels that distance.

The best method of population control available to stone age hunter-collectors was to prolong the span of years during which a mother nursed her infant. Recent studies of menstrual cycles carried out by Rose Frisch and Janet McArthur have shed light on the physiological mechanism responsible for lowering the fertility of lactating women. After giving birth, a fertile woman will not resume ovulation until the percentage of her body weight that consists of fat has passed a critical threshold. This threshold (about 20–25 percent) represents the point at which a woman's body has stored enough reserve energy in the form of fat to accommodate the demands of a growing fetus. The average energy cost of a normal pregnancy is 27,000 calories — just about the amount of energy that must be stored before a woman can conceive. A nursing infant drains about 1,000 extra calories from its mother per day, making it difficult for her to accumulate the necessary fatty reserve. As long as the infant is dependent on it mother's milk, there is little likelihood that ovulation will resume. Bushman mothers, by prolonging lactation, appear to be able to delay the possibility of pregnancy for more than four years. The same mechanism appears to be responsible for delaying menarche — the onset of menstruation. The higher the ratio of body fat to body weight, the earlier the age of menarche. In well-nourished modern populations menarche has been pushed forward to about twelve years of age, whereas in populations chronically on the edge of caloric deficits it may take eighteen or more years for a girl to build up the necessary fat reserves.

What I find so intriguing about this discovery is that it links low fertility with diets that are high in proteins and low in carbohydrates. On the one hand, if a woman is to nurse a child successfully for three or four years she must have a high protein intake to sustain her health, body vigor, and the flow of milk. On the other hand, if she consumes too many carbohydrates she will begin to put on weight, which will trigger the resumption of ovulation. A demographic study carried out by J.K. Van Ginneken indicates that nursing women in underdeveloped countries, where the diet consists mostly of starchy grains and root crops, cannot expect to extend the interval between births beyond eighteen months. Yet nursing Bushman women, whose diet is rich in animal and plant proteins and who lack starchy staples, as I have said, manage to keep from getting pregnant four or more years after each birth. This relationship suggests that during good times hunter-collectors could rely on prolonged lactation as their principal defense against overpopulation. Conversely, a decline in the quality of the food supply would tend to bring about an increase in population. This in turn would mean either that the rate of abortion and infanticide would have to be accelerated or that still more drastic cuts in the protein ration would be needed.

I am not suggesting that the entire defense against overpopulation among our stone age ancestors rested with the lactation method.

Among the Bushmen of Botswana the present rate of population growth is 0.5 percent per annum. This amounts to a doubling every 139 years. Had this rate been sustained for only the last 10,000 years of the old stone age, by 10,000 B.C. the population of the earth would have reached 604,463,000,000,000,000,000,000.

Suppose the fertile span were from sixteen years of age to forty-two. Without prolonged nursing, a woman might experience as many as twelve pregnancies. With the lactation method, the number of pregnancies comes down to six. Lowered rates of coitus in older women might further reduce the number to five. Spontaneous abortions and infant mortality caused by disease and accidents might bring the potential reproducers down to four — roughly two more than the number permissible under a system of zero population growth. The "extra" two births could then be controlled through some form of infanticide based on neglect. The optimal method would be to neglect only the girl babies, since the rate of growth in populations that do not practice monogamy is determined almost entirely by the number of females who reach reproductive age.

Our stone age ancestors were thus perfectly capable of maintaining a stationary population, but there was a cost associated with it — the waste of infant lives. This cost lurks in the background of prehistory as an ugly blight in what might otherwise be mistaken for a Garden of Eden.

34
Eating Christmas in the Kalahari

RICHARD BORSHAY LEE

Editor's note: The !Kung and other Bushmen speak click languages. In the story, three different clicks are used:

1. *The dental click (/), as in* /ai/ai, /ontah, *and* /gaugo. *The click is sometimes written in English as tsk-tsk.*
2. *The alveopalatal click (!), as in* Ben!a *and* !Kung.
3. *The lateral click (//), as in* //gom.
Clicks function as consonants; a word may have more than one, as in /n!nu.

The !Kung Bushmen's knowledge of Christmas is third-hand. The London Missionary Society brought the holiday to the southern Tswana tribes in the early nineteenth century. Later, native catechists spread the idea far and wide among the Bantu-speaking pastoralists, even in the remotest corners of the Kalahari Desert. The Bushmen's idea of the Christmas story, stripped to its essentials, is "praise the birth of white man's god-chief"; what keeps their interest in the holiday high is the Tswana-Herero custom of slaughtering an ox for his Bushmen neighbors as an annual goodwill gesture. Since the 1930s, part of the Bushmen's

annual round of activities has included a December congregation at the cattle posts for trading, marriage brokering, and several days of trance-dance feasting at which the local Tswana headman is host.

As a social anthropologist working with !Kung Bushmen, I found that the Christmas ox custom suited my purposes. I had come to the Kalahari to study the hunting and gathering subsistence economy of the !Kung, and to accomplish this it was essential not to provide them with food, share my own food, or interfere in any way with their food-gathering activities. While liberal handouts of tobacco and medical supplies were appreciated, they were scarcely adequate to erase the glaring disparity in wealth between the anthropologist, who maintained a two-month inventory of canned goods, and the Bushmen, who rarely had a day's supply of food on hand. My approach, while paying off in terms of data, left me open to frequent accusations of stinginess and hard-heartedness. By their lights, I was a miser.

The Christmas ox was to be my way of saying thank you for the cooperation of the past year; and since it was to be our last Christmas in the field, I determined to slaughter the largest, meatiest ox that money could buy, insuring that the feast and trance dance would be a success.

Through December I kept my eyes open at the wells as the cattle were brought down for watering. Several animals were offered, but none had quite the grossness that I had in mind. Then, ten days before the holiday, a Herero friend led an ox of astonishing size and mass up to our camp. It was solid black, stood five feet high at the shoulder, had a five-foot span of horns, and must have weighed 1,200 pounds on the hoof. Food consumption calculations are my specialty, and I quickly figured that bones and viscera aside, there was enough meat — at least four pounds — for every man, woman, and child of the 150 Bushmen in the vicinity of /ai/ai who were expected at the feast.

Having found the right animal at last, I paid the Herero £20 ($56) and asked him to keep the beast with his herd until Christmas day. The next morning word spread among the people that the big solid black one was the ox chosen by /ontah (my Bushman name; it means, roughly, "whitey") for the Christmas feast. That afternoon I received the first delegation. Ben!a, an outspoken sixty-year-old mother of five, came to the point slowly.

"Where were you planning to eat Christmas?"

"Right here at /ai/ai," I replied.

"Alone or with others?"

"I expect to invite all the people to eat Christmas with me."

"Eat what?"

"I have purchased Yehave's black ox, and I am going to slaughter and cook it."

"That's what we were told at the well but refused to believe it until we heard it from yourself."

"Well, it's the black one," I replied expansively, although wondering what she was driving at.

"Oh, no!" Ben!a groaned, turning to her group. "They were right." Turning back to me she asked, "Do you expect us to eat that bag of bones?"

"Bag of bones! It's the biggest ox at /ai/ai."

"Big, yes, but old. And thin. Everybody knows there's no meat on that old ox. What did you expect us to eat off it, the horns?"

Everybody chuckled at Ben!a's one-liner as they walked away, but all I could manage was a weak grin.

That evening it was the turn of the young men. They came to sit at our evening fire. /gaugo, about my age, spoke to me man-to-man.

"/ontah, you have always been square with us," he lied. "What has happened to change your heart? That sack of guts and bones of Yehave's will hardly feed one camp, let alone all the Bushmen around /ai/ai." And he proceeded to enumerate the seven camps in the /ai/ai vicinity, family by family. "Perhaps you have forgotten that we are not few, but many. Or are you too

blind to tell the difference between a proper cow and an old wreck? That ox is thin to the point of death."

"Look, you guys," I retorted, "that is a beautiful animal, and I'm sure you will eat it with pleasure at Christmas."

"Of course we will eat it; it's food. But it won't fill us up to the point where we will have enough strength to dance. We will eat and go home to bed with stomachs rumbling."

That night as we turned in, I asked my wife, Nancy: "What did you think of the black ox?"

"It looked enormous to me. Why?"

"Well, about eight different people have told me I got gypped; that the ox is nothing but bones."

"What's the angle?" Nancy asked. "Did they have a better one to sell?"

"No, they just said that it was going to be a grim Christmas because there won't be enough meat to go around. Maybe I'll get an independent judge to look at the beast in the morning."

Bright and early, Halingisi, a Tswana cattle owner, appeared at our camp. But before I could ask him to give me his opinion on Yehave's black ox, he gave me the eye signal that indicated a confidential chat. We left the camp and sat down.

"/ontah, I'm surprised at you; you've lived here for three years and still haven't learned anything about cattle."

"But what else can a person do but choose the biggest, strongest animal one can find?" I retorted.

"Look, just because an animal is big doesn't mean that it has plenty of meat on it. The black one was a beauty when it was younger, but now it is thin to the point of death."

"Well I've already bought it. What can I do at this stage?"

"Bought it already? I thought you were just considering it. Well, you'll have to kill it and serve it, I suppose. But don't expect much of a dance to follow."

My spirits dropped rapidly. I could believe that Ben!a and /gaugo just might be putting me on about the black ox, but Halingisi seemed to be an impartial critic. I went around that day feeling as though I had bought a lemon of a used car.

In the afternoon it was Tomazo's turn. Tomazo is a fine hunter, a top trance performer (see "The Trance Cure of the !Kung Bushmen," *Natural History*, November 1967), and one of my most reliable informants. He approached the subject of the Christmas cow as part of my continuing Bushmen education.

"My friend, the way it is with us Bushmen," he

began, "is that we love meat. And even more than that, we love fat. When we hunt we always search for the fat ones, the ones dripping with layers of white fat: fat that turns into a clear, thick oil in the cooking pot, fat that slides down your gullet, fills your stomach and gives you a roaring diarrhea," he rhapsodized.

"So, feeling as we do," he continued, "it gives us pain to be served such a scrawny thing as Yehave's black ox. It is big, yes, and no doubt its giant bones are good for soup, but fat is what we really crave and so we will eat Christmas this year with a heavy heart."

The prospect of a gloomy Christmas now had me worried, so I asked Tomazo what I could do about it.

"Look for a fat one, a young one … smaller, but fat. Fat enough to make us //gom ('evacuate the bowels'), then we will be happy."

My suspicions were aroused when Tomazo said that he happened to know of a young, fat, barren cow that the owner was willing to part with. Was Toma working on commission, I wondered? But I dispelled this unworthy thought when we approached the Herero owner of the cow in question and found that he had decided not to sell.

The scrawny wreck of a Christmas ox now became the talk of the /ai/ai water hole and was the first news told to the outlying groups as they began to come in from the bush for the feast. What finally convinced me that real trouble might be brewing was the visit from u!au, an old conservative with a reputation for fierceness. His nickname meant spear and referred to an incident thirty years ago in which he had speared a man to death. He had an intense manner; fixing me with his eyes, he said in clipped tones:

"I have only just heard about the black ox today, or else I would have come here earlier. /ontah, do you honestly think you can serve meat like that to people and avoid a fight?" He paused, letting the implications sink in. "I don't mean fight you, /ontah; you are a white man. I mean a fight between Bushmen. There are many fierce ones here, and with such a small quantity of meat to distribute, how can you give everybody a fair share? Someone is sure to accuse another of taking too much or hogging all the choice pieces. Then you will see what happens when some go hungry while others eat."

The possibility of at least a serious argument struck me as all too real. I had witnessed the tension that surrounds the distribution of meat from a kudu or gemsbok kill, and had documented many arguments that sprang up from a

real or imagined slight in meat distribution. The owners of a kill may spend up to two hours arranging and rearranging the piles of meat under the gaze of a circle of recipients before handing them out. And I also knew that the Christmas feast at /ai/ai would be bringing together groups that had feuded in the past.

Convinced now of the gravity of the situation, I went in earnest to search for a second cow; but all my inquiries failed to turn one up.

The Christmas feast was evidently going to be a disaster, and the incessant complaints about the meagerness of the ox had already taken the fun out of it for me. Moreover, I was getting bored with the wisecracks, and after losing my temper a few times, I resolved to serve the beast anyway. If the meat fell short, the hell with it. In the Bushmen idiom, I announced to all who would listen:

"I am a poor man and blind. If I have chosen one that is too old and too thin, we will eat it anyway and see if there is enough meat there to quiet the rumbling of our stomachs."

On hearing this speech, Ben!a offered me a rare word of comfort. "It's thin," she said philosophically, "but the bones will make a good soup."

At dawn Christmas morning, instinct told me to turn over the butchering and cooking to a friend and take off with Nancy to spend Christmas alone in the bush. But curiosity kept me from retreating. I wanted to see what such a scrawny ox looked like on butchering, and if there *was* going to be a fight, I wanted to catch every word of it. Anthropologists are incurable that way.

The great beast was driven up to our dancing ground, and a shot in the forehead dropped it in its tracks. Then, freshly cut branches were heaped around the fallen carcass to receive the meat. Ten men volunteered to help with the cutting. I asked /gaugo to make the breast bone cut. This cut, which begins the butchering process for most large game, offers easy access for removal of the viscera. But it also allows the hunter to spot-check the amount of fat on the animal. A fat game animal carries a white layer up to an inch thick on the chest, while in a thin one, the knife will quickly cut to bone. All eyes fixed on his hand as /gaugo, dwarfed by the great carcass, knelt to the breast. The first cut opened a pool of solid white in the black skin. The second and third cut widened and deepened the creamy white. Still no bone. It was pure fat; it must have been two inches thick.

"Hey /gau," I burst out, "that ox is loaded with fat. What's this about the ox being too thin to bother eating? Are you out of your mind?"

"Fat?" /gau shot back, "You call that fat? This wreck is thin, sick, dead!" And he broke out laughing. So did everyone else. They rolled on the ground, paralyzed with laughter. Everyone laughed except me; I was thinking.

I ran back to the tent and burst in just as Nancy was getting up. "Hey, the black ox. It's fat as hell! They were kidding about it being too thin to eat. It was a joke or something. A put-on. Everyone is really delighted with it!"

"Some joke," my wife replied. "It was so funny that you were ready to pack up and leave /ai/ai."

If it had indeed been a joke, it had been an extraordinarily convincing one, and tinged, I thought, with more than a touch of malice as many jokes are. Nevertheless, that it was a joke lifted my spirits considerably, and I returned to the butchering site where the shape of the ox was rapidly disappearing under the axes and knives of the butchers. The atmosphere had become festive. Grinning broadly, their arms covered with blood well past the elbow, men packed chunks of meat into the big cast-iron cooking pots, fifty pounds to the load, and muttered and chuckled all the while about the thinness and worthlessness of the animal and /ontah's poor judgment.

We danced and ate that ox two days and two nights; we cooked and distributed fourteen potfuls of meat and no one went home hungry and no fights broke out.

But the "joke" stayed in my mind. I had a growing feeling that something important had happened in my relationship with the Bushmen and that the clue lay in the meaning of the joke. Several days later, when most of the people had dispersed back to the bush camps, I raised the question with Hakekgose, a Tswana man who had grown up among the !Kung, married a !Kung girl, and who probably knew their culture better than any other non-Bushman.

"With us whites," I began, "Christmas is supposed to be the day of friendship and brotherly love. What I can't figure out is why the Bushmen went to such lengths to criticize and belittle the ox I had bought for the feast. The animal was perfectly good and their jokes and wisecracks practically ruined the holiday for me."

"So it really did bother you," said Hakekgose. "Well, that's the way they always talk. When I take my rifle and go hunting with them, if I miss, they laugh at me for the rest of the day. But even if I hit and bring one down, it's no better. To them, the kill is always too small or too old or too thin; and as we sit down on the kill site to cook and eat the liver, they keep grumbling, even with

their mouths full of meat. They say things like, 'Oh this is awful! What a worthless animal! Whatever made me think that this Tswana rascal could hunt!'"

"Is this the way outsiders are treated?" I asked.

"No, it is their custom; they talk that way to each other too. Go and ask them."

/gaugo had been one of the most enthusiastic in making me feel bad about the merit of the Christmas ox. I sought him out first.

"Why did you tell me the black ox was worthless, when you could see that it was loaded with fat and meat?"

"It is our way," he said smiling. "We always like to fool people about that. Say there is a Bushman who has been hunting. He must not come home and announce like a braggart, 'I have killed a big one in the bush!' He must first sit down in silence until I or someone else comes up to his fire and asks, 'What did you see today?' He replies quietly, 'Ah, I'm no good for hunting. I saw nothing at all [pause] just a little tiny one.' Then I smile to myself," /gaugo continued, "because I know he has killed something big.

"In the morning we make up a party of four or five people to cut up and carry the meat back to the camp. When we arrive at the kill we examine it and cry out, 'You mean to say you have dragged us all the way out here in order to make us cart home your pile of bones? Oh if I had known it was this thin I wouldn't have come.' Another one pipes up, 'People, to think I gave up a nice day in the shade for this. At home we may be hungry but at least we have nice cool water to drink.' If the horns are big, someone says, 'Did you think that somehow you were going to boil down the horns for soup?'

"To all of this you must respond in kind. 'I agree,' you say, 'this one is not worth the effort; let's just cook the liver for strength and leave the rest for the hyenas. It is not too late to hunt today and even a duiker or a steenbok would be better than this mess.'

"Then you set to work nevertheless; butcher the animal, carry the meat back to the camp, and everyone eats," /gaugo concluded.

Things were beginning to make sense. Next, I went to Tomazo. He corroborated /gaugo's story of the obligatory insults over a kill and added a few details of his own.

"But," I asked, "why insult a man after he has gone to all that trouble to track and kill an animal and when he is going to share the meat with you so that your children will have something to eat?"

"Arrogance," was his cryptic answer.

"Arrogance?"

"Yes, when a young man kills much meat he comes to think of himself as a chief or a big man, and he thinks of the rest of us as his servants or inferiors. We can't accept this. We refuse one who boasts, for someday his pride will make him kill somebody. So we always speak of his meat as worthless. This way we cool his heart and make him gentle."

"But why didn't you tell me this before?" I asked Tomazo with some heat.

"Because you never asked me," said Tomazo, echoing the refrain that has come to haunt every field ethnographer.

The pieces now fell into place. I had known for a long time that in situations of social conflict with Bushmen I held all the cards. I was the only source of tobacco in a thousand square miles, and I was not incapable of cutting an individual off for noncooperation. Though my boycott never lasted longer than a few days, it was an indication of my strength. People resented my presence at the water hole, yet simultaneously dreaded my leaving. In short I was a perfect target for the charge of arrogance and for the Bushmen tactic of enforcing humility.

I had been taught an object lesson by the Bushmen; it had come from an unexpected corner and had hurt me in a vulnerable area. For the big black ox was to be the one totally generous, unstinting act of my year at /ai/ai, and I was quite unprepared for the reaction I received.

As I read it, their message was this: There are no totally generous acts. All "acts" have an element of calculation. One black ox slaughtered at Christmas does not wipe out a year of careful manipulation of gifts given to serve your own ends. After all, to kill an animal and share the meat with people is really no more than Bushmen do for each other every day and with far less fanfare.

In the end, I had to admire how the Bushmen had played out the farce — collectively straight-faced to the end. Curiously, the episode reminded me of the *Good Soldier Schweik* and his marvelous encounters with authority. Like Schweik, the Bushmen had retained a thoroughgoing skepticism of good intentions. Was it this independence of spirit, I wondered, that had kept them culturally viable in the face of generations of contact with more powerful societies, both black and white? The thought that the Bushmen were alive and well in the Kalahari was strangely comforting. Perhaps, armed with that independence and with their superb knowledge of their environment, they might yet survive the future.

35

When the Turtle Collapses, the World Ends

BERNARD NIETSCHMANN

In the half-light of dawn, a sailing canoe approaches a shoal where nets have been set the day before. A Miskito turtleman stands in the bow and points to a distant splash that breaks the gray sheen of the Caribbean waters. Even from a hundred yards, he can tell that a green turtle has been caught in one of the nets. His two companions quickly bring the craft alongside the turtle, and as they pull it from the sea, its glistening shell reflects the first rays of the rising sun. As two men work to remove the heavy reptile from the net, the third keeps the canoe headed into the swells and beside the anchored net. After its fins have been pierced and lashed with bark fiber cord, the 250-pound turtle is placed on its back in the bottom of the canoe. The turtlemen are happy. Perhaps their luck will be good today and their other nets will also yield many turtles.

These green turtles, caught by Miskito Indian turtlemen off the eastern coast of Nicaragua, are destined for distant markets. Their butchered bodies will pass through many hands, local and foreign, eventually ending up in tins, bottles, and freezers far away. Their meat, leather, shell, oil, and calipee, a gelatinous substance that is the base for turtle soup, will be used to produce goods consumed in more affluent parts of the world.

The coastal Miskito Indians are very dependent on green turtles. Their culture has long been adapted to utilizing the once vast populations that inhabited the largest sea turtle feeding grounds in the Western Hemisphere. As the most important link between livelihood, social interaction, and environment, green turtles were the pivotal resource around which traditional Miskito Indian society revolved. These large reptiles also provided the major source of protein for Miskito subsistence. Now this priceless and limited resource has become a prized commodity that is being exploited almost entirely for economic reasons.

In the past, turtles fulfilled the nutritional needs as well as the social responsibilities of Miskito society. Today, however, the Miskito depend mainly on the sale of turtles to provide them with the money they need to purchase household goods and other necessities. But turtles are a declining resource; overdependence on them is leading the Miskito into an ecological blind alley. The cultural control mechanisms that once adapted the Miskito to their environment and faunal resources are now circumvented or inoperative, and they are caught up in a system of continued intensification of turtle fishing, which threatens to provide neither cash nor subsistence.

I have been studying this situation for several years, unraveling its historical context and piecing together its past and future effect on Miskito society, economy, and diet, and on the turtle population.

The coastal Miskito Indians are among the world's most adept small-craft seamen and turtlemen. Their traditional subsistence system provided dependable yields from the judicious scheduling of resource procurement activities. Agriculture, hunting, fishing, and gathering were organized in accordance with seasonal fluctuations in weather and resource availability and provided adequate amounts of food and materials without overexploiting any one species or site. Women cultivated the crops while men hunted and fished. Turtle fishing was the backbone of subsistence, providing meat throughout the year.

Miskito society and economy were interdependent. There was no economic activity without a social context and every social act had a reciprocal economic aspect. To the Miskito, meat, especially turtle meat, was the most esteemed and valuable resource, for it was not only a mainstay of subsistence, it was the item most commonly distributed to relatives and friends. Meat shared in this way satisfied mutual obligations and responsibilities and smoothed out daily and seasonal differences in the acquisition of animal protein. In this way, those too young, old, sick, or otherwise unable to secure meat received their share, and a certain balance in the village was achieved: minimal food requirements were met, meat surplus was disposed of to others, and social responsibilities were satisfied.

Today, the older Miskito recall that when meat was scarce in the village, a few turtlemen would put out to sea in their dugout canoes for a day's harpooning on the turtle feeding grounds. In the afternoon, the men would return, sailing before the northeast trade wind, bringing meat for all. Gathered on the beach, the villagers helped drag the canoes into thatched storage sheds. After the turtles were butchered and the meat distributed, everyone returned home to the cooking fires.

Historical circumstances and a series of boom–bust economic cycles disrupted the Miskito's society and environment. In the seventeenth and eighteenth centuries, intermittent trade with English and French buccaneers — based on the exchange of forest and marine resources for metal tools and utensils, rum, and firearms — prompted the Miskito to extend hunting, fishing, and gathering beyond subsistence needs to exploitative enterprises.

During the nineteenth and early twentieth centuries, foreign-owned companies operating in eastern Nicaragua exported rubber, lumber, and gold, and initiated commercial banana production. As alien economic and ecological influences were intensified, contract wage labor replaced seasonal, short-term economic relationships; company commissaries replaced limited trade goods; and large-scale exploitation of natural resources replaced sporadic, selective extraction. During economic boom periods the relationship between resources, subsistence, and environment was drastically altered for the Miskito. Resources became a commodity with a price tag, market exploitation a livelihood, and foreign wages and goods a necessity.

For more than 200 years, relations between the coastal Miskito and the English were based on sea turtles. It was from the Miskito that the English learned the art of turtling, which they then organized into intensive commercial exploitation of Caribbean turtle grounds and nesting beaches. Sea turtles were among the first resources involved in trade relations and foreign commerce in the Caribbean. Zoologist Archie Carr, an authority on sea turtles, has remarked that "more than any other dietary factor, the green turtle supported the opening up of the Caribbean." The once abundant turtle populations provided sustenance to ships' crews and to the new settlers and plantation laborers.

The Cayman Islands, settled by the English, became in the seventeenth and eighteenth centuries the center of commercial turtle fishing in the Caribbean. By the early nineteenth century, pressure on the Cayman turtle grounds and nesting beaches to supply meat to Caribbean and European markets became so great that the turtle population was decimated. The Cayman Islanders were forced to shift to other turtle areas off Cuba, the Gulf of Honduras, and the coast of eastern Nicaragua. They made annual expeditions, lasting four to seven weeks, to the Miskito turtle grounds to net green turtles, occasionally purchasing live ones, dried calipee, and the shells of hawksbill turtles (*Eretmochelys imbricata*) from the Miskito Indians. Reported catches of green turtles by the Cayman turtlers generally ranged between 2,000 and 3,000 a year up to the early 1960s, when the Nicaraguan government failed to renew the islanders' fishing privileges.

Intensive resource extraction by foreign companies led to seriously depleted and altered environments. By the 1940s, many of the economic booms had turned to busts. As the resources ran out and operating costs mounted, companies shut down production and moved to other areas in Central America. Thus, the economic mainstays that had helped provide the

Miskito with jobs, currency, markets, and foreign goods were gone. The company supply ships and commissaries disappeared, money became scarce, and store-bought items expensive.

In the backwater of the passing golden boom period, the Miskito were left with an ethic of poverty, but they still had the subsistence skills that had maintained their culture for hundreds of years. Their land and water environment was still capable of providing reliable resources for local consumption. As it had been in the past, turtle fishing became a way of life, a provider of life itself. But traditional subsistence culture could no longer integrate Miskito society and environment in a state of equilibrium. Resources were now viewed as having a value and labor a price tag. All that was needed was a market.

Recently, two foreign turtle companies began operations along the east coast of Nicaragua. One was built in Puerto Cabezas in late 1968, and another was completed in Bluefields in 1969. Both companies were capable of processing and shipping large amounts of green turtle meat and by-products to markets in North America and Europe. Turtles were acquired by purchase from the Miskito. Each week company boats visited coastal Miskito communities and offshore island turtle camps to buy green turtles. The "company" was back, money was again available, and the Miskito were expert in securing the desired

commodity. Another economic boom period was at hand. But the significant difference between this boom and previous ones was that the Miskito were now selling a subsistence resource.

As a result, the last large surviving green turtle population in the Caribbean was opened to intensive, almost year-round exploitation. Paradoxically, it would be the Miskito Indians, who once caught only what they needed for food, who would conduct the assault on the remaining turtle population.

Another contradictory element in the Miskito–turtle story is that only some 200 miles to the south, at Tortuguero, Costa Rica, Archie Carr had devoted fifteen years to the study of sea turtles and to the conservation and protection of the Caribbean's last major sea turtle nesting beach. Carr estimates that more than half the green turtles that nest at Tortuguero are from Nicaraguan waters. The sad and exasperating paradox is that a conservation program insured the survival of an endangered species for com-mercial exploitation in nearby waters.

Green turtles, *Chelonia mydas*, are large, air-breathing, herbivorous marine reptiles. They congregate in large populations and graze on underwater beds of vegetation in relatively clear, shallow, tropical waters. A mature turtle can weigh 250 pounds or more and when caught, can live indefinitely in a saltwater enclosure or for a

Number of Green Turtles Exported Annually from Eastern Nicaragua

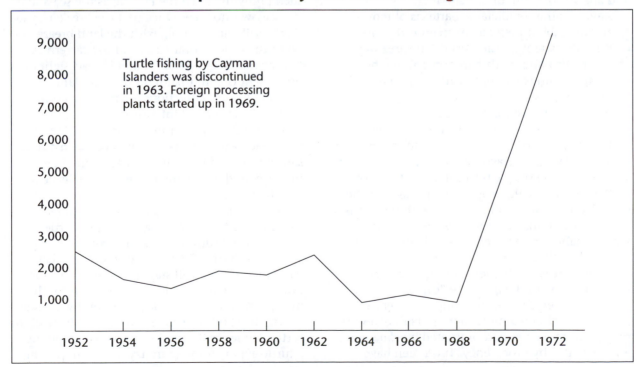

couple of weeks if kept in shade on land. Green turtles have at least six behavioral characteristics that are important in their exploitation: they occur in large numbers in localized areas; they are air breathing, so they have to surface; they are mass social nesters; they have an acute location-finding ability; when mature, they migrate seasonally on an overlapping two- or three-year cycle for mating and nesting; and they exhibit predictable local distributional patterns.

The extensive shallow shelf off eastern Nicaragua is dotted with numerous small coral islands, thousands of reefs, and vast underwater pastures of marine vegetation called "turtle banks." During the day, a large group of turtles may be found feeding at one of the many turtle banks, while adjacent marine pastures may have only a few turtles. They graze on the vegetation, rising periodically to the surface for air and to float for awhile before diving again. In the late afternoon, groups of turtles will leave the feeding areas and swim to shoals, some up to four or five miles away, to spend the night. By five the next morning, they gather to depart again for the banks. The turtles' precise, commuterlike behavior between sleeping and feeding areas is well known to the Miskito and helps insure good turtling.

Each coastal turtling village exploits an immense sea area, containing many turtle banks and shoals. For example, the Miskito of Tasbapauni utilize a marine area of approximately 600 square miles, with twenty major turtle banks and almost forty important shoals.

Having rather predictable patterns of movement and habitat preference, green turtles are commonly caught by the Miskito in three ways: on the turtle banks with harpoons; along the shoal–to–feeding area route with harpoons; and on the shoals using nets, which entangle the turtles when they surface for air.

The Miskito's traditional means of taking turtles was by harpoon — an eight- to ten-foot shaft fitted with a detachable short point tied to a strong line. The simple technology pitted two turtlemen in a small, seagoing canoe against the elusive turtles. Successful turtling with harpoons requires an extensive knowledge of turtle behavior and habits and tremendous skill and experience in handling a small canoe in what can be very rough seas. Turtlemen work in partnerships: a "strikerman" in the bow: the "captain" in the stern. Together, they make a single unit engaged in the delicate and almost silent pursuit of a wary prey, their movements coordinated by experience and rewarded by proficiency. Turtlemen have

mental maps of all the banks and shoals in their area, each one named and located through a complex system of celestial navigation, distance reckoning, wind and current direction, and the individual surface-swell motion over each site. Traditionally, not all Miskito were sufficiently expert in seamanship and turtle lore to become respected "strikermen," capable of securing turtles even during hazardous sea conditions. Theirs was a very specialized calling. Harpooning restrained possible overexploitation since turtles were taken one at a time by two men directly involved in the chase, and there were only a limited number of really proficient "strikermen" in each village.

Those who still use harpoons must leave early to take advantage of the land breeze and to have enough time to reach the distant offshore turtle grounds by first light. Turtlemen who are going for the day, or for several days, will meet on the beach by 2:00 a.m. They drag the canoes on bamboo rollers from beachfront sheds to the water's edge. There, in the swash of spent breakers, food, water, paddles, lines, harpoons, and sails are loaded and secured. Using a long pole, the standing bowman propels the canoe through the foaming surf while the captain in the stern keeps the craft running straight with a six-foot mahogany paddle. Once past the inside break, the men count the dark rolling seas building outside until there is a momentary pause in the sets; then with paddles digging deep, they drive the narrow, twenty-foot canoe over the cresting swells, rising precipitously on each wave face and then plunging down the far side as the sea and sky seesaw into view. Once past the breakers, they rig the sail and, running with the land breeze, point the canoe toward a star in the eastern sky.

A course is set by star fix and by backsight on a prominent coconut palm on the mainland horizon. Course alterations are made to correct for the direction and intensity of winds and currents. After two or three hours of sailing the men reach a distant spot located between a turtle sleeping shoal and feeding bank. There they intercept and follow the turtles as they leave for specific banks.

On the banks the turtlemen paddle quietly, listening for the sound of a "blowing" turtle. When a turtle surfaces for air it emits a hissing sound audible for fifty yards or more on a calm day. Since a turtle will stay near the surface for only a minute or two before diving to feed, the men must approach quickly and silently, maneuvering the canoe directly in front of or behind the turtle. These are its blind spots. Once harpooned, a turtle explodes into a frenzy of action, pulling

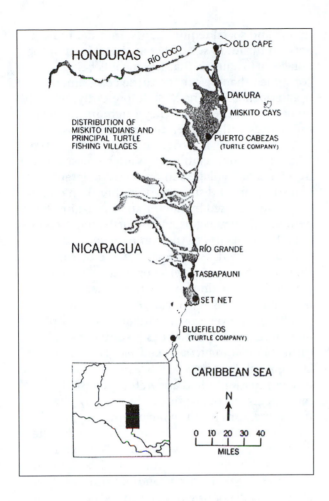

HONDURAS

Río Coco

OLD CAPE

DAKURA

MISKITO CAYS

DISTRIBUTION OF
MISKITO INDIANS AND
PRINCIPAL TURTLE
FISHING VILLAGES

PUERTO CABEZAS
(TURTLE COMPANY)

NICARAGUA

RÍO GRANDE

TASBAPAUNI

SET NET

BLUEFIELDS
(TURTLE COMPANY)

CARIBBEAN SEA

N

0 10 20 30 40
MILES

Catching turtles with nets requires little skill; anyone with a canoe can now be a turtleman. The Miskito set thousands of nets daily, providing continuous coverage in densely populated nocturnal habitats. Younger Miskito can become turtlemen almost overnight simply by following more experienced men to the shoal areas, thus circumventing the need for years of accumulated skill and knowledge that once were the domain of the "strikermen." All one has to do is learn where to set the nets, retire for the night, remove the entangled turtles the next morning, and reset the nets. The outcome is predictable; more turtlemen, using more effective methods, catch more turtles.

With an assured market for turtles, the Miskito devote more time to catching turtles, travelling farther and staying at sea longer. Increased dependence on turtles as a source of income and greater time inputs have meant disruption of subsistence agriculture and hunting and fishing. The Miskito no longer produce foodstuffs for themselves; they buy imported foods with money gained from the sale of turtles. Caught between contradictory priorities — their traditional subsistence system and the market economy — the Miskito are opting for cash.

The Miskito are now enveloped in a positive feedback system where change spawns change. Coastal villages rely on turtles for a livelihood. Decline of subsistence provisioning has led to the need to secure food from local shopkeepers on credit to feed the families in the villages and the men during their turtling expeditions. Initial high catches of turtles encouraged more Miskito to participate, and by 1972 the per person and per day catch began to decline noticeably.

In late 1972, several months after I had returned to Michigan, I received a letter from an old turtleman, who wrote: "Turtle is getting scarce, Mr. Barney. You said it would happen in five or ten years but it is happening now."

Burdened by an overdependence on an endangered species and with accumulating debts for food and nets, the Miskito are finding it increasingly difficult to break even, much less secure a profit. With few other economic alternatives, the inevitable step is to use more nets and stay out at sea longer.

The turtle companies encourage the Miskito to expand turtling activities by providing them with building materials so that they can construct houses on offshore cays, thereby eliminating the need to return to the mainland during rough weather. On their weekly runs up and down the coast, company boats bring food, turtle gear, and

the canoe along at high speeds in its hopeless, underwater dash for escape until it tires and can be pulled alongside the canoe.

But turtle harpooning is a dying art. The dominant method of turtling today is the use of nets. Since their introduction, the widespread use of turtle nets has drastically altered turtling strategy and productivity. Originally brought to the Miskito by the Cayman Islanders, nets are now extensively distributed on credit by the turtle companies. This simple technological change, along with a market demand for turtles, has resulted in intensified pressure on green turtle populations.

Buoyed by wooden floats and anchored to the bottom by a single line, the fifty-foot-long by fourteen-foot-wide nets hang from the surface like underwater flags, shifting direction with the current. Nets are set in place during midday when the turtlemen can see the dark shoal areas. Two Miskito will set five to thirty nets from one canoe, often completely saturating a small shoal. In the late afternoon, green turtles return to their shoals to spend the night. There they will sleep beside or beneath a coral outcrop, periodically surfacing for air where a canopy of nets awaits them.

cash for turtles to fishing camps from the Miskito Cays to the Set Net Cays. Frequent visits keep the Miskito from becoming discouraged and returning to their villages with the turtles. On Saturdays, villagers look to sea, watching for returning canoes. A few men will bring turtle for their families; the majority will bring only money. Many return with neither.

Most Miskito prefer to be home on Sunday to visit with friends and for religious reasons. (There are Moravian, Anglican, and Catholic mission churches in many of the villages.) But more and more, turtlemen are staying out for two to four weeks. The church may promise salvation, but only the turtle companies can provide money.

Returning to their villages, turtlemen are confronted with a complex dilemma; how to satisfy both social and economic demands with a limited resource. Traditional Miskito social rules stipulate that turtle meat should be shared among kin, but the new economic system requires that turtles be sold for personal economic gain. Kin expect gifts of meat, and friends expect to be sold meat. Turtlemen are besieged with requests forcing them to decide between who will or will not receive meat. This is contrary to the traditional Miskito ethic, which is based on generosity and mutual concern for the well-being of others. The older Miskito ask why the turtlemen should have to allocate a food that was once abundant and available to all. Turtlemen sell and give to other turtlemen, thereby insuring reciprocal treatment for themselves, but there simply are not enough turtles to accommodate other eco-

nomic and social requirements. In order to have enough turtles to sell, fewer are butchered in the villages. This means that less meat is being consumed than before the turtle companies began operations. The Miskito presently sell 70 to 90 percent of the turtles they catch; in the near future they will sell even more and eat less.

Social tension and friction are growing in the villages. Kinship relationships are being strained by what some villagers interpret as preferential and stingy meat distribution. Rather than endure the trauma caused by having to ration a limited item to fellow villagers, many turtlemen prefer to sell all their turtles to the company and return with money, which does not have to be shared. However, if a Miskito sells out to the company, he will probably be unable to acquire meat for himself in the village, regardless of kinship or purchasing power. I overheard an elderly turtleman muttering to himself as he butchered a turtle: "I no going to sell, neither give dem meat. Let dem eat de money."

The situation is bad and getting worse. Individuals too old or sick to provide for themselves often receive little meat or money from relatives. Families without turtlemen are families without money or access to meat. The trend is toward the individualization of nuclear families, operating for their own economic ends. Miskito villages are becoming neighborhoods rather than communities.

The Miskito diet has suffered in quality and quantity. Less protein and fewer diverse vegetables and fruits are consumed. Present dietary staples — rice, white flour, beans, sugar, and coffee — come from the store. In one Miskito village, 65 percent of all food eaten in a year was purchased.

Besides the nutritional significance of what is becoming a largely carbohydrate diet, dependence on purchased foods has also had major economic reverberations. Generated by national and international scarcities, inflationary fallout has hit the Miskito. Most of their purchased foods are imported, much coming from the United States. In the last five years prices for staples have increased 100 to 150 percent. This has had an overwhelming impact on the Miskito, who spend 50 to 75 percent of their income for food. Consequently, their entry into the market by selling a subsistence resource, diverting labor from agriculture, and intensifying exploitation of a vanishing species has resulted in their living off poorer-quality, higher-priced foods.

The Miskito now depend on outside systems to supply them with money and materials that are

Distribution of Turtle Meat by Gift and Purchase

Percentage of Villagers*	Pounds Received per Person
18	10–14+
28	6–9
32	2–5
22	0–1.9

During the one-month period from April 15 to May 15, 1971, 125 green turtles were caught by the turtlemen of Tasbapauni, Nicaragua. Of these, 91 were sold to turtle companies; the remaining 34 were butchered and the meat sold or given to villagers. In all, 3,900 pounds of turtle meat were distributed, but 54 percent of the villagers received 5 pounds or less, an insufficient amount for adult dietary protein requirements.
*Population of 998 converted to 711 adult male equivalents.

subject to world market fluctuations. They have lost their autonomy and their adaptive relationship with their environment. Life is no longer socially rewarding nor is their diet satisfying. The coastal Miskito have become a specialized and highly vulnerable sector of the global market economy.

Loss of the turtle market would be a serious economic blow to the Miskito, who have almost no other means of securing cash for what have now become necessities. Nevertheless, continued exploitation will surely reduce the turtle population to a critical level.

National and international legislation is urgently needed. At the very least, commercial turtle fishing must be curtailed for several years until the *Chelonia* population can rebound and exploitation quotas can be set. While turtle fishing for subsistence should be permitted, exportation of sea turtle products used in the gourmet, cosmetic, or jewelry trade should be banned.

Restrictive environmental legislation, however, is not a popular subject in Nicaragua, a country that has recently been torn by earthquakes, volcanic eruption, and hurricanes. A program for sea turtle conservation submitted to the Nicaraguan government for consideration ended up in a pile of rubble during the earthquake that devastated Managua in December 1972, adding a sad footnote to the Miskito–sea turtle situation. With other problems to face, the government has not yet reviewed what is happening on the distant east coast, separated from the capital by more than 200 miles of rain forest — and years of neglect.

As it is now, the turtles are going down and along with them, the Miskito — seemingly, a small problem in terms of the scale of ongoing ecological and cultural change in the world. But each localized situation involves species and societies with long histories and, perhaps, short futures. They are weathervanes in the conflicting winds of economic and environmental priorities. As Bob Dylan sang: "You don't need a weatherman to tell which way the wind blows."

SECTION TWO
Kinship

Introduction

All societies have **kinship** systems, comprising beliefs, rules, and practices, but the nature of the rules and beliefs, as well as of the practices accompanying them, differ widely from group to group. All societies have rules of **descent**, which define the inheritance of name, group membership, or property, some emphasizing **matrilineal descent** (calculated through female links), and others, **patrilineal descent** (calculated through male links). Many others, including North American English-speaking societies, observe different for the inheritance of surnames (patrilineal) and property (**cognatic**). Some societies have different patterns of inheritance for different kinds of property. Among some peoples, ancestors are extremely important, long-remembered and incorporated into very large family trees, compared with which the family tree of a typical North American would appear relatively stunted. Kinship ties are also established through marriage, another institution associated with widely differing rules, beliefs, and expectations in different societies. Differences are evident in the number of spouses individuals may have at the same time, the ways in which spouses are chosen, and the ways in which conjugal unions are validated — with a **bride-price** or **dowry**, in a ceremony, or just by moving into a new dwelling.

Anthropologists seem to devote an inordinate amount of time and energy to the study of kinship, and students are sometimes discouraged by the complexities of **kinship systems** and the diagrams that depict them. The anthropologist's fascination with the study of kinship stems from the fact that, in many societies, nothing makes sense until one knows the kinship relations among group members. A typical example is found in Janet Siskind's ethnography (1973) of the Sharanahua Indians of the village of Marcos, in Peru: "To understand Marcos is to learn the kinship system, since the structuring of every action one might call economic, social, or political is organized by the categories imposed upon these people to whom one is related" (p. 54). Unlike the Sharanahua, who interact with their relatives all the time, most North Americans have family reunions that include relatives other than just the father and mother and their children, only on special occasions — Thanksgiving, Christmas, or New Year's Day. It is not uncommon for close relatives to send cards to one another apologizing for not keeping in touch during the past year! This is but one indication of the isolation and decreased social importance of the kinship unit that anthropologists call the **nuclear family**, composed of a man and woman, and the children they have had together. In fact, even the nuclear family — or, preferably, the **conjugal family** — is no longer (if it ever was) a statistically dominant type of family unit in the rich industrial societies. In Canada and the United States, 33 percent of children live with only one natural parent, or a natural parent and a step-

Elopement, Mexican-style. In many societies, instead of ensuing from a carefully negotiated and sanctioned request, marriage follows the elopement of the bride and groom. This 14-year-old Mazahua Indian eloped with the 17-year-old daughter of a rich man. They hid from her father's blazing guns for two weeks before getting the law on their side in the civil marriage ceremony shown here. In their village, most marriages follow an elopement. Source: Jean-Luc Chodkiewicz.

parent. The fastest-growing type of household in North America is the *matrifocal* household, in which the children live with their mother, who is divorced or has never been married.

All societies have rules that prohibit **incest**, that is, marriage or any kind of sexual interaction between certain kinds of relatives. The punishments for breaking these rules are often severe in *this* world, and many societies believe that they are no less severe in the next. In many societies, the rules stipulate a hierarchy of incest crimes, from those deemed merely improper to those considered crimes against nature, and unforgivable. The numerous sexual-abuse trials of the past decade in the United States and Canada have revealed what anthropologists had discovered long before in other societies: the crime is surprisingly common, but has often been covered up or denied, and consequently left unpunished, because it is experienced as too horrible to expose to public scrutiny. A typical pattern is described by May Diaz in her study of the Mexican village of Tonalá (Chapter 47). The villagers were indignant about the rape of a young girl by her father, and even talked about lynching him, but

nothing happened: "No one discussed the possibility of recourse to political authority. Incest is a crime against God and nature, according to the people of Tonalá, not a government matter. The supernatural forces finally took a hand, and the baby died at birth" (Diaz 1966, 82).

Similar cases are analyzed by Hymie Rubenstein in his essay on the punishment of incest in the Caribbean village of Leeward, in Chapter 36. His discussion highlights the multiplicity of social, political, and personal considerations involved when people living in poverty, in small villages, are put in the position of having to judge one another. After all, they have no recourse to the anonymity afforded by our megacities: they are forced to live the rest of their lives together, under one another's close scrutiny.

In Chapter 37, Melvyn C. Goldstein describes a kinship system in which Western concepts of jealousy, legitimacy of children, and nuclear family are directly challenged. The **polyandry** of many Tibetans is an original solution to their specific ecological and economic problems. Moreover, Goldstein finds that the native explanation for the practice is more accurate than many of those conceived by anthropologists. His position on this point is an example of agreement between the "emic" and "etic" explanations. **Emic** explanations are those defined as true if they are consistent with the perceptions, feelings, or beliefs of the people observed, whereas **etic** explanations are those considered true only if they are consistent with an existing body of scientific knowledge or with the observations and analysis of an independent scientific observer.

Robert Murphy's "What Makes Warú Run?" (Chapter 38) is a tragicomic account of kinship in action among the Mundurucú of Brazil. Warú was the son of a village chief, but had been raised by a Brazilian trader. Consequently, in his life among the patrilineal but *matrilocal* Mundurucú Indians, he was lost between two cultural worlds. His persistent blundering with respect to cultural norms threatened the stability of the Mundurucú social system. He tried to bolster his status through marriage, then jeopardized his position instead by engaging in **polygyny**: the villagers retaliated by plotting against his life and by attacking him through one of his wives. One of the important social rules made evident by Warú's story (though apparently not to Warú himself) is that, in a society that survives through the avoidance of conflict, direct confrontation of deviants and opponents is to be avoided at all costs.

In Chapter 39, Muriel Dimen-Schein compares the family life of the Yanomamö of Brazil and the Nuer of the Sudan with that of fictional families well known to North American soap opera fans. This fresh approach enables her to highlight cultural differences in expectations and customs related to kinship. In many societies, marriage is considered far too important to be left to the whims of inexperienced youth: parents make the decision. Romantic love may result from such a union, but it is not a prerequisite for it. Combined with the effects of industrialization in the nineteenth century, the belief that romantic love should be the basis for marriage contributed to the demise of the extended family and the rise of the modern nuclear family. Today's high rates of divorce and the frequent incidence of spouse abuse suggest that this may not have been the most desirable of developments.

Dimen-Schein makes it clear, however, that among both the very rich and the very poor in North America, kinship ties are still extremely important. A typical example of the *marriage alliances* made by wealthy Americans — one that any Yanomamö would understand — was the "bride market" on the French Riviera at the beginning of this century: in unions between impoverished European aristocrats and rich Americans, the former gained money, and the latter, respectability and social status. It has been estimated that, by 1909, 500 American heiresses and 220 million dollars had been exported to Europe for the improvement of the family name (Galbraith 1977, 68).

Works Cited

Diaz, M. 1966. *Tonalá: Conservatism, Responsibility and Authority in a Mexican Town*. Berkeley: University of California Press.

Galbraith, J.K. 1977. *The Age of Uncertainty*. Boston: Houghton Mifflin.

Siskind, J. 1973. *To Hunt in the Morning*. New York: Oxford University Press.

36
Dealing with Incest in a Caribbean Village

HYMIE RUBENSTEIN

Introduction

All human societies have rules restricting sexual intercourse between certain relatives. The ban on copulation between such kin is called the *incest taboo*. No known society permits widespread mating between mother and son, father and daughter, and brother and sister. Even in the few societies that allow or even encourage sexual relations among special members of their royal families, the exceptions only emphasize the force of the ban among the mass of common people. Confronted by few such universals in their study of human lifeways, anthropologists have been trying to account for the ubiquity of the incest taboo for over a hundred years. Many theories have been proposed to account for the origins of the prohibition, the reasons people observe it, and the social and biological functions it performs. Comparatively little attention has been paid to what happens when the taboo is actually broken. This is surprising since the generality of the rule against incest highlights the fact that it is almost always broken by some people in most known societies. If this were not so then there would be little need to ban

it in the first place. In the United States and Canada, for example, incest — often obliquely termed "the sexual abuse of children" — is the most recent skeleton to emerge from the closet of sexual perversion. If anthropology has anything important to say about the human condition it must confront practice as well as theory — concrete cases of breaches of the taboo in particular societies and how they are handled, not just abstract theories meant to apply to most sociocultural systems.

The aim of this paper is to describe and explain the way incest is dealt with in the peasant community of Leeward Village in the eastern Caribbean island of St. Vincent.[1] Incestuous mating is rare in Leeward Village, probably rarer, in per capita terms, than in North America. But when it does take place it prompts a distinctive punitive reaction. *Hangings*, the term employed by villagers to describe the mock trials and ritual executions of those found guilty of incest, seem easily explained as ceremonial expressions of community moral outrage and humiliating condemnations of those who would break such a taboo. But *hangings* are much more than ethical statements and communal reprimands; they are also arenas for the expression of beliefs and values about Vincentian family, community, and national life. It is these less visible features of *hangings* that determine their form and explain their content.

From Hymie Rubenstein (Department of Anthropology, University of Manitoba), original essay, 1992. Reprinted with permission.

Societal Community and Background

St. Vincent is a small island of some 108,000 English-speaking people in the southeastern part of the Caribbean. The island is one of the most underdeveloped in the West Indies, and most Vincentians are the poor rural descendants of Black African slaves forcibly transported to the country during the eighteenth and nineteenth centuries to labor on the sugar plantations that dominated the economy of the time.

Leeward Village is a compact settlement containing 2,300 people, nearly all of whom are Black members of the island's lower class.[2] Villagers dominate such unremunerative occupations as peasant and wage-labor agriculture, small-scale commercial fishing, petty-commodity retailing, semi-skilled and unskilled trades, and government manual wage-labor. Though the community is not characterized by a high level of solidarity, villagers are keenly interested in each other's behavior, especially activities that transgress local and national social norms. The deed that most arouses community moral outrage is the breach of the incest taboo. The worst violation of the taboo is copulation between parents and children and between brothers and sisters. Sexual relations between step-parents and step-children and between parents and informally adopted children are also considered *nasty*, although less so than between actual biological kin.

When word that incest has taken place becomes known through gossip networks, the community response is a mock trial and ritual execution of the guilty parties. *Hangings* are a feature of lower-class West Indian culture that has received no previous attention in the literature. In traditional social functionalist terms, *hangings* seem to be ritualized forms of social control in which villagers express their collective aversion to incest by symbolically punishing the guilty parties. But such an explanation is limited. The problem is to account for *hangings* given a fully developed and accessible national juridical system that defines incest as a criminal act and to which villagers readily turn to *gain satisfaction* [redress] in other situations. St. Vincent has had a system of British jurisprudence since 1763, and Leeward Villagers turn to it when sexual transgressions such as rape, unlawful carnal knowledge, and bestiality take place. The village Police Station is manned by a sergeant and four constables, and weekly hearings take place in the courthouse located on the upper storey of the station.

Three Cases of Incest

Three cases of incestuous mating in Leeward Village that were dealt with by conducting mock trials and ritually hanging effigies of the participants are described below, the second in the words of an informant indirectly involved in the events leading up to it.

Case No. 1. When John McIntyre (a pseudonym) began to live with Meatrice Lewis, all her children, except her youngest daughter, Pauline, had moved out on their own. When Pauline was about 14 years old, she and John began a clandestine affair resulting in her pregnancy three years later. Meatrice soon discovered her daughter's condition — like many mothers in the village, she regularly checked her daughter's *towels* [cloth menstrual pads] for signs of pregnancy — and forced the girl to admit John's responsibility for it. As Pauline's pregnancy became public knowledge and in the absence of any other suitor, Meatrice's neighbors began taunting her that her own *keeper* [common-law husband], John, had *breed* [impregnated] the girl. They were scandalized by Meatrice's refusal to throw John out of the house and give Pauline a severe beating for allowing her *father-in-law* [stepfather] to *live* [have sex] with her. Meatrice defended her inaction by proclaiming that John was not Pauline's real father, that he was supporting the girl, and that even if their accusations were true, this was none of their business. Villagers believed that what had happened was very much their business and concluded that Meatrice, John, and Pauline ought to be *hanged*.

Case No. 2. "I was *friendlin'* with [having an affair with] Walker's daughter, Linda, and I uses to, when she come on the beach and buy fishes, follow her up the road and we'd go through the fields and have our fun. Well, her father got to know and he keep telling her that he had to bust his tail, which means he had to work hard, to support her and she just lovin' man when she should a be lovin' him. Well, his daughter keep *turnin'* [shuffling from one foot to another with her head downcast] and ask him what do he mean by that and he turn around and said, 'You don't know what I mean by that? You have man carryin' you up the road every morning and me who *mindin'* [supporting you], I can't see you.' Well, this goes on for a period of time just talkin' and talkin' towards me and her being friendly. Well, one day she had to carry his lunch [to him]. He's a farmer, and while she carry his lunch he bring up the same conversation towards me, and so on, and ask her, out of me and him who does she love more, and she told him, 'Well, I have to love you more; you is my father. You caused me to be here in the world and I have to love you more. But the things Bill [the boyfriend] can do to me you can't do.' And he began to fuss about it. He said, 'Why? I'm the same man like Bill,' and so on, and he tried to hold on to her and have sex with her. When she was *shame* [ashamed] about it she tried to cry and tug away from him, and so on. He cut her with a *cutlass* [machete], lash her with a cutlass and cut her on the hand. And I'm not sure really but I don't think they make any children but they used to have sex. I find out by the girl telling me. She told me what was going on. And they had the *hanging*, the same *hanging* I was talking about towards it."

Case No. 3. Linda was Walker's eldest daughter. Villagers generally believe that he engaged in incestuous relations with all but one of his six other daughters over a 25-year period.[3] He began relations with his last daughter, Nesta, in the early 1980s, when the girl was about 14 years old. They were discovered early one afternoon when one of Nesta's older brothers unexpectedly entered the house and began yelling, "Papa, what are you doing on Nesta! Papa, get off Nesta!" Though villagers consider Walker's behavior as extremely perverse, they also jokingly attribute it to his statement that, "Before any man taste um, I had to taste um." Of course, this could not excuse such debauchery and resulted in his being hung in effigy for a second time.

In none of these three cases was the violation of the mating prohibition ever reported to the police. Since *hangings* are conspicuous public ceremonial events and are even publicized on the radio to attract members from other communities, the village constables were doubtless aware of what was going on but took no action since no formal complaint was lodged. More importantly, being members of the Black lower class themselves, they would have condoned the community-level handling of the breach of the incest taboo.

A *hanging* consists of two interrelated activities, a stylized jury trial that follows the form and content of mainstream criminal proceedings and a mock hanging of full-scale life-like images constructed by village carpenters to resemble the accused parties. One or more village men of outgoing personality, administrative ability, and good reputation organize and sponsor hangings

for personal amusement, to punish the guilty parties by publicly humiliating them in a dramatic fashion, to enhance their own community standing by demonstrating the skill needed to conduct such an elaborate enterprise, and for personal financial benefit.[4]

The sponsors select villagers to play the various roles in the trial. These include a judge, policemen, jury members, a bailiff, a prosecuting attorney, a defense attorney, the accused parties, witnesses, and members of the family of the defendants. An effort is made to fill the positions with witty and articulate persons. The Crown witnesses are chosen for their familiarity with the facts of the case. Ideal witnesses are those with firsthand knowledge of the transgression. Most of the actors, including the jury, are given farcical pseudonyms for comic relief and to "hide" their true identities. The most hilarious of these are reserved for the defendants and are chosen to highlight the breach of sexual morality associated with the case. "Miss Upholder" was the name given to the mother in Case 1, who failed to show outrage when she discovered that her daughter was carrying her common-law husband's child. "Father Habit" was assigned to Walker in his second *hanging* because of his chronic incestuous behaviour. His daughter was termed "Miss No Shame" since it was believed that she did not sufficiently resist her father's vile advances.

Sittings of the trial, which lasts for up to two months, are held a couple of times a week in the late evening in a large public meeting hall. At the opening session the judge, who is dressed in a black suit and wig, requests the facts of the case. The prosecutor reads out the charge that on a given date the male defendant had sexual relations with his daughter. Although the hearings deliberately follow societal jural process, the multipurpose nature of *hangings* encourages spontaneous departure from mainstream procedures. This includes uproarious verbal duels between competing attorneys, hilarious testimonies from the witnesses and other players, and constant interjections from the audience. At the final sitting, the jury, composed of six or seven villagers, hands down the written verdict of guilty as charged. The judge announces the sentence — "The defendants shall be hung by the neck until they are dead. May God have mercy over their souls" — and signs the death ban. This acts as a signal for those who have acted as members of the family of the accused to express their grief with loud wailing and crying.

The end of the trial marks the beginning of a period, sometimes lasting up to two weeks, during which the *images* [effigies], whose faces have been carved from coconut husks, are available for private viewing. Occasional dances are also held at this time.

To provide illumination for the events, the hanging of the effigies takes place during the first full moon following the handing down of the verdict. A steel band or other musical group leads a procession composed of several hundred people to the site — the grounds of the village primary school or the graveyard — and plays throughout the evening. Bamboo poles some 20 feet long are employed as gallows, and the images are pulled by ropes to their tops. This is followed by several hours of dancing to the music of the band while the gallows are continuously paraded through the assembled crowd, the images manipulated in a comical fashion. Finally, the ropes are sharply jerked, breaking the necks of the mannequins, while the village marksman fires at them with a rifle. Again, a public dance follows. No fee is charged for attending the effigy hanging, and most villagers try to attend, finding it a rare and enjoyable occasion in village life.

Explaining *Hangings*

As collective forms of ritual punishment, *hangings* represent a reaction to a serious breach of family and community morality. But they also serve as a medium for the expression of beliefs and values that are distinctive to rural lower-class black Vincentians.

Slander. Though villagers readily appeal to the police and courts when they feel they have been *advantaged* [taken advantage of], they manifest the widespread concern among lower-class Vincentians about being *actioned* [taken to court] or *complained* [reported to the police] for slanderous assault. Since accusations of incest are almost never supported by the public testimony of the participants, there is no proof that it has really occurred. Villagers handle the opposition between wanting to condemn incestuous behavior and the concern of being sued by the actual parties by using pseudonyms for them. Though this hardly has the desired effect — indeed, if no one knew who was being referred to, the whole exercise would be pointless — villagers believe that if they do not use the actual names of the parties, they cannot be charged with slander. Likewise, this helps the actual parties to remain effective, albeit somewhat marginalized, members of their community despite the manner in which their fellow community members have treated their behavior.

Family Business. Villagers succinctly express the lower-class conviction that *family business* is private business as follows: "When *family and family* [members of the same nuclear or extended family, especially those residing in the same household] have *boderation* [trouble], no outsider have no right to *come inside* [involve themselves in the matter]." Villagers are, therefore, faced with the dilemma of wanting to punish incestuous behavior, yet respecting the high value placed on family privacy. *Hangings* offer a neat solution to this contradiction. They are a form of punishment purposely confined to a unit, the village community, composed of individuals who "all suck from the same *bubbie*" [breast]. In other words, even if *family business* has been taken out of the domestic unit, it continues to be restricted to a domain in which most people are related by kinship and marital ties.

Nature. There is much talk about sex in the village, and it is agreed that *nature* [sexual desire] is often dangerous and sometimes uncontrollable. Sexual desire becomes particularly dangerous for both men and women when it manifests itself in mating between those for whom it is prohibited. If they are discovered, they will suffer a permanent loss of community respect and risk irretrievably damaging extant kinship relations. But often "sex can't wait," and some men are eager "to eat the *zaboca* [avocado pear] and eat the seed too [copulate with both a mother and daughter]." A few women are even reluctant to engage in a common-law union if they have a teenaged daughter at home for fear that their partner will find his new *daughter-in-law* [stepdaughter] too much of a temptation. Indeed, when a teenaged member of a household becomes pregnant and the genitor is not readily recognized, a father or stepfather is occasionally held responsible for the girl's condition.

Hangings give dramatic expression to both the danger and uncontrollability of *nature*. They do so by implying that whereas villagers consider incest *nasty* and *wicked*, they nonetheless believe it to be part of *nature*, albeit a disreputable part that ought to be kept under strict control. The proceedings are carried out in an almost frivolous fashion not because incest is something to be treated lightly but because it is almost too serious to be dealt with in any other manner (save being reported to the authorities). Moreover, by transforming the guilty parties into comic figures, incest becomes somewhat more manageable, part of the behavior not of those who are rational but of fools, *dotish* [mentally defective] people, and other misfits. This feature also protects the guilty parties from being fully ostracized. They have taken to an extreme — albeit an unacceptable one — a feature of the human condition that has an almost independent power of its own. To be sure, they must forever carry the stigma of their transgressions and they will be gossiped about long after the events have been concluded. But they are never treated as pariahs.

Mainstream Institutions. Villagers are generally ambivalent when it comes to most government bodies. On the one hand, state institutions are respected because they are the main sources of island power and authority, because they symbolize some of the most prestigious norms of the society, and because they may be personally useful, even profitable, from time to time. On the other hand, these same bodies are feared because their operation is imperfectly understood, because they are politically nepotistic (a distinct disadvantage when one's party is out of power), and because of unsatisfactory dealings with them. In particular, the police and courts are respected for offering the best way to gain satisfaction in such cases as theft, assault, and direct verbal abuse. But they are feared because one can always become the victim of their unpredictability or perceived favoritism and because of a bewilderment as to the formal rules governing their operation.

Hangings nicely resolve this dialectic between respect and fear. Although much of their form is patterned on mainstream court procedures, that *hangings* take place at all and the comical way in which they are carried out is symptomatic of a marked dissatisfaction with societal jurisprudence. The arbitrariness of the government courts is emphasized, for example, by the defendants always being found guilty, and their aloofness and formality are parodied in the farcical and disorganized conduct of the trial. More important, perhaps, the very fact that these mainstream institutions are singled out for hilarious treatment places them, if only temporarily and ritually, under the control of that unit that controls them least, the rural peasant community.

Notes

1. See Rubenstein, "Incest, Effigy Hanging, and Biculturation in a West Indian Village," *American Ethnologist* 3 (1976): 765–81, for a fuller discussion of incest and effigy hanging in St. Vincent.
2. I have conducted nearly four years of field research in Leeward Village since 1969. For a full discussion of social life and economy in the community, see Rubenstein, *Coping with Poverty: Adaptive Strategies in a Caribbean Village*, (Boulder, Colo.: Westview Press, 1987).
3. The only one who escaped his unwanted advances was informally adopted by another family at an early age.
4. There are small fees charged for attending each court sitting and for previewing the effigies between the end of the trial and the actual "execution."

37
When Brothers Share a Wife

MELVYN C. GOLDSTEIN

Eager to reach home, Dorje drives his yaks hard over the 17,000-foot mountain pass, stopping only once to rest. He and his two older brothers, Pema and Sonam, are jointly marrying a woman from the next village in a few weeks, and he has to help with the preparations.

Dorje, Pema, and Sonam are Tibetans living in Limi, a 200-square-mile area in the northwest corner of Nepal, across the border from Tibet. The form of marriage they are about to enter — fraternal polyandry in anthropological parlance — is one of the world's rarest forms of marriage but is not uncommon in Tibetan society, where it has been practiced from time immemorial. For many Tibetan social strata, it traditionally represented the ideal form of marriage and family.

The mechanics of fraternal polyandry are simple. Two, three, four, or more brothers jointly take a wife, who leaves her home to come and live with them. Traditionally, marriage was arranged by parents, with children, particularly females, having little or no say. This is changing somewhat nowadays, but it is still unusual for children to marry without their parents' consent. Marriage ceremonies vary by income and region and range from all the brothers sitting together as grooms to only the eldest one formally doing so.

From *Natural History*, March 1987, pp. 39–48. Copyright 1987 American Museum of Natural History. Reprinted with permission.

The age of the brothers plays an important role in determining this: very young brothers almost never participate in actual marriage ceremonies, although they typically join the marriage when they reach their midteens.

The eldest brother is normally dominant in terms of authority, that is, in managing the household, but all the brothers share the work and participate as sexual partners. Tibetan males and females do not find the sexual aspect of sharing a spouse the least bit unusual, repulsive, or scandalous, and the norm is for the wife to treat all the brothers the same.

Offspring are treated similarly. There is no attempt to link children biologically to particular brothers, and a brother shows no favoritism toward his child even if he knows he is the real father because, for example, his other brothers were away at the time the wife became pregnant. The children, in turn, consider all of the brothers as their fathers and treat them equally, even if they also know who is their real father. In some regions children use the term "father" for the eldest brother and "father's brother" for the others, while in other areas they call all the brothers by one term, modifying this by the use of "elder" and "younger."

Unlike our own society, where monogamy is the only form of marriage permitted, Tibetan society allows a variety of marriage types, including monogamy, fraternal polyandry, and polygyny. Fraternal polyandry and monogamy are the most common forms of marriage, while polygyny typically occurs in cases where the first wife is barren. The widespread practice of fraternal polyandry, therefore, is not the outcome of a law requiring brothers to marry jointly. There is choice, and, in fact, divorce traditionally was relatively simple in Tibetan society. If a brother in a polyandrous marriage became dissatisfied and wanted to separate, he simply left the main house and set up his own household. In such cases, all the children stayed in the main household with the remaining brother(s), even if the departing brother was known to be the real father of one or more of the children.

The Tibetans' own explanation for choosing fraternal polyandry is materialistic. For example, when I asked Dorje why he decided to marry with his two brothers rather than take his own wife, he thought for a moment, then said it prevented the division of his family's farm (and animals) and thus facilitated all of them achieving a higher standard of living. And when I later asked Dorje's bride whether it wasn't difficult for her to cope with three brothers as husbands, she laughed and

echoed the rationale of avoiding fragmentation of the family and land, adding that she expected to be better off economically, since she would have three husbands working for her and her children.

Exotic as it may seem to Westerners, Tibetan fraternal polyandry is thus in many ways analogous to the way primogeniture functioned in nineteenth-century England. Primogeniture dictated that the eldest son inherited the family estate, while younger sons had to leave home and seek their own employment — for example, in the military or the clergy. Primogeniture maintained family estates intact over generations by permitting only one heir per generation. Fraternal polyandry also accomplishes this but does so by keeping all the brothers together with just one wife so that there is only one *set* of heirs per generation.

While Tibetans believe that in this way fraternal polyandry reduces the risk of family fission, monogamous marriages among brothers need not necessarily precipitate the division of the family estate: brothers could continue to live together, and the family land could continue to be worked jointly. When I asked Tibetans about this, how-

Tibetan Family Planning Chart

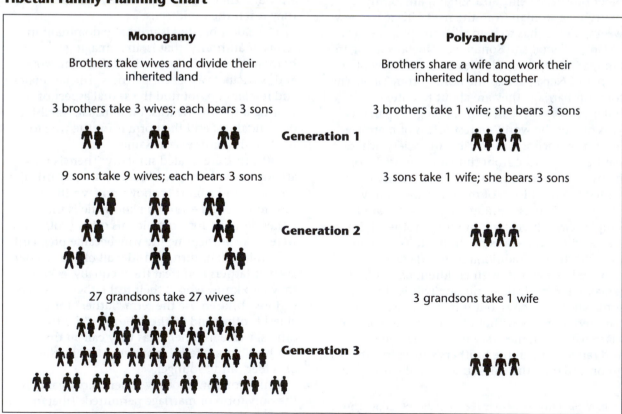

Monogamy	Polyandry
Brothers take wives and divide their inherited land	Brothers share a wife and work their inherited land together
3 brothers take 3 wives; each bears 3 sons	3 brothers take 1 wife; she bears 3 sons
Generation 1	
9 sons take 9 wives; each bears 3 sons	3 sons take 1 wife; she bears 3 sons
Generation 2	
27 grandsons take 27 wives	3 grandsons take 1 wife
Generation 3	

Source: Joe LeMonnier, Natural History, *March 1987. Courtesy of Natural History Magazine.*

ever, they invariably responded that such joint families are unstable because each wife is primarily oriented to her own children and interested in their success and well-being over that of the children of the other wives. For example, if the youngest brother's wife had three sons while the eldest brother's wife had only one daughter, the wife of the youngest brother might begin to demand more resources for her children since, as males, they represent the future of the family. Thus, the children from different wives in the same generation are competing sets of heirs, and this makes such families inherently unstable. Tibetans perceive that conflict will spread from the wives to their husbands and consider this likely to cause family fission. Consequently, it is almost never done.

Although Tibetans see an economic advantage to fraternal polyandry, they do not value the sharing of a wife as an end in itself. On the contrary, they articulate a number of problems inherent in the practice. For example, because authority is customarily exercised by the eldest brother, his younger male siblings have to subordinate themselves with little hope of changing their status within the family. When these younger brothers are aggressive and individualistic, tensions and difficulties often occur despite there being only one set of heirs.

In addition, tension and conflict may arise in polyandrous families because of sexual favoritism. The bride normally sleeps with the eldest brother, and the two have the responsibility to see to it that the other males have opportunities for sexual access. Since the Tibetan subsistence economy requires males to travel a lot, the temporary absence of one or more brothers facilitates this, but there are also other rotation practices. The cultural ideal unambiguously calls for the wife to show equal affection and sexuality to each of the brothers (and vice versa), but deviations from this ideal occur, especially when there is a sizable difference in age between the partners in the marriage.

Dorje's family represents just such a potential situation. He is fifteen years old and his two older brothers are twenty-five and twenty-two years old. The new bride is twenty-three years old, eight years Dorje's senior. Sometimes such a bride finds the youngest husband immature and adolescent and does not treat him with equal affection; alternatively, she may find his youth attractive and lavish special attention on him. Apart from that consideration, when a younger male like Dorje grows up, he may consider his wife "ancient" and prefer the company of a woman his own age or younger. Consequently, although men and women do not find the idea of sharing a bride or a bridegroom repulsive, individual likes and dislikes can cause familial discord.

Two reasons have commonly been offered for the perpetuation of fraternal polyandry in Tibet: that Tibetans practice female infanticide and therefore have to marry polyandrously, owing to a shortage of females; and that Tibet, lying at extremely high altitudes, is so barren and bleak that Tibetans would starve without resort to this mechanism. A Jesuit who lived in Tibet during the eighteenth century articulated this second view: "One reason for this most odious custom is the sterility of the soil, and the small amount of land that can be cultivated owing to the lack of water. The crops may suffice if the brothers all live together, but if they form separate families they would be reduced to beggary."

Both explanations are wrong, however. Not only has there never been institutionalized female infanticide in Tibet, but Tibetan society gives females considerable rights, including inheriting the family estate in the absence of brothers. In such cases, the woman takes a bridegroom who comes to live in her family and adopts her family's name and identity. Moreover, there is no demographic evidence of a shortage of females. In Limi, for example, there were (in 1974) sixty females and fifty-three males in the fifteen-to thirty-five-year age category, and many adult females were unmarried.

The second reason is also incorrect. The climate in Tibet is extremely harsh, and ecological factors do play a major role perpetuating polyandry, but polyandry is not a means of preventing starvation. It is characteristic not of the poorest segments of the society, but rather of the peasant landowning families.

In the old society, the landless poor could not realistically aspire to prosperity, but they did not fear starvation. There was a persistent labor shortage throughout Tibet, and very poor families with little or no land and few animals could subsist through agricultural labor, tenant farming, craft occupations such as carpentry, or by working as servants. Although the per person family income could increase somewhat if brothers married polyandrously and pooled their wages, in the absence of inheritable land, the advantage of fraternal polyandry was not generally sufficient to prevent them from setting up their own households. A more skilled or energetic younger brother could do as well or better alone, since he would completely control his income and would not have to share it with his siblings. Consequently, while there was and is some polyandry among the poor, it is much less frequent and more prone to result in divorce and family fission.

An alternative reason for the persistence of fraternal polyandry is that it reduces population growth (and thereby reduces the pressure on resources) by relegating some females to lifetime spinsterhood. Fraternal polyandrous marriage in Limi (in 1974) average 2.35 men per woman, and not surprisingly, 31 percent of the females of child-bearing age (twenty to forty-nine) were unmarried. These spinsters either continued to live at home, set up their own households, or worked as servants for other families. They could also become Buddhist nuns. Being unmarried is not synonymous with exclusion from the reproductive pool. Discreet, extramarital relationships are tolerated, and actually half of the adult unmarried women in Limi had one or more children. They raised these children as single mothers, working for wages or weaving cloth and blankets for sale. As a group, however, the unmarried women had far fewer offspring than the married women, averaging only 0.7 children per woman, compared with 3.3 for married women, whether polyandrous, monogamous, or polygynous. While polyandry helps regulate population, this function of polyandry is not consciously perceived by Tibetans and is not the reason they consistently choose it.

If neither a shortage of females nor the fear of starvation perpetuates fraternal polyandry, what motivates brothers, particularly younger brothers, to opt for this system of marriage? From the perspective of the younger brother in a landholding family, the main incentive is the attainment or maintenance of the good life. With polyandry, he can expect a more secure and higher standard of living, with access not only to his family's land and animals but also to its inherited collection of clothes, jewelry, rugs, saddles, and horses. In addition, he will experience less work pressure and much greater security because all responsibility does not fall on one "father." For Tibetan brothers, the question is whether to trade off the greater personal freedom inherent in monogamy for the real or potential economic security, affluence, and social prestige associated with life in a larger, labor-rich polyandrous family.

A brother thinking of separating from his polyandrous marriage and taking his own wife would face various disadvantages. Although in the majority of Tibetan regions all brothers theoretically have rights to their family's estate,

in reality Tibetans are reluctant to divide their land into small fragments. Generally, a younger brother who insists on leaving the family will receive only a small plot of land, if that. Because of its power and wealth, the rest of the family usually can block any attempt of the younger brother to increase his share of land through litigation. Moreover, a younger brother may not even get a house and cannot expect to receive much above the minimum in terms of movable possessions, such as furniture, pots, and pans. Thus, a brother contemplating going it on his own must plan on achieving economic security and the good life not through inheritance but through his own work.

The obvious solution for younger brothers — creating new fields from virgin land — is generally not a feasible option. Most Tibetan populations live at high altitudes (above 12,000 feet), where arable land is extremely scarce. For example, in Dorje's village, agriculture ranges only from 12,900 feet, the lowest point in the area, to 13,300 feet. Above that altitude, early frost and snow destroy the staple barley crop. Furthermore, because of the low rainfall caused by the Himalayan rain shadow, many areas in Tibet and northern Nepal that are within the appropriate altitude range for agriculture have no reliable sources of irrigation. In the end, although there is plenty of unused land in such areas, most of it is either too high or too arid.

Even where unused land capable of being farmed exists, clearing the land and building the substantial terraces necessary for irrigation constitute a great undertaking. Each plot has to be completely dug out to a depth of two to two-and-a-half feet so that the large rocks and boulders can be removed. At best, a man might be able to bring a few new fields under cultivation in the first years after separating from his brothers, but he could not expect to acquire substantial amounts of arable land this way.

In addition, because of the limited farmland, the Tibetan subsistence economy characteristically includes a strong emphasis on animal husbandry. Tibetan farmers regularly maintain cattle, yaks, goats, and sheep, grazing them in the areas too high for agriculture. These herds produce wool, milk, cheese, butter, meat, and skins. To obtain these resources, however, shepherds must accompany the animals on a daily basis. When first setting up a monogamous household, a younger brother like Dorje would find it difficult to both farm and manage animals.

In traditional Tibetan society, there was an even more critical factor that operated to perpetuate fraternal polyandry — a form of hereditary servitude somewhat analogous to serfdom in Europe. Peasants were tied to large estates held by aristocrats, monasteries, and the Lhasa government. They were allowed the use of some farmland to produce their own subsistence but were required to provide taxes in kind and corvée (free labor) to their lords. The corvée was a substantial hardship, since a peasant household was in many cases required to furnish the lord with one laborer daily for most of the year and more on specific occasions such as the harvest. This enforced labor, along with the lack of new land and the ecological pressure to pursue both agriculture and animal husbandry, made polyandrous families particularly beneficial. The polyandrous family allowed an internal division of adult labor, maximizing economic advantage. For example, while the wife worked the family fields, one brother could perform the lord's corvée, another could look after the animals, and a third could engage in trade.

Although social scientists often discount other people's explanations of why they do things, in the case of Tibetan fraternal polyandry, such explanations are very close to the truth. The custom, however, is very sensitive to changes in its political and economic milieu and, not surprisingly, is in decline in most Tibetan areas. Made less important by the elimination of the traditional serf-based economy, it is disparaged by the dominant non-Tibetan leaders of India, China, and Nepal. New opportunities for economic and social mobility in these countries, such as the tourist trade and government employment, are also eroding the rationale for polyandry, and so it may vanish within the next generation.

38
What Makes Warú Run?

ROBERT F. MURPHY

I

Warú,[1] the young chief of the Mundurucú[2] village of Uarí, visited the village of Uakuparí with great frequency. So frequently in fact that he once made the ten-hour round trip in one day. Inquiry revealed that Warú was on the horns of a dilemma. Though he was chief of Uarí, he kept a young and pretty wife in the house of his father, the chief of Uakuparí. Whenever he visited his wife, his "followers" in Uarí busied themselves in plotting against him. Hearing of these threats to his authority, he would immediately dash back to reassert his position of leadership. But as soon as he was out of sight of Uakuparí, the men of that community sought to tarnish the virtue of his wife; this was not a difficult task, and half the men of the village ultimately enjoyed her favors. Their exploits were well publicized, and Warú, hearing of his cuckoldry, would hurriedly retrace his steps. During most of the time we lived in Uakuparí, Warú gravitated between the two communities — to the great amusement and deep satisfaction of his fellow Mundurucú.

On the lowest level of explanation, I have already stated what makes Warú run. But the key questions of why the men of Uarí plotted against him and why those of Uakuparí pursued his wife can only be answered through an analysis of Mundurucú society and culture and of Warú's position within it. For Warú was a marginal man trying to play traditional social roles to which he had not been socialized, and he failed to define correctly the nature of the role expectations or the values that pertained to specific social situations. His cumulative blunders finally threatened the stability of this small society, and certain processes were set in motion to reestablish the normal flow of social interaction. Anthropologically, this is a study in deviance and social control. Humanistically, it is a tragedy, but like many tragedies, one that has overtones of comedy.

II

Warú's personality was most deviant, and I shall spell this out in terms of his manifest behavior, as it compared with the normal behavior of Mundurucú men and their chiefs. I know nothing of the socialization of Warú, only that at an early age he went to live in the household of a local Brazilian who traded in the village headed by Warú's father. He came back to live among his people, but he was no longer a Mundurucú, any more than he was a Brazilian. When I first met Warú, he addressed me in backwoods Portuguese

From Robert F. Murphy, "Deviance and Social Control I: What Makes Warú Run?" in *The Kroeber Anthropological Society Papers*, No. 24, Spring 1961, pp. 55–61. Reprinted with the permission of Yolanda Murphy.

and in a swaggering manner introduced himself as "Warú, son of José [the chief of Uakuparí] and chief of Uarí." This contrasted markedly to the diffident and self-effacing way in which most Mundurucú addressed me, and each other. Though I was an outsider, I had at the time been several months with the group and this departure from what I expected of a tribesman upset me considerably. Warú turned out to be a great problem in other ways. He cited his own importance as a justification for the demands that he made on me for gifts. And he bragged continually of his ability to deal with whites, to lead his followers, to hunt, or to do almost anything in either the realm of traditional Mundurucú activity or in their relationships with the outside world. He strove desperately and openly towards the acquisition of prestige and of material goods, which he had accepted as indicators of prestige. For this reason our mosquito boots were admired greatly, as this would surely differentiate him from his barefoot Indian fellows — shortly after one of his visits my wife discovered that her boots were missing. And we met no other Mundurucú so brash. They felt free to enter our house at all times, but only Warú would demand a cup of coffee and then lie in our hammocks; he was quite offended when we pointed out to him that his body paint was staining them. Warú had other unusual characteristics. He spoke freely and critically of other men to us and did this even in the presence of third parties. Nor did he bother to conceal his hostility and contempt when someone inimical to him was near. But underneath this facade, Warú was a frightened and anxious man. He would often confide to me darkly that "people are talking about me." Lest this be interpreted as paranoia in the clinical sense, I should stress that people were indeed talking about him, and Warú had every reason to be anxious. Not only his ego but his very life was in danger.

III

Warú's behavior grated against almost every single point of Mundurucú expectations regarding how a chief should act and how men, in general, should behave. Mundurucú society is intensely egalitarian and based upon the principle of maintenance of solidarity among a group of males who are conceived to be peers. It has a peculiar structure in that it is divided into patrilineal moieties, which in turn are differentiated into a number of patrilineal clans. But the normal mode of residence is matrilocal, and men generally move to the villages of their wives. This disperses the clans throughout all the villages, for a young man, when he marries, leaves the father from whom he obtains clan membership. It also produces a dualism of loyalties in which the man maintains a clan identity and, with it, defined role obligations, and also acquires membership and roles in the village of his wife. This produces a classic form of organic solidarity, for the society is bound together by cross-cutting segments. But it is a very simple form of organic solidarity and an extremely brittle one. Social cohesion must be vigorously maintained and individual strivings muted, for alliances in cases of conflict cannot range along simple segmental lines. To support a fellow-clansman in a crisis may pit a person against his village mates and vice versa. In a society with a population of only 1,200, living in communities of 60 to 100 persons, such stresses are serious threats to social stability in any event; in one of the Mundurucú type they may be totally disruptive. The social system not only produces solidarity but also requires it for maintenance.[3] Given the structure of Mundurucú society, the effective social actor was one who was cooperative, unaggressive, serene, quiet, and willing to place the will of the collectivity before his own. It may be immediately perceived that Warú presented a threat to propriety and to the social system. He was belligerent, loud, self-centered, and acquisitive — all the things that a Mundurucú should not be.

Like all people, the Mundurucú are, to an extent, prestige-seekers, but there are cultural differences in the coinage of status. The traditional culture placed no value upon material acquisitions, and, although this was slowly changing, Warú's tastes were inordinate and clearly derived from his experience among the Brazilians. He thus violated a value standard and at the same time offended the entire community by self-consciously and openly trying to raise himself above his fellows.

Warú not only misconstrued the ends of Mundurucú prestige but he also misunderstood the means for their attainment. The primary rule, and the one he most flagrantly violated, was that one should not *seek* prestige but let it come to him naturally. For example, bravery in war was highly valued but the posture of bravado was ridiculed. A coward was relegated to the lowest end of the status scale, but one who boasted of the damage he intended to inflict upon the enemy in the coming battle was placed in the vanguard of the attack. To attain prestige a man should be modest and unassuming, while observing all the traditional expectations of what constitutes valued behavior. But primarily, he should act always as if he had only the collective well-being and goals in mind. Warú's braggadocio, individualism, and competitiveness had violated every rule of the game, and he won dislike and contempt, rather than the esteem and power he wanted so badly.

Disturbing though all this was to the delicate adjustment of Mundurucú social structure and contrary though his behavior was to the values that bound this adjustment, Warú had committed *the* cardinal error. He had allowed his grievances against certain individuals and groups to come out into the open and alignments emerged for and against him that cut across both village and clan-linked role commitments. Hostilities and latent factions are part of the tribal life of the Mundurucú, but they are carefully repressed — a requisite for the functioning of Mundurucú society. The average Mundurucú is well trained in disguising aggression and presenting the bland face of neutrality, but Warú's own socialization was in part derived from Brazilians and was not adjusted to the functional needs of the Indian society. Like any cuckold, he had some cause to feel aggrieved. His error was in openly objecting to the offense against him, a normal course for a Brazilian cuckold, but not for a Mundurucú victim.

IV

Warú's alienation from Mundurucú society induced severe anxiety and intensified his quest for a favorable identity. He sought this through his role of chief of the village of Uarí. The contemporary Mundurucú chieftaincy must be understood as a boundary role. The dependency of the Indians on manufactured goods, obtained through the sale of wild rubber, has given the Brazilian traders a position of great influence among them, which they exercise through the chief. When the trader wants increased production he tells the chief, who then is supposed to exhort his followers to greater effort. Correspondingly, the chief acts as bargaining agent for the village in trade negotiations, and the people interpret his role to be in large part that of their representative to the outer world. If the trader is sufficiently well established with a village, he can do much to influence the choice of a chief. But since he cannot completely counter the patrilineal rule of inheritance of the chieftaincy, it is common practice to select one or two possible

heirs and rear them in his household; this is what happened to Warú. This is agreeable to the chief, for he gains the favor of the trader and, with it, preferential treatment in sales and purchases. It is clearly beneficial to the trader, as he hopes thereby to install a chief who will be responsive to his wishes, even at the expense of the Mundurucú villagers.[4]

The contemporary Mundurucú chief is in a dilemma. If we look upon a boundary role as one in which both ends have to be played against the middle, we see the chief caught between the interests of the trader and those of his followers; these interests rarely coincide. It is a difficult position, but one that can be maintained by maximal adherence to the traditional behavior expected of chiefs and minimal acquiescence to the demands of the traders. Warú's father, José, played a comparatively successful role. If the trader told him that the villagers were heavily in debt to him, José would communicate this fact and suggest that it would be well to collect more rubber; he never attempted even verbal coercion. He also sincerely sought to obtain the maximum return for his people.

José embodied many characteristics of the traditional chief. An older man, he carried himself with a modest and unassuming dignity. He guided, persuaded, and cajoled, but he carefully refrained from ordering people, and all decisions of communal significance were made in consultation with the mature men of the village. Beyond this, José knew Mundurucú traditional knowledge and lore and attempted to perpetuate it.

Warú's position was very different from that of his father, for he was the prototype of the Indian boy who had been "educated" by a trader and later installed as a chief. He had no legitimate claim to the position, and it was necessary for the trader to insist that he would recognize only Warú in dealings with Uarí. The residents grudgingly assented, but they regarded him as chief only in trade relations. The most influential man of the village was, in reality, a renowned shaman who was the son of the last chief and was considered the legitimate heir to the office.

Warú's precarious situation was made worse by the fact that he was under thirty years old and the junior of many men in the village. To complicate matters, he had no supporting group of kinsmen in Uarí. Matrilocality, I have said, is the normal mode of residence among the Mundurucú, but the sons of chiefs generally remain with their fathers after marriage. From the point of view of conscious motivation, the sons of chiefs remain patrilocal because their fathers are influential enough to persuade men to relinquish their daughters to them as a means of solidifying relations with them. By the same line of reasoning, a young man who marries the daughter of a chief is willing to join the prestigious father-in-law. But from the point of view of social structure, the function of the patrilocality of the chief's family is twofold. By keeping the sons, the chief is able to transmit authority to them without the discontinuity that would result if they were resident in the villages of their wives. Moreover, the chief is surrounded by a group of patrilineally related kin, a small and solidary patrilineage. His position is further enhanced by the fact that he has sons-in-law within the village. Much as this may reinforce his prestige, it does not enable him to exercise unilateral authority, for the rest of the village men are ever-watchful and jealous of the chief's family and would be quick to resist, however passively, what they considered to be high-handedness. Warú, however, did not have the surrounding group of relatives that might have given even minimal support to his claim to leadership. Rather, he depended upon the trader and his father and relatives in Uakuparí to buttress his position.

Given his delicate status, Warú proceeded to worsen it through a misinterpretation of the chieftaincy. He had listened to his father's nostalgic tales of the role of the chief in times past, and one might say that he had some knowledge, in a purely cognitive sense, of the traditional culture. It is highly dubious, however, that Warú had internalized sufficient culture to make him an effective actor within the system of social relationships. Warú knew that "in the old days, chiefs were powerful men who directed their people and bought goods for them." This view of the past may or may not have been true, but it surely did not apply to the present. Warú, nonetheless, announced at large that he was eminently qualified to be chief, as only he knew how to deal with the trader and only he had the force to tell the people how, when, and where to work. I was a special recipient of this information, for Warú found it most important to gain stature in the eyes of a prestigeful outsider. But Warú also told all the others of his importance, and the people of Uarí stated that he indeed relayed the demands of the trader in forceful terms. His "followers" saw him solely as an agent of the trader in their village, and they were certain that his only function was to promote their exploitation and defraudment. Their analysis was correct, but I doubt that Warú thought his role to be at all

antisocial. There is no evidence to substantiate this, for only he could tell me whether he was aware of the machinations of the trader, and he did not. But I believe that Warú saw the trader as a paternal figure, many of whose values he had internalized and subscribed to as legitimate. And he also saw himself to be in the position of a strong and traditional leader.

Warú had learned something else about the chiefs of times past, and this was the fact that many were polygynous. Polygyny was possible only for chiefs, for the matrilocality that applied to most of the population made it most difficult to have plural wives unless they were sisters. Even for a chief, however, polygyny was a difficult and stormy relationship, and it was evidently never of very great frequency.

Warú did not have the implicit and unconscious ability to understand the fine points of Mundurucú social structure that a man raised in a village would have, and he made some of his most serious blunders in marriage. Soon after assuming the chieftaincy of Uarí, he married a woman of the village, a widow several years older than himself who, through the situational variability of post-marital residence, had a strong nucleus of kin in the village. Though I have no data upon which to make a firmer statement, it is quite probable that he married the woman — frankly a crone — in order to enlist the sympathies of her relatives. But Warú was a young, handsome, and virile man, and he subsequently sought a wife more to his liking. He located a pretty girl of about sixteen years in the village of Kapikpík and brought her home to Uarí. This enraged the first wife, who berated Warú, assaulted the girl, and complained to her brothers. The latter expressed their disapproval of the polygynous union to Warú, and the rest of the village supported them. Warú's general behavior and his exercise of his "chieftaincy" had already outraged them, and this offense against his first wife, a native daughter of the village, was beyond their endurance. Warú refused to divorce the new wife, to whom he was greatly attached, but took her to Uakuparí where he left her in the care of his father. He validated his polygyny by pointing to the tradition that this was a prerogative of chiefs.

##

This brings us through most of the key features of Mundurucú culture and social structure and to the point at which this paper began. And since this is in essence a tragic tale, we will see in this final section how the ring must inevitably close on Warú. He had offended all the Mundurucú canons of taste and ethics and had become a source of strain in this small and tightly knit society. Now the forces of social control became operative and he felt the heavy pressure of his fellow men.

Having left his pretty bride in the "safe" confines of his father's house, Warú returned to Uarí to set matters right and quiet the discontent. But he continued in his arrogant and demanding ways and the sentiments of the villagers became further inflamed, with no small assistance from his first wife and her family. There grew among them a firm determination to kill him, and the intention might have been immediately carried out were it not for his ties in Uakuparí. This was an important collective decision by the residents of Uarí, for his execution would set off a train of repercussions that would seriously disrupt their relations with Uakuparí and with the trader. Moreover, Warú did not have shamanistic power and the usual post-hoc explanation for the killing of a deviant — that he was a perpetrator of black magic — could not be used in this case. But his continued presence was even more disruptive, and Warú's life was placed in serious jeopardy.

In the meantime, the person of the young wife was not as secure as Warú thought it would be. Her husband was away and she was a rather wayward girl; whatever rectitude she possessed was certainly no match for the insistent attempts of the men of Uakuparí. Soon, all of the men of the village except those prohibited by incest regulations — and there were some exceptions even to this — were enjoying the favors of Warú's young wife in the underbrush surrounding the village, at the stream, in the forest, in the gardens, or wherever they might find her alone. The enthusiasm of the men was understandable from her physical attractiveness, but there was another component to their attentions. Whenever they related their exploits to me, the men would express great satisfaction *at what they were doing to Warú*, for the Uakuparí men, too, disliked Warú with some intensity. Even in his father's village, his presence threatened the smooth tenor of social relations, and he was considered unbearable. But physical sanctions against Warú would have been impossible in the village in which his father was a chief, and the men of Uakuparí attacked his manhood instead. There could be no doubt about the aggressive character of their seductions, nor of its success in dealing a mortal blow to Warú's prestige by reducing him to a helpless butt of laughter.

Warú soon heard of the events in Uakuparí from members of his family and immediately returned. He made frontal accusations against many of the men and even mentioned my Brazilian assistant as being among those who had cuckolded him. The village reacted to his charges ambivalently. They were highly amused at his discomfiture and humiliation, but they were seriously concerned about the open accusations and threats of violent reprisal. Not only was this a breach of fundamental rules of deportment, but if violence were to break out the social system would be seriously threatened. The village soon became ranged on two sides. Warú's family supported him, but the majority of the population were ranked solidly against him. Thus, the threat of conflict had spread from Uarí to Uakuparí. And Warú ran back and forth between Uarí, where they plotted against his life, and Uakuparí, where they took more covert measures against him through his wife.

The balance of power and of moral correctness lay with Warú's opponents, and the task of his supporters was made most difficult by virtue of the fact that Warú had almost ceased to be a social person — the rules no longer applied to him. We left the field before the curtain fell on our little drama, but one could already predict the conclusion. This was seen most clearly when, shortly before our departure, José fell from a palm tree and lay seriously injured for several days. Knowing that the people of Uarí would kill him as soon as they were assured of his father's death, Warú came immediately to Uakuparí and remained there until the old man's recovery was certain. During this period, Warú approached me and said, "You know, if my father dies, I will leave this land and go to live on the banks of the Tapajós River." I asked him why, and in fine Warú style, he answered, "Because it is so beautiful there." Warú knew that his life as a Mundurucú was finished.

Notes

1. All proper names are fictitious.
2. The Mundurucú Indians are a Tupian-speaking people of the upper Tapajós River in the state of Pará, Brazil. My wife and I carried out a one year fieldwork program there in 1952–53 with the support of the William Bayard Cutting Traveling Fellowship granted by Columbia University, and a Research Training Fellowship of the Social Science Research Council.
3. A more complete description and analysis of the relation between Mundurucú social structure and the positive evaluation of male solidarity has already been published in my article, "Intergroup Hostility and Social Cohesion," *American Anthropologist*, 1957.
4. I have discussed the general structure of authority and its relation to Brazilian society in detail in my book, *Headhunter's Heritage*, 1960.

39
Domesticity and Politics

MURIEL DIMEN-SCHEIN

If we were to write a soap opera about the Yanomamö or the Nuer, we would have to include conflicts and characters that differ from those in American soaps — the decisions of lineage elders instead of the wills of rich uncles; breakaway nuclear families instead of runaway children; a priest's curse for unpaid bride-wealth instead of social snubs; jealousy not of the new woman in town but of a co-wife; hatchet wounds inflicted by jealous Yanomamö males instead of emotional ones by neurotic Western spouses. The domestic scene would still be our focus, but it would be embedded in larger, more permanent units of people. The neighborhood would consist of consanguineal and affinal kinship, and there would be no non-kin. The ongoing economic and political affairs of life would still form the background, but both domestic foreground and public background would be couched in the same metaphors, that is, those of multifunctioned kinship.

Even if kinship is not about biology, and marriage is an affair of politics rather than of love, kinship and marriage do, nevertheless, everywhere intersect to create social groups within which procreation takes place and love can develop. Kinship and marriage do for most other cultures what they do for ours: They organize people spatially and socially into households that perform maintenance functions, providing shelter and rest, a reliable and regular source of food, a place where people of different generations care for and learn from each other, and, often, "space" for psychological self-renewal. In most cultures, one domestic unit carries out all these functions, and each person in it has not one role but several. This is so in our own also, where long lists have been made, in fatuous praise, wry despair, or militant anger, of the many jobs of suburban American housewives: angel in the kitchen, harlot in the bedroom, solicitous hostess, loving mother, child psychologist, chauffeur, nurse, and so on.

Cultural differences between domestic groups come from the way these multiple functions and tasks are carried out. Whereas in our small nuclear family, we are socially and emotionally burdened with them all, the Nuer's *extended* family parcels them out. The coresidence of their corporate lineages makes at least three generations live together — a husband and wife, one or more married sons, and these sons' wives and children. Tasks are allocated according to the principles of sex, age, and marital ties. The men care for the cattle, cultivate a few crops, and take over the education of boys when they reach puberty and can begin to herd. The women raise

From Muriel Dimen-Schein, *The Anthropological Imagination*, McGraw-Hill, 1977, pp. 127–33. © 1977 Muriel Dimen-Schein. Reprinted with the permission of The Charlotte Sheedy Literary Agency, Inc.

children and cook, aided by growing daughters. In monogamous marriages, each woman cooks and raises her children separately; if there are co-wives, they may work together even if they live in separate huts, and their mother-in-law may also sometimes baby-sit for their infants. Women share play as well, for co-wives and mothers-in-law and daughters-in-law provide companionship for one another.

One of the reasons, then, why love between two individuals is a minor criterion for marriage in these societies is that spouses have to get along with other people besides each other; in fact, the Nuer woman may spend more time with her co-wives and mother-in-law than with her husband, who may work more with his father and brothers than with her. The Euro-American emphasis on romantic love is a consequence of different arrangements of people in spatial and social relationships. Our domestic scene does not incorporate the married couple into ongoing kinship and/or territorial units; it isolates them in accordance with our dominant cultural principles.

In the Euro-American system of kinship, marriage is the only principle to establish domestic groups, because our descent rules do not distinguish concrete groups from one another. Although we inherit our surnames from our fathers, we consider ourselves to be equally related to both sides of our family. This system of *bilateral* descent tracks relationships through both sexes, or on both the mother's side and the father's side, without limit. Along with marriage, it creates only two cognatic descent groups. One is the *kindred*. This group consists of all kin traced on both mother's and father's sides through both males and females; the distance one traces varies, usually ending at second cousins (the children of one's parents' first cousins), that is, all those with great-grandparents in common. Another way is to conceive of this group as all those people whom one would invite to one's wedding if one were on equally good terms with both sides of one's family.

The second descent group is the nuclear family, whose core is created by the conjugal couple's usual establishment after marriage of its own *neolocal* residence. Since the nuclear family is equally related to the families of both spouses, it is part of neither. We signal its separateness by our kinship terms, in which it is an island of uniqueness in a sea of classificatory kin: All those outside the two-generation nuclear family and the two generations immediately above and below it receive classificatory terms. Thus, both

father's brother and mother's brothers are *uncle*; we do not have separate terms for each separate uncle. Or, to put it another way, where the Yanomamö make distinctions, we do not: Their classificatory "brothers" and "sisters" are only one part of the group we call first cousins, within which group we also include people whom the Yanomamö call spouse and sibling-in-law. The only people to whom we apply special, *descriptive* terms are our parents, siblings, children, grandparents, and grandchildren.

The linguistic symbolization of the nuclear family's closure reinforces its structural isolation and its culturally preferred economic independence. The only built-in regulations that force it outward are incest prohibitions, which, in our culture, stipulate that one may not have sexual relations with primary kin, grandparents, and grandchildren. All cultures share an incest taboo on the nuclear family, but from then on, nothing is sacred. What we judge to be rather incestuous, such as marriage to a first cousin, the Yanomamö prefer (though they prohibit marriage to parallel cousins, that is, to those cousins who are classificatory siblings, and prefer marriage to the other first cousins, called cross cousins, to whom the term of "spouse" is applied). Marriages which we permit, such as to a distant relative linked through males to one's father, the Yanomamö outlaw. But unlike the Yanomamö, we have no explicit positive marriage rules; emically, there are no particular kinship groups or individuals whom we are supposed to marry.[1]

Structurally, this means that the nuclear family household lacks defined relationships to any other continuing group. Such stable connections, which elsewhere are prescribed by the kinship system and guarantee economic aid and companionship, must instead be carved out of the rest of social life by each generation. The only institutionalized ties for the older generation of the nuclear family are the affinal links created by their children's marriages; but even these are voluntary and not often maintained. As we saw, people seek other connections from informal groups, but friends provide little security. Kin are the only reliable source of ties in the sense that one's relationship to them is in some sense given. But even between them, the means of communication are flimsy; as "Somerset" showed, parents and married children have a hard time relating to one another.

Yet such links are often forged. For example, although a married couple will live neolocally, they very frequently will choose a house near the bride's family (on "Mary Hartman, Mary

Hartman," Mary lived next door to her mother). This is like *matrilocal* residence in which spouses live with the bride's matrilineal group (her mother and father, her mother's sisters and their husbands and children, and her own sisters and their husbands and children). It differs because the rule of descent differs. Nevertheless, it is similar in that it results in mutual aid between consanguineally related women. By living near her mother, a woman reduces the loneliness and workload of keeping house and caring for children. After the birth of children, for example, closer relations tend to develop between the two households as she calls on her mother for advice and baby-sitting services; the latter may permit her to take a full-time job to bring in additional income or pin money.

But the kinship network, etically considered, is extremely important for the poor and the rich. Those who do not have, and/or cannot get, permanent, adequate employment depend for their economic survival on a group of kin — paternal, maternal, or both. *Matrifocal* households, held together by a line of mothers and daughters, represent one type of extended family that appears among the poor in nineteenth-century European industrial cities as well as contemporary North American ones. Kin also may live separately and yet help one another out, as Elliot Liebow describes for black working-class people in Washington, D.C., and as Michael Young and Peter Willmott do for the London working class. Indeed on "All in the Family," Gloria and Mike moved in with Archie and Edith, her parents, when they got married; but even when they moved out after the birth of their son, they only moved next door, and continued to request and to get baby-sitting services and meals.

The extended family thus appears in another guise, not as a concrete household or a corporate group, but as a network of mutual aid relations that may expand and include more than just mother and daughter. Our ideology does not really acknowledge this network; instead, it idealizes the middle-class nuclear family as it idealizes the individual who makes it on her/his own, and this emic view is what soap operas portray.

Paradoxically, the wealthy also use the extended kin group for financial security; but they do it to live even better, not merely to stay alive. Family lines with large holdings of stock, for example, can dominate major corporations. The Rockefeller family has much of its wealth, though separately owned by each individual, jointly managed by corporations, trust funds, and foundations. And people in such families manage their nationally and internationally vital businesses to their mutual advantage.

The wealthy also use marriage, another kinship principle, to retain their position. In a system of bilateral descent, marriage extends inheritance claims to an unlimited number of people. But if marriages are kept within a small circle of friends, the goods will also remain within that circle. And so they are; the newspaper society page shows that the wealthy very often marry the wealthy. They practice the opposite of exogamy, *endogamy*, or marriage within a group. Other societies, too, have preferential endogamy, even within lineages, as a means to consolidate wealth. By these principles, of course, endogamy is not to the financial advantage of the underclasses, although it may reinforce or create a sense of subcultural solidarity and thereby enhance political leverage.

In our culture, endogamy happens without our willing it. Although our ideal marriage preference is to "fall in love," the lives of different classes of people are socially structured so that people are bound to fall "helplessly" in love with someone not only of their own class, but also of their own religion, race, ethnic group, and even geographical area. For example, religion, race, and ethnicity form the social bases of neighborhoods, which are common meeting grounds for lovers. Clubs perform the same match-making function, and their membership rules, often restricted on religious or racial grounds, in effect keep their young from meeting the "wrong" people. Like some colleges, clubs may charge very high membership fees, which also effectively limit their patrons to one class.

The rule of endogamy becomes conscious when someone breaks it: In Somerset, when Andrea, heiress to Delaney Brands, fell in love with David, a fledgling middle-class lawyer, her mother did her best to break up the relationship. But the engagement finally ended only when Andrea gave David a car for his birthday. Since he was poorer than Andrea, he couldn't accept it — it made him seem less of a man. And even if such values don't break up the engagements, marriages can always be arranged, bending the rules a little to allow first cousins to marry, a traditional technique of European royalty to conserve their power.

It has long been thought that the principles of descent and marriage no longer integrate the social system in industrial, complex societies. Perhaps they have declined in emic importance for all of us, and in etic importance for the middle-class nuclear family household, to its misfortune. But the wealthy and the poor use extended kinship to their advantage; the wealthy manipulate marriage to maintain their power; and many of us try to better ourselves by marrying up and out of our class. The few who achieve upwardly mobile marriages are quickly assimilated by the upper class. They acquire its trappings of behavior, values, and relationships, and drop their old ones. David couldn't do this and so he didn't make it. Kinship, of course, does not structure our social lives all by itself. Whereas the Nuer and the Yanomamö separate people by rules of descent and marriage, we do so by rules of wealth and power as well. The fact that those who do marry up soon cut their ties to their poorer kin reinforces the internal socio-economic uniformity within each class and the differences between classes.

Note

1. Unless one counts races, ethnicities, and so on, as kinship groups, which in a sense they are.

SECTION THREE
Political Systems

Introduction

Humans are social animals: this characteristic made possible the survival of these hairless, clawless, fangless, and otherwise rather helpless apes. The kinds of social groups formed by humans vary enormously in size, complexity, and the amount of control that they exert over individuals. At one extreme are small egalitarian bands, like those of the Mbuti Pygmies (Chapter 40); at the other are powerful empires, such as the Chinese empire or that of the Incas of Peru (Chapter 44), in which the state exerts complete control over a highly stratified society.

In **egalitarian societies**, all individuals of the same age and sex have similar chances of gaining prestigious status, be it that of headman, best curer, or best story teller. Of course, not everyone is absolutely equal, and, typically, women are "less equal," but overall, in such societies, all benefit about equally. This means that all members of egalitarian societies have a roughly equal interest in maintaining order: there is no need for law-and-order "specialists," such as police officers, since everyone is something of a cop! Certain individuals may possess a little more **authority** than others — the ability to suggest, and persuade others to follow, their advice or requests — but, ultimately, all decisions are made by *consensus* (a compromise to which all agree). Any member of the group who does not agree is free to vote with his feet — to go

off and join another group. Maurice Godelier's analysis of the dynamics of Mbuti bands, in Chapter 40, illustrates the great importance of kinship in formalizing what we would call political activity. Besides providing a good description of the social processes that promote cooperation, help prevent open conflict, and let the forest punish deviants, Godelier's essay is attractive from the point of view of its method. He suggests that respect for three constraints — dispersion, cooperation, and fluidity — make possible the maintenance of the Mbuti social and ecological order.

One cannot read Douglas Oliver's account of the life and deeds of Soṇi, the Big Man of Siuai (Chapter 41), without wondering how long it would take him to seize power if he lived in Ottawa or Washington! The most egalitarian of societies have among their members gifted people whose strong personality stands out. Many agricultural societies of Melanesia allow a special status for a forceful individual of this sort: they let him be a "Big Man," as long as he is willing to work for it. The Big Man is a "redistributor," who gathers and combines the fruits of his labor and that of many others in order to redistribute the goods in a lavish feast for all. Typically, the egalitarian nature of the society is protected by the condition that prestige be granted only on the basis of generosity. An incentive to increase production is built into the process of **redistribution**: additional prestige is granted to the redistributor who donates the most. The Siuai can afford a Soṇi only because it

259

is possible for them to intensify production without endangering their resources. A similarly ambitious leader among the !Kung, coaxing and plotting to make group members hunt more, would wreak havoc in short order: overhunting would result in starvation. The !Kung could not afford the kind of leadership associated with redistribution; for that reason, they ridicule extraordinary gifts and deny the giver any of the prestige that a redistributor like Soni could gain in Bougainville.

Most people alive today do not live in egalitarian societies, but have been incorporated into stratified societies. A **stratified society** is divided into classes, which differ from one another in terms of wealth and control over resources, energy, and other people. Unlike egalitarian societies, stratified societies do not reward generosity: they grant prestige and power to the rich, not to those who give their wealth away. The dominant characteristic of a stratified society is that most of its members are poor and work hard, and that their efforts contribute to maintaining the power and luxury of a small elite. **Power** is often consolidated in the military, the church, and various administrations for the collection of taxes and the maintenance of the stratified order. This sort of political organization constitutes a **state**. Robert Carneiro's search for the origins of the state, as presented in Chapter 42, leads him to reject theories that assume that most people voluntarily became slaves and members of the lower classes. Archaeological evidence proves that the state was invented independently by various different peoples, and that, in all cases, the rise of the state was preceded and accompanied by war. While this may imply that violence is necessary for state formation, it does not suggest that the latter is an inevitable result of the former: anthropologists know of many societies, like that of the Yanomamö, that have remained egalitarian in spite of warfare.

Under what circumstances, then, would warfare have led to stratification and, subsequently, to the creation of the state? One of the major factors identified by Carneiro is ecological **circumscription**. Consider, for example, a fertile valley that is surrounded by desert. If the people living in that valley were defeated in war, they would have no reasonable alternative but to stay, face subjugation, and pay the taxes levied by their conquerors. However, Carneiro's explanation involves a myriad of factors: circumscription, agricultural use of fertile land, population increase, warfare, and social stratification. To these important factors, many anthropologists add grain production, for the following reason: Unlike yams, sweet potatoes, and many other crops that cannot be stockpiled because

they will spoil, grains can and must be stored. A state can arise only under circumstances that allow for the accumulation of wealth, and one can become rich in grains, but not in rotting yams and sweet potatoes. This explains in part why the state could not have arisen in places such as New Guinea, where it was impossible to store foods for extended periods.

Carneiro's analysis deals only with *pristine states*, such as Sumer, which arose independently, without influence from, or even knowledge of, any other state. Another important contribution to the study of pristine states was that of Kent Flannery. Unlike Carneiro's essay, which attempts to explain *why* and *where* states arose, Flannery's essay entitled "The Cultural Evolution of Civilizations" (1972) describes *how* certain systemic changes transformed and perverted previous institutions. Similar analyses of the properties of systems came to be used with increasing success by archaeologists such as the Binfords and by anthropologists with approaches and interests as different as Roy Rappaport's (1968) in his ecological anthropology and Claude Lévi-Strauss's (1987) in his structuralist works.

Chapter 43, entitled "Cyclical Conquests," by Julian Steward and Louis Faron, complements Carneiro's analysis of the origins of the state. It describes the functions of the state and the stages of instability that gradually lead either to its disintegration and collapse or to the militaristic acquisition of new territories and the subsequent creation of an *empire*. More specifically, although a state is an integrating and coordinating agency that provides public services, it is also a consuming institution that increases taxes as political, military, and religious institutions gain more power. When the tax burden becomes too great, the state either collapses in revolt or conquers other states to extract new taxes from them: thus, an empire is born. When the empire finally collapses under the heavy burden of local, state, and imperial taxes, all public services — irrigation, transportation, storage, and so on — collapse with it, and many people starve. Eventually, the survivors gather into villages, which, in time, amalgamate into chiefdoms, which in turn develop into states, which eventually either collapse or build a new empire...

Steward and Faron illustrate their thesis with examples from American pre-Columbian civilizations; in Chapter 44, Pedro Carrasco's essay documents further the achievements of those empires. Unlike most scholars, Carrasco emphasizes the similarities rather than the differences between the empire of the Incas of Peru and the Aztec empire in Mexico. He analyzes social stratification in much more detail than do the authors of the preceding chapters, and shows that ethnicity and kinship provided some of the mechanisms used for the creation of social stratification. In spite of the lack of written records from these civilizations, their political systems were no less sophisticated and no less effective than those of the Spaniards who destroyed them, in only a few years, with the aid of horses, new weapons, and new diseases such as smallpox.

From Carrasco's article, we learn some of the mechanisms that contributed to the appearance of social stratification. It is also important, however, to consider some of the effects that social stratification has had on contemporary societies. Poverty and homelessness are found in the wealthiest of modern industrial societies. In spite of their democratic ideals, these wealthy societies are highly stratified, benefiting the majority of people far less than they do a small, privileged minority. When the ancient Greeks invented *democracy* (literally, "power to the people"), they defined who "the people" were, and they were *not* the slaves, the women, the children, or the poor workers of Greek society. "The people" were mostly privileged men.

The extreme poverty of the people one meets on skid row in Winnipeg (Chapter 45) and other North American cities is not the result of an alleged "culture of poverty." It cannot be explained by laziness or state of mind. Christopher Hauch's eloquent testimony documents the hard work and complex strategies for coping with poverty used by these victims of social stratification. Involved with the social welfare agencies of Winnipeg, Hauch is an "action anthropologist," who uses his anthropological knowledge to solve practical human problems. He focuses his analysis on the apparently wasteful, drunken binges in which skid row residents indulge from time to time, when they receive an unexpected windfall. Hauch shows that these episodes are nearly archetypal examples of *reciprocity*, providing the residents with a type of social security similar to that afforded the !Kung by the sharing of meat. His explanation of the causes of poverty and the adjustments to it made by skid row residents has obvious implications for the selection of successful strategies for helping the destitute.

Works Cited

Flannery, K. 1972. "The Cultural Evolution of Civilizations." *Annual Review of Ecology and Systematics* 4: 399–426.

Lévi-Strauss, C. 1987. *Anthropology and Myth: Lectures, 1951-1982*. Translated by Roy Willis. New York: Oxford.

Rappaport, R. 1968. *Pigs for the Ancestors: Ritual in the Ecology of a New Guinea People*. New Haven: Yale University Press.

40 Mbuti Politics

MAURICE GODELIER

The Mbuti Pygmies inhabit a generalised ecosystem of a simple type, the equatorial forest of Zaïre. They are hunter-gatherers. They use the bow and net for hunting game, consisting mainly of different varieties of antelope and occasionally elephant. The women collect mushrooms, tubers, and other wild plants as well as molluscs and thus contribute more than half the food resources. Honey is collected once a year and its harvest is the occasion for the division of each band into smaller groups, which come together again at the end of the honey season. Hunting is done collectively. Married men in a semicircle hold their individual nets (about thirty metres in length) end to end, while unmarried women and children head the game back toward the nets. These activities are repeated every, or nearly every, day and, in the evening, the produce from hunting and gathering is divided and consumed by all members of the camp. Each month, if game becomes scarce round the camp, the band moves to another site, but always within the same territory, which is known and respected by neighbouring bands. Kinship and family relations, such as they are, play a secondary role in production because work is divided according to sex and generation. Individuals frequently leave the band where they were born and go to live in neighbouring bands, sometimes for good. Wife exchange is practised, and the spouse is sought preferably in a distant band; never in the mother's or paternal grandmother's band. Bands do not have chiefs, and authority is divided according to generation and sex; old and renowned hunters do, however, enjoy greater authority than other members of the band. War does not occur between bands but murder and severe punishment are very rare within the band. The death of all adults, men and women, and girls' puberty are accompanied by ritual and festivity; *molimo* in the former case and *elima* in the second. In these, the forest becomes the object of intense worship and "makes its voice heard" through the intermediary of sacred flutes. Bands number between seven and thirty hunters and their families; hunting with less than seven nets is ineffective, while with more than thirty hunters there would not be sufficient game to provide regular supplies for the group; and the organisation of hunting with nets, normally performed without a real leader, would have to be modified in order to remain effective.

When these economic and social relations are analysed closely, we see that the conditions of production determine three internal constraints

From Maurice Godelier, translated by Robert Grain, *Perspectives in Marxist Anthropology*, pp. 51–59. Copyright 1977 Cambridge University Press. Reprinted with permission. (Bibliographic documentation contained in the original text is omitted here. Interested readers should consult the original publication.)

on the modes of production and that these constraints express the conditions of reproduction for these modes of production together with the restricted possibilities of this reproduction.

- Constraint No. 1 is a "dispersion" constraint on hunting groups and on the minimal and maximal numbers limiting each group.
- Constraint No. 2 is a "cooperation" constraint on individuals according to sex and age in the process of production and in the practice of hunting with nets.
- Constraint No. 3 is a "fluidity" constraint, a "non-closure," or as Turnbull puts it, the maintenance of a state of permanent "flux" within the bands; this flux is expressed by the frequent and rapid variation of their strength and social composition.

These three constraints express the *social* conditions of the reproduction of the process of production, given the existing nature of the productive forces (special techniques for hunting and gathering) and the nature of the biological conditions for reproduction of animal and plant species which go to make up the generalised ecosystem of the equatorial forest of Zaïre. These constraints create a system, that is to say, each intervenes along with the others. Constraint No. 2, for example, the "cooperation" constraint on individuals according to sex and age, which assures their own existence and reproduction as well as that of the band, assumes a form determined by the action of Constraint No. 1, since the size of the band must be kept within certain limits, and by the action of Constraint No. 3, since the necessity to keep bands in a state of flux constantly modifies a group's size and social composition, that is to say, ties of kinship, affinity, or friendship between those called upon to cooperate each day in the process of production and redistribution of hunting and gathering produce. Equally, one could show — and this should be done — the effects of Constraints 1 and 2 on 3, and Constraints 2 and 3 on 1. We should also note that these constraints (particularly those of "dispersion" and "flux") are such that both the individual's and the band's social conditions of reproduction are equally and immediately conditions of reproduction in Nbuti *society* as a whole and are always present in all parts of it. They are, therefore, internal conditions for each band and at the same time *common* conditions for *all* the bands; this makes for the reproduction of the socioeconomic system in its entirety.

These three constraints, therefore, make for a system. This system is born from the very process of production whereby it expresses the material and social conditions of reproduction. And the system itself is at the basis of a number of simultaneous structural effects on *all* the other instances of Mbuti social organisation, effects which we can only list, since a full demonstration would take too long. All these effects consist in the determination of the *elements of content and form* of instances which are *compatible* with these constraints, therefore assuring the reproduction of the Mbuti mode of production. Thus, these constraints, *internal* to the mode of production, are at the same time channels by which the mode of production determines, in the final analysis, the nature of the different instances of Mbuti society and, since the effects of these constraints are *simultaneously* active on all instances, by the action of the system of constraints, the mode of production determines the *relation* and *articulation* of all the instances among them and in relation to itself, that is, determines the general *structure* of the society as it is, the specific form and function of each of these instances which go to compose it. To search and find the system of constraints determined by a social process of production, is to proceed epistemologically in such a way that one can show the structural causality of the economy on society and, at the same time, the general specific structure of this society, its logical ensemble, even though this economic causality, this general structure of society and this specific logical ensemble are never directly observable phenomena as such, but facts which have to be reconstructed by thought and scientific practice. Proof of the "truth" of this reconstruction can only be that it offers to explain *all* observed facts and poses new questions to the student in the field, questions which require fresh research and new ways of finding answers; this is the very process and progress of scientific knowledge.

Having demonstrated and analysed this system of constraints, we are now ready to take account and reveal the *necessity* of all *major* facts observed and recorded in the works of Schebesta and Turnbull.

The idea of *distinct* territories is explained by the dispersion constraint; using the flux constraints, the "non-closure" of bands can be explained by the inexistence of *exclusive* rights of bands to their territory. What is invariable is not the internal composition of bands, but the existence of *stable* relationships *between* bands, therefore a relationship which reproduces and permits the reproduction of all bands. Now we can explain the reason for the *form* and *content* of the social relations of ownership and the employment of this basic resource which is the hunter's and gatherer's territory — that part of nature which constitutes "a store of primitive goods" or a "laboratory for the means of production" (Marx). What we wish to reveal here is the origin of rules and the customary laws of appropriation in the very process of production and the use to which nature is put. Now a revelation of the origins, outside consciousness, of the system of conscious norms of the social practices of production agents, operating within determined means of production, is a fundamental step ahead in the use of Marx's methods, but it is generally neglected or caricatured by Marxists. Here we should like to express our agreement with C. Bettelheim in his critical analysis of the confusion reigning in the theory and practice of both economists and rulers in socialist countries as far as the juridical aspect and the real content of relations of production is concerned.

The "juridical" sphere also penetrates to norms of action of individuals and groups regarding their territory for hunting and gathering and their production resources; we cannot, however, elaborate this point; instead we shall make a rapid analysis of the structural effects of the mode of production on Mbuti kinship relations. Here again, the facts and norms coincide with the structure of the mode of production and with the constraints imposed, particularly Constraint No. 3, the "non-closure" of bands, which maintains a structure of flux between them. Kinship terminology mainly stresses generational and sex differences, reproducing forms of cooperation in the process of production (Constraint No. 2). When relations of affinity are analysed, we find a preference for marrying into distant bands and the prohibition of marrying within your mother's or paternal grandmother's band. These are positive and negative norms which accord with Constraint No. 3, because they prevent "closure" of groups and their constitution as *closed* units exchanging women in a *regular* and *directed fashion*; since in taking a woman from his mother's or grandmother's band, he would be *reproducing* the marriage of his father and/or his grandfather, therefore reproducing former and older relations which would make relations between bands *permanent* — each generation would be linked apropos the exchange of women necessary for the reproduction of society and each individual band.

Moreover, by *simultaneously* prohibiting marriage between neighbouring bands on adjacent territories, the formation of closed bands (Constraint No. 3) is made even more impossible.

Thus, Constraints 1 and 3 affect forms of affinity and at the same time explain the fact that marriage is primarily an exchange between individuals and nuclear families; all this preserves the fluid structure of bands. It also explains why the band as such interferes only in order to regulate the new couple's place of residence; this is of great importance since a young man receives a net ("made by his mother and maternal uncle") and shares fully and individually in hunting activities only after marriage, thereby becoming a full agent of production in the reproduction of the band. Then again, the relative weakness of any collective control over the individual (Constraint No. 3) and over the couple explains the relative *precariousness* of marriage among the Mbuti.

The structural effects of the mode of production on descent are perfectly complementary with those on affinity. The Mbuti, as Turnbull has shown admirably, do not have a true lineage organisation, and when we refer to lineage "segments" in order to indicate groups of brothers living in the same band, this is awkward and a misuse of terminology. The fact that there are no regular or directed matrimonial exchanges between bands, which would mean each generation following its ancestors' example, prohibits continuity and the formation of consanguinal groups of any high genealogical degree or groups which could control their continuity by an essential segmentation. At the same time, in order for society to reproduce itself through matrimonial exchanges, there must be at least four bands in order for these matrimonial relations to exist. Band A (of self), band B (the mother's band), band C (the paternal grandmother's band), and band D (the spouse's band, which as we know must not be a neighbouring one).

From a methodological point of view, it is clear that it would be a mistake to imagine that a logical study of the functioning of a society can be made by analysing only one band or a single local unit.

Other effects of the constraints imposed by the mode of production appear when we analyse the political relations existing between and within bands. These effects are different in their content because they have an effect on a different aspect, irreducible to elements of the process of production, but they are *isomorphic* to the effects produced on other instances of Mbuti society. This isomorphy derives from the fact that all the different effects come from the *same* cause acting simultaneously on all levels of society. This method of carrying out a structural analysis within a Marxist framework, as distinct from ordinary cultural materialism or some people's so-called Marxism, does not *reduce* the various instances of a society to economics nor does it represent economics as the only true reality, whereby all other features reflect differing and phantasmic effects. Our way of using Marxist theory takes fully and strictly into account the specificity (and the relative autonomy) of all things.

Two features characterise political rule and practice among Mbuti Pygmies: (1) lack of any significant inequality in political status or authority between individuals, men and women, or between generations, the old, the adult, and the young. Inequality does exist, favouring adult men in relation to women; old men in relation to individuals; and men over women in younger generations; (2) a systematic refusal of all kinds of violence or any collective repression in the regulation of conflicts between individuals or bands.

In the first case, should inequality threaten to develop — for example, if a great elephant hunter wishes to convert his prestige as a hunter to one of authority over the group, the institutional response is one of mockery, public gibes; in brief, a systematic erosion of all attempts to develop inequality over and beyond certain limits compatible with the voluntary (Constraint No. 2) and always provisional (Constraint No. 3) cooperation between individuals and within a band. In the second case, the response to all conflict which may *seriously* threaten the unity of the band or relations between bands results in a systematic recourse to compromise or diversion. In each band one person plays the role of buffoon (Colin Turnbull, in the first months of his stay among the Mbuti, played this role unawares), and this person is responsible for avoiding all serious conflicts which could lead to a dramatic event such as murder or the band's fission, thus threatening the internal goodwill and understanding necessary for cooperation and reproduction (Constraint No. 2). To avoid conflicts getting out of hand, the buffoon systematically draws attention away from them. Say, two individuals, *a* and *b*, are in serious conflict because one has committed adultery with the other's wife, and their confrontation threatens to lead to physical violence or murder, the buffoon (who may be male or female), using artifice, exaggerates the importance of a minor tiff which other individuals, *c* and *d*, for example, are having; after several

hours of shouting and quarrelling, *a* and *b* will find themselves on the same side against *d*. All this tends to diminish the intensity of their own particular quarrel. In two instances only does the band practise repressive violence: first, if a hunter secretly places his personal net in front of all the other nets which are placed end to end, and thus improperly appropriates a greater share of game. This means that he is transforming the communal effort of the band, hunters and beaters (women and children), to his own personal advantage; second, if, during a *molimo* festival in the forest's honour, a man goes to sleep and forgets to sing the sacred songs in unison when the forest is replying to the men's call (the voice of the forest being heard through the intermediary of the sacred flutes carried by the young men of the camp).

In both these cases, the thief and the man who goes to sleep, the internal solidarity of the group is disturbed and the real or imaginary conditions for reproduction are threatened (Constraint No. 2). In both cases the guilty one is abandoned, left alone and defenceless in the forest, where he will soon die unless the band who exiled him comes to find him again. It is the forest therefore which is entrusted with the task of sanctioning ultimately the major violations of the band's rules regarding social reproduction. Although it is, in fact, the band who has in practice condemned a guilty man, it is as though the forest were punishing him. Here, we find ourselves in the presence of a process of fetishisation of social relations, a process we shall return to when we analyse the religious practice of the Mbuti forest cult.

In interband conflict, violence is also avoided, and all observers have pointed out, as a remarkable fact, the absence of war among the Pygmies. When a band captures game on another's territory, it sends a portion of the slaughtered game to this band; the conflict is thus regulated by compromise and sharing. Why is it that war is eliminated from Mbuti political experience? Because it would bring about oppositions which would crystallise groups and create rigid frontiers, excluding other groups from the use of certain territories and resources, increasing or decreasing the numbers of victorious or vanquished groups, respectively, and breaking the delicate equilibrium necessary for the reproduction of each band and for society as a whole. War is therefore incompatible with Constraints Nos. 1, 2, and 3 of the mode of production, taken separately or in their reciprocal relationships. The absence of witchcraft among the Mbuti can be explained by the same reasons, because witchcraft presupposes suspicion, fear, and hate between individuals and groups, preventing a good understanding or collective and continued cooperation between members of a band. If it did not lead us so far away from our theme, we should make a comparison between Mbuti hunters and Bantu farmers — their neighbours — who practise witchcraft avidly.

We might extend these different analyses further; for example, we could account for *all* the reasons why the existence of personal authority, such as "big-men," or the existence of a permanent and centralised political hierarchy are incompatible with the conditions of reproduction or the mode of production. The possibility that individuals may, at any moment, leave one band and join another, the non-existence of lineal kinship relations, of continuity in the marriage alliance, are converging factors which make it impossible for authority to remain in the hands of a single individual who would eventually pass it on to his descendants — thus resulting in the formation of a hierarchy of political power in favour of closed groups, kinship, lineage, or any other kind of group. At this theoretical stage, our aim is to show the specific action of each instance, combined with the action of internal constraints of the mode of production, as, for example, the effect of the content and form of Mbuti kinship relations (non-lineal) on social forms of authority combined with the direct effects the mode of production can have on all political relations (absence of war, fluidity in a band's memberships, etc.). We are now faced with a complex epistemological question concerning the analysis of *reciprocal* effects, convergent or divergent, which increase or limit themselves reciprocally, and analysis of the mutual effect of all instances on the basis of their specific relationships, their *general articulation* determined finally by the mode of production. Such an analysis is absolutely necessary in order to explain the content, form, and function of Mbuti religion, a religion which dominates their ideology and symbolic actions.

Let us now consider those data which are almost impossible to decipher — religious facts. Among the Mbuti, religious practice takes the form of a forest cult. It is observed every day and in all their actions: in the morning, before leaving for the hunt, in the evening when they return and prior to dividing the game, etc. The more exceptional circumstances in the life of individuals or bands — birth, girls' puberty, death — are occasions for ritual. The most important are the *elima* festival for girls and the great *molimo*

festival for the death of a respected adult. In the case of epidemics, a succession of poor hunts, or serious accidents, the band carries out "little *molimos*." In all everyday or more exceptional events in the life of both the individual or the community, the Mbuti turn to the forest and worship it, that is to say, they dance and, especially, sing in its honour.

The forest, for the Mbuti, is "Everything." It is the ensemble of all inanimate and animate beings; it is a higher reality which exists as a person, a divinity to whom one speaks as to a father, mother, friend, even lover. The forest insulates and protects them from their Bantu neighbours; it is bountiful with gifts of game and honey; it scares away illness, punishes the guilty. It is Life. Death overtakes men and other living things because the forest goes to sleep and therefore it must be awakened to persuade it to carry on providing nourishment, health, goodwill — in short, happiness and social harmony for the Mbuti in whatever band they may happen to live. Mbuti affirmation of dependence on, and trust in, the forest culminates in the great *molimo* ritual. Over a period of as long as a month, the band spends every day hunting with extra special ardour. There is an abundance of captured game; and it is shared out and eaten at a feast which is followed by dancing and singing lasting almost till dawn and, in the morning, the voice of the forest summons the Mbuti to fresh hunts and more dancing. Woe betide anyone whose tiredness from the night's activities prevents him from waking when the forest voice is heard and the sacred trumpets enter the camp on the shoulders of strong excited young men. The guilty person who has spoiled this communion, this unison, with the forest, may immediately be put to death or banished to the forest which punishes him by letting him die. One finds here an isomorphism involving two violations of the law which provoke punishment. To refuse to hunt with everybody or to sing with everyone is to disrupt the vital cooperation and unity of the band for the reproduction of its real and imaginary conditions of existence (Constraint No. 2).

What the forest represents, then, is both a supralocal reality — the natural ecosystem within which the Pygmies reproduce themselves as a society — and the totality of the material and social conditions for the reproduction of their society (the forest, as a god, provides game, health, social harmony, etc.). Mbuti religion therefore is an ideological instance where the conditions of reproduction of their mode of production and their society are represented; but they are represented *upside-down*, as "fetishised," "mythical." It is not the hunters who catch game, it is the forest which provides them with a certain quantity for them to subsist and reproduce. Everything takes place as if a reciprocal relationship existed between persons of different power and status, since as distinct from men, the forest is omnipresent, omniscient, and omnipotent. Toward it, men adopt attitudes of gratitude, love, respectful affection. When they forbid the needless killing of animals, the destruction of animal and plant species, it is the forest they are respecting (representation of the consciousness of Constraint No. 1 and the conditions of renewal in the process of hunting and gathering natural, determined species).

But Mbuti religion is not just a system of representations, it is also social practice and plays a fundamental role in the very reproduction of society.

Can we use this method to construct a "theory of the process of fetishisation" in social relations and — going further than different kinds of ideological, religious, or political fetishism — tackle, in scientific manner, the domain of symbolic practice? These different realities have been badly mishandled by materialists, who appeal to a cultural ecology or to Marxism, even passing over these realities without a word. These studies are usually pursued from an idealistic point of view, associated with functionalism (as in Turner's work) or structuralism. From this point of view, relations between a society's symbolic actions and its mode of production are practically never explored, since idealism is powerless to reveal or reconstruct them, even if it does not dogmatically deny them. Yet this is one of our major theoretical problems and its solution would contribute to an explanation of the conditions and reasons for the origins of class and state societies, and, as a result, the historical reasons for the disappearance of most classless societies.

41
The Rise of a Big Man

D O U G L A S   L .   O L I V E R

The Rise of Soŋi

Soŋi was born around 1893 in Turuŋom; his mother was a Rukaruinai Tree-rat, his father a Whistler Kingfisher; both parents were also born in Turuŋom and their marriage conformed to a long-standing local tradition of "straight" cross-cousin intermarriage between local Rukaruinais and Whistlers. Soŋi was orphaned during early childhood, and for the next few years he was cared for by his own maternal uncle. Later on one of Soŋi's own paternal uncles took over the job of sponsoring Soŋi's rise to *mumi*-hood — the young man having begun to show promise at an early age. Meanwhile Soŋi slept about in the houses of several kinsmen and was provided with food by a matrilineage *sister* of his deceased father.

In terms of material possessions the young Soŋi was comparatively well off. His own matrilineage, the Turuŋonai branch of Rukaruinai Tree-rats, had settled in Turuŋom several generations previously and acquired much land in the course

Excerpted from Douglas L. Oliver, *A Salomon Island Society: Kinship and Leadership among the Siuai of Bougainville*. Cambridge, Mass.: Harvard University Press, 1955, pp. 423–30, 431, 432–39. Reprinted with the permission of the author. (Bibliographic documentation contained in the original text is omitted here. Interested readers should refer to the original publication.)

of time; it also possessed a large hoard of heir-looms. In addition, Soŋi had access to the resources of his father's matrilineage, much of whose property had become practically combined with his own matrilineage's through the many cross-cousin marriages that had taken place between members of the two units. Moreover, enough inheritance was left over from his father's private capital (*pure*) to start his accumulation of pigs. Soŋi purchased a few small pigs and turned them over to his sponsoring paternal uncle to fatten for sale. The uncle also solicited the aid of neighboring kinsmen, telling them: "Let us all help this boy Soŋi become a *mumi*. He has the ambition and industriousness but is an orphan and hence cannot depend on his father for help. Let us all make pots and sell them, then give the money to Soŋi for buying pigs." Several men did as the uncle suggested, even fattening the pigs that were purchased with the money earned for Soŋi.

Then, when Soŋi was about fifteen, his uncle mobilized all the men in Turuŋom to help build a small club-house for the boy, and thus he was launched on his feast-giving career. It should be mentioned that the paternal uncle had a son of his own about Soŋi's age, but that individual showed no promise of becoming a *mumi* and hence received no special assistance from his father or others. This man later moved to a neighboring settlement and although he appears to harbor no resentment against Soŋi, neither has he assisted him in any way.

Another event cleared the way for Soŋi's continued advance. The maternal uncle who cared for Soŋi during the latter's early childhood was then the most prominent man in Turuŋom itself. The latter's son, Koŋkoma, was several years older than Soŋi, showed fair promise, and was beginning to be pushed ahead by his father until an interruption occurred. A resident of nearby Hiuannai died, and divination singled out a Turuŋom native, Ham, as responsible for the death. The Hiuannai *mumi* then paid Koŋkoma's father to kill Ham, which he did. The only thing wrong with this action was that Ham happened to be a kinsman of the great Jeku *mumi*, Tokura, and when Tokura heard of the murder he set out with a few followers to kill Koŋkoma's father. The latter received ample warning and escaped with Koŋkoma to a distant settlement where kinsmen provided haven for them until Tokura died many years later. This episode left the field open for Soŋi's advance, there having been no other young man in Turuŋom with comparable promise or support. (Later, when Koŋkoma returned to Turuŋom, Soŋi was already firmly established as highest-ranking leader there. Koŋkoma was jealous and angered by what he considered to be Soŋi's usurpation, but could do nothing about it. On one occasion, when Soŋi had just completed a new club-house, Koŋkoma cleared a new path so as to make a wide detour around the club-house, hoping thus to deflect some of the traffic. This tactic backfired, causing Koŋkoma much embarrassment; Soŋi called the new path "empty-stomach trail," signifying that people who traveled along Koŋkoma's pathway would miss being fed at Soŋi's frequent club-house feasts. Eventually Koŋkoma contracted what appears to be tuberculosis, and now is a frail old widower dependent upon relatives for food and shelter.)

Soŋi consolidated his preeminence in Turuŋom by building, successively, two large club-houses and filling them with gongs, thereby keeping his neighbors actively working on his behalf and rewarding them with numerous pork banquets — pork, it should be added, which they themselves helped to fatten for him. Natives still tell of Soŋi's readiness, during that period, to contribute generously at the baptisms of their children and the funerals of their kinsmen. When the Patrol Officer wished to appoint a Headman for Turuŋom, Soŋi was offered the position, but he would have no truck with the new regime and arranged for the Hat to be given to his elder matrilineage mate, Siham.

Soŋi has reportedly given scores of feasts but his adherents single out fourteen of these as having been especially large and significant for his socio-political career. The first seven of these were given to reward leaders of neighboring settlements for their assistance in building Soŋi's club-houses and carrying slit gongs. For the seventh, Soŋi had intended asking his rival, Konsei, the Paramount Chief, to assist in carrying his largest gong from an old club-house to a new one, but Konsei rejected the bid, terming it insolent. ("That Turuŋom is a place of no consequence. If they want me to honor them with my presence, they will have to pay me in shell money.") On hearing this, Soŋi redoubled his efforts and prepared a huge feast to which he invited all of Rataiku and none of Mokakaru. This episode served to publicize Soŋi's name throughout Siuai and caused him to be identified with Rataiku sentiment against the hated Konsei.

The four subsequent feasts were *mumi*-honoring affairs (*muminai*) given for neighboring Rataiku leaders. Two of these leaders reciprocated, while making it clear that they did not wish to compete further. The two others did not even attempt to repay and accepted defeat philosophically. Thanks to Soŋi's tact, all four of these erstwhile rivals became Soŋi's faithful allies. Later, on the death of Moki, the last of the great war-making *mumis*, Soŋi became tacitly recognized as highest-ranking leader of Rataiku, and he began to prepare to extend his activities beyond Rataiku.

Mokakaru was the logical place to begin, but after Konsei's death there was no one left in Mokakaru to offer suitable competition. Soŋi disposed of Konsei's Chief Interpreter, the opportunistic U'ta (who, by the way, is, like Soŋi, a Rukaruinai Tree-rat), with a feast which U'ta could never hope to repay; but Soŋi did this more as an amusement than as a serious social-climbing tactic. U'ta is universally disliked on account of his conceit and officiousness, and Rataikuans make a great joke of him by imitating his exaggerated salutes and his insistence upon giving orders in pidgin English. They dub him "the *kou*," in reference to a long-necked, supercilious looking bird, which is described in a folk tale as acting as if all feasts it attended were being given in its honor. Nor was young Tomo, Konsei's successor as Paramount Chief, a suitable rival for Soŋi to compete with; hence Soŋi turned towards central Siuai for the next stage of his career. It was at this point that we moved to his village and were thus on hand to witness his most ambitious enterprise.

*   *   *

Soŋi the Man

And now for Soŋi himself. He is about forty-five years old, of medium height and slender. He usually wears a conical fiber hat (*ohkuna*) and a dirty, ragged calico loincloth, seldom troubling to bathe — in fact, he is rather contemptuous of the fastidiousness of his Methodist neighbors. His manner is usually solemn, without appearing unfriendly, and his rare smiles are benign and infectious. His voice is high-pitched but he seldom speaks loudly. Occasionally his anger flares up, but manifests itself in masterfully worded sarcasm rather than in shouts or threats.

Soŋi has no intimate friends. Aside from his quest for renown, the joy of his life is his two young sons by his first wife. This wife died in childbirth when the younger son was still an infant, and Soŋi has lavished care and affection on the two little boys, explaining that he pities them because they have no mother. Soŋi's third wife also died in childbirth during our stay there, leaving only his second wife, with her young son and infant daughter. Because of the nature of the deaths of these two wives, Soŋi appears convinced that some envious man has carried out *tao* sorcery, and often speaks of moving away from Turuŋom in order to escape this evil and thus be able to sire more children without risking their mothers' lives. It is often suggested to Soŋi that he take measures to divine the identity of the *tao* sorcerer, but he refuses, saying that his enemies would have him jailed if they learned of it, and that even if he learned the man's identity the Australian regime would not permit him to punish him.

While other men gad about visiting kinsmen or attending ceremonies and court hearings, Soŋi remains in his club-house or pottery shed, restringing shell money or making pottery. Now and then he disappears to his hamlet house and remains secluded there with his wife and children for days at a time. Few people visit him at his village house and even fewer venture near his hamlet house.

Soŋi is a *mikai*-magician and states candidly that he practices mainly in order to earn money. A few years back his services were in considerable demand but when his failures multiplied, clients dropped away. Now, Koura is considered a more skillful *mikai* than Soŋi by his Turuŋom neighbors. Soŋi's spirit-familiar is the ghost of his younger brother (and only sibling), Mokekui, who died in infancy. Mokekui's ghost walks around with Soŋi and is given regular food offerings. Soŋi asserts that Mokekui's tender age

may account for his run of failures as a *mikai*, and talks of acquiring a more effective familiar. Soŋi's club-house demon is said to have resided in the Turuŋom area for a long time, but prior to Soŋi it was unattached to any individual for as far back as informants can recall. This demon spends most of its time in Soŋi's club-house but occasionally appears (to Soŋi) at the latter's village house demanding food. Soŋi usually prevails upon the demon to return to the club-house by staging there a small pork feast for his adherents, with the essence of the pig's blood going to the demon. (It is, of course, a danger to women and children for the demon to lurk near the place where they stay.)

Soŋi's *Muminai* Feast

The first overt action signalizing the preparations for Soŋi's new *muminai* feast occurred when he tabooed his coconut trees. This event took place in February 1938, and was described to us by a Turuŋom resident: "Soŋi slaughtered a pig, placed some of the pork in a pot along with a banana leaf and cooked them. When the stew was done he removed the leaf and fastened it around the trunk of one of his coconut palms, saying: 'Hey, there, you *horomorun*. Smell this food I offer you and look out for my coconuts. If a thief steals any of them, kill him.'"

After this, Soŋi began to formulate plans for financing the feast and obtaining a record number of pigs. First of all, in late October, he mobilized his Hand-money men (*aŋuraranopo*), telling Tamaŋ, Maimoi, Asinara, Pitaino, Koiri, Tampa, Ronsa, Tahiŋ, and To'osi to pen up the pigs he had farmed out to them and hold them ready for the feast. "The hand-money payment," he told them, "will come later." (Afterwards Maimoi told me: "The only hand-money we ever get is the smell of the cooking pig.")

Farming out pigs was one of the simplest methods used by Soŋi to accumulate animals for his feast. Some of his transactions were far more complex, as illustrated by the following example.

In May 1938, Soŋi said to Koura: "I am going to single you out as one of my principal *mouhes* (supporters) at the next feast. So you give to me now the pig which you would eventually give when I honor you." Koura went to Opisa and asked him to repay a pig lent to him months previously. Koura then gave this pig to Soŋi, who in turn presented it to Pitaino for slaughtering on the occasion of the baptism ceremony of Pitaino's infant daughter. Pitaino owned a fine tusker pig which Soŋi coveted. When Soŋi began to collect pigs for his own feast he turned to Pitaino and asked for the tusker in return for his earlier (coercive) gift. This tusker was then sent to Kaopa, leader of Noronai village, to induce him to lend Soŋi several hundred spans of shell money.

* * *

Among all Soŋi's adherents, Koura was most heavily indebted to him for past loans, and Soŋi asked him to repay his debt of five pigs so that they could be used at the big feast. Koura, who is one of Soŋi's most ambitious adherents, decided to make the loan repayment into something of a renown-winning occasion. He invited residents of several neighboring hamlets to attend a feast and help him transfer a fine old gong from his abandoned club-house to his new one. This feast was held in January, only a few days before the big feast, and Soŋi was requested to attend and receive his pigs. The other guests received four small pigs for their help in carrying the gong. Soŋi expressed mixed feelings about this affair of Koura's. On the one hand, he was somewhat annoyed at Koura for using up pigs which might have been saved for the big feast to come. On the other hand, he was pleased to have an adherent of his put on a feast and thereby increase both the adherent's and, indirectly, his own renown — but in this connection Soŋi complained that the four pigs distributed among the guests were inadequate and did not reflect enough renown upon Turuŋom.

After Soŋi had made initial preparations for collecting pigs, he decided to go hunting opossums. He sent word to every able-bodied adult male in the village and set a date for starting out.

On the preceding night, Siha-the-Cripple dreamt that a man fell from a tree. He told several villagers of his dream and warned them not to go opossum-hunting. Opisa, Pitaino, and Tamaŋ were sitting in the club-house discussing the advisability of hunting in the face of Siha's warning, when Soŋi arrived and said, very angrily: "You are a crowd of women, all of you. True, Siha is a dream prophet but who cares about his dreams? If I dream, that's different, that's something real." That night they all set out as scheduled, with Siha included.

As soon as they had arrived in the forest, Ho'oma went off alone in the direction of the Mivo River; he was armed with hunting spears and took his dogs with him. "He wants to taste pork," I was told. "He's a real bush demon, that one; and he will surely bring back a wild pig."

Sure enough, three days later, after all the men had returned loaded down with opossums, Ho'oma stalked in with the carcass of a wild pig slung across his back.

"Now," he said, "I'm going to have *my* feast." Whereupon he sent Ronsa, Pitaino, and Tampa off to get firewood, Siha and To'osi to get cooking pots, and Koiai to take out some taro from his garden. Meanwhile, he singed and butchered the pig, and joked about himself: "I've become a *mumi* now, a *mumi* with one pig!"

When everyone had returned, Ho'oma supervised the cooking. For my benefit, he swaggered around in imitation of an officious Administration appointee, and enjoyed his joke immensely. Then he invited all men in the village to come and eat. When a crowd had gathered he distributed the pork — it was a typically thin wild pig, and didn't go far — and jokingly told his guests: "Just try and surpass my feast!"

When the materials were being assembled for his feast Soŋi commissioned a talented musician from Mokorino village to compose a eulogy to be sung and piped at the feast by the hosts and defenders. Soŋi provided the theme, a lament which he himself had earlier composed in the form of a complaint against an ulcer which had malformed one of his feet; in substance:

> You sore, demon, if you were a man I would rise and slay you and place your skull in the club-house. But alas, you are only a sore, and I can only look at you and weep from pain. [Meaning: I am a powerful warrior and a club-house owner and can work my will on mortal men, but against a little sore I too am powerless.]

The composer elaborated somewhat on the theme and adapted it to music. He chose a panpipe of five reeds, cutting them in lengths to suit the required tones. Then he passed around his master panpipe for copying by Soŋi's adherents and Kaopa's co-defenders.

Prior to this, in mid-October, preparations for the feast were temporarily interrupted when Soŋi's third wife died in childbirth. Soŋi was visibly and probably sincerely grieved by her death, but he was also annoyed by its untimeliness and resolved not to allow it to interfere with his feast preparations. As he said: "People here are always dying and causing me to use up my resources on funeral feasts. That's why my other feasts were not as large as I wanted them to be." He did, however, taboo sounding the gongs in his club-house for a while. Then, in mid-December, he held a *tureko* feast to celebrate the re-beating of his gongs, and to this feast he invited the male residents from all his *tuhia*s, asking them to bring along their panpipes to practice singing and dancing the song intended for the big feast. He butchered seven small pigs and distributed baskets containing stone-baked pork, taro, sweet potatoes, and cooked greens among all the guests, giving one large basket to the leader of each contingent. After the food had been consumed, two of the *mikai*-magicians present removed the taboo by beating each gong with coconuts, which were then broken open and eaten. Then hosts and guests joined together in panpipe practice.

After this, practice sessions were held at several club-houses. The Siuai show tireless enthusiasm when actually performing at a feast, but become very bored and tired when learning and practicing.

* * *

Next, the time arrived for preparing puddings, but before this could be done Soŋi had to remove the taboo placed earlier on his coconut palms. He secured a live opossum for a scapegoat, and forced it to climb into one of the palms. Then he called out to his club-house demon: "Go away now." The opossum was then recaptured, killed, and cooked, and its essence was offered to the club-house demon. In explanation of this event an informant stated: "The club-house demon seized the soul of the opossum, and perceiving that it is no longer necessary to guard the palms, the demon called off all his demon followers."

It was decided to make *anitapu* (sago and almond) and *kihanu* (taro and coconut) puddings for the big feast. First of all, sago had to be secured.

During the second week of December, Soŋi sent for Ronsa and Maimoi to arrange for cutting sago palms. Ronsa, it transpired, had none ripe enough, so Soŋi "bought" two from Maimoi, and promised to pay later. Then Soŋi set a date for the tree-felling and sent To'osi and Opisa to get some helpers. To'osi engaged the "shredders," while Opisa engaged the "washers." Maimoi — they were his palms and his job to fell them — asked Tampa, Siha, Ho'oma, and Ronsa to assist him with the felling. When the palms had been felled, Maimoi reported to Soŋi, who passed the word on to the "shredders." Early the following morning, the "shredders" removed the bark from one side of the palms and began to chop away the pith. Soŋi sent Ho'oma to beat a gong to summon the "washers." Soon they all appeared with Opisa, and when the shredders gave them a signal they set about washing the shredded sago

pith. When the "washers," had finished the job they called out to several "packers," who joined them and compressed the starch into leaf packages. When they had finished with this, Soŋi directed them to store the packages in the club-house and in their own houses.

Even though the adult males of the village were busily employed preparing food for the feast, the ordinary affairs of everyday life had to drone on, but with this difference: women had to perform much of the work ordinarily done by men. Such differences were evident in many families and resulted in some temporary changes in the relationships among family members. The case of Ho'oma is informative.

Ho'oma is a faithful subject of Soŋi's and at the same time is generally regarded as a good family man. He usually works very hard in the garden, even assisting his wife with planting and weeding, a task which most men consider undignified. His wife, Pirume, is a regular Xanthippe, but she was once overheard telling a group of women that her husband, Ho'oma, is a good husband: "He is unselfish; he divides his pork among us all."

The men of Turuŋom like Ho'oma — they always laugh at his buffoonery — but they do not have much respect for him. Younger men would not hesitate to send him on errands, and Ho'oma — anxious to please — generally does as he is told. As one would expect, Soŋi began to depend more and more upon him when preparing for his feast. By December 7, Soŋi was referring directly to Ho'oma whenever he wanted some important task done. He started conferring with Siham and Ho'oma preliminary to starting a job and left much of the business of preparation to them; consequently, Ho'oma began to give orders to other natives. At the same time, he slept more often at the club-house and returned to his own home only for meals.

This behavior obviously annoyed Pirume because she railed at Ho'oma whenever he appeared, screaming to him to "try sounding wood (cutting down trees) in his garden rather than waste time sounding wood (beating wooden gongs) in Soŋi's club-house." After one of these squabbles, Ho'oma stayed away from home for a week, during which time Pirume forced her lazy sons, Koiai and Minsipi, to do more work than was their custom.

In spite of the redoubled efforts of men like Ho'oma, in mid-December it became obvious to the Turuŋom natives that there were not enough local laborers to carry out all the work of food preparation. Thereupon Soŋi acted as he had on many previous occasions and sent word to Tukem, leader of Rennu village, to assist. Hitherto Soŋi and Tukem used to meet in each other's club-house and make arrangements for exchanging pigs or money. Each treated the other with greatest deference, addressing each other as "friend" (ŋonosim) and sharing betel nut. Tukem and his Rennu villagers stood in the same relationship to Soŋi and Turuŋom villagers as Kaopa and his Noronai adherents, and many other leaders and their adherents. When Soŋi, acting in his capacity as the leader of Turuŋom village, wanted outside assistance, he went directly to the leader of another village. Not even in his most expansive mood had he seriously attempted to usurp authority in another village. This situation is aptly illustrated by an incident that occurred in Rennu.

One of Tukem's old followers had, as a result of an old feud, borne a grudge against Soŋi since boyhood, and he has always resented Soŋi's visits to Rennu. Once while Soŋi was there, he addressed the old fellow and his son and jokingly asked them to contribute a pig for the coming feast. The old man remained stolidly silent, not even bothering to look in Soŋi's direction. After Soŋi left, Tukem asked the ancient why he had not spoken to Soŋi, and the old man replied: "I'm not his fool. One mumi's enough for me." Later Tukem suggested to Soŋi: "I will ask the ancient stone-heart for a pig, perhaps he will give it to me." Soŋi replied: "Never mind, if I had really wanted his pig, I would have asked you in the first place." And there the matter rested.

After Soŋi had received Tukem's assurance that Rennu villagers would assist in the food preparations, he turned to Siham and asked him to supervise. Siham is the most knowledgeable cook in Turuŋom. Besides knowing all the recipes, he controls a large number of magical techniques which insure successful baking and boiling. The cooking lasted for six days. During this time nearly every adult male from the two villages was on hand, even decrepit Kanasai and Koŋkoma. Only the bitter old man of Rennu remained at home, sulking.

Finally the time came for making sago-almond pudding. Siham set various individuals to do certain things, and the work proceeded apace. Stone-heaters called out to sago-and almond-grinders when the oven was prepared. Grinders, working with mortar and pestle, reduced, mixed, and thinned the ingredients, and passed on the mash to packers. Packers poured it into leaf-lined frames; then placed the pudding in the oven.

Meanwhile Siham supervised nearly every step, regulating the speed and pointing out deficiencies. Soŋi also hovered around, and on several occasions sent numbers of Turuŋom and Rennu men to get more firewood and to refill the bamboos with water. This change in relations surprised me but, apparently, not the Rennu villagers. Having become so accustomed to the formality and restraint between Soŋi and those natives, I was not prepared to see the former order the Rennu villagers about as if they were his own adherents.

From this time on, Rennu villagers frequented Soŋi's club-house and aided Turuŋom natives with all their communal tasks.

The first striking evidence of the "political" merger of Rennu with Turuŋom occurred just before the social-climbing feast, when Soŋi deputized Ho'oma to direct the construction of a display platform. Tukem complained that he had expected to supervise that job himself; and spent the rest of the day at his hamlet house, disappointed and sulky.

But Tukem or no Tukem, the display platform was finished under Ho'oma's direction, and was decorated with food. The completion of these events was a signal for the feast invitation to be sent.

As early as September it was rumored about that "all the big leaders in Siuai are nervous over Soŋi's choice of a guest of honor for his feast; they would all be shamed by so much generosity." Soŋi appeared to enjoy the suspense he was creating, then, one day, just after the display platform had been decorated with coconuts, he announced that he had made his choice, and without recourse to divination. This was the news that Siuai had been waiting for.

"Siham," ordered Soŋi, "collect as many men as you need and carry invitation pigs to Sipisoŋ of Kinirui."

This was a great surprise to the curious natives; that is, until they realized the significance of the gesture. Earlier, while Soŋi was making arrangements to collect pigs for his feast, he had a bitter quarrel with this Sipisoŋ, an Administration appointee of little renown. Soŋi had been frustrated in his effort to secure one of Sipisoŋ's great tuskers and obviously wished to humiliate him. Soŋi knew that to refuse an invitation to a muminai is to suffer contempt, but to accept without hope of reciprocating is to court even worse disaster. His move was successful. Siham returned with the invitation pigs and recounted how humiliated Sipisoŋ had been: "He felt so much shame that he vowed he would never again set foot in Turuŋom." (Nor did he — until the feast, which he attended and seemed to enjoy thoroughly!)

After having rebuked Sipisoŋ, Soŋi conducted divination and sent the invitation pigs to Kope, most influential leader and Paramount Chief of central Siuai. Wiseacres claimed they knew that he was going to be the choice from the beginning. Kope accepted and they agreed on a date. Messages passed to and fro, with Soŋi begging Kope's pardon for the presumption shown by inviting such a great man to so modest a repast; and with Kope expressing gratitude that a *mumi* as big as Soŋi would deign to notice him, and prophesying that he would never be able to reciprocate such a bountiful gift.

Kope slaughtered the invitation pigs sent to him by Soŋi, cut them in strips, and sent the strips around to all the leaders of central, southern, and western Siuai, as well as to a few leaders from the neighboring ethnic areas of Banoni and Nagovisi. They were invited to attend the feast with Kope, who designated them as his *allies* and urged them to join in the *attack* on Turuŋom.

While this was going on, Soŋi sent out other invitation pigs to Kaopa of Noronai and some other Rataiku natives designated to be his defenders. Kaopa, in turn, invited many other leaders to attend with their adherents as his co-defenders. He invited all Siuai leaders and Hat-men not directly asked by Soŋi or Kope, including Moŋko of Kupiŋku, the Paramount Chief and highest-ranking leader of northwest Siuai; Tomo, the Paramount Chief of northeast Siuai; and even some leaders from Terei.

In other words, this was to be not only a whole tribal affair and probably the first such ever given, but was also intended to reach out beyond the borders of Siuai.

Now there remained only one decision to make. Should or should not Soŋi appear at the feast and be seen by his guests? Hitherto on several occasions he had made all preparations for his feasts and then retired to his hamlet house in order to hide from envious sorcerers. The matter was not decided until Kope himself sent a message saying that "he would only come to the feast — Turuŋom is so far away! — provided he could be assured of seeing his renowned host." Soŋi decided to remain and he was assured that every device known to his followers would be used to protect him.

All was in readiness. The curious and excited Defenders strolled in hours before dawn on January 10, 1939, and took part in the final *pig-counting*. Koura claimed he saw Soŋi's *horomorun* dancing along the ridgepole, vastly pleased with the noise and the smell of food. Women huddled together around minute fires in the village and discussed the great event with animation; some of the bolder ones actually stole up to the edge of the dancing ground and peered through the reeds at the drummers.

The morning was spent by all the men applying cosmetics and decorating weapons, preparing themselves as if they were making ready for war. Spears were oiled and bows restrung and polished. Faces and torsos were painted both with powdered lime, sign of invulnerability in battle, and with red ocher, sign of warfare and festivity. Protective charms were distributed about the body to guard against sorcery.

By noon all the Defenders had massed around the front of the club-house and were straining to hear the faraway shouts that announced the approach of the Attackers. While some of the tardier ones quickly applied ocher and lime, there was a last-minute consultation to reconsider whether Soŋi should remain or hide. He remained, and sat upon his largest wooden gong alongside the spot believed to be occupied by his *horomorun*.

Then, like a shot, a single spearman rushed into the clearing, ran up to the front of the club-house, threatened the natives lined up there, and retired. A second followed suit, then a third, and so on until scores of howling natives had rushed in brandishing their spears and axes and twanging arrows against bowstrings. More men entered at a run carrying pigs, for the guest must reciprocate the invitation pigs previously sent to him.

The rush then slackened off and the Attackers began to mill around the southern end of the dancing ground, while the Defenders formed a revolving circle nearer the club-house. Then the piping began. Every native performed so strenuously that he could not hear the rival melody above the din of his own. The Turuŋom natives discovered that their song, the lament for Soŋi's sore, now seemed too complicated and slow, so after halting along with it for a while they abandoned it for a more spirited tune.

The music went on for an hour before the guests began to move gradually in the direction of the club-house. As they pressed forward, the Defenders thinned out in order to give the guests a chance to see their host. Soŋi reluctantly slid down from his perch and stood upright while his guests stared at him.

Then, at the signal from Soŋi, some of his men rushed to the pens and dragged in the squealing pigs. Others climbed the display platform, whisked away with bundles of leaves the demons guarding it, and began to hand down baskets of food.

After the pigs and puddings had been lined up on the ground, Soŋi motioned to Kope to accept them. This was the signal for a stampede. Puddings were ripped into, drinking nuts broken open. Meanwhile Kope recorded on a fern frond tally the value of the pigs, and distributed them among his allies. The pigs were quickly strangled and tied to poles, and the whole company of Attackers and Defenders moved off. The exit was as sudden and dramatic as the entry. The whole affair had lasted only two hours.

Some 1100 natives attended the feast and received 32 pigs, distributed as follows: 17 pigs worth a total of 1070 spans of *mauai* to Kope; 7 pigs worth a total of 450 spans to Kaopa; 4 pigs worth a total of 220 spans to those Rataiku leaders who were directly invited; 3 pigs worth 160 spans given directly to Soŋi's principal *taovu* partners; and one pig worth 20 spans given to the Australian Patrol Officer, whom Soŋi invited in order to show him "how *Siuai* leaders act."

Every Turuŋom native seemed to sense the depression of anticlimax. A few of them strolled around the dancing ground, now red with betel juice. Some of them kept up a disconsolate piping. No pudding remained for them — "We shall eat Soŋi's renown for a day or two" — so the only thing left to them was talk about the feast, particularly about the number of guests who had been present. And of course by nightfall, these numbers had been exaggerated to legendary proportions, as had accounts of everything else concerned with the feast.

"Now we shall rest," To'osi told me hopefully. "Now we can attend our gardens." I agreed with him, just as hopefully, and went away to sleep.

Yet early the next morning the wooden gongs boomed out again and they seemed louder than ever, probably because the noise was so unexpected. A few sleepy natives strolled in the direction of the club-house and heard Soŋi storm out:

Hiding in your houses again; copulating day and night while there's work to be done! Why, if it were left up to you, you would spend the rest of your lives smelling yesterday's pig. But I tell you, yesterday's feast was nothing. The next one will be really big. Siham, I want you to arrange with Konnu for his largest pig; and you, Maimoi, go to Mokakaru and find a pig for Uremu; and — etc.

Opisa turned to me and whispered: "*That's* the fashion of a *mumi!*"

42
A Theory of the Origin of the State

ROBERT L. CARNEIRO

For the first two million years of his existence, man lived in bands or villages which, as far as we can tell, were completely autonomous. Not until perhaps 5000 B.C. did villages begin to aggregate into larger political units. But, once this process of aggregation began, it continued at a progressively faster pace and led, around 4000 B.C., to the formation of the first state in history. (When I speak of a state I mean an autonomous political unit, encompassing many communities within its territory and having a centralized government with the power to collect taxes, draft men for work or war, and decree and enforce laws.)

Although it was by all odds the most far-reaching political development in human history, the origin of the state is still very imperfectly understood. Indeed, not one of the current theories of the rise of the state is entirely satisfactory. At one point or another, all of them fail. There is one theory, though, which I believe does provide a convincing explanation of how states began. It is a theory which I proposed once before,[1] and which I present here more fully. Before doing so, however, it seems desirable to discuss, if only briefly, a few of the traditional theories.

Explicit theories of the origin of the state are relatively modern. Classical writers like Aristotle, unfamiliar with other forms of political organization, tended to think of the state as "natural," and therefore as not requiring an explanation. However, the age of exploration, by making Europeans aware that many peoples throughout the world lived, not in states, but in independent villages or tribes, made the state seem less natural, and thus more in need of explanation.

Of the many modern theories of state origins that have been proposed, we can consider only a few. Those with a racial basis, for example, are now so thoroughly discredited that they need not be dealt with here. We can also reject the belief that the state is an expression of the "genius" of a people,[2] or that it arose through a "historical accident." Such notions make the state appear to be something metaphysical or adventitious, and thus place it beyond scientific understanding. In my opinion, the origin of the state was neither mysterious nor fortuitous. It was not the product of "genius" or the result of chance, but the outcome of a regular and determinate cultural process. Moreover, it was not a unique event but a recurring phenomenon: states arose independently in different places and at different times. Where the appropriate conditions existed, the state emerged.

Voluntaristic Theories

Serious theories of state origins are of two general types: *voluntaristic* and *coercive*. Voluntaristic theories hold that, at some point in their history, certain peoples spontaneously, rationally, and voluntarily gave up their individual sovereignties and united with other communities to form a larger political unit deserving to be called a state. Of such theories the best known is the old Social Contract theory, which was associated especially with the name of Rousseau. We now know that no such compact was ever subscribed to by human groups, and the Social Contract theory is today nothing more than a historical curiosity.

The most widely accepted of modern voluntaristic theories is the one I call the "automatic" theory. According to this theory, the invention of agriculture automatically brought into being a surplus of food, enabling some individuals to divorce themselves from food production and to become potters, weavers, smiths, masons, and so on, thus creating an extensive division of labor. Out of this occupational specialization there developed a political integration which united a number of previously independent communities into a state. This argument was set forth most frequently by the late British archeologist V. Gordon Childe.

The principal difficulty with this theory is that agriculture does *not* automatically create a food surplus. We know this because many agricultural peoples of the world produce no such surplus. Virtually all Amazonian Indians, for example, were agricultural, but in aboriginal times they did not produce a food surplus. That it was *technically feasible* for them to produce such a surplus is shown by the fact that, under the stimulus of European settlers' desire for food, a number of tribes did raise manioc in amounts well above their own needs, for the purpose of trading.[3] Thus the technical means for generating a food surplus was there; it was the social mechanisms needed to actualize it that were lacking.

Another current voluntaristic theory of state origins is Karl Wittfogel's "hydraulic hypothesis." As I understand him, Wittfogel sees the state arising in the following way. In certain arid and semiarid areas of the world, where village farmers had to struggle to support themselves by means of small-scale irrigation, a time arrived when they saw that it would be to the advantage of all concerned to set aside their individual autonomies and merge their villages into a single large political unit capable of carrying out irrigation on a broad scale. The body of officials they created to devise and administer such extensive irrigation works brought the state into being.[4]

This theory has recently run into difficulties. Archeological evidence now makes it appear that in at least three of the areas that Wittfogel cites as exemplifying his "hydraulic hypothesis" — Mesopotamia, China, and Mexico — full-fledged states developed well before large-scale irrigation.[5] Thus, irrigation did not play the causal role in the rise of the state that Wittfogel appears to attribute to it.[6]

This and all other voluntaristic theories of the rise of the state founder on the same rock: the demonstrated inability of autonomous political units to relinquish their sovereignty in the absence of overriding external constraints. We see this inability manifested again and again by political units ranging from tiny villages to great empires. Indeed, one can scan the pages of history without finding a single genuine exception to this rule. Thus, in order to account for the origin of the state we must set aside voluntaristic theories and look elsewhere.

Coercive Theories

A close examination of history indicates that only a coercive theory can account for the rise of the state. Force, and not enlightened self-interest, is the mechanism by which political evolution has led, step by step, from autonomous villages to the state.

The view that war lies at the root of the state is by no means new. Twenty-five hundred years ago Heraclitus wrote that "war is the father of all things." The first careful study of the role of warfare in the rise of the state, however, was made less than a hundred years ago, by Herbert Spencer in his *Principles of Sociology*. Perhaps better known than Spencer's writings on war and the state are the conquest theories of continental writers such as Ludwig Gumplowicz, Gustav Ratzenhofer, and Franz Oppenheimer.

Oppenheimer, for example, argued that the state emerged when the productive capacity of settled agriculturists was combined with the energy of pastoral nomads through the conquest of the former by the latter. This theory, however, has two serious defects. First, it fails to account for the rise of states in aboriginal America, where pastoral nomadism was unknown. Second, it is now well established that pastoral nomadism did not arise in the Old World until after the earliest states had emerged.

Regardless of deficiencies in particular coercive theories, however, there is little question that, in one way or another, war played a decisive role in the rise of the state. Historical or archeological evidence of war is found in the early stages of state formation in Mesopotamia, Egypt, India, China, Japan, Greece, Rome northern Europe, central Africa, Polynesia, Middle America, Peru, and Colombia, to name only the most prominent examples.

Thus, with the Germanic kingdoms of northern Europe especially in mind, Edward Jenks observed that, "historically speaking, there is not the slightest difficulty in proving that all political communities of the modern type [that is, states] owe their existence to successful warfare." And in reading Jan Vansina's *Kingdoms of the Savanna* (1966), a book with no theoretical ax to grind, one finds that state after state in central Africa arose in the same manner.

But is it really true that there is no exception to this rule? Might there not be, somewhere in the world, an example of a state which arose without the agency of war?

Until a few years ago, anthropologists generally believed that the Classic Maya provided such an instance. The archeological evidence then available gave no hint of warfare among the early Maya and led scholars to regard them as a peace-loving theocratic state which had arisen entirely without war.[7] However, this view is no longer tenable. Recent archeological discoveries have placed the Classic Maya in a very different light. First came the discovery of the Bonampak murals, showing the early Maya at war and reveling in the torture of war captives. Then, excavations around Tikal revealed large earthworks partly surrounding that Classic Maya city, pointing clearly to a military rivalry with the neighboring city of Uaxactún. Summarizing present thinking on the subject, Michael D. Coe has observed that "the ancient Maya were just as warlike as the ... bloodthirsty states of the Post-Classic."

Yet, though warfare is surely a prime mover in the origin of the state, it cannot be the only factor. After all, wars have been fought in many parts of the world where the state never emerged. Thus, while warfare may be a necessary condition for the rise of the state, it is not a sufficient one. Or, to put it another way, while we can identify war as the *mechanism* of state formation, we need also to specify the *conditions* under which it gave rise to the state.

Environmental Circumscription

How are we to determine these conditions? One promising approach is to look for those factors common to areas of the world in which states arose indigenously — areas such as the Nile, Tigris-Euphrates, and Indus valleys in the Old World and the Valley of Mexico and the mountain and coastal valleys of Peru in the New. These areas differ from one another in many ways — in altitude, temperature, rainfall, soil type, drainage pattern, and many other features. They do, however, have one thing in common: *they are all areas of circumscribed agricultural land*. Each of them is set off by mountains, seas, or deserts, and these environmental features sharply delimit the area that simple farming peoples could occupy and cultivate. In this respect these areas are very different from, say, the Amazon basin or the eastern woodlands of North America, where extensive and unbroken forests provided almost unlimited agricultural land.

But what is the significance of circumscribed agricultural land for the origin of the state? Its significance can best be understood by comparing political development in two regions of the world having contrasting ecologies — one a region with circumscribed agricultural land and the other a region where there was extensive and unlimited land. The two areas I have chosen to use in making this comparison are the coastal valleys of Peru and the Amazon basin.

Our examination begins at the stage where agricultural communities were already present but where each was still completely autonomous. Looking first at the Amazon basin, we see that agricultural villages there were numerous, but widely dispersed. Even in areas with relatively dense clustering, like the Upper Xingú basin, villages were at least 10 or 15 miles apart. Thus, the typical Amazonian community, even though it practiced a simple form of shifting cultivation which required extensive amounts of land, still had around it all the forest land needed for its gardens. For Amazonia as a whole, then, population density was low and subsistence pressure on the land was slight.

Warfare was certainly frequent in Amazonia, but it was waged for reasons of revenge, the taking of women, the gaining of personal prestige, and motives of a similar sort. There being no shortage of land, there was, by and large, no warfare over land.

The consequences of the type of warfare that did occur in Amazonia were as follows. A defeated group was not, as a rule, driven from its land. Nor did the victor make any real effort to subject the vanquished, or to exact tribute from him. This would have been difficult to accomplish in any case, since there was no effective way to prevent the losers from fleeing to a distant part of the forest. Indeed, defeated villages often chose to do just this, not so much to avoid subjugation as to avoid further attack. With settlement so sparse in Amazonia, a new area of forest could be found and occupied with relative ease, and without trespassing on the territory of another village. Moreover, since virtually any area of forest is suitable for cultivation, subsistence agriculture could be carried on in the new habitat just about as well as in the old.

It was apparently by this process of fight and flight that horticultural tribes gradually spread out until they came to cover, thinly but extensively, almost the entire Amazon basin. Thus, under the conditions of unlimited agricultural land and low population density that prevailed in Amazonia, the effect of warfare was to disperse villages over a wide area, and to keep them autonomous. With only a very few exceptions, noted below, there was no tendency in Amazonia for villages to be held in place and to combine into larger political units.

In marked contrast to the situation in Amazonia were the events that transpired in the narrow valleys of the Peruvian coast. The reconstruction of these events that I present is admittedly inferential, but I think it is consistent with the archeological evidence.

Here too our account begins at the stage of small, dispersed, and autonomous farming communities. However, instead of being scattered over a vast expanse of rain forest as they were in Amazonia, villages here were confined to some 78 short and narrow valleys.[8] Each of these valleys, moreover, was backed by the mountains, fronted by the sea, and flanked on either side by desert as dry as any in the world. Nowhere else, perhaps, can one find agricultural valleys more sharply circumscribed than these.

As with neolithic communities generally, villages of the Peruvian coastal valleys tended to grow in size. Since autonomous villages are likely to fissure as they grow, as long as land is available for the settlement of splinter communities, these villages undoubtedly split from time to time.[9]

Thus, villages tended to increase in number faster than they grew in size. This increase in the number of villages occupying a valley probably continued, without giving rise to significant changes in subsistence practices, until all the readily arable land in the valley was being farmed.

At this point two changes in agricultural techniques began to occur: the tilling of land already under cultivation was intensified, and new, previously unusable land was brought under cultivation by means of terracing and irrigation.

Yet the rate at which new arable land was created failed to keep pace with the increasing demand for it. Even before the land shortage became so acute that irrigation began to be practiced systematically, villages were undoubtedly already fighting one another over land. Prior to this time, when agricultural villages were still few in number and well supplied with land, the warfare waged in the coastal valleys of Peru had probably been of much the same type as that described above for Amazonia. With increasing pressure of human population on the land, however, the major incentive for war changed from a desire for revenge to a need to acquire land. And, as the causes of war became predominantly economic, the frequency, intensity, and importance of war increased.

Once this stage was reached, a Peruvian village that lost a war faced consequences very different from those faced by a defeated village in Amazonia. There, as we have seen, the vanquished could flee to a new locale, subsisting there about as well as they had subsisted before, and retaining their independence. In Peru, however, this alternative was no longer open to the inhabitants of defeated villages. The mountains, the desert, and the sea — to say nothing of neighboring villages — blocked escape in every direction. A village defeated in war thus faced only grim prospects. If it was allowed to remain on its own land, instead of being exterminated or expelled, this concession came only at a price. And the price was political subordination to the victor. This subordination generally entailed at least the payment of a tribute or tax in kind, which the defeated village could provide only by producing more food than it had produced before. But subordination sometimes involved a further loss of autonomy on the part of the defeated village — namely, incorporation into the political unit dominated by the victor.

Through the recurrence of warfare of this type, we see arising in coastal Peru integrated territorial units transcending the village in size and in degree of organization. Political evolution was attaining the level of the chiefdom.

As land shortages continued and became even more acute, so did warfare. Now, however, the competing units were no longer small villages but, often, large chiefdoms. From this point on, through the conquest of chiefdom by chiefdom, the size of political units increased at a progressively faster rate. Naturally, as autonomous political units increased in size, they decreased in number, with the result that an entire valley was eventually unified under the banner of its strongest chiefdom. The political unit thus formed was undoubtedly sufficiently centralized and complex to warrant being called a state.

The political evolution I have described for one valley of Peru was also taking place in other valleys, in the highlands as well as on the coast.[10] Once valley-wide kingdoms emerged, the next step was the formation of multivalley kingdoms through the conquest of weaker valleys by stronger ones. The culmination of this process was the conquest[11] of all of Peru by its most powerful state, and the formation of a single great empire. Although this step may have occurred once or twice before in Andean history, it was achieved most notably, and for the last time, by the Incas.[12]

Political Evolution

While the aggregation of villages into chiefdoms, and of chiefdoms into kingdoms, was occurring by external acquisition, the structure of these increasingly larger political units was being elaborated by internal evolution. These inner changes were, of course, closely related to outer events. The expansion of successful states brought within their borders conquered peoples and territory which had to be administered. And it was the individuals who had distinguished themselves in war who were generally appointed to political office and assigned the task of carrying out this administration. Besides maintaining law and order and collecting taxes, the functions of this burgeoning class of administrators included mobilizing labor for building irrigation works, roads, fortresses, palaces, and temples. Thus, their functions helped to weld an assorted collection of petty states into a single integrated and centralized political unit.

These same individuals, who owed their improved social position to their exploits in war, became, along with the ruler and his kinsmen, the nucleus of an upper class. A lower class in turn emerged from the prisoners taken in war and employed as servants and slaves by their captors. In this manner did war contribute to the rise of social classes.

I noted earlier that peoples attempt to acquire their neighbors' land before they have made the fullest possible use of their own. This implies that every autonomous village has an untapped margin of food productivity, and that this margin is squeezed out only when the village is subjugated and compelled to pay taxes in kind. The surplus food extracted from conquered villages through taxation, which in the aggregate attained very significant proportions, went largely to support the ruler, his warriors and retainers, officials, priests, and other members of the rising upper class, who thus became completely divorced from food production.

Finally, those made landless by war but not enslaved tended to gravitate to settlements which, because of their specialized administrative, commercial, or religious functions, were growing into towns and cities. Here they were able to make a living as workers and artisans, exchanging their labor or their wares for part of the economic surplus exacted from village farmers by the ruling class and spent by members of that class to raise their standard of living.

The process of political evolution which I have outlined for the coastal valleys of Peru was, in its essential features, by no means unique to this region. Areas of circumscribed agricultural land elsewhere in the world, such as the Valley of Mexico, Mesopotamia, the Nile Valley, and the Indus Valley, saw the process occur in much the same way and for essentially the same reasons. In these areas, too, autonomous neolithic villages were succeeded by chiefdoms, chiefdoms by kingdoms, and kingdoms by empires. The last stage of this development was, of course, the most impressive. The scale and magnificence attained by the early empires overshadowed everything that had gone before. But, in a sense, empires were merely the logical culmination of the process. The really fundamental step, the one that had triggered the entire train of events that led to empires, was the change from village autonomy to supravillage integration. This step was a change in kind; everything that followed was, in a way, only a change in degree.

In addition to being pivotal, the step to supracommunity aggregation was difficult, for it took two million years to achieve. But, once it was achieved, once village autonomy was transcended, only two or three millennia were required for the rise of great empires and the flourishing of complex civilizations.

Resource Concentration

Theories are first formulated on the basis of a limited number of facts. Eventually, though, a theory must confront all of the facts. And often new facts are stubborn and do not conform to the theory, or do not conform very well. What distinguishes a successful theory from an unsuccessful one is that it can be modified or elaborated to accommodate the entire range of facts. Let us see how well the "circumscription theory" holds up when it is brought face-to-face with certain facts that appear to be exceptions.

For the first test let us return to Amazonia. Early voyagers down the Amazon left written testimony of a culture along that river higher than the culture I have described for Amazonia generally. In the 1500s, the native population living on the banks of the Amazon was relatively dense, villages were fairly large and close together, and some degree of social stratification existed. Moreover, here and there a paramount chief held sway over many communities.

The question immediately arises: With unbroken stretches of arable land extending back from the Amazon for hundreds of miles, why were there chiefdoms here?

To answer this question we must look closely at the environmental conditions afforded by the Amazon. Along the margins of the river itself, and on islands within it, there is a type of land called *várzea*. The river floods this land every year, covering it with a layer of fertile silt. Because of this annual replenishment, *várzea* is agricultural land of first quality which can be cultivated year after year without ever having to lie fallow. Thus, among native farmers it was highly prized and greatly coveted. The waters of the Amazon were also extraordinarily bountiful, providing fish, manatees, turtles and turtle eggs, caimans, and other riverine foods in inexhaustible amounts. By virtue of this concentration of resources, the Amazon, as a habitat, was distinctly superior to its hinterlands.

Concentration of resources along the Amazon amounted almost to a kind of circumscription. While there was no sharp cleavage between productive and unproductive land, as there was in Peru, there was at least a steep ecological gradient. So much more rewarding was the Amazon River than adjacent areas, and so desirable did it become as habitat, that peoples were drawn to it from surrounding regions. Eventually crowding occurred along many portions of the river, leading to warfare over sections of river front. And the losers in war, in order to retain access to the river, often had no choice but to submit to the victors. By this subordination of villages to a paramount chief there arose along the Amazon chiefdoms representing a higher step in political evolution than had occurred elsewhere in the basin.[13]

The notion of resource concentration also helps to explain the surprising degree of political development apparently attained by peoples of the Peruvian coast while they were still depending primarily on fishing for subsistence, and only secondarily on agriculture. Of this seeming anomaly, E.P. Lanning has written: "To the best of my knowledge, this is the only case in which so many of the characteristics of civilization have been found without a basically agricultural economic foundation."

Armed with the concept of resource concentration, however, we can show that this development was not so anomalous after all. The explanation, it seems to me, runs as follows. Along the coast of Peru, wild food sources occurred in considerable number and variety. However, they were restricted to a very narrow margin of land.[14] Accordingly, while the *abundance* of food in this zone led to a sharp rise in population, the *restrictedness* of this food soon resulted in the almost complete occupation of exploitable areas. And when pressure on the available resources reached a critical level, competition over land ensued. The result of this competition was to set in motion the sequence of events of political evolution that I have described.

Thus, it seems that we can safely add resource concentration to environmental circumscription as a factor leading to warfare over land, and thus to political integration beyond the village level.

Social Circumscription

But there is still another factor to be considered in accounting for the rise of the state.

In dealing with the theory of environmental circumscription while discussing the Yanomamö Indians of Venezuela, Napoleon A. Chagnon has introduced the concept of "social circumscription." By this he means that a high density of population in an area can produce effects on peoples living near the center of the area that are similar to effects produced by environmental circumscription. This notion seems to me to be an important addition to our theory. Let us see how, according to Chagnon, social circumscription has operated among the Yanomamö.

The Yanomamö, who number some 10,000, live in an extensive region of noncircumscribed rain forest, away from any large river. One might expect that Yanomamö villages would thus be more or less evenly spaced. However, Chagnon notes that, at the center of Yanomamö territory, villages are closer together than they are at the periphery. Because of this, they tend to impinge on one another more, with the result that warfare is more frequent and intense in the center than in peripheral areas. Moreover, it is more difficult for villages in the nuclear area to escape attack by moving away, since, unlike villages on the periphery, their ability to move is somewhat restricted.

The net result is that villages in the central areas of Yanomamö territory are larger than villages in the other areas, since large village size is an advantage for both attack and defense. A further effect of more intense warfare in the nuclear area is that village headmen are stronger in that area. Yanomamö headmen are also the war leaders, and their influence increases in proportion to their village's participation in war. In addition, offensive and defensive alliances between villages are more common in the center of Yanomamö territory than in outlying areas. Thus, while still at the autonomous village level of political organization, those Yanomamö subject to social circumscription have clearly moved a step or two in the direction of higher political development.

Although the Yanomamö manifest social circumscription only to a modest degree, this amount of it has been enough to make a difference in their level of political organization. What the effects of social circumscription would be in areas where it was more fully expressed should, therefore, be clear. First would come a reduction in the size of the territory of each village. Then, as population pressure became more severe, warfare over land would ensue. But because adjacent land for miles around was already the property of other villages, a defeated village would have nowhere to flee. From this point on, the consequences of warfare for that village, and for political evolution in general, would be essentially as I have described them for the situation of environmental circumscription.

To return to Amazonia, it is clear that, if social circumscription is operative among the Yanomamö today, it was certainly operative among the tribes of the Amazon River four hundred years ago. And its effect would undoubtedly have been to give a further spur to political evolution in that region.

We see then that, even in the absence of sharp environmental circumscription, the factors of resource concentration and social circumscription may, by intensifying war and redirecting it toward the taking of land, give a strong impetus to political development.

With these auxiliary hypotheses incorporated into it, the circumscription theory is now better able to confront the entire range of test cases that can be brought before it. For example, it can now account for the rise of the state in the Hwang Valley of northern China, and even in the Petén region of the Maya lowlands, areas not characterized by strictly circumscribed agricultural land. In the case of the Hwang Valley, there is no question that resource concentration and social circumscription were present and active forces. In the lowland Maya area, resource concentration seems not to have been a major factor, but social circumscription may well have been.

Some archeologists may object that population density in the Petén during Formative times was too low to give rise to social circumscription. But, in assessing what constitutes a population dense enough to produce this effect, we must consider not so much the total land area occupied as the amount of land needed to support the existing population. And the size of this supporting area depends not only on the size of the population but also on the mode of subsistence. The shifting cultivation presumably practiced by the ancient Maya required considerably more land, per capita, than did the permanent field cultivation of, say, the Valley of Mexico or the coast of Peru.[15] Consequently, insofar as its effects are concerned, a relatively low population density in the Petén may have been equivalent to a much higher one in Mexico or Peru.

We have already learned from the Yanomamö example that social circumscription may begin to operate while population is still relatively sparse. And we can be sure that the Petén was far more densely peopled in Formative times than Yanomamö territory is today. Thus, population density among the lowland Maya, while giving a superficial appearance of sparseness, may actually have been high enough to provoke fighting over land, and thus provide the initial impetus for the formation of a state.

Conclusion

In summary, then, the circumscription theory in its elaborated form goes far toward accounting for the origin of the state. It explains why states arose where they did, and why they failed to arise elsewhere. It shows the state to be a predictable response to certain specific cultural, demographic, and ecological conditions. Thus, it helps to elucidate what was undoubtedly the most important single step ever taken in the political evolution of mankind.

Notes

1. R.L. Carneiro, in *The Evolution of Horticultural Systems in Native South America: Causes and Consequences; A Symposium*, edited by J. Wilbert, *Antropológica (Venezuela)*, Suppl. 2 (1961): 47–67, see especially pp. 59–64.

2. For example, the early American sociologist Lester F. Ward saw the state as "the result of an extraordinary exercise of the rational ... faculty" which seemed to him so exceptional that "it must have been the emanation of a single brain or a few concerting minds...."

3. I have in my files recorded instances of surplus food production by such Amazonian tribes as the Tupinambá, Jivaro, Mundurucú, Tucano, Desana, Cubeo, and Canela. An exhaustive search of the ethnographic literature for this region would undoubtedly reveal many more examples.

4. Wittfogel states: "These patterns [of organization and social control — that is, the state] come into being when an experimenting community of farmers or protofarmers finds large sources of moisture in a dry but potentially fertile area.... a number of farmers eager to conquer [agriculturally, not militarily] arid lowlands and plains are forced to invoke the organizational devices which — on the basis of premachine technology — offer the one chance of success; they must work in cooperation with their fellows and subordinate themselves to a directing authority."

5. For Mesopotamia, Robert M. Adams has concluded: "In short, there is nothing to suggest that the rise of dynastic authority in southern Mesopotamia was linked to the administrative requirements of a major canal system." For China, the protypical area for Wittfogel's hydraulic theories, the French Sinologist Jacques Gernet has recently written: "although the establishment of a system of regulation of water courses and irrigation, and the control of this system, may have affected the political constitution of the military states and imperial China, the fact remains that, historically, it was the pre-existing state structures and the large, well-trained labour force provided by the armies that made the great irrigation projects possible." For Mexico, large-scale irrigation systems do not appear to antedate the Classic period, whereas it is clear that the first states arose in the preceding Formative or Pre-Classic period.

6. This is not to say, of course, that large-scale irrigation, where it occurred, did not contribute significantly to increasing the power and scope of the state. It unquestionably did. To the extent that Wittfogel limits himself to this contention, I have no quarrel with him whatever. However, the point at issue is not how the state increased its power but how it arose in the first place. And to this issue the hydraulic hypothesis does not appear to hold the key.

7. For example, Julian H. Steward wrote: "It is possible, therefore, that the Maya were able to develop a high civilization only because they enjoyed an unusually long period of peace; for their settlement pattern would seem to have been too vulnerable to warfare."

8. In early agricultural times (Preceramic Period VI, beginning about 2500 B.C.), human settlement seems to have been denser along the coast than in the river valleys, and subsistence appears to have been based more on fishing than on farming. Furthermore, some significant first steps in political evolution beyond autonomous villages may have been taken at this stage. However, once subsistence began to be based predominantly on agriculture, the settlement pattern changed, and communities were henceforth concentrated more in the river valleys, where the only land of any size suitable for cultivation was located.

9. In my files I find reported instances of village splitting among the following Amazonian tribes: Kuikuru, Amarakaeri, Cubeo, Urubú, Tuparí, Yanomamö, Tucano, Tenetehara, Canela, and Northern Cayapó. Under the conditions of easy resettlement found in Amazonia, splitting often takes place at a village population level of less than 100, and village size seldom exceeds 200. In coastal Peru, however, where land was severely restricted, villages could not fission so readily, and thus grew to population levels which, according to E.P. Lanning, may have averaged over 300.

10. Naturally, this evolution took place in the various Peruvian valleys at different rates and to different degrees. In fact it is possible that at the same time that some valleys were already unified politically, others still had not evolved beyond the stage of autonomous villages.

11. Not every step in empire building was necessarily taken through actual physical conquest, however. The threat of force sometimes had the same effect as its exercise. In this way many smaller chiefdoms and states were probably coerced into giving up their sovereignty without having to be defeated on the field of battle. Indeed, it was an explicit policy of the Incas, in expanding their empire, to try persuasion before resorting to force of arms.

12. The evolution of empire in Peru was thus by no means rectilinear or irreversible. Advance alternated with decline. Integration was sometimes followed by disintegration, with states fragmenting back to chiefdoms, and perhaps even to autonomous villages. But the forces underlying political development were strong and, in the end, prevailed. Thus, despite fluctuations and reversions, the course of evolution in Peru was unmistakable: it began with many small, simple, scattered, and autonomous communities and ended with a single vast, complex, and centralized empire.

13. Actually, a similar political development did take place in another part of Amazonia — the basin of the Mamoré River in the Mojos plain of Bolivia. Here, too, resource concentration appears to have played a key role. In native North America north of Mexico the highest cultural development attained, Middle-Mississippi, also occurred along a major river (the Mississippi), which, by providing especially fertile soil and riverine food resources, comprised a zone of resource concentration.

14. Resource concentration, then, was here combined with environmental circumscription. And, indeed, the same thing can be said of the great desert river valleys, such as the Nile, Tigris-Euphrates, and Indus.

15. One can assume, I think, that any substantial increase in population density among the Maya was accompanied by a certain intensification of agriculture. As the population increased, fields were probably weeded more thoroughly, and they may well have been cultivated a year or two longer and fallowed a few years less. Yet, given the nature of soils in the humid tropics, the absence of any evidence of fertilization, and the moderate population densities, it seems likely that Maya farming remained extensive rather than becoming intensive.

43
Cyclical Conquests

JULIAN H. STEWARD and LOUIS C. FARON

Cyclical Conquests: Prehistoric Empires

A state functions in two capacities: first it is an integrating and coordinating agency that serves the needs of its people; second, it is a consuming institution that demands goods and services from the people. In the first capacity, it arranges that a certain portion of the effort of its component communities and classes be channeled into projects that are beneficial to everyone. An irrigation state plans, creates, and manages waterworks that increase the yield of farm land, and it brings new land under cultivation. In order to do this, however, it must devise a political organization and a power structure. In a prescientific era, it may back its power with supernaturalism, that is, with a state church or cult; and it may have to employ military force if the groups that it seeks to bring into cooperation resist rational or supernatural appeals.

Once state political, religious, and military institutions are created, they exist of their own right and for their own sake as well as to serve the public. Special classes of people — lords, priests,

From Julian H. Steward and Louis C. Faron, *Native Peoples of South America*, McGraw-Hill, 1959, pp. 100–109. (Bibliographic documentation contained in the original text is omitted here. Interested readers should consult the original publication.)

soldiers, or bureaucrats, as the case may be — become identified with state institutions and functions and have to be supported by the public. In the irrigation civilizations of the north coast of Peru, the warrior-priests were, in effect, the state. So long as an economy is expanding through improved technology and the exploitation of new and abundant resources, the state may demand a constantly increasing amount of productive output without endangering itself. During the Era of Regional Florescence, as we have seen, the state exacted ever larger portions of national productive effort, as is witnessed by the construction of larger and larger mounds, temples, palaces, and forts and the manufacture of mounting quantities of ceremonial and luxury goods. When technological progress ceases and new resources are not available to support larger numbers of specialists, demands upon the society cannot be augmented indefinitely. Apparently, however, no state has ever been content to live within its own productive capacity, to remain in a condition of economic and cultural equilibrium or *status quo*. When the state rulers have finally exacted all that the local traffic will bear, their only recourse is to acquire a portion of the output of other states. A predatory primitive society may carry out sporadic raids against its neighbors and bring home the loot. More developed states, such as those of the Central Andes, however, insist upon continued and assured access to their neighbors as tribute-paying vassals, or they expand their own political structure and incorporate their neighbors into a multistate empire.

An empire by this definition is a group of states — size is less important than the nature of the structure — which have been forcibly subjugated by a single, more powerful state in order that a portion of their produce may be appropriated to the institutions of the dominant state, that is, to the classes which in effect are the state. The empire may increase the security of its people through socialistic measures, as the Inca did, but its principal reason for being is to control and appropriate production. This is an economic definition of empire, but it is required by the facts. It is doubtful whether history discloses any true empires that were built primarily to impose their religion on alien peoples or to afford an outlet to militarism for its own sake.

In the early irrigation civilizations, independent states were qualitatively different from empires. Whereas the state existed in an expanding economy and primarily served public interest, the empire was a phenomenon of a rather frozen economy. While it endeavored to increase production and may have brought a slight population increase, expansion was reaching its limits. In time, the standard of living of the general population was lowered through greater demands for goods and services. The native empire had then to develop a strong political and legal system to control its people. Centralization of administrative, military, and religious controls led to large centers of population concentration, or cities.

Imperial warfare was carried on primarily for conquest. Inca warfare contrasted with that of the Regional Florescent cultures in that captive taking to supply the temple with sacrificial victims was given up. It also contrasted with that of the Circum-Caribbean peoples in that the latter, who evidently resembled the Regional Florescent cultures in their military patterns, not only took prisoners but allowed individual soldiers an opportunity to improve their social status. The custom of building walled cities instead of relying on hilltop forts as refuges also shows a change in warfare. Service in the army is but one of the many services required by the empire of the common man, whose inability to achieve upward social mobility is a characteristic of imperial society. As population pressures increased, class distinctions became frozen. Military, political, and religious statuses became fixed in a complex, hereditary hierarchy. Conquered states were not dissolved; they were fitted into the imperial

hierarchy under the overlordship of their conquerors. Manufactured products also reflect imperial social regimentation. Local styles and a fairly free and vigorous art gave way to forms and designs which, though technically excellent, were standardized and mass-produced.

This analysis of empires may be stated differently by saying that an empire represents a level of sociocultural integration that is higher and qualitatively different from the state level, just as the latter is different from the community level. An empire, therefore, can be viewed in terms of at least three different levels of internal integration. The folk communities form the lowest or basic level. They carry on the primary functions of producing goods for their own consumption, procreating and rearing children, and living day by day in the context of local social and religious life. The archaeological evidence shows that domestic house types, utensils, shamanism, and family organization changed comparatively little during the long sequence of prehistoric periods. The multicommunity, theocratic state represents the second level. The state developed wholly new forms of religion, political and economic organization, and militarism. The folk of the local communities contributed goods and services to the state, participated in the ceremonialism, and probably profited by the trade which followed local specialization. But their community activities were very similar to those of independent folk villages. The empire, an amalgamation of states, constitutes the third level. It is like an additional layer of culture superimposed upon the other two layers. The states were not destroyed; their institutions and leaders were incorporated into the larger hierarchy.

It is admittedly difficult to recognize the patterns of empire and the processes of their formation with certainty in archaeological data. We know, however, that the Inca had built a tremendous empire by the time of the Spanish Conquest, and there must have been some point at which the conditions leading to empire appeared. The end of the Era of Regional Florescence seems to be this point.

During the Era of Regional Florescence, the states developed internally. Production was expanding, population increased, more and more individuals became specialists, and the socio-politico-religious structure became well defined. The technical and aesthetic achievements of the era were direct responses to the stimulus of state elaboration.

Toward the end of the Era of Regional Florescence, the conditions of imperialism were beginning to appear. Irrigation agriculture had been brought near maximum productiveness in most regions, the basic technologies were fully established, and the population had expanded close to its limits. A very large proportion of the productive effort was being devoted to state institutions. Militarism was strongly developed, and while it served religion through supplying sacrificial victims, it had also become an implement of imperialism.

As W.C. Bennett and J.B. Bird interpret the archaeological data, the Mochica had already occupied five of the major north-coast valleys; the Lambayeque, still farther north, were spreading their influence to neighboring regions; the Recuay and Cajamarca cultures of the north highland were expanding their territories even as far as the coast; and the central coastal valleys were united stylistically, if not politically. "This widespread expansion resulted in considerable conflict and confusion. In some regions, the irrigation systems seem to have broken down and the populations diminished and scattered. In fact, the peoples of the central Andes apparently became engaged in serious internecine warfare."

Changes in the Virú Valley during the Tiahuanaco period are illustrative of those which occurred widely throughout Peru under the domination of an empire. There are about a hundred communities of this period, but the total population is little, if any, larger than previously. The difference lies in a tendency of some of the population to concentrate in planned centers. Such sites often consist of walled compounds, the houses being laid out in rows. The larger sites, or cities, have mounds and temples inside the walls.

The Virú Valley people had probably already been members of a state which included neighboring valleys. It was part of the Mochica-culture area, which had distinctive types and styles of materials and included a number of states. During the Tiahuanaco period, however, a new culture abruptly appeared. It is found not only in the Virú Valley and the Mochica area but throughout most of Peru, where it partly replaced local styles. The Tiahuanaco culture is characterized mainly by an art style, by certain religious motifs, and by a considerable number of distinctive cultural objects.

How can we account for these sudden innovations? The Tiahuanaco culture certainly consisted in part of new religious concepts and practices. For this reason, some authorities are disposed to regard it as primarily a cult movement, which somehow caught on and was readily adopted throughout the country. They consider it comparable to the Formative period cult with its feline god, which made the Central Andes fairly homogeneous in ceremonial manifestations but failed to unite it politically. That Tiahuanaco influences brought a new cult cannot be doubted, but its comparability to the Chavín-Cupisnique-Ancón religion is very questionable.

The religious pattern of the Formative Era was introduced to people who had previously had no state level of religious organization. Pre-Formative ceremonialism was limited to a simple complex involving community shrines. Village acceptance of the Formative Era mounds, temples, and feline deity met with no opposition from an established state or cult religion. The readiness with which the ceremonialism was accepted is indicated by the spread of mounds, temples, and even the rather distinctive style of pottery through Meso-America northward into the Mississippi Valley. The Tiahuanaco cult, on the other hand, confronted firmly entrenched local state cults or religions in every valley. These local religions, moreover, were strongly integrated with state structure. Local societies would not be likely to acknowledge the supremacy of new gods and to adopt new forms of worship merely because these had become fashionable among their neighbors or because they were advocated by some proselytizing priests.

The fundamental conditions of empire formation were present when the Tiahuanaco period started, and the most convincing explanation for the spread of this culture is that it was imposed upon Peru by a military conquest. If the Tiahuanaco Empire seems large, we have only to remember that the Inca Empire was much larger, extending some two thousand miles along the Andes, and that it was built up in less than a hundred years. We cannot prove, of course, that the area affected by the Tiahuanaco culture was an empire, but there is no equally good explanation why so many regions rather suddenly abandoned local practices or why, after a fairly short period, the Tiahuanaco features themselves were given up and the local customs resumed. The fact that symbols of local regions were revived after a short time strongly suggests that the local religions had been forcibly suppressed.

The Tiahuanaco culture took form in the southern Andean highlands, although it is not certain that this region is the center of dispersal for the culture or the seat of its empire. The site of Tiahuanaco, which lies in the Altiplano some 12,000 feet above sea level 12 miles south of Lake Titicaca in Bolivia, however, contains what is considered a "pure" Tiahuanaco culture, a culture that developed locally and was not mixed with features derived from other regional cultures. Therefore, presumably, it shows in unadulterated form the elements which characterize this culture.

The site covers a large area and contains a tremendous number of platforms, courts, mounds, stone structures, and carved stones which probably date from several periods. The "classical" complex is represented by a group of four major structural units consisting of courts, stairways, gates, and buildings. These are notable both for the architectural skill evidenced in large-scale planning and for the vast regimentation of sheer manpower involved in construction. Several features are diagnostic of Tiahuanaco architecture. Many of the stones, some of which weigh up to 100 tons, have been transported more than three miles from the quarry. Prior to construction, the stones were wrought into rectangular forms with complicated angles, yet they were somehow fitted together and joined by copper cramps. Some of the construction was monolithic. In a number of cases, a huge gateway or a gateway and stairs were carved from a single stone. What amounted almost to a compulsion for stonecutting led these builders to carve out stone seats and other forms even in solid rock.

The major construction at Tiahuanaco was erected around a low natural hill that was shaped into a faced mound, some 700 feet square and 50 feet high, surmounted by house sites and a reservoir. Perhaps this served as a fortress. Another structure is a rectangular platform about 450 feet square, faced with large vertical slabs between which are smaller stones. An inner court, 190 by 130 feet, was entered by a megalithic stairway. This contains stone statues and the famous monolithic gateway, the "Gateway of the Sun." This last is a single huge rectangular piece of stone, 10 feet tall, carved with human, condor, and sun symbols.

Construction similar to that at the site of Tiahuanaco has been found elsewhere in Peru, but a more widespread diagnostic of the period is the stone carving. Carved forms include statues, friezes on gateways and buildings, and human and animal heads attached to buildings by tenons. Human statues are squarish, rigid figures of standing men with their hands on their bellies. The identifying stylistic features of the flat carvings were also represented on ceramics and textile designs. The eyes are shown with one or two tear streaks. This "weeping god," who first appeared in the Regional Developmental Era in a different style, is very characteristic of the Tiahuanaco culture. In full face, the eyebrows meet to form a T with the nose. Front views depict human beings with a staff in each hand. Side views show men wearing a puma or condor mask and often running with a cape flying out behind. Designs characteristically have appendages, which end in puma, condor, or fish heads. Geometric designs include rectilinear, stepped elements.

Ceramics, which are made in a number of distinctive forms, bear similar decorations in polychrome on a red background. The design is outlined in one or two colors. Textiles have not been found at Tiahuanaco, but they are represented in the dress of the carved figures and show the same designs as these figures. Tie dyeing, the tying of portions of cloth so that dye will not penetrate, and ikat, the tie dyeing of individual threads, were processes introduced at this time.

The Tiahuanaco culture attained a very wide distribution, although it did not equal the Inca. It spread to Cochabamba in eastern Bolivia, Arequipa in southern Peru, Calama in northern Chile, and all of Peru except Huamachuco and Cajamarca in the north highlands and Lambayeque and Piura on the north coast. The center from which this cultural and political conquest emanated is not known. Tiahuanaco is an impressive site, but it was not necessarily the capital of the empire. The highlands have been so incompletely explored that every few years major spectacular ruins are discovered, after which comes the exacting work of examining them scientifically so as to ascertain their chronological and cultural position.

The center of the empire, however, was certainly in the highlands, which were more deeply affected by the Tiahuanaco culture than the coast; for it is there that the full complex of structural remains as well as ceramic and textile styles are found. Wari, in the central highlands, has large pillars, statues, dressed stone tombs, and other lithic features. The coastal sites, on the other hand, show Tiahuanaco influence more in the ornamentation of ceramics, textiles, and other goods than in major constructions. Evidently the conquerors had not had time to build in their own style on the coast and used existing mounds and temples. It should be noted, however, that the highland had always built more with stone and the coast with adobe. Each material requires special constructional methods.

A.L. Kroeber pointed out many years ago that the major cultural impulses in Peruvian development seemed to emanate from the highlands. It is certainly true that all the Pan-Peruvian cultures are most strongly represented in the highlands. The Formative Era Chavín culture, though found on the coast, had it most impressive site in the north highland. Tiahuanaco was of highland origin and fades somewhat on the coast. The Inca were also of highland origin.

It is probable that geographical factors account for the wide spread of culture in the highlands. It is fairly continuously settled country, whose major deep valleys run north and south and are not a barrier to communication. Culture can spread rapidly throughout this area, except in the extreme south, where deserts are encountered. The coast, on the other hand, is completely arid and uninhabitable except where rivers reach the sea. The oasislike valleys had easier communication with the interior highland than with one another.

The Tiahuanaco culture undoubtedly reached all parts of the coast from the interior. As the empire did not endure more than two hundred years, its failure to introduce architectural styles to the coast may mean that there was insufficient time. The Tiahuanaco conquest, however, probably also encountered rather serious resistance, for the isolation of the north coast valleys from one another had begun to break down during the Regional Florescent Era, when coastwise roads and seacoast navigation put the small valleys in touch with one another and furthered political amalgamation of this region.

The Tiahuanaco conquest by no means gave complete cultural unity to the Central Andes. The north coast not only preserved its local architecture and some of its art styles, but it improved its metallurgy through using copper-arsenic alloys and silver plating. The north highlands continued to construct temples or to use older temples in the general architectural tradition of the castillos of the Formative Era Chavín culture, and it buried its dead in stone grave boxes. The south coast practiced urn burial, manufactured silver-copper alloys, and maintained its excellence in textile manufacture. The central highlands were distinguished by their two-color negative-painted pots. None of these regional characteristics is found at the classical site of Tiahuanaco.

Toward the end of the Tiahuanaco period, a new style of painting ceramics in black, white, and red attained a minor vogue throughout the empire, but it was not accompanied by other cultural features of significance.

The rise and fall of empires is the inexorable result of cultural forces and not the unpredictable consequence of military encounters, political maneuvers, and other factors which depend fortuitously upon individual decisions. The conditions and processes which led to the formation of the Tiahuanaco Empire also contained the seeds of its destruction and of the rise of another empire.

An empire as conceived here is a device for concentrating goods and services in the hands of a ruling hierarchy. It regiments and organizes production, but the ancient irrigation empires had little scope for expanding production. When population pressure relative to a fixed amount of production becomes serious and the standard of living of the common man has decreased to the point of threatening his survival, the political and economic patterns of empire can no longer be supported. Local revolts overthrow alien cults and rulers, despite every effort to maintain order through armed force. In the ensuing chaos, it is probable that irrigation works are not kept up, production drops off, and famine decimates the population. There is an interim of dark ages. Local sovereigns finally return to power, irrigation works are repaired, local religious cults are resurrected, and there follows a period of regional states, or lesser empires, before one or another of these gains supremacy in the constant struggle for power. China and the Near East both endured some two thousand years of cyclical conquests — periods of warring states followed by imperial growth — after their florescent ages. The Central Andes had reached the peak of its second empire, that of the Inca, when the Spaniards arrived.

The rise and fall of empires entailed cultural changes only to a minor extent. Essentially, the cycles represented social change within the framework of a fairly fixed cultural pattern and complex. The basic technologies and productive processes of the Central Andes were unaltered after the Era of Regional Florescence. During the Era of Conquests, each peak of empire brought a florescence of cultural features associated with the imperial institutions. While Inca architecture, religious concepts, and art styles differed from those of Tiahuanaco, both empires made outstanding achievements. But considerable state culture survived the Tiahuanaco Empire and reinstated itself when the empire fell. The folk or community culture survived all these changes comparatively intact; in fact, it lasted well into the Spanish period in spite of national or imperial institutions introduced from the Old World.

44
The Political Economy of the Aztec and Inca States

PEDRO CARRASCO

Comparisons of the Aztec and Inca systems have often stressed their differences in order to define the individuality of each case. This chapter emphasizes their similarities. The shared features that make up a common type of economic organization are first formulated and the points of contrast are later discussed in terms of this common system.

My interpretation of both the Inca and Aztec economic organizations being of a common type depends to a large extent on my theoretical basis. I hold that production is the key area in the organization of any economy and that the understanding of any economic system and the establishment of any typology has to take as its central point the analysis of production. In the process of production converge, first, the material factors of production, that is, the natural resources exploited and the tools employed; second, the relations of production, that is, the social relations that occur in the process of production; and third, the property system, in other words, the rights that men have over material goods. In this way, the analysis of production compels us from the start to examine ecology, technology, and social structure as well

as the relations among them. It is thus a key to all basic social processes.

Economic Organization

The basic and most significant characteristic of the Aztec and Inca economies is that they were politically organized economies; that is, the economic process was embedded in the political institutions of a stratified society. The common system can be briefly defined as follows.

The basic subsistence technique is intensive agriculture on permanent fields relying exclusively on human energy with the use of simple tools. The basic factors of production, land and labor, are controlled by the political organization. Two major categories of land exist. One is in the possession of the peasants, who produce for their own support as household units with supplementary help from labor exchange and cooperation at the community level. These peasant producers are always subject to the rendering of labor services and in some places also of tribute in kind. The peasant household, therefore, is one of the major units of production in these societies. The other type of land is held by institutions or members of the ruling level and is worked with the labor services of peasants. It is thus the basis for other production units; these are managed by institutions or members of the upper social level who use public lands and the labor services of the commoners assigned to them. The labor for units larger than the household is always provided as politically required services from determined status groups. Craft production takes place along similar lines either in household units or under the management of upper level institutions based on public resources and the labor services required from artisans.

Circulation takes place primarily in accord with administrative decisions, and wealth is distributed on the basis of status. In the case of the ruling estate, income is received primarily in the form of products from public lands and shares from other forms of revenue. The market mechanism exists to fill the gaps left by the politically defined distribution. It is of secondary importance because it does not enter into the process of production; land and labor are not handled as commodities.

The surplus appropriated by the ruling estate is used in maintaining its members and their privileged status, in the support of public works for the common good (such as irrigation works), and in ostentation (much of it in religious ceremony).

Let us examine these various features in more detail.

As in all archaic civilizations, intensive agriculture was the material basis of Mesoamerican and Andean societies. Generally, intensive methods of cultivation with high levels of productivity permit a more complex division of labor and the existence of a numerous population. Intensive cultivation also results in permanent utilization of the soil and in forms of ownership and control of the land that will direct part of what is produced to persons other than the cultivator himself.

A variety of techniques was used in both Mesoamerica and the Andes, according to the nature of the lands and of the plants under cultivation: irrigation, fertilization, and modifications of the natural configuration of the land (by such means as terraces and raised or sunken fields). These techniques make cultivated land itself partly a product of human effort.

Agriculture was carried on with only rudimentary tools, and an intensive investment of labor was of greater importance than the complexity of the tools employed. The number of cultigens was very high and provided both food and raw materials for crafts. Given the great environmental variety in these two areas of civilization, almost all the plants that had been domesticated in the Americas could be cultivated in both areas.

In contrast with the great number of cultigens, very few domestic animals were kept, and their use was less varied and more restricted geographically than in Old World civilizations. In any case, with the exception of the partial use of llama manure as fertilizer, domestic animals were not integrated into the agricultural technology.

Industry was at a technical level similar to that of agriculture. The most highly developed were characterized by intensive and highly skilled human effort using simple tools. The slight utilitarian use of metal and the absence of the wheel and of work animals make clear the technical limitations of both industry and agriculture.

A characteristic of both centers of civilization in the New World was large-scale construction using great masses of workers. This is seem most memorably in the monumental architecture of public buildings such as temples, palaces, and storehouses; other examples include fortresses, roads, irrigation systems, dikes, and terracing that utilized and conserved hilly terrain. All such works constitute either the infrastructure necessary for the production and circulation of goods that are fundamental to the society, or else the means of demonstrating and maintaining the power of the rulers.

In spite of important differences, Mesoamerica and the Andean region present similar environmental factors: Both lie within the tropics and are crossed by high mountain ranges. This means in both cases that the land is divided into a great number of clearly separated natural regions that present different ecological conditions and resources.

The environmental diversity was related to the ethnic multiplicity and regionalism that were characteristic of both areas. From an economic point of view the diversity of resources in contiguous zones encouraged relations of interdependence among the inhabitants of different econiches. This was achieved through a variety of procedures. At times a given social unit utilized different environments directly; in other cases, different social groups exploited different environmental resources and were connected through systems of exchange based either on political relations or on commerce.

For the conservation and transmission of information certain techniques, such as the Inca *quipus* and the Mesoamerican pictographs, were used. These served as mnemonic aids and permitted the recording of numerical data necessary for the management of the economy. However, neither area had a true writing system, that is, a means of reproducing oral texts in their entirety. Only when Maya inscriptions have been completely deciphered will we know to what extent there may have been an exception in their case.

In both Mesoamerica and the Andes the sixteenth-century writers tell us that peasants were jacks-of-all-trades who could take care of all the basic necessities of their households, in agriculture as well as in craft production. Members of the family group constructed the simple peasant house and wove cloth for the family's clothes. To a large extent, therefore, the peasant household was organized as a self-sufficient unit. Some of the artisans who produced for the use of others were only part-time specialists, who also cultivated some land for their own subsistence. Thus, like the farmers, they were producing both for their own needs and also for local exchange; in addition, they either paid tribute or gave labor services in their specialized activities. The more intensive specialization was associated with the highly skilled crafts of artisans working for the upper level of society. In this case their products would be luxury objects for the rulers or buildings and ceremonial objects for state activities.

The cultivation of lands assigned to members and institutions of the ruling class and the construction of public works were effected through the personal services exacted from the mass of peasants. There are two basic elements in this system: First, the workers rendered their services during limited periods of time; second, because of the lack of draft animals and machinery a great number of workers were needed to accumulate sufficient work energy. These two elements were especially true in construction works, which is where the simple cooperation of great masses of workers was most used. Therefore, a form of labor organization prevailed similar to a military organization. It was based on the classification of the whole population in units arranged according to the numbering system of each region (vigesimal in Mesoamerica, decimal in the Andes), the age of the workers, and their territorial or social unit. Teams were formed to work in community projects, in production for their chiefs, and in public works according to the principle labeled in Spanish *rueda y tanda* ("turn and team"). Each team of workers discharged its obligations in turn, thus sharing the work load evenly among the available workers and at the same time maintaining a steady labor supply. This system was related to well-developed time counts in terms of which the work periods due from each group or individual were specified.

Social Stratification

The social division of labor in these two societies also included a distinction between those occupied in the different lines of material production and those who, supported by the former, were devoted to managerial and other nonproductive activities; in other words, these were stratified societies. As in other early civilizations, stratification was of the *estate* type. By this I mean a system in which there are politically defined social categories whose members have particular sets of rights and obligations in economic, political, and other social fields. Thus, in Aztec and Inca societies members of each estate had different property rights, tribute obligations, sumptuary rules, political rights, and so on. However, the classification of every individual within an estate system did not eliminate social mobility. Within each estate there were distinctions as to the distribution of economic resources or political functions not strictly ascribed by estate rules. Also, social mobility could take the form of moving from one estate to another with the accompanying loss or acquisition of the rights and obligations pertaining to one or another estate.

This estate system was the basis in these societies of a power structure that controlled the distribution of land and labor and that also defined and regulated the production units.

In both civilizations social stratification was characterized by the existence of two major estates. The mass of the population were the commoners, organized in local communities that had the use of certain lands for their own sustenance but with the obligation of rendering personal services or tribute. Commoners participated in local government at the community level but not, as a rule, in the higher levels of wider political entities.

The dominant or ruling estate consisted of a hereditary nobility whose members had rights to the tribute and personal services rendered by the commoners. They also enjoyed privileges within the political organization, in effect constituting the personnel of government in all the higher administrative, military, and religious levels.

In both the areas we are comparing, one also finds intermediate social strata whose estate position was less precisely defined. Members of such strata might belong to lower levels of the noble estate, or they might be individuals or groups chosen from among the common people; sometimes they had a particular ethnic affiliation. They carried out functions pertaining to the organization of the state or were included in the households of the members of the ruling estate. They included the artisans who specialized in the production of luxury goods, the merchants, and lower level officers of the military and governmental organizations.

On another social level in both regions were certain menial groups; they were in a position inferior to that of the average common people because they were subject to a great economic dependency. They included farmhands on state lands and those who worked as porters, servants, or clowns in state palaces or for members of the dominant estate. In some cases their position has been compared to serfdom or slavery. To a more limited extent individuals of this menial or semislave level may have also been in the service of commoners, but these are fewer in number and are incorporated into the households of their masters.

Corporate Groups

The existence of corporate groups with important economic functions was basic in these societies; they appeared within both social levels, the nobility and the commoners. They may also have been internally differentiated within each of the two ranks. These corporate groups were usually labeled *calpulli* in Mexico and *ayllu* in the Andes. Much has been speculated about the meaning of these terms from the point of view of kinship. I would emphasize, however, that descent simply regulated the composition and the recruitment process of the corporate groups. What matters most in an analysis of economic and political structure are the activities of such groups. They were corporate segments within a given political unit that functioned collectively as holders of a corporate title to land, in the setting up of cooperative work teams, in their collective responsibility for the presentation of labor services or tribute, and in the division of labor in productive, administrative, or ceremonial activities.

The different corporate groups were coordinated into larger social and political units by a division of labor that included either specialization in different activities or the procedure of taking turns in order to provide the same activity at different time periods. This latter procedure required the existence of numerical schemes for the coordination of human groups and time periods. Such schemes were an important characteristic of these societies, and were also related to

natural forces, world directions, or calendrical periods.

In some way, these corporate groups were bound together by concepts of common descent; whether such concepts had to do with ethnic origin or a particular type of kinship is in this discussion of secondary importance. At any rate, there are differences as to the extent to which terms such as *ayllu* and *calpulli* refer directly to kinship. The term *ayllu* is clearly applied in old sources to a kin group; *calpulli* is used primarily for a social subdivision, although the idea of common origin of its members may also be present. The main point, however, is that these terms were applied to social subdivisions of various kinds, such as small rural communities or the wards or quarters into which cities were divided. Kinship rules were not necessarily uniform within the large areas and the many ethnic groups included in the Aztec and Inca empires.

Ethnicity and kinship are both of considerable importance in the definition of the estates and corporate groups that make up the system of social stratification in our two areas. Almost all regional political units — the dependent kingdoms (*tlatocayotl*) in Mexico or the provinces (*waman*) of the Inca empire — were pluriethnic societies, and the different ethnic units occupied somewhat different positions in the stratification scale. In the case of the wider political units, the ruling estate and the royal dynasty were clearly identified with a given ethnic element. This was the case of the Inca in Peru or of the Mexica and various Chichimeca ruling lineages in Mexico, which were superimposed on other ethnic groups. In these large polities, too, certain ethnic groups specialized in particular activities — such as various crafts, trade, or military service — that placed them on the intermediate levels of the social scale. Other ethnic groups were almost exclusively at the peasant level.

The ruling estate coincided almost entirely with the lineage of the ruler or with a series of noble lineages, that is, the ruling estate was organized into corporate groups defined on the principle of descent. Kinship, therefore, played a part in defining estate membership and in the transmission of offices, titles of nobility, and wealth.

The royal lineages of the Inca (*panaca*) and the palaces or chiefly houses (*tecpan, teccalli*) of Mexico are comparable corporate lineages that make up the composition of the upper levels of society. Differences in rank within the royal lineages and within the upper levels of society were also connected with the kinship principle because they were defined in terms of the different ranks of the royal wives or on the basis of relative distance from the direct line of the ruling sovereign.

All this shows that it is not possible to think that social stratification and the state arose in these societies through the growth of a civil type of organization based solely on property relations, moving away from a kinship based or gentile organization. In the native civilizations of the New World, as in some societies in Asia and Africa, the very principle of kinship provides the framework for the ascription of individuals to the different statuses in the stratification system, and kinship acts as an integrating factor in the definition of the corporate groups that make up the stratification structure.

* * *

Political System

Since we are dealing with politically directed economies, it is essential to assess similarities and differences on the basis of the respective political systems of the two areas.

As regards political organization, Mesoamerica and the Andean zone presented a clearly defined contrast at the time of the conquest. The Incas had unified all the areas of high culture in one centralized state; the whole civilized world known to Andean man had entered into a common political unit. In Mesoamerica different political units of a comparable level of civilization and with common cultural antecedents coexisted. The so-called Aztec empire consisted of what might be called a confederation of three political entities that were at least theoretically equal, and the greater part of the conquered territories had been integrated into the empire only in regard to tribute payments. The degree of political centralization was therefore much less than in the Andean world. In spite of this difference, however, there were important resemblances between the two regions in their forms of political organization.

In Mesoamerica, as in the Andes, the dominant estate coincided with the personnel of government. There was no distinction between an economically dominant class and those who governed. This identity of the economically powerful with the governing personnel is only one aspect of what has been called "primitive fusion," characteristic of primitive societies and archaic civilizations. To use a different terminol-

ogy, there is no distinction between state and society, or indeed between private and public life. In these types of societies, activities that would be specialized functions of separate institutions in more complex societies occur in combined form within multifunctional institutions. In the civilized societies of Mesoamerica and the Andes, economic, political, military, and ceremonial activities were closely integrated both as to institutions and personnel. The economy was directed by the state; economic relations in the production and distribution of goods were based on political relations of subjection and control. An essential part of the economic surplus was used for public works and the ceremonial expenses of political and religious institutions. Militarism was closely connected with religion; warriors and young men about to begin their military careers were the main participants in major rites and ceremonial observances of the yearly cycle. High-ranking government officers performed duties that were not only civil but military and religious as well.

Levels of politico-territorial integration also show fundamental similarities in Mesoamerican and Andean civilizations. In both areas the political entities of greatest size, which we call "empires," were constituted on the basis of a whole series of local units; each one had its own ethnic composition and particular internal organization based on the existence of peasant communities. When examined separately, these regional units reveal organizational traits similar to what has been described as characteristics of the chiefdom (*cacicazgo*) level. The local ruler had ethnic and sometimes kinship ties with his subjects; between him and them there were also economic relations based on reciprocity and redistribution that supported the common interests of the entire group. All this created feelings of community solidarity in opposition to other regions that constituted similar units. In the marginal areas of the empires, on the frontier or in the interior, there were minor political entities of this type similar to the chiefdoms of the circum-caribbean zone in their degree of social complexity. In the periods of political disintegration, which seem to have alternated with those of imperial integration, the number of political units of the chiefdom type would presumably increase.

Therefore the social transformation of the original Inca and Mexica (and Chichimeca) groups, which has often been described as an evolution from "tribe" to "empire," has to be seen in light of the fact that the wider political structures coexisted with their component regional units as well as with their marginal neighbors, whose organization was close to that of the chiefdom level of integration.

The distinction between the ruling estate and the commoners is most clearly seen when considering the empire as a whole. The chiefs of the various regions, related through descent or affinity to the imperial lineage, formed the upper social level of the whole empire. Within each regional unit, the ruling element consisted of the chief together with his relatives and attendants; local government was based on the functions that these persons assumed in the administration of the economy and the political organization. The household or palace of the chief was the central point of local public administration. Political unification came about when one or several of these regional units, previously independent, managed to acquire control over a great number of other regions. The resultant empire than accumulated its economic surplus from all of them, and the members of the dominant estate of the conquering region made up the highest level of the imperial government as a whole. Regional governments in subject areas were kept to the extent that the previously existing political entities became regional administrative units, and the native chiefs of each region continued to hold authority in local affairs. No matter how centralized an empire might appear to be, the survival of these local ethnic and political units was always evident; it is on the basis of these units that the empire had taken shape through processes of confederation and conquest. Furthermore, given the lack of physical and economic mobility (the lack both of efficient means of transportation and of a generalized use of money), the geographic extent of the empires compelled the formation of politico-territorial subdivisions with a considerable degree of autonomy.

The central government of these empires, then, was in effect similar to that of a single territory placed over all the others that it had conquered. The administration of the empire was closely related to the household of the ruler, for the highest imperial officials were chosen from among the ruler's closest relations. Local chiefs, by being kept in place as local governors, came to form part of the imperial administration. They became related through marriage with the imperial dynasty, and the chiefs or their sons attended the capital for certain ceremonial occasions. The heirs to local chieftainships went to the capital to be educated. Thus, they became culturally assimilated to the ruling group, while at the same time they served as hostages in case of conflict. On the other hand, provincial administration did not remain entirely in the hands of the local chiefs. In the various conquered regions, the central power established governmental mechanisms that it controlled directly. This is most highly developed in the Inca empire, but it is also found in a rudimentary form in the Aztec. Certain officials were placed above the local chiefs, on either a permanent or temporary basis, as tribute collectors and visiting judges or inspectors. Garrisons, tribute depositories, or rest houses were controlled directly from the center.

Conquered groups were moved from one part of the empire to another, and colonies of the dominant ethnic group were established in strategic points. Rebellion was thus made more difficult. Ethnic groups were scattered about the country, located far from the area they knew best, and mixed in with other ethnic groups with whom they had no ties of solidarity. Furthermore, these movements of population created governmental organs controlled directly by the central power. This was especially true if the people thus moved were colonies of the dominant ethnic group or of selected ethnic groups with specialized functions such as military responsibilities or the collection and storing of goods intended for the central power.

The means of increasing and maintaining the extension of the empire was always war and militarily imposed control. Occasionally booty may have been the principal object of a campaign, but there was always something more at stake than immediate plunder. A system of controls was set up that permitted the regular extraction of the economic surplus of conquered regions through the payment of tribute and labor services.

45
Reciprocity on Skid Row

CHRISTOPHER HAUCH

Introduction: The Myth of the Squandering Squatter

It is seemingly all but a law of nature that whenever a skid row resident encounters money, in relative bulk, his first and overriding inclination is to squander it. Receiving a welfare cheque or other lump sum, such as might be earned from a short-term job or income-tax refund, the skid row man will typically commence swift and unrestrained consumption of the most frivolous, extravagant purchases, treating himself and his companions to long episodes of apparently relentless inebriation. The phenomenon is known as "binge spending," and by every account it is a pan–North American skid row tradition.

In light of the severe depth and prevalence of poverty on skid row, the practice of binge spending seems economically irrational. Western social scientists have traditionally interpreted it as evidence of a sort of psychopathology. The "symptom" is repeated failure at planning for the long term. This disorder, typically associated with the "culture of poverty" model, is characterized as a pathological fixation on life-in-the-present, and it is called "nondeferred gratification."

The concept of nondeferred gratification has fairly dominated explanations of spending practices in urban poverty areas for nearly three decades. As a result, many treatment facilities for skid row alcoholics take great pains to incorporate rudimentary money-management training into their programs. Furthermore, most welfare departments in the United States and Canada maintain a policy of withholding aid from known practitioners of this "aberrant" spending behavior. As a result, skid row people seldom benefit from income security programs.

Nevertheless, there may be more to binge spending than meets the distant critical eye. In the course of several years' ethnographic research of skid row in the City of Winnipeg, Canada, I discovered evidence suggesting that binges may provide selective advantages to their practitioners. The base for this research was the Main Street Project, a government-funded outreach program and emergency shelter. This agency is both long-lived and credible in Winnipeg's skid row community: this facilitated unusually close contact with its residents. As a result, it was possible to gather longitudinal demographic data, and the ethnographer had an accepted status that justified and made easier sustained observations of community life.

From Christopher Hauch (Senior Clinical Consultant, Mental Health Division of Manitoba Health), original essay, 1992. Reprinted with permission. (The views expressed in this essay are those of the author and do not necessarily represent the policy of Manitoba Health.)

In spite of the importance of Christmas shopping-till-you-drop in the American retail industry, binges are unlikely to become dominant features of the economy in the mainstream society. Nevertheless, as the study progressed, the ecology of skid row emerged as one so radically different from that of the world surrounding it that differences in behavior became more understandable. In some ways, the adaptive pressures on residents of skid row resembled those which are imposed upon a foraging society like that of the !Kung San. Not only the constraints were similar, but several survival strategies were common to these very different groups. Analogues to several of skid row's economic customs, including binge spending, are found in the ethnography of many foraging peoples.

Hard Work Does Not Pay

The skid row district of Winnipeg is similar to most of those found elsewhere in North America. As attested by its decaying turn-of-the-century buildings, it is the city's historic center, the onetime nucleus of its trade. Like so many of its counterparts, its decline over the decades since the Depression followed the expansion of business away from the city's core and the growth of residential districts far beyond its original borders. Many early structures remain, and, on its periphery, a few have witnessed brilliant restoration. Of the hundred or so small businesses included in the twenty-four square blocks of skid row proper, few enjoy more than remnants of an earlier prosperity. Now, most survive only by virtue of grossly depreciated rent or tax assessments, and a small but steady stream of low-income customers.

Skid row is the home of the city's most poor and disaffiliated, among whom many drunkards and a few of the mentally ill are conspicuous. The population of skid row was defined as including all the homeless frequenters of the area during the five-year period of the study. The population was quite homogeneous and displayed its characteristics with remarkable consistency over time.

Among the most prominent of those characteristics was a lack of marketable skills. In Winnipeg, skid row residents tended to have marginal schooling, and were able to compete only for scant short-term laboring positions. Few had enjoyed much better times. Unskilled labor experiences dominated typical "pre–skid row" employment histories.

Almost all residents were male, most of them between the ages of 35 and 50. Close to three-quarters of the population was composed of Native peoples, a statistic that remained stable over the years. Most were Cree- and Saulteaux-speaking men, along with a few women, from nearby reserves. Of the whites, by far the majority were transient laborers whose first homes had been in traditionally impoverished parts of the country.

While the demography remained stable, the constituency did not. The turnover in personnel was surprising, amounting in some years to 60 percent of the entire population. Avenues of mobility were myriad, if not all upward. Native residents who were able to, returned to their home reserves from time to time. Some found full-time work, or simply relocated to other skid rows. More fell victim to horrible sickness, and thus were absorbed into an otherwise inaccessible social service support system. Others were imprisoned, and during my stay, many died. Literally, tens of thousands came and went over the few years' duration of the research. Apart from a very few colorful and effectively permanent habitués, there was no large lingering membership.

Even with so fluid a population, there was rarely any variety in the most salient expressions of lifestyles. Notably, residents were always poor — or rather, destitute. Besides, a popular image of "the sagacious and self-styled hobo" was shown to be a myth of the well-to-do. All my informants were well acquainted with homelessness and, recounting their experiences, expressed fear at its prospects. The homeless endured sickness, injury, and death as ordinary consequences both of the severe Winnipeg winters and of violence in all its conceivable forms. No sane person would volunteer for all this suffering. The business of securing shelter and provision and, ultimately, an escape from skid row dominated daily life.

While life-threatening poverty came as no surprise, the "business" of circumventing it did. Initially, the presumption was that petty crime, social agency usage, and scavenging provided the baseline skid row subsistence. It turned out that all were indeed part of the broad repertoire of local survival strategies. Beyond that, it was discovered that the population was also a working one, almost to a man. Moreover, unlike crime, for example, which appeared to be largely against each other, and hence redistributive in nature, legitimate employment seemed by far the most common means of actually creating wealth for the society.

As expected, steady jobs were nonexistent. Securing one usually implied the worker's departure from skid row. Everyone worked, however sporadically, for the very specialized network of casual-labor offices. Survival depended on it. It was in the structure of this skid-row-based industry that part of the explanation for local spending behavior lay.

The men were retained by a casual-employment office — usually for arduous and repetitive jobs — and they were both paid and dismissed at day's end. There was no job security and few of the benefits that normally attend full-time employment. Other scholars have pointed out that this type of labor recruitment is typical in skid row regions. It is often mentioned in the literature as "spot jobs" — the work of urban nomads.

Though typically recruiting in skid row, casual labor is never an indigenous invention. It is always organized by nonresident entrepreneurs who seek profit by orchestrating brief deals between conventional, mainstream business, with its fluctuating labor requirements, and skid row men, with their hopeless inability to secure full-time jobs. This is how it appeared during my study of Winnipeg's skid row.

First, casual-labor agents enlisted skid row men to work, offering them minimum wages, as a rule. The labor of these men was then "sold" — by the day — to secondary purchasers for fees roughly equivalent to what the market hourly wage might be, were the position permanent and unionized. The secondary purchaser never had any obligation beyond the one-day contract and thus, over the long term, was able to adjust wage output closely to subtle variations in staffing requirements.

Due to the poverty prevalent on skid row, nearly all men, including the chronically ill, made at least periodic use of the market for casual labor. As early as four o'clock in the morning (or two to three hours before the workday begins), dozens could be seen staking positions near office entrances, at times huddled against brutal cold.

For the few fortunate who were hired, the jobs available varied in the extreme. Some small businesses required snow removal; others wanted flyers to be delivered or simple construction tasks to be performed. On better days, large contracts might be posted. The major rail companies, for example, are, by necessity, regular customers. A train entering Winnipeg may be required to pick up or discharge a single large load quickly. The task is labor intensive and it involves far more men than could be retained on a permanent basis.

Always, jobs trickled in from a host of marginal, spur-of-the-moment enterprises. Many

businesses solicited the most desperate workers by preference, impressed both by their willingness to perform demeaning labor and by their reluctance to complain to authorities about unsafe working conditions.

At one point in the study, for example, a local business was discovered salvaging metal from discarded automobile batteries, purchased in lots from nearby junk dealers. Many of my informants were hired through a casual-labor office to work whole days splitting the batteries open with sledge hammers, on exposed concrete pads. To spare costs, the company neglected to provide the required protective gloves, eyeglasses, trousers, and so on. Such items were considered optional and thus no one who could not afford them was ever prohibited from working. Soon, all those hired for the work suffered acid burns. At first, some were injured sufficiently to require hospitalization; released, they were again destitute, and for their debilities only less capable of competing for work. But most simply stayed on, day after day, in pain. In six cases that I knew of, men toiled for nearly five weeks, until eventually their wounds, new ones layered upon old, made it physically impossible for them to continue.

Casual jobs were both temporary and unpleasant; in addition, they were almost invariably futureless. One's work site was forever changing. In consequence, one rarely enjoyed an opportunity to impress supervisors and ascend any single organizational hierarchy. Surprisingly, casual-labor office managers suggested in interviews that it was still necessary to impede the natural, upward mobility process. Business would suffer, they said, if customers hired permanently their best workers, having tested them during casual labor for their suitability to assume full-time positions. To avoid this problem, a supplemental contract was implemented. Each time a laborer was sent to a work site, the referring office insisted that the customer refrain from hiring him for a permanent position for at least six months. This contract was of dubious legality and owed its strength more to universal, tacit agreement than to any judicial enforcement. Still, even the most ambitious on skid row soon discovered that it made them ineligible to apply for certain full-time openings. Even if they were sent to the same work site for weeks running, they were often helpless to penetrate the permanent work force. As a rule, their job assignments were varied frequently by the referring offices, so tenured labor opportunities diminished day by day.

Work was sparse and poorly paid. A review of annual income records revealed that the successful laborers earned about half the minimum wage for 52 weeks. Dependence upon casual labor was a condemnation to a clearly marginal subsistence.

How the Poor Pay More

Even so, the characteristically low incomes of skid row habitués were not alone responsible for the widespread chronic homelessness. Although modest, they were rarely much lower than those which many university students, living in residence, subsist on. And like university campuses, skid row was replete with outlets in which all manner of goods and services could be purchased at modest prices. Monthly rentals for hotels and rooming houses were low. Meals were inexpensive, as were the clothing and housewares sold in local thrift stores.

Rather, casual labor was only one of the necessary conditions for extreme poverty. Another was skid row's sheltering industry, the sum of all rented accommodations, which ironically not only profited from homelessness but actively promoted it, in certain creative ways.

To appreciate the interaction, it is necessary to distinguish two distinct groups of shelter consumers on skid row — in a sense, two types of severely poor. One, not normally identified with the skid row populace, consists of all those who receive income in orderly, predictable disbursements. Some are elderly men, in particular those whose sole income derives from federal pension programs. Others are the recipients of long-term disability payments, modest trust funds, and so on.

The second, larger group, consists of all those who rely on sporadic incomes. Its membership is somewhat less varied. Some are professional, or rather full-time, criminals (interestingly, these are rare on skid row). But by far the majority are casual laborers — the true, conspicuous skid row residents.

On the face of it, the distinction seems trivial. Neither group can boast a superior average income. Yet the latter's poverty is ostensibly the deeper. Among laborers, homelessness is the norm, while steady earners, though generally doomed to squalid conditions, appear all but immune to the experience.

The paradox was explained during this study, in that each group was charged rent at a different rate. Steady earners were able to raise capital once per month. Like all such people, they shopped for the best accommodations that a reasonable portion of their incomes allowed for. Accordingly, skid row landlords set monthly rates that were equitable, or at least befitting of their products' characteristically substandard quality.

Casual laborers, on the other hand, were paid intermittently throughout the month. They would have preferred the stability of leasing arrangements, but the most lucrative strategy for landlords was to charge rent with equal intermittence. No man was ever advanced a room against his agreeing to pay at that month's end. If unable to make full payment in advance, he was forced to a daily rate. On the average, daily hotel rates in the area reached up to seven times those normally paid by steady earners, or about 65–80 percent of a laborer's net daily income.

If a laborer worked one day, then he was able to secure one day's shelter; if not, he was homeless. The dichotomy was inexorable, since the two-tiered system profited hotel owners even when it resulted in apparently high vacancy rates. For all intents, basic shelter is an inelastic commodity, especially in winter. As long as rentals were kept within the average daily wage, therefore, no real benefit ever accrued to the owner for their reduction.

Rooming houses of the region provided no sanctuary. No daily rate was offered, and worse, tenants were required to supply damage deposits in advance of occupancy. The only remaining option was to stay at the Salvation Army hostel, which, unlike the hotels, did provide a reasonable daily rate. But even here, we observed only a variation on hotel policies. Those who could provide 30 days rent in advance were entitled to a private, locked room, a place where they could store possessions. All others were crowded into open dormitories where storage was impossible and theft inevitable. Whatever portable surplus one had when one entered, be it money remaining from the day's wages, or expensive belongings, was quickly lost to equally needy men. In consequence, for their meager comforts, hotels were usually preferred.

Giving and Receiving

One might speculate that, in the midst of such dire and seemingly intractable circumstances, little but brutality and fierce individualism — Hobbes's "war of all against all" — could prevail. Brief visits to skid row strengthen the notion. The people we saw seemed all but inured to life's daily perils. Their society at once strikes us as tenuous and unstructured in the extreme.

Penetrating skid row's salient hostile aspect, however, one finds widespread evidence of altruistic behavior. The culture contains only a few proscriptions regarding violence. At the same time, there is an intense, universal commitment to philanthropy, articulated in the expression "you can't turn people down on the street."

The expression is more than a platitude: it almost summarizes economic life. Gestures of seeming kindness, of sharing, among men so uniformly impoverished, were routinely observed. Unlike what can be observed among middle-class people, prior relationship is rarely a factor in the decision to give, so long as the remotest affiliation with skid row is confirmed. Such gestures are not as a rule even accompanied by sentiment. No message of obligation, even to return thanks, is imposed on the receiver. Similarly, when receiving, no sense of obligation is displayed.

At first, this made for tremendously frustrating ethnography. Poverty on this scale, it was expected, would surely stimulate some sort of internal economic organization — taking the form perhaps of intragroup support networks and stratification and commodity distribution rules. Such groups and their rules would have been the natural objects of social research.

No such formal culture or organization availed itself. By all evidence, goods flowed freely throughout the community, altogether unhampered by any discernible structure. For the most part, residents simply provided for one another unhesitatingly in times of need. No direct mode of repayment was ever implicit in transactions: sometimes all parties reasonably presumed that they would never meet again.

Yet, there were two pervasive constants in the economy, unspoken practices that appeared to govern all exchange-related behavior. First, while generosity was valued, severe punishments were always exacted on misers. Everyone seemed aware that deprivation had the potential for occasioning great hazards, even death. On this basis, most tended to interpret hoarding as an act of extreme hostility and isolationism. Those who came upon wealth and did not share it were routinely brutally beaten and robbed. If caught several times, they were additionally subjected to ostracism.

The second was that skid row people were willing to tolerate prolonged asymmetrical exchange. For example, those few who were physically incapable of working, but who had not yet qualified for state aid, could be sustained for lengthy periods solely by the generosity of their fellows. In time, of course, this would tend to strain relations. Such was inevitable in so marginal an economy. Here, the remedial sanction was more subtle in nature. Violence was never automatic; nor, after suffering near countless requests for aid, did anyone conspicuously act the miser. Instead, gossip would ignite and, feeding upon widespread discontent, would punish its victims with increasingly mean criticisms. Mental status was most frequently targeted. Longtime suppliants would suddenly earn reputations as "crazies," dangerous and unpredictable lunatics. As such a reputation swelled, so too usually did ostracism. Progressive poverty, illness, and ultimate rescue by welfare agencies, or hospitals, marked the typical downward sequence.

In essence, this was the extent of economy. On the one hand there was one overriding cultural value: that wealth ought always to be shared and that the act of sharing justifies neither complacence nor gratitude. Two powerful sanctions prevailed: one was directed at enforcing the former law and another at curtailing its abuse.

At first, the system appeared disorganized, or at best, rife with cultural contradictions. In fact, the concurrent existence of these traits literally defines a well-known economic institution: generalized reciprocity. Furthermore, there seems to be an almost eerie likeness between the fundamental material constraints of skid row and those typically found in the egalitarian foraging societies where anthropologists document generalized reciprocity. In each case, the sustaining conditions of the system seem the same.

Generalized reciprocity was likely the earliest form of human economic organization. Wherever it exists, the institution displays essentially the features described above (with the incitement to rumor usually taking the form of accusations of witchcraft). Most characteristically, there are no ironclad rules of private ownership. All members of the society are producers, in one specialty or another. All goods entering the society are viewed as belonging to all people. No overt mechanism exists to calculate debt or capital. No immediate reckoning of any kind occurs to figure out one's right of access in relation either to ascribed status or ostensible productivity.

At once, the system reveals a somewhat innate beneficence. Despite severely marginal ecosystems, all inhabitants contribute to the welfare of the nonproductive members as well as their own. No one prospers over his fellows. Rather, residents cling to one another for daily support, as sparse resources are distributed to a meager but usually comfortable and equitable baseline.

The driving force of this arrangement is not pure altruism. Everyone is expected to both produce and distribute at least intermittently — to maintain balance over the long term. Failing this, hard sanctions are eventually brought to bear. Also, generalized reciprocity is sustained under material conditions that severely frustrate the accumulation of surplus and the appearance of social and economic stratification.

One of these is the nondurability of subsistence goods. Most foraging societies tend to lack the technological means to preserve naturally occurring wealth. Most foodstuffs will spoil. Even those that do not spoil are difficult to transport over the great distances that foragers must travel. Nor, usually, can they be stored in any stationary locale in such a way as to be inaccessible to needy insects, beasts, or people. With small reserves and no concrete insurance against shortfalls, one is best served by cultivating a reputation for generosity.

So it is too on skid row, although here the analogue lies in the nature of business practices. One "buys" one's subsistence with sporadic income at prices more or less geared to a full day's earnings. Surplus is an oddity. Even if it does appear, it is almost impossible to protect it from robbery. Banking, of course, might be used. But each time one brings a portion of one's savings into the community, fellow residents in need are encountered. In such an event, there are only two options. One may refuse requests for aid and be beaten and ostracized. Or one may share in the remote hope of accumulating social credits for use at a time when the roles will be reversed.

I observed over five years that skid row was extremely fluid in its membership: only very few residents remained there as long as I did. The consequence was that formalized subsocietal groups were never able to congeal successfully in this setting. Few residents ever chose to associate themselves too closely with any given group, out of a rational fear that designated aid-partners would soon vanish into any of the various avenues of mobility. Some tried. On several occasions, kin from nearby Indian reserves were observed to enter the region simultaneously. They would survive, initially, by mutual and exclusive support, working and living together and occasionally menacing local residents as a gang. Inevitably, their numbers would diminish. Once there were only a few remaining, these few would routinely incur the most brutal retribution for their past stinginess and gang-style behavior. In every case, the sequence was painfully predictable: violent punishments always followed social deviancy.

Drunken Binges Are Shrewd Investments

So far in the discussion, the mechanics of generalized reciprocity have been described only as they bear on normally meager subsistence conditions. Situations of imbalance are inevitable and tax the normal exchange process. The situation of a skid row man getting a windfall would be similar to that of a forager encountering sudden spectacular wealth in the form, for example, of large delectable game. A problem of scale and hence protocol arises. In such an instance, many people must be summoned for the wealth to be equitably divided. How is the summoning to be done without broadcasting the giver's importance? How is apportionment to take place such that the unlikelihood of immediate recompense is not dramatized? Always, in a society that loathes debt, the management of windfalls is a delicate business.

In his now classic research of the !Kung San, Richard Lee illustrated what turns out to be a typical solution in egalitarian societies. Fearful of exhibiting aspirations to leadership, an ambition that is perilous at best in such a society, successful hunters always tend to trivialize the value of a major kill. Colleagues will usually concur with the judgment and, on the face of it, will participate only begrudgingly in the tasks of retrieving a carcass and rendering it to portions.

Analogous problems on skid row were resolved in a similar way — through binges. Upon acquiring any large amount of money, perhaps as an income-tax refund, the skid row resident found himself in the odious position of having to do something with it. Skid row offered few alternatives in such an instance: one could attempt to conceal it, only to end up beaten and robbed, or one could share — generously. These being the only choices, sharing, especially in the form of a quick and thorough binge, was clearly the wiser.

The ecology of skid row imposes certain minor stylistic differences on the solution. Whereas, for example, one might anticipate binging to be evident in a broad distribution of funds consumed at once in the form of needed commodities, the practice typically involved few people and notoriously frivolous purchases. Alcohol was especially favored, often being the focus of days-long parties from which participants occasionally required clinical detoxification.

Further, unlike the usual modesty one finds characteristic of givers in most smaller transactions, the hosts to a sizeable binge often exhibited great braggadocio. Announcing new-found wealth, the men boasted of their limitless philanthropy, distributing cash on the street, in bars, and even throwing it away and proclaiming (the frequent expression) "It means nothing to me." Attracting a circle of friends and relatives, in short order, the generous host would vent self-aggrandizement, spending furiously as if to confirm each claim of greatness.

Much of this seems uncharacteristic of the usual quiet, practical, and unassuming nature of gift giving in everyday life. The sheer size and impoverishment of the skid row population made for unusual stresses in the normal distribution process. Even so, binging reflected no essential deviation from the basic characteristics of reciprocity.

A comparatively large sum (for example, a $500 income-tax refund) afforded no special advantage to the individual skid row resident since it could never be saved, given the omnipresent threat of robbery. Nor was it sufficient to make possible a permanent relocation away from skid row to a place where miserliness would not have been a cultural taboo. The expression "Money means nothing to me" was an astute appraisal of the dilemma. Unlike possible analogues in smaller egalitarian societies, such windfalls are useless in meeting even the most basic immediate needs of the group, because of the great number of potential, nearby receivers.

Of course, this created no problem in most instances in which only small sums passed hands. If encountering someone in need, one simply relinquished everything one had then; because he was at once penniless, the giver could not be blamed for failing to assist the next applicant.

Large windfalls had to be redistributed to many, so that no one became conspicuously wealthier than another. The giver was in a tenuous social position. He might have attempted to make like-sized donations to a few people of his choice, but this would invariably appear as the intended exclusion of those who received nothing. Besides, should one so overlooked wish to avenge violently the giver's snub, no one would come to his assistance for fear of appearing "paid off."

Binge spending was the perfect solution. Coming into a large sum, the recipient commenced a swift and indiscriminate distribution. As quickly as possible he purchased food, liquor, and gifts of myriad description, showing no preference for binge participants, but donating randomly to anyone who happened by. Further, as if abrogating publicly any subsequent obligation of receivers, the host boasted of his great generosity, impressing upon all his belief in the virtues of sharing and fellowship, and showing contempt for money. The host almost insisted that no one leave feeling in any way indebted to him. Thus, the louder his boasting the better, as those friends and relatives who heard too late of his spree to get their share could bear no grudge based on miserliness.

The use of alcohol during a binge provided an additional advantage. Often, former hosts would report having "lost a couple of days" during a binge, meaning that their memory of the episode had been impaired by sustained drinking. On occasions on which relatives protested their exclusion from binges, this would frequently be used as a defense. Common reports were "I was on a wild drunk ... I didn't know what I was doing." Often this would placate the accuser.

Binges are very adaptive responses to the problem of distributing large sums on skid row. Quick wealth is an accident on skid row, one which places the recipient in great physical danger. Thus, the spontaneous spending of it is a matter of group enforcement, having no greater purpose than to afford the safest and most equitable division, and swiftest consumption.

Binges are clearly not exercises in frivolous indulgence, or evidence of the skid row people's inability to plan for the long term. A memorable skid row spending spree witnessed during the research illustrates this point. The host, V, had sustained serious and permanent injury to both legs because of an accident during casual labor. Hoping to avert a lawsuit, the purchasing industry offered, while V was still hospitalized, a single lump sum, some $3,000, in compensation. V quickly agreed to the offer and, discharging himself from care at the encouragement of friends, began a long and unrestrained bout of partying in the skid row hotel district.

Well aware of his history of drinking, Main Street Project workers naturally became concerned by this — especially since V's physicians suggested that V was unlikely to work again and that a period of sustained drinking might impede his recovery. Nonetheless, no efforts of Project staff would deter him: within a week, V was both penniless and unemployable.

The episode might well have been attributed to a lack of money-management skills and disregard for personal health. My experience with V then, and for three years subsequently, proved very much the contrary. Immediately after distributing his windfall, V applied for and received permanent welfare assistance for reasons of physical disability. Every month he received a cheque, again a lump sum. He used this to leave skid row. Although he occasionally visited the skid row area later, he was seldom observed intoxicated, or even patronizing the local taverns. Instead, given a secure income, V managed a largely sedentary style of life, living alone, and exhibiting great aptitude for budgeting a decidedly modest income.

And so it was for most people. Sudden, finite wealth invariably ordained madness, while opportunities for permanent income were more likely to result in health, as the fundamental ingredients of a working class world view.

Conclusions

This observation may have interesting implications for applied research and social programming. We can appreciate, for example, why counseling has usually failed whenever it was designed to restructure the patterns of spending of skid row residents. Many of the behaviors that this counseling attempted to elicit were maladaptive on skid row.

Contrary to such psychological explanations as the "culture of poverty" model, the causes of poverty on skid row are almost always material and ordinary. During the course of my work I often helped residents to prepare income-tax returns. It turned out that many of them earned more than welfare recipients who were permanent residents of area hotels and rooming houses. Why, then, were they homeless? The simple answer is that those who relied on work paid by the day were forced to rent shelter by the day, at rates so high that periodic homelessness was inevitable.

This explains why life-threatening poverty in this setting cannot be eliminated until social programs target the basic material conditions of the local economy. This may not mean costly job-creation initiatives or across-the-board increases in income security benefits. Rather, the more effective strategies are likely to be small and local: typical examples would be some regulation of the local labor and housing businesses, together with flexible provisions for income security. A better understanding of the problems of skid row residents and the provision of more effective help will require much commitment, but also a sustained attention to the ecology of seemingly deviant patterns of behavior.

References

Hauch, Christopher. 1985. *Coping Strategies and Street Life: The Ethnography of Winnipeg's Skid Row*. Winnipeg: Institute of Urban Studies.

Lee, Richard. 1979. *The !Kung San: Men, Women and Work in a Foraging Society*. New York: Cambridge University Press.

Liebow, Elliot. 1967. *Tally's Corner*. Boston: Little, Brown and Co.

Orwell, George. 1940. *Down and Out in Paris and London*. New York: Penguin.

Spradley, James. 1970. *You Owe Yourself a Drunk: An Ethnography of Urban Nomads*. Boston: Little, Brown and Co.

Wiseman, Jacqueline P. 1970. *Stations of the Lost: The Treatment of Skid Row Alcoholics*. Englewood Cliffs, N.J.: Prentice-Hall, Inc.

SECTION FOUR
Status and Role

Introduction

Poets and philosophers have often compared the world to a stage, on which each of us is the unwitting performer of many roles. Sir Henry Maine (1861) was an early sociologist who explored the theoretical implications of this notion. His contribution was to distinguish *ascribed statuses*, resulting from one's birth, sex, or age, from *achieved statuses*, which one acquires as a result of some behavior, activity, or accomplishment. The statuses of "son," "member of the Eagle clan," "young girl," or "old man," are examples of ascribed statuses; those of "headman," "wife," or "university student" are achieved.

In *The Study of Man* (1936), anthropologist Ralph Linton clarified the difference between status and role. According to him, a **status** is a collection of rights and duties; it is an abstraction representing the place of a given individual in the structure of the many social groups of which he or she is a part. Each individual has many statuses. Linton viewed a **role** as the dynamic aspect of a status, the performance of the potential for action represented by the status. Linton was quick to point out that role and status are so inseparable that the distinction between them is solely of academic interest. Many sociologists, such as Robert Merton and Erving Goffman, found the distinction too static and artificial. They emphasized that individuals, in the course of their interactions, are constantly modifying their behavior, adjusting it to their perception of the

situation, of themselves, and of the expectations that they assume others have of them.

The popular, everyday conception of the term *status* mistakenly associates it only with positions of privilege and authority. Just as one can have the status of "king" or "hero," one may have the status of "traitor," "sick person," or "cripple." Robert F. Murphy's *The Body Silent*, from which an excerpt is presented in Chapter 46, is a deeply moving account of the frustrations and the ambiguous social status of sick people and wheelchair-bound paraplegics and quadriplegics in our culture. For fifteen years, Murphy continued to teach, at Columbia University, and to write, despite the progress of the tumor that was causing his body to become less and less responsive to his active mind. Such a "silence of the body" is not only a physiological and personal problem: the victims of this kind of disability find themselves becoming social outcasts, embarrassing disproofs of the American Dream, and frightening reminders of that dream's fragility. Murphy's ultimate form of "participant observation" imbues his account with an emotional immediacy that no formalistic analysis could attain. His incisive descriptions of the change in roles that the sick must endure and of the way in which disabled people are made outcasts are offered in what is the first systematic, book-length analysis of these phenomena by an anthropologist.

In most societies — even egalitarian societies — another disadvantaged status is that of women. Men frequently assume the most prestigious statuses, and there is no society in which women have greater power than men. Indeed, **matriarchy** — rule by women — is a myth. As Murphy suggested once in a discussion of the Mundurucú Indians of Brazil, this myth may be an expression of men's insecurity. After all, from a purely biological point of view, the number of women in a population determines its reproductive potential. With a hundred men and one woman, the population would be on its way to extinction, whereas if only a single man survived a war, and there were a hundred war widows, the population would bounce back in no time. From this perspective, the majority of men can be seen as unnecessary, disposable pets: small wonder they are the ones sent off to perform such dangerous tasks as hunting and fighting wars.

In many societies, men overcompensate for their insecurity by loudly proclaiming their superiority. The latter is confirmed by religious beliefs, that construe God to be male and men to be truer images of him than women, while depicting women as polluting and the cause of men's loss of sacred-

ness. For nearly a century, claims such as these from around the world have been dutifully reported by male anthropologists. Sigmund Freud, the father of psychoanalytic theory, explained further that anatomy is destiny: women, he claimed, are condemned by their penis envy to remain submissive.

How much of this male talk is believed by the women of any given society is debatable. Women ethnographers, revisiting the people studied earlier by men, have often found that the latter had asked only the opinion of "well-informed informants" — that is to say, old men. We see in May Diaz's ethnography of Tonalá, a Mexican village, that *machismo*, the ideology of male superiority, is indeed alive among the men (Chapter 47). Diaz also finds, however, that their wives, mothers, and sisters manipulate them so consistently and to such an extent that the control of "macho" men over "weak" women is revealed as something of an amusing illusion. The strict separation and interdependence of family roles are explicit in Tonalá. The apparently overwhelming power of the father is enjoyed without responsibility; other members of the family avoid him, and the mother, in fact, heads the household.

Closer to home, and in a very different style, Marvin Harris proposes an explanation for the startling changes in the status of American women during the last few decades (Chapter 48). In the 1950s, the church, business, unions, and women themselves still agreed that the place of a woman was in the home, caring for her contribution to the baby boom, and pampering her husband. What happened? New kinds of jobs came on the market for which women, with their high levels of education and modest acceptance of low wages, were desirable, while at the same time, persistent inflation was causing families to need the money. Harris shows how American women were forced by continuing inflation to remain in these jobs, and how this led to the restructuring of the role of women in their families and in society as a whole. One of the consequences of the new consciousness that emerged was the so-called women's liberation movement: the liberation of many of its followers consisted of the opportunity to work a double shift — one in the workplace and one, no lighter than before, in the home.

Stalking the ferocious butterfly. Among the Wayana Amerindians of South America, gender roles are learned early in life. Little boys learn the art and lore of hunting from an early age. While they play, their sisters are busy helping their mothers to cook and to work in the garden. Source: Jean-Luc Chodkiewicz.

Works Cited

Goffman, E. 1959. *The Presentation of Self in Everyday Life*. Garden City: Doubleday Anchor Books.

Linton, R. 1936. *The Study of Man: An Introduction*. New York: Appleton-Century.

Maine, H. 1861. *Ancient Law*. London: J. Murray.

46
The Body Silent

ROBERT F. MURPHY

A person's ordinary social roles — mother, father, lawyer, baker, student, and so forth — all become temporarily suspended when he or she falls ill. The individual becomes a "sick person," which relieves him or her of some or all of the ordinary obligations, depending on the severity of the illness.

The suspension of his other duties does not mean that the person playing the sick role has none at all. Quite the contrary; he is saddled with one big obligation: He must make every effort to get well again. In our own doctor-ridden culture, this means that he must seek medical advice; he must take his medicine and follow the doctor's orders. This expectation mandates the proper role of the sick as one of passivity. The sick person is excused from work or school, household duties are suspended or at least limited, and connubial relations may be put on ice. But in return, he must devote full time to getting better.

There are rules for being sick. If one is only slightly ill, he or she may be criticized for taking too many liberties from ordinary duties. Anyone who [complains of minor ailments] acquires a reputation as either a shirker or a hypochondriac. We treat the former with contempt or punishment and the latter with derision. At the other extreme is the heroic stance, adopted by the person who ignores pain and suffering and goes about his or her ordinary business. Such types, however, receive only limited honors. The mother who cares for children and household despite serious illness is admired as long as she makes a good recovery. If her condition worsens, she "has brought it on herself," and those who formerly praised her courage will say that "a woman with three young children has an obligation to take care of herself." The mother thus moves from heroine to child neglecter and is regarded as the cause of her own condition. She has violated the first commandment of sickness: Get well.

As with all other social roles, a person can succeed or fail at sickness. A key rule for being a successful sick person is: Don't complain! The person who smiles and jokes while in obvious physical misery is honored by all. Doctors and nurses are especially appreciative of this kind of patient, for he usually follows orders and seldom files malpractice suits. Hospital visitors also value cheeriness, and the sick person soon finds that he is expected to amuse them, and thus relieve their guilt at being well. These are front-area, or on-stage, performances — to use sociologist Erving

Excerpted from Robert F. Murphy, *The Body Silent*, Henry Holt Co., 1987, pp. 19–22, 90–91, 108, 116–17, 131. Copyright 1987 Robert F. Murphy. Reprinted with the permission of Yolanda Murphy. (Bibliographic documentation contained in the original text is omitted here. Interested readers should consult the original publication.)

Goffman's celebrated theatrical metaphor for social interaction. The backstage behavior may be totally different, however, and the public hero may become a whiner at home. The bad patient is either tyrannical or a crybaby, or both at once. But above all, the bad patient is one who does not follow orders. There are, then, social skills in sickness.

Contrary to popular fears, the overwhelming majority of people who enter hospitals come out not only alive, but also in better health than when they entered. What one loses in the hospital is not life but freedom of choice, for the patient must submit to the requirements and routines of the institution. When an individual is additionally removed from his normal habitat and is placed under custodial care, his passivity is complete. He is shorn of all other social roles and is regarded as one sick body among many. Some attention is given to age, sex, and social standing, but this has less effect on care than might be imagined. In general, hospitals are more democratic toward their patients than is society at large; they withhold honor with an even hand. This is particularly irritating to medical people when they become patients and find themselves treated as minors in the same establishments in which they normally reign supreme. The hospital inmate soon learns that he must conform to the routine imposed by the establishment. If dinner is scheduled for 4:30 P.M., as it was on a floor in which I once spent two months, then that's when you eat. And if your bowels don't move often enough to suit the nursing staff, laxatives are the answer. The infamous routine that demands that all temperatures be taken at 6:00 A.M. is well known to all who have been patients. I even spent five weeks on one floor where I was bathed at 5:30 every morning because the daytime nurses were too busy to do it.

The patient conforms in still other ways. There is a chain of authority that goes down from attending physician to nurse to patient, with obedience expected at each level. All of this is understandable, however onerous. Given its problems of size and complexity, the average general hospital must work according to a thoroughly "rationalized" system. There is an elaborate division of labor, a meticulous allocation of responsibilities, and a careful scheduling of activities. The hospital has all the features of a bureaucracy, and, like bureaucracies everywhere, it both breeds and feeds on impersonality. It should be cautioned, however, that the "rationality" of a bureaucracy refers only to the attempt to impose order, not to its actual operation. To the

contrary, as the sociologist Robert Jackall has demonstrated brilliantly, the practical results of these careful designs are often exercises in madness, and hospitals are case studies of the awesome disparities between theory and practice. They are places in which both Florence Nightingale and Nurse Ratched of *One Flew Over the Cuckoo's Nest* could feel at home.

To a certain degree, the hospital is a "total institution," a custodial place within which the inmates live out all aspects of their lives; it is an island of social relations. The totality is not as great as that of the military or the prison, but in long-term care facilities, such as mental hospitals and physical rehabilitation centers, it comes close. The truly closed-off total institution generally tries to expunge prior identities and to make the individual assume one that is imposed on him by authority. Prisons and the military give the newly inducted close haircuts and a number. The hair grows back, but the numerical identity is more enduring; I once absentmindedly listed my Navy serial number instead of my Social Security number — twenty-five years after my discharge. The purpose of all that is to make the individual forget that he is somebody's son or husband and think of himself instead as a soldier or convict. The Navy had brilliant success in my own case, and my early professorial career was colored by an uneasy feeling that I was a seaman who had gotten on the wrong ship. I had been so thoroughly imbued with the sailor role that I had a hard time adjusting to the academic style.

The hospital requires that the inmate think of himself primarily as a patient, for this is a condition of conformity and subservience. This allows the medical staff to treat the patient with a degree of distance and dispassion, to view him or her as a case rather than as a person. The patient may not like this treatment, this evenhanded pleasantness, but he is in fact a co-conspirator in the process; after all, his other roles and duties have already been suspended. This is all common-sense knowledge to most people, and it has been the subject of countless scholarly papers, but it bears repeating because I knew exactly what kind of social morass I was getting into.

*   *   *

Of all the psychological syndromes associated with disability, the most pervasive, and the most destructive, is a radical loss of self-esteem. This sense of damage to the self, the acquisition of what Erving Goffman called a "stigma," or a "spoiled identity," grew upon me during my first months in a wheelchair, and it hit me hardest when I returned to the university in the fall of 1977. By then, I could no longer hold on to the myth that I was using a wheelchair during convalescence. I had to face the unpalatable fact that I was wedded permanently to it; it had become an indispensable extension of my body. Strangely, I also felt this as a major blow to my pride.

The damage to my ego showed most painfully in an odd and wholly irrational sense of embarrassment and lowered self-worth when I was with people on my social periphery. Most of my colleagues in the anthropology department were old friends, some even from our undergraduate years, and they generally were warm and supportive. But people from other departments and the administration were another matter. During my first semester back at the university, I attended a few lunch meetings at the Faculty Club, but I began to notice that these were strained occasions. People whom I knew did not look my way. And persons with whom I had a nodding acquaintance did not nod; they, too, were busily looking off in another direction. Others gave my wheelchair a wide berth, as if it were surrounded by a penumbra of contamination. These were not happy encounters.

My social isolation became acute during stand-up gatherings, such as receptions and cocktail parties. I discovered that I was now three-and-a-half feet tall, and most social interaction was taking place two feet above me. When speaking to a standing person, I have to crane my neck back and look upward, a position that stretches my larynx and further weakens my diminished vocal strength. Conversation in such settings has become an effort. Moreover, it was commonplace that I would be virtually ignored in a crowd for long periods, broken by short bursts of patronization. There was no escape from these intermittent attentions, for it is very difficult to maneuver a wheelchair through a crowd. My low stature and relative immobility thus made me the defenceless recipient of overtures, rather than their instigator. This is a common complaint of the motor-disabled: They have limited choice in socializing and often must wait for the others to come to them. As a consequence, I now attend only small, sit-down gatherings.

Not having yet read the literature on the sociology of disability, I did not immediately recognize the pattern of avoidance. Perhaps this was for the best, as my initial hurt and puzzlement ultimately led me to research the subject. In the meantime, I stopped going to the Faculty Club.

*   *   *

At the beginning of [the chapter in *The Body Silent* from which this text is taken], I spoke of the feeling of aloneness, the desire to shrink from society into the inner recesses of the self, that invades the thoughts of the disabled — a feeling that I attributed in part to the deep physical tiredness that accompanies most debility and the formidable physical obstacles posed by the outside world. But we have added other elements to this urge to withdraw. The individual has also been alienated from his old, carefully nurtured, and closely guarded sense of self by a new, foreign, and unwelcome identity. And he becomes alienated from others by a double-barreled mechanism: Due to his depreciated self-image, he has a tendency to withdraw from his old associations into social isolation. And, as if in covert cooperation with this retreat, society — or at least American society — helps to wall him off.

*   *   *

In summary, from my own experience and research and the work of others, I have found that the four most far-reaching changes in the consciousness of the disabled are: lowered self-esteem; the invasion and occupation of thought by physical deficits; a strong undercurrent of anger; and the acquisition of a new, total, and undesirable identity. I can only liken the situation to a curious kind of "invasion of the body snatchers," in which the alien intruder and the old occupant coexist in mutual hostility in the same body. It is a metamorphosis in the exact sense. One morning in the hospital, a nurse was washing me when she was called away by another nurse, who needed help in moving a patient. "I'll be right back," she said as she left, which all hospital denizens know is but a fond hope. She left me lying on my back without the call bell or the TV remote, the door was closed, and she was gone for a half hour. Wondering whether she had forgotten me, I tried to roll onto my side to reach the bell. But I was already quadriplegic, and, try as I might, I couldn't make it. I finally gave up and was almost immediately overcome by a claustrophobic panic, feeling trapped and immobile in my own body. I thought then of Kafka's giant bug, as it rocked from side to side, wiggling its useless legs, trying to get off its back — and I understood the story for the first time.

*   *   *

America is a land of shrinking resources and families, a society whose culture glorifies the body beautiful and youthfulness, while barely tolerating youths. It is small wonder that it harbors people increasingly turned in on themselves in rampant narcissism. To make matters worse, the increased affluence of the upper middle class and upper class is offset by the growing despair of the lower class. The economic plight of their men is eroding the black family, and once proudly independent blue-collar workers now line up in soup kitchens, their jobs sent overseas by American capital. Our cities are littered with homeless people sleeping in bus stations and doorways, rummaging for food in garbage cans, abandoned by a society that dodges responsibility by telling itself that such people choose to live that way. The successful simply shrug their shoulders and say, "I'm alright, Jack." Our cities present scenes that are almost reminiscent of Calcutta. Europeans are appalled, but to most urban Americans the homeless have become invisible. They walk around the human rag piles, they avert their eyes, and they maintain the myth that they dwell in what some politicians have called "a shining city on a hill."

They do the same thing with the disabled.

*   *   *

The kind of culture the handicapped American must face is just as much a part of the environs of his disability as his wheelchair. It hardly needs saying that the disabled, individually and as a group, contravene all the values of youth, virility, activity, and physical beauty that Americans cherish, however little most individuals may realize them. Most handicapped people, myself included, sense that others resent them for this reason: We are subverters of an American Ideal,

just as the poor are betrayers of the American Dream. And to the extent that we depart from the ideal, we become ugly and repulsive to the able-bodied. People recoil from us, especially when there is facial damage or bodily distortion. The disabled serve as constant, visible reminders to the able-bodied that the society they live in is shot through with inequity and suffering, that they live in a counterfeit paradise, that they too are vulnerable. We represent a fearsome possibility.

*   *   *

We owe a great deal of our understanding of ritual to Arnold van Gennep and Emile Durkheim, and to Durkheim's students Henri Hubert and Marcel Mauss, but it is the anthropologist Victor Turner who has done most to bring their ideas into line with modern cultural and social theory. The title of one of his essays, "Betwixt and Between," is actually a neat description of the ambiguous position of the disabled in American life. The long-term physically impaired are neither sick nor well, neither dead nor fully alive, neither out of society nor wholly in it. They are human beings but their bodies are warped or malfunctioning, leaving their full humanity in doubt. They are not ill, for illness is transitional to either death or recovery. Indeed, illness is a fine example of a nonreligious, nonceremonial liminal condition. The sick person lives in a state of social suspension until he or she gets better. The disabled spend a lifetime in a similar suspended state. They are neither fish nor fowl; they exist in partial isolation from society as undefined, ambiguous people.

47
Machismo and Impotence

MAY N. DIAZ

In the Mexican town of Tonalá, the social distance which characterizes the way in which marriages are made, as well as the interrelationships within the family, both derives from and is daily supported by the division of economic roles. By using the criteria of sex and age, economic activities are divided so that there is little overlap between what different persons do. The one possible exception is in pottery-making, but even then, although the definition of male and female roles may differ from one household to another, the separation of tasks in any one family tends to be consistent, clearly understood by all members, and to involve the minimum overlap of functions. For most economic tasks what is done by a woman is not done by a man; what is done by a man is not done by a boy. Boys perform peripheral male activities, while girls perform subordinate female ones. The two criteria and the subsequent division of labor provide two themes or ideas about social relationships that are found permeating most social interaction in the village: (1) the sphere of man and the sphere of woman are strictly separate, and (2) statuses are arranged hierarchically by age. In addition, the fact that there is little overlap of activities makes for a rigid system. If the role-player normally assigned to a task is absent, the task may have to go unperformed. If mother is ill or out of the house, no one else can take the responsibility of preparing the meal. In a patrilocal household the problem is solved by eating with one of the other nuclear families, but the general feeling is that no one else can do the job. A death in the family puts great strain on the system of role allocations. Usually a family tries to fill the void with another person to take over the economic role — the father's sister may move in, so she can cook and clean, the mother's brother may take over as head of the household if the sons are not yet grown, or the son-in-law if there are only grown daughters. It is important to have all the family roles filled, for members are dependent upon one another for the maintenance of the family unit.

The family system runs by interdependence and strict role separation. It is integrated on this basis, but such a mode of integration is precarious and threatened by new behavior patterns. Everyone understands what a man does and what a woman does as long as the activities are the traditional ones. As soon as one introduces new activities, one raises the question of whether they are properly masculine or feminine. For many village individuals it is easier to avoid making a

From May Diaz, *Tonalá: Conservatism, Responsibility, and Authority in a Mexican Town*. Berkeley: University of California Press, 1966, pp. 84–92. Copyright © 1966 the Regents of the University of California. Reprinted with permission. (Bibliographic documentation contained in the original text is omitted here. Interested readers should consult the original publication.)

decision than to withstand a threat to one's sex identity. New behavior patterns also raise the possibility that paternal authority is threatened.

The third general theme of family organization is that of a split between the locus of power and that of responsibility. In the formal structure the mother is responsible for the actions of the members of the family, but she has no direct power. This creates a situation that is conflict-ridden and frustrating for the mother. There are ways out: social chaos in the household, dependence on the saints, the priests and the Church, and manipulation. All take place, of course, but only the last is of interest here. Through manipulation, a role-player with little overt authority — the mother — is able to gain her own ends when she is able to use accepted rules of behavior and role expectations to support her. An example will perhaps make the matter clearer.

Lupita, a young unmarried woman, was telling me how difficult it was to arrange to talk to one's boyfriend, since fathers and brothers object to any courting that they see going on. She had been talking to her boyfriend at the front window of the house when her married brother arrived on the scene. The boy left immediately, but her brother had caught sight of him and was angry. "Who was that here at the window?" he asked.

"No one that concerns you," she snapped back.

"Of course it concerns me," he replied.

"That's only because you don't mind your own business. After all, you are married now, and you are not my boss," she said. But she evidently felt that she was on shaky ground, for she said that she halfway expected him to slap her for her impertinence, but somehow, from somewhere she got the courage to face him.

At this point the father came to the door to find out what the shouting was about. Lupita told him that her brother was being impossible. The brother tried to explain what the fight had been about and ended by saying, "Why don't you keep better watch over your daughters?" The father only shooed them both into the house. Although the brother let the matter drop, Lupita was afraid that the incident would not end there, for she felt that her sister-in-law would needle her brother, who would in turn talk to her father and get him aroused enough to lay down an ultimatum. And her father's ultimatum she would have to obey.

She decided to take a little action of her own. She went to help her mother with supper and started to complain about how her brother's wife would nag him, and he in turn would put pressure on the father. Her mother was a willing

listener; she had other scores to settle with her daughter-in-law; for she felt that the younger woman was an interloper who had come between mother and son; she felt that her husband was too sympathetic to the daughter-in-law; and that the daughter-in-law tried to alienate the grandchildren from the grandparents. As soon as the father came to be served his dinner, the mother began to scold him for letting his sons take over his authority and for not wearing the pants in his family. He responded in the way mother and daughter had anticipated. He decided to let the incident drop and went out immediately after dinner, rather than stopping to talk to his son.

The incident demonstrates several points: in the first place, a person with little authority (the mother, a person with responsibility but little overt power) was able to achieve her ends; she was willing to maneuver the father, the power-holder, because of her desire to frustrate the daughter-in-law's manipulations; she was able to do so by appealing to the formal structure (namely, the father holds the power, not the daughter-in-law) put in terms of the easily understood cultural symbol of who wears the pants. Note also that the father's decision is dramatized as withdrawal.

Another kind of manipulation relies upon the effective tie between mother and offspring in combination with her overt lack of power in the formal structure. By words, gestures, and mien she transmits the message, "Look how I suffer as a result of your misdeeds." This is a very powerful weapon indeed, for it plays upon the vast buried sea of guilt feelings of the children. As the mother weeps silently, withdraws, refuses to go out of the house, ceases eating, hides her face behind a shielding rebozo, she is engaged in a passive resistance campaign that is quite successful in forcing her children to conform to her wishes. It is a less effective weapon in handling her husband, but it works there sometimes too.

In the incident of Lupita and her family, who was the decision-maker? On the surface everyone is. The father wears the pants and decides not to take direct action. The brother initiates action. The sister-in-law moves the brother to take action (or perhaps it is only the sister's image of her brother's wife that is an actor in the scene). The mother precipitates a decision in the direction she wants it made. The sister gives just the right cues to mother so that things move her way. One is left with the impression that the women are maneuvering busily.

It is important to note that the women's decision-making is implicit and hidden; since according to the formal structure women do not hold power, enforcing their decisions on others must be done by means other than direct commands. If power is the ability to have others do what you want them to, then manipulation is an alternative mode of behavior in respect to power. The dichotomy of expressive and instrumental leadership when applied to the family is often taken to mean this division between formal and informal leaders, but it is somewhat misleading to see the two sets of terms as coterminous.

For one thing, the informal decision-maker may manipulate the situation and the role-players in order to make decisions concerned with instrumental and adaptive goals — that is, those goals concerned with the relationship of the collectivity, in this case the family, to the outside world; decisions in this adaptive area are made by the instrumental leader. The fact that a Tonaltecan mother can manipulate the situation in such a way that she decides whether a piece of property should be sold, or what occupation the son should go into, means that there are possible modes of action whereby she becomes the *de facto* instrumental leader. Secondly, since our model ties together mother, expressive leader, and integrative functions, we tend to see her in the leader role as some kind of clucking hen, keeping things calm, peaceful, and running smoothly. Of course, at least part of the time she does this. But part of the time she is also creating conflict and enlarging the social divisions in the household in order to attain other goals — sometimes personal ones, at times other integrative goals that she considers of more importance — somewhat like stopping a prairie fire by building a fire in front of it.

Up until now we have been talking about implicit and unrecognized decision-making. How do things work in reference to explicit authority?

All the members of the family are expected to behave with respect toward the father. This means that a member does not drink in his presence except on ceremonial occasions; that sex, lovers, boyfriends, and sweethearts are never mentioned when he is around; that one does not quarrel or fight when he is in the house. Failure to show respect is quickly punished with a slap or a beating, depending on the temperament of the particular father and how much face he has lost. Consequently, the social distance of the respect relationship is underscored often by physical distance. Young girls go about their female chores in the kitchen or a corner of the patio; boys soon learn that things are more comfortable when they are out of the house. Except when small boys are busy at specific chores, they spend their days in the street or the plaza. They play away from home; they run in to snatch a bite of food whenever they are hungry. One might label this the phenomenon of the "absent child" in contradistinction to the absent father.

As a result of the need for maintaining distance between the father and other members of his family, daily life is arranged in such a way that there are few occasions for validating group unity through common activities. Meals are not the structured sit-down affairs we are used to; partaking of dinner transmits a kind of message other than togetherness. Rather it is an occasion in which authority is validated in that father is served preferentially vis-à-vis sons, while women serve the men first and themselves afterward. This pattern is quite different from that of the urban middle class, where the dining room forms the nucleus of the house, and, of the time the family is together, the greatest amount is spent there. Leisure time in Tonalá is likely to be spent in sex-differentiated groups. Women and small children cluster in doorways on warm evenings and gossip and tell stories; men play billiards in the billiard parlors or stand around street corners and talk politics. Even church-going underscores the divisions rather than ceremonially supporting family unity, for family members go to church separately, men and women sit on different sides of the church and usually belong to different religious associations.

Since daily life emphasizes the fact that society consists of intermeshing series of relationships between pairs of individuals, the responsibility component of authority, that is, responsibility to a bounded group, tends not to be very obvious.

Within the family the child sees the mother as the responsible person both in daily behavior and in the ideal picture of family relations. Indeed, the structure is such that the responsible person and the power holder are not the same. In the final result, responsibility is seen to be part of female role behavior.

What is seen as the attribute of power and of the male role, of the father the child wants to be like, is power divorced of responsibility. In all societies, the child probably first learns the authority role in respect to the obvious attributes of his father: he smokes or he can stay up late or he handles the magic flutes, or some other surface behavioral clue. But this view is overlaid by other propositions as the child grows in understanding and adds to his knowledge of what father does: he works, he supports the family, he makes decisions. But if what goes on within the walls of the house is patterned in such a way that the small boy does not see these responsibility attributes of the authority figure in action, he tends to make the equation: authority = power without responsibility. In this instance the father does not undertake actions within the walls of the house; as the person responsible for the nuclear family unit in a larger context, he is completely absent, distant, or removed from what the child is allowed to see. The father's behavior outside the walls of the house is as mysterious to the child as what goes on in a *kiva* for a five-year-old Hopi.

Ideally speaking, the Tonaltecan father is responsible to the government for the actions of his family members and his power over them, and also to the Church. In practice, responsibility toward governmental agencies in this sphere is minimal, for governmental action in reference to family units is well-nigh nonexistent except in large cities. In Tonalá there is no government agency with jurisdiction over matters of family and child welfare except the Court of First Instance, a part of the state judicial system. Few Tonaltecans use the court for suits involving kinsmen; they are thought of as private matters, not the business of the government. A father's maltreatment of a son may result in the personal action of a relative or other individual plus informal social sanctions, but it is unlikely to result in court action. With respect to the Church, the responsibility component tends to fall on the mother; she is the one who both formally and actually is considered to bear the responsibility for her children's Christian upbringing and behavior. As the *Hoja Parroquial* put it, "Her duty to cultivate in her children the Christian virtues is most fundamental and indispensable."

Two factors contribute heavily to the stereotype of authority that the child learns. The first of these is the distant relationship with the father. The child does not observe his father's making of decisions within the walls of the house, for the respect owed the head of the family channels day-to-day authority into the hands of the mother. Respect also demands that the child be away from the father whenever he is on adult male business outside the house; the boy does not gradually learn the role as a result of observing how his father acts vis-à-vis other grown men, for the rules are such that when his father is somewhere outside the house, he is not in the same place. The second factor has to do with the structure of the family itself, its internal splintering, its lack of solidarity within; the father tends to be seen as a free agent rather than as the representative of a nuclear family in reference to the outside world. Solidarity with men in general or with one's leisure companions may have preference.

As a consequence of these factors, the child sees authority as power shorn of responsibility and clothed in the outward symbols of the male role — *machismo* if you will; to be physically strong, careless of consequences and dangers, jealous of one's honor, and able to enforce one's wishes and desires on others. Power is seen as unpredictable, based on personal whims, shaped by *voluntad* (will); the powerful person can bring gifts or mete out punishment, but which he will choose to do cannot be foretold.

48
Women in America

MARVIN HARRIS

All the industrializing nations found that the best way to preserve and increase the quantity and quality of their laboring classes was to prohibit or discourage the employment of married women in factory jobs. In the United States, the temptation to push married women into factory work was never as strong as in Europe because the great current of immigration into the New World provided ample numbers of qualified men, at least until the immigration laws were changed in the 1920s.

Prior to World War II, the material and procreative imperative and married woman's homebody role suited the government, churches, and employers of labor. Traditionally, the government held that the more people, the bigger the armed forces, the greater the security of life and property. Also, the more people, the greater the tax base, the better equipped the armed forces, and the greater the available wealth for the government bureaucracy. From the industrialist and merchant point of view, the more people, the bigger the market for real estate and goods and the cheaper the supply of labor. Similarly, for organized religion, the more people, the more

From Marvin Harris, *Why Nothing Works: The Anthropology of Daily Life*, Chapter 5, 86–97. A Touchstone Book published by Simon & Schuster, Inc. (updated with a new preface), 1987. Copyright © 1981 Marvin Harris. Reprinted with the permission of Simon & Schuster, Inc.

souls to save and pray for, the higher the level of economic support, and the greater the political influence of each denomination.

Women's homebody role also suited the male breadwinner. Wives who went to work posed a double threat: They undermined the basis of the husband's dominant role in family and society and they drove male wages down by increasing the supply of workers. These incentives explain why the unions were once one of the great bastions of antifeminism: The men who ran the unions wanted women to stay home for the same reason they wanted blacks to stay on the farms and immigrants to stay across the ocean — to force up the price of labor. For unionized men a worker's wage had at least to be "sufficient to keep his wife and children out of competition with himself." In the words of a turn-of-the-century Boston labor union leader: "The demand for female labor is an insidious assault upon the home; it is the knife of the assassin aimed at the family circle."

Throughout most of America's past, therefore, men from all social classes joined forces to keep married women at home where they were unpaid maidservants for their husbands and unpaid baby-makers for everybody else. The employment figures for the beginning of the century bear this out. In 1890 women made up 17 percent of the paid labor force. But the overwhelming majority of these women were single, widowed, or divorced. The typical and preferred pattern was for a married woman never to work for pay. If a girl's family could afford it, she stayed home until she got married. If not, she went to work until she got married and then quit immediately. The typical women workers were girls waiting to get married, "spinsters" unable for one reason or another to get married, women who had been abandoned by their husbands, and widows. In 1890 only 14 percent of the women in the job force were married and these women represented only 5 percent of working-age women. Most of these married working women were blacks and recent immigrants. For a married, native-born white woman to work outside the home for money was a phenomenal rarity: only 2 percent of them did it. In contrast, 23 percent of married adult black women in 1890 already held jobs (and not because they were "liberated" but because they were poor!).

Except for a tiny group of privileged female doctors, lawyers, college teachers, and other professionals, scarcely any native-born married white women went to work unless their husbands died or abandoned them. A woman simply did not get married to a man who could not "support" her, which meant that many women had to postpone getting married and that many remained single for life. Although we think of the present feminist situation as characterized by a new tendency to delay marriage, the record for late marriages was actually achieved in 1900. Over 40 percent of American women that year between the ages of twenty and twenty-nine had never had a husband. But unlike the somewhat smaller group of single women in their twenties today, the unmarried women of the past could not live alone or with male or female age mates; they remained instead with their parents or they moved in with married brothers or sisters, and were frequently looked down upon and humiliated for their lack of success in capturing a breadwinner husband.

Until World War II, therefore, the proportion of *married* women who participated in the workforce remained small. In 1940, despite a sharp increase in working wives during the Great Depression, only 15 percent of married women who had a husband present held an outside job. But this was soon to change. By 1960 the proportion of employed married women with husbands present had risen to 30 percent and by 1980 to about 50 percent. More than half of married women in the prime reproductive age of thirty-five years or younger now hold jobs. As one might expect, the proportion of married women who go to work is highest among those who have no small children to take care of at home. This proportion has climbed to a phenomenal 80 percent among married women less than thirty-five years old. But the proportion of young married women who go to work even though (or because) they have small children to take care of is also astonishingly high: 40 percent of those under thirty-five who have one or more children under six; and over 60 percent of those who have a child at home between six and eighteen.

Has this drastic change in the participation rate of married women in the labor force finally broken the back of the marital and procreative imperative? I think so. The traditional pronatal system could tolerate increased participation by *unmarried women* in the labor force; but it could not survive increased participation by *married women*. The fulfillment of the marital and procreative imperative hinged on women staying home in order to raise children. While one can easily think of alternative arrangements such as day-care centers which might resolve the contradiction between jobs and babies, no such arrangements were or are available on the requisite national scale, primarily because day care has to be paid in cash, while home care was paid with sentiment. As married women poured into the labor force, all the dire warnings that procreation and employment outside the home were incompatible suddenly came true. The baby boom collapsed, and the fertility rate began its historic plunge, reaching zero-population-growth levels in 1972 and falling still further to an average of 1.8 children per woman by 1980. Incidentally, the idea that the baby boom collapsed because of the introduction of the "pill" can easily be dismissed, since the bust began in 1957 while the pill was not released for public use until June 1960. As late as 1964, when fertility was falling with unprecedented speed, only 10 percent of married women of childbearing age were using the "pill."

I think the most misguided notion about the end of the baby boom and the transformation of housewife into wage laborer is the belief that women's liberation made the housewife dissatisfied with her homebody baby-making role and so she went out and found a job. Women's liberation did not *create* the working woman; rather the working woman — especially the working housewife — created women's liberation. As we have just seen, the massive shift of married women into the labor force had already taken place *before* the period of intensive consciousness-raising. In the words of University of Florida anthropologist Maxine Margolis,

Thus, while the past fifteen years have witnessed the entry of women, particularly wives and mothers, into the labor force in unprecedented numbers, popular opinion only belatedly recognized the importance of this phenomenon. While the media devoted much space to "bra burning" and other supposed atrocities of the women's movement, little attention was paid to the reality of women's work, which had set the stage for the revival of feminism.

Moreover, it is a great deception to believe that women went out and found jobs. Given the nature of the U.S. economy and its chronically high levels of unemployment, the mere desire to find a job is not enough to land one. The jobs have to be there. Between 1947 and 1978, twenty-five million new jobs were filled by women. And by 1979 two out of every three new jobs were being taken by women. Feminists have often neglected to say that these jobs find the women as much as the women find the jobs. To understand why the feminist rebellion took place precisely when it did, we must understand both sides of the equation: what it was that compelled or enticed married women to want to look for work, and what it was in the national economy that created vast numbers of new jobs that went looking for married women.

On the worker's side, married women's initial motivation was to provide a supplement to their breadwinner-husband's income. The 1950s and early 1960s were a period of consumer expectations aimed at the ownership of clothing, household furnishings, automobiles, telephones, and many new or previously prohibitively expensive product lines such as washing machines, dryers, dishwashers, and color TV sets. Much of married women's initial surge toward the job market was keyed toward purchasing specific products deemed important for a decent standard of living in what was then being called the affluent society. To achieve these limited goals married women were quite willing to accept part-time, temporary, and dead-end jobs.

As all the polls and surveys of the 1950s showed, the baby-boom mothers had no intention of giving up their homebody role. At first, the married women who moved into the labor force were primarily housewives over forty-five whose children had "left the nest." But a decisive break came in the early 1960s when younger married women, with children under eighteen, began to enter the labor force in droves. This break was not caused by a rise in feminine consciousness; rather it was caused by the beginning of the Great Inflation.

By the early 1960s the baby-boom parents were finding it increasingly difficult to achieve or hold on to middle-class standards of consumption for themselves and their children, and the wife's job had begun to play a crucial role in family finances. As the first of the baby-boom children approached college age, the burden of medical care, schooling, clothing, and housing for the average family increased far faster than the male breadwinner's salary.

Official government statistics place the beginning of the inflationary surge after 1965 and indicate that spendable weekly earnings (in constant dollars) of workers with three dependents fell by only about 1 percent between then and 1970. But inflation does not affect all parts of a family's budget equally. It hits especially hard at food, health care, housing, and education. Moreover, there is something seriously wrong with the official index of purchasing power: It takes no account of the quality of goods and services. One can infer that women were going to work as much to replace or repair their cars, washing machines, and dishwashers as to acquire them. There was, after all, despite all the protestations of managerial innocence, an iron fist inside the glove of planned obsolescence. What good was it to own cars or dishwashers that kept breaking down? Critics of the American consumer's apparently insatiable appetite for cosmetic model changeovers fail to consider that while "new" seldom meant "better," "old" usually meant "broken." More and more, therefore, the wife's earnings had to be used for essentials rather than for frills and luxury items. Soon more and more baby-boom parents began to discover that if they wanted to enlarge their slice of the pie, or to just hold on to what they had, they could not do so on one salary. More and more the redemption of middle-class parenthood came down to one thing: a second income.

While I think I have now shown that there were strong economic pressures on women to break out of the homebody role, we must not forget the other side of the equation. Pressures to join the labor force have always existed, but married women had previously not yielded to them because there were simply no jobs they could or would take — no jobs that they themselves and their husbands and the other partisans of the marital and procreative imperative regarded as suitable for married women. Suitable jobs — jobs compatible with the traditional goals of procreation and marriage — would allow women to work part-time or to move in and out of the workforce in order to meet family needs.

And if married women had to work, they should try not to compete with men and thereby cheapen the breadwinner's wages. They ought to work at occupations and industries in which women predominated.

Precisely these specifications characterize the jobs that went looking for women workers after World War II. The great bulk of the new jobs were of two types: low-level information-processing jobs such as file clerks, secretaries, typists, and receptionists; and low-level people-processing jobs such as nurses, primary school teachers, retail sales help, medical and dental assistants, guidance counsellors, and social workers. These were woman-dominated occupations, mainly part-time, in-and-out, temporary or dead-end, and almost always poorly paid as evidenced by the fact that the average employed woman in the United States makes only 58 percent of the average male's wages. Most of the new jobs were white- or "pink"-collar jobs and the great bulk of these, in turn, were secretarial, clerical, or sales jobs situated within or dependent on some branch of government or the bureaucracy of some large corporation or retail chain. In brief, the kinds of jobs that went looking for women were the jobs that were being created as an integral part of the process leading to the current bureaucratized and oligopolized impasse with its inconveniences, disservices, and misinformation, and its inflationary inefficiencies.

In broad perspective, the call-up of women for duty in the service-and-information job market represents a curious replay of the call-up of women into manufacturing early in the industrial revolution. But there is one crucial difference: This time the recruitment of women for employment outside the home did not seem to threaten the livelihood of male workers since the kinds of jobs involved had long been dominated by women rather than men. They were jobs — at least at the beginning — that men didn't want and that married women took as a temporary expedient with their husband's approval in order to preserve the ideals of the marital and procreative imperative.

With the generation of immigrant "coolies" fading from the scene, the dormant white American housewife was the service-and-information employer's sleeping beauty. Her qualifications were superb. She was available in vast numbers. She had been trained for her entire life to be unaggressive and to take orders from men. Her husband earned more than she did so she would take a job that was neither permanent nor secure. She had little interest in joining a union and still less in struggling to form one. She would accept temporary jobs, part-time jobs, jobs that let her go home to cook or take care of the children, jobs that were boring, jobs that had no future. And she could read and write. All she needed was an office manager, agency head, financial vice president, or some other "service-and-information-boss charming" to kiss her into life.

The timing of the feminist outburst at the end of the 1960s marks the moment of collective realization that women, married or not, would have to continue to work as a consequence of inflation and of the growing dearth of males who held genuine breadwinner jobs, and that unless they rebelled they would continue to get the worst of all possible worlds: dull, boring, dead-end jobs at work, and cooking, cleaning, child care, and chauvinist males at home. At the end of the 1960s, women were being drawn through a pneumatic tube. At one end of the tube there was inflation squeezing them out of the home and into the job market; at the other end there was the expanding service-and-information job market, sucking them into a niche specifically designed for literate but inexpensive and docile workers who would accept 60 percent or less of what a man would want for the same job.

The pillars of the male-dominated breadwinner family now stood hollow and near collapse. Neither the interests of big business or government lay as before in a united defense of the marital and procreative imperative. In an age of nuclear arms, high birthrates were no longer a military priority, while for government and business the immediate assured benefits of employing women overshadowed the long-run penalties of a falling birthrate. The only real opposition came from the organized churches. But here the struggle was waged with weapons of sentiment, and not those of material costs and benefits; and while the churches could make some couples feel guilty for not getting married and having children, they could scarcely offer to pay the bills for wives who felt guilty enough to stay home.

As for the male breadwinner, he least of all could resist the new role society was preparing for him. The Carnegie Corporation reports that "a family with an annual income of $10,000 must spend more than $50,000 to raise a child to the age of 18, not including savings put aside for higher education." Anthropologist Wanda Minge estimates that a moderate income family (with less than $20,000 after taxes) will have to spend $195,000 to rear a child from birth through four years of college, allowing for 10 percent annual inflation but no extras such as piano lessons or orthodontics. While married men on the average still contribute about three times as much as their working wives to family income, wives' salaries now make the difference between just getting by or falling into poverty; or between a barely middle-class versus a workingman's family budget. As the *Wall Street Journal* put it: "The workingman breadwinner who doesn't have a wife on a payroll just may wind up not having enough bread." Or, one might add, breaking his back moonlighting on a second job.

To be sure, men wanted to keep women home and to have their wives' paychecks too; they wanted wives to take care of the kids *and* to go to work to help pay for them. And, to make matters worse, they wanted the deference due the bread-winner without winning the bread. They wanted the kowtowing and pandering of the old order to go on, as if a woman's wellbeing still depended on finding, pleasing, and keeping a man who could afford to get married.

Women were being asked to work in two places at once: to work for half a man's pay on the job and for no pay at all off the job, and to remain submissive and obedient to sexist hus-bands who no longer supported them. And so it was women who had most to gain and least to lose by kicking at the hollow pillars of the temple of marriage and childbirth.

The demise of the marital and procreative imperative has brought about a rapid and irre-versible restructuring of American domestic life and of the American way of love and sex. Although authorities like historian Carl Degler and sociologist Mary Jo Bane have tried to reassure the older generation that the "family is here to stay," the family that remains is not the family that the older generation wanted to preserve. Like it or not, the lifetime male-domi-nated, two-parent, multichild, breadwinner family has virtually ceased to exist. While it is true that most children will continue to be born into some kind of family situation, the kind of domestic unit involved and the typical pattern of life experiences with respect to residence, mar-riage, and child-rearing that Americans can look forward to as they grow up are fundamentally new additions to American culture.

Much conservative thought about the preser-vation of traditional family patterns hinges on the notion that the precipitous drop in fertility is an aberration that will soon give way to another baby boom. Nothing of the sort is likely to occur. The baby boom was the aberration, the last

hurrah of the marital and procreative imperative. As women struggle to achieve career parity with men and get ever more deeply involved in the job market, the historic downward trend in birthrates will continue for a long time to come. The rate mentioned earlier, the first-time marriage rate, has also been moving downward, falling from ninety per thousand single women in 1950 to about sixty-five in 1976. Most of this drop can be attributed to the aging baby-boom children who have been postponing marriage or not getting married at all. In 1960 only 28 percent of women between the ages of twenty and twenty-four were single; in 1974 the figure was 40 percent. And those who have gotten married have been getting divorced in astonishing numbers. Between 1965 and 1978 the country's divorce rate more than doubled, with the highest frequency found again, significantly, among the younger, twenty-to-twenty-four age group. With one out of three marriages ending in divorce — an all time high — it is farfetched to point to a high rate of remar-riage among older couples (now also starting to decline) as evidence for the "preservation of the family." Very little is being preserved. Simultaneous with the rise in the divorce rate, the postponement of marriage, and the fall in the birthrate, there has been an 81 percent increase in the number of families headed by women — either separated, divorced, widowed, or never-married — since 1960. About 17 percent of all children now live in such families at any one time, and the odds that children born today will at one point be living in such families is well over 40 percent. As families grow smaller, as divorce rates rise, and as marriage and birth rates fall, more and more Americans will find themselves living alone for a good portion of their lives. The growth in the number of single persons in the age group twenty-five to thirty-four is a forecast of things to come. In 1950 only one out of twenty men and women in this age group was living alone; in 1976, one out of three of them was living alone! Among elderly widowed women (sixty-five years and older), the frequency rose from one out of four to an astonishing two out of three. Already in 1980 only 6 percent of all American families fit the traditional normative pattern of full-time homebody wife and mother, breadwinner father and husband, and two or more dependent children. Far more Americans are living alone or in single-parent, remarried, or childless families than in the traditional nuclear family into which the baby-boom generation was born.

SECTION FIVE
Religion

Introduction

All human societies have sets of beliefs concerning supernatural beings and forces, and anthropologists have spent considerable effort in attempting to define them. There are so many different varieties of beliefs and rituals that an all-encompassing definition of religion is bound to be very vague. For instance, a belief in gods (powerful or not) is not universal; neither is the practice of praying nor the concept of sin. Many of the distinctions made by early anthropologists, such as the opposition of magic and religion, are viewed as ethnocentric and of little validity by many modern anthropologists. Even the distinction of a "natural" world from a "supernatural" world makes little sense to many people: for instance, a Trobriand Islander would not distinguish the weeding of his garden as a "technique" from garden magic as a "ritual." To him, both are practices instrumental in getting yams.

A significant contribution to the understanding of religious phenomena was Émile Durkheim's suggestion in his *Elementary Forms of Religious Life* (trans. 1915) that the gods we worship are made in the image of our societies. This implies that in egalitarian societies, such as that of the Yuquí and the !Kung, or those of the Australian Aborigines discussed by Durkheim, the supernatural realm does not contain superior gods to be worshiped. The spirit world of these people extends and confirms the egalitarian nature of their society. Praying to superior, whimsical gods, who may or may not grant one's prayers, is a phenomenon found in stratified societies: the hierarchy of gods, angels, and saints confirms and sanctifies social stratification.

A missionary attempting to impose the religion of a stratified society on a small egalitarian society is, in a sense, like a biologist attempting to graft the head of an elephant onto the body of a mouse. The prognosis in both cases is equally poor. In his famous ethnography *Yanomamö: The Fierce People*, N. Chagnon (1977) comments on various qualities of missionary zeal: "Where the Protestants impatiently attack the whole culture [of the Yanomamö] and try to bring salvation to all, including adults, the Catholics are more patient and focus on the children" (p. 159). In her recent work on the Yuquí (see Chapter 30), Allyn M. Stearman (1989) devotes an entire chapter to this issue. She comments that, "Because the missionaries are so intent on erasing old ideologies, preserving what is Yuquí is seen as counter to the mission's ultimate objective of conversion. Ethnocide can be a slow, insidious process, the gradual eating away of a people's culture until they are no longer distinguishable from the society around them" (p. 148).

Most modern ethnographies discuss at length both the beneficial and detrimental effects of mission activity. Anthropologists are often impressed by the dedication of many missionaries, who risk — and often lose — their lives in the defense of

Mazahua altar for the dead. Religious rituals surrounding death are found in all societies. The Mazahua Indians of Mexico prepare offerings for the spirits of their dead relatives on Hallowe'en. Special bread is baked in shapes associated with the patrilineal ancestors of the master of the house. Fruit and liquor are also offered on this altar. The dead consume the spirit of the offerings during the night, and the rest is given away the next day in a village-wide reciprocal exchange. Source: Jean-Luc Chodkiewicz.

indigenous people. Nevertheless, anthropologists underline the disruption of social and ideological systems generated by missionary activity. An example of the anthropological debates on this issue is found in Section Six (Chapters 53 and 54), where the predictions of Lauriston Sharp in his famous essay "Steel Axes for Stone-Age Australians" are challenged by another anthropologist, John Taylor, who visited the same people several decades later, and found that their culture had been transformed rather than disrupted.

In spite of the many obvious differences among world religions, anthropologists point out that most religions agree on sanctifying the domination of men over women. Women are often denied access to both the priesthood and religious rituals, such as going into trance. Women are described in the beliefs of many egalitarian, as well as stratified, societies as impure, polluting temptresses. And major Christian thinkers, such as St. Augustine, in

The City of God, expressed doubts as to whether women have souls.

There are, however, many societies, including our own, in which some women are religious practitioners. Even in China, where the status of women is often low, some women are respected **shamans**, as described in Chapter 49. The term *shaman* is used by anthropologists to refer to a wide variety of religious practitioners. Here, we shall refer to shamanism to describe a set of religious beliefs and practices found in most parts of the world. Most shamans share the belief that the world is made up of several layers, like an onion. Humans live on one layer, and ordinary people can perceive only this layer. In trances, the shaman's soul leaves his or her body, and visits spirits living on other, parallel layers, or worlds, obtaining their support for restoring to a patient his or her soul, or for stealing the soul of an enemy. Diviner, curer, adviser, the shaman is an important person in many communities, not only in

Rite of passage. In many societies, the transition from childhood to adulthood is marked by a public ritual. Among the Wayana Amerindians of South America, the transition from boyhood to adulthood is marked by the Maraké, a series of rituals culminating, after several months, in a night-long dance, followed by an ordeal in which ants with a very painful bite are applied all over the boy's body. The boys are pictured here getting dressed for the occasion. Source: Jean-Luc Chodkiewicz.

egalitarian, but also in stratified societies, like that of the Cantonese. Jack Potter's vivid description of the rituals, and his analysis of a crafty, manipulative shaman illustrate how difficult it is for an outsider to distinguish faith from politics, social control, and entertainment.

Anthropologists have studied religions from many different perspectives: the psychological, evolutionist, functionalist, structuralist, and symbolic, to name a few. They all agree on the importance of religion in the lives of the people they study. Most anthropologists since Émile Durkheim have shown the contribution of religious beliefs and rituals to the continued existence of the sociocultural systems of the peoples they study. Materialist anthropologists such as Marvin Harris point out further that religious beliefs may also make a significant contribution to the adaptation of a population to its ecosystem. Harris discusses this notion in his essay "The Origin of the Sacred Cow," in Chapter 50. It has not been

only misinformed people, but also sophisticated anthropologists such as Robert Lowie, who have claimed that the sacred cows of India were typical examples of economic mismanagement and irrationality. Why do India's hungry masses not eat the beef and buy tractors? Is it just because of an irrational religion? Lowie's view that religion and not economics explains the "sacred cow complex" in India arises from his opposition to materialistic explanations, and his preference for *emic* analyses, in which the informants' perceptions and explanations are privileged (Lowie 1960). Since the Hindus claimed that they did not kill and certainly did not eat cows, this is what was reported as fact.

Harris, however, points out that the Hindu religion once required the sacrifice of cows, which were then consumed, in large numbers, in redistributive feasts. This practice came to an end with overpopulation: steaks became a luxury enjoyed only by the rich. Cows competed with poor pea-

Ritual beating. During this ritual beating, part of the Maraké of the Wayana, the initiates are supposed to smile to show that they are disdainful of pain. The Maraké saves Wayana boys from the indignities and uncertainties of North American teenagers, who achieve the privileges of adulthood only gradually, over many years. Source: Jean-Luc Chodkiewicz.

sants for scarce land and food, so the poor kept only enough cows for pulling plows and carts and for milk. Even now, there are not enough cows in India, where they are used seven times more efficiently than in North America, producing labor, milk, and dung. Cows don't rust the way tractors do, and, unlike tractors, they are able to reproduce. Their "exhaust" is a precious manure, and also serves as cooking fuel in this deforested country. Statistics show that bovicide (the culling of cow herds) is routine, efficient, and closely correlated with local needs for traction or milk. Moreover, the untouchables, as well as many non-Hindus, actually eat many of the cows. Harris shows that the belief in the sacredness of the cows has been essential to protecting the cows of poor farmers both from meat-packing industries and from their owners' hunger in times of famine. While it may not be the best solution to India's ecological problems, the sacredness of the cow has made perfectly good ecological and economic sense. This analysis of the sacred cow has sparked a lively debate between materialist anthropologists and those who still emphasize the symbolic and cultural aspects of cow worship. For the most part, the latter remain unaware that, rather than contradicting it, their analysis complements Harris's. An *etic* reality need not contradict its *emic* reflection in the mirror of the mind.

Everywhere, when oppressed peoples cannot find any earthly way to gain relief from injustice and oppression, they turn to their gods for help. First they attempt armed resistance, as did the Jews when they were dominated by the Romans; the Melanesians, who were colonized by the British, the French, and the Germans; the North American Indians; and, more recently, the Shiite Moslems of Iran. When a people are defeated, they retreat into ritual action, inventing **revitalization movements**, among which we may count such diverse belief systems as Christianity, **cargo cults**, and the Ghost Dance. Because the new cults appear to the invading outsiders as ridiculous and irrelevant to immediate political action or uprisings, they provide tolerated shields, for a minimum of organization, against oppression. Revitalization movements can thus be described as religions of the oppressed. Peter Farb's essay in Chapter 51 analyzes the phases in the evolution of such cults. He describes the bloody wars of extermination against North American Indians, the military response of the Native peoples, then the rise of such new cults as that of the Dreamers and that of the Ghost Dance. After reinventing and giving new life to old beliefs (revitalization), these cults may evolve into a new phase of accommodation with the dominant society, often in the form of an acceptance of subjugation. In the Roman empire, the case of Christians rising from the level of oppressed and persecuted victims to the status of emperors is exceptional.

Today, religion is far from dead in North America: the best evidence to support this claim is that religion is a booming business worth billions of tax-free dollars annually. All traditional churches, however, are confronting difficulties. The Catholic church, for example, has had to close many seminaries, for lack of recruits, and many churches, for lack of priests. At the same time, new and aggressively expanding religious groups have appeared. Although not all of the contemporary "gurus" have a fleet of 80 Rolls-Royces (as did the guru Rajneesh), utilitarian motives can generally be attributed to most of the leaders of cults, from EST or the Church of Scientology to the Unification Church of the Moonies or the various brands of television evangelism. The Gospel of Wealth is taught by the modern electronic church, whose leaders explicitly flaunt their luxurious life styles as proof of God's blessing.

In this new jungle of religions, God may be alive and well in America, but he goes by many aliases. This is the point developed by Reginald Bibby in his book *Fragmented Gods*, excerpted in Chapter 52. In his study of the changing patterns of religious activity in Canada, Bibby discovered that Canadians pick and choose beliefs, values, and moral rules the way they shop in their supermarkets. The fragmentation of Canadians into many social, cultural, and linguistic groups is reflected in their religious attitudes. Furthermore, the separation between the realms of the sacred and the profane has increased: traditional churches are used mostly to mark rituals of passage, such as birth, marriage, and death, but are largely ignored between those ceremonial occasions.

Works Cited

Augustine, St. 1957. *The City of God against the Pagans*. Cambridge: Harvard University Press.

Chagnon, N. 1977. *Yanomamö: The Fierce People*. Second edition. New York: Holt, Rinehart and Winston.

Durkheim, E. 1915. *The Elementary Forms of Religious Life*. Translated by J.W. Swain. London: Allen and Unwin.

Lowie, R. 1960. *Lowie's Selected Papers in Anthropology*. Edited by C. Dubois. Berkeley: University of California Press.

Stearman, Allyn Maclean. 1989. *Yuquí: Forest Nomads in a Changing World*. New York: Holt, Rinehart and Winston.

49 Cantonese Shamanism

JACK M. POTTER

The *mann seag phox* (alternatively, *mann mae phox*) act as intermediaries between the villagers and the supernatural worlds of heaven and hell. Assisted by their familiar spirits, the *seag phox* send their souls to the supernatural world, where they communicate with deceased members of village families. They also know how to recapture the kidnapped souls of sick village children, and they can predict the future. They care for the souls of girls who die before marriage, and protect the life and health of village children by serving as *khay mha*, fictive mothers.

The Group Séance

In 1962, at the time of the Moon Cake Festival on the fifteenth day of the eighth month, the three spirit mediums of Ping Shan held their annual free group séance open to all the villagers. At dusk the villagers, young and old, men and women, gathered on the cement rice-threshing floor in the open area west of Ping Shan's central

ancestral halls. As darkness fell and the full moon filled the sky with light almost as bright as day, the most accomplished shaman of the three, known as the Fat One, took her place on a low stool before a small, impoverished altar table. As the incense sticks on the altar burned down, the Fat One, her head covered with a cloth, went into a trance. She jerked spasmodically and mumbled incoherent phrases. Then she started to sing a stylized, rhythmic chant, as her familiar spirits possessed her and led her soul upward, away from the phenomenal world into the heavens. Their destination was the Heavenly Flower Gardens.

Many of the villagers were less interested in the Fat One's destination than in the ghosts (*kuei*) she met along the way. These were the souls of their deceased relatives and neighbors, who took advantage of this opportunity to commune with the living. They asked for news, gave advice, and sometimes voiced complaints.

The first ghost the medium encountered spoke as follows: "It was not time for me to die. My head was severed by a Japanese sword. I am angry and lost because my bones are mixed with those of other people." The assembled villagers immediately recognized this as the voice of Tang Tsuen's younger brother, who was one of ten villagers executed by the Japanese for smuggling during World War II. The villagers believe that anyone who meets such an unnatural death has an understandable grievance against the living, and his ghost is greatly feared. Tang Tsuen's wife, who was attending the séance, beseeched the ghost in a frightened voice to "protect the luck and safety of my husband." Tang Tsuen and his wife had worried for years about this ghost. To pacify him, they had planned to buy a silver plaque with the brother's name engraved on it, place it in a *kam taap*, a ceramic funerary vessel, and bury it in a permanent tomb where, they hoped, the brother's spirit would rest in peace.

The ghost of the dead brother, speaking through the medium, told Tang Tsuen that a costly permanent tomb was unnecessary because he had died unmarried and an elaborate burial was therefore inappropriate. All Tang Tsuen and his wife had to do, the ghost said, was to write his name on a piece of silver paper and hang it beside their ancestral altar. "If you do this," the ghost said, "I will try to help you, my brother, and your wife to have good luck and many children." As an afterthought, the spirit mentioned how pleased he was that his elder brother's wife had burned so much gold paper for him to spend and had offered him such excellent fruit during festival worship.

Later, while discussing the séance with a villager, I learned that the matter went much deeper than I had realized. Shortly after the war ended, Tang Tsuen's mother had, in fact, been bothered by the restless ghost of her younger son. As the villagers explain it, people accept death without resentment if they have lived a full, normal life and their death mandate is entered in the King of Hell's book in the usual fashion; this is fate, and nothing can be done about it. Executed in his youth by the Japanese, Tang Tsuen's brother had been deprived of the normal balance of his lifespan. The result was a troubled ghost, who could neither find peace himself nor leave his family any. Plagued by her son's ghost, Tang Tsuen's mother became physically and mentally ill, and died less than a year after her son's execution. Convinced that the ghost had driven the old lady to her grave and fearing for their own lives, Tang Tsuen and his wife tried to placate this restless family spirit. On the first and fifteenth days of every month, they made elaborate offerings in the doorway of their house, calling out to the bothersome ghost, "We are giving you money and offerings; take them and be satisfied! Don't come back to bother our family." Tang Tsuen also had gone to the expense of having his brother's spirit exorcised by a famous Taoist priest in the nearby market town during the Hungry Ghost Festival, when great quantities of food and paper money were offered

the wandering ghosts of the countryside in hopes of appeasing restless spirits and driving them away.

Nothing seemed to work, however. The ghost continued to haunt the couple's household, causing Tang Tsuen and his wife to fall ill repeatedly, and, they believed, to remain childless. Trips to spirit mediums confirmed that the couple's tragic barrenness was the work of the dead brother's jealous ghost. Tang Tsuen's wife was terrified when she heard the family ghost begin to speak through the medium that night.

Then, suddenly, the voices of children were heard through the medium, quarreling and fighting over the orange and peanuts that were part of the offering. One child's voice said, "These are mine"; another, a little girl's, screamed angrily, "No! These things are not for you; they were purchased as an offering!" Shrilly she continued, "These things belong to my parents and you stole them." The village women shouted in reply, "No, money was spent for this food; go away and don't bother us." By this time all the villagers had recognized the stubborn little girl as the deceased daughter of Tang Kau, the shopkeeper from whom Tang Tsuen's wife had purchased the offerings.

Suddenly the ghost of the girl spoke again: "When I took sick you did not call a doctor; after I became seriously ill you finally called one, but by then it was too late and I died." Speaking through the medium, the voice repeated this accusation again and again. Finally the women of the village grew angry and scolded the ghost, saying, "We don't want to hear any more of this; you are too young to know about things like this." The little girl had, in fact, died four years earlier, when she was two years old.

Tang Kau and his wife, the dead girl's parents, stood among the villagers without saying a word. They were ashamed to have the circumstances of their daughter's death rehearsed before the entire village, and they now feared that the girl's unhappy ghost would return to make her brothers and sisters ill. From the night of the séance on, Tang Kau and his wife dutifully burned silver paper for her on the first and fifteenth of every month. If the family's luck turns bad, they will blame their misfortune on their daughter's angry ghost. Resentment at their failure to call a doctor in time and jealousy of her surviving brothers and sisters are considered sufficient grounds for her returning to haunt the family.

The interview with the child's ghost ended as her final plaintive words drifted across the darkened village: "My parents were careless.

When I died, they hired someone who buried me so shallowly that my body was not completely covered and the dogs got at me. I cannot rest."[1]

The other villagers believed that the Fat One had deliberately brought up the case to frighten the guilt-ridden Tang Kau into placing the soul of his dead daughter under the medium's care. The villagers predicted that Tang Kau would wait and see if ordinary ritual procedures pacified his revengeful child's spirit. At the first sign of illness in the family or financial reverses, he probably will ask the Fat One to take charge of his daughter's spirit, a service for which she would of course charge a sizable fee.

The next village spirit the Fat One encountered on her heavenly voyage was Tang Mok-leung's father. The old man had died years earlier, when he was over sixty years old. He was, in the terminology sometimes used by the villagers, an old ghost. Young ghosts, that is, ghosts of the newly dead, are very powerful beings; if dissatisfied, they usually return to harry people. Like an aging person, the ghost grows progressively weaker as he ages, and he also becomes increasingly disposed to help rather than harm the living. Once a person has been dead more than sixty years, his ghost no longer inspires much fear; he may even be born again as a different person. Occasionally spirit mediums are unable to locate an aged ghost because it has been reborn into another life. Thus supernatural potency diminishes as the personality of the ghost dims in the minds of the living.

Tang Mok-leung and his aged mother were present at the séance. They heard the old man speak through the medium: "Everyone is well; my eldest son, I see, has sent $1,000 from abroad to help the family." Tang Mok-leung remained silent at this, so everyone present assumed that he had in fact received such a sum from his elder brother, who had emigrated to Europe. The old ghost continued speaking in a good-humored vein, now addressing his wife: "You, old 'ghost' [kuei], are very lucky, aren't you? Now that our son has sent you all this money, you have money to gamble with every day." The conversation represented an affectionate exchange between an old married couple; the old man was clearly pleased that his wife and family were doing so well. The good fortune of the family, until now just unsubstantiated gossip, was publicly confirmed, and the fortune and status of the aged woman recognized. In such cases the annual séance served to take stock of the gossip about villagers that has accumulated during the year and deal with it in a public manner.

The interview ended with the old ghost counseling his son and daughter-in-law: "Daughter-in-law, obey your mother-in-law; son, obey your mother. Be careful in doing things; do not quarrel," he said as his voice faded away. Benevolent old family ghosts typically give their families such advice during these séances. Their message affirms the society's normative structure.

The next spirit the medium encountered was the younger brother of Tang Soo's father. Through the medium he admonished his widow: "No matter how much money you make working for your nephew, you always give it to your daughter. You must keep some back for yourself." The old woman would have none of this, and scolded her husband's ghost: "Don't tell me what to do! If I'd known you were going to die so young, I wouldn't have married you because now I am left alone and have to work as a servant to support myself." Good-naturedly the old ghost replied, "But you are very happy now. Your nephew lets you stay with his family and so you have a new house to live in." The old woman scolded her husband again and he riposted. The dialogue continued for some time, until the entire audience was laughing at this incongruous quarrel between the old woman and her husband's ghost.

The shaman continued on her trip to the Heavenly Flower Gardens, describing the beautiful scenery she saw along the way. As she traveled on, she suddenly met a woman's ghost holding three children's souls in her hands. The medium asked the ghost who the three souls belonged to and why she had stolen them. The ghost replied that she was starving and had kidnapped the three children's souls in hopes of receiving ransom money for them. The medium summoned her tutelary spirits — the souls of her own dead children — to question the children's souls in hopes of eliciting their identity. When the spirits asked the children who their fathers and mothers were and how many brothers and sisters they had, the answers made it plain to all that they were the souls of village children whose mothers were in the audience. The mothers berated the woman ghost. "You must be crazy! Why have you stolen our children's souls?" The women asked the medium to send spirit soldiers to recover their children's souls. The ghost, unintimidated by this prospect, defiantly insisted on ransom money before she would release the souls.

The three mothers ran back to their homes to fetch gold paper to burn as ransom, and an article of their child's clothing to be used in retrieving its soul. Once home they examined the children and found they were not well. Their complexions were yellowed, their appetites gone — symptoms of soul loss. If the souls were not recovered, the children would sicken and eventually die.

The three mothers rushed back into the arena and burned the gold paper as an offering to the ghost. After the ransom was paid, the ghost released the children's souls, and the medium's tutelary spirits brought them back down to earth with a loud, whistling sound. The medium then placed the soul of each child in its garment, which the women clutched tightly as they ran right home. As they ran they called their child's name, urging the rescued souls not to worry, they would soon be home and be given sweets to eat. The mothers rushed into their houses still repeating these assurances. Then, after hurriedly bowing before the ancestors, they each laid the garment beside the child it belonged to, so that the soul would easily recognize and reenter the body.

It turned out later that most of the villagers knew from the ghost's description that it was the notorious wife of Bean Curd Jong. Many years earlier, Bean Curd Jong married an evil young woman. From the beginning, the household was unhappy because the wicked daughter-in-law worried and scolded her mother-in-law night and day. Finally, the old lady could bear no more, and hanged herself dressed in a bridal costume. The villagers believe that a woman who dies dressed this way will become a fierce and powerful ghost; perhaps Bean Curd Jong's mother had this in mind. After her death — as the daughter-in-law learned when she consulted a spirit medium about an illness — the old lady complained to the King of Hell about her daughter-in-law's wickedness, and she and the King of Hell together plotted the untimely death of the whole family.

First the ghost of the old lady stole the soul of her son, who had violated his filial obligations by supporting the wife against her. Bean Curd Jong died shortly after his mother. His daughter was the next to die, then the evil daughter-in-law, and finally the son. Although the old lady had killed off the entire family, the villagers said the root cause of the family's troubles was the wickedness not of the mother, but of the daughter-in-law. As a ghost she has been even more ferocious than her mother-in-law, repeatedly bringing harm to the villagers, who are still terrified of her. Her favorite haunt is her family's old house. After the family died out, it was rented to outsiders because no village family would live there for fear of the ghost.

After the children's souls had been ransomed and returned to their owners, the medium and the village women scolded the ghost. "Don't do this again. If you do, spirit soldiers will be sent to catch and beat you. All those children have their own parents, why do you bother them? You must stop doing these evil things."

The evening wore on, with the spirit medium continuing her travels until well past midnight. She continued to run across the villagers' family spirits. Rather than identifying them directly by name, she questioned the spirits, asking such questions as how many daughters-in-law they had, how many siblings, how many children. Given a few general clues, the villagers were able to guess the spirit's identity. Among the spirits there was much quarrelsome jockeying for the opportunity to talk with their families. The questions typically asked of the spirits were the same as those that would be asked in a private consultation with the medium. The most common questions were about the dead person's well-being. This is a matter of great concern because if family spirits are not content and comfortable, their descendants will not prosper.

Finally, after an eventful journey through the heavens, the spirit medium passed through the portals leading to the four Heavenly Flower Gardens, where every living person is represented by a potted flowering plant. The East and South Gardens are large, the North and West Gardens small. When a woman conceives a child, a heavenly flower is planted in one of the small gardens, and a seed is sent down from heaven into the uterus of the woman. The villagers liken the uterus to a flower that begins to enlarge and open after conception. The growing life flowers remain in the small gardens until the people they represent are between twelve and sixteen years old, when they are transplanted into one of the large gardens. When a person's plant is moved to a large garden, it is placed alongside that of his or her future spouse. The villagers believe that the old, arranged marriages were fixed in heaven in this manner.

Two female deities, Lee Paak and Zap Yih Nae Neung, tend the flowers while they are in the small gardens. The two deities watch over all the world's children, deciding which shall flourish and which shall die. They also decide which women shall have children and which shall remain barren. Understandably, they are very important deities to Cantonese women. There is an image of Zap Yih Nae Neung in the Hang Mei Village temple of Ping Shan. Women pray to it that they may have children and that their children may be protected from harm.

The medium journeys to the Heavenly Flower Gardens in order to inspect the villagers' flowers. This "inspection of the flowers," or *chan fa*, is a form of fortune-telling. The medium examines the condition of a person's flower: are there yellowed leaves or spider webs on the plant, does the flower seem in poor condition? The medium examines the flower to see how many red flowers (representing daughters) or white flowers (representing sons) are in bloom; unopened buds on the plant represent future offspring. If the pot contains bamboo, a woman will be barren; if it holds tangerines, she will have many children. The condition of a villager's flower tells the medium important things about that person's future.

When she had reached the Heavenly Gardens, the Fat One began to tell the villagers' fortunes by *chan fa*. One of the many villagers whose flowers she inspected was Tang Soo-kwai, a 48-year-old man. Soo-kwai did not attend the séance, but his mother and his wife were there. Soo-kwai's mother gave the Fat One the eight characters denoting the year, month, and day of her son's birth. This was necessary so the medium could locate Soo-kwai's pot, which has the same eight characters written on it. Soo-kwai's plant, the Fat One reported, had one white and three red flowers, representing his three daughters and one son, plus an unopened white bud, indicating that eventually he would have another son.

Suddenly, the Fat One called out that she saw a woman's ghost hovering around Soo-kwai's plant, an announcement that riveted the villagers' attention. Speaking through the medium, the ghost informed the spectators that this flowerpot belonged to her husband. Everyone then knew that the ghost was Tang Soo-kwai's deceased first wife. From the look on the face of Soo-kwai's second wife, this was a bad omen.

The ghost assured her, however, that she would not bother her husband or his family and was merely visiting his plant because she was lonely. Soo-kwai's second wife relaxed a bit. The ghost conversed with several women in the audience. She expressed anxiety about her son and daughter, and admonished the second wife to take good care of them and see that they were well brought up and properly educated. Soo-kwai's younger brother's wife was also at the séance, and the ghost told her that since they had known and liked each other in life, she had nothing to fear. "Now I am a ghost [*kuei*]," she said, "but I have a good heart and will not bother you. When I was alive we were good friends, and now we are still like sisters." This was a relief to the brother's wife, and Soo-kwai's second wife was also pleased to hear the ghost expressing good will rather than malevolence.

The final event of the séance was a remarkable attempt by the spirit medium to preserve traditional religious beliefs and practices among the younger generation, which is increasingly affected by modern secular ideas. A young couple had just built a modern-style house in the village without installing the paper images that represent the traditional guardian deities of village houses. The spirits of the new household spoke through the medium. They said they had nothing to eat and no permanent place of their own, and so had to flit around restlessly. The spirit generals of the doors, the guardian spirit of the house, and the kitchen god all said that if a suitable resting place and proper worship were not arranged for them, the household would soon meet with disaster. So effective was this warning that the modern young couple installed the traditional deities and began to worship them the very next day.

The Regular Duties of the Spirit Medium

The dramatic group séance takes place only once a year, during the eighth month, which is an especially propitious time for communicating with spirits. Throughout the rest of the year the spirit mediums cure illness, converse with villagers' family spirits, tell fortunes, and care for their fictive children.

The professional headquarters of the spirit mediums are their altar houses or shrines, *pay dhaan*. Each *pay dhaan* contains an altar on which the medium's special tutelary deities are enshrined, sometimes along with the souls of girls who died unmarried, other spirits entrusted to her special care, and assorted religious paraphernalia. It is here that people come to consult the spirit medium, and it is here that she customarily goes into trances and communicates with the supernatural world. When the medium's altar house serves as a repository for the souls of unmarried village girls as well as the medium's tutelary spirits, it is called a *dsox zan dhaan*, or "shrine where spirits reside."

In 1963 there were two *dsox zan dhaan* in Hang Mei Village, belonging to Kao Paak-neung and the Fat One, the two spirit mediums of Hang Mei; and there was a *pay dhaan* in the adjacent village of Hang Tau, which belonged to the elderly spirit medium from China proper. The altar houses of the Fat One and the Old Woman from China were dingy lean-tos, built against walls of their houses. Kao Paak-neung's altar house was a recently built little one-room shrine, situated between the fish pond and the Hang Mei Village temple. Kao Paak-neung had formerly practiced in a lean-to like those of the two other mediums, but in 1957 Tang Nai-men, in gratitude for her efforts on behalf of his many children, had built her a new one.

Kao Paak-neung's altar house was sparkling white inside and out, with colorful testimonial banners given her by Tang Nai-men hanging on the wall. The most striking feature of the shrine was the altar itself, a large piece of orange-red paper, which was affixed to the wall and had written on it in bold black characters the names of the spirits and deities who aided Kao Paak-neung in her profession. Before the altar was a large table, which held a variety of ritual objects: vases of plastic flowers intended to brighten the shrine and please the spirits of the altar; mirrors to gratify the souls of the young girls who dwelled in the altar; tea and fresh fruit for the spirits to eat along with incense that the villagers considered the spiritual equivalent of rice; a bowl of fresh water so the spirits could wash their hands before eating; and a copper incense burner and candlesticks used in the medium's ritual performance.

Alongside the altar hung five dresses, belonging to five young girls whose spirits dwelled in the altar. These were placed there because the villagers are uncertain how to treat the spirits of women who die before marriage. The spirit tablets of adult men and married women are kept on their family's ancestral altar, and those of unmarried men are placed either on the altar or on a wall beside the altar (as in the case of Tang Tsuen's unmarried brother). Women who die before marriage present a problem because they have no husband and are not members of their father's lineage. People are afraid to put their tablets in the home because they might haunt the family. The solution is to put the spirits of unmarried daughters under the shaman's charge. The medium has the names of her spiritual charges written on her altar, where she worships them twice daily and on festival days. When village parents place a daughter's spirit under the medium's care, they usually bring one of the deceased child's garments to hang near the altar so the child's spirit knows the shrine is her home. Parents visit their dead daughters' spirits during the Spring and Autumn Festivals, when the villagers worship the spirits of their dead kin.

On Kao Paak-neung's altar are written the names of seven deities, the names of her dead son and two dead daughters, who serve her as spirit helpers, the names of six young female spirits entrusted to her care, and the name of Tang Fang-cheung, her husband's younger brother, who died before marriage. Fang-cheung's name appears on the altar because he ended an unhappy life as an opium addict by committing suicide in his lineage's ancestral hall. His spirit was presumed to have been made so unhappy by his unfortunate way of life and manner of death that it was greatly feared. Kao Paak-neung propitiated it daily.

* * *

When a sick person or a concerned relative comes to the altar house to seek the spirit medium's help, she begins by ascertaining the patient's home village and eight characters. Because the supernatural world is organized bureaucratically, the spirits need the name of the person's village so they know where to start their investigations. The eight characters help them identify the specific soul that is lost. If the patient is seriously ill, the medium then throws the divination blocks to determine whether a cure is possible; if the blocks say the illness is mortal, there is no use proceeding further.

A village woman who was an apprentice shaman told me about one of Kao Paak-neung's untreatable cases. A man from Mai Po Village fell ill, and his wife asked Kao Paak-neung to come to their house and treat him. When Kao Paak-neung called down her tutelary spirits, they told her that the man was dying and there was nothing she could do for him. The ailing man refused to accept this verdict. Speaking through Kao Paak-neung, he promised her tutelary deities that he would establish a fictive kinship relation with them if they restored his health. But the spirits reiterated that his case was hopeless: his sister in hell had prepared his coffin and he was doomed. The sick man and his family still doubted Kao Paak-neung, but soon afterward she learned that he had died as predicted. (Kao Paak-neung attributes the man's death to his evil sister. Married off to a very poor farmer, she had had a hard life. When she fell sick her husband had no money for a doctor, and she died. After her death her husband did not worship her. Her lonely, dissatisfied soul returned to her father's house, where her brother lived. She caused her brother to die so that his soul would keep her company.) An able spirit medium like Kao Paak-neung should always know whether or not a person can be treated. Kao Paak-neung claimed that of the many cases she had treated over the previous decade, only about ten of her patients had died, and that in each case she had predicted the outcome beforehand with the aid of her tutelary spirits.

If the divination blocks indicate that treatment is possible, the spirit medium proceeds to go into a trance, call down her familiar spirits, and begin a search for the ghost who has stolen the sick person's soul. First she lights two ritual candles and burns three sticks of incense. Then she settles herself in front of her altar. She covers her head and face with a scarf because when she sings she opens her mouth very wide. The scarf spares onlookers the painfully ugly sight of her distorted face.

Usually by the time the three incense sticks have burned down, the medium is already entranced and has called down her familiar spirits to enter her body. She always calls the spirits of her dead children first because she is powerless without their help. They are the intermediaries through whom she contacts the more powerful deities on her altar. Sometimes the children's spirits refuse to enter their mother's body, in which case she can do nothing. The children's spirits are very young and sometimes would rather go off and play. They also may be uncooperative or even vindictive when they feel slighted. For example, about five or six years earlier two women came to play cards with Kao Paak-neung. Her guests arrived early, and Kao Paak-neung, who had not had time to buy party food, took some cakes from the altar to offer them. A few minutes later her eyes suddenly turned glassy and she went into a trance. The souls of her children had retaliated for the misappropriation of their cakes by possessing the medium. For several days she either stared fixedly without speaking or talked gibberish, giving nonsensical answers to questions put to her. She had no appetite, her head ached, and she was always exhausted. She recovered only after she had propitiated the spirits with special offerings.

Usually, however, the medium is on good terms with her tutelary spirits and is able to go into a trance whenever she holds a curing séance. She begins to shake and her body grows cold — signs that the spirits are entering her. As she trembles, she cries out the names of the spirits on her altar, asking them to find the soul of her patient. In searching for the patient's soul they follow a route much like the route to the Heavenly Flower Gardens followed in the annual group séance. Almost always the lost soul is discovered in the hands of a ghost that has kidnapped it. The spirit medium tries to learn the identity of the malevolent ghost and its relation to her client. She asks leading questions, drawing upon her intimate knowledge of village families. The client searches his memory for family ghosts with reason to bother their living relatives. Usually he has a good idea who the ghost might be and helps the medium in her search. At other times, the medium puts leading questions to the client until he cries out, "It must be — ." The medium outlines the steps necessary to achieve a cure. If the illness is not serious and the ghostly kidnapper not very powerful, the medium tells the child's mother or some other female relative the kinds of food and amount of paper money required to ransom the ailing person's soul. She uses her divination blocks to find out how long the patient will take to recover. The medium ends the session by scattering rice around to feed her tutelary spirits, and giving her callers rice to take home to the patient.

If the illness is serious or the offending ghost exceptionally powerful, the medium arranges for a ceremony at the patient's home. Lasting from nine in the evening until four in the morning, such a ceremony is very expensive and is usually a last resort. For a ceremony at a patient's home, the medium arrives in the evening. Incense, candles, offerings, and so on have been prepared for her use. She goes into a trance and calls on her spirit helpers to wrest the soul away from the ghost and return it safely home. The battle is often prolonged and difficult. The medium calls on powerful deities, spirit soldiers, and spirit policemen to help her rescue the soul. If she has not located the lost soul in earlier sessions, much of the evening is devoted to the quest. If she already knows where the lost soul is and who has taken it, she concentrates on wresting it away from the kidnapper. By midnight the medium has found the patient's soul and secured its release with offerings of paper money; from then until about 4 A.M. the medium escorts the soul home through the heavens.

Note

1. Young children are not given an elaborate funeral the way older people are. Usually they are perfunctorily buried in a makeshift coffin.

50
The Origin of the Sacred Cow

MARVIN HARRIS

In India today only untouchables freely partake of red meat. Observant high-caste Hindus limit their diets to vegetable foods and dairy products. To eat meat is always undesirable, but the worst of all is to eat beef. High-caste Hindus feel about eating beef as an American feels about eating the family poodle. And yet there was a time when meat, especially beef, appealed to the inhabitants of India as much as steak and hamburgers now appeal to the inhabitants of North America.

Village life in India during the Neolithic period was based on the production of domestic animals and grain crops. Much like Middle Eastern villagers, the earliest Indians raised cattle, sheep, and goats in combination with wheat, millet, and barley. At about 2500 B.C., when the first large settlements began to appear along the Indus River and its tributaries, vegetarianism was still a long way off. Among the ruins of the earliest cities — Harappa and Mohenjo-Daro — half-burned bones of cattle, sheep, and goats are mixed in with the kitchen debris. In the same cities, archaeologists have also found bones of pigs, water buffalo, hens, elephants, and camels.

From Marvin Harris, *Cannibals and Kings: The Origins of Cultures*, Chapter 12, pp. 141–52. Copyright © 1977 Marvin Harris. Reprinted with the permission of the author and Random House, Inc.

The cities of Harappa and Mohenjo-Daro, notable for their fired-brick buildings and their extensive baths and gardens, seem to have been abandoned sometime after 2000 B.C., partly as a result of ecological disasters involving changes in the course of the river channels upon which they depended for irrigation. In their weakened condition they became vulnerable to "barbarian tribes" moving into India from Persia and Afghanistan. These invaders, known as Aryans, were loosely federated, semimigratory pastoralist-farmers who first settled in the Punjab and later fanned out into the Ganges Valley. They were late Bronze Age peoples who spoke a language called Vedic, the parent tongue of Sanskrit, and whose way of life strongly resembled that of the pre-Homeric Greeks, Teutons, and Celts beyond the pale of the centers of state formation in Europe and Southwest Asia. As Harappa and Mohenjo-Daro declined, the invaders took over the best lands, cleared the forests, built permanent villages, and founded a series of petty kingdoms in which they set themselves up as rulers over the region's indigenous inhabitants.

Our information about what the Aryans ate comes largely from the holy scriptures written in Vedic and Sanskrit during the second half of the first millennium B.C. This literature shows that during the early Vedic period — up to 1000 B.C. — they dined on animal flesh, including beef, frequently and with considerable gusto.

Archaeological investigations at Hastinapur also strongly suggest that cattle, buffalo, and sheep were among the animals eaten by these earliest settlers of the Gangetic plain.

Om Prakash, in his authoritative study *Food and Drinks in Ancient India*, sums up the situation in the early Vedic period as follows:

> Fire is called the eater of ox and barren cows. The ritual offering of flesh implied that the priests would eat it. A goat is also offered to fire to be carried to forefathers. A barren cow was also killed at the time of marriage obviously for food.... A slaughter house is also mentioned. The flesh of horses, rams, barren cows, and buffaloes was cooked. Probably flesh of birds was also eaten.

In the later Vedic period,

> it was customary to kill a big ox or a big goat to feed a distinguished guest. Sometimes a cow that miscarried or a sterile cow was also killed. *Atithigva* also implies that cows were slain for guests. Many animals — cows, sheep, goats, and horses — continue to be killed at sacrifices, and the flesh of these sacrificial animals was eaten by the participants.

The later Vedic and early Hindu texts contain many inconsistencies concerning the consumption of beef. Along with numerous descriptions of cattle being used for sacrifice are passages indicating that cows must never be slaughtered and that beef eating should be abandoned altogether. Some authorities — A.N. Bose, for example — claim that these inconsistencies can best be explained by the hypothesis that orthodox Hindu scholars interpolated the anti-beef-eating, anti-cow-slaughtering passages at a later date. Bose feels that "beef was the commonest flesh consumed" throughout most of the first millennium B.C. Perhaps a less controversial solution to the contradictions in the sacred texts is that they reflect gradual changes of attitudes over an extended period during which more and more people came to regard the eating of domesticated animals — especially cows and oxen — as an abomination.

What emerges with crystal clarity is that the late Vedic–early Hindu Ganges Valley kingdoms had a priestly caste analogous to the Levites among the ancient Israelites and the Druids among the Celts. Its members were called Brahmans. The duties of the Brahmans are described in the Sanskrit works known as *Brahmanas* and *sutras*. There is no doubt that early Brahman ritual life, like that of the Druids and Levites (and the earliest religious specialists of every chiefdom and statelet between Spain and Japan), centered on animal sacrifice. Like their counterparts all over the Old World, the early Brahmans enjoyed a monopoly over the performance of those rituals without which animal flesh could not be eaten. Brahmans, according to the *sutras*, were the only people who could sacrifice animals.

The *sutras* indicate that animals should not be killed except as offerings to the gods and in extending "hospitality to guests" and that "making gifts and receiving gifts" were the special duties of Brahmans. These prescriptions precisely duplicate the regulatory provisions for the consumption of meat characteristic of societies in which feasting and animal sacrifice are one and the same activity. The "guests" honored by early Vedic hospitality were not a handful of friends dropping by for dinner but whole villages and districts. What the *sutras* are telling us, in other words, is that the Brahmans were originally a caste of priests who presided over the ritual aspects of redistributive feasts sponsored by "open-handed" Aryan chiefs and war lords.

After 600 B.C. the Brahmans and their secular overlords found it increasingly difficult to satisfy the popular demand for animal flesh. Like priests and rulers in the Middle East and elsewhere, they were unable to maintain high rates of animal slaughter and bountiful redistributions without the wasteful eating of animals needed to plow and manure the fields. As a result, meat eating became the privilege of a select group comprising Brahmans and other high-caste Aryans, while the common peasants, lacking the power to tax or confiscate other people's animals, had no choice but to preserve their own domestic stock for traction, milk, and dung production. Thus the Brahmans gradually came to be part of a meat-eating elite whose monopoly over the privilege of slaughtering animals for redistributive feasts had been transformed into a monopoly over the privilege of eating them. Long after ordinary people in northern India had become functional vegetarians, the Hindu upper castes — later the most ardent advocates of meatless diets — continued to dine lustily on beef and other kinds of meat.

I base my argument for this widening gulf between a pampered meat-eating aristocracy and an impoverished meatless peasantry partly on the fact that toward the middle of the first millennium B.C. a number of new religions began to challenge the legitimacy of the Brahman caste and its sacrificial rituals. Of these reformist religions, the best-known are Buddhism and Jainism. Founded in the sixth century B.C. by charismatic holy men, both Buddhism and Jainism outlawed caste distinctions, abolished hereditary priesthoods, made poverty a precondition of spirituality, and advocated communion with the spiritual essence of the universe through contemplation rather than through the sacrifice of animals. In their condemnation of violence, war, and cruelty, and their compassion for human suffering, both of these movements anticipated key elements of Christianity.

For the Buddhists, all life was sacred, although it could exist in higher and lower forms. For the Jains, not only was all life sacred but it shared a common soul: there were no higher and lower forms. In either case, priests who sacrificed animals were no better than murderers. Buddhists tolerated the eating of animal flesh, provided the eater had not participated in the killing. The Jains, however, condemning the killing of all animals, insisted on a pure vegetarian diet. The members of some Jainist sects even deemed it necessary to employ sweepers to clear the path in front of them in order to avoid the calamity of accidentally extinguishing the life of a single ant.

As I suggested earlier, the end of animal sacrifice coincided with the growth of universalistic, spiritualized religions. With the erstwhile "great providers" increasingly unable to validate their majesty through popular displays of open-handed generosity, people were encouraged to look for "redistributions" in an afterlife or in some new phase of being. I have also pointed out that the image of the ruler as great protector of the weak against the strong arose as a matter of practical statecraft during periods of imperial expansion. Buddhism, like Christianity, was ideally suited, therefore, for adoption as an imperial religion. It dematerialized the obligations of the emperor at the same time that it obligated the aristocracy to show compassion to the poor. This explains, I think, why Buddhism became an official religion under Asoka, one of the most powerful emperors in the history of India. Asoka, grandson of the founder of the north Indian Maurya Dynasty, converted to Buddhism in 257 B.C. He and his descendants forthwith set about creating the first and still the largest ever of Indian empires — a shaky realm stretching briefly from Afghanistan to Ceylon. Asoka was thus possibly the first emperor in history to set out to conquer the world in the name of a religion of universal peace.

Meanwhile, Hinduism was profoundly affected by the new religions and began to adopt some of the reforms which had made its Buddhist rival politically successful. Eventually, the widespread opposition to animal sacrifice came to be represented within Hinduism by the doctrine of *ahimsa* — nonviolence based on the sacredness of life. But this change did not come all at once nor did it proceed in a single direction. After the collapse in 184 B.C. of the Maurya Dynasty, Brahmanism revived and meat eating among the elite flourished once more. As late as A.D. 350, according to Prakash, "flesh of various animals" was served to Brahmans at Sraddhas, the redistributive ceremonies commemorating the dead. "The Kurma Purana goes to the extent of saying that one who does not take flesh in a Sraddha is born again and again as an animal."

No one is able to say precisely when cows and oxen became distinct objects of veneration among Brahmans and other high-caste Hindus. It is impossible to assign precise dates to changes in Hindu ritual because Hinduism is not a single organized religion but an immense number of loosely affiliated congregations centering on independent temples, shrines, deities, and castes, each with its own doctrinal and ritual specialties. One authority, S.K. Maitz, claims that the cow had already become the most sacred of animals by A.D. 350, but his evidence is a single canto in an epic poem which describes a certain king and his queen as "worshipping cows with sandal paste and garlands." There is also the inscription of King Chandragupta II, dated to A.D. 465, which equates the killing of a cow with the killing of a Brahman. But the modern Hindu point of view may be intruding. The Gupta emperors issued royal decrees aimed at preventing the consumption of various animals by commoners. Hindu royalty fussed over horses and elephants as well as cows. They garlanded their animals, bathed them, provided them with carpeted stalls, and set them free to roam in protected reserves. It may have been only after A.D. 700 and the Islamic conquest of India that the sacred cow complex acquired its familiar modern form. The followers of Islam had no compunctions about eating beef. Hence under the Moguls, the Islamic emperors of India, cow protection may have become a political symbol of Hindu resistance against the beef-eating Moslem invaders. At any rate, the Brahmans — for centuries the sacrificers and consumers of animal flesh — gradually come to regard it as their sacred duty to prevent the slaughtering or eating of any domestic animals, especially cows and oxen.

To the best of my knowledge, no one has previously been able to offer a rational explanation as to why India, unlike the Middle East or China, became the center of a religion that forbade the consumption of beef and venerated the cow as the symbol of life. Let us see if the general principles concerning the establishment of animal taboos that I suggested in the previous chapter [of *Cannibals and Kings: The Origins of Cultures*] are applicable. Ancient Indian beliefs and practices were initially similar to beliefs and practices common to most of Europe, Asia, and North Africa. As predicted, the general transformation from redistributive animal sacrifice to the taboo on the consumption of previously valuable and abundant species followed upon the intensification of agriculture, depletion of resources, and growth of population density. But these generalities do not explain the particular emphasis on cattle and vegetarianism in India or the particular religious complexes associated with animals in other regions.

The place to start, I think, is in the Ganges Valley, where the rate of population growth appears to have been much greater than in the Middle East — or, indeed, than anywhere else in the ancient world. During the Vedic period population was scanty and spread out in small villages. As late as 1000 B.C. population density was low enough to permit each family to own many animals (the Vedic texts mention twenty-four oxen harnessed to a single plow), and as in pre-Roman Europe cattle were regarded as the principal form of wealth. Less than 700 years later the Ganges had probably become the most populous region in the world. Estimates by Kingsley Davis and others give India a population of between 50 and 100 million in 300 B.C. At least half of that total must have been living in the Ganges Valley.

We know that during the early Vedic period the Gangetic plain was still covered with virgin forests. Scarcely a tree remained by 300 B.C. While irrigation provided a secure base for many farm families, millions of peasants received either insufficient flows of water or none at all. Because of fluctuations in monsoon rains, it was always risky to depend on rainfall alone. Deforestation undoubtedly increased the risk of drought. It also increased the severity of the floods which the Holy River Ganges unleashed when the monsoons dumped too much rain all at once onto the Himalayan foothills. Even today droughts that endure in India for two or three consecutive seasons endanger the lives of millions of people who depend on rainfall to water their crops. From the *Mahabharata*, an epic poem composed sometime between 300 B.C. and A.D. 300, we know of one drought that lasted twelve years. The poem tells how lakes, wells, and springs dried up, and how agriculture and cattle rearing had to be abandoned. Markets and shops were left empty. The sacrifice of animals came to a halt, and the very stakes for tying up the animals disappeared. There were no festivals. Everywhere heaps of bone could be seen and cries of creatures could be heard. People left the cities. Hamlets were abandoned and set on fire. People fled from one another. They feared each other. Places of worship were deserted. Old people were driven from their houses. Cattle, goats, sheep, and buffalo turned into ferocious beasts that attacked one another. Even the Brahmans died without protection. Herbs and plants withered. The earth looked like a crematorium and "in that dreadful age when righteousness was at an end, men began to eat one another."

As population density grew, farms became increasingly smaller and only the most essential domesticated species could be allowed to share the land. Cattle were the one species that could not be eliminated. They were the animals that drew the plows upon which the entire cycle of rainfall agriculture depended. At least two oxen had to be kept per family, plus one cow with which to breed replacements when the oxen wore out. Cattle thus became the central focus of the religious taboo on meat eating. As the sole remaining farm animals, they were potentially the only remaining source of meat. To slaughter them for meat, however, constituted a threat to the whole mode of food production. And so beef was tabooed for the same reason that pork was tabooed in the Middle East: to remove temptation.

The respective interdictions against beef and pork, however, reflect the different ecological roles of the two species. The pig was abominated; the cow was deified. Why this should have been the case seems obvious from what I've said about the importance of cattle in the agricultural cycle. When pork became too costly to be raised for meat, the whole animal was rendered useless — worse than useless — because it had only been good as something to eat. But when cattle became too costly to be raised for meat, their value as a source of traction did not diminish. Hence they had to be protected rather than abominated, and the best way to protect them was not only to forbid the eating of their flesh but to forbid their slaughter. The ancient Israelites had the problem of preventing the diversion of grains to the production of pork. The solution was to stop raising pigs. But the ancient Hindus could not stop raising cattle since they depended on oxen to plow the land. Their main problem was not how to refrain from raising a certain species but how to refrain from eating it when they got hungry.

The conversion of beef into forbidden flesh originated in the practical life of individual farmers. It was the product neither of a superhuman culture hero nor of a collective social mind brooding over the cost/benefits of alternative resource management policies. Culture heroes express the preformed sentiments of their age and collective minds don't exist. The tabooing of beef was the cumulative result of the individual decisions of millions and millions of individual farmers, some of whom were better able than others to resist the temptation of slaughtering their livestock because they strongly believed that the life of a cow or an ox was a holy thing. Those who held such beliefs were much more likely to hold onto their farms, and to pass them on to their children, than those who believed differently. Like so many other adaptive responses in culture and nature, the "bottom line" of the religious proscriptions on the use of animal flesh in India cannot be read from short-term cost/benefits. Rather, it is the long term that counted most — performance during abnormal rather than normal agricultural cycles. Under the periodic duress of droughts caused by failures of the monsoon rains, the individual farmer's love of cattle translated directly into love of human life, not by symbol but by practice. Cattle had to be treated like human beings because human beings who ate their cattle were one step away from eating each other. To this day, monsoon farmers who yield to temptation and slaughter their cattle seal their doom. They can never plow again even when the rains fall. They must sell their farms and migrate to the cities. Only those who would starve rather than eat an ox or cow can survive a season of scanty rains. This human forbearance is matched by the fantastic endurance and recuperative powers of the Indian zebu breeds. Like camels, Indian cattle store energy in their humps, survive for weeks without food or water, and spring back to life when favored with the slightest nourishment. Long after other breeds have expired from disease, hunger, and thirst, zebus continue to pull plows, bear calves, and give milk. Unlike European cattle breeds, zebus were selected not for their strength, beefiness, or copious flow of milk, but largely for their ability to survive severe dry seasons and droughts.

And this brings us to the question why the cow rather than the ox has come to be the most venerated animal. The flesh of either sex is equally taboo, but in ritual and art Hinduism emphasizes the sacredness of cows far more than that of male cattle. Yet practice belies theory. Oxen outnumber cows two to one in the Gangetic plain — a sex ratio which can be accounted for only by the existence of systematic selection against female calves through malign neglect and indirect "bovicide" (exactly paralleling the *sub rosa* treatment of female human infants.) This lopsided ratio reflects the greater value of oxen over cows as a source of traction for plowing the fields. Despite all the fuss made over the holy mother cow, under normal circumstances oxen are, in fact, treated much better. They are kept in stalls, fed by hand, and given grain and oil cake supplements to make them strong and healthy. Cows, on the other hand, are treated in everyday rural life the way American Indians treated their dogs or the way European farmers used to treat their pigs. They are the village scavengers. They are not kept in stalls and fed on fodder crops. Instead, they are let loose to roam around the village to pick up whatever scraps of garbage they can find. Having licked the village clean, they are permitted to wander off in search of a few blades of grass that somehow survived their last tour of a roadside ditch or that have sprouted in the spaces between the railroad ties. Because cows are treated as scavengers, they are likely to show up in such inconvenient places as the gutters of busy thoroughfares and the edges of airport runways, giving rise to the foolish charge that India has been overrun by millions of "useless" cattle.

If the cow more than the ox is the symbol of *ahimsa*, the sacredness of life, perhaps it is because the cow more than the ox is endangered by the sentiment that it is "useless." During times of hunger the cow stands more in need of ritual protection than the draft oxen. Yet from the point of view of the resumption and continuity of the agricultural cycle the cow is actually more valuable than the male draft animal. Although it is not as strong as an ox, it can in emergencies pull the plow as well as someday produce replacements for animals that succumb to thirst and hunger. Under duress, therefore, the cow must be treated as well as — if not better than — the ox, and that is probably why it is the principal object of ritual veneration. Mohandes Gandhi knew what he was talking about when he said Hindus worshiped the cow not only because "she gave milk, but because she made agriculture possible."

Why beef came to be forbidden flesh in India cannot fully be explained unless one can also account for its not becoming taboo in the other early centers of state formation. One possibility is that Indian farmers were more dependent on irregular monsoon rainfall than were farmers in other regions. This may have made it more urgent to protect cows and oxen during times of hunger. In Egypt and Mesopotamia, where cattle were venerated and their sacrifice prohibited in late dynastic times, beef continued to be eaten. But both Egypt and Mesopotamia, unlike India, were totally dependent on irrigation agriculture and never had large numbers of farmers who relied on drought-resistant cattle to get through the dry season.

China presents a more difficult problem. Although they also used ox-drawn plows, the Chinese never developed a cow-love complex. On the contrary, female cattle in China have long been held in rather low esteem. This is reflected in Chinese cooking. Whereas in northern India the traditional cuisine relies heavily on milk or milk products and the basic cooking fat is clarified butter, or ghee, Chinese recipes never call for milk, cream, or cheese and the basic cooking fat is lard or vegetable oil. Most adult Chinese have a strong dislike for milk (although ice cream has gained increasing popularity in recent years.) Why are the Indians milk-lovers and the Chinese milk-haters?

One explanation for the aversion of the Chinese to milk is that they are physiologically "allergic" to it. Adult Chinese who drink quantities of milk generally get severe cramps and diarrhea. The cause is not really an allergy but a hereditary deficiency in the ability of the intestines to manufacture the enzyme lactase. This enzyme must be present if the body is to digest lactose, the predominant sugar found in milk. Between 70 and 100 percent of Chinese adults have a lactase deficiency. The trouble with this explanation is that many Indians — between 24 and 100 percent, depending on the region — also have a lactase deficiency. And so do most human populations, Europeans and their American descendants being the exception. Moreover, all the unpleasant consequences of lactase deficiency can easily be avoided if milk is drunk in small quantities or if it is consumed in any one of a number of soured or fermented forms such as yogurt or cheese, in which the lactose is broken down into less complex sugars. In other words, lactase deficiency is only a barrier to the drinking of large quantities of milk American-style. It can't explain the aversion to butter, sour cream, cheese, and yogurt — all of which are conspicuously absent from Chinese cuisine.

What stands out in the comparison of Chinese and Indian ecosystems is the virtual absence in China of the cow as a farm animal. John Lasson Buck's authoritative survey of pre-Communist Chinese agriculture showed that in northern China there were on the average 0.05 oxen but less than 0.005 cows per farm. This indicates a cattle sex ratio of more than 1,000 males to 100 females, as compared with a ratio of between 210:100 and 150:100 in the Central Gangetic Plain and 130:100 for all of India. This difference reflects the fact that the cow had virtually no role in the northern Chinese domestic economy other than to breed oxen, which explains at least one aspect of the Chinese distaste for milk: there were no cows around the typical northern Chinese village. No cows, no milk; no milk, no chance to acquire a taste for milk products.

The livestock picture in China was always characterized by considerable regional variation in the use of large draft and pack animals. In the north central and northeastern provinces the sum of all the horses, donkeys, and mules was almost as great as the number of cattle. This contrasts with the states of Uttar Pradesh, Bihar, and West Bengal in the Ganges Valley, where horses, donkeys, and mules occur in insignificant numbers.

The greatest difference between the Chinese and Indian livestock situations, however, lies in the vast number of pigs in China and the virtual absence of pigs from most of the Gangetic Plain. Buck estimated that on the average each farm in northern China had 0.52 pigs. A member of a recent delegation to China, G.F. Sprague of the Department of Agronomy of the University of Illinois, estimates that China produced between 250 and 260 million swine in 1972. This is more than four times the amount produced in the Unite States, "a nation noted for extensive swine production." If the Chinese produced these animals the way they are produced in the United States, Sprague writes, they "would represent a severe drain on the available food supply." But there is little resemblance between the production practices in the two countries. Swine production in the United States depends upon providing the animals with corn, soya meal, vitamin and mineral supplements, and antibiotics. In China swine are raised primarily as a household enterprise and, like cows in India, are "fed on waste materials not suitable for human food; vegetable refuse, ground and fermented rice hulls, sweet potato and soya bean vines, water hyacinths and so forth." Just as Indian cows are valued for their manure, so Chinese swine are valued "almost as much for manure as for their meat." In other words, the pig is and was the main village scavenger for the Chinese. It provided them with crucial supplements of fats and proteins and much-needed fertilizer just as the Indians derived such essentials from their village scavenger, the cow. With one big difference: since the pig cannot be milked, it has to be eaten if it is to serve as a source of dietary fats and proteins. This means that as long as swine filled the niche of village scavenger, the Chinese would never accept a religion such as Islam, which specifically prohibits the consumption of pork.

But why did the Chinese adopt the pig as the village scavenger while the Indians adopted the cow? Several factors were probably involved. First of all, the Gangetic Plain is less desirable as a habitat in which to rear pigs than is the Yellow River Basin. The fierce spring heat and the recurrent droughts to which the zebu cattle breeds have adapted render the moisture-loving pig a risky investment. In Uttar Pradesh, India's largest food-producing state, 88 percent of the rainfall occurs in four months, while average daily high temperatures in May and June hover well over 100 degrees Fahrenheit. Northern China, on the other hand, has cool springs, moderate summers, and no marked dry season.

Another important factor is the comparative availability of grazing lands on which traction animals can be reared. China, unlike India, has a large area that is suitable for pasturing traction animals and that cannot be used for growing food crops. In China only 11 percent of the total land area is under cultivation, while in India almost 50 percent of the total area is cropland. According to Buck, the northern spring wheat region of China contains "considerable public grazing land where low rainfall and broken topography make cultivation difficult." By contrast, less than 2 percent of the total cropland area of the Central Gangetic Plain is permanent pasture or grazing land. Thus in India the breeding of the basic traction animal had to take place in zones that were already tightly packed with human beings — zones lacking nonarable lands suitable for forage. The traction animal, therefore, had to be fed primarily on waste products such as those available to a village scavenger. In other words, the traction animal and the scavenger had to be one and the same species. And it had to be cattle, because neither horses, donkeys, nor mules could perform satisfactorily in the blistering heat and aridity of the monsoon climate, while water buffalo were useless to farmers who lacked irrigation.

Perhaps the best way to view the treatment of animals in India as opposed to China is in terms of different phases of a single great convergent process of intensification. Neither China nor India could afford large-scale exploitation of animals primarily for flesh or dairy products because of the immense human population densities and the severe caloric losses entailed in animal husbandry carried out on arable lands. In pre-Communist China the rural population lived on a diet that derived 97.7 percent of its calorie ration from plant foods and only 2.3 percent from animal products — mainly pork. The species used primarily as draft animals were seldom eaten in rural China, any more than they were eaten in India. Why, then, wasn't beef prohibited by a religious taboo?

In fact, there was such a taboo in some regions. No less an authority than Mao Tse-tung made the following observations when he was in Hunan:

> Draught-oxen are a treasure to the peasants. As it is practically a religious tenet that "Those who slaughter cattle in this life will themselves become cattle in the next," draught oxen must never be killed. Before coming to power, the peasants had no way of stopping the slaughter of cattle except the religious taboo.

And T.H. Shen writes:

> The butchering of cattle for beef is against Chinese tradition. It is only near the large cities that any cattle are butchered to furnish meat, and then it is done when they are no longer needed on the farms.

While both China and India have suffered the effects of millennia of intensification, the process seems to have been carried to the greater extreme in India. Chinese agriculture is more efficient than Indian agriculture primarily because of the greater area cultivated under irrigation — 40 percent of Chinese croplands versus 23 percent of Indian croplands. Average yields per acre of rice are therefore twice as high in China as in India. Given the viability of the pig, donkey, mule, and horse in China, and the topographical and climatic factors of production, intensification did not reach levels necessitating a total ban on the slaughter of animals for meat. Instead of milking their traction animals, the Chinese slaughtered their pigs. They settled for a little less animal protein in the form of meat than they could have gotten in the form of milk — had they used the cow rather than the pig in the scavenger niche.

Hindus and Westerners alike see in the meat-eating taboos of India a triumph of morals over appetite. This is a dangerous misrepresentation of cultural processes. Hindu vegetarianism was a victory not of spirit over matter but of reproductive over productive forces. The very same material process that promoted the spread of empty-handed religions in the West, the end of animal sacrifice and redistributive feasts, and the interdiction of the flesh of such domestic species as the pig, horse, and donkey led India inexorably in the direction of religions that condemned the eating of all animal flesh. This did not happen because the spirituality of India surpassed the spirituality of other regions; rather, in India the intensification of production, the depletion of natural resources, and the rise in the density of population were pushed further beyond the limits of growth than anywhere else in the preindustrial world except for the Valley of Mexico.

51
The Hopes of the Oppressed

PETER FARB

Revivalistic Movements

A culture that is in the process of being swamped by another often reacts defensively by physically grappling with the outsiders. But it may wage a cultural war as well. Such defensive reactions have been given various labels by anthropologists: nativism, revivalism, revitalization, and messianism. All are deliberate efforts to erect a better culture out of the defeat or decay of an older one. They may be as fanciful as the attempt in Ireland at the end of the last century to revive the moribund Irish Gaelic form of the Celtic language in the face of British rule. Or, in the case of some minority groups in the United States exposed to Americanization, the defensive reaction may consist of ethnic get-togethers, at which foods from the old country are eaten, native costumes worn, folk dances performed, and the language of the homeland spoken.

The reactions of primitive peoples overpowered by Eurasian colonial empires have usually

Excerpted from Peter Farb, *Man's Rise to Civilization: The Cultural Assent of the Indians of North America*, pp. 260–73. Copyright © 1968 Peter Farb. Reprinted with the permission of Dutton, an imprint of New American Library, a division of Penguin Books USA Inc. (Bibliographic documentation contained in the original text is omitted here. Interested readers should consult the original publication.)

been much more extreme. Their lands appropriated, their social system ripped apart, their customs suppressed, and their holy places profaned — they tried to resist physically, but they were inevitably defeated by the superior firepower and technology of the Whites. As hopelessness and apathy settled over these people, the ground was prepared for revivalistic and messianic movements that promised the return of the good old days. North America has been the scene of many dozens of these movements, in one place after another erupting sporadically and then dying down. And they resulted almost every time in bloodshed and additional defeats, which produced further disillusionment to spark the next revival.

The Indians, as well as well other peoples who came under colonial rule, have more recently experienced the same sort of acculturation that took place among the Jews and early Christians in the ancient Near East. There are strong parallels between the hope for salvation among the Jews and the hopes of Indians who followed native prophets, between the early Christian martyrs and the Indian revolts against United States authority, between the Hebrew and the Indian prophets. Particularly fascinating, and it is a story not often told, is the way in which the Jews and early Christians have served as models for oppressed peoples from primitive cultures far from the Near East. Almost wherever the White missionary has penetrated, primitive peoples have borrowed from his bible those elements in which they saw a portrayal of their own plight; and most often this has been an identification with the Jews. The roots of many nativistic movements — among such groups as the Maori of New Zealand, the Kikuyu of Kenya, the Bantu of South Africa, and the Ghost Dancers of North America — can be found in the appeal that the story of the Jews held for these people. Because of such identification, some primitive peoples have claimed descent from one of the ten lost tribes of Israel. In their yearning to escape from servitude, they have found a model in Moses, whose name is a popular cognomen among many colonial peoples. They regard the arrest and execution of a native on charges of being a rebel against White authority in the same terms as the trials undergone by the Hebrew prophets or the passion of Jesus.

The First Phase: Recovery of Lost Cultures

The succession of revivalistic and messianic movements that took place among the American Indians used to be looked upon merely as stubborn resistance by Indian heathens to the obvious blessings the Whites wanted to bestow. But anthropological studies have shown it was not that simple. All the Indian revivalistic movements fall into two phases. One, which will be discussed in this section, attempts the recovery of an old and lost culture; the other attempts to accommodate itself to Whites.

As their cultures began to disintegrate under military and cultural assault by Whites, the Indians yearned to restore a way of life that was fast disappearing. Such a situation was particularly favorable for the rise of prophets who promised the disappearance of the White intruders and the retrieving of the past. In 1680 the Pueblo Indians, led by a prophet named Popé who had been living at Taos, expelled the Spaniards. Catholic priests were slaughtered in their missions and their bodies piled high on church altars. About one-fifth of the total Spanish population of 2,500 was killed outright, and the rest fled to El Paso, Texas. Everything of Spanish manufacture or ownership — not only churches, houses, furniture, and art, but even swine and sheep — was destroyed. The god of the Spaniards was declared dead, and the old religious ways came out into the open again. But Popé's attempt to become complete dictator over all the Pueblo

Indians was clearly an impossible fantasy since they were organized only on the tribal level, and tribes are extremely fragile. The Pueblo confederation broke apart and the people warred among themselves. In 1692 the Spaniards marched back in victory.

The Pueblo Rebellion was primarily a revolt against alien authority, but the next major Indian uprising, which took place in 1762, was clearly messianic. A Delaware Indian prophet appeared in Michigan and preached a doctrine that he said had been revealed to him in a vision. He called for the cessation of strife by Indian against Indian, and a holy war against Whites to be carried on only with bows and arrows. Foolishly, in his rejection of all White culture, he rejected also the use by Indians of White firearms, which might have tipped the balance in his favor. This prophet (whose name no one ever bothered to record) inflamed the Indians around the Great Lakes, and finally a practical man, an Algonkian named Pontiac, arose to lead them. He formed a confederation and attacked English forts all along the Great Lakes until he was ambushed and his forces utterly defeated. But his unsuccessful holy war festered like a wound. Forty years later the Shawnee Prophet (whose Indian name translates as "The Rattle"), twin brother of Chief Tecumseh, repeated the promises of the Delaware Prophet: liberation of Indians and extirpation of the Whites. Indians from many dozens of tribes and bands sent emissaries to the Shawnee to listen to his teachings, and they returned home to excite the entire frontier.

Tecumseh established the greatest Indian alliance that ever existed north of Mexico. He and his emissaries visited almost every band, tribe, and chiefdom from the headwaters of the Missouri River in the Rocky Mountains to as far south and east as Florida. Indians everywhere were arming themselves for the right moment to attack the Whites when, in 1811, Tecumseh's brother, the Shawnee Prophet, launched a premature attack at Tippecanoe, on the banks of the Wabash. In the battle that ensued, the Indians were defeated by General William Henry Harrison, who later was elected President of the United States under the slogan of "Tippecanoe and Tyler, Too." Tecumseh rallied his remaining forces and joined the British in the War of 1812. He fought bravely in battle after battle, but in 1813 his 2,500 warriors from the allied tribes were defeated decisively, once again by General Harrison, in Ontario. He was killed, but his followers spirited away his body, and for years thereafter the frontier was plagued by rumors that he would soon return. He never did, and the prophecy of his brother had been dramatically disproved by White bullets.

There is a sequel, ironic and tragic, to the story of the Shawnee Prophet. One of his followers, named Kanakuk, became a prophet among the Kickapoo, but his teachings were entirely different. Instead of being an advocate of war against Whites, he called upon the Kickapoo to abjure killing, lying, the use of liquor, and all other sins; their reward, he said, would be the discovery of new green pastures where they could settle in peace. But these proposals did not save his people from being forced out of their small area of land in Missouri and onto another in Kansas that was both smaller and less green. There, in 1852, he died of smallpox. His band of faithful, convinced that he would rise again on the third day, gathered in a close group around his body — in spite of all medical warnings about the dangers of infection. The cult, almost down to the last follower, was wiped out by smallpox.

Dreamers

The Dreamers originated among the Indians who lived along the lower reaches of the Columbia River in Oregon and Washington. This cult, too, sought recovery of the lost culture, but it differed from the previous revivalistic movements in that it had strong Roman Catholic overtones. Smohalla ("Preacher") was born about 1820 in the Rocky Mountains and was educated by Roman Catholic missionaries. He proclaimed a cult largely influenced by Catholic doctrine; he also became known as a great shaman and worker of miraculous cures. But about 1860 he was challenged by another shaman — named Moses, ironically enough — who left him bleeding and presumed dead on the banks of a river.

He was carried downstream by rising flood waters, and a White farmer rescued him. Once he had recovered from his ordeal, Smohalla wandered through the Southwest and into Mexico. When he returned finally to his own people, he maintained that he had actually been dead and that the Great Spirit had conversed with him. The Great Spirit told Smohalla how disgusted he was that the Indians had forsaken their native religion for that of the Whites. Smohalla's miraculous return was sufficient proof for many that the Great Spirit had chosen him as a messenger of revelation to the Indian people.

Because he went into frequent trances, Smohalla became known as the Dreamer, and so his followers were known collectively as Dreamers. Upon awakening from one of his trances, he would report to them the visions he had had; out of these visions he pieced together a remarkable cosmogony. In the beginning, the Great Spirit created the earth, the animals, and all living things, including mankind. The first men he created were Indians, followed next by Frenchmen, then priests, Americans, and finally Negroes — which was pretty much Smohalla's opinion about the hierarchy of the portion of mankind he knew. Therefore the earth belonged to those first men, the Indians, who must take care not to defile it as the Whites had. "You ask me to plow the ground!" said Smohalla. "Shall I take a knife and tear my mother's bosom? You ask me to cut grass and make hay and sell it and be rich like white men! But how dare I cut my mother's hair?" Smohalla's preaching posed a major obstacle to the United States government at a time when its official policy was to force all Indians to become farmers.

Inspired by the teachings of Smohalla, Chief Joseph of the Nez Percé in Idaho rebelled in 1877. Before he was trapped only thirty miles short of refuge in Canada, he had consistently outwitted and outfought a superior United States Army across a thousand miles of Rocky Mountain terrain. It was also one of the most honorable of the Indian wars — at least on Chief Joseph's side; for, although he forbade his warriors to scalp or to torture, the Whites massacred his women and children. Finally, with most of his warriors dead, his people starving, freezing, and maimed, Chief Joseph walked toward the White generals, handed his rifle to them, and said: "I am tired of fighting ... My people ask me for food, and I have none to give. It is cold, and we have no blankets, no wood. My people are starving to death. Where is my little daughter? I do not know ... Hear me, my chiefs. I have fought; but from where the sun now stands, Joseph will fight no more forever."

Despite the promises contained in the surrender agreement, the United States Army did not permit the survivors to return to their lands. Instead, they were sent to the malarial bottomlands of the Indian Territory, where the six of Chief Joseph's children who had managed to survive the rebellion all died of disease, along with most of his band. Chief Joseph and those few who remained alive were then allowed to walk, in winter, to a new reservation in northern Washington, fifteen hundred miles away. They were given no supplies of clothing or food for the trip. Despite Chief Joseph's defeat, and the defeat of several other Indian leaders who were inspired by Smohalla, the cult of the Dreamers survived for some time thereafter. It even had a minor resurgence in 1883 in response to the increasing frustration brought by the building of the Northern Pacific Railroad.

The Ghost Dance

The climax of the many revivalistic movements was the Ghost Dance of 1890. It first appeared about 1870 among the Northern Paiute who lived on the California–Nevada border. The Union Pacific Railroad had recently completed its first transcontinental run, and no doubt that inspired the vision of the prophet Wodziwob that a big train would bring back his dead ancestors and announce their arrival with an explosion, an idea probably inspired by the steam whistle. He proclaimed that a cataclysm would swallow up all the Whites but miraculously leave behind their goods for those Indians who joined his cult. Also, a heaven on earth would be created, for at that time the Great Spirit would return to live with the Indians. These miracles were to be hastened by ceremonial dancing around a pole and by singing the songs that Wodziwob had learned during a vision. But no benefits ever resulted from these dances, and they were abandoned.

The Ghost Dance that erupted twenty years after Wodziwob, in 1890, resulted from the intertwining of several strands, one of which was the founding in 1831 by Joseph Smith of the Latter-Day Saints of Jesus Christ (Mormons). He prophesied that a New Jerusalem would arise in the desert, where all those with faith would gather, including the lost tribes of Israel. After the Mormons settled in Utah, it became part of their belief that the Indians represented the remnants of the Hebrew tribes taken into captivity by the Assyrians some 2,500 years earlier. The Mormons sent emissaries to the Indians, whom they dubbed Lamanites, inviting them to join the Mormon colonies and to be baptized. Joseph Smith was also supposed to have prophesied in 1843 that when he reached his eighty-fifth year — that is, in 1890 — the messiah would appear in human form.

The various threads now begin to come together. The Indian prophet Wodziwob had an assistant, and the assistant had a son who became known as Wovoka the prophet. In that year awaited by the Mormons — 1890 — Wovoka appeared and preached the Ghost Dance religion. The Mormons found it perfectly understandable that in the promised year the messiah should appear first among the Indians rather than among Whites, for the Indians were the descendants of Jews and thus possessed priority.

James Mooney, who is responsible for most of our information about the Indian revivalistic and messianic movements, never doubted the sincerity of Wovoka. Mooney talked with him at length in 1892 and appraised him as being the usual sleight-of-hand shaman but by no means a fraud. Wovoka never claimed to be the messiah awaited by the Mormons (although his followers did). He personally made no attempt to spread his teachings, and in fact he never even left Walker Lake, Nevada. Wovoka had led an obscure life until he suddenly fell into a trance during a solar eclipse. When he awoke, he reported that God had taken him by the hand and shown him all the dead Indians happy and young again. God then told Wovoka about a dance that the people must perform to bring the dead Indians back to life again, for the dance generated energy that had the power to move the dead. The dance was spread quickly both by Paiute missionaries and by other Indians who came to visit Wovoka. His teachings took hold among many Paiute and related Shoshonean groups, but not among Indians in California and Oregon, who had already been immunized by the failure of the first Ghost Dance of Wodziwob in 1870. The Pueblo theocracy, of course, rejected it.

Ethnographers have puzzled over why the Ghost Dance of 1890 made almost no impression at all among the Navaho, who are usually regarded as emotional, and who had been subjected to much the same deprivation, defeat, starvation, disease, and forcible removal as the other Indian groups that enthusiastically adopted the Ghost Dance. There is no doubt that news of the Ghost Dance was carried to the Navaho by Paiute missionaries and that they were familiar with all its teachings, yet they totally rejected it. A goodly number of explanations have been offered. Some anthropologists have argued that the Navaho are skeptical by nature, whereas others state that the Navaho were comparatively wealthy in livestock at the time and no longer undergoing the stress of deprivation.

One aspect of Navaho culture, its religion, does suggest a valid explanation. The most significant element in the Ghost Dance complex was the promised return of the dead Indians. Ghost Dance missionaries tried to win over the Navaho by stating that at that moment the Navaho ancestors were on their way back to the reservation. If there is a single aspect of Navaho religion that clearly separates it from that of the surrounding Pueblo Indians, it is the Navaho's fear of the dead and of ghosts. What to other Indians was welcome news — the return of their ancestors — to the Navaho represented a calamity. Even though the Navaho undoubtedly desired the Ghost Dance's promises of the disappearance of the Whites and the restoration of the old ways of life, they were also frightened that the teachings about ghosts might be true.

After the Ghost Dance spread across the Rockies to the Plains tribes it ran amok. The Cheyenne and the Arapaho in Oklahoma started dancing immediately. The fervor attacked other Plains tribes virulently, particularly the Sioux, who were at that time the largest and most intransigent of them all. The Sioux had been forced to submit to a series of land grabs and to indignities that are almost unbelievable when read about today. At the very time that news of the Ghost Dance reached them, they were being systematically starved into submission — by the White bureaucracy — on the little that was left of their reservation in South Dakota. The spark to ignite the Sioux was also present in the person of their White-hating leader, Sitting Bull, a veteran of Custer's last stand in 1876.

The Sioux sent delegates to speak to Wovoka, who advised them to work hard and to make peace with the Whites. By the time the messengers reported back to the Sioux, though, Wovoka's advice had become corrupted and his teachings distorted by confusion with earlier and more violent nativistic movements. The Sioux's version of Wovoka's teachings was that dancing would not only bring back the ancestral dead and the herds of bison, but also exterminate the Whites by causing a landslide. And, best of all, the Indians would be invulnerable to White firepower, for their "ghost shirts" — dance shirts fancifully decorated with designs of arrows, stars, birds, and so forth — were capable of warding off bullets.

Interestingly enough, the Ghost Dance took its most virulent form on the Rosebud Sioux reservation; and the Rosebud population has continued to this day to harbor strong feelings against the authority of the United States government. (For example, on April 15, 1967, when approximately a quarter of a million people marched on the United Nations to protest the Vietnam War, the only Indian group to send a large delegation was the Rosebud Sioux.) From Rosebud, the Ghost Dance spread like a prairie fire to the Pine Ridge Sioux and finally to Sitting Bull's people at Standing Rock. The Sioux rebelled; the result was the death of Sitting Bull and the massacre of the

Indians (despite their ghost shirts) at Wounded Knee in 1890. As quickly as it had set the plains aflame, the Ghost Dance was extinguished.

Only a few months after the massacre at Wounded Knee, while the Sioux were still confused and embittered by their defeat, a deranged White man visited their reservations. He declared himself to be the messiah and he predicted the millennium when the star-pansy flowers bloomed that spring. When the star pansies did bloom and the millennium did not come, the Sioux disillusionment was complete. The last hope of a return to the old days was replaced by resignation to whatever future trials the Whites had in store for them.

A further irony is that the Ghost Dance spread rapidly for only one reason: White culture. English, as the only language common to the various tribes, was the means by which Wovoka's teachings were communicated among the Indians. And the Indians who spread the word of the new movement were able to get from place to place quickly because they took advantage of the rapid transportation provided by the White man's railroads.

The Ghost Dance movement of 1890 died at Wounded Knee, and with it died something else. The Ghost Dance represented the last futile attempt by the American Indians to retrieve the old ways, to save their fast-disappearing culture. From that time on, Indians turned to movements that sought accommodation with Whites.

The Second Phase: Accommodation

The Indians' hope of bring back the old days had proved an illusion, but the second response — adaptation to an alien White world — was rooted in firmer ground. Perhaps the earliest of the accommodation movements was that founded in 1799 by a Seneca named Handsome Lake. Whites called his cult the "New Religion" of the Iroquois, but its name translated into English really meant "Good Tidings" or "Good Message." It combined traditional Iroquois beliefs with those of the Quakers, among whom Handsome Lake had been reared, and it quickly spread from the Seneca to the rest of the Six Nations.

Handsome Lake was regarded as a prophet at a time when Iroquois fortunes seemed on the rise again after a period of hopelessness. The American Revolution had divided the allegiance of the Six Nations, causing them to fight among themselves; Jesuit missionaries had instigated mass migrations of these people to Canada; their population had been further diminished by warfare, disease, and rampant alcoholism, and they had been deprived of most of their lands. By the time of Handsome Lake, though, they had faced the reality of the White conquest, and they were putting the pieces back together again. They had made peace with the new American republic, and they believed themselves to be protected by their solemn treaties with it. That Thomas Jefferson while President had called the religion of Handsome Lake "positive and effective" gave the Iroquois a new sense of security, as well as pride in the high esteem Whites had for their prophet.

The Quaker influence is evident in Handsome Lake's teachings. He renounced witchcraft and instead emphasized introspection, compassion for those who were suffering, and good deeds even in thought. He believed in silent prayer and the confession of sins, and he recommended the White man's bible as a good guide for any Iroquois to follow through life. Although Handsome Lake accepted the idea of monotheism, which was easily grafted onto the Iroquois concept of a Great Spirit, he rejected the New Testament; and Jesus played no role in his religion. Wherever the two pieces could be fitted together, traditional Iroquois festivals and beliefs were combined with Christian rituals. For example, the Iroquois had a feast resembling the Eucharist to mark the New Year, at which time a white dog was sacrificed to the Great Spirit. The place of worship looked like a church but was called a longhouse, thus recalling the traditional Iroquois dwelling and the hallmark of the Iroquois League.

*   *   *

Messiahs: Indian and Others

Several decades ago, reproductions in miniature of a sculpture called "The End of the Trail," which depicted a doleful Indian horseman, were commonly seen in White American living rooms. They seemed to signify the final victory over the vanishing Red man. In the years since, the Indian has not only refused to vanish, but has, thanks to the various messianic movements, managed to find a way to survive in a White world and to salvage a part of his native culture.

The scene of messianic movements has now switched from North America to other frontiers of the world — to South America, to Africa and Asia, and to the islands of the Pacific. Since the Second World War, with much of the world in turmoil,

with the emergence of new nations and the spread of White influence, new messianic movements have sprung up vigorously, even within the context of such well-established religions as Islam, Buddhism, and Taoism. The dozens of messianic movements that have arisen among North American Indians can shed light on how and why they originate, the course they take, and the response Whites make to them.

Every messianic movement known to history has arisen in a society that has been subjected to the severe stress of contact with an alien culture — involving military defeat, epidemic, and acculturation. The bewildered search for ways to counteract the threat may actually increase the stress, arousing anxiety over whether new solutions will be any better than the old. Once doubts arise about any aspect of the ancestral cultural system, there is yet increased stress due to fear that the entire cultural system may prove inadequate. At this point, the culture as a whole begins to break down, manifested by widespread alcoholism, apathy, disregard of kinship obligations and marriage rules, and intragroup violence.

Such behavior comes at the very time when the culture is least able to cope with it, and so the intensity of the stress increases still more. Ultimately, the inadequacy of the culture becomes apparent even to the most conservative of its members, and the culture may deteriorate to such an extent that it literally dies. The birth rate drops and the death rate rises; the society no longer possesses the will to resist, and it is fallen upon by predatory neighbors; the few survivors scatter and either gradually die out or are absorbed by other groups. The collapse may be forestalled or even averted if a revitalization or messianic movement arises that is acceptable to the culture. Such a movement depends upon the appearance of a particular personality at a certain precise time in the disintegration of the culture.

Almost every messianic movement known around the world came into being as the result of the hallucinatory visions of a prophet. One point must be emphasized about the prophet of the messianic movement: He is not a schizophrenic, as was so long assumed. A schizophrenic with religious paranoia will state that he is God, Jesus, the Great Spirit, or some other supernatural being. The prophet, on the other hand, never states that he is supernatural — only that he is or has been in contact with supernatural powers. (Of course, after his death, his disciples tend to deify him or at least to give him saintly status.)

Invariably the prophet emerges from his hallucinatory vision bearing a message from the supernatural that makes certain promises: the return of the bison herds, a happy hunting ground, or peace on earth and good will to men. Whatever the specific promises, the prophet offers a new power, a revitalization of the whole society. But to obtain these promises, the prophet says that certain rituals must be followed. These rituals may include dancing around a ghost pole or being baptized in water, but usually numerous other duties must be attended to day after day. At the same time that the prophet offers promises to the faithful, he also threatens punishment and catastrophe, such as world destruction or everlasting damnation. The prophet now declares the old ways dead and shifts attention to a new way or to a revised conception of an old part of the culture. To spread the word of what he has learned from his visions, he gathers about him disciples and missionaries.

The various prophets known to world history differed in their preaching methods, just as the American Indian prophets differed from each other. Some prophets spoke emotionally to large crowds, whereas others addressed themselves to small groups and left it to their disciples to carry the message. Some, like the Qumran sect that copied out the Dead Sea scrolls, appealed to a religious elite of particularly devout people, whereas others concerned themselves only with the downtrodden and exploited who shall inherit the earth.

What most impresses the people around the prophet is the personality change he has undergone during this time. In most cases, he lived in obscurity until he suddenly emerged as a prophet; the Indian prophets became cured of previous spiritual apathy, and those who had been alcoholics gave up the habit. The sudden transformation in personality may be due to changes produced in the body under physical and emotional stress, although more research on this point is needed. It is known, though, that individuals vary a great deal in the reaction of their metabolisms to stress. That alone would explain why, when stress reaches a certain intensity in the culture, only certain individuals feel called forth to become prophets while most do not. In any event, the prophet has emerged in a new cultural role, and his personality is liberated from the stress that called his response into being in the first place. Immune to the stress under which his brethren still suffer, he must to them appear supernatural.

The disciples who gather around the prophet also, like him, undergo a revitalizing personality change — as did Peter, to name one very familiar

example. The prophet continues his spiritual leadership, but the disciples take upon themselves the practical tasks of organizing the campaign to establish the new movement. They convert large numbers of people, who in turn also undergo revitalizing personality transformations. If the messianic movement has been allowed to survive to this point by the oppressive, dominant culture that called it into being in the first place, a vital step must now be taken. The prophet must emphasize that he is only the intermediary between the converts and the supernatural being whose message he has been spreading. This step is essential, for it ensures the continuity of the new movement after its founding prophet dies. The prophet puts the converts and the supernatural being into close touch with each other by calling for certain symbolic duties the faithful must perform toward the supernatural being, such as eating peyote or partaking of bread and wine.

The new movement often has to resist both the oppressive alien culture and the opposition of factions within itself. The successful messianic movement meets this resistance by resorting to any one of a number of adaptations. It may change its teachings, as did the early Christians who gradually gave up Jewish rituals, such as circumcision. It may resort to political maneuvering and compromise. Most messianic movements, though, make the disastrous mistake that almost all Jewish and American Indian messianic movements did: They choose to fight. Islam alone succeeded by force of arms, whereas the success of the early Christians was their choice of universal peace as their weapon.

Once the messianic movement has won a large following, a new culture begins to emerge out of the death of the old — not only in religious affairs but in all aspects of economic, social, and political life as well. An organization with a secular and a sacerdotal hierarchy arises to perpetuate the new doctrine. The religion in that way becomes routinized in a stable culture. All routinized religions today (whether they be the Native American Church, Mohammedanism, Judaism, or Christianity) are successful descendants of what originated as messianic movements — that is, one personality's vision of a new way of life for a culture under extreme stress.

These steps apply equally to the messianic movement in Soviet Russia, even though it denies belief in the supernatural. Czarist Russia in 1917 was a society under extreme stress, disintegrating both on the war front and at home; in the previous decade it had suffered a humiliating defeat by the Japanese. There was unrest, and repressive measures were stern. A prophet, Lenin, arose; and he made a miraculous return from exile in Switzerland in a railroad car that traversed enemy territory. He preached his vision of Utopia, and he referred constantly to a revered, almost supernatural being named Karl Marx. The missionary fervor excited Lenin's close followers, and they in turn won adherents even among their former enemies in society. One element of the population in particular — the economically downtrodden — was appealed to, and it was promised a reward here on earth. But first these people had to perform certain rituals: convert to the new doctrine of Marx–Lenin; change the economic way of life; publicly confess errors, even if such confession resulted in martyrdom. After the prophet's death, a political organization of key disciples (Stalin, Trotsky, and others) continued his teachings and prepared a complex doctrine that admitted of no revisionism or deviation. The prophet himself was deified after death, as demonstrated today by the people paying homage at Lenin's tomb to the embalmed cadaver that, miraculously, is not heir to the corruption of the flesh.

52
Servicing Religious Consumers in a Multicultural Society

REGINALD W. BIBBY

While the question of the reality of the gods cannot be addressed by the sociologist, the question of the nature of culture can. And if there is little difference between the nature of culture and the nature of the gods, we are left with two possibilities: either the gods are not "getting through" or they don't exist at all. In either event, they are insignificant to everyday life.

As Canada approaches the dawn of the twenty-first century, the gods are in trouble. There is little difference between the look of culture and the look of religion. Whereas Pierre Berton's primary criticism two decades ago in *The Comfortable Pew* was that the Church was playing it safe by lagging behind culture, the Church of today has largely caught up to culture, but has in no way passed it. *The Comfortable Pew* has been replaced by The Cultural Pew.

For some time now, a highly specialized, consumer-oriented society has been remoulding the gods. Canadians are drawing very selectively on religion, and the dominant religious groups are responding with highly specialized items —

isolated beliefs, practices, programs, and professional services, notably weddings and funerals.

The problem with all of this is that religion, instead of standing over against culture, has become a neatly packaged consumer item — taking its place among other commodities that can be bought or bypassed according to one's consumption whims. Religion has become little more than a cultural product and is coming precariously close to acknowledging that culture creates the gods.

The possibility that culture will devour religion has always existed. Indeed, the reason that the question of "who created whom" has been raised in the past is that people have frequently worshipped gods that strikingly resembled their own personal and cultural characteristics. Psychologists like Gordon Allport have noted how people tend to emphasize supernatural features that reflect their own needs — if they are weak, then God is all-powerful; if they are friendless, then God is a companion; if they need guidance, then God is all-knowing. Sociologists since at least Max Weber have pointed out that the conceptions of the gods closely resemble the characteristics of societies and groups — agricultural peoples develop gods of sun and rain and ocean peoples worship gods of the sea; masters and slaves, the rich and the poor, the upper class and the lower class — all have very different views about God, life, and death.

When rival nations go into battle with simultaneous claims that "God is on our side"; when advocates of capitalism and socialism use the same "God" to legitimize their own position and condemn the other; when homosexuality is denounced as "sin" by Christian heterosexuals and declared "acceptable to God" by homosexuals who say they too are Christians; when people within the same denomination or even the same congregation say they have sought the will of God and have come to opposite conclusions — in such cases the neutral onlooker can be excused for wondering, "Where does the human contribution stop and the non-human begin?"

Some people conclude that no such division exists, that it's all human-made. The match-up between human and divine characteristics is so tight that there is no need to consider an intervening supernatural factor. Sigmund Freud argued that the hopes of humans resemble the alleged characteristics of "God" so closely that people simply transfer their hopes and wishes to an imaginary being. Émile Durkheim concluded that the characteristics of social groups are so similar to those of "God" that "God" is nothing more than the groups' experience of themselves. Karl Marx found that the nature and will of the gods closely reflected power relations. He declared, "Man makes religion; religion does not make man," and man has "found only his own reflection in the fantastic reality of heaven, where he sought a supernatural being."

Historically, Judeo-Christian religion has claimed to be much more than individuals and culture. It has asserted that there is a God back of life who, as the German theologian and preacher Helmut Thielicke put it, brought history into being, oversees it, and will be there at its end. This God is more than a mirror image of individuals and culture; indeed, "It" speaks to all of personal and social life, pronouncing and, when necessary, denouncing.

The extensive research unveiled in [Bibby's *Fragmented Gods*] suggests that a religion with this kind of God is largely dead in Canada. Consumers tell religion what type of religion they would like; culture accordingly tells religion how to update and upgrade its content and forms. But, ironically, in trying to get in step with the modern age, organized religion — by dismantling the gods and serving them up piecemeal — is running the risk of becoming increasingly trivial. However, there is hope. As Berton wrote in his important critique twenty years ago, "If the Christian Church is ailing, it is certainly worth reviving." Rejuvenation is not beyond the realm of possibility.

Religion as History and Memory

The gods weren't always so fragmented. In the beginning, religion was a central feature in the lives of Canada's Native peoples. They may not have produced systematic theologies in European terms. But our founding Indians and other indigenous Canadians have been described as "deeply committed to religious attitudes, beliefs and practices" that were grounded in "communion with nature and a connectedness with all of life."

Along the way, religion in Roman Catholic and Protestant form sailed across the Atlantic from France and England and became an integral part of the earliest settlements. Religion has been an important travelling companion of virtually every other newly arriving group. Its presence has been physically acknowledged in the myriad churches, synagogues, mosques, and temples that dot the urban and rural landscapes of the nation to this day.

Accordingly, religion has had a significant place in Canadian history. As one thinks of the past, it is impossible to imagine Quebec with no Roman Catholics, Ontario with no Anglicans or Presbyterians, the Prairies with no evangelical Protestants, and British Columbia and the Atlantic region without the Church of England.

Religion has also claimed a place in most of our personal lives. Two in three of us were attending services almost every week or more when we were growing up. Religion calls forth various memories of grandparents and parents, white shirts and dresses, Sunday schools and Latin Masses, after-service meals, and, in many cases, a reduced level of activity that was strangely becoming to that different day in the week.

For some, religion is associated with good feelings — a family alive and together, close friends, a world that seemed peaceful and somehow less complex than the one we know today. For others, the thought of religion brings back memories of forced attendance, rigid morality, unbelievable beliefs, and contact with people who often seemed different from everybody else — and were aptly dubbed, by some clergy, "God's peculiar people."

Today, in the twilight of the twentieth century, things have changed. Religion no longer occupies centre stage in our society. Protestantism is not a pivotal feature of Anglo culture; Roman Catholicism is no longer at the heart of Québécois culture. Religion's importance to other cultural groups has similarly declined as those groups have become increasingly integrated into mainstream Canadian life.

It is true that our society continues to give lip service to the importance of religion. The Canadian Charter explicitly states that "Canada is founded upon principles that recognize the supremacy of God and the rule of law." We welcome visits by the Pope and other figures such as Bishop Desmond Tutu, Mother Teresa, Coretta King, and Billy Graham.

But it is also readily apparent that religion has little influence when it comes to political and economic decision-making, higher education, entertainment, and even personal morality. At the level of the federal government, for example, Robertson Davies, the novelist and Master emeritus of Massey College, maintains:

> Our houses of Parliament open their sessions with daily prayers, asking for divine guidance, but what they discuss is necessarily broadly materialistic, sometimes quasi-scientific, and when prayers are over God is rarely invoked.

In trying to tell us what we are like in his best-selling 1985 book, *The Canadians*, Andrew Malcolm gives virtually no attention to religion. The Anglican Archbishop of Toronto, Lewis Garnsworthy, has summed up the situation well in his 1984 Charge to the Synod:

> We survive — great at Coronations, charming at weddings and impressive at funerals as long as we don't eulogize. We are welcome mascots at family do's and offer respectability to the Christmas cocktail circuit. We grace any community as long as we stay out of social issues and do not change a jot or tittle of well-worn liturgy.

Religion has also ceased to be life-informing at the level of the average Canadian. For most, it is extremely specialized in content and influence. People hold some beliefs and pray at least once in a while. They occasionally find themselves at a wedding, perhaps a funeral, and maybe a christening. But for the majority of Canadians, religious commitment is a former acquaintance rather than a current companion. In the poetry of Kris Kristofferson, the things that remind them of religion, such as a church bell or a Sunday School chorus, tend to "take them back to something that they lost somewhere, somehow along the way."

The implications of it all are not clear. Many Canadians say they are no worse off, and are maybe even better off, without religious involvement. Still, I suspect that many silently wonder if they really are — if something beyond just religion has been "lost somewhere along the

way." A good number also wonder if their children in turn will experience any loss, aware that, because of their choices, that old-time religion that was "good enough for grandma, their parents, and them" is frequently a stranger to their sons and daughters.

*   *   *

The findings are in and the message is clear. Religion, Canadian-style, is mirroring culture. A specialized society is met with specialized religion. Consumer-minded individuals are provided with a smorgasbord of fragment choices. Culture leads; religion follows. While the situation is not unique to Canada, it *is* nonetheless the Canadian religious reality.

In this country, religion gives every indication of being something we create rather than something with a non-human dimension. To return to the question we raised at the beginning of the book [*Fragmented Gods*], the Canadian situation strongly suggests not that the gods created us, but that we are creating the gods. The specifications are handed down by culture.

This, I stress, is not a subjective or theological observation. On the contrary, it is an objectively observable conclusion based on a simple examination of the nature of culture on the one hand and the nature of religion on the other. The correlation between the two is unmistakably strong. Few would argue that the relationship is due to religion's impact on culture. Indeed, to the extent that religion is regarded as a life-embracing system of meaning, the reality of its fragmentation leaves little doubt as to which is the artist and which the canvas.

The situation may well continue basically unchanged as we move into the next century. If so, a number of features can be expected.

Religion in the Twenty-First Century

If religion continues to be so highly dependent upon culture, it will be moulded by national and global developments. Social forecasters seem to agree that, in the future, two central features will be prominent — the acceleration of both available information and technological innovation. For example, the chairman of the board of the Microsoft Corporation, Bill Gates, says, "In twenty years, the Information Age will be here, absolutely. The dream of having the world database at [our] fingertips will have become a reality." By the early twenty-first century, the experts say, a personal computer will be owned and operated by every child, as common as a pair of Nikes; television will give way to "sensavision," allowing us not only to see and hear but also to feel and smell; many of today's diseases, including cancer and arthritis, will disappear.

As Gates points out, history is far from being in the process of merely repeating itself. Technology is leading us into unprecedented territory at an unprecedented pace. He argues that we cannot begin to extrapolate from the past in establishing the rate of change in even the next twenty years: "The leap will be unique. I can't think of any equivalent phenomenon in history."

The increase in information and innovation will only intensify specialization both by institutions and by individuals. Religion will feel the consequences.

Fragment Consumption

Specialized offerings from a wide variety of sources will be available to Canadians performing a variety of roles. The consequent consumer attitude to goods and services will continue to be applied also to religion and religious organizations. The tendency to adopt fragments will be pervasive.

This is no groundless speculation. Analyses of religious styles by age cohort have shown that the consumption of belief, practice, and service fragments — versus identifiable commitment — is considerably more prevalent among younger Canadians than others. As the population ages, the consumption segment of the population can accordingly be expected to increase. Religious influence will consequently be minor at the individual level.

Socially, the Churches can be expected to follow their twentieth-century pattern of officially speaking out on many matters, yet having limited impact. The editor of *The Presbyterian Record*, James Dickey, in discussing the need for closer ties among religious groups, recently observed: "Perhaps we have accomplished little because we operate from the top of the institutional structures, not the base." The Canadian Conference of Catholic Bishops has similarly noted that the background preparation of statements is often limited to "dialogue with specialized elites." They stress that "unless [the background work] is constantly nurtured by the actions and reflections of popular movements and grass-roots communities, it will prove inadequate." In view of the declining participation of Canadians in the churches, the statements of religious groups will increasingly lack the endorsement of a sizeable committed

constituency and will therefore have less political clout and social impact.

The Roman Catholic sociologist, author, and priest Andrew Greeley predicts that the power of the Pope will shrink.

> Today we are experiencing the last gasp of a dying order, and in twenty years most of it will be gone. There will be a new leadership more interested in listening to what the people and what the local bishops say. The present condition in the church is transitional.

Religion will without question be with us as we move into the twenty-first century. Despite his skepticism about the future influence of the papacy, Greeley predicts that in twenty years "no one is going to claim ... that we don't need religion, even though some people obviously will not have strong 'religious sensibilities.'" If anything, according to Greeley, there will be an increased emphasis upon the non-rational aspects of religion — the emotional, mystical, and poetic.

Freud was wrong in expecting that "the illusion," as he called it, would be left "to the angels and the sparrows" as civilization increasingly opted for science and reason. But in fairness to Freud, it is obvious that the religions of the present age, characterized by "fragmented gods," are extremely abridged versions of the life-embracing systems envisaged by their founders.

Old and New Companies

The twenty-first century should see the continued presence of organized religion, primarily in its present dominant forms. But there will be no lack of an ongoing stream of new companies. Proponents of "consumer cults" can be expected to work hard to legitimize their "products." Because of the profit potential in dollars and human lives, aggressive promotion through the varied available means of mass marketing can be expected. Harvey Cox of Harvard University suggests that, in order to be popular in the United States, at least, the new entries will "have to offer a mixture of religion, scientific theories, psychological techniques, and ecological lore." Cox cites Scientology as an example of such a viable market candidate.

But the Canadian religion market, beyond the possibility of supernatural fragment contributions, is extremely tight, and there are few signs that it will open up. Further, because of the specialized nature of our society, rivals of the established religious groups will probably fare no better than Christianity in attempting to have an impact on the whole of people's lives. Some of the new competitors — the New Age Movement, for example — may be resisted and strongly opposed as too different. Most, however, will probably be either ignored or allowed a retail outlet to supplement the prevailing beliefs and practices.

Decreasing Involvement

If religious groups continue to operate essentially as they are at present, what can be projected with a high degree of confidence is a continued drop-off in regular attendance at services. The most notable determinant of adult affiliation and attendance is parental and church socialization in childhood. Sean O'Sullivan's observation receives solid support from research: "Faith, after all, is not something that comes suddenly or grows in isolation; it is passed on in large measure by the simple, devout faith of parents and others." Bruce Hunsberger, a psychologist at Wilfrid Laurier University in Waterloo, Ontario, is among those who, for some time, have been finding that "the reported emphasis placed on religion in one's childhood home is one of the best predictors of later religiosity." But the surveys have revealed that the regular attendance levels of both adults and school-age children have decreased from two-thirds to one-third over the second half of this century.

Some will argue that many Canadians will return to church — that the "baby-boomers" will eventually find their way back. However, the *Project Canada* surveys have found very little support for such an argument. They have included a core of more than a thousand people who participated in 1975 and 1980 and almost six hundred people who have participated in all three surveys. What we have found is that there is a slight increase in attendance for some who marry and have children. But such an increase does not characterize the majority.

*   *   *

The truth of the matter is that large numbers of Canadians are not going to return to the churches because they have little to which to return — many were never really there. The religious socialization that so many of us experienced when young is simply not as common among our children.

What might future attendance levels look like? If the rate of attrition of the 1950s, 1960s, and 1970s continues, it will mean that the drop from two-thirds to one-third between 1945 and 1985 will be followed by a drop from one-third to one-sixth in another forty years (by around the year 2025). That's a very big "if," since much of Canada's attendance drop-off resulted from the modernization of Quebec. Still, it's interesting and perhaps significant that, at present, the proportion of Canadians between the ages of 18 and 29 who attend services weekly stands at about 16 percent — one-sixth of that cohort.

Although attendance projections are bleak, religious organizations are assured of continued contact with Canadians. The desire of people to have churches perform rites of passage surrounding birth, puberty, marriage, and death guarantees the religious groups at least a service role well into the twenty-first century — that is, if they want it.

SECTION SIX
Endangered Societies and Cultures

No man is an island, entire of itself;

every man is a piece of the Continent, a part of the main;

if a Clod bee washed away by the sea, Europe is the lessee,

as well as if a Promontories were,

as well as if a Mannor of thy friends or of thine own were;

any man's death diminishes me, because I am involved in Mankinde;

And therefore never send to know for whom the bell tolls; it tolls for thee.

John Donne
(1573–1631)

Introduction

Since their first appearance during the late Neolithic, state societies have been encroaching upon smaller, self-sufficient groups. We started this reader with a discussion of Darwin's theory of evolution, which suggests that, in general, it is the reproductively fittest, best adapted that survive. A fundamental aspect of the history of humankind since the Neolithic seems to contradict Darwin: Well adapted, sustainable societies, capable of maintaining a reasonably consistent culture for millennia without damaging their ecosystem, were wiped out by unstable state societies, which waxed and waned in rapid succession, each time leaving the earth the poorer for it. The explanation for the puzzling success of state societies is not that they are "fit" but rather that they are powerful. Through warfare, the powerful replace the weak. Of course, such success is very momentary. Ecologists compare the self-satisfied gloating of the prophets of "progress" to that of a man who has jumped from the Empire State building: When last heard from, he was passing the tenth-floor window, shouting: "Everything's all right, so far!"

Most tribal and village people alive today face extinction as expanding state systems encroach upon their territories. Their forests have been burned down, their natural resources taken away, and their social and religious systems ridiculed, persecuted, or "missionized" out of existence. The brutality and hypocrisy of this process of destruction have been well documented by groups such as Cultural Survival and Amnesty International (Davis 1977). The process has continued relentlessly, and has gained momentum with technological innovations such as airplanes, helicopters, and bulldozers, which have facilitated access and encroachment. The aggressor states have used the excuse of overpopulation and the myth of progress to justify **ethnocide** and **genocide**. One is reminded of the story of Gandhi's response to a snobbish reporter who asked him what he thought of Western civilization. Gandhi appeared thoughtful for a while, then exclaimed: "*Western* civilization? That would be a good idea!"

When they lament the extinction of small egalitarian societies of the past and present, anthropologists are not being hopeless dreamers, willing to sacrifice progress in order to conserve obsolete relics of the past. Each time a human society or culture is destroyed, one of humanity's ways of adapting is extinguished, and, along with it, the solutions to a wide variety of ecological, economic, social, psychological, and religious problems disappear forever. The adaptation of any species of plants or animals must involve great diversity to make natural selection without the threat of extinction possible. To preserve humanity, it is critical, as President John F. Kennedy said, that we "make the world safe for diversity."

If the Great Coca-Cola Culture of the rich and powerful Western societies succeeds in supplanting all the world's cultures, when it fails — and it is too unstable not to fail — there will be no alternative for natural selection, and the extinction of the species will ensue. Each time one of the "powerful" societies "missionizes," "integrates," "develops," or otherwise destroys a people or a sociocultural system, humanity is diminished, and we all die a little because of it. The verse from John Donne that opens this section expresses a profound truth: "any man's death diminishes me, because I am involved in Mankinde; / And therefore never send to know for whom the bell tolls; it tolls for thee."

Especially since the colonial expansions of the nineteenth century, the rich and powerful nations of Europe and America have forcefully promoted the wholesale export of their ideas, customs, and beliefs to the rest of the world. However, various peoples throughout the world have *not* been eager to receive the new gods and gadgets. They have often rejected the foreign ideas and customs that have been proposed to them in the name of "progress" or "civilization." Developers, business-people, and even some anthropologists have deemed such rejections conservative and ethnocentric. The models presented by Oscar Lewis (1968) — the "Culture of Poverty" — and by Georges Foster (1967) — the "Image of Limited Good" — suggested that the value systems of the poor and powerless prevented them from taking advantage of development opportunities.

All human populations have different cultures because each culture is a product of the adaptive adjustments of the members of a particular society to their own particular social and ecological environments. Ethnocentrism causes people to reject the cultural traits of other cultures — which, in many cases, they neither need nor can afford — thereby protecting their diversity from the attempts of conquerors, developers, and missionaries to elimi-

nate it. Ethnocentrism contributes to the isolation and diversity of human cultures: it is the cultural equivalent of our bodies' immune systems, which protect them from foreign germs. Much as they oppose attempts to eliminate diversity, however, anthropologists do not argue against *contact* between peoples of different cultures. (Such an attitude was justifiably ridiculed in a poster published by Cultural Survival, which pictured a "native" inside a bell jar, over the caption "Preserving Cultures?") All societies change all the time, and diffusion is an important process of cultural cross-fertilization, as we saw in Ralph Linton's essay, in Chapter 29.

As we have suggested, however, forced diffusion is often destructive. Some consider the "gifts" of the powerful to the powerless a contemporary **Trojan Horse.** Such gifts can threaten the integrity of the recipients' social system and culture the way a virus threatens a biological organism. Lauriston Sharp's eloquent example of the unforeseen consequences of a gift of steel axes to Australian Aborigines (Chapter 53) is most instructive. It not only confirms that the road to hell may be paved with good intentions, but also, and more importantly, reveals the complexity and functional interdependence of all the parts of a sociocultural system. We must not, however, be too quick to cry "doom" or to perceive the less powerful societies as helpless victims with too little cultural vitality to survive foreign intrusions into their lives. This is the point that John Taylor makes in Chapter 54. Taylor revisited the Yir Yoront 33 years after Sharp had conducted his study, and found many examples of vitality and adaptability in the culture of the Yir Yoront. Although the culture had changed, it had not been destroyed, as Sharp predicted it would be.

It is important to emphasize examples of cultural resilience and, in some cases (see Chapter 58), at least partly successful resistance. Nevertheless, it would be a gross distortion of history to forget that most of the small egalitarian societies that existed at the beginning of this century have now disappeared, and that this relentless process is still under way today in Asia, Africa, and the Americas. Ultimately, it matters little whether the gift-giver or "innovator" is a missionary or a conqueror: when the powerful meet the powerless, it is a case of the robin romancing the worm. Bishop Desmond Tutu described the process as it manifested itself in South Africa this way:

When the White missionaries arrived, they had the Bible and we had the land. They said: "let us pray" and we closed our eyes and prayed. When we opened our eyes, we had the Bible and they had the land!

Bishop Tutu proposed this concise summary of the history of colonial Africa in a radio interview when he was awarded the Nobel Peace Prize. It accurately reflects the source of the poverty of the countries in Africa and elsewhere that we, adding insult to injury, call "underdeveloped." In Chapter 55, Richard Lee and Susan Hurlich describe how, since the early 1970s, the South African military and missionaries of the Dutch Reformed Church have destroyed the successful hunting-and-gathering way of life of the !Kung. The process of rapid and forced **acculturation** to which the !Kung have been subjected is described by other anthropologists as *ethnocide*, the killing of a culture. In addition to providing an "update" on a group of people discussed in every anthropology textbook, Lee and Hurlich's essay raises challenging issues pertaining to methodology. As a byproduct of imperialism, anthropology often contributed to the concealment of colonial domination and power. Does its use of concepts such as "ethnicity" and "acculturation" amount to a convenient avoidance of issues of class and conquest? In the context of South Africa, has the discipline's emphasis on the precious diversity of cultures inadvertently supported apartheid and stood in the way of black African nation building?

Joseph G. Jorgensen proposes an answer to such questions in Chapter 56, "Indians and the Metropolis." Acculturation studies have confirmed the aggressive government policy of integrating the American Indians into the dominant white society. The source of their poverty is not in their failure to become integrated into the national economy: they were fully integrated into that economy the day they were conquered. Rather, their poverty and "underdevelopment" were the price of the development of the dominant white society. Jorgensen shows how the Bureau of Indian Affairs actively contributed to the worsening economic, health, and legal problems of the Indians. He demonstrates that the appalling poverty of most Indian reservations is maintained by current government and business practices. The reservations are the poor "satellites" of the wealthy "metropolis" — that is, of urban centers of finance and political power.

In Chapter 57, Doris Young's brief account of the impact of hydroelectric megaprojects on the Cree of Northern Manitoba is written in a restrained and matter-of-fact style that makes it all the more eloquent and convincing. The projects brought southern Manitobans and other Canadians cheap electricity, but had dire consequences for the Indians, who lost their trapping areas and their balanced diet, were forced to become welfare recipients, suffered the effects of pollution, and lost their very way of life.

Finally, in Chapter 58, a short report from *Cultural Survival Quarterly* shows that, at last, small victories are being achieved by Amerindians seeking redress and compensation for the illegal destruction of their resources and their way of life. One strategy that has proved very successful in this regard is the coordination of the agendas and activities of Amerindian groups and environmentalists. A similar strategy helped the Australian Aborigines obtain a critical reversal in the legal status of their claims: in 1992, the High Court of Australia conceded for the first time that land occupied by Aborigines was not "empty land" and that they had the right to prevent the loss of their land and resources, as well as the right to get compensation for their losses. South American Indians have also gained international support for their protest against the construction of hydroelectric dams, which destroys their forests and leaves them homeless and destitute, through well-publicized demonstrations and visits to the United States and Canada. In Guatemala, where, during the 1980s, tens of thousands of Indians were victims of violent repression by the armed forces, Rigoberta Menchu, a Maya orphaned in the civil war, was awarded the Nobel Peace Prize in October 1992. This was the first time that the prize had been awarded to a native American. In Canada, the settlement of land claims is finally progressing. Furthermore, the acquittal of the First Nation warriors who mounted an armed resistance to the takeover of their land at Oka (for the purpose of building a golf course) may be a sign of the times. Finally, the involvement of the First Nation peoples in Canada's constitutional debate earned them a high profile and much respect and public support. Such examples offer some hope that, one day, we will learn that when the bell tolls, it tolls for us all.

Works Cited

Davis, S. 1977. *Victims of the Miracle: Development and the Indians of Brazil*. New York: Cambridge University Press.

Lewis, O. 1968. "The Culture of Poverty." In *Poverty in America*, edited by L. Ferman, J. Kornbluh, and A. Haber, pp. 405–15. Ann Arbor: University of Michigan Press.

Foster, G. 1967. *Tsintzuntzan: Mexican Peasants in a Changing World*. Boston: Little, Brown.

53
Steel Axes for Stone-Age Australians

LAURISTON SHARP

I

Like other Australian aboriginals, the Yir Yoront group, which lives at the mouth of the Coleman River on the west coast of Cape York Peninsula, originally had no knowledge of metals. Technologically, their culture was of the Old Stone Age, or Paleolithic, type. They supported themselves by hunting and fishing, and obtained vegetables and other materials from the bush by simple gathering techniques. Their only domesticated animal was the dog; they had no cultivated plants of any kind. Unlike some other aboriginal groups, however, the Yir Yoront did have polished stone axes hafted in short handles, which were most important in their economy.

Towards the end of the nineteenth century metal tools and other European artifacts began to filter into the Yir Yoront territory. The flow increased with the gradual expansion of the white frontier outward from southern and eastern Queensland. Of all the items of western technology thus made available, the hatchet, or short-handled steel axe, was the most acceptable to and the most highly valued by all aboriginals.

From *Human Organization*, Vol. 11, Summer 1952, pp. 17–22. Reprinted with the permission of the Society for Applied Anthropology. (Bibliographic documentation contained in the original text is omitted here. Interested readers should consult the original publication.)

In the mid 1930s an American anthropologist lived alone in the bush among the Yir Yoront for thirteen months without seeing another white man. The Yir Yoront were thus still relatively isolated and continued to live an essentially independent economic existence, supporting themselves entirely by means of their Old Stone Age techniques. Yet their polished stone axes were disappearing fast and being replaced by steel axes which came to them in considerable numbers, directly or indirectly, from various European sources to the south.

What changes in the life of the Yir Yoront still living under aboriginal conditions in the Australian bush could be expected as a result of their increasing possession and use of the steel axe?

II: The Course of Events

Events leading up to the introduction of the steel axe among the Yir Yoront begin with the advent of the second known group of Europeans to reach the shores of the Australian continent. In 1623 a Dutch expedition landed on the coast where the Yir Yoront now live. In 1935 the Yir Yoront were still using the few cultural items recorded in the Dutch log for the aboriginals they encountered. To this cultural inventory the Dutch added beads and pieces of iron which they offered in an effort to attract the frightened "Indians." Among these natives metal and beads have disappeared, together with any memory of this first encounter with whites.

The next recorded contact in this area was in 1864. Here there is more positive assurance that the natives concerned were the immediate ancestors of the Yir Yoront community. These aboriginals had the temerity to attack a party of cattle men who were driving a small herd from southern Queensland through the length of the then unknown Cape York Peninsula to a newly established government station at the northern tip. Known as the "Battle of the Mitchell River," this was one of the rare instances in which Australian aboriginals stood up to European gunfire for any length of time. A diary kept by the cattle men records that: "...10 carbines poured volley after volley into them from all directions, killing and wounding with every shot with very little return, nearly all their spears having already been expended. ...About 30 being killed, the leader thought it prudent to hold his hand, and let the rest escape. Many more must have been wounded and probably drowned, for 59 rounds were counted as discharged." The European party was in the Yir Yoront area for three days; they then disappeared over the horizon to the north and never returned. In the almost three-year long anthropological investigation conducted some 70 years later — in all the material of hundreds of free association interviews, in texts of hundreds of dreams and myths, in genealogies, and eventually in hundreds of answers to direct and indirect questioning on just this particular matter — there was nothing that could be interpreted as a reference to this shocking contact with Europeans.

The aboriginal accounts of their first remembered contact with whites begin in about 1900, with references to persons known to have had sporadic but lethal encounters with them. From that time on whites continued to remain on the southern periphery of Yir Yoront territory. With the establishment of cattle stations (ranches) to the south, cattle men made occasional excursions among the "wild black-fellows" in order to inspect the country and abduct natives to be trained as cattle boys and "house girls." At least one such expedition reached the Coleman River, where a number of Yir Yoront men and women were shot for no apparent reason.

About this time the government was persuaded to sponsor the establishment of three mission stations along the 700-mile western coast of the Peninsula in an attempt to help regulate the treatment of natives. To further this purpose a strip of coastal territory was set aside as an aboriginal reserve and closed to further white settlement.

In 1915, an Anglican mission station was established near the mouth of the Mitchell River, about a three-day march from the heart of the Yir Yoront country. Some Yir Yoront refused to have anything to do with the mission, others visited it occasionally, while only a few eventually settled more or less permanently in one of the three "villages" established at the mission.

Thus the majority of the Yir Yoront continued to live their old self-supporting life in the bush, protected until 1942 by the government reserve and the intervening mission from the cruder realities of the encroaching new order from the south. To the east was poor, uninhabited country. To the north were other bush tribes extending on along the coast to the distant Archer River Presbyterian mission, with which the Yir Yoront had no contact. Westward was the shallow Gulf of Carpentaria, on which the natives saw only a mission lugger making its infrequent dry season trips to the Mitchell River. In this protected environment for over a generation the Yir Yoront were able to recuperate from shocks received at the hands of civilized society. During the 1930s their raiding and fighting, their trading and stealing of women, their evisceration and two-or three-year care of their dead, and their totemic ceremonies continued, apparently uninhibited by western influence. In 1931 they killed a European who wandered into their territory from the east, but the investigating police never approached the group whose members were responsible for the act.

As a direct result of the work of the Mitchell River mission, all Yir Yoront received a great many more western artifacts of all kinds than ever before. As part of their plan for raising native living standards, the missionaries made it possible for aboriginals living at the mission to earn some western goods, many of which were then given or traded to natives still living under bush conditions; they also handed out certain useful articles gratis to both mission and bush aboriginals. They prevented guns, liquor, and damaging narcotics, as well as decimating diseases, from reaching the tribes of this area, while encouraging the introduction of goods they considered "improving." As has been noted, no item of western technology available, with the possible exception of trade tobacco, was in greater demand among all groups of aboriginals than the short-handled steel axe. The mission always kept a good supply of these axes in stock; at Christmas parties or other mission festivals they were given away to mission or visiting aboriginals indiscriminately and in considerable numbers. In addition, some steel axes as well as other European goods were still traded in to the Yir Yoront by natives in contact with cattle stations in the south. Indeed, steel axes had probably come to the Yir Yoront through established lines of aboriginal trade long before any regular contact with whites had occurred.

III: Relevant Factors

If we concentrate our attention on Yir Yoront behavior centering about the original stone axe (rather than on the axe — the object — itself) as a cultural trait or item of cultural equipment, we should get some conception of the role this implement played in aboriginal culture. This, in turn, should enable us to foresee with consider-able accuracy some of the results stemming from the displacement of the stone axe by the steel axe.

The production of a stone axe required a number of simple technological skills. With the various details of the axe well in mind, adult men could set about producing it (a task not consid-ered appropriate for women or children). First of all a man had to know the location and proper-ties of several natural resources found in his immediate environment: pliable wood for a handle, which could be doubled or bent over the axe head and bound tightly; bark, which could be rolled into cord for the binding; and gum, to fix the stone head in the haft. These materials had to be correctly gathered, stored, prepared, cut to size, and applied or manipulated. They were in plentiful supply, and could be taken from any-one's property without special permission. Postponing consideration of the stone head, the axe could be made by any normal man who had a simple knowledge of nature and of the techno-logical skills involved, together with fire (for heating the gum), and a few simple cutting tools — perhaps the sharp shells of plentiful bivalves.

The use of the stone axe as a piece of capital equipment used in producing other goods indicates its very great importance to the subsist-ence economy of the aboriginal. Anyone — man, woman, or child — could use the axe; indeed, it was used primarily by women, for theirs was the task of obtaining sufficient wood to keep the family campfire burning all day, for cooking or other purposes, and all night against mosquitoes and cold (for in July, winter temperature might drop below 40 degrees). In a normal lifetime a

woman would use the axe to cut or knock down literally tons of firewood. The axe was also used to make other tools or weapons, and a variety of material equipment required by the aboriginal in his daily life. The stone axe was essential in the construction of the wet season domed huts which keep out some rain and some insects; of platforms which provide dry storage; of shelters which give shade in the dry summer when days are bright and hot. In hunting and fishing and in gathering vegetable or animal food, the axe was also a necessary tool, and in this tropical culture, where preservatives or other means of storage are lacking, the natives spend more time obtaining food than in any other occupation — except sleeping. In only two instances was the use of the stone axe strictly limited to adult men: for gathering wild honey, the most prized food known to the Yir Yoront; and for making the secret paraphernalia for ceremonies. From this brief listing of some of the activities involving the use of the axe, it is easy to understand why there was at least one stone axe in every camp, in every hunting or fighting party, and in every group out on a "walk-about" in the bush.

The stone axe was also prominent in interper-sonal relations. Yir Yoront men were dependent upon interpersonal relations for their stone axe heads, since the flat, geologically recent, alluvial country over which they range provides no suitable stone for this purpose. The stone they used came from quarries 400 miles to the south, reaching the Yir Yoront through long lines of male trading partners. Some of these chains terminated with the Yir Yoront men, others extended on farther north to other groups, using Yir Yoront men as links. Almost every older adult man had one or more regular trading partners, some to the north and some to the south. He provided his partner or partners in the south with surplus spears, particularly fighting spears tipped with the barbed spines of sting ray, which snap into viscous fragments when they penetrate human flesh. For a dozen such spears, some of which he may have obtained from a partner to the north, he would receive one stone axe head. Studies have shown that the sting ray barbs increase in value as they move south and farther from the sea. One hundred and fifty miles south of Yir Yoront, one such spear may be exchanged for one stone axe head. Although actual investi-gations could not be made, it was presumed that farther south, nearer the quarries, one sting ray barb spear would bring several stone axe heads. Apparently people who acted as links in the middle of the chain and who made neither spears nor axe heads would receive a certain number of each as a middleman's profit.

Thus trading relations, which may extend the individual's personal relationships beyond that of his own group, were associated with spears and axes, two of the most important items in a man's equipment. Finally, most of the exchanges took place during the dry season, at the time of the great aboriginal celebrations centering about initiation rites or other totemic ceremonials which attracted hundreds and were the occasion for much exciting activity in addition to trading.

Returning to the Yir Yoront, we find that adult men kept their axes in camp with their other equipment, or carried them when travelling. Thus a woman or child who wanted to use an axe — as might frequently happen during the day — had to get one from a man, use it promptly, and return it in good condition. While a man might speak of "my axe," a woman or child could not.

This necessary and constant borrowing of axes from older men by women and children was in accordance with regular patterns of kinship behavior. A woman would expect to use her husband's axe unless he himself was using it; if unmarried, or if her husband was absent, a woman would go first to her older brother or to her father. Only in extraordinary circumstances would she seek a stone axe from other male kin. A girl, a boy, or a young man would look to a father or an older brother to provide an axe for their use. Older men, too, would follow similar rules if they had to borrow an axe.

It will be noted that all of these social relationships in which the stone axe had a place are pair relationships and that the use of the axe helped to define and maintain their character and the roles of the two individual participants. Every active relationship among the Yir Yoront involved a definite and accepted status of superordination or subordination. A person could have no dealings with another on exactly equal terms. The nearest approach to equality was between brothers, although the older was always superordinate to the younger. Since the exchange of goods in a trading relationship involved a mutual reciprocity, trading partners usually stood in a brotherly type of relationship, although one was always classified as older than the other and would have some advantage in case of dispute. It can be seen that repeated and widespread conduct centering around the use of the axe helped to generalize and standardize these sex, age, and kinship roles both in their normal benevolent and exceptional malevolent aspects.

The status of any individual Yir Yoront was determined not only by sex, age, and extended kin relationships, but also by membership in one or two dozen patrilineal totemic clans into which the entire community was divided. Each clan had literally hundreds of totems, from one or two of which the clan derived its name, and the clan members their personal names. These totems included natural species or phenomena such as the sun, stars, and daybreak, as well as cultural "species": imagined ghosts, rainbow serpents, heroic ancestors; such eternal cultural verities as fires, spears, huts; and such human activities, conditions, or attributes as eating, vomiting, swimming, fighting, babies and corpses, milk and blood, lips and loins. While individual members of such totemic classes or species might disappear or be destroyed, the class itself was obviously ever-present and indestructible. The totems, therefore, lent permanence and stability to the clans, to the groupings of human individuals who generation after generation were each associated with a set of totems which distinguished one clan from another.

The stone axe was one of the most important of the many totems of the Sunlit Cloud Iguana clan. The names of many members of this clan referred to the axe itself, to activities in which the axe played a vital part, or to the clan's mythical ancestors with whom the axe was prominently associated. When it was necessary to represent the stone axe in totemic ceremonies, only men of this clan exhibited it or pantomimed its use. In secular life, the axe could be made by any man and used by all; but in the sacred realm of the totems it belonged exclusively to the Sunlit Cloud Iguana people.

Supporting those aspects of cultural behavior which we have called technology and conduct is a third area of culture which includes ideas, sentiments, and values. These are most difficult to deal with, for they are latent and covert, and even unconscious, and must be deduced from overt actions and language or other communicating behavior. In this aspect of the culture lies the significance of the stone axe to the Yir Yoront and to their cultural way of life.

The stone axe was an important symbol of masculinity among the Yir Yoront (just as pants or pipes are to us). By a complicated set of ideas the axe was defined as "belonging" to males, and everyone in the society (except untrained infants) accepted these ideas. Similarly spears, spear throwers, and fire-making sticks were owned only by men and were also symbols of masculinity. But the masculine values represented by the stone axe were constantly being impressed on all members of society by the fact that females borrowed axes but not other masculine artifacts. Thus the axe stood for an important theme of Yir Yoront culture: the superiority and rightful dominance of the male, and the greater value of his concerns and all things associated with him. As the axe also had to be borrowed by the younger people it represented the prestige of age, another important theme running through Yir Yoront behavior.

To understand the Yir Yoront culture it is necessary to be aware of a system of ideas which may be called their totemic ideology. A fundamental belief of the aboriginal divided time into two great epochs: (1) a distant and sacred period at the beginning of the world when the earth was peopled by mildly marvellous ancestral beings or culture heroes who are in a special sense the forebears of the clans; and (2) a period when the old was succeeded by a new order, which includes the present. Originally there was no anticipation of another era supplanting the present. The future would simply be an eternal continuation and reproduction of the present, which itself had remained unchanged since the epochal revolution of ancestral times.

The important thing to note is that the aboriginal believed that the present world, as a natural and cultural environment, was and should be simply a detailed reproduction of the world of the ancestors. He believed that the entire universe "is now as it was in the beginning" when it was established and left by the ancestors. The ordinary cultural life of the ancestors became the daily life of the Yir Yoront camps, and the extraordinary life of the ancestors remained extant in the recurring symbolic pantomimes and paraphernalia found only in the most sacred atmosphere of the totemic rites.

Such beliefs, accordingly, opened the way for ideas of what *should be* (because it supposedly *was*) to influence or help determine what actually *is*. A man called Dog-chases-iguana-up-a-tree-and-barks-at-him-all-night had that and other names because he believed his ancestral alter ego had also had them; he was a member of the Sunlit Cloud Iguana clan because his ancestor was; he was associated with particular countries and totems of this same ancestor; during an initiation he played the role of a dog and symbolically attacked and killed certain members of other clans because his ancestor (conveniently either anthropomorphic or kynomorphic) really did the same to the ancestral alter egos of these men; and he would avoid his mother-in-law, joke with a mother's distant brother, and make spears in a certain way because his and other people's ances-

tors did these things. His behavior in these specific ways was outlined, and to that extent determined for him, by a set of ideas concerning the past and the relation of the present to the past.

But when we are informed that Dog-chases-etc. had two wives from the Spear Black Duck clan and one from the Native Companion clan, one of them being blind, that he had four children with such and such names, that he had a broken wrist and was left-handed, all because his ancestor had exactly these same attributes, then we know (though he apparently didn't) that the present has influenced the past, that the mythical world has been somewhat adjusted to meet the exigencies and accidents of the inescapably real present.

There was thus in Yir Yoront ideology a nice balance in which the mythical was adjusted in part to the real world, the real world in part to the ideal pre-existing mythical world, the adjustments occurring to maintain a fundamental tenet of native faith that the present must be a mirror of the past. Thus the stone axe in all its aspects, uses, and associations was integrated into the context of Yir Yoront technology and conduct because a myth, a set of ideas, had put it there.

IV: The Outcome

The introduction of the steel axe indiscriminately and in large numbers into the Yir Yoront technology occurred simultaneously with many other changes. It is therefore impossible to separate all the results of this single innovation. Nevertheless, a number of specific effects of the change from stone to steel axes may be noted, and the steel axe may be used as an epitome of the increasing quantity of European goods and implements received by the aboriginals and of their general influence on the native culture. The use of the steel axe to illustrate such influences would seem to be justified. It was one of the first European artifacts to be adopted for regular use by the Yir Yoront, and whether made of stone or steel, the axe was clearly one of the most important items of cultural equipment they possessed.

The shift from stone to steel axes provided no major technological difficulties. While the aboriginals themselves could not manufacture steel axe heads, a steady supply from outside continued; broken wooden handles could easily be replaced from bush timbers with aboriginal tools. Among the Yir Yoront the new axe was never used to the extent it was on mission or cattle stations (for carpentry work, pounding tent pegs, as a hammer, and so on); indeed, it had so few more uses than the stone axe that its practical effect on the native standard of living was negligible. It did some jobs better, and could be used longer without breakage. These factors were sufficient to make it of value to the native. The white man believed that a shift from steel to stone axe on his part would be a definite regression. He was convinced that his axe was much more efficient, that its use would save time, and that it therefore represented technical "progress" towards goals which he had set up for the native. But this assumption was hardly born out in aboriginal practice. Any leisure time the Yir Yoront might gain by using steel axes or other western tools was not invested in "improving the conditions of life," nor, certainly, in developing aesthetic activities, but in sleep — an art they had mastered thoroughly.

Previously, a man in need of an axe would acquire a stone axe head through regular trading partners from whom he knew what to expect, and was then dependent solely upon a known and adequate natural environment, and his own skills or easily acquired techniques. A man wanting a steel axe, however, was in no such self-reliant position. If he attended a mission festival when steel axes were handed out as gifts, he might receive one either by chance or by happening to impress upon the mission staff that he was one of the "better" bush aboriginals (the missionaries' definition of "better" being quite different from that of his bush fellows). Or, again almost by pure chance, he might get some brief job in connection with the mission which would enable him to earn a steel axe. In either case, for older men a preference for the steel axe helped change the situation from one of self-reliance to one of dependence, and a shift in behavior from well-structured or defined situations in technology or conduct to ill-defined situations in conduct alone. Among the men, the older ones whose earlier experience or knowledge of the white man's harshness made them suspicious were particularly careful to avoid having relations with the mission, and thus excluded themselves from acquiring steel axes from that source.

In other aspects of conduct or social relations, the steel axe was even more significantly at the root of psychological stress among the Yir Yoront. This was the result of new factors which the missionary considered beneficial: the simple numerical increase in axes per capita as a result of mission distribution, and distribution directly to younger men, women, and even children. By winning the favor of the mission staff, a woman might be given a steel axe which was clearly intended to be hers, thus creating a situation quite different from the previous custom which necessitated her borrowing an axe from a male relative. As a result a woman would refer to the axe as "mine," a possessive form she had never been able to use of the stone axe. In the same fashion, young men or even boys also obtained steel axes directly from the mission, with the result that older men no longer had a complete monopoly of all the axes in the bush community. All this led to a revolutionary confusion of sex, age, and kinship roles, with a major gain in independence and loss of subordination on the part of those who now owned steel axes when they had previously been unable to possess stone axes.

The trading partner relationship was also affected by the new situation. A Yir Yoront might have a trading partner in a tribe to the south whom he defined as a younger brother and over whom he would therefore have some authority. But if the partner were in contact with the mission or had other access to steel axes, his subordination obviously decreased. Among other things, this took some of the excitement away from the dry season fiesta-like tribal gatherings centering around initiations. These had traditionally been the climactic annual occasions for exchanges between trading partners, when a man might seek to acquire a whole year's supply of stone axe heads. Now he might find himself prostituting his wife to almost total strangers in return for steel axes or other white man's goods. With trading partnerships weakened, there was less reason to attend the ceremonies, and less fun for those who did.

Not only did an increase in steel axes and their distribution to women change the character of the relations between individuals (the paired relationships that have been noted), but a previously rare type of relationship was created in the Yir Yoront's conduct towards whites. In the aboriginal society there were few occasions outside of the immediate family when an individual would initiate action to several other people at once. In an average group, in accordance with the kinship system, while a person might be superordinate to several people to whom he could suggest or command action, he was also subordinate to several others with whom such behavior would be tabu. There was thus no overall chieftainship or authoritarian leadership of any kind. Such complicated operations as grass-burning animal drives or totemic ceremonies could be carried out smoothly because each person was aware of his role.

On both mission and cattle stations, however, the whites imposed their conception of leadership roles upon the aboriginals, consisting of one person in a controlling relationship with a subordinate group. Aboriginals called together to receive gifts, including axes, at a mission Christmas party found themselves facing one or two whites who sought to control their behavior for the occasion, who disregarded the age, sex, and kinship variables of which the aboriginals were so conscious, and who considered them all at one subordinate level. The white also sought to impose similar patterns on work parties. (However, if he placed an aboriginal in charge of a mixed group of post-hole diggers, for example, half of the group, those subordinate to the "boss," would work, while the other half, who were superordinate to him, would sleep.) For the aboriginal, the steel axe and other European goods came to symbolize this new and uncomfortable form of social organization, the leader–group relationship.

The most disturbing effects of the steel axe, operating in conjunction with other elements also being introduced from the white man's several sub-cultures, developed in the realm of traditional ideas, sentiments, and values. These were undermined at a rapidly mounting rate, with no new conceptions being defined to replace them. The result was the erection of a mental and moral void which foreshadowed the collapse and destruction of all Yir Yoront culture, if not, indeed, the extinction of the biological group itself.

From what has been said it should be clear how changes in overt behavior, in technology and conduct, weakened the values inherent in a reliance on nature, in the prestige of masculinity and of age, and in the various kinship relations. A scene was set in which a wife, or a young son whose initiation may not yet have been completed, need no longer defer to the husband or father, who, in turn, became confused and insecure as he was forced to borrow a steel axe from them. For the woman and boy the steel axe helped establish a new degree of freedom which they accepted readily as an escape from the unconscious stress of the old patterns — but they, too, were left confused and insecure. Ownership became less well defined, with the result that stealing and trespassing were introduced into technology and conduct. Some of the excitement surrounding the great ceremonies evaporated and they lost their previous gaiety and interest. Indeed, life itself became less interesting, although this did not lead the Yir Yoront to discover suicide, a concept foreign to them.

The whole process may be most specifically illustrated in terms of totemic system, which also illustrates the significant role played by a system of ideas, in this case a totemic ideology, in the breakdown of a culture.

In the first place, under pre-European aboriginal conditions, where the native culture has become adjusted to a relatively stable environment, few, if any, unheard of or catastrophic crises can occur. It is clear, therefore, that the totemic system serves very effectively in inhibiting radical cultural changes. The closed system of totemic ideas, explaining and categorizing a well-known universe as it was fixed at the beginning of time, presents a considerable obstacle to the adoption of new or the dropping of old culture traits. The obstacle is not insurmountable and the system allows for the minor variations which occur in the norms of daily life. But the inception of major changes cannot easily take place.

Among the bush Yir Yoront the only means of water transport is a light wood log to which they cling in their constant swimming of rivers, salt creeks, and tidal inlets. These natives know that tribes 45 miles further north have a bark canoe. They know these northern tribes can thus fish from mid-stream or out at sea, instead of clinging to the river banks and beaches, that they can cross coastal waters infested with crocodiles, sharks, sting rays, and Portuguese men-of-war without danger. They know the materials of which the canoe is made exist in their own environment. But they also know, as they say, that they do not have canoes because their own mythical ancestors did not have them. They assume that the canoe was part of the ancestral universe of the northern tribes. For them, then, the adoption of the canoe would not be simply a matter of learning a number of new behavioral skills for its manufacture and use. The adoption would require a much more difficult procedure; the acceptance by the entire society of a myth, either locally developed or borrowed, to explain the presence of the canoe, to associate it with some one or more of the several hundred mythical ancestors (and how decide which?), and thus establish it as an accepted totem of one of the clans ready to be used by the whole community. The Yir Yoront have not made this adjustment, and in this case we can only say that for the time being at least, ideas have won out over very real pressures for technological change. In the elaborateness and explicitness of the totemic ideologies we seem to have one explanation for the notorious stability of Australian cultures under aboriginal conditions, an explanation which gives due weight to the importance of ideas in determining human behavior.

At a later stage of the contact situation, as has been indicated, phenomena unaccounted for by the totemic ideological system begin to appear with regularity and frequency and remain within the range of native experience. Accordingly, they cannot be ignored (as the "Battle of the Mitchell" was apparently ignored), and there is an attempt to assimilate them and account for them along the lines of principles inherent in the ideology. The bush Yir Yoront of the mid-thirties represent this stage of the acculturation process. Still trying to maintain their aboriginal definition of the situation, they accept European artifacts and behavior patterns, but fit them into their totemic system, assigning them to various clans on a par with original totems. There is an attempt to have the myth-making process keep up with these cultural changes so that the idea system can continue to support the rest of the culture. But analysis of overt behavior, of dreams, and of some of the new myths indicates that this arrangement is not entirely satisfactory, that the native clings to his totemic system with intellectual loyalty (lacking any substitute ideology), but that associated sentiments and values are weakened. His attitudes towards his own and towards European culture are found to be highly ambivalent.

All ghosts are totems of the Head-to-the-East Corpse clan, are thought of as white, and are of course closely associated with death. The white man, too, is closely associated with death, and he and all things pertaining to him are naturally assigned to the Corpse clan as totems. The steel axe, as a totem, was thus associated with the Corpse clan. But as an "axe," clearly linked with the stone axe, it is a totem of the Sunlit Cloud Iguana clan. Moreover, the steel axe, like most European goods, has no distinctive origin myth, nor are mythical ancestors associated with it. Can anyone, sitting in the shade of a *ti* tree one afternoon, create a myth to resolve this confusion? No one has, and the horrid suspicion arises as to the authenticity of the origin myths, which failed to take into account this vast new universe of the white man. The steel axe, shifting hopelessly between one clan and the other, is not only replacing the stone axe physically, but is hacking at the supports of the entire cultural system.

The aboriginals to the south of the Yir Yoront have clearly passed beyond this stage. They are engulfed by European culture, either by the mission or cattle station sub-cultures or, for some natives, by a baffling, paradoxical combination of both incongruent varieties. The totemic ideology can no longer support the inrushing mass of foreign culture traits, and the myth-making process in its native form breaks down completely. Both intellectually and emotionally a saturation point is reached so that the myriad new traits which can neither be ignored nor any longer assimilated simply force the aboriginal to abandon his totemic system. With the collapse of this system of ideas, which is so closely related to so many other aspects of the native culture, there follows an appallingly sudden and complete cultural disintegration, and a demoralization of the individual such as has seldom been recorded elsewhere. Without the support of a system of ideas well devised to provide cultural stability in a stable environment, but admittedly too rigid for the new realities pressing in from outside, native behavior and native sentiments and values are simply dead. Apathy reigns. The aboriginal has passed beyond the realm of any outsider who might wish to do him well or ill.

Returning from the broken natives huddled on cattle stations or on the fringes of frontier towns to the ambivalent but still lively aboriginals settled on the Mitchell River mission, we note one further devious result of the introduction of European artifacts. During a wet season stay at the mission, the anthropologist discovered that his supply of tooth paste was being depleted at an alarming rate. Investigation showed that it was being taken by old men for use in a new tooth paste cult. Old materials of magic having failed, new materials were being tried out in a malevolent magic directed towards the mission staff and some of the younger aboriginal men. Old males, largely ignored by the missionaries, were seeking to regain some of their lost power and prestige. This mild aggression proved hardly effective, but perhaps only because confidence in any kind of magic on the mission was by this time at a low ebb.

For the Yir Yoront still in the bush, a time could be predicted when personal deprivation and frustration in a confused culture would produce an overload of anxiety. The mythical past of the totemic ancestors would disappear as a guarantee of a present of which the future was supposed to be a stable continuation. Without the past, the present could be meaningless and the future unstructured and uncertain. Insecurities would be inevitable. Reaction to this stress might be some form of symbolic aggression, or withdrawal and apathy, or some more realistic approach. In such a situation the missionary with understanding of the processes going on about him would find his opportunity to introduce his forms of religion and to help create a new cultural universe.

54
Goods and Gods

A Follow-up Study of "Steel Axes for Stone-Age Australians"

JOHN TAYLOR

In 1952 Lauriston Sharp published "Steel Axes for Stone-Age Australians" in *Human Organization*. The paper has become a classic of its kind. It has been reprinted many times and is highly respected as a model analysis of the dynamic relationship between technology and aspects of sociocultural systems. It also says something about missionaries.

Because of its wide availability I will not present (yet another) précis of the paper. But I will remind readers of the conclusion that Sharp drew from his analysis, and the prediction that followed from the conclusion. Sharp, it will be recalled, was demonstrating how even indirect and unintended acculturative pressures could precipitate cultural collapse. To epitomise these pressures and represent the insidious effects of all western material culture on the bush-dwelling people, he chose the steel hatchet which was being distributed by missionaries in large numbers. He concluded that the indigenous myth-making process would be unable to come to

terms with, and account for, not just the hatchet, but the myriad new traits being accepted into the bush natives' way of life. He predicted that they would abandon their totemic ideology entirely. "The steel axe, shifting hopelessly between one clan and the other," he said, "is not simply replacing the stone axe physically, but is hacking at the supports of the entire cultural system." The future would become confused, uncertain and fraught with anxiety causing perhaps symbolic aggression (such as increased levels of sorcery), or withdrawal and apathy (which Sharp had witnessed among Aboriginal groups to the south). Sharp saw the missionaries as providing the realistic solution to this dilemma. "In such a situation," he concluded, "the missionary with understanding of the processes going on about him would find his opportunity to introduce religion and to help create the constitution of a new cultural universe."

Like many undergraduates, I found "Steel Axes ..." exciting. The analysis was clear-cut; the writing was vivid and compelling. I was led to ask, no doubt like many others before me: What happened to the Yir Yoront? It seemed to me that Sharp's analysis presented an ideal scenario for follow-up research. Accordingly, as a doctoral candidate with the University of Queensland, I persuaded my supervisor to allow me to find the "Yir Yoront" and, using Sharp's materials as an

From T. Swain and D.B. Rose, eds., *Aboriginal Australians and Christian Missions: Ethnographic and Historical Studies*. Adelaide: Australian Society for the Study of Religions, 1988, pp. 438–91. Reprinted with permission. (Bibliographic documentation contained in the original text is omitted here. Interested readers should consult the original publication.)

364

ethnographic baseline, chart the adoption of their new way of life and the reconstitution of their world view.[1]

Sharp spent 29 months in the field between 1933 and 1935 working with Aboriginal groups still in possession of their own lands in the country between the Mitchell and Edward Rivers on the western side of Cape York Peninsula. This country had been set aside as a reserve for Aborigines by the Queensland State Government. He called the groups he worked with Yir Yoront, Yir Mel, Taior, and Ngentjin. In his 1952 paper Sharp refers only to the Yir Yoront. However earlier papers indicate that this was merely a descriptive convenience. His predictions for the Yir Yoront could be held to be equally true for the other groups he studied.

My enquiries, prior to going into the field, revealed that Sharp's Taior and Ngentjin (more properly referred to as Kuuk Thaayorre and Kuuk Yak) and some Yir Yoront people had gravitated to the Edward River mission that was set up by the Anglicans in 1938, three years after Sharp had left the field. This settlement also attracted a number of other bush-dwelling peoples hailing from the country between the Holroyd and Edward Rivers. The remainder of the Yir Yoront were to be found at Kowanyama some 65 km to the south. Kowanyama, established in 1915 by the Church of England, had a long history, and a large population with a good deal of linguistic heterogeneity. By contrast Edward River, whose population in 1968 numbered approximately 280, was a far more attractive research proposition. The records of missionary endeavour presented a picture of just the kind of cultural reconstitution Sharp predicted.

Edward River received its first ordained minister eleven years after its founding. Shortly after his arrival in 1949, the chaplain baptised fifty older children and adults and commenced formal religious instruction. In September of the following year, nine young adults were confirmed in the Christian faith. The ensuing years showed a record of evangelical success. The chaplains busied themselves with baptisms and held daily church services. One of them translated the Creed, the Lord's prayer, and the Ten Commandments into Kuuk Thaayorre and, at the request of the people, wrote a hymn in that language. 1955 saw the celebration of the first Christian marriage ceremony. In 1962 the superintendent of the time could record that there had been 417 celebrations of the Holy Eucharist, 4,824 communions (a figure which implies a rate of 30 communions a year for each confirmed Christian), 55 baptisms, 56 confirmations, 6 marriages, and 8 burial services. If these figures were any guide, then the major Christian sacraments seemed securely institutionalised. In 1967, the Anglican Church ceded its administrative control over the Edward River community to the Queensland State Government. By the time of the takeover, some 270 people had been baptised. About 45 per cent of the recognised marital unions (25 out of 53) had been celebrated in a Church wedding. There appeared to be an enthusiastic congregation attending church services, and plans were afoot to build a new Church. The Edward River people gave every appearance of having become a devout Christian community.

But appearances can be deceptive. When I commenced fieldwork at Edward River in 1968 not long after the government takeover, attendance at church services had fallen away dramatically. I quickly discovered that, contrary to Sharp's predictions, the totemic ideology had not disappeared. Youngsters and adults alike could recite their major totemic affiliations without hesitation. Totemic sites could be mapped, and even linked to similar maps Sharp himself had made during his fieldwork. Whenever I accompanied Aboriginal people out into the bush, their behaviour palpably demonstrated that they were moving in a landscape imbued with supernatural entities, powers, and associations. Further, the Christian sacraments had not replaced Aboriginal ritual. It was true that the traditional calendar of ceremonial activity revolving around initiation and species increase was no longer observed. There was, however, a calendar of non-Christian ceremonies operating within the settlement which focussed on death and mourning. It required little analysis to show that this ritual was generated by the same totemic world view that Sharp had described. In many respects, Edward River people behaved as if they had just stepped from the pages of Sharp's papers. Indeed, men still owned the axes and women had to borrow them!

Three broad questions arise from these observations. First, how did Edward River people manage to accommodate to Christian ideology? Second, why was Sharp so mistaken about the resilience of Aboriginal ideology? Third, what was the real impact of missionary endeavour on the Edward River people?

I will deal in turn with each question in the following sections.

Reconfiguring Beliefs

Before they had that fight at Kirkyoongknakarr, the Old People had gone way up there to the east to learn to be like white people. God was there. He was teaching the people book learning. One of the Old People said, "No, it's too hard. We can't manage these letters and these pencils. It's too hard for us. We have to go back to our own home."

"Alright," said God. "You give me back all those pencils and letters. You keep your spears but give me back those guns you have been using."

So the people gave God back the guns, the books, and the pencils.

God said, "Alright, now you keep those spears. I give them to you. You must kill bush animals for your food, wallabies and possums, and you must eat bush tucker like yams, lilies, and bulguru (*Eliocharis* sp). When you want to hunt anything, or kill something, then you must make your own spears and use them."

"Alright," said the Old People.

God gave the Old People some farewell gifts of tobacco, sugar, and bread and they went back to their homes where there were no white people. That was when they began to make spears and to use them to fight each other.

The content of the above myth shows it to be clearly spun out of the realities of mission life at Edward River. When I recorded it in 1969, it was appended to the beginning of a long saga owned by the Spear/Duck clan that deals with the institution of spear fighting. The manufacturing of a new myth was one way in which the Edward River people sought to reconcile present states-of-affairs and mythic verities.

As Sharp had pointed out, there were many novel phenomena to challenge the mythic verities. First, there was the problem simply of accounting for the presence of non-black humans, of new kinds of animals (for example, horses, cattle, feral pigs, cats, and so on), as well as the introduced material culture. Then there was the challenge posed by the ideologies of the missionaries, who were actively proffering alternative theories about the nature of supernatural beings and the place of humankind within the cosmos.

Manufacturing a new myth like the one above, and linking it in sequence to a corpus of other myths to legitimate it, was one way of expanding the Edward River cosmology. But there were other ways. For instance, the content of existing myths could be changed. Sometimes just a small alteration could account for some very large facts. The

Wallaby/Lightning clan possess a "Big Humpy" totem (or "story," as the phrase is on the western side of Cape York Peninsula). The term "Big Humpy" really labels an important mythological event that occurred in the Wallaby/Lightning estate. Like many of the Edward River myths, it has to do with the adventures of two brothers who are simply known as The Two Men. The "story" goes like this:

The Two Men were preparing to hold an initiation ceremony at Murka, but the people would not cooperate with them. They went instead to hold the ceremony in Wallaby/Lightning country. The Two Men were very angry to have been so openly ignored and they determined on revenge. They set out to go to the other initiation ceremony, but on the way they stopped at Pupurrkathman, where they made a firestick. Each man produced some glowing ash from the firestick and encased it in a ball of dry grass and attempted to hold it in his hand. The older brother's ball of grass burst into flames and burnt him. His younger brother's ash smouldered without flame in his hand. With the glowing coal secreted in the younger brother's hand, the two went on from Pupurrkathman (whose name signifies this event) to the initiation ground. Feigning cooperation, The Two Men sang, danced, and clapped with the others.

After the dances concluded, everyone went inside an enormous humpy that had been built of grass to shelter the participants. When everybody else was asleep, The Two Brothers stole outside. The younger brother fanned his glowing coal into a flame and set the humpy ablaze. The roaring of the fire aroused the sleepers and they all scrambled to get away from the flames. Those who escaped serious burning went from there to make their homes in other places. *Those who jumped out of the fire first were white people. They were not burnt at all. Those who were a little bit burnt were half-castes and Chinese. Others were charred fairly badly, and these became the ancestors of other Aborigines and Torres Strait Islanders.* Some were badly burned and jumped into the water of a nearby pool to ease the pain. There they sank down and their ashes became the conception spirits of the present Wallaby/Lightning clan members.

We may treat this myth in one of two ways. It may be, as the first myth seems, something totally new. Or else the italicised section is an interpolation. I think it is the latter because if we remove it, the remnant of the myth which is restricted to the pre-contact Aboriginal world still seems perfectly meaningful. Consider then what the interpolation accomplishes: nothing less than the origin of all races in four sentences.

If the races of humankind could be so easily accounted for, how then to deal with the Christian concept of God? I imagine that the fundamental problem for Edward River people was to make sense of what it was the missionaries were saying about this deity. In attempting to do this, they assumed that behind the lessons and biblical stories that were part of their Christian religious instruction, there was a belief system not greatly different from their own. The features of the Christian mythology were obscured, of course, by communication problems. However, from the Edward River point of view, deciphering the structure was no different from coming to terms with the mythologies of neighbouring groups of Aborigines. Christian mythology could be rendered understandable if part of it at least could be seen as composed of versions of myths that had parallels in the Edward River mythology.

A characteristic of the mythologies of the western side of Cape York Peninsula is that certain of them tend to repeat themselves at intervals. Thus the myth of the brolga and the emu occurs in the Aurukun area, at Edward River, and also in the Mitchell River Trust Area. Each version was firmly embedded in its own geography but in essence they were the same. The repetition creates no puzzles for Aborigines. The shared myths are known, and they provide major frames of reference for forming alliances between groups and individuals when other commonalities of interest were tenuous.

The myth of the water rat also existed in several versions. Its central character, Poonchr, as he is called in the Kuuk Thaayorre version, lived in a sky-world and came to earth occasionally in the form of a man by means of a magical rope. I will not describe the myth in detail. It is long and involved. What is important is that the Edward River people made a clear identification between God, who dwelt in heaven, and the creative figure Poonchr, who dwelt in the sky-world. In talking about the indigenous culture hero, men often referred to him as "Poonchr-God." It was not simply a matter of making mental equations. "Poonchr-God" intervened actively in people's lives. It was said that one old man, now dead, had actually had an encounter with him. From his description, "Poonchr-God" was large, black, and the possessor of massive genitals.

When people talked about "God," analysis revealed that it was often the syncretic character "Poonchr-God" that they had in mind. Consider the following set of opinions I recorded from one

informant about the arguments over the liaisons of the young single people that occasionally disturbed the tenor of the settlement:

Why should people want to fight over girlfriends and boyfriends? Parents should not be jealous of what their children do. It only leads to rows and *puri puri*.

When they are born, parents do not own their children's genitals. Their fathers do not cut their daughters with a knife to make them women. Men can't make the sex of a child the way they make their spears. They can't do that. Genitals come from God. He made a story and genitals belonged to the children. They don't belong to men the way spears do. Therefore, no one should worry about the way single girls carry on. God gave them genitals. Girls should use them in any way they want to.

On the surface, the reference to God making genitals might be seen as a slightly garbled account of the creation of Adam and Eve. In fact, it pertains directly to an episode in the Poonchr myth where Poonchr, finding that the women in the sky-world had no genitals, obligingly created them by making an incision in an appropriate part of their anatomy.

It follows that if the Christian beliefs of missionaries and others could be equated with Aboriginal cosmology, then there was no need to attempt to account for all artefacts, ideas, and animals that lay outside the purview of local belief systems. No one clan (or tribal group for that matter, as I shall argue below) possessed a universal compendium of all that there was in the world. Provided someone had the "story" was all that mattered. For instance, when I taxed an informant about the existence of a "story" place for the ubiquitous feral pig, I was told that there was no such place on the Edward River reserve. But it was confidently asserted that "There must be one somewhere" and that it probably belonged to a white man. Edward River people clearly thought Europeans possessed a fund of "stories" that explained their things, animals, and ideas which in turn provided a charter for their actions. Thus when some item of European manufacture caused trouble in the settlement (for example, alcohol) people in berating others would say, "We don't have the story for that thing (that is, alcohol). We don't know how to use it yet." How strong this belief in the stories of Europeans is may be demonstrated by the following example.

I had invited one of the closest of my Edward River informants to visit me in Brisbane in 1971. It was his first trip in a jet plane and his first experience of a large city. When I met him at the airport, he was plainly impressed, and not a little confused by the enormity of the place and numbers of Europeans. As we drove towards the city, he looked about him at the tall residential buildings and asked, "Brother, did man make these things? I think they must be from story," he prompted.

I said that the buildings were indeed man-made, and further along our route I showed him a building under construction. By the time we reached a central business district of Brisbane known as Fortitude Valley, the size of the buildings had increased considerably and Eddie was once again having doubts about the origins of the buildings. I assured him they were indeed man-made and not the product of some whitefellow "story."

To get to my home, we had to cross the Brisbane River. I chose to go via Brisbane's (then) largest bridge. It was a massive suspended steel arch. My informant had never seen anything so big. "What do they call this one, brother?" he asked. Without quite realising the implications of my reply, I said, "It's the Story Bridge." (It was named after a prominent Queensland citizen, J.D. Story.)

"Ah," said my informant, totally misconstruing my use of the label "story." He looked up at the fretwork of interlacing girders flashing by and found a comparison from his own Edward River environment where marvelous things may spring from the earth. He said, "It must have grown up like a mangrove, I reckon." Then he sat back with great satisfaction and contemplated the rest of Brisbane's marvels without puzzlement. His cognitive orientation was restored and his faith in the power of "stories" reasserted. The European environment was clearly interpretable through the categories of the Edward River cosmology.

Modifying Ritual

The pre-settlement cosmology found specific expression in rituals. Through ritual observances, Edward River people sought to communicate with, and to some degree control, the supernatural powers and beings that inhabited their mythic landscape. Ritual observances can be divided into three kinds — routine rituals and increase ceremonies, both of which were performed at the level of individuals and families, and the large-scale ceremonies, mostly centring on initiation, that involved the cooperation of many clans. The purpose of routine rituals was to introduce newcomers to particular tracts of land by identifying them with the owners. Such introductory rites offered a protective mantle against the harmful effects of potent and dangerous places and warded off the unwelcome attentions of ghosts, demons, and unpredictable mythic beings. Increase rites were aimed at conserving the material conditions of the hunter-gatherer mode of production. Large-scale ceremonies required a high degree of organisation and preparation. They culminated in dramatic celebrations of the actions of the mythic beings of the creative epoch through song and sacred dance. At one level they were rites of passage that marked important transition points in the careers of individuals (for example, from boy into man, progression in ritual status). At the social level ceremonial ritual provided a supernatural charter for clans as the primary landholding groups by linking them through conception filiation to the ceremonial responsibilities that had been instituted by the personalities of the mythic past.

These days (1988) three broad types of ritual activity occur at Edward River. First there are rituals that take place in the bush and are identical with those performed prior to the establishment of the settlement. Rites of introduction are still meticulously observed by Aboriginal travellers. People are still said to be manipulating places of power and malevolence in order to produce rain and storms, epidemics and annoying plagues of insects. However, the routine ritual connected with food species increase is no longer performed. The settlement store provides the bulk of foodstuffs. The bush is now seen as a place of abundance where many kinds of game and fish are simply waiting to fall to the firearms, spears, and fishing tackles of anyone who cares to go out and hunt them. The bush is no longer viewed as a habitat whose food supplies need to be assured through ritual control. Notably absent are the large-scale ceremonies revolving around initiation. The last of these was performed at the settlement in 1946.

The second kind of ritual activity comprises the ceremonies of the Christian church: the round of daily services, holy communion, baptism, confirmation, marriage, and burial. For the moment I will postpone discussion of these. The third sort of ritual activity revolves around death and mourning. Its most spectacular public manifestation is the "house opening," a ceremony performed to prepare the house of a deceased person for re-occupation. Despite its apparently "traditional" character, house openings have relatively tenuous links with pre-settlement ritual. They are, however, part of a sequence of activities that evolved under the impact of the exigencies of settlement life. Based upon the durable postulates of the Edward River cosmology concerning social relationships, death, and the after-life, this sequence of mortuary rituals fuses elements of Torres Strait Islander custom and Christian ritual to create a new kind of ceremonial complex. How this came about is worth describing in detail. Pre-settlement funerary ritual and mourning observances for the western side of Cape York Peninsula have been dealt with by a number of researchers. I shall describe Edward River practices only briefly here.

When a person's death was notified, the members of his/her kindred adopted the mourning behaviour appropriate to their relationship to the deceased (for example, the wearing of mourning regalia, observance of food taboos, going into seclusion), and undertook duties associated with the disposal of the corpse. The dead body was slung between forked poles and a camp composed of all those who knew the dead person gathered around at the site to grieve. When the body had reached a suitable state of decay, it was taken down from the poles, gutted (the viscera being buried), and the body fluids expressed from the remains until the cadaver was reduced to a thing of bone, hair, tendon, and desiccated flesh. It was then wrapped up in a bark parcel so that it could be carried about by female kin pending its final disposal. If magical death was suspected as the cause for demise, a divination ceremony was held over the place where the viscera were buried. At about the same time, people who had committed some dereliction against, or who had some unresolved dispute with, the deceased offered themselves for punishment by the dead person's close kin in order to clear the grievance and avoid being suspected of complicity in procuring the death. If the sorcerer's identity was established, then several young warriors might be secretly sworn to carry out a revenge expedition at a later time.

When the mourning camp broke up, access to the tract of land containing the death camp, and to other places particularly associated with the dead person, was prohibited to facilitate the severing of the ties between the dead person's spirit and the surviving family. After an interval of time the physical remains were finally interred or cremated in a public ceremony. The deceased's personal effects were usually left to decay at the final resting place, although certain items might be given to particular kin. A feast was provided by the mourning close kin for those who attended the last obsequies. The mortuary prohibitions on kin and places at this time were also lifted. Sometimes the final rites were used as an opportunity for identifying and killing the presumed sorcerer. As a result, they occasionally concluded in wild fights and fatalities.

Clearly there were features of this process that were objectionable to the missionaries, and incompatible with the sedentary lifestyle adopted by the Aborigines. The missionaries forbade corpse exposure. They insisted on immediate burial with Christian rites. They also actively suppressed the violence associated with grievance clearing and sorcery accusations, although they left intact other customs such as widow seclusion, the assumption of food taboos, and the closing of tracts of land. While areas out in the bush could be closed, it was of course not possible to close the tract associated with the site of death without evacuating the mission village. The first solution to this problem was to abandon the house in which a person died. Since the houses of the early mission were constructed out of bush materials (palm thatch and rough timber) which required frequent renovation, abandonment caused no great hardship. However, when the State Government began to provide modern, prefabricated housing, permanent abandonment could no longer be entertained. As a consequence the Edward River people developed "house openings."

The evolution of this ceremonial solution to the re-occupation of a dwelling took as its starting point a pre-settlement custom revolving around wet-season huts (or humpies), the only substantial shelters likely to last from one year to the next. If a person died in one of these, the abandoned shelter became the focus of the ceremony to open the tract. At a given time, a group of close kin and friends would gather about it to wail, to stamp on the ground, and to shake the structure in a final display of grief before declaring the place open. The humpy itself was left abandoned. The post-settlement ceremony, whose purpose was to open the house, was a greatly elaborated version embellished by the performance of "Island" and "Old Paten" dances. In pre-settlement times, the only occasion when people danced in funerary rites occurred during cremations. The dances of the post-settlement house opening ceremonies were not modelled on cremation dances. The inclusion of "Island" dancing drew its inspiration from the customs of Torres Strait Islanders. They were often held up as the precedent for doing new things at Edward River. It was said that Torres Strait Islanders opened their houses with singing and dancing. This was the main reason for incorporating "Island" dancing in the ceremony. In these dances, the melodies, instruments, dancing regalia, and stylised dance movements are based upon Torres Strait Islander models. The songs and the mass choreographing of the dancers' movements are locally devised. Another reason offered for the inclusion of these dances is that it gives the younger men who have not learnt "Old Paten" dances a part to play in the proceedings.

The origin of the term "Old Paten" is obscure. It refers to the performance in dance and song of episodes from the mythic creative period, called *woochorrm* by Thaayorre speakers. Some of the dances are post-settlement creations, but most of them are reproductions of portions of pre-settlement dance dramas that used to be performed in large-scale ceremonial rituals, especially the initiation ceremonies. In the case of house openings, the content of the dances generally draws on that segment of the *woochorrm* that belonged to the deceased. The addition of "Old Paten" dance segments came about through a traditional innovatory process, dreaming. The first dances that were performed were ones that had been created by the spirits of the dead themselves. They were passed on to their living kin in dreams with the request that they be performed in their memory at house openings. When it was realised that performing "Old Paten" was pleasing to the ghosts of dead kin, it was a small but significant step to include sections from the repertoire of initiation dances and other pre-settlement ceremonial dramatisations.

House openings are large-scale public activities requiring the cooperation of many people. They are not easy to organise, but there are always strong pressures from settlement staff and other community members to hold them as soon as possible to clear the way for re-occupation. They are usually held on weekends and staff are particularly invited to attend the proceedings. When everyone is assembled, and the performer's preparations complete, the "Island" dancers commence singing and emerge from the bush, or from behind a screen, and advance in a dancing line towards the house. As they draw near, people fall in behind them and follow them in procession around it. Next the dancers go inside the house. At a given signal, the neighbours and close relations of the deceased rush inside to cry for the dead person. This grief display is marked by heavy stamping and a great deal of banging on the walls of the dwelling. It is called the "house

bumping." Then follows a lull in the proceedings while a feast is held.

After the feast there follows the highlight of the ceremony, the "Old Paten" dancing. Each "Old Paten" segment consists of a discrete mythic event described in song. The dancers, their bodies decorated with bush paints, mime, with a masterly sense of theatre, the actions of the mythic characters involved. The dances are watched with rapt attention by the Aboriginal audience. Even most of the children know by heart the events being re-enacted. The "Old Paten" dances give vivid expression to the Edward River world of myth. The dramatic presentation of primal events in song and dance makes the Edward River cosmology tangible and therefore believable. When the last dance has been performed, the gathering breaks up in a high state of euphoria. Because the performers have been close to the sources of supernatural power, they will sleep late next day. The house is now ready for re-occupation, usually by a family not closely related to the dead person.

The "house opening" ceremony that I have just sketched is a part, albeit a spectacular part, of a sequence of funerary rituals that begin, as the pre-settlement sequence did, with public grieving and the assumption of customary taboos and statuses among the close kin. The body is now prepared for immediate burial, usually in a coffin. A church service and burial according to Christian rites is an established and expected part of the sequence. Divination may still be carried out although nowadays the divination vigil is kept over the new grave. Sorcery accusations are no longer made openly, but suspicions may be voiced privately, and may even sometimes emerge publicly in the heat of other disputes. The "house opening" releases a major set of mortuary restrictions. It is followed at a later date by the "look rubbish" ceremony.

The "look rubbish" ceremony has its origins in a part of the pre-settlement ritual that accompanied the final disposal of a body. Prior to burial or cremation, the kindred viewed the dead person's possessions and wept over them. Some items of value might be given away to distant kin, but mostly they were left to rot. In the "look rubbish" ceremony, there was no weeping over the dead person's possessions. Instead they were distributed among close relations. The major intent of the ceremony was to validate ritually the inheritance of a dead person's effects by members of the kindred. This was a new need that had arisen in the wake of the growing affluence of Edward

River society and the accumulation of consumer durables.

In brief, the Edward River cosmology has survived the challenge to its relevance and continues to function powerfully in the everyday life of the community. It has responded to changed needs and altered contexts by economically renovating beliefs and generating new rituals. While these renovations incorporate introduced elements, it has also maintained clear links with the past so that Edward River people can truly say, as they often do, "We follow on from old custom."

How was it then that Sharp came to predict a cultural collapse for the Yir Yoront?

A Critique of Sharp's Analysis

The primary object of Sharp's researches was to come to a clearer understanding of the nature of totemism in at least one relatively homogeneous Aboriginal society. At the time of Sharp's fieldwork there was already a voluminous literature extant on totemism. It was an area of such confusion that A.C. Haddon, in 1934, had been forced to conclude that, "Nearly every writer on the subject expresses different views from those of other writers but scarcely one of them has any original facts to offer." One might add that the position seems little clearer nowadays, for as R.M. Berndt and C.H. Berndt observe, "*Totemism* is a confusing term because it has been used in so many different ways." Sharp's purpose was to offer new facts and attempt to explain one particular Aboriginal totemic system. He was not concerned to integrate his findings and interpretations with the wider domain of theories of totemism.

As Sharp described it for the Yir Yoront, totemism was an association between classes of things, activities, and states (the totemic phenomena) and particular groups of people (clans or lineages). The associations were established by a set of myths. While Sharp provided abundant evidence of such associations among the Yir Yoront, the most important piece of evidence he submitted was a list in his doctoral thesis of the totems belonging to the Freshwater/Rain clan. For this group Sharp enumerated in excess of 220 totems. Included in it were 74 kinds of natural species comprising insects, birds, fish and other aquatic creatures, plants, crustaceans, amphibians, reptiles, and marsupials. Twenty-seven of the items referred to general environmental

phenomena such as clouds, dawn, stars, and thunder. Another 30 items referred to artefacts and material things associated with human activities such as camping places, axes, ashes, shelters, and pointing bones. All of these things were common enough in other lists of totems.

What was unusual about the list was the inclusion of things such as parts, states, and conditions of the human body (for instance, anus, blood vessels, sores, intellect, and so forth), as well as human emotions and activities (for example, marriage, copulation, shame, and so on). There were 91 items of this type. Even more remarkable was the fact that this large number of totems belonged to a single clan which in 1933 numbered about 40 people. The Freshwater/Rain tracts occupied less than 6 per cent of the total area owned by the 26 clans Sharp studied. Less than 8 per cent (17) of the totems associated with the Freshwater/Rain clan were shared with other clans. There is no doubt that Sharp meant his readers to take the example of the Freshwater/Rain clan as an apt illustration of the distribution of totems across the remaining clans. Suppose we make this inference. It follows that if the other 25 clans had equally large sets of multiple totems covering the same wide range of things, events, and states, and if there was the same degree of sharing of totemic items (that is, less than 8 per cent) between clans, then for all practical purposes the totems of the Yir Yoront present themselves as a kind of universal compendium of natural and cultural phenomena. Such a compendium would contain by my calculation some 5000 items.

Why were there so many totems? Sharp argued that the Aboriginal cosmology was ordered about a tripartite division of the perceived world of experience. These classes consisted of tracts of land, social groupings, and totemic objects. Tracts and totems had naturally distinctive characteristics and enduring identities. Social groups, on the other hand, were relatively changeable. Sharp argued that a strong objective reality could be imparted to otherwise ephemeral social groupings if they could be related to the unchanging landscape and the well-defined totems. This was the real purpose of the totemic system of the Yir Yoront.

Thus social groups, totems, and tracts were welded into a set of mutually dependent conceptual relationships. Small changes in the sets could be accounted for without upsetting the basic stability of the system. However, because the interweaving of the elements appeared to be on such a cosmic scale, any major change in any of the sets, Sharp argued, would have repercussions for the others. The result could only be social and cultural disintegration. Because of the tightness of the conceptual structuring, there was simply no room in the Aboriginal cosmology for Europeans and their enormous inventory of things. Contact with Europeans and European material culture must therefore cause the collapse of the entire cultural system itself. It was a courageous prediction. Few anthropologists have had such faith in their models that they have actually set the conditions for testing them against future events.

As it happens, Sharp was wrong about the way in which things would eventually occur. I believe I have presented enough evidence to indicate a vital and continuing cultural tradition which has coped exceedingly well with major changes in settings, activities, and artefacts, as well as coming to terms with foreign ideologies and rituals. I doubt if Sharp is the least bit dismayed to learn that the totemic belief system he patiently described with such accuracy has turned out to have such resilience.

I must acknowledge that the evidence for a universal compendium of totemic items seemed very strong in Sharp's data for the Freshwater/Rain clan. Yet 35 years later, try as I might, I could not produce clan lists of totems that came anywhere near the numbers that Sharp recorded for that single clan. Have whole sets of totems disappeared from people's minds in the space of 35 years? Was the Freshwater/Rain clan an extraordinary or atypical example? I cannot answer either question because I have not attempted to collect totemic lists for present-day Freshwater/Rain clan members.

I prefer another interpretation for the meaning of totemism. It is one that is profoundly influenced by the way in which the Edward River people themselves view those things anthropologists call "totems," Aborigines call "dreamings" or "stories," and the Kuuk Thaayorre call *woochorrm*. Such terms, I argue, refer to a set of symbols that represent mythological events at particular places. In other words, the totems are primarily tags for identifying segments of a mythological record. The association between social groups, totemic objects, and tracts does not come about, as Sharp suggested, because of the inherent features of the totems and tracts themselves (that is, their perdurability). Rather it is the ownership of a set of totems by particular clans denoted by the ownership of a ritual estate which in turn justified, or provided a charter for, a clan's primary entitlements to tracts of land within the Edward

River domain. This interpretation sits easily with Sharp's general description for the totemic system of the Yir Yoront. It does not require the system to break down when confronted with the presence of Europeans and their material culture.

The anxieties, ambivalences, and bizarre behaviour that Sharp noted in his classic paper were not so much indicators of culturally fatal cognitive disorientation, but rather, I submit, a short-run perturbation about the means for regularising the supply of European artefacts. The Edward River solution to the problem was achieved by inviting the Anglicans to establish a mission.

Conclusion

It is tempting to see Edward River Christianity as a veneer thinly laid over Aboriginal traditions. It would be wrong, however, to think that Christian rites have no place in the fabric of everyday life. Certainly some sacraments such as marriage do not appear to be popular. In the last ten years there have been no church marriages at all despite the formation of a number of stable *de facto* unions. The principal reason underlying the reluctance to marrying in church seems to be the expense involved in cementing unions that have already achieved community endorsement through the operation of the marriage system which is little changed in its operation from the one Sharp described for the Yir Yoront.

On the other hand Edward River parents almost without exception take their infants for baptism. The ritual of baptism is as important to them as the pre-settlement rites of introduction, which, interestingly enough, often included splashing newcomers to a place with water from a well or lagoon. Adult Aboriginal newcomers to Edward River seeking to settle permanently there offer themselves for baptism to demonstrate that they are now part of the community. I have already described how Christian burial rites are perceived as an integral part of Edward River funerary behaviour.

There is only a handful of Aboriginal people who can now be described as regular church attenders. One of them, a most tradition-oriented old man, continues to worship daily because he feels that frequent application to the sacramental wine will enhance his life span. At a more serious level, another, younger man, who is a lay preacher, is much concerned about Edward River's current social problems. It is beyond the scope of this paper to discuss the origins of these problems but they include widespread alcohol abuse, conflict and fighting (that not infrequently ends in homicide), rape, theft, and the neglect of children and old people. Tradition clearly has no remedy for these unwelcome and disturbing manifestations. The lay preacher looks to the Church as the one organisation capable of providing training for leadership and moral inspiration. Whether the Church can meet his expectations and play a significant role in addressing these issues remains to be seen.

Unlike Sharp, I do not have the courage to make a prediction.

Note

1. I undertook the fieldwork upon which this paper is based in three periods: as a postgraduate scholar with the University of Queensland from 1968 to 1971; as medical anthropologist with the Queensland Institute of Medical Research, 1971–1975; during fieldwork in 1988 financed by James Cook University of North Queensland. I acknowledge with gratitude the funds provided by the above institutions.

55
Colonialism, Apartheid, and Liberation

RICHARD LEE and SUSAN HURLICH

We know SWAPO. They won't kill us. We'd share the pot with SWAPO.

— a !Kung elder at Chum!kwe

If we go, the Bushmen will go with us.
— South African commander of !Kung army base

Generations of students in anthropology and social science classes have been introduced to the Kalahari San (Bushmen) as examples of hunter–gatherer societies. They are told that the hunting or foraging way of life was once the universal mode of human existence. Many of the case studies anthropologists use to illustrate their lectures were carried out ten to fifty or more years ago, before the penetration of European colonialism and capitalism. Too often, what they are *not* told is what these hunter–gatherers are doing today.

Several of the papers in [*Politics and History in Band Societies*, the volume from which this article is taken] document the political mobilization of the foraging peoples in the face of threats to their land base and cultural identity.

The !Kung San of Namibia have not yet mobilized and the threat they face is not to their land but to their very lives. Since the early 1970s, some of the !Kung have been drawn into the military orbit of the South African Defence Forces. Their militarization, ostensibly to fight against the freedom fighters of SWAPO (South West African People's Organization) illustrates in graphic terms the techniques used by South African imperialism to preserve at any cost the interests of capital in southern Africa.

The goal of this paper is to document this militarization and to show that just as history does not stand still, neither does the subject matter of anthropology come to an end when the last hunter–gatherer lays down his bow. The challenge to anthropologists is twofold, to understand the dangerous realities facing native peoples, and also to do something about them.

The San as Hunter–Gatherers

The devastating impact of European "civilization" on the small-scale societies of the non-Western world is well known. The Aborigines of Tasmania and the West Indies, the Beothuk Indians of Newfoundland, and the Xam Bushmen of South Africa were all exterminated by land-hungry

Excerpted from Richard Lee and Susan Hurlich, "From Foragers to Fighters: South Africa's Militarization of the Namibian San," in Eleanor B. Leacock and Richard B. Lee, eds., *Politics and History in Band Societies*. New York: Cambridge University Press, 1982, pp. 327–36, 342–43. Reprinted with permission. (Bibliographic documentation contained in the original text is omitted here. Interested readers should consult the original publication.)

374

European settlers before 1900. Hundreds of other aboriginal societies in Canada, the United States, Australia, and South America, having survived the initial onslaught, have continued into the present but with reduced numbers and a shrunken land base. In a very few parts of the world favoured by extreme isolation, hunting and gathering peoples managed to survive into the mid-twentieth century with their numbers, social organization, and economy essentially intact.

The interior !Kung San of the northern Kalahari of Botswana and Namibia (South West Africa) were one such people. Living at a ring of pans and natural springs around the Aha Mountain range and surrounded by a belt of waterless uninhabited country 50–150 kilometres wide, the 1,000 interior !Kung San were almost entirely unknown to outsiders until the 1950s.

In late 1950, an anthropological team led by Lorna and Laurence Marshall entered the area from the east and over the next two decades produced a superb series of ethnographic studies and films of the Nyae Nyae !Kung. A decade later another group of anthropologists, led by Irven DeVore and Richard Lee, initiated a fifteen-year programme of studies among the closely related Dobe area !Kung in Botswana.

As a result of these two long-term projects involving over thirty scientists from a variety of fields, the interior !Kung San of Nyae Nyae, Dobe, and /Xai/xai are now among the best-documented hunter–gatherers in the history of social science.

Far less well known to the world, however, are the traumatic events that have overtaken the !Kung in the 1970s, *after* the bulk of the anthropological studies were completed. Starting out as the most isolated hunter–gatherers in southern Africa, the !Kung San have been drawn by the South African Army into the middle of a shooting war. Having survived for thousands of years in the desert, the !Kung's very physical survival is now threatened by the South African military machine.

The San and Apartheid

The mineral-rich territory of Namibia, also known as South West Africa, has an area of 318,000 square miles and a population of 1.5 million. Its major exports include copper, nickel, uranium, diamonds, fish, and karakul sheep furs. Germany ruled South West Africa from 1885 to 1915. After the First World War, South Africa took over the colony under a League of Nations Mandate. During the 1920s and '30s, South Africa moved thousands of White settlers into South West Africa and

developed a thriving economy based on the abundant natural resources and a plentiful supply of cheap black labour. Following the Second World War, when all the mandate powers turned their mandates over to the jurisdiction of the United Nations Trusteeship Council, South Africa alone refused to relinquish its control over South West Africa. It continued to administer the colony as if it were a fifth province of the Union. With the complicity of a number of multinational companies, including Canada's Hudson's Bay Company and Falconbridge Nickel, South Africa continued to exploit the mineral, fishery, and agricultural wealth of South West Africa.

Throughout the 1950s and '60s, the people of the country petitioned the UN, the World Court, and international public opinion for redress for their intolerable situation. Only token support for their struggle was given by the West, while inside the country peaceful protests were met by more and more violence and repression.

In the isolated border regions, however, peoples such as the !Kung were only peripherally involved in these events. Until the 1930s the !Kung San were a single people moving freely from east to west in search of food and friends. In 1965 a fence was built along the Botswana–Namibia border dividing the population into what the !Kung themselves called the "Boer San" and "British San." As was the case with so many African peoples, the imposition of colonialism led formerly united groups to follow different historical paths.

As its claim to South West Africa (SWA) was increasingly being called into question at the UN, South Africa sought to strengthen its grip on the border regions and to establish a colonial infrastructure where none had existed before. South Africa built a series of government stations in northern SWA in the period 1960–65, and all the !Kung in Nyae Nyae were summoned to come and settle at a station called Chum!kwe with the promise of free rations and medical care. In the first few years of the settlement some seven hundred people were gathered in, far more than had been expected, and the South Africans were faced with the problem of whom to accept and whom to exclude. The neighbouring Botswana blacks were rigidly excluded and their cattle and other livestock were shot on sight if they were caught straying across the border from the Botswana side. But how were they to distinguish between !Kung from SWA and !Kung from Botswana when in their eyes all !Kung looked alike, were related by kinship, and moved freely back and forth?

The South West African Department of Native Affairs had compiled data on !Kung geographical place names in Botswana (BP) and SWA. The administrators hit upon the idea of using these data to determine who was a bona fide SWA !Kung and who was not. When !Kung men and women reported to the settlement's office for their weekly ration of maize meal, the clerk looked them up in these data; if they qualified as a resident of a waterhole on the SWA side of the border they were issued a metal dog-tag; each was stamped with a unique number and had to be presented each time food was handed out. If their place did not happen to fall in SWA, they were told, in the words of one informant: "You are not our Bushmen. Go back to BP side; the British will take care of you."

The strong !Kung institutions of sharing and gift exchange initially foiled this crude attempt at Divide and Rule. A lively trade in dog-tags sprang up on both sides of the border. Dog-tags bearing specific numbers were frequently passed from hand to hand as Chum!kwe residents offered their BP relatives a month or more of Boer hospitality at the settlement scheme.

Gradually the South Africans instituted a system of payments for wage-labour and phased out food hand-outs; the traffic in dog-tags declined but visiting and sharing of food rations continued despite the ban on BP !Kung.

In the mid-1960s other techniques of domination were introduced by the South Africans. A Dutch Reformed Church missionary-linguist was sent to Chum!kwe. To gain the confidence of the !Kung at first he simply handed out food and medical care. Later he began to preach the gospel in the !Kung language and to be openly hostile to !Kung traditional healing dances, calling them the work of the devil. Next a school was opened offering instruction in the lower primary grades. !Kung was the language of instruction with Afrikaans, but not English or Oshiwambo, offered as a second language (Oshiwambo is the majority language of Namibia). The exclusive use of !Kung and Afrikaans was part and parcel of the system of domination: (1) It opened up an exclusive channel of communication for ruling-class (that is, Afrikaner) ideology; (2) it limited communication between the !Kung and their Bantu-speaking neighbours in other parts of South West Africa; and (3) it limited the !Kung ability to listen to radio broadcasts in English or in African languages from the countries of black Africa which offered alternative political viewpoints to those of Afrikanerdom.

Once the full apartheid apparatus was in place, other developments followed quickly. Religious instruction for adults and children became part of the programme of the Chum!kwe school and some of the gospels were translated into !Kung. Christian ideas were a long time in taking root among the !Kung, but in September 1973 the Windhoek newspapers reported mass conversions at Chum!kwe, as many !Kung renounced the old ways and embraced Jesus Christ as their saviour.

Economically the !Kung were introduced to the "value" of wage-labour and the importance of consumer goods. Transistor radios, Western clothing, powdered milk, and commercial baby foods became popular items in the Chum!kwe store. With the new consumerism and exposure to racist advertising, the !Kung rapidly grew to be contemptuous of their own personal appearance. The Chum!kwe storekeeper reported to Lee that hair-straightening and skin-lightening creams had become the most popular items and the store could barely keep them in stock because of the great demand. Much of the remaining !Kung income went into ingredients for brewing home-brew beer. The Chum!kwe settlement in the late 1960s became the site of marathon drinking bouts, brawls, and absenteeism and child neglect caused by drinking. (It was the devastating effect of the drinking that the !Kung claimed drove them to religious conversion; a good example of the capitalist system providing both the cause of the corruption and its "cure.")

The full apartheid system also made provision for political "leaders" to be appointed from the native community. The traditional !Kung had lacked all forms of chieftainship or headmanship; what leaders there were exerted their influence in subtle and indirect ways; in a strongly egalitarian society they could persuade but not command. The new leaders appointed by the Native Affairs Department therefore had little credibility with the people and there was a rapid turnover of the occupants of these positions.

The San inhabitants of Chum!kwe enthusiastically took to the ideas of free food and medical care but remained, in general, suspicious or uncertain about the security of their new life and about the Afrikaners' long-term intentions. An indication of this reserve was the continuing importance that the SWA !Kung attached to maintaining links with their hunting and gathering relatives across the border in Botswana. Rarely a month passed when there weren't forty or fifty Chum!kwe residents paying visits to their kin at the Dobe area waterholes.

The Struggle for Liberation

The !Kung San are only one of a dozen ethnic groups in the territory of Namibia. The bulk of the population is made up of Bantu-speaking peoples such as the Ovambo, Kavango, Kwanyama, and Herero, as well as the Khoikhoi-speaking Nama, Damara, and other groups. San people like the !Kung in fact constitute only about 2 per cent of the black population of the country. And in many ways the fate of the !Kung under the apartheid system was vastly different from that of their compatriots.

While the !Kung enjoyed some material benefits from the South African occupation, the great majority of the people of Namibia were moved into overcrowded reserves from which they were forced in ever-increasing numbers to migrate out in order to find work in the mines and ranches of the territory. The low pay, harsh working conditions, and lack of political freedom, coupled with illegality and intransigence of the South African regime, drove the working people increasingly towards militant nationalist political organizations as their main salvation. After years of unsuccessful peaceful appeals to the South African regime, it became clear to the bulk of the people that armed struggle was the only way that Namibia could become free. In 1966, SWAPO — the liberation movement representing the vast majority of the Namibian people and recognized as their authentic representative by the UN and the Organization of African Unity (OAU) — initiated an armed liberation struggle with a series of attacks on South African military installations in the Caprivi Strip. Since then SWAPO has won the support of the great majority of the people in the urban centres and larger reserves. Most Western observers agree that if a free election were held in Namibia, SWAPO would get between 70 and 90 per cent of the vote.

With the opening of the resistance movement, South Africa's occupation tactics entered a new phase. In many parts of the Third World, European powers have tried to hold on to colonies and neo-colonies by force. From the British experience in Malaya, the French and later American experience in Indo-China, and the Portuguese in Angola, Guinea, and Mozambique, the Western powers gradually have built up a textbook of counter-insurgency warfare techniques to attempt to stifle or forestall the coming to power of progressive and popular revolutionary movements in the Third World. This kit of techniques now came into play with the South African occupation forces of Namibia. The story is eerily reminiscent of the use that the American Special Forces units (Green Berets) made of the Montagnard tribesmen of the strategic central highlands of Vietnam.

Paramilitary Tracking Units

After a decade of experience administering the San settlement at Chum!kwe, the South African Police (SAP), around 1970, began the wholesale incorporation of some of the bands into paramilitary tracking units directly involved in the anti-guerrilla war. The SAP chose the most isolated and politically least sophisticated of the bands, and they set these units up in isolated border posts where they are "protected" against outside influences, and are virtual prisoners of the army, dependent on them for their water and their weekly rations and for other supplies.

These units are spaced at camps, 40–60 kilometres apart along the border fence, and they follow a regular routine. Every morning two trackers set out from each post, one to the north the other to the south, scanning the sand for fresh tracks. Two trackers meet in the middle of the sector, compare notes, and may spend the night camped on the road. The next day they return to their respective posts, and another set of trackers set out. Thus any incursion into the territory is reported to the Police within hours.

The duties of the trackers also include frequent visits to !Kung villages inside Botswana. The South Africans have instructed them to tell nothing of what they may know of troop movements on the Namibian side but to observe closely any unusual behaviour on the Botswana side. The result is that the Namibian San exploit their kin ties, and the trust explicit in them, to feed information to the South Africans. This is bizarre behaviour by !Kung standards; they expect other !Kung to engage in greetings and share fully news of what they have seen of interest along the way. Just as the !Kung and other hunter–gatherers place a high value on sharing and reciprocity of food, so do they emphasize sharing and reciprocity of information. When this is interrupted, the fabric of !Kung society is threatened.

The Final Solution? The Military Takes Over

The second phase of militarization has been the actual recruitment of the San into the South African Defence Forces. This has been accompanied by a virtual replacement of civilian by military administration as the whole of northern Namibia has been declared "an operational" zone.

1975 marked a turning point for South Africa. Its colonial rule of Namibia was doomed and it sought to "Africanize" its regime by creating puppet institutions of government through "elected" black leaders from the ten non-white homelands into which Namibia had been divided. This resulted in the Turnhalle negotiations for independence under the Democratic Turnhalle Alliance (DTA). The puppet nature of the Turnhalle leaders is very apparent and this internal settlement attempt, bypassing SWAPO, has never achieved any credibility outside South Africa, except in the Reagan administration in the USA.

South Africa also sought to Africanize further its anti-guerrilla war by training puppet troops to do more of the actual fighting themselves. After 1974 !Kung soldiers were recruited directly into the South African Defence Forces. Although paramilitary tracking units continued to exist, the bulk of the !Kung recruits were put into regular army units at special bases where they were issued automatic weapons and taught to use them. As a result the !Kung have begun to die in increasing numbers in skirmishes in the Caprivi Strip and in incursions into Angola.

Two South African battalions are manned largely by "Bushman" troops. Battalion 31 was set up in the Caprivi Strip in 1974, composed of both !Kung and Barakwengo, or River "Bushmen." And in 1978, Battalion 36 was created with headquarters at Chum!kwe, in the heart of the Marshalls' Nyae Nyae area. In 1980, 31 Battalion (also known as Base Omega) had a strength of 600 Bushmen soldiers and 250 white officers. In addition, 700 women, 1,200 children, and 200 older dependants also live on the base. 36 Battalion's numbers are lower and instead of a single base, the soldiers and their dependants are spread out at 20 smaller camps at boreholes dotted throughout Bushman land.

For a number of years South Africa's secret war and its manipulation of the San and other ethnic groups were unknown to the outside world. In late 1977, however, the South African Defence Forces made known for the first time the existence of their secret Bushman military bases in the Caprivi Strip and took South African newsmen on a tour of some of them. The picture presented provides a chilling account of forced acculturation and how it is packaged by the media:

Deep in the dense Caprivi bush a colony of Bushmen are being taught a new culture and a new way of life by the White man. More than a thousand Bushmen have already discarded the bow and arrow for the R1 rifle and their wives are making clothes out of cotton instead of skin.

Gone are their days of hunting animals for food and living off the yield. They now have "braaiveis" and salds with salt and pepper while the men wear boots and their ladies dress in the latest fashions. Their children go to schools and sing in choirs.

A handful of South African soldiers started the Colony some time ago, attracting the children of the veld to a secret Army Base where they are teaching them the modern way of life.

"The most difficult thing to teach them is to use a toilet," the Commander of the Base said. Money and trade is something completely new to them but they are fast learning the White man's way of bickering.

In their small community they now have a store, hospital, school, and various other training centres. The men are being trained as soldiers while their womenfolk learn how to knit, sew, and cook. Well built wooden bungalows in neat rows are their homes although some of them still prefer to erect shanties next to them.

Medicine is also something new to them. It is estimated that Bushmen in the area were dying at a rate of 35 a month whereas they now have an average of three deaths a month.

Most of them died of disease and by the hands of witchdoctors.

It is an open camp and the people may come and go as they please, but most of them prefer to stay.

(*Windhoek Advertiser*, 19 September 1977)

*   *   *

Because the San population is relatively small and isolated compared to the other Namibian groups, the South Africans can exercise an even more total control over every aspect of the lives of the San.

The military bases function as "total" institutions. San women and children are brought into the camps along with the men and are given a comprehensive package of programmes ranging from sewing and cooking lessons to weapons training and martial arts. In their isolation these camps are closed societies like the "protected villages" or "strategic hamlets" set up by the Americans in Vietnam, or more recently by the Ian Smith regime in pre-1980 Rhodesia. The ostensible purpose is to "protect" the inhabitants from the guerrillas but in reality the goal is to prevent the inhabitants from giving support to the freedom fighters.

* * *

What's to Be Done?

Anthropology came into its own largely in the late nineteenth century, when Western industrial nations were beginning to administer colonial empires in their search for new sources of raw materials, cheap labour, and markets. Early anthropological studies provided colonial administrations with valuable information they could turn to their own use in controlling local land use, labour supplies, and commodity production. As a child of imperialism, anthropology's intellectual and ideological underpinnings are much the same as the Western tradition of which it is a part — a tradition which has been concerned with the politics of domination and control, and with the ideological concealment of this fact. As an example, anthropologists and sociologists have always been more comfortable with the study of *ethnicity* than with the study of *class*, and with the concept of *acculturation* than with the concept of *capitalist penetration*. On the other hand, many individual anthropologists have grasped the larger issues and have put their energies to work on behalf of oppressed Third and Fourth World peoples.

The South African regime, in pursuit of its policy of Apartheid and Separate Development, is attempting to channel and "freeze" local communities in ways which keep them artificially divided. To the extent that anthropologists continue to respond to the San (or Ovambo or Herero) merely as San (or Ovambo or Herero), tacit support is given to the South African policy of Apartheid.

The people of Namibia, under the leadership of SWAPO, have made it clear that they are fighting as Namibians for control of their nation, and not as San for control over their San communities or as Herero for control over their Herero communities.

SWAPO's commitment to national unity rather than ethnic divisions is clearly expressed in its Constitution, adopted by the meeting of the Central Committee, August 1976, in Lusaka, Zambia. Among the ten basic aims and objectives which SWAPO espouses, the following are of special note here:

2. To unite all the people of Namibia, irrespective of race, religion, sex, or ethnic origins, into a cohesive, representative, national political entity;

3. To foster a spirit of national consciousness or a sense of common purpose and collective destiny among the people of Namibia;

4. To combat all reactionary tendencies of individualism, tribalism, racism, sexism, and regionalism.

(SWAPO 1976)

The theoretical challenge posed to anthropologists is also a contradiction. With our use of the culture concept we claim our expertise in the study of *specific* cultures. Yet to advocate the preservation of a specific culture places us on a politically shaky footing. We can only begin effectively to use our knowledge and skills on behalf of our "cultures" if we learn the lesson that the late Amilcar Cabral sought to teach to the people of Guinea Bissau, a lesson summed up in the phrase, "die a tribe to be born a nation." Only then, by supporting the *national* political struggles of peoples in Namibia and elsewhere can we regain our role as students of humanity for the party of humanity.

56
Indians and the Metropolis

J O S E P H   G .   J O R G E N S E N

Introduction

How modern American Indians are integrated into the American political economy has received some anthropological analysis during the past thirty years. Anthropologists who have concerned themselves with *contemporary* Indian life have usually disregarded the political economic causes of Indian conditions and have employed an "acculturation" schema to explain why living Indian societies differ from their precontact forbears and from the dominant contemporary white or "Anglo" society as well. Stages, contexts, or levels of acculturation achieved by Indians are usually loosely defined and measured in relation to the hypothesized norms for white society. Though actual measurements of white society are seldom made and variation in white society is almost never accounted for, in general, the more similar an Indian society is said to be to white society, the more "acculturated" the Indian society is. In this view the dominated society accommodates itself to the dominant society in stages.

The underlying assumption in these studies is that the direction change takes is from a primi-

From Jack O. Wadell and O. Michael Watson, eds., *The American Indian in Urban Society*, pp. 67–111. Boston: Little, Brown and Co., 1971. (Bibliographic documentation contained in the original text is omitted here. Interested readers should consult the original publication.)

tive, underdeveloped society — that is, a society with low economic output and low standard of living — to a civilized, developed society that becomes fully integrated into the dominant white society. Integration is achieved when "acculturation" is complete. The actual steps involved vary from context to context. There is no single path.

The acculturation framework provides a rather euphoric way to think and talk about what has happened to American Indians since contact. It assumes that before white contact Indians were "underdeveloped" and avoids analysis of why Indians are as they are today. Because this framework assumes that Indians will eventually become fully integrated into the United States polity, economy, and society just like whites, it is also meaningless. No matter what the condition of Indian society is when analyzed by the anthropologist, it is always somewhere along the acculturation path, headed toward full acculturation. Because acculturation explains everything, it explains nothing.

Recently the clichés and erroneous concepts of acculturation research have been challenged by Vine Deloria, Jr., an Indian author. Although Deloria's criticisms are sound, he does not adequately explain why Indians are as they are. It is clear, however, that the political, economic, and social conditions of American Indians are not improving, and this is the nub of the issue.

Underdevelopment, in my view, has been caused by the *development* of the white-controlled national economy, and the political, economic, and social conditions of Indians are not improving because *the American Indian is, and has been for over one hundred years, fully integrated into the national political economy*. Underdevelopment, paradoxically then, has been caused by the development of the capitalist political economy of the United States. This postulate is in direct opposition to the postulate that seems to underlie acculturation and also suggests a basic contradiction in the American political economy. Before exploring this postulate, let us survey Indian conditions in the past several decades since they have *become* underdeveloped, and in a very cursory way, let us develop some idea of what the basic features of modern Indian life have been for these "acculturating" or "developing" people.

The Problem: The Persistence of Indian Poverty

The History of Indian Deprivation

In 1926 Lewis Meriam was commissioned by Secretary of Interior Hubert Work to survey Indian administration and Indian life. His report demonstrated that federal legislation and the niggardly funds allocated for Indian programs had injured rather than helped American Indians. It also showed that the Bureau of Indian Affairs (BIA), the government agency responsible for implementing federal policies and managing Indian affairs, had a long tradition of dry rot — that is, unimaginative and undereducated mismanagers caught up in red-tape procedures — that had made it incapable of helping Indians, particularly with their economic, health, education, housing, and legal problems.

Since the passage of the General Allotment Act (Dawes Act) of 1887, which was intended to civilize Indians and "free" them from communal land ownership, Indian reservation land had been drastically reduced by allotting acreage to each Indian family head and, in some instances, to other living Indians. The unallotted land became part of the public domain. By 1926, much Indian land was tied up in complicated heirship status, much had been sold or leased by Indians to whites, and Indian economic conditions, in general, were deplorable. Employment was almost nonexistent; family farming and ranching were not meeting subsistence needs. Thus, between 1887 and 1926 the underdeveloped Indians became more underdeveloped.

Meriam and his associates further showed that Indian health was particularly poor, with a high incidence of disease — especially diseases that are correlated with poverty, like tuberculosis and trachoma — and a high infant mortality rate. Indian housing was so substandard — dirt floors, no doors, wretched sanitation, no running water — and Indian diet so poor that the two coalesced greatly to exacerbate Indian health problems.

Federal education policy since the 1880s took preadolescent children away from their homes and the so-called restrictive backward influences of tribal life, and educated them in all-Indian boarding schools. The intention of the policy was to force rapid acceptance of white ways, and the optimistic notion behind it was that if a man is given an education, he will, ipso facto, make his own way successfully as a wage earner or capitalist-farmer or shopkeeper in white society. The Meriam report was critical of this education policy as well as the General Allotment Act of 1887, which was intended to bring the education-economic program to fruition and in a short time, to achieve the desired effects.

The Meriam report criticized the current state of Indian affairs, especially land and education policies, and made suggestions to solve the problems: Indian health and housing were to be improved; preadolescents were to educated on home reservations; loss of Indian land through sale or lease was to be stopped; and greater federal appropriations were to be made to increase salaries to entice better qualified people to join the BIA. Characteristically, the report did not cover such questions as the need for massive funds to develop industries — agricultural or otherwise — under the ownership and control of Indians. Rather, it directed itself to the symptoms of the Indians' problems and to cleaning up the bumbling, underfunded BIA, hoping that good advice administered through this special appendage of the federal welfare enterprise would improve the individual Indian's lot until he became self-sufficient.

During the Hoover administration, federal appropriations doubled from 1929 to 1932, but slackened by nearly 20 percent in 1933, during the depths of the Depression. Most of the money went for education expenses, salaries of better trained personnel, and health and medical expenses, including the salaries of doctors, nurses, nutrition experts, and others involved in Indian health programs. Thus, funds were provided for the education dream, for a larger and better trained welfare bureaucracy to administer Indian affairs, and for maintaining and hopefully improving Indian health. This welfare program served to expand the BIA, improve health slightly, and keep the Indian education system going.

In 1934, during Roosevelt's first administration, the Wheeler-Howard Act, known best as the Indian Reorganization Act (IRA) was passed. The IRA provided for sweeping changes in Indian policies. Following the recommendations of the Meriam report it allowed for consolidation of Indian land and purchase of more land; development of tribal governments with constitutions and charters; financial loans to the tribal governments for the development of tribal resources; and development of day schools for Indian children on home reservations. John Collier was appointed Commissioner of Indian Affairs to implement these policies, which were considered "radical" at the time.

The IRA did *not* decrease the powers of the BIA over Indian lives, even though tribal governments with constitutions were created. In fact, the IRA actually *increased* the powers of the Secretary of Interior over Indians. Many Congressmen and many lobbyists became irritated at Collier's implementation of the IRA, but their irritations and fears were premature. Because the program allowed land to be purchased for Indians, thus removing the land from state tax rolls, and because it was thought that it would be more difficult for private corporations to exploit resources on those lands if they fell into Indian ownership, state governments as well as agribusiness and mineral lobbies were opposed to the IRA and to Collier. Actually, mineral, farm, and rangeland exploitation became cheaper on Indian-owned land than on company-owned or leased federal land because a special tax exemption was implemented for lessees of Indian lands.

Shortly after World War II, Commissioner Collier was replaced and the Indian Claims Commission Act was passed allowing Indian tribes to sue the United States for redress of grievances, particularly for the loss of lands and broken treaties. Many thought that legal redress for these things and for inhumanities perpetrated against the American Indians was only just.

The Indian Claims legislation also paved the way for a new federal policy whose goal was the dissolution of the BIA and the termination of all treaty obligations of the United States to American Indians. It was argued that once the old scores over land thefts and other inhumanities had been settled and Indians were taught how to spend money wisely, they could make their own way as responsible citizens.

*   *   *

The results of the commission's [Commission on the Rights, Liberties, and Responsibilities of the American Indian] investigation showed the economic position of the Indian about 1960 to be less favorable than that of any other American minority group. Indian income was scandalously low; employment was meager, unstable, and temporary; and the Indian land base was smaller than in the previous decade. Indian health was poor compared with that of whites, as was Indian housing, education, and local government. Relatively nothing had changed for the American Indian since 1934, except that some land had been reacquired, schools had been developed near reservations — about *half* of all funds went to education — the BIA staff had grown, and Indian governments exercised a modicum of control over reservation societies which were poverty-ridden and often pervaded with factionalism.

*   *   *

These statistics lay bare the discrepancy between the non-Indian and Indian norms. In the mid-1960s, as in the mid-1920s, despite all programs, the American Indians were relatively as underdeveloped as in the past. Even in a statement of averages, as opposed to contrasting the Indian minimum to the non-Indian maximum in education, skills, employment, income, and comforts, Indian conditions are extremely low on all measures and suggest extreme deprivation. The *acculturation* has been to rural poverty and, more recently, urban poverty as well. Surprisingly, the Indians of California on all these measures of the quality of life are *much* better off than their counterparts in other states and *much* closer to the standards of living considered adequate for the average United States citizen than their congeners.

The Endemic Poverty of Contemporary Indians

To consider the endemic poverty of United States' Indians generally, we shall contrast California Indians with other groups and assess how Indian family household organizations have adjusted to economic deprivation.

The relative "prosperity" of California Indians is partly due to the self-selected migrants to major urban areas, many of whom have some employment, and to generally high welfare standards observed in that state. For the nation as a whole, the average family income of Indians is $1500 per year, $1300 *less* than for California Indian families and about $2000 *under* the currently specified "poverty line." The unemployment rate is between 40 and 50 percent on almost all reservations; that rate is calculated on the BIA's narrow definition of employability. That pegs the employment rate at 50–60 percent; over half represents temporary or part-time employment, that is, underemployment.

According to the President's Task Force on American Indians, the present poverty on Indian reservations and among urban ghetto Indians is deplorable. Housing is grossly dilapidated; the incidence of disease, especially upper respiratory and gastrointestinal forms, is seven or eight times the national average; Indian life expectancy is only two-thirds the national expectancy; and one-third of all adult Indians are illiterate. As youthful populations grow on the reservations, many spill off into the ghettos of urban areas, replacing rural poverty with urban poverty. Though adequate statistics on urban Indians are not available, particularly from the BIA — the agency responsible for sending many of them to the cities — it is estimated that 200,000 of the 600,000 American Indians currently live in urban areas.

In contrast to California Indians, 38 percent of whom use contaminated water, the national average of such usage by Indians is 74 percent. Forty-eight percent of California Indian families haul all domestic water, whereas 81 percent is the national average. Seventy-three percent of California Indians have unsatisfactory facilities for disposal of excreta: 83 percent is the national average. All Indian households, as well as the California Indian household, average more than five (5.4) occupants. The average size of Indian houses nationally is less than two rooms. The non-Indian household, however, averages only 2.9 occupants and occupies more than four rooms.

The composition of Indian households differs significantly from the nuclear-family, conjugal-pair, and single-person types that predominate in white America. In California 30 percent of all Indian households are composite, including such combinations of kin and non-kin as grandchildren, nieces and nephews, brothers or sisters of the husband or wife, a married child with spouse or children or both, and even more distantly related kin and affines (in-laws). Sixty-one percent of all California household heads are men and 39 percent are women — the latter being widowed, separated, or divorced. The composition of California Indian households is not an anomaly, but is a regular feature of Indian poverty and poverty in the Western Hemisphere generally.

Though there are no national statistics on the subject, the research of M. Munsell among the Salt River Pima-Papago of Arizona, L.A. Robbins among the Blackfeet of Montana, and J.G. Jorgensen among Shoshones and Utes on five reservations in Idaho, Wyoming, Colorado, and Utah confirms the California Indian household composition distribution. A difference is that these recent studies demonstrate that there are relatively *more* composite Indian households outside of California than in California, and that those outside of California are also larger. This is to be expected, given the greater average family income for California Indians.

The studies cited above clearly demonstrate that household size varies inversely with the amount and stability of income. The less stable and lower the amount of income among American Indian family households, the larger the households. The explanation for this phenomenon is that people with meager means join together to pool resources. It is better to crowd together under a single roof, or adjacent roofs, and share resources than it is to live apart in less crowded households where resources are less predictable. This grouping together characterizes poverty-stricken households among other ethnic and racial minorities within, as well as outside of, the United States.

Through sharing funds from several diverse sources — welfare (for example, Aid for Dependent Children, Old-Age Assistance, Federal Aid to the Blind), per capita payments from Indian Claims Commission judgments, lease income from land, wages from part-time labor, cash from piece work, goods received as welfare commodities or procured in hunting and fishing — these composite family households have adjusted to their lack of resources. Where nuclear family households occur among American Indians, they usually have a *stable* source of income, males tend to be the household heads, and, to a lesser extent, someone in the household is employed.

American Indian family household compositions tend to change in a rather predictable cyclic manner from composite to nuclear. If a son gains regular employment, he and his wife and children move out of his father's home and establish a separate household. In fifteen years or so, this man's nuclear family is likely to become a composite household as his own or his wife's parents move in to share his resources, or as his own children marry and establish temporary residence in the household.

American Indian composite households and family household cycle are not retentions of aboriginal customs, but are products of their meager and unstable incomes, lack of skills, and lack of control over resources. They do not have money or resources to allow them to cope with life as do the gainfully employed and nonpaternalistically guided lower (working), middle, and upper classes of United States' society. Indian family households change from composite to nuclear to composite as their economic conditions change, making the Indian family similar to other families living in poverty in the Western world. Yet the peculiar niche occupied by the Indians in the American culture of poverty — that of superexploited and paternalistically guided wards of neocolonialism, the vast majority of whom reside on reservations — separates them, say, from the Mestizo in Mexico, the Callampa dwellers in Chile, the rural poor and the Black urban ghetto dwellers in the United States, and the Black Caribs of Latin America and the West Indies.

Although the major problems of American Indians are rooted in economy and polity as are the problems of the other groups mentioned, a difference is that Indians often have resources. But the *access* of American Indians to their resources is severely restricted, and the major exploitation of these resources is carried out by non-Indian local, national, and multi-national corporations.

The Political Economic Niche Occupied by American Indians

A brief survey of the niche of reservations in the national economy reveals that reservations generally have land bases that are arid or semi-arid, and because some segments of the land are tied up in heirship, they are not feasible for development of profitable agribusiness. Moreover, most reservations do not have sufficient land, even if all of it were consolidated, to provide decent livelihoods from agriculture for all inhabitants on those reservations (the rural economies surrounding most reservations are basically agricultural). Reservations are generally located long distances from major markets, big cities, and industrial plants, so there are no large job markets. Moreover, the greater the distance to market, the less profitable, generally, the agribusiness on reservations. Reservations are also often located considerable distances from railroads and major highways, making transportation expensive and profitable development of heavy industry on reservations unlikely. Industrial development has been further inhibited because Indian populations are undereducated and underskilled.

Rural economies adjacent to reservations in most of the western half of the United States have withered, as large farms in the midwest with access to capital and improvements in technology, including hybrid crops, fertilizers, and pesticides, have become more productive and have grown at the expense of small agricultural operations everywhere. Federal farm policies have worked with the large farm corporations to protect them through price supports and soil-bank payments, encouraging further expansion of large farm corporations to gobble up small farms. In general, the greater the productivity, the greater the government assistance. Since 1920 the farm population of the United States has decreased by two-thirds and its percentage of the total population has plummeted from 30 to 6. Although the average size of all farms has increased, the number of farms has decreased by more than half since 1920. Since 1940 alone the average size of farms in the United States has increased by well over 200 percent. As examples of federal benefits, in 1967, 43 percent of United States farmers with incomes of less than $2500 per year received 4.5 percent of the federal farm subsidies. On the other hand, 65 percent of federal subsidies went to the *top* 10 percent of earners in the farm production pyramid, most of them being large corporations or food processing trusts.

The livestock business has followed a similar course in the past decade as quasi-cartels are beginning to control all aspects of beef production from feeder lots, to packing houses, to supermarket distribution. Grass-fed (range-fed) mature beef is less and less marketable because of the time needed for fattening the animals for slaughter and the difficulty in controlling the size of range-fed beef. Weight can be controlled on feeder lots, yielding animals of standardized size, and greatly easing slaughtering and packing because the animals can also be fattened more quickly. In addition, there is a dwindling demand for grass-fed beef by packing houses and distributors (both processes often carried out by the same corporation) because, they allege, the meat is not sufficiently marbled with fat, and the increased production costs, including transportation for range-fed beef, are pushing the producers of grass-fed beef off the market. This squeezes small operators out of business, especially those in the western United States who are long distances from the main markets.

Though the rural economies around Indian reservations are dwindling and farm consolidation is occurring at a rapid rate, there is some money to be made in agriculture on reservations. The BIA reports that $170 million was grossed from agriculture on all reserves (50 million acres) in 1966. These figures are rather liberal as they include the *estimated* value of all fish and game taken by Indians on their reservations (perhaps $20 million) and consumed by the procurers, but this modest amount of overestimating is not the critical point. Of the $170 million, the Indians realized only $58.6 million, $16 million of which was derived from rents and permits to non-Indians. This means that $127.4 million, or 75 percent of the gross from agriculture, went to *non-Indians* who paid Indians $16 million, or roughly 12 percent of their gross, for exploitation of Indian lands.

The BIA statistics clearly reveal what can happen to Indian resources when Indians have neither access to capital nor the skills or adequate counsel to exploit their own resources. Of the estimated $170 million from agriculture in 1966, the Indian share approximates $58.6 million, of which $16 million (27 percent) is from leasing to non-Indians, $23 million (39 percent) is from farming and ranching (this too is an estimate and includes all goods produced *and* consumed by Indians), and $19.6 million (34 percent) is from hunting and fishing for their own consumption. There is no way to know how inaccurate the latter two estimates are.

The BIA statistics on further exploitation of Indian resources are also revealing. In 1967 about 803 million board feet of lumber were cut. Only 100 million board feet, or about 12 percent, were processed in tribal sawmills. Indians were selling their natural resources yet maintaining practically no control over production. Timber sale brought $15 million to Indian tribes in 1967. There are no figures pertaining to the non-Indian gross, non-Indian profits, or the costs to Indian tribes to maintain their resources.

As for oil and all other minerals, including uranium, sand, gravel, phosphate, gilsonite, gypsum, coal, limestone, copper, lead, and zinc, the exploitation of these resources by national and multi-national corporations brought $31 million to tribal coffers in 1967 through bids and lease royalties. Again, the tribes do not control production and few jobs are generated for Indian employees. Though there are no figures on corporate profits or gross income, the corpora-tions are generating capital for themselves and offering Indian tribes carrots in the form of lease and royalty incomes, and the Indians are losing their resources.

Finally, since the early 1950s, the BIA has encouraged the location of industries on or near reservations to provide employment for Indians. The emphasis has not been on development of Indian-owned and -controlled industries. Tribes have been urged to use their modest amount of capital from land-claims judgments and mineral royalties to build plants and lease them to private corporations at low rates. The corporations, the Indians have been told, will then move onto the reservations, even though they are a great distance from markets, because they can operate at low costs and use cheap Indian labor.

Nothing much came of this program until 1962, when a few industries moved onto reserves to take advantage of provisions made for them. Between 1962 and 1968, 10,000 jobs were created through the development of industries on or near reserves. Characteristically, 6,000 (60 percent) of these jobs have gone to *non-Indians*. Private corporations are using Indian capital to expand, yet using Indian labor only when it is adequate to the task. Indians do not maintain ownership or control.

"Industrial development" has been mostly talk: development has accrued to industry and not to Indians or Indian-owned and controlled industry. In 1967 private non-Indian development of Indian lands on a lease basis, including all industrial, commercial, and recreational uses, brought $4 million to Indian tribes. Recreation brought $1.9 million of that total. The irony of this is that whites are paying low-lease fees to exploit Indian lands for white leisure use.

Why are things as they are, even after so much has been done to improve the Indians' lot? From 1955 to 1968, the BIA has grown from 9,500 employees to 16,000. From 1949 to 1969, federal government appropriations for American Indian affairs have increased from $49 million to $241 million. In fact, in the 1968–69 fiscal year, about $430 million was spent on federal programs intended to benefit Indians; yet the average annual income for all Indian families was about $1500.

Part of the failure of Indian policies is attributable to mismanagement by the BIA. For example, the BIA has encouraged the development of livestock operations at a time when quasi-cartels have been taking over the industry, and the bureau has advised tribes to allow non-Indian corporations to exploit Indian resources. But the causes of persistent Indian problems cannot be attributed solely to the BIA. Indeed, the growth of the BIA and the federal budget for Indian affairs are indicative of the more important causes of Indian poverty. Federal welfare institutions and funds have increased as exploitation has continued. The growth of the BIA is an effect of the way in which the national political economy has grown. Poverty is perpetually created and welfare measures are used to heal the most gaping wounds.

A Hypothesis about Indian Underdevelopment: The Metropolis–Satellite Political Economy

The Indians of the United States, in my opinion, have been integrated into the United States political economy since they were conquered. As shown above, Indians are currently deprived and have been deprived for the past several decades. This is not a coincidence or a fortuity; Indian poverty does not represent an evolutionary "stage of acculturation" somewhere between the underdeveloped tabula rasa and the developed non-Indian polity, economy, and society. In my hypothesis, Indian underdevelopment is the product of the full integration of United States Indians into the United States political economic society — albeit as super-exploited victims of that society.

*   *   *

The conditions of the "backward" modern American Indians are not due to rural isolation or a tenacious hold on aboriginal ways, but result from the way in which United States' urban centers of finance, political influence, and power have grown at the expense of rural areas. The rapid development of urban areas after the mid-nineteenth century brought the Indian social ruin, as measured in status and self-worth; poverty, as measured in access to strategic resources, the distribution of surpluses from one's own region, employment, housing, and general welfare; and political oppression and neocolonial subjugation, as measured by decimation of Indian populations through warfare, the dissolution of aboriginal polities, the loss of self-direction, the lack of access to the locus of political power, the general denial of citizenship (with a few exceptions) until 1924, and the increasing role of the BIA and the Secretary of Interior in approving the conduct of Indian affairs.

These results were brought about by expropriation of Indian land and resources by the railroads, mining corporations, farmers, and ranchers. Economic surpluses were taken from the rural areas, and used for the growth of the metropolis. For instance, from an estimated 16 million bison on the American plains in 1860, the bison population was reduced to about one thousand in 1885 through systematic killing by whites because there was a market for tongues and skins in the eastern United States, and more importantly because the plains could then be farmed and cattle raised without interference from the bison or the Indians who lived off them. The railroads, which received vast amounts of right-of-way — that is, Indian territory — free from the United States government, in turn sold this land to farmers and ranchers. The railroad profited from the sales and later began moving products from these farms and ranches to markets in the east. Indians were the first rural inhabitants to suffer from this development and the first people to be forced into underdevelopment from their previous condition of self-support and self-governance. Mining industries expanded throughout the west from the 1850s to the turn of the century, and they too expropriated Indian land and resources.

With the growth of technology influenced and controlled by the metropolis, particularly as it affected agribusiness and the mineral industries, non-Indian ranchers, farmers, and miners in rural areas, too, became "underdeveloped." For instance, the beef production industry, once based on range-fed cattle, has been revolutionized by development of hybrid crops, feeder lots, mechanized packing techniques, and the growth of large supermarket quasi-cartels which are beginning to control all aspects of production. Since 1935 the man-hours (labor-time) to produce beef (measured in live weight) has been cut nearly in half, and it has been cut by one-fourth since 1959 alone. Only those producers who control the greatest amount of capital are able to survive. Technology has influenced the grain, vegetable, and cotton industries through mechanization and fertilizers. Again, only the largest producers are able to survive. The small producer is losing his land due to costs or taxes, or both. He cannot get loans because he is a bad risk, and the large producer, in turn, is consolidating the land made available through the former's liquidation. But this trend is not a product solely of technology and capital; political influence and power, too, are critical in maintaining this trend.

Underdevelopment of rural areas is a product of the development of urban centers of finance and the latter wield considerable influence in enacting legislation to maintain their growth. The mineral industries have long lived under special tax-privilege umbrellas; they have profited from the special-use tax (allowance) applicable to the exploitation of Indian lands, as well as the tax-depletion allowances offered to oil, gas, and mineral producers generally. The influence of the mining lobbies prior to the General Allotment Act and the multi-national oil and mineral corporations in maintaining the privileged tax-depletion and protective import laws that have sheltered them for decades is solid evidence of the relationship between polity and the growth of the metropolis.

*   *   *

As the metropolis grows and the resources of the satellites nourish that growth, many people living in rural areas choose to better their conditions by moving to urban areas. Some are successful, especially if they are white, yet many trade rural poverty for urban poverty. For Indians who stand in a special neocolonial relationship to the rest of society, the latter is usually the case. This is not to say that all Indians are doomed to poverty. Just as some native Africans once living in colonial Kenya can, for example, be educated at Oxford and through help open businesses in London or Nairobi or even enter the British colonial service, so can some United States Indians move from reservations, gain university educations, and become popular authors or high-ranking officials in the Indian Service. But the odds and the context in which both colonial Africans and neocolonial Indians live weigh heavily against such happenings.

*   *   *

To summarize the hypothesis presented here, the growth of the metropolis caused the Indians of the United States to be underdeveloped; Indians did not begin that way.

57

Northern Manitoba Hydroelectric Projects and Their Impact on Cree Culture

DORIS YOUNG

I will be speaking about the cultural values of the Cree Nation, the socialization process, the economy, spirituality, and health. To connect these important institutions to the culture, it will be necessary to show:

- how the participation of the people was necessary to the survival of the community;
- the interdependence of the land and people, as well as of the people on one another;
- how people and nature are an integral part of the whole;
- how roles are defined by necessary activities;
- that all persons must be respected, regardless of age;
- that work is done according to physical ability; and
- that water is the life giver of the Cree nation, and has a special significance for woman, who is also a life giver.

First of all, the Cree Nation occupies the northern regions of Manitoba, Ontario, Quebec, Saskatchewan, and small portions of northern British Columbia and the Northwest Territories. The Cree is the largest Aboriginal nation in Canada.

From *People and Land in Northern Manitoba*, Department of Anthropology, University of Manitoba, 1992, pp. 13–19. Reprinted with the permission of the author.

My community, The Pas Reserve, has a population of about two thousand people and Cree was our first language. Our economic base was characterized mainly by hunting, fishing, trapping, and gathering. Our cultural values were transmitted through our history, story telling, and daily living.

Our land was vital to our well being. Everyone participated in the economy of our community and there was order to this activity. For example, the women and children gathered the earth's abundant harvest in the fall. The men trapped in the winter, hunted in spring and fall, and fished in the summer. All the members of my community were useful and valuable, including women and children. Our interdependence on one another was an ongoing life process. The earth was what gave us our life, breath, energy, and food. Our food was plentiful and our lives were meaningful and orderly. In all of our activity, we practised our traditional values of sharing, caring, and respecting one another and our surroundings.

Learning Native Values

My earliest childhood memories are the lessons that my grandmother taught me. She took care to teach us the spiritual riches of my culture. She maintained that all life was sacred. She taught us that the earth, the fish, as well as plant and animal life, were as important as men, women, and children. In my culture there was no hierarchy system. We were all important.

I remember my grandmother's first and last functions of each day were to pray. She was thankful for life. She would put her scarf on her head and bow her head to say her prayers. This spiritual outlook influenced me in a deep and meaningful way. I knew that my grandmother was sacred, just as the earth was sacred. I loved them both in a very special way. Today, I too am conscious of the sacredness of life.

My mother, on the other hand, taught us the practical things about life — how to work and how to relate to one another in a kind and respectful way. Her teachings were also centred around caring, sharing, kindness, and being respectful of one another.

This socializing process could be seen clearly during the gathering season. Every fall, the women and children of my community would go out to gather the abundant harvest of berries and moss in preparation for the winter season. Women and children were the gatherers and we worked side by side, in a co-operative way. Gathering season was also the time when we caught up on the summer's news. My mother and aunts enjoyed each other's company and during lunch break they would exchange stories about life in general. There was an order to the way in which the work was carried out. We all contributed to the berry pot. Each person, even the young children, was expected to put their berries into the pot. At the end of the day we would feel that we had made a substantial contribution to our food supply. When we were allowed to play, we did so knowing that our job had been done. We enjoyed ourselves.

Berry-picking season was always a time for working, learning, and having fun. Prayers were said and tobacco was offered before we picked. My mother taught us discipline and diligence in our work, as well as giving back to Mother Earth. When we worked, we worked. We were not allowed to be noisy until our job was done. I learned that it was not good to carelessly grab a handful of berries and shove them into my pail. We learned to be clean pickers. When I pick berries now I think about how the plant would feel if I were to pull its branches too harshly. We were taught at a very early age to be clean pickers and to be respectful to the plants.

We were also taught silence. My mother would tell us to sit down and just listen, be quiet for a while, listen to what is going on. Through silence, we learned the value of being attentive to our surroundings, to feel the interconnectedness of Mother Earth to the universe. I learned how to look and see how much life the bush actually had. I learned to be respectful to the plants and to be kind.

The berry-picking season also gave us children a chance to climb trees and have lots and lots of fun. Swinging from the very top of the trees was great. Sometimes we weren't heavy enough to bring the tree all the way down to the ground, so an older sister or brother would have to rescue us and bring us safely to the ground. We learned to get along and to care for one another. This was a valuable teaching because the berry-picking area was also filled with danger. We were always mindful of bears, or of the fact that one of us might wander off in the wrong direction and get lost. I always remember being told to take care of one another and we did. If we were fighting and quarrelsome, someone always told us that this was not good behavior. I remember the kindness with which we were told, and we listened. Today, I now tell my children to take care of one another.

Every fall we also gathered moss to keep the babies dry and warm, and to prevent diaper rash as well. Once the moss was picked, it was hung on the trees to dry. The children would then have time to play again. Moss picking was a very important job and everyone was expected to contribute to this activity. The moss was left on the shrubs for a few weeks and when we went back to pick up our moss, it would always be there. No one ever took it. We always seemed to know which was ours and which wasn't. We were respectful of others and did not touch their moss. My mother taught us to respect someone else's property. She always knew just how much moss to gather, as we had enough to last us till the next gathering season; no more, no less. She knew how to conserve and passed this knowledge down to us.

Water is a very important and sacred item to Aboriginal People and is a component of our spiritual ceremonies. Some significant reasons are these:

- all living things are dependent on water;
- human beings are made up mainly of water;
- life begins by the breaking of the water, just before a baby is born;
- women are life givers and are crucial to the survival and continuation of our culture.

It therefore follows that in my culture, women are the carriers and protectors of water. At our ceremonies, women bless the water and carry it around to each person to drink so that we are all blessed by this sacred gift.

I now understand why the women in my family carried the water from the streams and rivers for our cooking, drinking, and washing. The pails were heavy and I would often complain about this. My mother would help me by taking some of the water out of the pail, but she didn't take away my responsibility. I still had to do my share and carry some water. Before we took the water, my mother would be silent in prayer. She gave thanks to the Creator for the gift of the water that we would be using. Today, I give thanks to the Creator whenever I see the river or the lakes.

Our Land and Values

When I was young, my community was a safe and healthy place to live. We were relatively happy and confident people because we were able to sustain ourselves from the land. The land from which we received our food supplies was also the place where we learned our traditional values of caring, sharing, and respecting. The socialization process in which we learned and accepted these wonderful values was so evident in everything that we did. We learned to use these tools in our work and in our play.

The Impacts of the Flooding

The flooding of our land [resulting from a hydro-electric megaproject] altered our culture and changed our lives forever. Our economy, as well as our physical and spiritual health, has been drastically affected. The land where my mother gathered our berries and our moss was destroyed. The land where my father trapped was flooded. The lakes where my father fished are now contaminated. The hunting is less and less plentiful.

First of all, when my father lost his trapping area, a big part of our economy was gone. It's been about 30 years now since the flooding took place, and only recently has my reserve received some compensation for this loss. The lucrative summer fishing is all but a memory. Hunting has been affected in that the moose have moved further and further away. We find that it may now be dangerous to eat moose because they too appear to be contaminated. It is most distressing to read notices not to eat moose, particularly the liver, because of mercury contamination. The liver was the delicacy that we all looked forward

to eating. Gathering berries or moss as a vital economic activity of the community is a dim memory.

Our physical health has been affected because we no longer eat balanced meals. We have not been able to bridge the costs between the food we harvested from the land and store-bought food. The expense is too much for many community members who are now unemployed. People buy whatever they can afford and sometimes it's not always what's healthy. As well, we have not adequately learned to convert the nutrition of our former diets into the present way of shopping at convenience stores and shopping centres. Both my mother and grandmother had diabetes, and so have many, many others in my community. My mother and grandmother both died from diabetes complications.

Many people become welfare recipients. This position broke their pride and their generous spirits. My community suffered, as families became quarrelsome and agitated with one another. The welfare system does not encourage sharing; in fact, I have seen people being chastised because they had shared their store-bought food with others. Besides, the welfare money can never be stretched adequately to share our groceries with other members of our community. Many people have not come to terms with this situation. Shopping from a grocery store also does not provide the same satisfaction to a hunter in providing a meal for the family. The hunter is, in fact, removed entirely from the process.

Our connectedness to the earth became less and less because it's hard to feel connected to the earth when one is picking up food from store shelving, or when one turns on the tap for water.

Our spirituality was also altered because we no longer practised the values we learned when we were out on the land. Going to the store for food doesn't teach us about the universe in which we live, or how to care for it.

There's a gap in our generation with respect to our culture. My children don't know what living off the land means. Urban living prevents my children from knowing how to be connected to the earth. Picking berries is now a fun day, and is really no different from going to a city park for a picnic. It's not the same as knowing that our winter supply of food is dependent on that activity. The utility of picking berries is not the same today. The generation gap is, in fact, substantial when one considers the socialization process that is learned from living off the land. It's harder for my children to have a humanistic view of the land.

Conclusion

There is a saying that when you destroy nature, you are destroying yourself. I believe that this is true. When our land was destroyed, my culture was immeasurably altered. The lessons that my family taught me about life, when I was young, were lessons that were related directly to Mother Earth: the plants, the animals, the fish, the water. Our socialization process was thus connected to our relationship with the universe. We learned to be respectful and to care for Mother Earth and one another. We learned to share the abundance that she provided. Yes, the flooding of our lands altered our culture and changed our lives forever.

In spite of all of our best efforts, there is a gap between myself and my children. The tragedy of this gap is that we will never share the same kind of understanding about life from the universe that my mother, grandmother, and great-grandmother were able to share with their children. There is also a large gap in my own life knowing that that part of my culture has been destroyed. My generation appeared to be the last to know what living off the land really means. For this, we are immeasurably poorer.

The Aboriginal People have paid a high price for these mega hydro projects. Our spirituality has been weakened. Our communities were healthy, confident, and economically independent. Today, many members are on welfare and feel bitter and angry. The dams and the electricity have not made life better. Although we are working hard to restore what we have lost, the job is difficult when our lands are continually being destroyed.

58
Saving a Refuge

MICHAEL BEDFORD

In late 1991, 7,000 Gwich'in, working alongside environmentalists and conservationists, won a long battle over the future of 125 miles of pristine Alaskan coast. Waged in Washington, D.C., and small villages of Alaska, the classic David and Goliath fight pitted the Gwich'in and their allies against the financial and political power of oil companies and Alaska's political establishment.

The struggle began in 1987 when the U.S. Department of the Interior announced its intention to open for oil exploration Alaska's coastal plain in the Arctic National Wildlife Refuge, one of the few remaining wildernesses in the United States. President Eisenhower had protected the area's wildlife and environment by establishing the Arctic Wildlife Range in 1960. Twenty years later, Congress had enlarged the preserve to over 18 million acres and renamed it the Arctic National Wildlife Refuge.

Left unprotected, however, was Tract 1002, 1.5 million acres of coastal wetlands that U.S. Fish and Wildlife Service has called the refuge's heart, "the center of wildlife activity." For years, oil companies had pressured Congress for permission to explore for and exploit reserves along Tract 1002's coast. The lure was tempting to oil companies and Alaska politicians even though govern-ment studies estimate only a 20 percent chance of finding oil there, and any likely reserves would contribute just 200 days' worth of U.S. fuel needs. Oil and gas fields have pumped almost $2 billion into the Alaska treasury, 85 percent of the state's revenues. In 1987, oil companies reaped some $41 billion in profits from North Slope oil.

For the Indians of the region, the struggle over Tract 1002 has deep cultural and social implications. The Gwich'in inhabit fourteen communities bordering the refuge in Alaska and Canada's Northern Yukon National Park. These villages sit alongside the migration paths of the Porcupine caribou. The 180,000 caribou in the herd travel each spring from Canada to the coast, giving birth to their calves within Tract 1002. For thousands of years, the Gwich'in have depended on the caribou for food, cultural identity, spirituality, and a connection to the earth. "Our route to God is through the caribou," says Lincoln Tritt of Arctic Village, 120 miles above the Arctic Circle.

A failed hunt no longer means the Gwich'in go hungry. Food and other supplies are regularly flown in from Fairbanks to Arctic Village and other communities. Log houses have replaced caribou-hide shelters, and jeans are preferred to caribou skins. Still, any threat to the caribou directly challenges the Gwich'in way of life. Caribou remain the main source of protein, and a good hunt means ample food. Perhaps most important, the Gwich'in life passed down from

From *Cultural Survival Quarterly*, Spring 1992, pp. 38–42. Reprinted with the permission of Cultural Survival, Inc.

generations is the one they wish to carry forth through their children. Caribou grace Gwich'in stories and songs, and are considered the very center of Gwich'in life.

Oil Hunger

Since 1968, oil exploration and drilling have turned the nearby Prudhoe Bay area into an ecological nightmare. Over 1,100 miles of pipeline and 350 miles of road crisscross the landscape. Drilling stations and waste pits pockmark the ground; oil residue contaminates the land under the permafrost.

According to a 1991 Natural Resources Defense Council report, the Arctic ecosystems are very sensitive to disruption, with "air and water pollution ... of special concern." The impact of oil spills is reportedly more long term and far reaching than in more temperate climates. Noted naturalist and author Peter Matthiessen says in the NRDC report that "millions of gallons of oil industry waste and tens of thousands of air pollutants are pumped each year into the vulnerable arctic environment." The Prudhoe Bay area, "once the heart of the largest unspoiled wilderness in the United States ... [is] now an immense industrial facility strewn across hundreds of square miles."

The Prudhoe industrial complex has already destroyed thousands of Arctic acres, leading to a dramatic decline in wolves, birds, and bears. According to a 1990 Alaska Department of Fish and Game study:

> Oilfield complexes directly influence the distribution and movement of the CAH (Central Arctic Herd) caribou. Parturient [calving] and post-partum females are particularly sensitive to disturbance and tend to avoid areas of human activity.... Continued expansion and intensification of oil development within the central Arctic region could result in large-scale displacement of caribou with the potential for major impacts on herd productivity.

The Gwich'in closely watched development in Prudhoe Bay, especially as it approached the refuge and threatened the caribou. Gwich'in leader Jonathan Solomon, who has worked diligently to expand the refuge, perceives oil company plans to develop Tract 1002 as the beginning of a time of great trouble.

The fight over Tract 1002 gave the impetus to the first Gwich'in tribal meeting in over 100 years. The idea for this emerged during a 1987 tour of Gwich'in villages organized for the Colorado-based Institute for Resource Management, which actor Robert Redford had created to mediate environmental conflicts. Discussions with IRM on how to respond to oil company plans led to a decision to hold such a traditional Gwich'in gathering.

At first, however, no one knew how to proceed because many Gwich'in customs had been forgotten. Fortunately, Mary Kaye, sick in a Fairbanks hospital, remembered being told as a child some 80 years earlier about the last traditional Gwich'in meeting. She also knew that the traditional way to call for a meeting was to first gather the chiefs. Tribal meetings, she remembered, were called when times of "great trouble lay ahead."

In January 1988, chiefs from the United States and Canada met in Fort Yukon, Alaska, and laid plans for all Gwich'in to come together. IRM input at this planning session was critical, says Gwich'in Steering Committee staff director Bob Childers. Instead of holding a meeting exclusively for the Gwich'in, IRM suggested inviting the leaders of major environmental groups as observers. This way, the message would spread beyond northern Alaska. IRM also promised to raise money to help the Gwich'in tell their story.

The Gwich'in rejected another part of IRM's vision, however. IRM wanted to bring oil executives and Indians together to settle the conflict over Tract 1002. The Gwich'in refused, believing they must first strengthen their own awareness and resolve. Eventually, IRM was marginalized from the Gwich'in's plans, as strains arose over such issues as who was in charge, what language to hold the tribal meeting in, and who could speak at it.

Held in June 1988, the seven-day tribal meeting at Arctic Village closely followed tradition. Elders spoke first, with long stories and dire warnings on losing their customs. All discussions, which began at four in the afternoon and often lasted until midnight, were in Gwich'in. Dancing followed until 5 A.M. Alaska Governor Cowper was the only non-Gwich'in to address the gathering.

While the subject of protecting the caribou and the refuge dominated the week's discussions, the meeting was valuable for other reasons, too. Some relatives from either side of the U.S.–Canadian border met for the first time, many men publicly swore off alcohol, and a commitment was made to strengthening Gwich'in identity. The meeting covered issues of caribou and the Arctic Refuge, the international border, education and language rights, and alcohol abuse.

The meeting reaffirmed Gwich'in unity as a people and a nation. Two strong resolutions emerged: a united opposition to oil development in Tract 1002 and a decision to establish the Gwich'in Steering Committee. In the words of one of the resolutions, the committee would "tell the world what is at stake" in the refuge struggle.

In the midst of the Gwich'in's cultural reawakening, the 1989 Exxon Valdez disaster illuminated the threat of oil development in Alaska and led to wider awareness of and support for the Gwich'in. All summer, journalists from the lower 48 flooded Alaska. After exhausting the Valdez story, they visited Arctic Village. *Time, National Geographic, People*, and the *New York Times* all published articles sympathetic to the Gwich'in.

According to Bob Childers, environmental groups had carried the weight of protecting the refuge for ten years. The Washington-based Alaska Coalition, founded in 1976 to push for the 1980 Alaska Lands Act, had "fought the oil companies to a standstill." Yet, says Childers, the environmentalist analysis lacked an understanding that this was fundamentally a fight for human rights. The issue was about protecting a 1,000-year-old way of life, about "the last chance to do it right the first time."

For the Gwich'in Steering Committee, 1990 was a turning point, as support for protecting Tract 1002 grew. U.S. churches, especially the Episcopal Church, contributed by bringing potential allies together, educating constituents, and lobbying in Washington, D.C. The National Congress of American Indians and Indigenous Survival International reaffirmed their support. And the Gwich'in strengthened their alliance with the Alaska Coalition, the Wilderness Society, the Alaska Friends of the Earth.

According to observers among both the Gwich'in and environmentalists, stress as well as curiosity filled this alliance. Tension arose over definitions of success, suspicion about who defined the issues, and the difficulty Washington-based groups had in knowing how to deal with Native peoples.

Gwich'in versus Inupiat

Much deeper tensions were coming up in Alaska. In contrast to the Gwich'in, most coastal residents actually support oil exploration of the Arctic Refuge, and heightened tensions between the Gwich'in and the coastal peoples of Tract 1002 emerged over development plans. The Gwich'in traditionally inhabit the forested interior, while coastal Inupiat are tied to the sea for food and cultural identity. On top of that, Gwich'in and Inupiat had long fought over caribou hunting. Gwich'in came down into Inupiat territory to hunt caribou during the summer, while Inupiat also intruded Gwich'in areas to slay the animals.

Oil companies capitalized on these contrasts, arguing that drilling would take care of northern Alaska's poverty. The companies drew the media's attention to the Inupiat coastal village of Kaktovik, where residents proudly point to the local fire department, a free van for elderly citizens, and a modern medical clinic, all paid for with oil money. The 225 people of Kaktovik still hunt, fish, and boat among the ice floes to kill seal and bowhead whales, but motors power their boats and four-wheel-drive vehicles. The Kaktovik Inupiat Corp., which controls over 92,000 acres adjacent to Tract 1002, strongly supports development. It joined forces with the Arctic Slope Regional Corp., which owns the subsurface rights to the land.

Herman Aishanna, vice-president of the Kaktovik Inupiat Corp. and mayor of Kaktovik, says the village could reap a healthy return from service contracts and surface leases, as well as a 2 percent royalty on oil pumped. "We have a lot of young, energetic people here who don't have jobs," he told the *Anchorage Daily News*. "We need better snow removal, better docking facility for boats. We need natural gas hooked up to every house and better doors and windows. All of these cost lots of money." He dismisses the idea that drilling will harm caribou. "When they were having the first hearings about the [Arctic Refuge] lease sales, everyone was against them, but it appears the fears aren't valid anymore."

On the other hand, Kaktovik residents strongly oppose offshore drilling. "I don't mind drilling [in the Arctic Refuge] but not in the ocean," remarks Jimmy Soplu, one of Kaktovik's ten whaling captains. Although their economy is closely tied to oil, like the Gwich'in they can't accept development that threatens their traditions.

Arctic Slope Regional Corp. director Brenda Itta-Lee says the best way to steer oil companies away from the Chukchi and Beaufort seas is to open up the 1.5 million acres of the Arctic Refuge. "We are opposed to offshore drilling until all of our oil and gas deposits onshore are depleted, and that includes the Arctic Refuge," she says.

Still, according to the *Daily News*, some Inupiat fear that massive oil money may push Kaktovik into Alaska's mainstream, with all the attendant problems. "What we don't want to lose is tradition," Mayor Aishanna remarks. "The transition is already under way, and we're trying to deal with it as best as we can."

However, Bob Childers, from the Gwich'in Steering Committee, cynically refers to a fight between the human rights of the Gwich'in and the monied interests of the Kaktovik Inupiat and Arctic Slope corporations. He roots the Kaktovik endorsement of Tract 1002 development in a campaign orchestrated by oil company attorneys and public-relations firms. Until the early 1980s, people in Kaktovik had opposed oil development throughout the Arctic Refuge, but after the companies offered lucrative contracts to the village, Inupiat sentiments were divided.

Winning in Washington

Pressure to exploit the refuge intensified in February 1991, when the Interior Department released a report more than doubling the estimated oil reserves there. In response, the Gwich'in sued U.S. Interior Secretary Manuel Lujan, charging that the report avoided critical points, especially how exploration would affect the caribou. According to Gwich'in Steering Committee head Sarah James, "The Interior Department never had a hearing with the Gwich'in community, never talked to Gwich'in people, and we feel we got left out." In a second suit, the Natural Resources Defense Council and other environmental groups charged Lujan with filing a deficient Environmental Impact Statement.

Meanwhile, in the Senate, Energy Committee chair J. Bennett Johnston (D-LA) and Malcolm Wallop (R-WY) sponsored a proposal, supported by the Bush Administration, to open up Tract 1002. The bill also proposed streamlining the nuclear power licensing process and partially deregulating the electrical utility industry.

Joining the debate over the energy bill, Gwich'in traveled to Washington "not to lobby but to preach." They knew it would be hard to defeat the Johnston-Wallop bill, in part because the Alaska legislature had allocated $3 million for lobbying. Moreover, hundreds of industry lobbyists were pushing for passage.

Gwich'in concern was also based on having long been ignored in decisions about their homeland. "People come up week after week to visit Prudhoe Bay and the oil companies," James told Congress. "They fly over the refuge and go to Kaktovik, but they never stop in Arctic Village. They say transportation is too complicated, but they fly right by our village. There is never enough time, no matter how long they are in Alaska. Even when they are in Kaktovik, they are only allowed to talk with the people who support development. We are the ones who have everything to lose."

On November 1, 1991, the Senate defeated the Johnston-Wallop energy bill after one of the year's fiercest political fights. The Arctic Refuge had dominated the debate, as environmental groups waged a campaign of letter-writing, telephone calls to Senators, and lobbying, including bringing Gwich'in to Capitol Hill. The Indian testimony was a major factor in the victory, says Alaska Coalition chair Mike Matz. He suggests that Native people speaking for themselves meant more to Congress than white men in suits warning about development.

Unity, Identity, and Nationhood

Industrial nations have long sought natural resources on the lands of Native peoples. Perhaps with the growing awareness of the human and ecological devastation oil development has brought, this trend may slow. Sarah James thinks people's awareness has changed as she compares the Gwich'in struggle to that of the Sioux in *Dances with Wolves*. She values that movie as a tool for educating others about the price Native peoples pay in the name of progress.

Yet indigenous unity is not a given. Animosity between Native peoples is often deep, sometimes based in cultural differences, sometimes on contrasting agendas. Childers sees no easy resolution to the tensions between the Gwich'in and the Inupiat. Conflict between them could increase if pressures reemerge to develop Tract 1002.

When that may occur is not clear. Matz predicts a breathing space of five years until an energy bill that includes exploring the coastal plain could get through Congress. Changes in the world of international oil politics may place the region in jeopardy sooner.

Bob Childers of the Gwich'in Steering Committee is more hopeful. He sees the Gwich'in position as stronger than at any time in recent years. And time can only help the Gwich'in, he believes, as more is learned about the caribou and the effects of oil development. Moreover, all land disputes among the Gwich'in have been resolved, fostering a greater sense of unity, identity, and nationhood. As a result, political and cultural self-identity evolving parallel to the fight to protect the caribou could even lead to Indian efforts to protect the entire herd and expand the Arctic Refuge.

Glossary

acculturation The adoption of many cultural characteristics of a dominant society by the members of a less powerful group. *See* **ethnocide**.

Acheulian Tool assemblages of the Lower Paleolithic, including hand axes, associated with *Homo erectus* fossils.

adaptation The process through which populations of plants and animals are modified over the generations, somatically or behaviorally, and become, through natural selection, better adjusted to their own specific ecosystem. Adaptation requires the operation of mechanisms for continuity, mechanisms for change, and natural selection, a random mechanism that weeds out the less successful, without purpose or direction.

affinal kin A relative by marriage; an in-law. One's spouse's parents and siblings are one's affinal relatives.

agnate A patrilineal relative; one who is related to **Ego** through male links.

agriculture Food production using domesticated plants; started during the Neolithic, around 10,000 B.P., in the Middle East. In a narrow sense,

agriculture is distinct from horticulture, which does not make use of plows.

allele The several possible forms in which the gene occupying a given locus in a chromosome may occur.

ambilineal descent A **cognatic** rule of descent that allows inheritance through either male or female links.

animatism A term introduced by Robert Marett in reference to the belief that a supernatural force resides in certain persons or objects. *See also* **mana**.

Anthropoidea One suborder of primates, including all living and extinct monkeys, apes, and humans.

anthropological linguistics *See* **linguistic anthropology**.

anthropology The comprehensive and comparative study of past and present human populations and their origins.

anthropometry A subdiscipline of biological anthropology specializing in the measurement of all parts of the body and in the statistical analysis of those measurements.

applied anthropology Also called *action anthropology*. The use of anthropological training to solve practical human problems. All subdisciplines of anthropology have practical applications, from forensic research to the planning and execution of development and foreign-aid schemes. An increasing number of anthropology graduates are becoming involved in applied anthropology.

archaeology A subdiscipline of anthropology specializing in the study of the material remains of the cultures of past societies.

aristocracy A hereditary privileged class, such as the feudal nobility of Europe.

artifact A man-made object.

assemblage All the artifacts found in association with one another in an archaeological site.

asymmetrical reciprocity Reciprocal exchange between people of unequal social or economic status.

Aurignacian An early Upper Paleolithic culture associated with Cro-Magnon *Homo sapiens sapiens* and characterized by fine-blade stone tools, bone and wooden tools, spears, and art; dated from 35,000 B.P. to 20,000 B.P.

australopithecine The term commonly used to refer to all members of the genus *Australopithecus*.

Australopithecus afarensis An early australopithecine, named in 1978 by D.C. Johanson in classifying new fossils found in Hadar and Laetoli; bipedal; dated 3.7 m.y.a.

Australopithecus africanus "Southern ape of Africa." The first australopithecine to be discovered, in 1925; dated from 3.0 to 2.5 m.y.a.; average brain size 440 cc.

Australopithecus boisei East African variety of *Australopithecus robustus*. Named *Zinjanthropus boisei* by Louis Leakey; had big molars, broad face, and sagittal crest; dated from 2 to 1 m.y.a.

Australopithecus robustus A later, heavier form of *Australopithecus*, with stronger jaws and larger molars than *A. africanus*; brain size averages 520 cc.

authority The ability to suggest, and persuade others to follow, one's advice or requests. The sanctions associated with authority are of a nonmaterial kind (praise or mockery, witchcraft, heaven or hell). *See also* **power.**

avunculocal residence The tradition whereby a couple goes to live with the husband's mother's brother after marriage.

Aztec The Aztec empire thrived in Central Mexico from the thirteenth century until the Spanish conquest in 1519. The capital was Tenochtitlán, with about 300,000 inhabitants, who relied on Lake Texcoco for the food and natural protection it provided.

band A small nomadic egalitarian society, normally comprising fewer than a hundred members. Bands disperse, regroup, and exchange members according to complex ecological and social calendars. The headman of a band has little **authority** and no **power**.

barter A type of market exchange that does not involve money. In barter, as opposed to reciprocity, the value of the items exchanged is calculated and negotiated.

Beringia A land-bridge between Asia and Alaska, 900 miles (1500 km) wide, which became exposed when the sea level dropped during Pleistocene glaciations. The first "Americans" were Asiatic peoples who crossed Beringia.

biface A stone tool made by chipping flakes from both sides of a flat core; characteristic of Acheulian tool assemblages and also found at some Mousterian sites.

bilateral descent A **cognatic** rule of descent, in which kinship is traced evenly and symmetrically through links of both sexes, on the father's and the mother's side.

biological anthropology Also called *physical anthropology*. A subfield of anthropology that includes studies of human evolution and human variation. Specialties include paleoanthropology, paleopathology, and primatology.

bipedalism Standing upright and walking on two legs.

blade A stone flake with two parallel edges, at least twice as long as it is wide; systematically produced by all the makers of Upper Paleolithic tool assemblages.

B.P. Before the present.

brachiation Swinging arm-over-arm under one branch or from branch to branch; characteristic of certain monkeys and apes.

breeding population In population genetics, the term refers to all members of a population who could mate with each other.

bride-price Also called *bride-wealth*. A gift, or series of valuable gifts made in installments, from the kin of the groom to the kin of the bride. It reinforces the alliance between the two groups.

brow ridge A bony ridge in the shape of a cap visor above the eye sockets and the bridge of the nose.

burins Long, thin stone blades used for engraving bone, antlers, and ivory; commonly associated with the Aurignacian stone-tool industry.

call system Many nonhuman primate species communicate through a series of different calls, each of which conveys a specific meaning.

capitalism An economic system in which natural resources, labor, and capital can be bought and sold in a market where prices vary according to forces of supply and demand.

cargo cult A type of revitalization movement found in Melanesia since the nineteenth century. All cargo cults include among their beliefs the expectation of shiploads or planeloads of Western goods (cargo) sent by their ancestors.

caste An **endogamous** class, with closed membership, in which class status is ascribed by birth. The caste system of South Africa was justified on the basis of racist claims; that of India, on religious grounds.

catastrophism A prescientific theory suggesting that the distribution of life forms and land features is explained by catastrophes (such as the great biblical flood).

cephalic index A formula used to calculate the proportions of the skull. A narrow skull has a low cephalic index.

Cercopithecoidea Old World monkeys, found in Africa and Asia; the living primates with the widest geographical range, except for humans.

ceremonial center An archaeological site at which most of the monuments and other structures were designed for religious purposes and few were associated with permanent residence.

Chavin A Peruvian civilization that dominated the societies of the Andean Highlands from about 1000 B.C. to 200 B.C.

chief The hereditary leader of a group comprising several settlements. Chiefs receive tribute but are still bound to be generous; they have **authority** and some limited **power**.

chimpanzee *Pan troglodytes*. One of the closest relatives of *Homo sapiens*, and, together with the gorilla and the orangutan, one of the groups of living great apes.

chopper The name given to crude core tools with a jagged cutting edge that is retouched only on one side; found in Olduvai Gorge in Tanzania; dated 1.9 m.y.a.; associated with *Homo habilis* in Africa.

chromosome The thread-like structure in every living cell that carries hereditary information. Humans have 23 pairs of chromosomes.

circumcision Cutting off the foreskin of a boy's penis. Circumcision is part of a ritual of passage in many societies. For girls, a less common practice consists in cutting off the tip of the clitoris.

circumscription Robert Carneiro proposed the theory that states arose independently in areas in which fertile agricultural land was surrounded (circumscribed) by deserts or mountains.

clan A unilineal descent group, usually **exogamous**, including people who claim to be descendants from a distant, mythical ancestor. Clans are often composed of several lineages.

class Stratified societies are divided into groups of people with similar amounts of wealth and power. These groups, called classes, usually differ from one another in other aspects as well (life style, speech, and so on).

cognatic descent A rule of descent that recognizes the transmission of ascribed rights and duties through both male and female links. The main varieties of cognatic descent are **bilateral** and **ambilineal** descent.

colonialism Direct domination of the political system and economy of another nation. When that domination becomes indirect, it is called imperialism.

compadrazgo From the Spanish word meaning "co-parent," *compadrazgo* refers to a ritual kinship between the parents and the godparents of a child. This is a very important social institution, especially in the Balkans, Italy, and Spanish-speaking countries. It can be used to reinforce or extend previous kinship ties. Horizontal *compadrazgo* is established between people of the same class; vertical *compadrazgo*, between social unequals.

composite family A household unit resulting either from polygamy or from residence of the new couple with the parents of the bride or the groom.

conjugal family A family unit comprising a man and a woman and the children they have had together. This descriptive term is preferred by many modern anthropologists to the term **nuclear family**, which implies, inaccurately, that conjugal families are the building blocks of the society.

consanguineal kin This term, which means "blood relative," is used to refer to kinship ties established by descent as opposed to those created by marriage alliances.

core tool Stones or big flakes with a working edge shaped by chipping off smaller flakes. Includes **Oldowan** choppers and **Acheulean** hand axes.

couvade A ritual "paternity leave," observed by many societies, wherein the father rests and observes certain taboos while his wife goes back to work after giving birth.

Cro-Magnon A variety of early *Homo sapiens sapiens* (40,000 B.P.) discovered in southern France. The oldest known *Homo sapiens sapiens* lived in Africa at least 200,000 B.P.

cross-cousin A cousin related to *Ego* by two links of opposite sex, for example, the mother's brother's child or the father's sister's child.

cross-cultural comparison One of the distinctive techniques of anthropology, cross-cultural comparisons are the discipline's equivalent of laboratory experiments. They are an essential element of any significant anthropological claim.

cultural anthropology A subdiscipline of anthropology that studies the social and cultural characteristics of human societies. Sometimes subdivided into **ethnology** and **ethnography**, it is traditionally distinguished from archaeology, which is the cultural anthropology of past societies.

cultural relativism A philosophical attitude suggesting that the social and cultural characteristics of other societies should be understood and evaluated only in relation to the sociocultural system of which they are a part.

culture All of the socially transmitted patterns of behavior, knowlege, thoughts, and feelings that characterize a group of people (rather than individuals).

demography The study of quantitative aspects of human populations, such as population size, density, sex ratio, age ratio, and fertility and mortality rates.

descent In kinship studies, the rules governing inheritance of name, property, status, group membership, and so on. A society may have different rules for the inheritance of different things: In America, surnames are inherited patrilineally, whereas property is inherited bilaterally.

development A term used by politicians and economists in reference to the growth of production and wealth, with the assumption that an improvement in the standard of living follows.

diachronic study Research focusing on change (for example, historical linguistics, history, the search for the origins of institutions). The alternative is a synchronic study, in which origins and change are ignored, while the relationships among the parts of the system at any given time become the focus.

diffusion The transmission of cultural characteristics from one culture to another.

diffusionism A theoretical approach used by some anthropologists at the start of the twentieth century, which suggests that cultural similarities are explained by diffusion. Its most extreme proponent was G. Elliot Smith, who claimed that civilization originated in Egypt and diffused from there to the rest of the world, including Mesoamerica.

diluvialism The theory that the Flood described in Genesis was the source of all fossils of extinct forms.

displacement A characteristic of language that enables humans to send or receive messages about realities with which they are not in sensory contact.

divination A magical procedure to discover the causes of certain events, such as a patient's illness, and to predict future events.

division of labor The assignment of designated tasks to different categories of members of a society. The simplest division of labor is based on age and sex, but stratified societies, particularly industrial societies, have a complex division of labor that creates many full-time specializations and even partitions jobs into small, meaningless bits that are ceaselessly repeated throughout the workday.

DNA (deoxyribonucleic acid) A complex molecule whose chemical structure constitutes a coded message specifying the structures (cells, organs) that the body will produce. The Double Helix model of the DNA molecule was proposed in 1953 by J. Watson and F. Crick.

dominant trait In genetics, a trait that is expressed even if the individual has only one **allele** for that trait (heterozygotes).

double descent Patrilineal descent on the father's side, and matrilineal on the mother's side.

dowry A gift made by the parents of the bride to the couple or to the bride on the occasion of a marriage.

Dryopithecus Extinct ape genus of the Miocene; fossils found in Africa, Asia, and Europe dated from 20 to 10 m.y.a.

duality of patterning Instead of having a different call for every idea, human languages are patterned at two different levels: that of the **phoneme** and that of the **morpheme**. A limited number of meaningless phonemes are combined on the basis of unconscious rules to form an unlimited number of morphemes, which carry meaning.

ecological anthropology An approach that considers human populations as one part of an ecosystem including other populations, of plants and animals, interacting in the same habitat.

ecology The study of the relationships and complex interactions of plant and animal populations with each other and with the habitat in which they live.

economic anthropology Subfield of cultural anthropology in which patterns of production and exchange of goods and services are described and analyzed using an approach that is different from that of economists because it is comparative and holistic.

egalitarian society A society in which there are no social classes, in which no individual or group has power or privileged access to natural resources, and in which the chances of achieving any prestigious status are roughly equal for people of the same age and sex.

Ego Latin for *me*. This term is used to designate an individual as a point of reference in discussions of kinship. Often, kinship diagrams focus on an *ego* who is the informant that provided information about relatives, or who is the point of reference for the classification of his or her relatives.

emic Emic *facts* are those that we can learn only by "getting into the informant's head." Emic *explanations* are those that we define as true if they are consistent with the conscious or unconscious knowledge, beliefs, and claims of the people observed. *See also* **etic**.

enculturation The transmission of the culture of a group from one generation to the next.

endogamy The rule or practice of marrying within a certain social group (for example, village endogamy, caste endogamy).

environment Usually refers to the physical surroundings of a group — the climate, geology, topography, and animal and plant life in the area. Ecologists prefer the more precise term *ecosystem*. The *habitat* is the nonliving part of the ecosystem.

estrus In female mammals, the period during which females are sexually receptive to males.

ethnic group A social group comprising people who share real or alleged similarities of race, ancestry, history, or culture. A society in which several such groups coexist and maintain their differences is called a plural society.

ethnoarchaeology A modern archaeological approach in which archaeologists study modern-day peoples and the material remains of their activities to guide their search and interpretation of older remains.

ethnocentrism The idea, supported by a mixture of beliefs and feelings, that one's own culture is superior to any other and that foreign ways, ideas, and values are less "human" or less rational.

ethnocide The systematic destruction of a culture by forced acculturation — for example, making the language and customs of the group illegal or forcing the children into mission schools, where they are severely punished for using their parents' language. Ethnocide is widely practiced today.

ethnographic analogy The interpretation of the functions of archaeological artifacts based on their similarity to artifacts used by modern peoples described by ethnologists.

ethnography Description of the society and culture of a group of people.

ethnology The comparative analysis of all aspects of all known societies and their cultures.

etic Etic *facts* are those that we can determine scientifically, without requiring that the people observed be aware of them. Etic *explanations* are those that we define as true if they are consistent with an existing body of scientific knowledge or scientifically observed facts, regardless of whether the people observed are aware of them or in agreement with them. Anthropologists want to know both emic and etic facts, and attempt to provide both emic and etic explanations.

evolution Transformation from one type into another; also, the reconstruction of the sequence in which the types defined in a given science appeared (for example, species in biology; types of technologies or types of political systems in cultural anthropology). Evolution is not the same as progress. In biology, Darwin showed that evolution is a byproduct of the process of **adaptation** through **natural selection**.

exogamy A rule or practice of marrying someone from outside a specified social group (for example, village exogamy, clan exogamy).

extended family Several **conjugal** (**nuclear**) families closely linked to one another, usually as a result of a rule of postmarital residence.

extrasomatic Not part of the body structure. **Culture** is an important adaptive characteristic of human populations that is not associated with any organ of the body.

family of orientation The family group in which one is born and reared; it is composed of one's parents and siblings.

family of procreation A new family group, composed of a husband, a wife, and their children, that starts with the marriage of the couple.

feudal society A stratified society in which a lord promises loyalty to the king in exchange for a permanent grant in land and the right to control and exploit the people living on that land. Europe during the Middle Ages and Bunyoro are examples of feudal societies.

fieldwork Research performed by anthropologists in the aim of gathering data. Archaeological fieldwork includes excavations; cultural anthropological fieldwork usually involves some participant observation.

flakes Stone tools obtained by striking a stone core, then shaping the resulting flakes to adapt them to specific tasks. The Mousterian–Levalloisian technique included a careful preparation of the core, in order to predetermine the shape of the flake.

foraging society A society whose subsistence is derived primarily from hunting and gathering; usually nomadic.

fossil The remains or impression of a plant or animal preserved in mineralized form.

functionalism A theoretical approach that analyzes customs and sociocultural characteristics in terms of their function, as defined by their contribution to the maintainance and stability of the social system.

functionalist anthropology A school of anthropology that emphasizes synchronic explanations of sociocultural characteristics based on the functions they fulfill. Associated in particular with the work of A.R. Radcliffe-Brown, for whom the main function was the maintenance of the social system, and B. Malinowski, who emphasized biological and psychological functions.

gender Every society creates social distinctions in the statuses of their members according to their sex. These gender statuses are social constructs, not the inevitable result of sexual differences.

gene A part of the **DNA** molecule that specifies the manufacture of a certain protein: it is a unit of hereditary potential. It may or may not be expressed in the **phenotype**, with modifications resulting from interactions with the rest of the **genotype** and with the environment of the organism.

genetic drift A random factor in evolution, associated not only with the **allele** frequencies in a population, but also with the size of the population.

genocide The systematic extermination of one people by another; examples include the Tasmanians by the British, the Beothuks of Newfoundland by the Canadians, and Jews and Gypsies by Nazi Germany. Genocide has been taking place in recent years in Iraq, Guatemala, Brazil, and many other countries.

genotype The hereditary potential of individual plants and animals. The genotype may contain potentials that are not expressed in the **phenotype**.

gorilla The largest nonhuman primate, this ape lives in the forests of Africa. Largely terrestrial (knuckle-walking), gorillas have large and complex brains; an endangered species.

government The specific set of laws, institutions, and personnel used by the **state** at any given time to administer and control the people within its borders. The state may remain intact when governments change, whether peacefully or by revolution.

grammar Rules in every language governing the combination of **phonemes** to make acceptable **morphemes**, and the combination of morphemes to form meaningful statements (*see* **syntax**).

hand axe A **bifacial** core tool with sharp edges, a pointed end, and a rounded top. One of the many types of tools associated with **Acheulian** sites of *Homo erectus*.

heterozygote Carrier of two different variants of a gene (**alleles**) at the corresponding loci of homologous chromosomes.

historical archaeology Archaeological research focusing on recent historical sites, such as forts and trading posts in North America or medieval cities in Europe.

holistic approach An effort to include in the same explanation many different aspects of the existence of a society. This approach is a fundamental characteristic of **anthropology.**

Holocene The current geological epoch, which started with the melting of the last glaciation (10,000 B.P.).

homeostasis Maintenance of the equilibrium of a system through the operation of negative feedback mechanisms.

Hominidae The primate family that includes the australopithecines and all present and extinct varieties of the genus *Homo*.

Homo erectus Extinct species of the genus *Homo*, fossils of which were found in African and Eurasian deposits of the Lower and Middle Pleistocene. Its mean brain size is 1020 cc, twice as large as that of the australopithecines. The oldest and most complete specimen found to date is KNM-WT (1.6 m.y.a.), found in 1984 in West Turkana.

Homo habilis Latin for *handyman*. Name given by Louis Leakey to hominid fossils with a mean brain capacity of 646 cc found in Olduvai Gorge; assumed to be the earliest tool makers; dated 1.86 m.y.a. to 1.6 m.y.a.

Homo neanderthalensis [*Homo sapiens neanderthalensis?*] Extinct hominid species that inhabited Europe and the Near East from about 100,000 B.P. to 30,000 B.P. Associated with the Mousterian–Levalloisian tool assemblages, and also with the Chatelperronian (which had been classified as Upper Paleolithic until recently).

Homo sapiens From Latin *Homo*, meaning *man*, and *sapiens*, meaning *wise*. The species to which all humans belong. Modern humans are usually classified as *Homo sapiens sapiens* to distinguish them from early hominid relatives such as **Homo sapiens neanderthalensis**. The taxonomic status of many specimens of early *Homo sapiens*, often decided on the basis of their skull and facial characteristics, is debated by specialists.

Homo sapiens sapiens Anatomically modern humans, who appeared first in Africa around 100,000 B.P. or earlier. They flourished in Eurasia after about 40,000 B.P., at which point they become associated with the Upper Paleolithic cultures.

homozygote When the **alleles** at a given genetic locus are identical on the **chromosome** inherited from the mother and on the chromosome inherited from the father, the individual is homozygous at that locus.

horticulture A cultivation technique that does not include the broadcasting of seeds or the use of plows.

hydraulic theory Theory explaining the origin of the state as a result of the need to construct and maintain large-scale irrigation projects. Presented in the works of Karl Wittfogel and Julian Steward.

hypothesis General statement proposing an explanation for known facts and others still to be observed. It must be consistent with the previous body of science and with logic. It must also include a description of derived implications that are testable.

imperialism Covert or indirect domination of the economy and political system of other countries.

Inca At its peak, the Inca empire stretched from Colombia to Chile. A rigidly stratified society, including about six million people, it existed from 1438 until its destruction and sacking by Pizarro in 1540.

incest taboo Rules, associated with harsh ritual and social sanctions, that forbid sex with certain kinds of relatives. All societies have incest taboos, but they differ considerably in their classifications and rankings of prohibited relatives.

Indus civilization A civilization that developed in about 4500 B.P. along the Indus River in India and Pakistan. It built great dams, canals, and the famous cities of Mohenjo-daro and Harappa.

industrial society A society whose economy is based on mass production, taking place in factories with machines, powered by nonrenewable energy sources, which increase production to the point at which economies of scale are achieved.

infanticide The killing of children, intentional or not. Female infanticide is more commonly practiced. Infanticide has played a major role in preventing overpopulation in many societies.

instinct Genetically inherited pattern of behavior, such as the web making typical of a certain species of spiders. Humans have no instincts.

interglacial period The warmer period between glaciations, when the glaciers melt partially and retreat.

irrigation The diversion of the natural flow of rivers toward agricultural land, to supplement insufficient rainfall. The building and maintainance of large-scale irrigation projects is usually associated with state societies.

kindred A group centered around an individual(*Ego*), and based on bilateral descent. Only *Ego*'s siblings have the same kindred. This is a significant kinship group in Western industrial societies such as Canada and the United States.

kinship Beliefs and social institutions, found in all human societies, that create a close bond among people who claim common ties of descent or affinity. Popular myths (including the notion of "blood relatives") notwithstanding, kinship is a social institution, not a biological fact.

kinship system   A set of rules, beliefs, and customs, found in all societies, concerning descent, affinity, postmarital residence, and kinship terminology.

kinship terminology   Classification of relatives into labelled categories called kin terms. The main types of kinship terminology distinguished by anthropologists are Eskimo, Iroquois, Sudanese, Hawaiian, Crow, and Omaha.

ky   Thousands of years; e.g., 24 ky = 24,000 years.

language   The exchange of symbolic messages through sounds, spoken and heard; a uniquely human mode of communication, characterized by semantic universality. All humans have the potential to learn a language. Languages are composed of meaningless **phonemes**, which are combined to form **morphemes**, which are, in turn, combined to make messages.

Levalloisian technique   The technique of preparing a stone core in such a way as to predetermine the shape of the flakes that would be chipped off it. The sharp flakes were then modified to make different tools. Associated with Neandertals. Named after the stone quarry of Levallois in France, where the first tools of this type were collected.

levirate   The custom whereby a widow is supposed to wed one of her dead husband's brothers.

lineage   A unilineal **descent** group composed of people who claim to know their genealogical connections to one another and to a common ancestor. **Clans** usually include several lineages. In **patrilineage**, descent is reckoned through male links; in **matrilineage**, through female links.

linguistic anthropology   A subdiscipline of anthropology that studies the mutual influences of language and culture, the origins of language, and the history of languages as it relates to the history of cultures.

linguistics   The scientific study of **language** and its characteristics.

Magdalenian   A culture of the Upper Paleolithic, found in France and Spain from 17,000 B.P. to 10,000 B.P. In addition to superb stone tools, the Magdalenians had harpoons, spear-throwers, and bows and arrows. The culture is famous for the engravings and frescoes found in the caves of Lascaux, in France, Altamira, in Spain, and several others.

magic   Beliefs and rituals connected with the manipulation of events and phenomena by nonphysical means, for instance, by casting a spell or making certain signs. James Frazer contrasted magic and religion, but modern anthropologists consider the distinction ethnocentric.

mana   A Polynesian word used to describe the belief, found in many societies, that certain objects or people are possessed of a special inner force that brings luck, health, charisma, and so on.

market exchange   A system in which goods and services are exchanged, with their value explicitly stated, and a return is expected; includes both barter and money exchange.

marriage   There is no universal and precise definition of marriage; in all societies, it includes (exclusively, or as one of several possibilities) the union of a man and a woman, with a degree of permanence and with a social sanction defining the status of the children issuing from the union as legitimate.

matriarchy   Rule by women, as in the myth of the Amazons. No society is known to have been organized in this way.

matrilateral   On the side of the mother. In matrilateral cross-cousin marriage, for example, a man marries his mother's brother's daughter, or any woman classified in the same category.

matrilineal descent   A rule of descent that recognizes inheritance only through female links.

matrilocal   A rule pertaining to postmarital residence whereby the bride and groom go to live in the same locality as the bride's mother's relatives.

Maya   In Belize, Honduras, Guatemala, and South Mexico (the Yucatan peninsula), the Maya grew maize and developed a distinctive culture.

Their maximum growth occurred between A.D. 300 and A.D. 900. It was marked by class stratification; probably the formation of states; the construction of cities and ceremonial centers, such as Tikal; and outstanding achievements in writing, mathematics, and astronomy.

medical anthropology A subdiscipline of anthropology that applies anthropological theory and method to the study of biological and cultural factors affecting human health, illness, and healing.

melanin Brown pigment found in skin and other organs.

Mesopotamia The area between the Tigris and Euphrates rivers where large-scale irrigation, cities, and states first developed. Uruk (5800 B.P.), Ur, and Babylon are some of the most famous neolithic cities of Mesopotamia.

messianic movement A **revitalization movement** promising spiritual or material salvation and drastic improvements in the lives of the followers of a charismatic leader.

microlith A small stone tool made from a flint blade during the Mesolithic period, from 11,000 B.P. to 6,000 B.P. Microliths were usually embedded in wooden or bone handles.

minority A social group discriminated against or exploited by other members of the society on grounds of real or alleged differences in race, gender, history, or culture. Despite the literal meaning of the term, it can refer to a majority of the people in a society, as it did in South Africa.

moiety One of two halves (from the French *moitié*). Used by cultural anthropologists to refer to two **exogamous** clans, or groups of clans, in one society that exchange women and ritual services.

money A medium of exchange, in coins and banknotes, used in certain market economies. It is easily portable, anonymous, interchangeable, and offered in units that are multiples of the smallest unit. "Shell money," "salt money," and other such "moneys" are not divisible, and what can be bought with one "unit" cannot be bought with any combination of other units; these are not deemed true money.

monogamy A rule permitting only one spouse at a time. Many Americans practice serial monogamy, that is, having several spouses, one after the other.

morpheme In **linguistics**, the smallest unit of sound that conveys a meaning in a language. Free morphemes can be understood when they stand alone (e.g., "cat"), whereas bound morphemes serve only to alter the meaning of the free morphemes to which they are bound (e.g., "s" in "cats").

morphology In **linguistics**, the study of word structure, focusing on the categories and rules involved in word formation.

mutation Appearance of a random change in a gene or chromosome. These changes are subject to natural selection; most are detrimental, but some are advantageous.

m.y.a. Millions of years ago.

myth A sacred story explaining why the world, society, and people are the way they are. Besides proposing a kind of explanation, a myth is often a charter for action, and illustrates one or more aspects of the value system of a society.

natural selection The process discovered by Wallace and Darwin through which, over the generations, the less fit are eliminated and the fittest reproduce more successfully. The measure of adaptive success is reproductive success.

Neolithic Derived from two Greek words meaning *New Stone Age*. No longer used to describe the beginning of stone polishing, the term now refers to the period of domestication of plants and animals, starting about 10,000 B.P. in the Middle East.

neolocal residence A rule allowing or requiring a newly married couple to live away from the residence of the relatives of the bride or groom.

neoteny The retention in adulthood of more generalized and earlier characteristics of infants or fetuses of the same species or an ancestral species.

New Archaeology A school of thought in archaeology, led by L. Binford and his students, requiring a more rigorous as well as more imaginative use of the scientific method in archaeology. Its main emphasis is on scientific methodology and ethnoarchaeology.

niche In ecology, the functional position of a population in a certain ecosystem, determined by behavior as well as food preferences or physiological and somatic characteristics. E. Odum calls the niche of a population its "profession," and the habitat, its "address."

nomad True nomads wander in a random pattern, like some bands of foragers. Many **pastoralists** practice transhumance, a precisely timed pattern of migration on a traditional route.

nuclear family A family unit comprising a couple and the children they have had together. Some anthropologists, such as G.P. Murdock, considered the nuclear family to be a universal phenomenon. In many societies, however, the members of nuclear families do not live in the same house, or they are incorporated in larger kinship groupings such as clans or extended families. Many anthropologists prefer the term **conjugal family**.

oasis hypothesis V. Gordon Childe formulated this theory, according to which a rapid climatic warming after the Pleistocene led humans, plants, and animals to congregate in oases, where their relationships changed, leading to agriculture and animal husbandry.

Oldowan From the name Olduvai Gorge (Tanzania), the term refers to the oldest stone tool assemblages, containing pebble tools (unifacial **core tools**) and crude **flakes**.

Olmec The earliest chiefdoms in Lowland Mexico, located in the states of Veracruz and Tabasco. They built pyramids (La Venta, 3000 B.P.), carved massive statues, and conceived the first version of the Maya calendar.

orangutan *Pongo pygmaeous*. Largely arboreal, this great ape is now found only in Borneo and Sumatra. A very distant relative of *Homo sapiens*.

Paleolithic Derived from two Greek words meaning *Old Stone Age*. Includes all human cultures before the **Neolithic** of the Old World, when polished stone tools and agriculture started. This classification, based on the techniques of stone tool manufacture, has been refined by modern archaeologists, who divide the Paleolithic into three major periods: the Lower Paleolithic,

the Middle Paleolithic, and the Upper Paleolithic. Another period — the Mesolithic — has also been inserted to describe European cultures that followed the Upper Paleolithic and preceded the Neolithic.

paleontology Human paleontology is a subdivision of anthropology specializing in the study of the fossil remains of hominids and prehominids.

parallel cousin A cousin related to *Ego* by two links of the same sex, as in father's brother's child, mother's sister's child, or any person called by the same kinship term as these children.

participant observation A method of observation whereby anthropologists do not remain detached, outside observers, but participate in the daily lives and activities of the group they study. Bronislav Malinowski introduced this research technique in his work with peoples of the Trobriand Islands.

pastoralism A subsistence strategy based on the herding of such herbivores as cows, camels, and horses, practiced in areas of Africa, Asia, and Europe that are not suitable for agriculture. Pastoral societies are always associated with agricultural societies.

patrilineage Descent group formed by people who claim to be genealogically related to one another and to a common male ancestor through demonstrable male links. There are several patrilineages in a patrilineal **clan**.

patrilineal descent A rule of descent that recognizes inheritance only through male links. Patrilineal descent is observed by many more societies than is **matrilineal descent**.

patrilocal A rule pertaining to postmarital residence whereby the bride and groom go to live in the same locality as the groom's patrilineal relatives.

peasant An agriculturalist in a stratified society, who does not use modern technologies and pays rent and taxes. As used by anthropologists, this term does not have negative connotations.

phenotype The characteristics of an individual that are the apparent manifestations of that individual's genetic programming. The phenotype results from the interaction of the **geno-**

type with its environment. Natural selection operates directly on phenotypes.

phoneme A distinctive unit of sound, that has no meaning by itself, but that, in combination with other phonemes, produces a **morpheme**, which does carry a meaning. Every language has only a fixed set of phonemes, forming a phonemic system.

phonology The study of the sounds of languages. It is subdivided into *phonetics*, the study of the production and the physical properties of the sounds, and *phonemics*, which identifies the sound characteristics that may be used to alter meaning in a given language (**phonemes**).

phratry Several clans or local lineages clustered to form a new unit, for marriage or ritual purposes. When there are only two phratries in the same locality, they form a **moiety** system.

phylogeny The tracing of the evolutionary relatedness of different species; often illustrated in the form of a branching tree or bush.

physical anthropology *See* **biological anthropology**.

pixel The "picture element" in computer-imaging programs; one of the many tiny illuminated units of which an image on a computer screen is composed.

Pleistocene The sixth geological epoch of the Cenozoic (which started 65 m.y.a.). The Pleistocene began 1.5 m.y.a. and lasted until 10,000 B.P. It was followed by the Holocene, the present geological period. There were several glaciations during the Pleistocene, separated by warmer periods.

pluralism The coexistence in the same society of several subgroups differing in their ethnic, cultural, and linguistic backgrounds. *See* **minority**.

political anthropology A subfield of anthropology concerned with the patterns of leadership, authority, and power in human societies; the management of public affairs; and the origins and functions of institutions such as social stratification and the state. The comparative and holistic approach of political anthropologists distinguishes their work from that of political scientists.

polyandry A custom allowing a woman to have several husbands at the same time. Polyandry is much less common than **polygyny**.

polygamy A custom allowing marriage to several spouses at the same time (plural marriage).

polygyny A custom allowing a man to have several wives at the same time.

Pongidae The family that includes all modern great apes: chimpanzees, bonobos, gorillas, and orangutans.

potassium-argon dating (KAr) An absolute dating technique based on the half-life of 1.3 billion years of argon 40 produced by potassium 40; has been used to date fossils 5 million to 1 million years old.

power The ability to force others to obey one's requests and orders. It is backed by threats of physical violence, fines, jail sentences, torture, and execution. Social stratification cannot be maintained without power and threats of violence.

prehistoric archaeology A subfield of anthropology studying the material remains and the culture of human populations from the origin of humankind to the period when written records appear for each population. As such, it studies a period of a million years — about 99 percent of human history — in an attempt to reconstruct cultural history and extinct lifeways.

Primates The highest order of mammals, including humans and all their ancestors, apes, monkeys, and prosimians.

punctuated equilibrium Contrary to the Darwinian theory of slow, gradual evolution, punctuated equilibrium holds that long periods of stability were followed by sudden changes. S.J. Gould suggests that regulator genes activate or deactivate entire biochemical processes, and genetic drift could fix the process if the carriers of a mutated regulator gene were both viable and able to reproduce.

race A large, geographically isolated population within an animal species, which has had little gene flow with other populations for a long time; a subspecies. This statistical and genetic definition of race does not coincide with the popular definitions, based on **phenotype**, which ignore not only clinal variations, but also the very fact that most human populations do not fit the popular racial categories.

racist A type of explanation of human behavior and cultural characteristics that assumes the existence of clearly identifiable human groups distinguished by discrete biological characteristics that affect and partly determine features of intelligence, personality, and behavior. Modern anthropologists find no scientific basis for these claims.

radiocarbon dating (C14) Absolute dating technique based on the known rate of decay of C14, absorbed during the organism's lifetime, into C12 after the death of the organism. Useful for dating organic material up to 75,000 years old.

Ramapithecus Until recently, this late Miocene Hominoidea (14 m.y.a. to 9 m.y.a.) was thought by some scientists to be the first of the Hominidae. Numerous fossils found in Africa, Europe, and, especially, India provided a more complete picture: we now consider it to be an ancestor of orangutans.

rank Usually an ascribed status, inherited according to one's place in a genealogy. Ranked societies have chiefs, who have **authority** and usually some **power**. Their fund for power is amassed as a result of stratified **redistribution**.

reciprocity A form of exchange found in all societies. It involves the exchange of gifts of goods and services, wherein the giver and receiver pretend to ignore the value of the gifts, and the giver claims not to expect a gift in return. In the long run, there tends to be a balance of gifts and counter-gifts. Some authors distinguish this type of exchange, which they call "generalized reciprocity," from "balanced reciprocity" and "negative reciprocity."

redistribution A type of exchange in which the goods and services of many people are pooled by an organizer who combines these inputs and redistributes them, usually during a feast. In *egalitarian redistribution*, the redistributor works hard and makes no material profit; in *stratified redistribution*, that person works less hard and makes a material profit.

relative dating A technique to determine which of two samples is older, without eliciting a precise

date. Stratigraphy and fluorine analysis are examples of such techniques.

revitalization movements Religions of the oppressed: these new religions attempt to reconstruct a more satisfying sociocultural system. Christianity, Islam, Mormonism, **cargo cults**, the Ghost Dance, and modern evangelical fundamentalism are examples of revitalization movements.

rites of passage Rituals that provide social sanction to crucial steps in an individual's life, such as birth, puberty, marriage, and death. Since the publication of A. Van Gennep's *The Rites of Passage* in 1960, anthropologists describe the three stages of these rituals as separation, transition, and incorporation.

ritual Culturally patterned, repetitive sequences of behavior, which are symbolically instrumental. The following useful classification of types of religious rituals was proposed by A. Van Gennep: rites of passage, intensification, transition, and incorporation.

RNA (ribonucleic acid) Very similar to DNA, but with a distinctive sugar; activates and positions amino acids in protein synthesis.

role The dynamic aspect of a **status**; the performance of the rights, duties, and expected behavior associated with any status.

sacred In contrast to ordinary, mundane, and profane events and realities, societies posit holy, occult, and mysterious forces and events: this is the realm of the sacred.

Sapir–Whorf Hypothesis The hypothesis holds that the language spoken by a group of people structures their perceptions and the way they think. Language is not just a code to express ideas; it determines, in part, the modalities of our thinking processes. This hypothesis is not generally accepted by anthropologists.

semantic universality The characteristic that distinguishes human language from other means of communication; the ability to talk (and lie) about any kind of possible or impossible reality, at any point in time and space.

semantics The study of meaning in language, particularly in terms of the relationships among signs and what they stand for. In anthropology, much study focused on native classifications. Cognitive anthropology, componential analysis, and ethnoscience are some of the specialties that explore this aspect of the relationship between language and culture.

sexual dimorphism   Biological differences between the males and females of one species.

shaman   A part-time religious specialist who acts as medium, curer, and diviner in many societies. In some societies, the shaman is a woman. The traditional shamans differ from other faith healers in that, during trances, it is believed that their soul travels to other layers of the universe, invisible to ordinary people.

sickle cell anemia   A genetically transmitted disease in which homozygous individuals produce an abnormal hemoglobin resulting in poorly shaped red blood cells that do not carry oxygen to body tissues properly.

slash-and-burn agriculture   Also known as *swidden agriculture*, and *shifting cultivation*. A technique that consists essentially of the cutting, drying, and burning of the trees in a small patch of forest, which is cultivated for two or three years, then left fallow for ten or fifteen years. Slash-and-burn gardens contain a great variety of plants growing at different heights and at different rates. In many tropical areas, this is a very efficient and very productive technique, more sustainable than the industrial techniques that have recently been introduced.

slavery   In ranked societies, slavery is not usually hereditary (the Kwakiutl are an exception), and the descendants of slaves become absorbed into the society in which they live. African kingdoms allowed for the incorporation of slaves into their owners' strata; the Greeks, Romans, and nineteeth-century Europeans reduced slaves to subhuman status.

social stratification   The organization of a society into different classes. There are at least two classes — that of the rich and that of the poor — distinguished by their power or lack of it, and by the degree of control they have over wealth and natural resources.

society   A group of people of both sexes, comprising at least three generations, who share a common territory and common institutions and who depend on one another for their survival and well-being. In pluralistic societies, such as Canada, all members do not have the same culture.

sociobiology   A controversial research strategy, first proposed by E.O. Wilson in *Sociobiology: The New Synthesis* in 1975, suggesting a genetic basis to certain patterns of human behavior such as male dominance or warfare. Includes a refinement of the concept of natural selection known as inclusive fitness.

sociolinguistics   The study of the interactions between language and culture, social system, and variations of speech associated with variations in social context.

somatic   From the Greek root *soma*, meaning "body"; of or relating to the body. Somatic cells are all the cells of the body except for reproductive cells.

sororate   The custom whereby a widower marries a woman classified by their kinship terminology as one of his deceased wife's sisters. This institution expresses that in marriage, the formation of alliances is more important than the personalities of the individual bride and groom.

species   A taxonomic category including organisms known to be, or presumed to be, capable of interbreeding and producing fertile offspring.

state   A stratified society with a centralized government that provides public services and has the power to collect taxes and impose laws.

status   The position of an individual in a social system or subsystem. Some statuses are *ascribed* (determined by birth, sex, age), whereas others are *achieved* (as a result of some behavior during one's lifetime). *See also* **role**.

stereotype   An overgeneralization; a prejudice attributing certain characteristics to all members of a certain group or category of people, distinguished on the basis of race, gender, national, or ethnic characteristics.

stratified society   A society divided into classes. There are always at least two classes — a wealthy minority and a poor majority — but in many societies, there are several intermediate classes as well.

stratigraphy An archaeological relative-dating technique, borrowed from geology, that makes use of the law of superposition (in undisturbed areas, older materials are buried under new ones) and the concept of an index fossil (a diagnostic artifact that helps match corresponding layers of different stratigraphies).

structuralism An approach that developed after the Second World War; it is associated in linguistics with the work of the Prague School, and in anthropology with that of the influential French anthropologist Claude Lévi-Strauss. Culture, social systems, and myths are considered as systems expressing in different ways the basic and unconscious mental structures that Lévi-Strauss attempts to discover through his structural analysis. Structuralism focuses on psychological similarities across cultures rather than on cultural differences.

symbol An arbitrary sign, such as a sound, an object, or a gesture, used by people who share a culture to refer to a certain meaning independent of the sign itself — for example, a flag is a symbol.

syntax In linguistics, the unconscious structural rules that govern the combination of **morphemes** to form meaningful statements in a given language.

synthetic theory of evolution A refinement of Darwin's theory that emerged in the 1940s; it resulted from a combination of the discoveries of Darwin and Mendel with findings in the fields of paleontology and population genetics, among others.

taboo An interdiction against touching certain objects or performing certain acts that is associated with the threat of magical punishment.

technology A combination of knowledge and tools used to acquire or transform matter and energy.

Teotihuacán Established in A.D. 100, this central Mexican city grew to a population of more than 100,000. Its pyramids were among the world's biggest monuments. When it was burned in A.D. 750, its inhabitants were suffering from malnutrition.

territoriality The defense of their home range by animals of many species. For example, mated pairs of gibbons defend their range from other gibbons. Several influential authors have presented this behavior pattern as an instinct that they claim is also found in humans. This claim is rejected by most anthropologists.

theory The most certain scientific explanation available on a given topic at a given time. One arrives at a theory through testing and revising the testable implications of hypotheses. The hypotheses that survive the most rigorous testing available to science can be called theories. Unlike a scientific law, which is only the statement of a correlation between phenomena, a theory explains such a correlation.

Third World As distinguished from the rich industrial economies of the *First World* (Western Europe, Japan, North America) and from the socialist industrial societies of the *Second World* (the former Soviet Union, Eastern Europe), the term *Third World* designates other countries with less industrialization and more poverty, mostly in Africa, Asia, Latin America, and the Middle East. Many of these Third World countries are former colonies of Western nations.

Tikal The largest of the Maya ceremonial centers, located in the Petén region of Guatemala. It has about two thousand pyramids, temples, and other buildings, some of which are being restored. Its population reached 50,000.

Toltec A civilization that flourished in Mexico between A.D. 900 and A.D. 1300. The capital city was Tula.

tool An object, not part of the user's body, that is carried and used to modify in some way the environment of the user. Birds, elephants, and chimpanzees use tools. The use of tools is socially learned, not genetically transmitted.

totemism The symbolic association of exogamous clans with certain objects or natural phenomena. Rituals of solidarity proclaim and reinforce the identification of clan members with their totem.

trance A state of altered consciousness achieved by many different means (controlled breathing, the use of tobacco or of hallucinogenic or narcotic drugs) to facilitate contact with the supernatural. Trances are culture-bound, and their functions and symbolic significance vary from culture to culture.

tribe A political unit including members of several bands or villages, and various kinship groups; it involves certain political statuses and institutions that are not bestowed or organized on the basis of kinship alone. Tribal organization is associated with the emergence of a sense of common ethnicity and language.

Trojan horse According to Homer's *Iliad*, the Greeks finally conquered the city of Troy after feigning retreat, but leaving behind a big wooden horse. Hauled inside the city by the Trojans, the horse contained soldiers who sacked the city. Beware of Greeks (and developers) bearing gifts.

underdevelopment A term referring to the great poverty, poor health, and short life expectancy of disadvantaged countries, which result from those countries' integration at the bottom of a global social stratification.

uniformitarianism A theory proposed by Georges Buffon and James Hutton in the eighteenth century, and by the geologist Charles Lyell in 1873, explaining landforms as resulting from geological processes that are still observable today and that have acted in a continuous and uniform manner for a very long time. "The present is the key to the past."

unilineal descent Descent calculated through links of one sex only: patrilineal descent (through males only) or matrilineal descent (through females only).

uxorilocal The custom whereby a new married couple takes up residence near the bride's family. *See* **matrilocal**.

value A socially patterned ideal defining acceptable and desirable goals and behavioral patterns.

virilocal The custom whereby a new married couple takes up residence near the groom's parents. *See* **patrilocal**.

witchcraft The supernatural powers that many societies believe some people to be born with. Willfully or even unwittingly, those who practice witchcraft may cause misfortune, illness, and even death.

Reader Reply Card

We are interested in your reaction to *Peoples of the Past and Present: Readings in Anthropology*, by Jean-Luc Chodkiewicz. You can help us to improve this book in future editions by completing this questionnaire.

1. What was your reason for using this book?

   ❑ university course   ❑ college course   ❑ continuing education course

   ❑ professional   ❑ personal   ❑ other _____
   development   interest

   _____

2. If you are a student, please identify your school and the course in which you used this book.

3. Which chapters or parts of this book did you use? Which did you omit?

4. What did you like best about this book?

5. What did you like least?

6. Please identify any topics you think should be added to future editions.

7. Please add any comments or suggestions.

8. May we contact you for further information?

   Name: _____

   Address: _____

   _____

   Phone: _____

(fold here and tape shut)

MAIL ➤ **POSTE**

Canada Post Corporation / Société canadienne des postes

Postage paid
If mailed in Canada

Port payé
si posté au Canada

**Business
Reply**

**Réponse
d'affaires**

0116870399 01

0116870399-M8Z4X6-BR01

Heather McWhinney
Publisher, College Division
HARCOURT BRACE & COMPANY, CANADA
55 HORNER AVENUE
TORONTO, ONTARIO
M8Z 9Z9